Lecture Notes in Computer Science 9836

Commenced Publication in 1973
Founding and Former Series Editors:
Gerhard Goos, Juris Hartmanis, and Jan van Leeuwen

More information about this series at http://www.springer.com/series/7410

Kazuto Ogawa · Katsunari Yoshioka (Eds.)

Advances in Information and Computer Security

11th International Workshop on Security, IWSEC 2016
Tokyo, Japan, September 12–14, 2016
Proceedings

Springer

Editors
Kazuto Ogawa
Japan Broadcasting Corporation
Tokyo
Japan

Katsunari Yoshioka
Yokohama National University
Yokohama
Japan

ISSN 0302-9743   ISSN 1611-3349 (electronic)
Lecture Notes in Computer Science
ISBN 978-3-319-44523-6   ISBN 978-3-319-44524-3 (eBook)
DOI 10.1007/978-3-319-44524-3

Library of Congress Control Number: 2016911462

LNCS Sublibrary: SL4 – Security and Cryptology

This Springer imprint is published by Springer Nature
The registered company is Springer International Publishing AG Switzerland

Preface

The 11th International Workshop on Security (IWSEC 2016) was held at Sola City Conference Center, in Tokyo, Japan, during September 12–14, 2016. The workshop was organized by the Special Interest Group on Computer Security of Information Processing Society of Japan (CSEC of IPSJ) and supported by the Technical Committee on Information Security in Engineering Sciences Society of the Institute of Electronics, Information and Communication Engineers (ISEC in ESS of IEICE).

This year, the workshop received 53 submissions. Finally, 15 papers were accepted as regular papers, and four papers were accepted as short papers. Each submission was anonymously reviewed by at least four reviewers, and these proceedings contain the revised versions of the accepted papers. In addition to the presentations of the papers, the workshop also featured a poster session. The keynote speeches were given by Christopher Krugel, by Engin Kirda, and by Yosuke Todo.

The best paper awards were given to "Analyzing Android Repackaged Malware by Decoupling Their Event Behaviors" by Zimin Lin, Rui Wang, Xiaoqi Jia, Shengzhi Zhang, and Chuankun Wu, and "On the Security and Key Generation of the ZHFE Encryption Scheme" by Wenbin Zhang and Chik How Tan. The best student paper award was given to "Hybrid Risk Assessment Model Based on Bayesian Networks" by François-Xavier Aguessy, Olivier Bettan, Gregory Blanc, Vania Conan, and Hervé Debar.

A number of people contributed to the success of IWSEC 2016. We would like to thank the authors for submitting their papers to the workshop. The selection of the papers was a challenging and dedicated task, and we are deeply grateful to the members of the Program Committee and the external reviewers for their in-depth reviews and detailed discussions.

Last but not least, we would like to thank the general co-chairs, Satoru Torii and Masahiro Mambo, for leading the local Organizing Committee, and we would also like to thank the members of the local Organizing Committee for their efforts to ensure the smooth running of the workshop.

June 2016

Kazuto Ogawa
Katsunari Yoshioka

IWSEC 2016

11th International Workshop on Security

Organization

Tokyo, Japan, September 12–14, 2016

Organized by
CSEC of IPSJ
(Special Interest Group on Computer Security of Information Processing
Society of Japan)

and

Supported by
ISEC in ESS of IEICE
(Technical Committee on Information Security in Engineering Sciences Society
of the Institute of Electronics, Information and Communication Engineers)

General Co-chairs

Masahiro Mambo	Kanazawa University, Japan
Satoru Torii	Fujitsu Laboratories Ltd., Japan

Advisory Committee

Hideki Imai	University of Tokyo, Japan
Kwangjo Kim	Korea Advanced Institute of Science and Technology, Korea
Günter Müller	University of Freiburg, Germany
Yuko Murayama	Tsuda College, Japan
Koji Nakao	National Institute of Information and Communications Technology, Japan
Eiji Okamoto	University of Tsukuba, Japan
C. Pandu Rangan	Indian National Academy of Engineering, India
Kai Rannenberg	Goethe University of Frankfurt, Germany
Ryoichi Sasaki	Tokyo Denki University, Japan

Program Co-chairs

Kazuto Ogawa	Japan Broadcasting Corporation, Japan
Katsunari Yoshioka	Yokohama National University, Japan

Local Organizing Committee

Koji Chida	NTT, Japan
Takuya Hayashi	National Institute of Information and Communications Technology, Japan
Takato Hirano	Mitsubishi Electric Corporation, Japan
Hiroyuki Inoue	Hiroshima City University, Japan
Masaki Kamizono	PricewaterhouseCoopers Corporation Ltd., Japan
Akira Kanaoka	Toho University, Japan
Yutaka Kawai	Mitsubishi Electric Corporation, Japan
Satoshi Obana	Hosei University, Japan
Toshihiro Ohigashi	Tokai University, Japan
Kazumasa Omote	Japan Advanced Institute of Science and Technology, Japan
Satomi Saito	Fujitsu Laboratories Ltd., Japan
Masakazu Soushi	Hiroshima City University, Japan
Yuji Suga	Internet Initiative Japan Inc., Japan
Koutarou Suzuki	NTT, Japan
Masayuki Terada	NTT Docomo, Japan
Isamu Teranishi	NEC Corporation, Japan
Yu Tsuda	National Institute of Information and Communications Technology, Japan
Sven Wohlgemuth	Hochschule Fresenius University of Applied Sciences - Business School, Germany
Naoto Yanai	Osaka University, Japan
Masayuki Yoshino	Hitachi Corporation, Japan

Program Committee

Mohamed Abid	University of Gabes, Tunisia
Mitsuaki Akiyama	NTT, Japan
Elena Andreeva	KU Leuven, Belgium
Nuttapong Attrapadung	National Institute of Advanced Industrial Science and Technology, Japan
Reza Azarderakhsh	Rochester Institute of Technology, USA
Josep Balasch	KU Leuven, Belgium
Gregory Blanc	Télécom SudParis/Université Paris-Saclay, France
Olivier Blazy	Université de Limoges, France
Aymen Boudguiga	Institute for Technological Research SystemX, France

External Reviewers

Contents

Permutation and Symmetric Encryption

Privacy Preserving

Hardware Security

Post-quantum Cryptography

Paring Computation

System Security

Analyzing Android Repackaged Malware by Decoupling Their Event Behaviors

Zimin Lin[1,2], Rui Wang[1(✉)], Xiaoqi Jia[1],
Shengzhi Zhang[3], and Chuankun Wu[1]

[1] State Key Laboratory of Information Security,
Institute of Information Engineering,
Chinese Academy of Sciences, Beijing, China
wangrui@iie.ac.cn
[2] University of Chinese Academy of Sciences, Beijing, China
[3] Florida Institute of Technology, Melbourne, USA

Abstract. Malware have threatened Android security for a long time. One of main sources of those Android malware is that attackers inject malicious payloads into legitimate apps and then republish them, called repackaged malware. In this paper, we propose a new dynamic approach to analyze and detect the behaviors of Android repackaged malware. Our approach mainly concerns the framework-level behaviors of apps with rich semantics and a special execution sandbox is firstly constructed to extract them. Then, assuming that malicious payloads are usually triggered by certain events, we reconstruct the execution dependency graph to distinguish different event behaviors of malware. Thus, based on the independent event behavior sequences, only a small amount of malware samples from the same family are required to accurately compare and locate their common behaviors, which can be further used as signatures to detect other suspicious Android apps or to analyze malware's activities. For evaluation, we have implement the prototype system and 9 families of real world repackaged malware are detected in our experiments. Although only 3 samples for each family are randomly chosen to extract their common malware behaviors, the results show that our approach still has a high detection accuracy (96.3 %). In addition, some attacks such as code encryption and delay attack are also studied in this work.

Keywords: Android · Repackaged malware · Malicious payload · Execution dependency graph · Execution sandbox · Framework-level behavior

1 Introduction

With the dominance of Android in mobile OS market, a large number of apps have been developed. Only on Google Play are there more than 1.8 million apps. The huge revenue successfully attracts the attention of attackers, and many security issues such as malware have been reported frequently. Repackaged

© Springer International Publishing Switzerland 2016
K. Ogawa and K. Yoshioka (Eds.): IWSEC 2016, LNCS 9836, pp. 3–20, 2016.
DOI: 10.1007/978-3-319-44524-3_1

malware, created by injecting malicious code modules into legitimate apps [23], is currently one kind of main malware on the third-party Android app markets. In a recent study [25], 86.0 % of collected malware (1083 out of 1260) were repackaged versions of legitimate apps with malicious payloads. Those repackaged malware severely threaten the security of mobile devices and effective approaches for analyzing and detecting their malicious behaviors are in demand.

In order to detect Android malware, a variety of approaches, including both static and dynamic ones, have been proposed. To static approaches, they usually decompile apps and detect them by extracting different code features such as API behavior feature [5], API modality [17], API dependency graph [22], abstract malware signature [11] and app context [18]. In addition, those static approaches [7–9,21,24] designed to scan repackaged apps are often used to find potential malware. In most cases, static approaches are effective to detect malware. But, they can be significantly weakened by code obfuscation techniques. The work in [14] introduced multiple code transformation techniques, and showed that static approaches can not analyze apps with appropriate protections such as code encryption and Java reflection.

As to resisting code obfuscation techniques, dynamic approaches are more effective than static ones. At present, they have some other drawbacks. Dynamic approaches [6,12,15,16] were mainly designed for the threat evaluation of apps, and the features extracted by them are often very coarse-grained. For example, Afonso et al. [6] detected malware based on the invocation frequencies of some critical APIs, which cannot be used to distinguish the type of malware and analyze the concrete activities of malware. Another problem of the approach in [6] is that it can not extract the behaviors in dynamically loaded code or encrypted code, because the approach needs to patch code into original malware in advance for logging API behaviors. There are also some other types of works such as [13], which adopted traditional Linux malware analysis techniques (e.g. extracting thread-level system call behavior sequences) to detect Android malware. It is well-known that Android apps are mainly developed in Java language and executed in Dalvik virtual machine (DVM). After the interpretation of DVM, kernel system call behaviors are usually lack of semantics, and hard to be understood and analyzed.

Moreover, Android apps heavily depend on the event mechanism, such as system events and UI events. According to the previous studies [18,19], malicious payload are also more likely triggered by some certain events. However, by default the code handling different events is executed in the same thread. Thus, when a repackaged app is executed, behaviors generated by code of original app and malicious payloads intersect together. Even in the thread granularity, it is still difficult to accurately distinguish malicious behaviors from benign ones. Especially when there are only a small amount of malware samples, understanding their execution logic is critical to locate and analyze their malicious behaviors.

Aiming at the above problems, we propose a new dynamic approach to analyze and detect Android repackaged malware, by decoupling their different event behaviors. Firstly, an execution sandbox is built to obtain dynamic behavior information of malware, consisting of both framework-level behaviors for Java code and system call behaviors for native code. Then, based on the execution information, we construct the execution dependency graph to distinguish behaviors triggered by different events. Thus, by comparing event behavior sequences of a few malware samples from the same family, behaviors generated by malicious payloads can be easily located and used as signatures to detect other suspicious apps. In summary, our major contributions are as follows.

- We propose a new dynamic approach to analyze and detect Android repackaged malware. By decoupling different event behaviors, our approach is easier to find out malicious behaviors with less malware samples.
- We implement the prototype system. An execution sandbox is constructed to extract dynamic behaviors of apps without any change of the original apps, and automatic process is implemented for malware detection.
- We evaluate our approach with real world malware. The experiments on 9 families of repackaged malware (770 malware) and 900 benign apps show that our overall detection accuracy is 96.3 %.

2 Overview

2.1 Problem Statement

Android apps are mainly developed in Java code and easy to be decompiled and repackaged. The infection process of repackaged malware is described in Fig. 1. Attackers firstly inject their malicious payloads into legitimate apps, and then upload them to Internet or the third-party app markets. Once users download and install these repackaged malware, their mobile devices are attacked. To increase the infection rate of this attack, attackers are inclined to inject their malicious modules into a large number of popular benign apps. Although malicious modules are distributed in different apps, malware instances from the same family have similar behaviors. Correspondingly, a series of detection approaches [13,17,22,23] can be used to detect Android repackaged malware. However, existing approaches have some drawbacks. For instance, effectiveness of static approaches is seriously affected by code obfuscation techniques such as code encryption, while dynamic methods are mainly used for anomaly detection or directly based on traditional Linux malware analysis techniques, ignoring the execution characteristics of Android system.

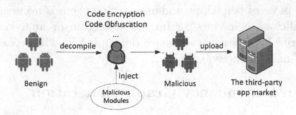

Fig. 1. Attack of Android repackaged malware.

2.2   Android Event-Based Execution Logic

Compared to executables with single entry in traditional operating systems, code of Android apps can be triggered by many different system and UI events. To support such feature, Android system defines numerous callback interfaces for developers. When one event happens, Android system tries to invoke the corresponding interface implemented by developers in callback way. Besides system events and UI events, the callback mechanism is also widely used to deal with internal events such as inter-component communication and handler message. By default, the processing code of those events is executed in the same thread, called main thread. As depicted in Fig. 2(a), when two events screen touch and SMS receiving happen, a series of callback interfaces implemented by developers is invoked. Although behaviors triggered by the two events are usually independent, it is difficult to distinguish them even in the thread granularity.

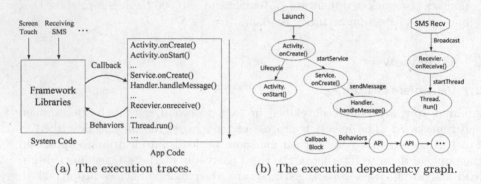

(a) The execution traces.   (b) The execution dependency graph.

Fig. 2. Example of execution dependency graph.

According to previous works [18,19], malicious payloads of repackaged malware are more likely to be triggered by some certain events. In order to avoid that behaviors generated by malicious payloads and by code of original app intersect together, we distinguish different event behaviors by reconstructing the execution dependency graph shown in Fig. 2(b). In the graph, every node represents a callback event and contains the corresponding function call behaviors generated by the event, while edges represent the dependencies between callback events. The dependency relationships are useful when every callback behavior block only contains a small piece of behaviors, and associating them is necessary to extract long enough malicious behaviors for further detection or analysis. Thus, once behaviors triggered by different events are decoupled, it will be easier to locate the behaviors of malicious payloads.

3   Execution Dependency Graph Generation

Assuming that execution information of malware has been extracted, Fig. 3 shows the workflow designed to reconstruct the execution dependency graph.

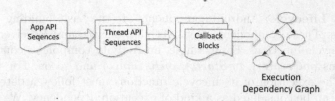

Fig. 3. Construction process of execution dependency graph.

Firstly, execution behaviors are split into sequences according to the thread identity. Then, based on the event callback mechanism, thread-level behavior sequences are divided into independent behavior blocks, which are called callback blocks in this paper. Finally, execution dependencies between callback blocks are built based on concrete execution parameters.

3.1 Callback Block Partition

When one event happens, the corresponding interface function is invoked in callback way, where functions of apps are invoked by system libraries. All behaviors in one callback block deal with the same event, so we consider them together and split thread-level behavior sequences into blocks based on the logic of callback interfaces.

To split callback blocks, we record the start and the end of each callback interface when apps are being executed. The concrete process is introduced in Sect. 5. During this process, some extra attributes of callback blocks are also collected. For example, if the callback interface function $onReceive(Intent)$ is invoked by the system function $ActivityThread.handleReceiver()$, we know that it is a lifecycle function of Receiver component, and parameters in $Intent$ need to be analyzed and stored as the attributes of this callback block. These attributes are useful to associate different behaviors.

There may exist a special case that multiple callback blocks are nested. Assuming that A is a callback block, it may contain another callback block B. Because all behaviors in B are still a part of A, we only consider the outermost callback block A.

3.2 Behavior Association

Although behaviors of malware are split into comparatively independent callback blocks, the execution of some callback blocks depends on some other behaviors. For instance, the callback block $Runnable.run()$ may be triggered by a thread creation behavior $Thread.start()$ in another callback block. To completely analyze malicious behaviors, we rebuild those execution dependencies. After studying some previous works and behaviors of several benign and malicious apps, we summarize major execution dependency relationships as follows.

Component Lifecycle. Android components are the basic building blocks of Android apps. Those components (e.g. Activity, Service and Receiver) consist of several lifecycle functions. For example, an Activity component contains lifecycle functions *onCreate()*, *onStart()*, *onResume()* and so on. For the same component, the execution of its lifecycle functions must follow a deterministic order, which can be considered as a kind of execution dependency. We associate lifecycle functions of the same component (with the same Java **this** reference) based on the guide of lifecycle logic [1].

Intent. Intent plays a key role in the inter-component communication (ICC) of Android apps. Based on the Intent mechanism, new components are created and callback interfaces are invoked. To build execution dependencies between different components, we analyze both function call behaviors and their Intent parameters.

Table 1. Part of interfaces related to Intent communication.

Activity	startActivity(Intent)
	startActivityIfNeeded(Intent,...)
	startNextMatchActivity(Intent)
	...
Service	startService(Intent)
	bindService(Intent,...)
Broadcast	sendBroadcast(Intent,...)
	sendOrderedBroadcast(Intent,...)
	sendStickyBroadcast(Intent)
	...

Table 1 shows part of system interfaces which are related to ICC. Once these interface behaviors are found in the execution process of malware, their Intent parameters are analyzed. The structure of Intent data is like key-value pairs. Two key fields *cmp* and *act* in Intent data are important to build the execution dependency. Key *cmp* specifies the package name of the target component that the Intent is supposed to send to. Nevertheless, when only key *act* is contained in the Intent data, all components registering this action may receive it and corresponding lifecycle functions will be invoked. By analyzing the behaviors and Intent parameters, execution dependencies between components are built.

Handler Message. Handler Message is widely used in Android apps to implement remote procedure calls (RPC). Figure 4 gives an example. A message is sent at line 10 with the function *sendMessage(Message)*, and it will be handled by the callback interface *handleMessage(Message)* defined at lines 2 to 5. There exists an execution dependency between the behavior *sendMessage(Message)* and the callback block *handleMessage(Message)*. Actually, if an *Runnable* data is integrated in *Message*, Android system will directly invoke the interface *Runnable.run()*, rather than *handleMessage(Message)*.

```
00:  public class MainActivity extends Activity {
01:    Handler handler = new Handler() {
02:      public void handleMessage(Message msg) {
03:        dosomething();
04:        ...
05:      }
06:    };
07:
08:    void onStart() {
09:      Message msg = new Message();
10:      handler.sendMessage(msg);
11:      ...
12:  }}
```

Fig. 4. Example of handler Message.

We build dependencies between message sending functions and handling functions by comparing the memory addresses of *Message* data, which is recorded in the system libraries.

Thread. In the Android apps, we observe two types of thread behaviors: single thread creation and thread pool. For the first case, a new thread is created to process an asynchronous task and all behaviors on the thread can be regarded as a whole. In terms of threads in the thread pool, they may be reused and behaviors on them need to be split.

Thread.start() and *AsyncTask.execute*() are two common interfaces used in the Android apps to create new threads. For *Thread.start*(), we directly associate this behavior with its callback block interface *Runnable.run*() according to the identity of new thread. While *AsyncTask.execute*() is invoked, callback interfaces *onPreExecute()*, *doInBackground()* and *onPostExecute()* will be executed in order. Those callback interfaces share the same object *AsyncTask*, whose memory address is used to build this type of execution dependency.

A thread pool is a collection of several worker threads, which can be efficiently reused to process multiple asynchronous tasks. For thread behaviors such as *ThreadPoolExecutor.execute(Runnable)* and *ScheduledThreadPoolExecutor.schedule(Runnable)*, we associate them with their corresponding callback blocks *Runnable.run*() based on the memory address of object *Runnable*.

Timer. Timer is used to handle delay events or to repeatedly execute the same task multiple times, which may generate many callback behavior blocks. Here, the function *Timer.schedule*(TimeTask)* is used to set a task, and the task will be finished by executing callback interface *TimeTask.run()*. We record the parameter *TimeTask* to build the execution dependencies of Timer events. Moreover, when the same task is executed multiple times, we directly associate these callback blocks based on their execution order.

User Interface. When apps are executed, numerous callback behavior blocks are also generated by user interface events such as screen update and button click. There exist execution dependencies between different UI behaviors. However, according to our understanding of the repackaged malware, their malicious behaviors are more likely to be executed in the background than to simultaneously relate multiple UI events. In this paper, we do not build the execution dependencies between UI events, and every UI event is a start node in the execution dependency graph.

4   Malware Detection

When the execution dependency graph is constructed, the execution logic of malware is clearly presented and execution behaviors of malware are split into a series of behavior sequences triggered by different events. Based on these event behavior sequences, we further locate and analyze those behaviors which are generated by the malicious payloads. In our approach, the basic element of event behavior sequences is the system interface call behavior. The main reason is that those system interface call behaviors are not easy to be changed and contain the information of other functions. Moreover, collecting them, rather than all function call behaviors, can reduce the overhead of execution sandbox dramatically.

4.1   Malware Common Behaviors Extraction

If two samples are from the same repackaged malware family, they should have similar malicious behaviors. Correspondingly, if many common behaviors or some dangerous behavior patterns are simultaneously found in two event sequences of different malware samples, these common behaviors may be generated by malicious payloads in a high probability. In this step, we use longest common sequence (LCS) algorithm to extract malicious behaviors. The complexity of LCS is $O(n * m)$, where n and m denote the length of the two compared sequences respectively. To ensure our approach is efficient, two optimizations are designed to reduce the length of behavior sequences. We introduce them as follows.

Loop Shrinkage. After observing behaviors of some samples, we find that massive redundant behaviors are generated by the loop structure and they account for a large proportion of the whole behavior sequences. These repeated behaviors excessively increase the complexity of our analysis and hide key behaviors. Therefore, before analysis, we combine repeated short sequences into one. For instance, the behavior sequence "ABCBCBCD" is converted into "ABCD".

Non-Critical Behavior Exclusion. Our goal is to analyze and detect Android malware, so some non-critical behaviors can be excluded to reduce the length of behavior sequences. Firstly, we execute and analyze some benign samples. If a function behavior is found in many benign samples, it may be not so important. Thus, we count and exclude those behaviors which occurs in more than a half of benign samples. To avoid that some critical behaviors such as permission-related functions are filtered, we manually check all excluded behaviors. Secondly, when malware samples are executed, we also exclude some their behaviors, which are invoked frequently but not critical in functional sense, such as UI behaviors with package name "Landroid/graphics".

After the two optimizations, the size of event behavior sequences dramatically decrease and common behaviors between malware from the same family can be efficiently extracted. Thus, we are able to further analyze malware activities, and use these behaviors to detect other suspicious apps.

4.2 Behavior Detection

When common behaviors of malware families are extracted, they can be further used as signatures to detect suspicious apps. The process contains two steps.

Signature Filter. Before detecting suspicious apps, we firstly filter some weak signatures and similar signatures. Weak signatures, included in both many malicious and benign apps, can cause a high false positive rate. Some benign apps are used to filter those weak signatures in advance. If any signature is contained in benign samples, it is considered as a weak signature and removed. Moreover, to speed up the detection, if the number of common behaviors of two signatures are more than 90 % of all their behaviors, we only keep one of them.

Behavior Detection. A suspicious malware is regarded as a malware if and only if the following condition is satisfied:

$$\frac{|LCS(sig_i, ts)|}{|sig_i|} > \theta$$

where sig_i denotes a malware signature, ts is the behavior sequence obtained from the suspicious app, $||$ is the length calculator of any behavior sequence and θ is the threshold. To speed up the detection, all behaviors are hashed into 32-bit integers, behaviors of target apps not contained in signatures are excluded, and behavior sequences of target apps are also processed with the loop shrinkage.

5 Implementation

We have implemented the prototype system. An execution sandbox is built to record the behaviors of malware. A python test script is written to automatically execute malware samples. A Java program is developed to reconstruct execution dependency graphs and detect malware.

5.1 Execution Sandbox Construction

Figure 5 presents the basic architecture of our Android execution sandbox. Both key framework-level interface call behaviors for Java app code and part of system call behaviors for native app code are extracted to analyze malware.

Framework-Level Interface Call. At the framework level, we record the information of interface calls, both interfaces in app code (callback) and interfaces in system libraries (behavior). To achieve this, we monitor the interpretation process of instructions *invoke-** in Dalvik virtual machine. If an interface is

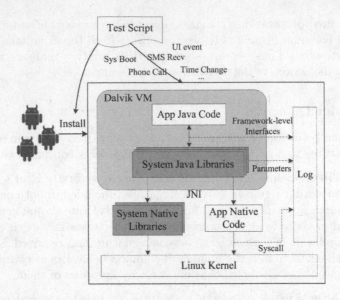

Fig. 5. The basic structure of execution sandbox.

invoked, its detailed information is logged. Similarly, to split callback blocks introduced in Sect. 3, we also obtain the end information of callback interfaces by analyzing the instructions *return-*.

We further explain how to distinguish framework-level interface call behaviors from the other function behaviors in DVM. A function invocation is an interface call behavior, if and only if either its caller function or its callee function belongs to the system libraries and the other is not. In advance, we collect all file signatures of system libraries (DEX format). When a function is invoked in DVM, the file signatures of caller function and callee function can be obtained as $(Method \rightarrow clazz \rightarrow pDvmDex \rightarrow pHeader \rightarrow signature)$. Thus, by comparing file signatures, we locate framework-level interface call behaviors.

Parameter Collection. To construct execution dependency graphs, some important behavior parameters have to be extracted. For simplicity, parameter information is mainly obtained by changing the code of framework-level libraries. For example, we patch our stub code into the system interface *startService(Intent)*, and the stub code will analyze and output the information in *Intent* data.

Java Reflection. When malware invoke their functions based on the Java reflection mechanism, we can only obtain the reflection behavior *Method.invoke()* rather than the real interface call behavior. We restore the behavior information by monitoring DVM interface *Java_lang_reflect_Method_invokeNative()*.

Native Code Behavior. Besides Java code, Android apps may contain a little native code. To analyze behaviors of native code, we also monitor some kernel system calls, carefully selected according to previous studies [12,16]. The source code of Linux kernel is changed to insert our stub code, which logs the selected system call behaviors and their parameters. Moreover, extra system calls are added in the Linux kernel to coordinate the behavior log process and avoid that repeated behaviors are logged at the framework level and Linux kernel.

5.2 Event Trigger

To trigger the behaviors of malware, we write a python script to automatically execute malware in Android emulator. Our script simulates both system events and UI events. For system events, we firstly statically analyze the configuration file *AndroidManifest.xml* of target apps to extract their permission information and registered system events. Based on these information, corresponding commands are generated to simulate system events. For example, system boot event is triggered with the shell command "am broadcast -a android.intent.action.BOOT_COMPLETED". For some special system events such as SMS receiving and updating location, we need to connect Android emulator via Telnet before sending commands. In terms of UI events, we directly generate random UI events with the tool Monkey [4].

Besides events, our script also changes some environment information to cater for malware. For instance, aiming at the delay attack (introduced in Sect. 6), our script frequently changes system time to trigger malware behaviors.

6   Evaluation

In this section, we evaluate our approach with real world repackaged malware.

6.1   Experiment Setup

To evaluate the effectiveness of our approach, 9 families of repackaged malware from Genome Project [3, 25] and 1250 benign apps are executed to extract their behaviors. For each malware family, 3 malware samples are randomly selected to extract malware signatures, which are used to detect the left samples. The benign apps are divided into two parts. 350 out of them are randomly chosen to filter weak signatures, and the other 900 apps are used to evaluate the false positive rate of our approach.

In the experiment, we construct execution sandbox with a low version of Android OS (2.3.4) to ensure that malware are executed correctly and demonstrate their malicious behaviors. It should be noticed that there is no problem to construct execution environment based on a higher version of Android source code. All experiments are conducted on a PC test machine equipped with Intel(R) Core(TM) i3 CPU, 6 GB of physical memory, and running the operating system of Ubuntu 14.04(64 bit).

6.2 Experiment Results

Table 2 shows the malware detection results under condition $\theta = 0.85$, where threshold θ is described in Sect. 4. We count the number of false negative (FN) and the number of false positive (FP) for every malware family, where an FN denotes that an app is a malware but our approach fails to report it and an FP denotes that an app is not a malware but it is labeled erroneously. Based on FP and FN, we further compute precision, recall rate and accuracy as follows.

$$Precision = \frac{MN - FN}{MN - FN + FP}$$

$$Recall = \frac{MN - FN}{MN}$$

$$Accracy = \frac{MN - FN + BN - FP}{MN + BN}$$

where MN is the number of evaluated malware samples and BN is the number of evaluated benign apps.

Table 2. The results of detecting repackaged malware under the condition $\theta = 0.85$.

Family	Malware number	FN	FP	Precision	Recall	Accuracy
ADRD	18	2	2	88.9%	88.9%	99.6%
AnserverBot	183	1	3	98.4%	99.5%	99.6%
BaseBridge	113	14	0	100%	87.6%	98.6%
DroidDream	13	1	5	70.6%	92.3%	99.3%
DroidKungFu3	200	3	5	97.5%	98.5%	99.3%
DroidKungFu4	89	15	0	100%	83.1%	98.5%
Geinimi	60	0	6	90.1%	100%	99.4%
GoldDream	41	0	3	93.2%	100%	99.7%
Pjapps	53	1	0	100%	98.1%	99.9%
In Total	770	37	24	96.8%	95.2%	96.3%

Taking DroidKungFu3 as an example, 3 out of 200 malware cannot be detected (FN = 3) and 5 out of 900 benign apps are erroneously labeled (FP = 5). So, the precision for detecting DroidKungFu3 is $(200-3)/(200-3+5) = 97.5\%$, recall rate is 98.5% and accuracy is 99.3%. In total, 37 out of 770 malware samples and 24 out of 900 benign apps are not detected correctly. The overall precision is 96.8%, recall rate is 95.2% and accuracy is 96.3%.

We further study some samples which are detected erroneously. False negatives are generated mainly because of two factors. Firstly, there exist multiple variants in some malware families such as BaseBridge. For each family, we only randomly select 3 malware samples to extract their behavior signatures. To deal with variants, more samples may be needed. Secondly, malicious behaviors of some malware may be not triggered completely, which will be discussed in the latter section. While for reducing the false positive rate, more benign samples can be used to filter weak signatures. However, a trade-off has to be made sometimes because some behaviors may really occur in both malicious and benign apps. Over-filter may lead to a high false negative rate.

Detection of Encrypted Malware. To verify the effectiveness of our approach for detecting encrypted malware, we also encrypt the code of several malware with the tool DexProtector [2]. Table 3 shows the results of detecting encrypted malware. For comparison, four families of encrypted malware are detected by both our approach and multiple famous antivirus softwares with static techniques (AVG, Norton, Kaspersky and Avast). When these malware are not encrypted, they can be correctly detected by the antivirus softwares. However, the antivirus softwares fail to detect those encrypted versions. Although AVG gives a report, it regards the encrypted malware as Adware erroneously.

Table 3. Detection results of encrypted malware.

Family	AVG	Norton	Kaspersky	Avast	Ours
KungFu3	×	×	×	×	√
Geinimi	×	×	×	×	√
Pjapps	×	×	×	×	√
GoldDream	×	×	×	×	√

From the table, all encrypted malware can be detected by our approach. There are also some exceptions during the experiments. We find that when malware are encrypted, some execution processes of samples crash and their malicious behaviors can not be extracted. This is not the problem of our approach.

6.3   Behavior Analysis

We use some real examples to explain our analysis and describe delay attacks found in our analysis.

Case Study 1: Behaviors of Pjapps malware. In the first case, we present the concrete analysis results for a Pjapps malware. Figure 6 shows its execution dependency graph, automatically drawn by the tool Graphviz [10]. Because the whole graph is very large, only part of it is presented. After comparing the behaviors of two Pjapps instances, we locate their malicious behavior sequences triggered by the event *android.intent.action.SIG_STR*. When the malware receives system event *SIG_STR*, it start a new service by invoking function *startService()*. And in the service, new broadcast events are registered and user sensitive information such as device identity are obtained. Finally, the malware connects to the website "http://log.meeego91.com/android" and uploads these information.

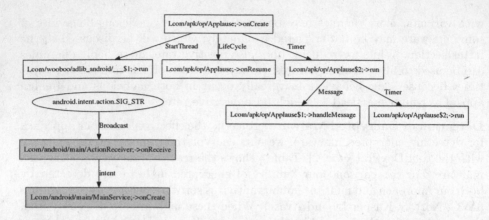

Fig. 6. A segment of the execution dependency graph of a Pjapps sample.

Case Study 2: Delay Attacks. We present delay attacks found in multiple malware families. Under the attack, malware can delay their malicious behaviors. Thus, if malware are not executed in a long time or during some specific time periods, we cannot extract their exact malicious behaviors. Obviously, to analyze more Android apps, it is impossible to allocate too much time for each app. In order to deal with delay attacks, our execution script frequently changes system time to cater for malware. Moreover, the key system delay function $Thread.sleep()$ is also changed to speed up the execution of Android apps. In our experiment, we find this type of attack in multiple malware families such as DroidKungfu, Geinimi and GoldDream.

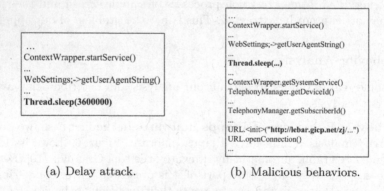

(a) Delay attack.   (b) Malicious behaviors.

Fig. 7. Delay attack in GoldDream.

Figure 7(a) shows an example of delay attack in malware GoldDream, the malware will suppress its malicious thread for 3600000 milliseconds (one hour) with the system function $Thread.sleep()$. To reduce the sleep time, we directly change this system interface. Thus, more malicious behaviors as shown in Fig. 7(b) can be extracted, e.g. sensitive personal information is obtained and uploaded to the host "http://lebar.gicp.net".

6.4 Performance

In our experiment, all malicious and benign samples are executed in the same execution sandbox, and their behaviors are triggered with the same policies. For each sample, about 3–5 min are taken to collect its behaviors. The main difference of execution time is because our script simulates system events according to the different registered information in the manifest files of Android apps. During the execution, we exclude system apps and only log the behavior information of target app to reduce the system overhead.

Table 4 shows the time taken to detect samples. In the first row, the process of malware common behavior extraction contains two parts: constructing execution dependency graphs and comparing malware behaviors with LCS algorithm. In total, 79 s are taken in this process and the average time required by every family is 8.8 s. Secondly, we filter the weak signature with 350 benign samples and the whole process takes 309 s. Finally, 1670 app samples (770 malicious and 900 benign samples) are detected in 313 s.

Table 4. Processing time (seconds) for detecting apps.

Phase	Number	Overall	Average
Common behavior extraction	9 families	79	8.8
Signature filter	9 families	309	34.3
Malware detection	1670 samples	313	0.2

7   Discussion

In this section, we compare our approach with related works and discuss the limitations of our approach.

7.1 Comparison

Compared to static approaches [5,11,17,18,22], our approach can detect those malware protected with code obfuscation techniques such as code encryption, which has been described in the previous section. In the existing dynamic approaches, the work in [13] is also designed to detect the repackaged malware. The previous approach extracts the malicious behaviors by comparing the thread-level system call behavior sequences of repackaged malware. However, our approach pays more attentions on the framework-level interface call behaviors with rich semantics. And we constructs the execution dependency graphs of repackaged malware to decouple the behaviors triggered by different events.

In the experiments, we use less malware samples to extract the malware signatures and our overall detection accuracy is not lower than that of the previous work [13]. Moreover, the previous work manually executes the malware, while our approach is completely automatic. The number of malware samples detected in our experiments is more than 15 times of that of previous work.

7.2 Limitation

Evasion. Our approach locates malicious behaviors by comparing event behavior sequences with LCS algorithm. If there is just a very small piece of malicious behaviors, our approach may be difficult to locate it accurately. Also attackers can split their malicious behaviors into small pieces and then inject them into different event behavior sequences. To deal with this problem, some more complicated features such as behavior dependency graph [22] designed for static analyses can also be referenced in the dynamic analysis. However, these approaches are usually based on statistical methods or machine learning techniques, which require enough malware training samples.

Behavior Trigger. In this paper, we simulates both system events and random UI events to trigger the behaviors of repackaged malware. However, how to automatically and effectively trigger malware behaviors is still one of main difficulties of dynamic approaches. If the behaviors of malicious payloads can only triggered by some hidden events such as user login, our approach will fail to detect them. In this aspect, there are some related works such as AppIntent [20]. Based on the symbolic execution technology, AppIntent generates event constraints to guide its dynamic analysis. At present, the low efficiency make it unpractical to use the type technique to automatically execute many apps.

8 Conclusion

We propose a new dynamic approach to analyze and detect Android repackaged malware. In our approach, an execution sandbox is firstly built to extract dynamic behaviors of malware. Then, the execution dependency graph of malware is constructed to decouple different event behaviors. Finally, based on these event behavior sequences, common behaviors of malware from the same family are extracted with the LCS algorithm and further used to detect other suspicious apps. Compared to other related dynamic approaches, our approach is easier to analyze the repackaged malware with less samples. In our experiments, 770 malware and 900 benign apps are detected by our approach, with 96.8 % precision, 95.2 % recall rate and 96.3 % accuracy.

Acknowledgement. This work was supported by National Key Research and Development Plan under Grant No. 2016YFB0800603, National Natural Science Foundation of China (NSFC) under Grant No. 61402477 and No. 61100228, the Strategic Priority Research Program of the Chinese Academy of Sciences under Grant No. XDA06010703.

References

1. App components. http://developer.android.com/guide/components/index.html
2. Dexprotector. https://dexprotector.com/
3. Genome project. http://www.malgenomeproject.org/
4. Monkey. http://developer.android.com/tools/help/monkey.html
5. Aafer, Y., Du, W., Yin, H.: DroidAPIMiner: mining API-level features for robust malware detection in android. In: Zia, T., Zomaya, A., Varadharajan, V., Mao, M. (eds.) SecureComm 2013. LNICST, vol. 127, pp. 86–103. Springer, Heidelberg (2013)
6. Afonso, V.M., de Amorim, M.F., Grégio, A.R.A., Junquera, G.B., de Geus, P.L.: Identifying android malware using dynamically obtained features. J. Comput. Virol. Hacking Tech. **11**(1), 9–17 (2015)
7. Chen, K., Liu, P., Zhang, Y.: Achieving accuracy and scalability simultaneously in detecting application clones on android markets. In: 36th International Conference on Software Engineering, ICSE 2014, Hyderabad, India, 31 May – 07 June 2014, pp. 175–186 (2014)
8. Chen, K., Wang, P., Lee, Y., Wang, X., Zhang, N., Huang, H., Zou, W., Liu, P.: Finding unknown malice in 10 seconds: mass vetting for new threats at the google-play scale. In: 24th USENIX Security Symposium, USENIX Security 2015, Washington, D.C. USA, 12–14 August 2015, pp. 659–674 (2015)
9. Crussell, J., Gibler, C., Chen, H.: Scalable semantics-based detection of similar android applications. In: Proceedings of Esorics, vol. 13. Citeseer (2013)
10. Ellson, J., Gansner, E.R., Koutsofios, L., North, S.C., Woodhull, G.: Graphviz - open source graph drawing tools. In: Mutzel, P., Jünger, M., Leipert, S. (eds.) GD 2001. LNCS, vol. 2265, pp. 483–484. Springer, Heidelberg (2002)
11. Feng, Y., Anand, S., Dillig, I., Aiken, A.: Apposcopy: semantics-based detection of android malware through static analysis. In: Proceedings of the 22nd ACM SIGSOFT International Symposium on Foundations of Software Engineering, (FSE-22), Hong Kong, China, 16–22 November 2014, pp. 576–587 (2014)
12. Isohara, T., Takemori, K., Kubota, A.: Kernel-based behavior analysis for android malware detection. In: Seventh International Conference on Computational Intelligence and Security, CIS 2011, Sanya, Hainan, China, 3–4 December 2011, pp. 1011–1015 (2011)
13. Lin, Y., Lai, Y., Chen, C., Tsai, H.: Identifying android malicious repackaged applications by thread-grained system call sequences. Comput. Secur. **39**, 340–350 (2013)
14. Rastogi, V., Chen, Y., Jiang, X.: Droidchameleon: evaluating android anti-malware against transformation attacks. In: 8th ACM Symposium on Information, Computer and Communications Security, ASIA CCS 2013, Hangzhou, China, 08–10 May 2013, pp. 329–334 (2013)
15. Shabtai, A., Kanonov, U., Elovici, Y., Glezer, C., Weiss, Y.: "Andromaly": a behavioral malware detection framework for android devices. J. Intell. Inf. Syst. **38**(1), 161–190 (2012)
16. Su, X., Chuah, M., Tan, G.: Smartphone dual defense protection framework: detecting malicious applications in android markets. In: 8th International Conference on Mobile Ad-hoc and Sensor Networks, MSN 2012, Chengdu, China, 14–16 December 2012, pp. 153–160 (2012)

17. Yang, C., Xu, Z., Gu, G., Yegneswaran, V., Porras, P.: DroidMiner: automated mining and characterization of fine-grained malicious behaviors in android applications. In: Kutyłowski, M., Vaidya, J. (eds.) ICAIS 2014, Part I. LNCS, vol. 8712, pp. 163–182. Springer, Heidelberg (2014)

18. Yang, W., Xiao, X., Andow, B., Li, S., Xie, T., Enck, W.: Appcontext: differentiating malicious and benign mobile app behaviors using context. In: 37th IEEE/ACM International Conference on Software Engineering, ICSE 2015, Florence, Italy, 16–24 May 2015, vol. 1, pp. 303–313 (2015)

19. Yang, W., Li, J., Zhang, Y., Li, Y., Shu, J., Gu, D.: Apklancet: tumor payload diagnosis and purification for android applications. In: 9th ACM Symposium on Information, Computer and Communications Security, ASIA CCS 2014, Kyoto, Japan, 03–06 June 2014, pp. 483–494 (2014)

20. Yang, Z., Yang, M., Zhang, Y., Gu, G., Ning, P., Wang, X.S.: Appintent: analyzing sensitive data transmission in android for privacy leakage detection. In: 2013 ACM SIGSAC Conference on Computer and Communications Security, CCS 2013, Berlin, Germany, 4–8 November 2013, pp. 1043–1054 (2013)

21. Zhang, F., Huang, H., Zhu, S., Wu, D., Liu, P.: Viewdroid: towards obfuscation-resilient mobile application repackaging detection. In: 7th ACM Conference on Security & Privacy in Wireless and Mobile Networks, WiSec 2014, Oxford, United Kingdom, 23–25 July 2014, pp. 25–36 (2014)

22. Zhang, M., Duan, Y., Yin, H., Zhao, Z.: Semantics-aware android malware classification using weighted contextual API dependency graphs. In: Proceedings of the 2014 ACM SIGSAC Conference on Computer and Communications Security, Scottsdale, AZ, USA, 3–7 November 2014, pp. 1105–1116 (2014)

23. Zhou, W., Zhou, Y., Grace, M.C., Jiang, X., Zou, S.: Fast, scalable detection of "piggybacked" mobile applications. In: Third ACM Conference on Data and Application Security and Privacy, CODASPY 2013, San Antonio, TX, USA, 18–20 February 2013, pp. 185–196 (2013)

24. Zhou, W., Zhou, Y., Jiang, X., Ning, P.: Detecting repackaged smartphone applications in third-party android marketplaces. In: Second ACM Conference on Data and Application Security and Privacy, CODASPY 2012, San Antonio, TX, USA, 7–9 February 2012, pp. 317–326 (2012)

25. Zhou, Y., Jiang, X.: Dissecting android malware: characterization and evolution. In: IEEE Symposium on Security and Privacy, SP 2012, San Francisco, California, USA, 21–23 May 2012, pp. 95–109 (2012)

Hybrid Risk Assessment Model Based on Bayesian Networks

François-Xavier Aguessy[1,2]($\boxtimes$), Olivier Bettan[1], Gregory Blanc[2],
Vania Conan[1], and Hervé Debar[2]

[1] Thales, 4 avenue des Louvresses, 92622 Gennevilliers, France
[2] SAMOVAR, Télécom SudParis, Université Paris Saclay,
9 rue Charles Fourier, 91011 Évry, France
francois-xavier.aguessy@telecom-sudparis.eu

Abstract. Because of the threat posed by advanced multi-step attacks, it is difficult for security operators to fully cover all vulnerabilities when deploying countermeasures. Deploying sensors to monitor attacks exploiting residual vulnerabilities is not sufficient and new tools are needed to assess the risk associated with the security events produced by these sensors. Although attack graphs were proposed to represent known multi-step attacks occurring in an information system, they are not directly suited for dynamic risk assessment. In this paper, we present the Hybrid Risk Assessment Model (HRAM), a Bayesian network-based extension to topological attack graphs, capable of handling topological cycles, making it fit for any information system. This hybrid model is subdivided in two complementary models: (1) Dynamic Risk Correlation Models, correlating a chain of alerts with the knowledge on the system to analyse ongoing attacks and provide the hosts' compromise probabilities, and (2) Future Risk Assessment Models, taking into account existing vulnerabilities and current attack status to assess the most likely future attacks. We validate the performance and accuracy of this model on simulated network topologies and against diverse attack scenarios of realistic size.

1 Introduction

Information systems concentrate invaluable information resources, generally composed of the computers and servers that process the data of an organisation. Given the number and complexity of attacks, security teams need to focus their actions on the most important attacks, in order to select the most appropriate security controls [20]. Importance in our context is related to the risk the attack induces on the missions of the information system. The most impacting attacks are multi-step attacks. A multi-step attack is a complex attack composed of several successive steps. Each step may be illegitimate (*e.g.*, the exploitation of a vulnerability in software) or legitimate (*e.g.*, a user with administrators privilege accessing sensitive data). For example, an attacker first subverts a client computer using a spear-phishing email exploiting a vulnerability, then attacks the

© Springer International Publishing Switzerland 2016
K. Ogawa and K. Yoshioka (Eds.): IWSEC 2016, LNCS 9836, pp. 21–40, 2016.
DOI: 10.1007/978-3-319-44524-3_2

Active Directory to get administrator privileges, and, thanks to this privilege, accesses a database server that contains sensitive data.

In order to defend against complex attacks, we need to model them and assess associated risks. But risk assessment, and in particular dynamic risk assessment (*i.e.*, regular update of risk assessment in operational time, according to the occurring attacks) is not easy. Several models have been proposed in the literature to formalise multi-step attacks, mainly tree- or graph-based models. An attack graph, for example, is a risk analysis model grouping all the paths an attacker may follow in an information system. Several tools to generate attack graphs exist. Their use is attractive because they leverage already available information (vulnerability scans and network topology). However, attack graphs are static and do not contain detections or attack status and thus are not fitted for dynamic risk assessment. Several extensions of static risk assessment models have been proposed in the literature to accommodate dynamic risk assessment, but they suffer from common limitations, such as existing cycles.

According to the National Information Assurance Glossary [18], a risk is "*a measure of the extent to which an entity is threatened by a potential circumstance or event, and typically a function of (1) the adverse impacts that would arise if the circumstance or event occurs; and (2) the likelihood of occurrence*". As a result, the risk is generally considered in Information Security Management Systems (ISMS) as the combination of the likelihood of the exploitation of vulnerabilities and their impact on the system. Determining the risk in a system is the result of a 5-step process detailed by the National Institute of Standards and Technology (NIST) in [19], as shown in Fig. 1. In this process, the step (2.c) is the determination of the likelihood of occurrence of the attacks. It takes as input the potential threat sources and the vulnerabilities and attack predisposing conditions. Once the likelihood of attacks has been assessed, the next step is to determine their magnitude of impact. Finally, from likelihood and impact, we can compute the risk. In order to make risk assessment dynamic, the process

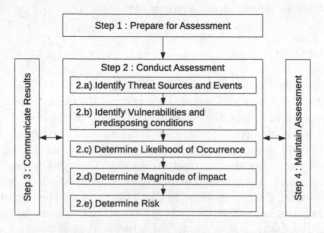

Fig. 1. Risk assessment process [19]

is maintained over time and its results have to be communicated regularly to security management operators.

At an organisational level, several methods help to analyse the risk of information systems and keep those systems secure. For example, ISO/IEC 27000 [10] is the ISMS Family of Standards providing recommendations on security, risk and control in an information system. In particular, ISO/IEC 27005 [9] describes a methodology to manage the risks and implement an ISMS. Another well-known method for the analysis of risks in information systems is EBIOS (Expression of Needs and Identification of Security Objectives) [5]. These standards present global methodologies to manage risks in organisations. They generally combine (1) technical tools (*e.g.*, vulnerability scanner) to assess, for example, the vulnerabilities and the likelihood of attacks and (2) organisational methodologies (*e.g.*, stakeholder interviews) to identify the critical assets and consequences of successful attacks.

The technical tools for dynamic risk assessment usually do not include a model to detect the occurring multi-step attacks and assess their likely futures. In this paper, we build such a model that aims at assessing the risk brought by the exploitation of technical vulnerabilities in a system. This model mostly focuses on the step (2.c) of the NIST's risk assessment process of Fig. 1: the determination of the likelihood of occurrence of attacks. Indeed, methodologies to estimate attacks likelihood do not depend on the system in which they are implemented, contrary to the impact assessment which may require adaptation for the target organisation. Thus, in our experimentations, we evaluate our risk model only by its likelihood results, by assuming that all compromised assets induce the same impact.

The model we propose in this paper is a new hybrid model combining attack graphs and Bayesian networks for dynamic risk assessment (DRA). This model is subdivided into two complementary models: (1) The Dynamic Risk Correlation Models (DRCMs) correlate a chain of alerts with the knowledge on the system to analyse ongoing attacks and provide the probabilities of hosts being compromised, (2) The Future Risk Assessment Models (FRAMs) take into account existing vulnerabilities and the current attack status to assess which potential attacks are most likely to occur. DRCMs aim at threat likelihood assessment, identifying where the attack comes from. It outputs probabilities that attacks are completed and that assets of the information system are compromised. These probabilities provide security operators with the capability to manage priorities according to the likelihood of ongoing attacks. FRAMs aim at threat mitigation, identifying the most likely and impacting next steps for the attacker. With respect to the current state of the art, our contributions are twofold. First, we provide an explicit model for DRA and a process for handling cycles. Second, our model provides a significant performance improvement in terms of number of nodes and vulnerabilities over the existing state of the art, enabling scalability. While classic Bayesian attack graph models are usually demonstrated over a few nodes, we show that our model can be realistically computed at the scale of an enterprise information system.

This paper is organised as follows: Sect. 2 presents the state of the art of the multi-step attack models. Section 3 presents topological attack graphs and expose the problem of cycles. Then, it presents the architecture of the Hybrid Risk Assessment Model, composed of DRCMs and FRAMs. Section 4 validates the design of the hybrid model on simulated topologies. Section 5 compares our work with the related work, before concluding and presenting our future work, in Sect. 6.

2   State of the Art

Initially proposed for risk analysis, attack graphs have been extended as Bayesian attack graphs, to include ongoing attacks probability information, which is required for dynamic risk assessment.

2.1   Attack Graphs

An attack graph is a model regrouping all the paths an attacker may follow in an information system. It has been first introduced by Phillips and Swiler in [24]. A study of the state of the art about attack graphs compiled from early literature on the subject has been carried out by Lippmann and Ingols [16], while a more recent one was made available by Kordy et al. [14]. Topological attack graphs are based on directed graphs. Their nodes are topological assets (hosts, IP addresses, etc.) and their edges represent possible attack steps between such nodes [11]. Attack graphs are generated with attack graph engines. There are three main attack graph engines: (1) *MulVAL*, the Multi-host, Multi-stage Vulnerability Analysis Language tool created by Ou et al. [21], (2) the Topological Vulnerability Analysis tool (*TVA*) presented by Jajodia *et al.* in [11,12] (commercialised under the name *Cauldron*) and (3) Artz's *NetSPA* [2].

Attack graphs are attractive because they leverage readily available information (vulnerability scans and network topology). However, they are not adapted for ongoing attacks, because they cannot represent the progression of an attacker nor be triggered by alerts. Thus, they must be enriched to provide the functionalities needed to perform dynamic risk assessment, for example using Bayesian networks.

2.2   Bayesian Attack Graphs

A Bayesian network is a probabilistic graphical model introduced by Judea Pearl [22]. It is based on a Directed Acyclic Graph, where nodes represent random variables, and edges represent probabilistic dependencies between variables [3]. For discrete random variables, these dependencies can be specified using a Conditional Probability Table associated with each child node. Bayesian networks are particularly interesting for computing inference, *i.e.* calculating the probability of each state of all nodes of the network, given evidences, *i.e.* nodes that have been set to a specific state. In the general case, exact inference is a NP-hard problem and can be done efficiently only on small networks, using the algorithm of Lauritzen and Spiegelhalter [15]. However, if the structure of the graph is a polytree, it can be done in quasi-linear time, using Pearl's Belief Propagation Algorithm [23].

A Bayesian attack graph, introduced by Liu and Man in [17] is an extension of an attack graph based on a Bayesian network, constituted of nodes representing a host in a specific system state (a true state means that the host is compromised) and edges representing possible exploits that can be instantiated from a source host to a target host. The major concern of building such a Bayesian network from an attack graph is due to the structure of a Bayesian network that must be acyclic, while attack graphs almost always contain cycles. To avoid cycles, Liu and Man assume that an attacker will never backtrack once reaching a compromised state, but do not detail how such assumption is used to build the model. In [7], Frigault and Wang use Bayesian inference in Bayesian Attack Graphs to calculate security metrics in an information system. Xie *et al.* present in [27] a Bayesian network used to model the uncertainty of occurring attacks. The Bayesian attack graph is enhanced with three new properties: separation of the types of uncertainty, automatic computation of its parameters and insensitivity to perturbations in the parameters choice. This model also adds nodes dedicated to dynamic security modelling: an *attack action node* models whether or not an action of the attacker has been performed, a *local observation node* models inaccurate observations (IDS alerts, logs, etc.). In [4], Cole uses a Credal network (a Bayesian network with imprecise probabilities) to represent parameters uncertainty and detect attack paths. He demonstrates that the uncertainty is too high for single-step attacks, but for multi-step attacks, it is possible to achieve high confidence in the detections. However, the computational costs of inferences in a Credal network are prohibitive to use it with real network topologies.

Bayesian networks add to the advantages of direct acyclic graphs powerful tools to compute and propagate probabilities between nodes of the graph. Moreover, the dependencies between nodes are not AND or OR relations anymore, but are probabilities of occurrence with a set of predecessors, which is much more expressive. It is thus a very interesting model for dynamic risk assessment. However, two important problems arise when we want to use Bayesian networks for modelling ongoing multi-step attacks: (1) performance, as the inference in a Bayesian network can be very complex, and (2) a Bayesian network must be based on an acyclic graph, which is generally not the case of attack graphs. Heuristics allow to suppress cycles, but they also suppress paths that could be followed by an attacker.

3   Hybrid Risk Assessment Model

Given the advantages brought by Bayesian Attack Graphs (expressiveness, dynamicity, powerful probability propagation tools), they provide a strong foundation for dynamic security modelling. Our proposal extends Bayesian Networks to be used for DRA with real-scale information systems.

3.1   Topological Attack Graph

We will first present the main input from which we build the HRAM: a topological attack graph. A *topological attack graph* (TAG) is a directed graph consisting of *topological assets*, the nodes representing the assets of an information system (*e.g.*, an IP address or a computer cluster), and *attack steps*, the edges representing an attack from the parent topological asset to the child one. A TAG is generated with an attack graph engine such as MulVAL [21] or TVA [12] from a vulnerability scan and a flow matrix. Each attack step features a *type* of attack, describing how the attacker can move between nodes (*e.g.*, exploitation of a vulnerability, credential theft). Depending on the type of attack, each attack step is associated with a set of *conditions*. A condition is a fact that needs to be verified, for an attack step to be possible (*e.g.*, "a vulnerability is exploited on the destination host"). It is associated with a *probability of successful exploitation*. For vulnerability exploitation conditions, in our experiments, we use an approximation of the probability of successful exploitation using information coming from the Exploitability Metrics of the Common Vulnerability Scoring System (CVSS) [6]. It is deduced from (1) the Attack Complexity (AC), (2) Privileges Required (PR), and (3) User Interaction (UI) values, as well as the Attack Vector (AV), which is taken into account when constructing the topological attack graph. Some attack steps and topological assets are associated with a *sensor*, an oracle raising an alert when the attack step has been detected as completed or the topological asset has been detected as compromised. A sensor represents, for example, a Host or a Network Intrusion Detection System, a Security Information and Event Management system, or a human report.

3.2   Solution to the Cycle Problem

A TAG is a directed graph model defined globally for a system, containing all potential attacks that may happen. It does not contain the position of the attacker and thus almost always contains cycles, for example inside local networks in which any host can attack any other one. A simple example of a cycle is shown in Fig. 2a.

The common assumption to break cycles in attack graphs is that an attacker will not backtrack, *i.e.*, attack again a node he has already successfully exploited. This is reasonable because backtracking does not bring new attack paths. It has been properly justified by Ammann *et al.* in [1] and by Liu and Man in [17]. However, the state of the art solutions for Bayesian modelling of an attack graph, such as the ones of Liu and Man [17] and Poolsappasit et al. [25], use this assumption to arbitrarily delete possible attack steps. In reality, in a single model containing all potential attacks, it is impossible to delete cycles without adding new nodes. It would require to know a priori which path the attacker will choose. A solution to break cycles while keeping all possible paths is to enumerate them, starting from all possible attack sources, or targeting all possible targets, keeping in nodes a memory of the path of the attacker. Figure 2b shows an example of such a cycle breaking process. In this figure, the node $tn_1tn_2tn_3$ means that

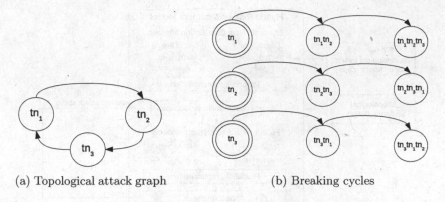

(a) Topological attack graph   (b) Breaking cycles

Fig. 2. Cycles in a topological attack graph

the attacker controls the node tn_3, having first compromised tn_1, then tn_2. We discuss, in Sect. 3.4, how we apply this process for Dynamic Risk Correlation Models and, in Sect. 3.5, for Future Risk Assessment Models. Unfortunately, this process causes a combinatorial explosion in the number of nodes of the model. We also describe in Sects. 3.4 and 3.5 how we deal with this challenge in HRAMs, thanks to pruning functions.

3.3 Hybrid Risk Assessment Model Architecture

Our approach distinguishes two sub-objectives of determining the likelihood of occurrence within dedicated models: Dynamic Risk Correlation Models (DRCMs) and Future Risk Assessment Models (FRAMs), combined to provide a complete Hybrid Risk Assessment Model (HRAM), whose architecture is presented in Fig. 3.

We take as input a TAG generated by an attack graph engine (*e.g.*, MulVAL [21] or TVA [12]). First, we build DRCMs from this TAG and the set of current alerts at time t. The reconciliation of the probabilities given by the several DRCMs gives the current attack status at time t. Then, we build FRAMs which give the likely futures of the system, according to this current status. The combination of these likely futures with an impact analysis results in the risk of the system.

3.4 Dynamic Risk Correlation Model

Building process. The goal of the DRCM is to provide explanations for the alerts that have been raised by intrusion detection sensors. By *explanation*, we mean the identification of the likely source nodes that have been compromised and that have enabled the attacker to launch the detected attack. A DRCM is built from the most recently received alert, the *target*, and explains why this alert has been generated, taking into account past alerts. As soon as a new alert

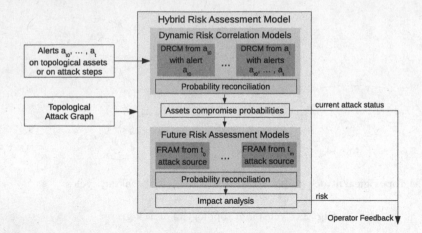

Fig. 3. Hybrid Risk Assessment Model architecture

is received, a new DRCM is built. Older DRCMs are kept in parallel with the newly generated DRCM, to manage scenarios with several distinct simultaneous attacks (*i.e.*, a new alert is not related to older ones). Probabilities of all kept DRCMs are reconciliated.

Following the process described in Sect. 3.2, we construct each DRCM in such a way as not to have any cycles, but to keep all possible attack paths "directed to" the target. The DRCM is built from the latest received alert. Then, we recursively add the attack steps and assets allowing to compromise the target. We store, in each DRCM Topological Asset, the path from this node to the target of the DRCM. This allows to ensure that the building process never comes back on a previously exploited node and thus the DRCM does not have cycles, but contains all possible causes of the latest received alert.

Moreover, we design this building process in order to generate a graph structure of the DRCM which is a polytree (*i.e.*, directed graph with no directed nor undirected cycles). This implies, for example, to duplicate the condition and sensor nodes (*i.e.*, new conditions and sensors for each added attack step). The DRCM being a polytree satisfies the requirements of Pearl's inference algorithm [23], which is quasilinear in the number of nodes. Thus, the inference in such a DRCM with a polytree structure containing duplicated nodes is much more efficient and consume less memory, in comparison with a directed acyclic graph structure with fewer nodes (no duplicates), for identical results.

Model nodes. A DRCM is a Bayesian network with 5 types of nodes. Each one represents a Boolean random variable and is associated with a conditional probability table (CPT), representing its probabilistic dependency toward its parents.

– A *DRCM Topological Asset* represents the random variable describing the status of compromise of a specific asset of the TAG, in order to exploit the DRCM

Target. It has one parent (DRCM Attack Step) of each type of attack that can be used to compromise it (*i.e.*, there may be as many parent nodes as there are different attack types) and a DRCM Attack Source representing that this node may be a source of attack. Its CPT is a *noisy-OR*: at least one successful attack is needed to compromise this node and it can also be compromised if it is the source of attack itself. Even if no parent is compromised, there is still a little chance that an unknown attack compromises this node.

- A *DRCM Attack Source* represents the random variable describing that a specific asset of the TAG is a source of attack. It is a node without parents. As such, it does not have a complete CPT, but only an a priori probability value. The *a priori* probability of having an attack coming from this asset has to be set by the operators knowing the probability that an attack starts from this threat source.
- A *DRCM Attack Step* represents the random variable describing that an attack step has been completed by an attacker. It has two types of parents: DRCM Conditions, and a DRCM Topological Asset. At a minimum, the DRCM Topological Asset is required, but the exact CPT depends on the type of attack step.
- A *DRCM Condition* represents the random variable describing that the condition of an attack step is verified. It does not have any parent. Its a priori probability is the probability of successful exploitation of the condition.
- A *DRCM Sensor* can either be attached to a DRCM Topological Asset or to a DRCM Attack Step. It represents the random variable describing that the sensor of an attack step or an asset has raised an alert. Its parent is the object monitored by the sensor. Its CPT represents the false-positive and false-negative rates of the sensor. The sensor corresponding to the latest received alert, and from which the DRCM is built, is the *target* of the DRCM.

Figure 4 shows an example of a DRCM built from an alert on host h_1 (the node in dotted line on the left) in a topology of 3 hosts. DRCM Topological Assets are represented by a rectangle shape, DRCM Attack Sources by a five-sided shape, DRCM Attack Steps by a diamond shape, and DRCM Conditions by an oval shape.

Model usage. As shown in Fig. 3, we build the structure of the DRCM according to the TAG, starting from the latest received alert. Then, we set the states of the DRCM Sensors according to the previous security alerts received from the sensors:

- If the sensor of an attack step or an asset exists and is deployed in the network, as long as it has not raised any alert, all related DRCM Sensors are set to the *NoAlert* state.
- If the sensor has raised an alert corresponding to this attack step or asset, the related DRCM Sensors are set to the *Alert* state.
- If the attack step or asset has no deployed sensor, there is *NoInfo* about this sensor. So, the related DRCM Sensors cannot be set in any state and these

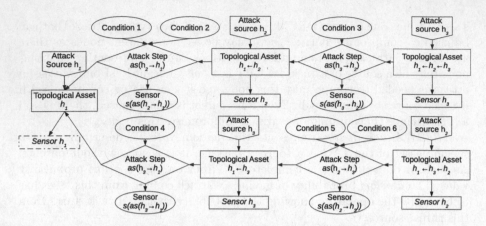

Fig. 4. Dynamic Risk Correlation Model

nodes can be safely deleted from the DRCM, with no impact on other nodes final probabilities.

Then, we use a Bayesian network belief propagation algorithm (*e.g.*, Pearl's) to update the probabilities of each state at all the nodes.

Probability reconciliation within a DRCM. The outputs of a DRCM are of two types: (1) the probabilities of attack sources, describing how likely an asset is to be the source of the attack impacting the target of the DRCM, and (2) the compromise probabilities, describing how likely it is that an asset has been compromised along the path of the attacker.

As a DRCM Topological Asset contains the attack path from its related asset to the target, many DRCM Topological Assets represent the same physical asset. Indeed, the attacker can potentially use several different paths to reach the target: for example, $h_1 \leftarrow h_2 \leftarrow h_4$ is different from $h_1 \leftarrow h_3 \leftarrow h_4$, but in both cases, the attacker starts from the same asset h_4 to attack the target h_1. In a DRCM $DRCM_i$, we thus have many DRCM Topological Assets and DRCM Attack Sources representing the same asset a. We chose to give the operator the worst case for compromise probability of assets. Thus, as output of a DRCM, we assign to an asset:

– a probability of compromise Pc that is the maximum of the probabilities of DRCM Topological Assets related to this asset:

$$Pc_{DRCM_i}(a) = max_{node \in \{\text{DRCM Topological Assets}(a)\}} Pc_{DRCM_i}(node)$$

– an attack source probability Ps that is the maximum of the probabilities of DRCM Attack Sources related to this asset:

$$Ps_{DRCM_i}(a) = max_{node \in \{\text{DRCM Attack Source}(a)\}} Ps_{DRCM_i}(node)$$

Probability reconciliation between DRCMs. As described at the beginning of Sect. 3.4, several older DRCMs are kept in parallel with the new ones generated each time a new alert is received. They can be related to different simultaneous attacks. These DRCMs $DRCM_i$ give different sources and compromise probabilities for the same asset a. Thus, the second level of probability reconciliation is done between all kept DRCMs. Similarly to the single DRCM case, we want to present the operator with a view of the worst case, and assign to an asset a a probability of compromise $Pc(a)$ and an attack source probability $Ps(a)$ that is the maximum of the related probabilities in all the DRCMs:

$$Pc(a) = max_{DRCM_i \in \{\text{kept DRCMs}\}} Pc_{DRCM_i}(a)$$

$$Ps(a) = max_{DRCM_i \in \{\text{kept DRCMs}\}} Ps_{DRCM_i}(a)$$

Pruning in a DRCM. The main limitation when implementing the DRCM is the combinatorial explosion of the number of nodes, due to the cycle breaking process. This process introduces a lot of redundancy which increases significantly the size of the model. In order to improve the performance and prevent this combinatorial explosion, we provide a practical way to cut useless paths (with extremely low probabilities) while preserving the other paths.

The probability of a DRCM Topological Asset represents the probability of the attacker having exploited the DRCM target, *by exploiting this topological asset*. As long as no attack has been detected on a path, the probability of an asset being compromised decreases rapidly as a function of the length of the path between the DRCM Topological Asset and the DRCM Target. Moreover, thanks to the several DRCMs that are kept, if a detected step is discarded in a DRCM, it will be present in another older DRCM, closer to its detection node, thanks to the redundancy of the model. According to the state of the sensors along a path, we have different pruning policies, summarised in Fig. 5.

The rules applied when building a DRCM are the following:

- We keep exploring and memorising the path from the target asset, as long as we find *Alert* sensors.
- For *NoAlert* sensors, when there are more than *MaxNumberNegativeDetectionsToExplore*, we discard the path and keep only *MaxNumberNegativeDetectionsToKeep* nodes.
- For *NoInfo* sensors, when there are more than *MaxNumberNoInfoToExplore*, we discard the path and keep only *MaxNumberNoInfoToKeep* nodes, but with values for the parameters bigger than for *NoAlert* sensors.
- As soon as an *Alert* sensor is found on an explored path, the counters of *NoAlert* and *NoInfo* are reset to 0.

Thus, the parameter *MaxNumberNegativeDetectionsToExplore* corresponds to the maximum number of successive false-negatives (missed detections) that we allow the model to take into account. The parameter *MaxNumberNoInfoToKeep* corresponds to the maximum number of successive undetectable steps that we allow the model to take into account.

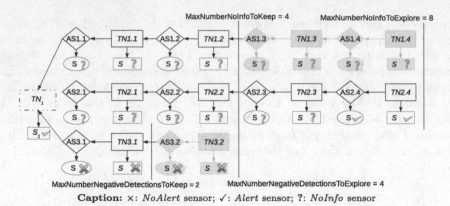

Caption: ×: *NoAlert* sensor; ✓: *Alert* sensor; ?: *NoInfo* sensor

Fig. 5. Pruning policies in Dynamic Risk Correlation Model

Selection of the DRCMs to keep. The last important thing about this model is the selection of the DRCMs to keep. Indeed, as one new DRCM is generated each time an alert is received, the number of models to keep can increase quickly. However, when several alerts are part of the same attack, they will be part of the DRCM whose target is the sensor that raised the latest alert. Moreover, there will be more *Alert* sensors in this DRCM (increasing probabilities of all nodes of the DRCM), and at most the same number of *NoAlert* sensors (decreasing probabilities) than in all previous DRCMs related to the same attack. Thus, all the previous DRCMs related to the same attack are useless, because they are included in the last generated DRCM and their probabilities will be lower so they do not change the maximum of asset compromise probabilities. The only different DRCMs that are useful to keep are those not related to the same attacks because they bring new information about the occurring attacks. They can be identified by having at least one DRCM Topological Asset, with a higher probability than all the ones of the latest DRCM, for the same asset. These attacks could be part of a more global attack scenario, starting from different sources, that has not yet converged or it might be distinct attacks that are happening simultaneously. That is why we may need to keep several DRCMs in parallel.

3.5   Future Risk Assessment Model

Building process and model usage. The second type of model constituting the HRAM is the Future Risk Assessment Model (FRAM). The goal of such model is to evaluate among all possible futures, the ones that are the most likely to happen. As indicated by Fig. 3, a FRAM is built from each attack source, according to the DRCMs' reconciled compromise probabilities. Then, we use a belief propagation algorithm to update the probabilities of all the nodes. When there is a completed attack step or a compromised asset, a FRAM taking this node as starting point is built or updated and the branches from this attack step are deleted in all other FRAMs. Indeed, this attack is no longer a possible future, as it has happened and will be investigated in its own FRAM. Even if the structure of a FRAM does not change with detections, its probabilities of conditions and attack sources can be updated. For example, the condition probability of a vulnerability that has already been exploited is set to "1".

The way FRAMs are built and cycles solved is identical to the DRCMs, starting from an attack source rather than from a target. See Sects. 3.2 and 3.4 for more details.

Model nodes. A FRAM is a Bayesian Network with 5 types of nodes, each one representing a Boolean random variable. Each node is associated with a conditional probability table (CPT), representing its probabilistic dependency toward its parents.

- A *FRAM Topological Asset* represents the random variable describing the future status of compromise of an asset of the TAG. Its CPT is the same as DRCM Topological Assets without the DRCM Attack Source parent.
- The *FRAM Attack Source* represents the random variable describing that an asset is the source of attack. It is the root of the FRAM. It does not have any parent and its a priori probability is provided by the reconciliation of probability of DRCMs.
- A *FRAM Attack Step* represents the random variable describing that an attack step can be successfully exploited by an attacker. Its CPT is the same as DRCM Attack Steps.
- A *FRAM Condition* represents the random variable describing that the condition of an attack step is verified. Its a priori probability is the same as DRCM Conditions.

Figure 6 shows an example of a Future Risk Assessment Model starting from host h_1 in a topology of 3 hosts. The FRAM Attack Source is represented by a five-sided shape, FRAM Topological Assets by a rectangle shape, FRAM Attack Steps by a diamond shape, and FRAM Conditions by an oval shape.

Probability reconciliation in FRAMs. Similarly to the DRCM, several FRAM Topological Assets can represent the same topological asset, when an attacker can use several paths. We chose to give to the operator the worst case, for the probability of the assets being compromised in the near future, just like in DRCMs. Thus, as output of a FRAM, we assign to an asset a probability of compromise in the future that is the maximum of the probabilities of FRAM Topological Assets targeting the same asset.

Pruning in a FRAM. As a FRAM does not include any evidence (*i.e.*, it does not contain sensor nodes which are set in a specific state), the Bayesian inference is much easier to compute. Moreover, it has fewer nodes than a DRCM, thus its combinatorial explosion of nodes is not as important. However, the combinatorial explosion of the number of nodes, due to the cycle breaking process is still

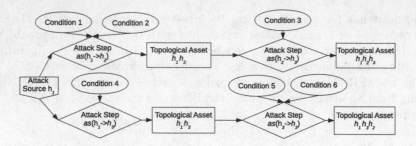

Fig. 6. Future Risk Assessment Model

present. If they are not built carefully, there is a lot of useless redundancy in all FRAMs, which increases significantly the size of the model. A major part of this redundancy can be deleted when building a new FRAM, by deleting all the paths started from all sources of other FRAMs. All these subtrees can be deleted safely, as their probabilities will be less than the probabilities of the FRAM started from the attack source. Moreover, as we only want to predict the near future, we can limit to a small number of steps (*e.g.*, 3) the next steps to compute.

3.6   Impact Analysis

The last component necessary to build our Hybrid Risk Assessment Model is the impact analysis function. The goal of this function is to take the assets of the information systems with their compromise likelihood computed by the FRAMs and an impact score associated with each asset to give a risk score to assets. We apply the usual equation to compute the risk R of a topological asset a, with the probability of compromise P of the asset computed by the FRAMs, and the impact I of its compromise:

$$R(a) = P(a) \times I(a)$$

In this work we focus on the likelihood computation ($P(a)$), whose methodology is independent of the system studied, whereas the impact analysis ($I(a)$) strongly depends on the organisation. Thus, we only associated with each asset a fixed impact score. Moreover, in order to validate the probabilistic results of the model, we assign to each asset the same impact value ($I(a) = 1, \forall a$) for the validation.

4   Validation

As a use case, to validate the performances and the results of the HRAM, we simulate network topologies, as shown in Fig. 7a, containing up to 120 hosts, divided in 7 subnets. These topologies are representative of a real network in

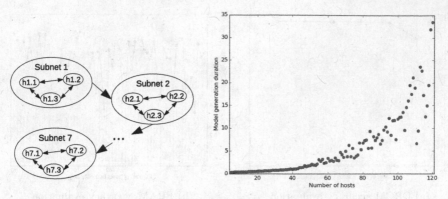

(a) Simulations network topology   (b) HRAM performance evaluation (seconds)

Fig. 7. Simulations of the Hybrid Risk Assessment Model

which defence in depth is implemented: all the hosts of a subnet have access to all the hosts of a deeper subnet. In each subnet, all accesses between hosts are authorised. Each host has 30 random vulnerabilities for a maximum total of around 3600 vulnerabilities.

4.1 Performances

To evaluate the performances of the model, we first generate the topological attack graphs of the simulated topologies. Then, for each simulation, we generate one random attack scenario of 7 successive attack steps, to which are added false positives and steps with no sensor information. Finally, we evaluate the HRAM.

Figure 7b shows the duration in seconds of the generation of the HRAM (TAG generation then DRCM and FRAM) on such topologies, with one scenario of 7 attack steps. This simulation shows that for medium-sized topologies (up to 120 hosts) the duration of the HRAM analysis is sufficiently small (< 35 s), for the operator to be able to properly understand the risk in operational time.

This could be extended to bigger information systems, by clustering together identical (in terms of vulnerabilities, roles, permissions, network accesses, *etc.*) templates of servers or of client machines in one topological asset, as they possess the same vulnerabilities and authorised accesses and thus behave in a similar way in the HRAM. Even with 60 assets in the topological attack graph with, for example, 20 templates of client machines, 15 of network servers, and 25 of business application servers, it is possible to model a real world large company information system.

4.2 Accuracy

To evaluate the accuracy of the results of the DRCMs (*i.e.*, how close the compromise probabilities are from the truth), we simulate attack scenarios of up to

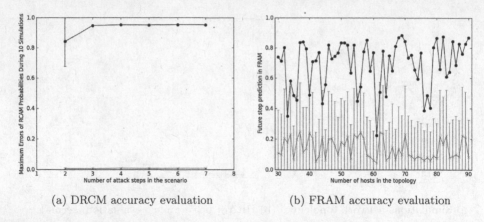

(a) DRCM accuracy evaluation   (b) FRAM accuracy evaluation

Fig. 8. Accuracy of the Hybrid Risk Assessment Model

7 successive steps on random topologies of 70 hosts, as presented in Sect. 4.1 (results are identical from 10 up to 120 hosts). We add to the 7 true positive alerts of these scenarios, 10 randomly located false positives and 10 sensors with no information (*i.e.*, a positive predictive value of $PPV = \frac{7}{7+10} \approx 0.4$).

The results of these simulations are shown in Fig. 8a. For each simulated scenario, we compare the theoretical results known in the scenarios with the results obtained as output of the DRCM started from the lastly raised alert. In the plot of Fig. 8a, the black curve on the top represents the compromise probabilities, with a confidence interval, during 10 simulations, of the hosts known as compromised in the scenarios, according to the number of attack steps in the scenario. The theoretical result would be a line with only "1" probabilities. The grey curve at the bottom represents the compromise probabilities, with a confidence interval, during 10 simulations, of the hosts known as healthy, according to the number of attack steps in the scenario. The theoretical result would be a line with only "0" probabilities. Note that after 3 attack steps in the scenario for the compromised hosts, and for all values for not compromised hosts, the confidence interval is so small that it cannot be noticed on the figure.

This experimentation shows that the greater the number of attack steps in the scenario, the larger the recognition probability and the smaller the confidence interval. Moreover, it shows a large free space between the curve of compromised hosts and the curve of healthy hosts. This means that there are no false negative and false positive introduced by the DRCM. Finally, even if there are false-positives and sensors without information, compared to the number of successive attack steps (up to 7), we retrieve only the real attack elements, thanks to our model built from the latest received alert and taking into account the order and relations between attack steps.

We use the same simulated topologies to evaluate the accuracy of the results of the FRAMs (*i.e.*, how close the possible futures are from the next step of attack). The results of these simulations are shown in Fig. 8b. We compare the next attack step known in each scenario with the results obtained as output of the FRAM started from the previous scenario (with one less attack step). In the plot of Fig. 8b, the black curve on the top represents the future risk probability computed by the FRAM of the future attack step (known in the next attack scenario). The grey curve on the bottom represents the average future risk probabilities, computed by the FRAM, of all other hosts of the topology, with confidence intervals.

This experimentation shows that the FRAM predicts quite well the next step of attack in the simulated scenarios, because its probability is generally much higher than the probabilities of other next steps. However, this is possible because in these simulations, the attacker takes the easiest attack steps (*i.e.*, attacks the most vulnerable machine). The FRAM is thus particularly interesting when few future attack steps are easier than the other possible futures.

5   Related Work

Many people have proposed enhancements to improve attack graphs or trees with Bayesian networks, in order to use them for dynamic risk assessment [17, 26,27]. However, they do not describe accurately how they address cycles that are inherent to attack graphs. For example, in [27], Xie *et al.* present an extension of MulVAL attack graphs, using Bayesian networks, but they do not mention how to manage the cycle problem, while MulVAL attack graphs frequently contain cycles. In the same way, in [7], Frigault and Wang do not mention how they deal with the cycle problem when constructing Bayesian attack graphs. In [17], Liu and Man assert that to delete cycles, they assume that an attacker will never backtrack. Poolsappasit *et al.* in [25] use the same hypothesis. However, as detailed in Sect. 3.2, they do not present how they deal with this hypothesis to keep all possible paths in the graph, while deleting cycles. We propose here novel models exploding cycles in the building process, in order to keep all possible paths, while deleting the cycles, to compute the Bayesian inference. Moreover, we also add several improvements (practical pruning, polytree structure, *etc.*) reducing the size of the graph structure and improving the performance of the inference. We thus constrain the size of the graph in which we do Bayesian inference, while conserving all paths by linearising cycles.

The model presented by Xie et al. [27] and the one of Liu and Man [17] are made of a single model to describe the compromise status of assets of the information system. In a single model, an increase of compromise probability of an asset due to an already happened attack is mixed up with an increase due to a very likely possible future. However, the distinction of these two causes is very valuable for a security operator, for example to select where to deploy a remediation. The hybrid model we propose separates the compromise information of the past alerts from those of the likely futures. It allows a security operator to know if a topological asset has already been compromised (thanks to DRCMs) or if it may be compromised in the near future (FRAMs).

In this work, we focus on the likelihood component of the risk assessment. Thus, we use a simple impact function as output of the FRAMs, matching each compromised topological asset with a fix impact value. Other works of the state of the art rather focus on the impact component. For example, Kheir *et al.* in [13] details how to use a dependency graph to compute the impact of attacks on Confidentiality, Integrity and Availability. This work is complementary to ours as we could add this kind of impact function after the FRAMs to compute a more accurate attack impact.

Models such as [8] use Dynamic Bayesian Networks to monitor and predict the future status of the system. It uses a sequence of Bayesian networks, which can be huge to process. The model we propose here keeps only the past information necessary to explain all alerts and to update the models to evaluate potential futures (FRAMs). Moreover, the building process and exploitation of DRCMs takes into account the temporality of raised alerts to determine attacks. Finally, contrary to other models based on Bayesian attack graphs, our model can distinguish several distinct simultaneous attacks in the alerts raised in a system, by analysing all kept DRCMs.

Our experimental validation uses simulated topologies far bigger than the state of the art. For example, Xie *et al.* assess their model on 3 hosts and 3 vulnerabilities [27], Liu and Man on 4 hosts and 8 vulnerabilities [17]. The real world examples used by Frigault and Wang in [7] contain at most 8 vulnerabilities on 4 hosts. The test network used by Poolsappasit *et al.* in [25] contains 8 hosts in 2 subnets, but with only 13 vulnerabilities. Thanks to our polytree models, we successfully run our HRAM efficiently on simulated topologies with up to 120 hosts for a total of more than 3600 vulnerabilities.

6   Conclusion and Future Work

We present in this paper a new Hybrid Risk Assessment Model, combining the dynamic risk correlation and the future risk assessment analysis. This model enables dynamic risk assessment. It is built from a topological attack graph, using already available information. Dynamic Risk Correlation Models are built according to dynamic security events, to update the compromise probabilities of assets. We use these probabilities to build Future Risk Assessment Models, to compute the most likely futures. This combination of two complementary models separates the compromise status of assets between past attacks and likely futures.

This model handles the cycles in attack graphs and thus is applicable to any information system, with multiple potential attack sources. The cycle breaking process significantly increases the number of nodes in the model, but thanks to the polytree structure of the Bayesian networks we build and practical pruning, the inference remains efficient, for big information systems. In order to be able to use the Hybrid Risk Assessment Model for even bigger information systems, future work will investigate how the usage of a hierarchical topological attack graph can be appropriate to build the Hybrid Risk Assessment Model. Another future work will be to use the ability of Bayesian networks to learn parameters from data, in order to update the values in the Conditional Probability Tables after the confirmation/negation of compromise by the operators.

References

1. Ammann, P., Wijesekera, D., Kaushik, S.: Scalable, graph-based network vulnerability analysis. In: Proceedings of the 9th ACM Conference on Computer and Communications Security, pp. 217–224. ACM (2002)
2. Artz, M.L.: Netspa: a network security planning architecture. Ph.D. thesis, Massachusetts Institute of Technology (2002)
3. Ben-Gal, I., Ruggeri, F., Faltin, F., Kenett, R.: Bayesian networks. In: Encyclopedia of Statistics in Quality and Reliability (2007)
4. Cole, R.: Multi-step attack detection via bayesian modeling under model parameter uncertainty. Ph.D. thesis, The Pennsylvania State University (2013)
5. Secrétariat Général de la Défense Nationale: Ebios-expression des besoins et identification des objectifs de sécurité (2004)
6. Forum of Incident Response and Security Teams: Common vulnerability scoring system v3.0: Specification document, pp. 1–21 (2015)
7. Frigault, M., Wang, L.: Measuring network security using bayesian network-based attack graphs, pp. 698–703, July 2008
8. Frigault, M., Wang, L., Singhal, A., Jajodia, S.: Measuring network security using dynamic bayesian network. In: Proceedings of the 4th ACM Workshop on Quality of Protection, pp. 23–30. ACM (2008)
9. ISO/IEC 27005:2011. Information technology - Security techniques - Information security risk management. ISO (2011)
10. ISO/IEC 27000:2014: Information technology - Security techniques - Information security management systems - Overview and vocabulary. Technical report (2014)
11. Jajodia, S., Noel, S., O'Berry, B.: Topological analysis of network attack vulnerability. In: Kumar, V., Srivastava, J., Lazarevic, A. (eds.) Managing Cyber Threats. Massive Computing, vol. 5, pp. 247–266. Springer, US (2005)
12. Jajodia, S., Noel, S., Kalapa, P., Albanese, M., Williams, J.: Cauldron mission-centric cyber situational awareness with defense in depth. In: Military Communications Conference, pp. 1339–1344. IEEE (2011)
13. Kheir, N., Debar, H., Cuppens-Boulahia, N., Cuppens, F., Viinikka, J.: Cost evaluation for intrusion response using dependency graphs. In: International Conference on Network and Service Security, N2S 2009, pp. 1–6. IEEE (2009)
14. Kordy, B., Piètre-Cambacédès, L., Schweitzer, P.: DAG-based attack and defense modeling: don't miss the forest for the attack trees. Comput. Sci. Rev. 13, 1–38 (2014)
15. Lauritzen, S.L., Spiegelhalter, D.J.: Local computations with probabilities on graphical structures and their application to expert systems. J. R. Stat. Soc. 50, 157–224 (1988)
16. Lippmann, R.P., Ingols, K.W.: An annotated review of past papers on attack graphs. Technical report, DTIC Document (2005)
17. Liu, Y., Man, H.: Network vulnerability assessment using bayesian networks. In: Defense and Security, pp. 61–71. International Society for Optics and Photonics (2005)
18. National Information Assurance Glossary: CNSS N 4009: Committee on National Security Systems. Technical report (2010)
19. National Institute of Standards and Technology: SP 800-30 Rev. 1: Guide for Conducting Risk Assessments. Technical report (2012)
20. National Institute of Standards and Technology: SP 800-53 Rev. 4: Security and Privacy Controls for Federal Information Systems and Organizations. Technical report (2013)

21. Ou, X., Govindavajhala, S., Appel, A.W.: Mulval: a logic-based network security analyzer. In: USENIX Security Symposium (2005)
22. Pearl, J.: Fusion, propagation, and structuring in belief networks. Artif. Intell. **29**(3), 241–288 (1986)
23. Pearl, J.: Probabilistic Reasoning in Intelligent Systems: Networks of Plausible Inference. Morgan Kaufmann, Massachusetts (1988)
24. Phillips, C., Swiler, L.P.: A graph-based system for network-vulnerability analysis (1998)
25. Poolsappasit, N., Dewri, R., Ray, I.: Dynamic security risk management using bayesian attack graphs. Dependable Secure Comput. **9**, 61–74 (2012)
26. Qin, X., Lee, W.: Attack plan recognition and prediction using causal networks. In: Computer Security Applications Conference, pp. 370–379, December 2004
27. Xie, P., Li, J.H., Ou, X., Liu, P., Levy, R.: Using bayesian networks for cyber security analysis. In: IEEE/IFIP International Conference on Dependable Systems and Networks, pp. 211–220. IEEE (2010)

Hooking Graceful Moments: A Security Analysis of Sudo Session Handling

Ji Hoon Jeong[1,2], Hyung Chan Kim[1(✉)], Il Hwan Park[1], and Bong Nam Noh[2]

[1] The Affiliated Institute of ETRI, P.O. Box 1, Yuseong,
Daejeon 34188, Republic of Korea
`kimhc@nsr.re.kr`

[2] Chonnam National University, Yongbong-ro 77, Gwangju 61186, Republic of Korea

Abstract. *Sudo* is a widely used utility program to temporarily provide the privileges of other users when executing shell commands in many UNIX and Linux systems. In conventional usage, a Sudo user who fulfills password authentication is eligible to execute a series of shell commands with system administrative privilege for a while. As Sudo enables privilege switchover, it has been the attractive target of attacks for privilege escalation in nature. Although Sudo source code have been reviewed by security researchers and patched accordingly, in this paper, we show that Sudo is still vulnerable to session hijacking attacks by which an attacker is able to achieve privilege escalation. We explain how such attacks are possible by spotlighting the inherently flawed session handling of Sudo. We also describe two attack designs – shell proxy and ticket reuse attack – by revisiting some known attack strategies. Our experimental results show that the recent versions of Sudo, in combination with the underlying shell program, are affected to the attack designs.

Keywords: Least privilege principle · Session hijacking · Privilege escalation · Software security

1 Introduction

Sudo [4], firstly developed at around 1980, is a utility program that enables temporal privilege switchover from one user to another in executing shell commands for UNIX and Linux systems. Sudo has been commonly used for administrative tasks, which require system *root* privilege, such as installing/updating software packages, editing system configuration files, adjusting kernel parameters, and so on. Sudo is vastly adopted to be used by default in widely deployed Linux distributions such as Debian, Ubuntu, and its derivatives. The other distributions mostly include Sudo package to be activated by choice. Mac OS X is also configured to use Sudo by default.

The opinions expressed herein reflect those of the authors, and not of the affiliated institute of ETRI.

© Springer International Publishing Switzerland 2016
K. Ogawa and K. Yoshioka (Eds.): IWSEC 2016, LNCS 9836, pp. 41–60, 2016.
DOI: 10.1007/978-3-319-44524-3_3

Sudo is usually encouraged as it provides several security benefits. With Sudo deployment, a user does not need to get, and stay with, interactive root shell session to execute a series of administrative commands. Otherwise, the user might input destructive commands inadvertently, thereby impairing the system under management. Moreover, multiple users assigned to administrative jobs do not need to share any root password and their rights to execute a specific set of privileged commands can be separated by configuration. As for accountability, Sudo instance actively logs whole issued commands while conventional root shell session does not.

Despite of the wide adoption, as for attackers, Sudo is the attractive target of attacks to achieve *privilege escalation* in nature. Sudo enables temporal privilege overriding: therefore, it is evident that if an attacker is able to compromise a Sudo user (Sudoer), the attacker has chances to set up an attack to surreptitiously execute shell commands with the additionally permitted privilege. The target privilege is of administrative (root) account in most cases. This kind of attack is feasible with the proxy execution strategy: *i.e.*, the attacker may be able to let the victim user to execute some commands of the attacker's flavor on behalf of the attacker by exploiting Sudo session weakness.

Sudo, in fact, has been considered to prevent this weakness with a ticket-based session management scheme together with some additional protective mechanisms. If a Sudo session is established after taking configured – mostly password based – authentication procedure, then a ticket is issued by which the following Sudo shell command can be executed with no additional authentication until the timestamp expiration in the ticket. Fundamentally, the attacker cannot invoke privileged shell commands directly from another terminal as Sudo checks *session ID* [8] and also validates whether the terminal in use is the place of ticket issue. Sudo also prohibits the well-known *library injection attacks* by throttling some environmental variables which can be abused for replacing a dynamic shared object (dso) with malicious one. This is intended to preclude the possible session hijacking attack by a modified shared object dynamically linked with Sudo. In addition, there are external defense measures provided at kernel layer: *Yama* Linux security module [6] as well as *SELinuxDenyPtrace* [3]. Both are helpful to make difficult or impossible *code injection attack*. Yama restricts the scope of `ptrace` system call and SELinux with ptrace control even turns off the system call facility. These two measures thus can protect shell process tied with valid Sudo session from adversarial code implanting.

Notwithstanding all the defense measures and mitigation efforts, in this paper, we show that it is still possible to achieve successful privilege escalation attack against the very recent versions of Sudo (1.8.16). There have been some previous works concerning the proxy execution and ticket constraint avoidance strategies [13,18,20] to tackle Sudo session handling issues. Basically, here we revisit the two strategies elaborating those to work on the recent Sudo versions. Unlike the previous works, we present more comprehensive and detailed review on session handling issues and also provide concrete attack examples. Note that we do not tackle vulnerabilities of code implementation. Our viewpoint is rather on highlighting the flawed session handling of Sudo.

To show the security impacts of our analysis, first of all, we examine the privilege semantics of Sudo session. The ticket-based session establishment is basically for the convenience: once a Sudo session is established, the validated Sudoer does not need to take repetitive authentication procedures for the following Sudo invocations until the session timeout. One fundamental security issue here is on that the invoking shell process gets to semantically have *dual privileges* which is definitely inappropriate in terms of the *principle of least privilege*.

Although the dually privileged session is inevitable for the purpose of using Sudo, great care must be taken in dealing with established session. The other problem is on that Sudo seems to be failed to prevent session hijacking attacks due to insufficient session protection mechanism. Throughout this work, we found that the following factors can lead to illegal reuse of established – in our views, dually privileged – Sudo session:

- **Lack of integrity check for issuing shell processes.** Sudo does not care whether issuing shell is trustworthy or not. An attacker, thus, is able to execute privileged shell commands by compromising the issuing shell process bypassing the most of Sudo protections.
- **Reusable ticket.** Although Sudo session ticket has been revised to prevent ticket reuse attack, it is still possible to reuse it. If an attacker is successful in matching out ticket parameters within a given session timeout, the ticket is reusable resulting in the illegal session reuse without valid authentication.

It is quite clear that the misuses of established Sudo session may result in escalation from the privilege of Sudo user – and also of the attacker – to that of another – normally administrative – one. Based on the problem review, we describe real world attack designs and conduct experiments on a Linux system installed with the recent versions of widely used distributions.

Contributions. In this paper we will analyze the security impacts of the flawed Sudo session handling and describe realistic attack designs.

1. A study of the improper session handling which may incur dually privileged state in terms of the privilege semantic.
2. Exploring weaknesses around Sudo which may lead to the possible misuse of established Sudo session.
3. Providing two proof-of-concept examples based on attack designs revisiting the shell proxy as well as ticket reuse strategies.

The source code package of our experimental tools, to demonstrate the attack designs, is available on a github project[1].

Paper Organization. Section 2 presents background of Sudo session handling and then, in Sect. 3, we show the problem issues around it. In Sect. 4, we describe attack designs to conduct realistic attacks for privilege escalation and show the experimental results in Sect. 5. In Sect. 6, we discuss on related work. Section 7 concludes this paper.

---

[1] https://github.com/binoopang/sudo.

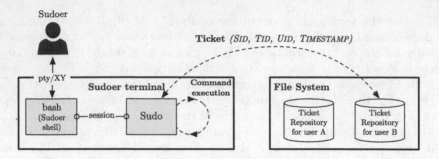

Fig. 1. The relation among Sudo session entities.

2   Background

2.1   Establishing Sudo Session

Sudo enables a configured user, usually assigned to administrator role, to invoke shell commands with root privilege. In order to invoke a series of privileged commands with Sudo, the user is required to be legitimately authenticated. As Sudo operates on a per-command basis [16], in fact, every command invocation should be passed through proper authentication. At the very first command execution under Sudo, a user is required to undergo, primarily, password based authentication procedure at first hand unless non-default authentication methods are included by configuring *Plugable Authentication Module (PAM)* [10]. Unlike *su* command, which requires the password of root account, Sudo requires the password of Sudoer.

For the sake of convenience, Sudo maintains the ticket-based session management so as not to put Sudoer through repetitive password inputs. After the successful initial authentication, Sudo establishes a session and issues the corresponding session ticket. The following privileged command invocations are legitimately permitted without further password authentication by checking the validity of the issued ticket. The session validity is hold during the *grace period* and it is 5 min in most default configurations.

Throughout this paper, we mean that *Sudoer shell* and *Sudoer terminal* are the respective entities associated with established session. Figure 1 illustrates the relationship among Sudo session entities and it is the conceptual situation after initial authentication.

2.2   Session Tickets

The established, thus valid, Sudo session is associated with a ticket. When a Sudoer passes through initial authentication, the corresponding session ticket is generated and it is stored in the per-user ticket repository. The repository is not allowed to be read and/or modified by non-root users: only root privileged user can access to the repository directly.

The parameters of Sudo ticket has been revised for many years to deal with security issues brought up by public communities. In the latest version of Sudo (version 1.8.16), the two types of tickets are involved: *tty_ticket* and *ppid_ticket*.

tty_ticket. When an user wants to perform a series of shell command executions interactively, the user have to log in into the given system directly via terminal devices such as local console (*tty*), serial (*ttyS*), pseudo terminal (*pty*), and the like. For brevity, here we use the term tty as the representative terminal device instance. When Sudo handles sessions with per-tty granularity, Sudo generates *tty_ticket* for each terminal which has completed initial authentication. The parameters of valid tty_ticket is comprised of quadruple (S_{ID}, T_{ID}, U_{ID}, $T_{IMESTAMP}$); The user U_{ID} associated with the session S_{ID} and the terminal T_{ID} is permitted to invoke privileged shell commands. The tty_ticket is valid during the *grace period*, *i.e.*, from the time of ticket issuing $T_{IMESTAMP}$ to the time $T_{IMESTAMP}$ + *timeout* where the *timeout* is 5 min in default configuration. S_{ID} is the session ID which is determined by the process ID of session leader. Note that shell process, such as `bash`, becomes session leader in usual Sudo usages. T_{ID} represents the actual device number of (pseudo) tty by which one can discriminate each terminal device in use. U_{ID} is the system user ID of ticket owner (Sudoer). The timestamp field $T_{IMESTAMP}$ records the time of the most recent shell command execution with Sudo. For every Sudo invocations, the $T_{IMESTAMP}$ value is updated accordingly.

ppid_ticket. It is also possible to deploy Sudo with non-interactive manner. Terminal devices therefore are not directly involved for this case. For example, a user can set up a script that includes login facility with the help of *sshpass* [2]. In such case, Sudo employs the P_{PID} (parent process ID, or ppid) instead of the T_{ID} to establish sessions with per-ppid granularity. The parameters of ppid_ticket are defined by (S_{ID}, P_{PID}, U_{ID}, $T_{IMESTAMP}$); The user U_{ID} associated with the session S_{ID} and the parent process P_{PID} is permitted to invoke privileged shell commands. As same with tty_ticket, ppid_ticket expires session if no further Sudo invocation follows within a given grace period.

3   Problems of Sudo Session Handling

We have conducted an empirical source code auditing as well as dynamic analysis on Sudo program. In this section, we explain our examination results around Sudo session handling issues.

3.1   Dually Privileged Session

The most good reason of Sudo deployment in terms of security is that Sudoer is relatively safe from inadvertent mistake in executing shell commands mixed with root and non-root privileges. This is evident compared to the case of just staying with root shell. Sudoer should be explicit when using the root privileged commands. In view of Sudoer, it looks like explicit privilege switchover between

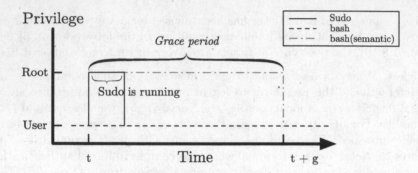

Fig. 2. The privilege transition in a Sudo session.

root and non-root modes. However, this is not true in terms of the privilege semantic. To clear out the privilege transitional semantic in a Sudo session, we illustrate the situation in Fig. 2. Here we define a function $max\_priv(a, b)$ which returns the maximum privilege between the time a and b. Then, $max\_priv(t, t + g)$, where t is the time of successful initial authentication (*i.e.*, session start time) and g is the configured grace time (5 min in default), will constantly returns the maximum privilege between the two time points. This implies that the established Sudo session is associated with *dual privileges*: the one of Sudoer and the other one of root account.

The session semantically tied with dual privileges is obviously problematic in terms of the classical *least privilege principle*. In other words, during the given grace period, although the Sudoer shell process is non-root privileged as for what the underlying OS kernel understands, it is actually dually privileged; therefore, the attacker may be able to misuse root privileged commands if one can properly set up the link point between the privileges.

As for the real world link point, the *code injection* technique using `ptrace()` system call could be a candidate in realizing Sudo session attack. More concretely, malicious code injection into Sudoer shell process will incur indirect root-privileged command executions by an attacker who set up the link point between the privileges. In Sect. 4.2, we will present an example scenario of this case.

3.2 Too Wide Subject Eligibility

When Sudo is invoked, in normal cases, there would be a shell process, such as *bash*, as its parent. The shell process might be initially created by `fork()` call from, *e.g.*, login, sshd, or gnome-terminal process or it can be created from another shell process, especially if Sudo is invoked from a script file. If a given shell process creates some child processes, these are tied with the same session ID (sid) [11][2]. Unless the process does not declare to be a new session leader, it will be included to the same session group with the invoking shell (parent process).

---

[2] Note that this is not the concept of Sudo session but that of process session.

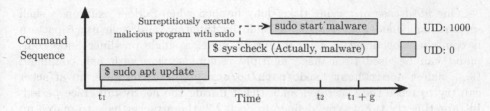

Fig. 3. Subject eligibility problem: the downloaded malware is able to execute Sudo shell command without authentication after one of the other child of parent shell process establishes a valid Sudo session.

Concerning with the two session concepts, there is the *subject problem*: if one of process once establishes a Sudo session, all the other processes in the same process session group are eligible to invoke Sudo commands without requiring any independent authentication during the given grace period. Evidently, it is not safe because an arbitrary child process with the same process session ID can invoke root privileged commands and it possibly leads to security problem if the child is compromised.

Let's take an example of such negative case, shown in Fig. 3, assuming that a user downloaded a system utility of one's flavor. Opening a terminal, the user makes system changes using some administrative commands (`apt`) with Sudo. Then, in the same terminal, the downloaded utility is invoked (`sys_check`) to evaluate newly changed environment *without Sudo* as it does not require root privilege. At this time, the utility, which is actually malware implanted by an attacker, can gain root privilege if it surreptitiously executes malicious Sudo commands because it has the same process session ID with the invoking shell. This situation is surely in contrast to the user's intention, in terms of privilege assignment, because the user executes the utility explicitly without involving Sudo. However, the malicious code in the utility is able to implicitly trigger the malicious commands with root privilege.

3.3   Reusable Ticket

If a session ticket is issued after authentication, it is stored in the local file-system until Sudo reissues the ticket or the system faces to shutdown. Meanwhile, the Sudo session can outlive the shell login session of Sudoer [5] and this means that the Sudo session information is still remained for a while as the ticket is accessible by the file system operations. As a result, an attacker can ride on the outlived Sudo session if the attacker is able to reuse the stored ticket.

Reusing Sudo ticket is trying to match up the shell environment of attacker to the parameters of Sudo session ticket currently saved in the file system: in fact, this is a well-known security issue. However, no complete fixes are yet applied to mitigate this issue as it is generally considered that reusing Sudo ticket is difficult to achieve. In this work, we highlight that Sudo session hijacking attack through ticket reuse trials can be practically achievable.

One ideal case of reusing ticket may happen when Sudoer exits one's shell session immediately after invoking Sudo legitimately, and such usage pattern is commonly occurred in general. For example, a single one-liner Sudo command can be used to manage multiple remote servers with `ssh` command (*e.g.*, `ssh-t admin@host "sudo/path/to/script"`). In this case, an attacker can try to reuse the generated Sudo ticket during the nearly full grace period. In targeting tty_ticket type, defined in Sect. 2.2, the attacker have to match up the two constraints, S_{ID} and T_{ID}, as the user ID of shell process of the attacker is same with U_{ID} by our assumption. The match up should be finished before the time constrained by $T_{IMESTAMP}$.

The attacker can be more aggressive if a Sudoer does not exit the login shell in use by which an attacker cannot resolve `tty` constraint T_{ID} as the Sudoer holds the `tty` by which the underlying OS cannot yield the `tty` value to the attacker. In such case, the attacker can forcibly eject the Sudoer shell process – thus the `tty` is released – and have a chance to resolve the T_{ID}. It would be more effective if the ejection is performed right after the successful Sudo invocation, as the attacker can have sufficient grace period to match up the related parameters for reusing the Sudo session ticket.

4   Attack Designs

This section presents the possible attack designs based on our examination. We basically revisit strategies discussed in some previous works as well as related communities around Sudo. Here we limit our environmental boundary to Linux systems and confine to the privilege escalation case – *i.e.*, from non-root to root – for the sake of succinctness.

4.1   Attacker Model and Assumptions

We assume that an attacker is successful in breaking into a victim system and gets the privilege of Sudoer via any possible scenarios except password sniffing. The scenarios may include performing APT style attacks such as sending malicious e-mail and/or performing watering hole scenarios [12,21]. By the first stage attack, the attacker is successful in driving to download an infected upgrade package, or any other methods to gain privilege of the victim account, so as to execute shell commands without the knowledge of the password of that account. The attacker's goal here is achieving privilege escalation from the victim account to the system root account. Real world attack campaigns may also have the similar goal.

Sudo attack designs require such a strong assumption as it is not a server-like remotely exploitable program. Rather, privilege escalation exploiting Sudo might be the second stage goal for attackers within a local system. Moreover, under this strong assumption, there would be alternative ways to get the root privilege excluding Sudo involvement such as inducing to execute a fake version

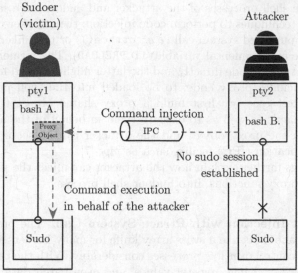

Ticket A : (pty1, bash A, UID=1000)
Sudo only accepts commands of the session with the ticket A.

Fig. 4. Shell proxy attack.

of Sudo. However, our aim is here to review the Sudo session handling issues, therefore, the attack models of our interests inevitably involve Sudo.

Specifically, if the attacker successfully access the target victim shell with any first stage attacks, the victim account should meet the following conditions:

– The account have read and write permissions in accessing local file system and this is normally true in most cases.
– The account is included in the Sudoer group. This means that the account is eligible to execute privileged shell commands with Sudo.

4.2 Shell Proxy Attack

Here we present a proxy style attack to invoke arbitrary shell commands with root privilege. Figure 4 depicts the flow of shell proxy attack. The core idea behind this attack is on compromising live Sudoer shell process so that make the Sudoer shell process execute some commands of the attacker's flavor. The attacker may set up the *shell monitor* that detects successful Sudo command invocations. The setup also includes the *proxy executor* that literally executes attacker's Sudo command. Whit this setup, the attacker's commands can be executed with root privilege bypassing tty_ticket constraint.

In order to achieve shell proxy attack, the attacker must be able to inject proxy code into the address space of the Sudoer shell process. This is basically permitted as the shell processes of the attacker and Sudoer have same user ID. There are a few techniques to perform code injection: the attacker can make use of the debugger purposed system call (*e.g.*, ptrace()) or the linker trick taking advantage of the environmental variable (LD_PRELOAD). The former enables the attacker to inject proxy code directly and the latter might be used for the shared object, which includes proxy code, to be loaded into the shell process of the victim. In our test case, we first build a proxy shared object to deliver the attacker's commands as well as to execute them in behalf of the attacker. The channel between the proxy object and the attacker can be set up with inter-process communication (IPC) facility such as *pipe* [7].

The followings further explain how the attacker can inject the shared object, which contains proxy functions, into Sudoer shell process.

Shared Object Injection with Ptrace System Call. The process tracing system call (ptrace()) is like a swiss army knife for many hackers as it provides rich interface to control over live processes considerably. With the ptrace(), one can pause a process, change register values, and even patch data and/or code part of the process. The daily use of debugging tools such as *gdb* and *strace* are implemented on top of the ptrace() system call. Meanwhile, attackers are also in favor of this facility to patch and/or inject malicious code/object.

As for injecting shared objects into a live process, there is a famous system API function in Windows world: CreateRemoteThread(). Attackers can use this function perform shared object injection very easily. On the other hand, in Linux/Unix world, there is no such system call or function supported by underlying OS or system libraries. However, there are some efforts to enable shared object injection such as Jugaad [9] and hotpatch [14]. These works also internally use ptrace() to inject shell code which eventually loads shared object into target process.

Shared Object Injection with Linker Trick. In Linux systems, there is a well known linker trick by which one can inject shared object into initiating process. The trick is supported by the linker (*ld*). It can be used with the environmental variable *LD_PRELOAD* that points to the path of shared object which is loaded preferentially. This is widely used to extend features or to modify behavior of pre-built application without re-compiling main executable.

In order to implant the proxy object into Sudoer shell, we modify the initialization script of the shell, .bashrc in case of the shell program *bash*. Whenever bash is started, by Sudoer login, .bashrc script in the Sudoer's home directory is read and the according initialization is applied for the bash process. Note that most other shell program such as *csh* and *ksh* also deploy such initialization script. By the attacker model of this work, the attacker can modify .bashrc file as the shell session of the attacker is associated with the same user ID (uid) with that of victim Sudoer.

```
1  if [ −z "$SUDO_EXP" ]; then
2      echo "First_execution_of_bash"
3      export LD_PRELOAD=/tmp/libshproxy.so
4      export SUDO_EXP=TRUE
5      bash
6  else
7      echo "Second_execution_of_bash"
8      unset LD_PRELOAD
9  fi
```

Listing 1.1. Code snippet that loads our proxy object automatically when a bash process is started.

In our attack setup, the code snippet in Listing 1.1, is inserted to `.bashrc` file of the victim Sudoer. After that, as soon as the Sudoer logs in into the system, two bash processes will be started in series: the first one will execute the second bash by our code resulting in the injection of our proxy object specified with LD_PRELOAD (*i.e.*, /tmp/libshproxy.so).

4.3 Ticket Reuse Attack

As explained in Sect. 3.3, Sudo session ticket is able to be reused, and therefore, Sudo session is also reusable under if successfully resolved. Let's assume that an attacker is targeting a just established Sudo session of the tty_ticket $(S_{ID}, U_{ID}, T_{ID}, T_{IMESTAMP})$, and then the Sudoer is logged out by oneself or kicked out by the attacker.

In order to reuse the Sudo session, the attacker needs to resolve the constraints of each parameters of the ticket before the ticket expiration. As the attacker has valid U_{ID} by the attacker model, the S_{ID} and T_{ID} should be resolved to be successful in session reusing. Basically, the attacker can resolve the two constraints by matching up the attacker's shell environment with a simple brute force manner. The attacker repeats terminal process creation until the values of the two parameters are matched up. During the match up procedure, the S_{ID} and T_{ID} can be compared with the values obtained from results of `ps` command invocation.

Resolving T_{ID}. T_{ID} is a minor number of pseudo terminal device and all pseudo terminals have the unique T_{ID} for them. That is why the T_{ID} is used as a index parameter for getting associated tty_ticket. In fact, Sudo stores both major numbers and minor numbers of pseudo terminal devices in the ticket storage. It is not necessary to match up major number as all those values are same. However, each pseudo terminal has unique minor number.

Since Linux system tries to assign the lowest value to T_{ID} like `open()` system call's fd assignment, we can predict the next T_{ID} value for the newly created pseudo terminal. Therefore, an attacker is able to match up the T_{ID} constraint by simply creating a new pseudo terminal after the shell process of victim Sudoer is just exited (or forced to be exited). This approach guarantees that the attacker will eventually get the same T_{ID} value for one of newly created terminals because all the non-assigned values can be tried by the attacker.

Resolving S_{ID}. S_{ID} is a session ID determined by the process ID of session leader. Sudo compares the current S_{ID} with the one in a given ticket and reject any Sudo invocation if the S_{ID} does not match to prevent the class of session hijacking attacks as well as session reuse attacks [18]. As the probability of having the same session ID is $\frac{1}{32767}$ in typical 32-bit systems, it is hard to reuse sessions with manual Sudo tactics. However, a simple brute force approach – which is similar with T_{ID} resolving – will also work for resolving the S_{ID}.

The domain of process ID is a finite totally ordered set $< P, \leq >$ where P is defined by $\{x \mid (1 \leq x) \wedge (x \leq 32767)\}$ in 32-bit Linux systems. The process ID assigning function f returns from the least element 1 and continues to increase, by consecutive calls, until it reaches to the greatest element 32767. If the return of f reaches to that value, then the next return value will roll over. Thus, the attacker is able to iterate the whole process ID domain except the ID values already assigned and the target ID value for S_{ID} will be matched up eventually.

A Brute Force Algorithm to Revive Sudo Session. Attackers can think of the process ID assigning function f to be `fork()` system call in Linux systems. `fork()` creates a child process and a new process ID will be assigned to the child. In order to resolve S_{ID} and T_{ID} constraints at the same time, attackers can deploy `forkpty()` which is a combination of `openpty()`, `fork()`, and `login_tty()`. Thus, it has the ability to generate the values for process ID as well as terminal ID. With the system call, attackers can try to perform the match up process for both S_{ID} and T_{ID}.

With the `forkpty()` system call, we devise a simple brute force algorithm (Algorithm 1) to resolve S_{ID} and T_{ID} constraints. At the first phase, T_{ID} resolving is performed with a simple brute force loop. If the target T_{ID} value is obtained, it is forced to close the terminal immediately so that the same T_{ID} value can be produced again in the very next `forkpty()` call. At the 2nd phase, `forkpty()` is called repeatedly to get the targeting value for S_{ID}. When it returns the right S_{ID}, the shell with the revived Sudo session will be ready. Note that this algorithm will not fail unless one of the other processes coincidentally pre-occupies the targeting values by assigning a new terminal or forking a new process in the middle of the loops.

5   Experimental Evaluation

This section reports our evaluation results of the two attack designs – shell proxy and ticket reuse attack – described in the previous section. To confirm the security impacts of the attacks, we implemented a set of tools to realize the two attacks and tested on a dozen of Linux systems. The Linux distributions were selected by the popularity referencing the distrowatch web site [1].

5.1   Experiment I: Shell Proxy Attack

Shell proxy attack (Fig. 4) can be performed with the linker trick explained in Sect. 4.2. One can build a shell proxy object, which is a basically dso with

---

Algorithm 1. Resolving S_{ID} and T_{ID} constraints.

S_{ID}: A target session ID.
T_{ID}: A target pseudo terminal ID.
fd : A file descriptor to communicate with the terminal of T_{ID}.

▷ 1st phase: try to resolve the T_{ID} first.
while true do
    tid ← CreatePseudoTerminal();
    if tid *equals to* T_{ID} **then**
        ClosePseudoTerminal (tid);
        break ;

▷ 2nd phase: here we have the valid T_{ID}, now resolve the S_{ID}.
while true do
    (sid, fd) ← forkpty();
    if sid > *0* **then**
        if sid *equals to* S_{ID} **then**
            return fd ;
        else
            close(fd);
    else
        ▷ If the two constraints are matched up, child process invokes **execve()**
        to make the shell environment for reusing Sudo ticket.
        if sid *equals to* S_{ID} **then**
            execve(*bash*);

---

position independent code (PIC) option enabled. When the proxy object is loaded into a shell process of interest, it first creates a thread to perform proxy activities while the host (shell) process is alive. The role of our proxy function is simple: it just monitors a pipe which is created to receive attacker's shell commands. If a command is pended to the pipe, the monitor just executes it by forking a child process. We also made a tiny commander, named as fwd, which actually pushes the monitored shell commands into the communication pipe.

On completion of the attack setup, now we can launch shell proxy attack just by waiting victim Sudoers. Once a Sudoer logs in into the system under test, the proxy object is loaded into the Sudoer's shell process. Now if the Sudoer executes a root shell command "sudo id" passing through successful password authentication (Fig. 5(a)), the attacker is also able to execute the same command in the different terminal without password authentication (Fig. 5(b)). To be practical, the very first forwarded shell command might be the one for being a root shell session so as to get the whole control of the system without requiring no more shell proxy attack stages.

Te investigate the possible attack deployment range, we have conducted the same experiment described above on some popular Linux distributions (Table 1).

```
user@local:~$ sudo id
Password: user_input_pass
uid=0(root) gid=0(root) groups
user@local:~$
```

```
user@local:~$ fwd "sudo id"
uid=0(root) gid=0(root) groups
user@local:~$
```

        (a) sudoer terminal   (b) adversary terminal

Fig. 5. After the victim user's sudo execution in terminal (a), the attacker placed in terminal (b) is also successful in invoking `sudo ID` command indirectly via `fwd`.

Table 1. The results of shell proxy attack (sorted by the distrowatch hit rank).

Distribution	Default Sudo version	Process protection	Vulnerable?
MintOS Cinnamon	1.8.9p5	ptrace_scope	yes
Ubuntu 15.10(stable)	1.8.15	ptrace_scope	yes
Ubuntu 15.04(stable)	1.8.9p5	ptrace_scope	yes
Debian 7(stable)	1.8.5p2	none	yes
Debian 8(testing)	1.8.10p3	none	yes
Debian 8(unstable)	1.8.11p2	none	yes
OpenSUSE 13.2	1.8.10p3	none	yes
Fedora Core 21(stable)	1.8.8	none	yes
Fedora Core 22(unstable)	1.8.12	ptrace_scope	yes
CentOS 7.0	1.8.6p7	none	yes
RHEL 7.1	1.8.6p7	none	yes

We could be successful in privilege escalation with shell proxy attack for all the distributions we have tested.

5.2   Experiment II: Ticket Reuse Attack

Based on the attack design described in Sect. 4.3, we have performed *ticket reuse attack* on the various versions of Sudo. Here we show our experimental results to answer the two questions: (1) whether it is possible to resolve constraints in Sudo session ticket, and (2) if so, whether attacker is able to finish resolving constraints assigned to session ticket within limited grace period.

Resolving Ticket Constraints. In order to reuse a session ticket, an attacker should be able to resolve all the constraints of the ticket during the grace period defined with $T_{IMESTAMP}$. It would be sufficient time if Sudoer exists or is kicked out from one's shell session just after invoking a valid Sudo command. Otherwise, it depends on the remaining time.

   To perform constraint resolving, we built a simple brute force program reflecting Algorithm 1 and applied the program for various Sudo versions compiled from

Table 2. Our experimental results for resolving Sudo ticket constraint (S: Session ID, T: Terminal ID, U: User ID, TS: Timestamp, G: Group ID, CT: Creation Time of PTY).

Version	Release date	tty_ticket	Resolved?
1.8.16	2016-03-17	(S, T, U, TS)	yes
1.8.15	2015-11-01	(S, T, U, TS)	yes
1.8.12	2015-02-09	(S, T, U, TS)	yes
1.8.10	2014-03-10	(S, T, U, TS)	yes
1.8.9	2014-01-06	(S, T, U, G, TS)	yes
1.8.6	2012-09-04	(S, T, CT, TS)	partial

respective official source archives. Table 2 shows our results. We could resolve ticket constraints completely with the version 1.8.7 and above. Meanwhile we were not fully successful with the version 1.8.6 and below. Especially matching up the CT constraint, which is the creation time of pseudo terminal, was not made. In order to match up the CT constraint, attackers should be able to control system local time, however, it deviates from our assumptions. Overall, ticket reuse attack is valid for the most recent versions of Linux distributions as they mostly deploy the vulnerable versions. Note that CentOS and RHEL systems with the major version 7 are not affected as those distributions still stay with Sudo version 1.8.6. However, at the time of this writing, we conjecture that it will be upgraded to some of the vulnerable versions.

As we mentioned in Sect. 2, the parameter constitution of Sudo ticket has been revised for a long time. The current constitution is concretized after the version 1.8.10 and this version newly introduces the *ppid_ticket*. This paper only deal with the tty_ticket case although we also have finished our tests for ppid_ticket case. The results were quite similar in many aspects with the tty_ticket case, thus, we do not include the ppid_ticket results due to the paper limit.

The Feasibility of Reusing Session Ticket. Even though one can resolve a given ticket constraints, it is useless if it takes too much time exceeding the limited grace period. It takes more time to resolve S_{ID} than T_{ID} since the domain of S_{ID} is greater than that of T_{ID}. Furthermore, attackers need to iterate the whole domain of S_{ID} in the worst case. The probabilities of successful reusing both tty_ticket and ppid_ticket are highly dependent on the size of S_{ID} domain and the remaining time until session expiration.

We have analyzed the size of S_{ID} domain for 32-bit and 64-bit Linux systems and it turns out that it was 32768 for 32-bit and 131072 for 64-bit systems respectively. As having larger domain size, attackers need more time to resolve ticket constraints in 64-bit systems.

To measure the constraint resolving time, we have performed our experiments on a virtual machine which has the specification of 2.7 GHz Intel Core i7 and

Table 3. Sudo vulnerabilities reported in the last 5 years

ID	Score	Details
CVE-2014-0106	6.6	Improper environment variable checking in env_reset
CVE-2013-2777	4.4	Improper controlling terminal validation
CVE-2013-2776	4.4	Improper controlling terminal validation
CVE-2013-1776	4.4	Improper controlling terminal validation
CVE-2013-1775	6.9	Bypass intended time restriction by setting the system clock
CVE-2012-3440	5.6	Allows overwriting arbitrary files via a symlink attack
CVE-2012-2337	7.2	Improper support of configurations that use a netmaks syntax
CVE-2012-0809	7.2	Format String Bug. Allows local user to execute arbitrary code
Bug #87023	-	Bypass *tty_ticket* by revisiting closed pseudo terminal

2 GB RAM. Our experiment results show that it takes no more than 20 s in a 32-bit system. With a 64-bit system, we could iterate whole S_{ID} domain within 80 s in our implementation. This means that we can resolve ticket constraints if the remaining time of grace period is greater than, roughly, 2 min in worst case.

However, attackers can set up an attack environment so as not to run the 1st phase of Algorithm 1 by forcibly kicking out Sudoer as soon as the valid Sudo session is detected. With such tactics, the brute force can be more feasible. Unfortunately the 2nd phase loop is hard to be eliminated due to frequent background process launchings and the loop iteration is required in most cases.

In Linux systems, the size of S_{ID} domain can be tuned as it is a kernel parameter (/proc/sys/kernel/pid_max). This kernel parameter can influence on the capability of Algorithm 1. In our test, if we set the kernel parameter greater than 451,000, then the constraint resolving iteration could not be completed until session expiration. However, note that the default value of the parameter rarely changed and most Linux distributions retain original value encoded in Linux kernel source code.

6   Related Work

6.1   Sudo Vulnerabilities and Fixes

Since the year 1999, several Sudo vulnerabilities have been reported and we list the related bug report items of the recent years in Table 3.

Bug #87023 [13] discussed the possibility of Sudo session reuse on tty_ticket with reusable T_{ID} which is of previously closed pseudo terminal. As the investigated Sudo version (1.6.8) checks only T_{ID} and U_{ID}, it is possible to reuse tty_ticket if one can reopen a terminal which is associated with the previously used T_{ID} before session expiration. This bug has been dealt with by introducing a new constraint, *i.e.*, the creation time of pseudo terminal (CT). We think that this fix trial can not effectively counter ticket reuse attack as the creation time of real tty is always same after system boot up. Furthermore, attackers may roll back the system time by exploiting *ntp* vulnerabilities [15] to avoid the constraint. Interestingly, the CT constraint is omitted from the version 1.8.9.

CVE-2012-0809, CVE-2012-2337, and CVE-2012-3440 are caused due to improper code implementation. In such cases, the respective code snippets were patched. CVE-2013-1775 is about bypassing ticket constraint in which clock resetting technique is introduced [17]: when a user issues sudo-k to expire one's ticket, the time-stamp is set to the UNIX epoch time value. If an attacker can reset the time-stamp to that value, then the attacker also can run Sudo command with escalated privilege without authentication. This vulnerability has been fixed in a way of ignoring timestamp of the epoch value instance.

Among the assigned items, CVE-2013-1776, CVE-2013-2776, and CVE-2013-2777 were related to session handling problems. These are basically the same vulnerability; namely, these have been discriminated because of differently affected versions. These items are related to ticket constraint avoidance issue in where terminal device ID spoofing technique is involved. This issue also has been fixed: session ID is included into the ticket data structure. Since attacker can not spoof his or her session ID, the applied fix is on right way to defeat the some ID spoofing attacks. However, it is possible to reuse ticket by restoring terminal ID and session ID at the same time conducting brute-force attack and, in the last section, we showed the attack setup is realistic through our experiments.

Sudo have been revised to deal with session hijacking problem. Before the version 1.7.3, Sudo does not enable *tty_ticket* by default and which means that one ticket is valid for all of terminal instances. An attacker, thus, could gain root privilege when an user establishes Sudo session. To address this problem, Sudo enables *tty_ticket* enforcing by default after that.

Another notable fix against ticket reuse attack is also made. Before the version 1.8.6, ticket does not includes S_{ID} to classify controlling terminal devices. Since the lack of S_{ID}, an attacker is able to hijack the Sudo session if the attacker can spoof any valid T_{ID}. A related work [18] described the possible T_{ID} spoofing issue in which techniques of redirecting standard file descriptors were presented. To deal with this problem, after the version 1.8.6, Sudo ticket contains S_{ID} and both T_{ID} and S_{ID} should be matched.

6.2   Works on Sudo Session Handling Issues

Sudo Session Hijacking. Napier discussed the issues of least privilege in using some automated tools including Sudo [20]. Especially, he pointed out the improper Sudo session handling: a single Sudo ticket can be used for multiple terminal instances and a established Sudo session can be reusable after the associated Sudoer has logged out. Before version of 1.7.3, Sudo does not enables tty_ticket policy by default. An user, thus, could invokes privileged command over all instance of terminal after one valid session is established. Before version of 1.8.6, tty_ticket does not contain session ID. An attacker, thus, could reuse ticket by login same terminal.

Authentication Bypass Using Terminal ID Spoofing. Castellucci presented that the use of ttyname() could lead to the potential bypass of the *tty_tickets constraints* [18]. Sudo deploys `ttyname()` function to discriminate among terminal devices. However, the function accepts file descriptors as inputs for its functionality. If an attacker is able to manipulate the mappings between file descriptors and active terminal devices, he or she can bypass the constraints on tty_ticket. This vulnerability is assigned to CVE-2013-1776.

Environmental Variable Injection. Macke reported that the `env_reset` option is disabled in Sudoers file of Sudo versions until 1.8.5 [19]. When the option is disabled, it is not possible to block out all dangerous environment variables. By this weakness, an attacker could deploy the notorious LD_PRELOAD environmental variable to execute arbitrary commands with escalated privilege. This vulnerability is assigned to CVE-2014-0106. As a workaround, the recent version of Sudo deploy the *proc file system* as well as `sysctl()` instead of relying on `ttyname()`.

Concerning the well-known weaknesses that we discussed above, the latest version of Sudo (1.8.16) activates tty_ticket, by default, to prevent the execution of Sudo from different terminal devices. Moreover, the data structure of session ticket has been revised to contain POSIX session ID to prohibit the known ticket reuse attack. Although such mitigation efforts have been discussed and patched in the related communities, we have shown that it is still possible to override Sudo session by elaborating the attack strategies.

6.3   Possible Mitigations

Disabling the concept of grace period in Sudo session may require consecutive authentication activities for every command invocations and that will lead to usability sacrifice. To sustain the current usage of Sudo, privilege escalation with the attack designs shown in this paper should be mitigated in some ways.

To protect Sudo from a class of shell proxy attacks, we need to disable code injection facilities, such as `ptrace`, more radically with the help of kernel layer component: *e.g.*, applying `ptrace_scope` to any launching Sudo instances. It may be difficult to protect code injection solely with user level solutions. Moreover, it is necessary to supplement invalidating procedure of the used tickets so as to properly counter ticket reuse attacks. For example, introducing some unrecoverable variables, such as nonce values or session creation time, into session ticket items may severely hinder attacker's reconstruction of valid ticket constraints.

Overall, it is certain that Sudo itself does not have whole responsibility to protect attacks for privilege escalation. Because it is quite difficult to protect Sudo itself especially against attacks involving code injection. Moreover, privilege information stored in places accessible by user level process may be susceptible to be recycled and that leads to possible session reuse. Fundamentally, it would be more appropriate to provide a facility for transient privilege switchover as a OS service.

7   Conclusion

In this paper, we presented our security analysis of the vastly used utility program, Sudo, for daily uses to perform some administrative tasks in UNIX/Linux systems. We have conducted empirical source code auditing as well as runtime testing, and noticed that there are still session handling problems in Sudo: dually privileged session, process subject eligibility, and reusable ticket problems. Based on the recognition of these problems, we described the two attack designs to demonstrate effective attacks to hijack live Sudo session so as to achieve privilege escalation. The attack strategies are basically based on previous studies, and we have revisited to make concrete example cases. We have also conducted experiments and confirmed that the attack designs are feasibly deployable by imaginary attackers if they can access to a victim Sudoer shell process but without knowing authentication password.

Possible future' work may include enhancing the security of Sudo session handling scheme to mitigate attacks demonstrated through this work possibly reflecting our remarks in Sect. 6.3. Moreover, another approach would involve designing a new scheme to support transient privilege escalation in more safe way replacing the current session handling scheme, and the effort should sustain both usability as well as security.

Acknowledgments. We would like to thank Kaan Onarlioglu, Erwan Le Malécot, and the anonymous reviewers for their suggestions and comments.

References

1. Distrowatch page hit ranking. http://distrowatch.com/dwres.php?resource=popularity
2. Non-interactive SSH password auth. http://sourceforge.net/projects/sshpass/
3. Selinuxdenyptrace (fedora features). https://fedoraproject.org/wiki/Features/SELinuxDenyPtrace
4. Sudo main page. http://www.sudo.ws/
5. Sudoers manual. http://www.sudo.ws/sudoers.man.html
6. Yama, limux security module. http://www.kernel.org/doc/Documentation/security/Yama.txt
7. pipe(7) linux user's manual (2005)
8. credentials(7) linux user's manual (2008)
9. Jugaad: Linux Thread Injection Kit. Defcon19 (2011)
10. Morgan, A.G., Kukuk, T.: The linux-pam system administrator's guide Ver. 1.1.2 (2010)
11. Kerrisk, M.: The Linux Programming Interface. No Strach Press, San Francisco (2010)
12. Kindlund, D.: Holyday watering hole attack proves difficult to detect and defend against. ISSA J. **11**, 10–12 (2013)
13. kko: sudo option "tty_tickets" gives false sense of security due to reused pts numbers (2007). https://bugs.launchpad.net/ubuntu/+source/sudo/+bug/87023
14. Kumar, V.N.: Hotpatch (2013). http://selectiveintellect.com/hotpatch.html

15. Malhotra, A., Cohen, I.E., Brakke, E., Goldberg, S.: Attacking the network time-protocol. IACR Cryptology ePrint Archive 2015, p. 1020 (2015). http://dblp.uni-trier.de/db/journals/iacr/iacr2015.html#MalhotraCBG15
16. Miller, T.C.: Sudo in a nutshell. http://www.sudo.ws/sudo/intro.html
17. Miller, T.C.: Authentication bypass when clock is reset (2013). http://www.sudo.ws/sudo/alerts/epoch_ticket.html
18. Miller, T.C.: Potential bypass of tty_tickets constraints (2013). http://www.sudo.ws/sudo/alerts/tty_tickets.html
19. Miller, T.C.: Security policy bypass when env_reset is disabled (2014). http://www.sudo.ws/sudo/alerts/env_add.html
20. Napier, R.A.: Secure automation: achieving least privilege with SSH, Sudo, and Suid. In: Proceedings of the 18th USENIX Conference on System Administration (LISA), pp. 203–212. USENIX Association, Berkeley (2004)
21. O'Gorman, G., McDonald, G.: The elderwood project. Technical report, Symantec (2012)

Security of Web of Things: A Survey
(Short Paper)

Wei Xie[✉], Yong Tang, Shuhui Chen, Yi Zhang, and Yuanming Gao

College of Computer, National University of Defense Technology,
Changsha, China
xiewei@nudt.edu.cn

Abstract. Web of Things (WoT) is the most promising application model of Internet of Things (IoT). Current IoT systems urgently need extendibility and loose coupling, which are easily provided by WoT. However, some concerns about WoT security have been raised by academic researchers as well as industrial engineers. This paper provides a review of WoT literature especially on security issues. Moreover, this paper proposes an architecture that regards smart gateways as ideal devices to achieve WoT security. Smart gateways are classified into five types, and security functions are suggested for each type.

Keywords: Web of things · Security · Architecture · Smart gateway

1 Introduction

Web of Things (WoT) is the most promising application model of Internet of Things (IoT). The relation between IoT and WoT is just like the relation between the Internet and the Web. IoT supports WoT at the network layer while WoT displays IoT at the application layer. If IoT is aimed to provide any device (computers, routers, phones, etc.) with an IP address, then WoT is aimed to provide any electronic item (including smart cards, sensors, etc.) with a URL (Uniform Resource Locater). There are three types of EPC (Electronic Product Code) with 64, 128 or 256 bit length, respectively. However, IPv4 can only provides 32 bit length addresses, and even IPv6 can at most provides 128 bit length addresses. It means making each EPC-tagged item with a unique IP address is infeasible. Therefore, expendability of IoT can be achieved only with the help of WoT that provides an unlimited amount of URLs.

WoT is loosely coupled, which is an urgently needed capability for current IoT systems. IoT is composed with a variety of heterogeneous devices, protocols and applications. It is difficult either to update tightly coupled components or to share resources among different systems. WoT is based on highly developed Web technologies that are loose coupled, easy to develop, and convenient for resource sharing. With the help of WoT, IoT systems can be easily developed, updated, and share resources among each others.

WoT is a new rising research field receiving more and more attentions from academic researchers to industrial engineers. On the academic aspect, a search result with a keyword "Web of Things" on the website "Web of Science" is displayed in Fig. 1. The result shows that dozens of papers have been published each year since 2008, and both

© Springer International Publishing Switzerland 2016
K. Ogawa and K. Yoshioka (Eds.): IWSEC 2016, LNCS 9836, pp. 61–70, 2016.
DOI: 10.1007/978-3-319-44524-3_4

of the published and cited paper numbers have upward tendencies. On the industrial aspects, Siemens has opened a research center in Berkeley in September 2013, primarily focusing on the WoT research; Google has launched an open standard project called "Physical Web" in October 2014, trying to access smart things through URL interfaces; W3C has also set up a WoT community group in July 2013 and an interest group in January 2015. The 1st international workshop on WoT is held by/W3C in June 2014, indicating the standardization process of WoT has begun.

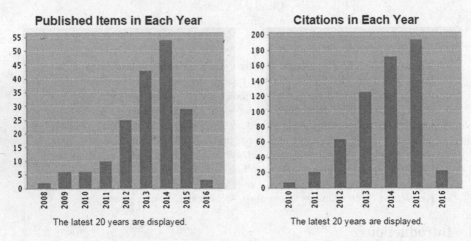

Fig. 1. Literature with the keyword "Web of things" (The searching time is in March 2016. The 2015 items are not completely included because there normally need several months for a published paper to be indexed.)

WoT brings new challenges to systems and users, therefore, security is an important research direction. Many embedded devices in WoT have constrained resources unable to support classical cryptographic algorithms such as RSA, SHA, AES, etc. As a result of this, the widely used HTTPS scheme, which is based on public key certificates, is infeasible for WoT scenarios. Moreover, there are more and more personal items accessible online, widely threatening users privacy. Thus, authorization schemes and access control methods become more and more important. However, current Web authentication schemes such as OAuth [1] are insufficient for WoT applications, because these schemes cannot provide secure ownership transfers that are necessary for the online personal items.

The major contents and contributions of this paper include: Sect. 2 analyzes present status and points out three limitations of current WoT security researches. Section 3 proposes an architecture that classifies smart gateways of WoT into five types and suggests security functions for each type. Section 4 gives a conclusion of this survey.

2   Reviews of WoT Security

This section classifies previous literature into eight research directions, and reviews present situations and limitations of exiting WoT security studies.

2.1 Classifications of WoT Literature

Previous literature of WoT can be classified into eight research directions. The classification is not according to logical relations but according to research hotspots. (1) The accessible device [2, 3] research direction focuses on a resource constrained device's capability and efficiency of accessing to an IP network and serving as a Web server or client. (2) The lightweight communication [4, 5] research direction focuses on improving existing protocols or designing new protocols that are lightweight and suitable for resource constrained devices in WoT scenarios. (3) The deliverable resource [6–10] research direction focuses on finding, searching, and mashups of WoT resources, which represent physical things. (4) The semantic data [11–13] research direction focuses on building semantic data that can be read and understood by smart devices in WoT, promoting M2M (Machine to Machine) interactions. (5) The social network [14, 15] research direction focuses on reusing currently highly developed Web social networks to serve WoT applications. (6) The architecture & framework [16–19] research direction focuses on abstractly modeling WoT architectures and frameworks composed of components and layers. (7) The prototype & application [23–25] research direction focuses on implementing WoT prototypes for current IoT applications such as RFID (Radio Frequency IDentification), IoV [20, 21] (Internet of Vehicles), WSN [22] (Wireless Sensor Network), smart home, smart city, etc. (8) The security and privacy research direction is important, however, only has few researches that have little relations with each others. This section reviews previous security works in three aspects as follow.

2.2 Encryption and Authentication

Encryption and authentication are usually implemented together, because they both use cryptographic techniques based on passwords and certificates. TLS [26] (Transport Layer Security) protocol is widely deployed to provide TCP-based applications like HTTP with encryption in transport layer and authentication of servers. Correspondingly, DTLS [27] (Datagram Transport Layer Security) protocol is aimed to provide UDP-based applications like CoAP [4, 5] (Constrained Application Protocol) with encryption in transport layer and authentication of servers.

Encryption in transport layer and authentication of servers for WoT have been basically solved by using DTLS-based solutions. The research [28] presents Lithe, which is an integration of DTLS and CoAP; and then proposes a novel DTLS header compression scheme significantly reducing the energy consumption by leveraging the 6LoWPAN [29] (IPv6 over Low-power Wireless Personal Area Networks) protocol. Similarly, to reduce DTLS traffics, the research [30] presents preliminary overhead estimates for the certificate-based DTLS handshake; and then proposes three techniques to reduce the overheads of the DTLS handshake based on pre-validation, session resumption and handshake delegation. Nevertheless, the survey [31] points out that it is infeasible to provide billions of WoT devices with different certificates by using PKI (Public Key Infrastructures). Instead, a feasible solution may be DCAF [32] (Delegated CoAP Authentication and Authorization Framework), which is an IETF internet draft.

It is also based on DTLS and CoAP, but using symmetric PSK (Pre-Shared keys) rather than public key certificates.

However, encryption in application layer and authentication of users for WoT have not been solved. There is no user concept in transport layer, as a result of this, DTLS can only authenticate servers and clients rather than users in WoT applications. Actually, authenticating a client device doesn't mean authentication its user, since different users may login on a single client. Furthermore, even if different users login on different clients, there may be still thousands of users using same brands and versions of devices that may have the same PSK. It enables a malicious user to decrypt other users' messages once he/she sniffs enough network traffics. Only encryption and authentication in application layer can solve the above problems. To our knowledge, however, there are few related works for lightweight WoT applications.

2.3 Authorization and Ownership Transfer

Authorization and ownership transfer are two main methods to preserve user's privacy in WoT. Because using and owning are two basic rights of a user toward a physical object. WoT should provide users with their using rights by authorization schemes and their owning rights by ownership transfer schemes.

There have been some works about access control and authorization in WoT, although these independent works have little relations with each others. For instance, the research [33] analyses access control considering the WoT characteristics and the RESTful resource oriented Web architecture. It proposes a mechanism utilizing not only a requester information (a typical identity, an internet addresses, etc.) but also contexts of a thing itself. It also presents a Web-resource structure for access control. The research [34] proposes a method that enables people to share their devices to others with flexible access control; illustrates how to rely on existing social networks to enable owners to leverage user profiles and social links in place for creating access control policies. It also integrates social network services into a role-based access control model. The research [35] proposes a context-aware usage control model (ConUCON) that leverages the context information to enhance data, resource, and service protection for WoT. On the basis of ConUCON, the research also designs and implements a context-aware usage control framework on the middleware layer in a smart home project to protect security and privacy. The research [36] introduces an architecture that utilizes features of a role-based access control model to specify access control policies for WoT by using cryptographic keys.

Ownership transfer is as essential as authorization for WoT, according to the research [31], however, there is currently no research aimed at this issue. Users are required to be authorized before accessing traditional Web resources (an electronic book, a private video, etc.), but they are rarely required to get ownerships of the recourses. It is because that the traditional Web resources can be easily copied and shared, its ownership is not an important issue. In contrast, WoT resources actually present physical things, which cannot be electronically duplicated. Therefore, it is necessary to maintain ownership attributes for WoT resources. Defining and designing ownership transfer schemes are quite essential for WoT applications. To our knowledge, however, there is currently no related works.

2.4 Other Security Issues

Besides encryption, authentication, authorization and ownership transfer, other security issues such as trust, risk, reputation have been also preliminary addressed in previous researches. For instance, the research [37] suggests to build trust management schemes of WoT nodes based on locations, brands, reputations, and etc. The research [38] introduces a security-enhanced reputation-based discovery model for WoT; and proposes a multi-layer architecture for high efficient discovery according to Chord protocol in Peer to Peer networks. The research also maps heterogeneous physical equipments to virtual nodes and separates them into different trust domains depending on reputation calculations. The research [39] discusses trusts, reputations and risks for CPS (Cyber Physical System), which involve the connections of real world objects into networked information systems including the WoT.

Besides the above issues, overall frameworks and architectures for WoT security are also valuable research topics, i.e. how to decomposes WoT systems into layers and components according to security requirements and solutions. WoT is a complex network composed with heterogeneous devices and protocols. Messages are transmitted between varieties of sensors, gateways, cloud nodes, mobile terminals, and transformed through varieties of protocols such as Zigbee/6LoWPAN, IPv4/IPv6, TCP/UDP, HTTP/CoAP. Different frameworks and architectures usually face different risks and require different protections. However, to our knowledge, there are few current researches on overall frameworks and architectures toward WoT security.

3 The Proposed Architecture for WoT Security

To address the issue described in Sect. 2.4, this section proposes an architecture that employs smart gateways to achieve WoT security. The architecture provides two perceptions:

- Smart gateways, which translate various protocols among heterogeneous networks, are ideal devices to provide WoT with security.
- Smart gateways can be classified into five types, which are recommended or deprecated to carry out certain types of security functions.

3.1 Role of Smart Gateways

Smart gateways are essential devices for WoT to translate various protocols that used in heterogeneous devices and networks. A typical WoT network is generally composed of two sub-networks: a sensor network and an IP network. A smart gateway in WoT is an adapter to receive, restructure, encapsulate and retransmit protocol packets between the two sub-networks. For instance, a wireless sensor device only supports Zigbee [40] communications, but its administrator uses a mobile Web browser to configure the device through an HTTP interface. In this case, a configuration message from the Web browser has to be repackaged several times before it arrives to the sensor device. At least, a Zigbee gateway and a Web server are required. They can be carried out by an embedded software, an dedicated hardware or a cloud service.

Smart gateways that are used in various kinds of WoT systems are classified into only five types in this paper. A conceptual example of utilizations of different smart gateways is illustrated in Fig. 2.

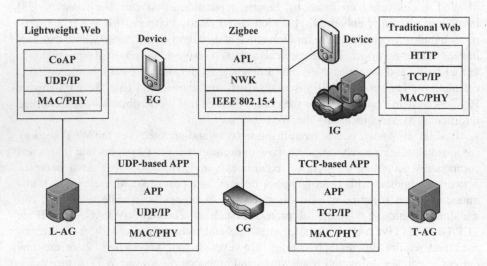

Fig. 2. Classifications of WoT smart gateways

3.2 Classification of Smart Gateways

On one hand, smart gateways can be classified into Embedded Gateways (EG) and Independent Gateways (IG). A EG is a software running on a sensor device and serving as a gateway. It is mainly designed to achieve a higher efficiency by a lower cost for a resource constrained environment. Normally, A EG can only provide lightweight Web protocols like UDP-based CoAP. An IG is a dedicated physical device specialized to convert protocols between heterogeneous networks. For instance, it is convenient to redesign a SOHO (Small Office Home Office) router as a specialized gateway for a smart house, making a sensor device in the house connect with a public cloud on the internet.

On the other hand, smart gateways can be classified into Communication Gateways (CG) and Application Gateways (AG). A CG generally converts protocols between a sensor network and an IP network, e.g. between Zigbee and IPv4. An AG is mainly a translator between Web and other protocols in the application layer, e.g. between HTTP and a private application protocol using a customized port.

Moreover, the AG can be further classified into two subtypes: the Traditional AG (T-AG) and the Lightweight AG (L-AG). A T-AG is used to translate a private application protocol to a powerful web protocol like HTTPS, which is widely deployed on the internet. A Lightweight AG (L-AG) is used to translate a private application protocol to a lightweight Web protocol like CoAP, which is more suitable for resource constrained environments.

3.3 Security Functions of Smart Gateways

Besides protocol conversion, smart gateways are also ideal devices to carried out security functionalities for WoT. Suggested gateway types of security functions are listed as Table 1. However, it is worth to note that, one type of smart gateways is only suitable for some kinds of security functions and unsuitable for others.

The IG and T-AG are recommended to employ classical cryptographic algorithms such as AES, RSA, etc., because these algorithms' security has been verified by widely deployed applications. On the contrary, the EG or L-AG is unfeasibly to implement the classical cryptography because of limitations in constrained resources.

The CG, which operates in transfer layer, can easily provide authentications of servers and encryptions in transport layer by using SSL. Firewalls based on package filters are also suitable for the CG. However, security functions like content audit, anti-malware, as well as authentication and authorization to users are recommended to be carried out by the AG rather than the CG, because only the AG can understand various messages packaged in application protocols.

Table 1. Suggested security functions for each type of smart gateways

Security functions		EG	IG	CG	AG	
					L-AG	T-AG
Encryption	Application layer	–	–	×	✓	✓
	Transport layer	–	–	✓	×	×
	Lightweight	✓	×	–	✓	×
	Classical	×	✓	–	×	✓
Authentication	To users	–	–	×	✓	✓
	To servers	–	–	✓	×	×
Authorization		–	–	×	✓	✓
Firewall	Package filter	–	–	✓	×	×
	Application proxy	–	–	×	✓	✓
Anti-malware		–	–	×	✓	✓

✓: Recommended ×: Deprecated –: Inconclusive

4 Conclusion

The contributions of this paper include: (1) This paper points out three limitations of current WoT security researches: i.e. few researches on encryption in application layer and authentication of users; no research on WoT ownership transfer; few researches on overall architectures and frameworks for WoT security. (2) This paper proposes an architecture that regards smart gateways as the ideal devices to provide WoT with security. Smart gateways are classified into five types (i.e. EG, IG, CG, L-AG and T-AG), each with recommended and deprecated security functions respectively.

Our future work is to design a layered framework and to implement a prototype to proof the concept of the proposed architecture.

Acknowledgments. This work is partially supported by the National Natural Science Foundation of China under Grant nos. 61379148 and 61472437.

References

1. Leiba, B.: OAuth web authorization protocol. Internet Comput. IEEE **16**, 74–77 (2012)
2. Duquennoy, S., Grimaud, G., Vandewalle, J.J.: The Web of Things: interconnecting devices with high usability and performance. In: International Conference on Embedded Software and Systems, 2009, ICESS 2009, pp. 323–330 (2009)
3. Castro, M., Jara, A.J., Skarmeta, A.F.: Enabling end-to-end CoAP-based communications for the Web of Things. J. Netw. Comput. Appl. **59**, 230–236 (2016)
4. Bormann, C., Castellani, A.P., Shelby, Z.: CoAP: an application protocol for billions of tiny internet nodes. IEEE Internet Comput. **16**, 62–67 (2012)
5. Levä, T., Mazhelis, O., Suomi, H.: Comparing the cost-efficiency of CoAP and HTTP in Web of Things applications. Decis. Support Syst. **63**, 23–38 (2014)
6. Guinard, D., Trifa, V.: Towards the web of things: Web mashups for embedded devices. In: Workshop on Mashups, Enterprise Mashups and Lightweight Composition on the Web (MEM 2009), in proceedings of WWW (International World Wide Web Conferences), Madrid, Spain, p. 15 (2009)
7. Guinard, D., Trifa, V., Pham, T., Liechti, O.: Towards physical mashups in the web of things. In: 2009 Sixth International Conference on Networked Sensing Systems (INSS), pp. 1–4. IEEE (2009)
8. Fielding, R.: Representational state transfer. In: Architectural Styles and the Design of Network-based Software Architecture, pp. 76–85 (2000)
9. Guinard, D., Trifa, V., Karnouskos, S., Spiess, P., Savio, D.: Interacting with the SOA-based internet of things: Discovery, query, selection, and on-demand provisioning of web services. IEEE Trans. Serv. Comput. **3**, 223–235 (2010)
10. Stirbu, V.: Towards a restful plug and play experience in the web of things. In: 2008 IEEE International Conference on Semantic Computing, pp. 512–517. IEEE (2008)
11. Pfisterer, D., Römer, K., Bimschas, D., Kleine, O., Mietz, R., Truong, C., Hasemann, H., Kröller, A., Pagel, M., Hauswirth, M.: SPITFIRE: toward a semantic web of things. IEEE Commun. Mag. **49**, 40–48 (2011)
12. Scioscia, F., Ruta, M.: Building a Semantic Web of Things: issues and perspectives in information compression. In: 2009 IEEE International Conference on Semantic Computing, pp. 589–594. IEEE (2009)
13. Ruta, M., Scioscia, F., Di Sciascio, E.: Enabling the semantic Web of Things: framework and architecture. In: 2012 IEEE Sixth International Conference on Semantic Computing, pp. 345–347. IEEE (2012)
14. Guinard, D., Fischer, M., Trifa, V.: Sharing using social networks in a composable web of things. In: 2010 8th IEEE International Conference on Pervasive Computing and Communications Workshops (PERCOM Workshops), pp. 702–707. IEEE (2010)

15. Cheng, C., Zhang, C., Qiu, X., Ji, Y.: The Social Web of Things (SWoT)-structuring an integrated social network for human, things and services. J. Comput. **9**, 345–352 (2014)
16. Guinard, D., Trifa, V., Wilde, E.: A resource oriented architecture for the web of things. In: Internet of Things (IOT), 2010, pp. 1–8. IEEE (2010)
17. Dillon, T.S., Zhuge, H., Wu, C., Singh, J., Chang, E.: Web-of-things framework for cyber–physical systems. Concurrency Comput. Pract. Exp. **23**, 905–923 (2011)
18. Lee, E.A.: Cyber physical systems: design challenges. In: 2008 11th IEEE International Symposium on Object Oriented Real-Time Distributed Computing (ISORC), pp. 363–369. IEEE (2008)
19. Ostermaier, B., Schlup, F., Romer, K.: Webplug: a framework for the web of things. In: 2010 8th IEEE International Conference on Pervasive Computing and Communications Workshops (PERCOM Workshops), pp. 690–695. IEEE (2010)
20. Chen, Y., Xu, M., Gu, Y., Li, P., Shi, L., Xiao, X.: Empirical study on spatial and temporal features for vehicular wireless communications. EURASIP J. Wireless Commun. Netw. **2014**, 1–12 (2014)
21. Lv, P., Wang, X., Xue, X., Xu, M.: SWIMMING: seamless and efficient WiFi-based internet access from moving vehicles. IEEE Trans. Mob. Comput. **14**, 1085–1097 (2015)
22. Lu, X., Dong, D., Liao, X., Li, S., Liu, X.: PathZip: a lightweight scheme for tracing packet path in wireless sensor networks. Comput. Netw. **73**, 1–14 (2014)
23. Guinard, D., Trifa, V., Mattern, F., Wilde, E.: From the internet of things to the web of things: resource-oriented architecture and best practices. In: Architecting the Internet of Things, pp. 97–129. Springer (2011)
24. Guinard, D., Floerkemeier, C., Sarma, S.: Cloud computing, REST and mashups to simplify RFID application development and deployment. In: Proceedings of the Second International Workshop on Web of Things, p. 9. ACM (2011)
25. Bröring, A., Remke, A., Lasnia, D.: *SenseBox* – a generic sensor platform for the web of things. In: Puiatti, A., Gu, T. (eds.) MobiQuitous 2011. LNICST, vol. 104, pp. 186–196. Springer, Heidelberg (2012)
26. Turner, S.: Transport layer security. IEEE Internet Comput. **18**(6), 60–63 (2014)
27. Rescorla, E., Modadugu, N.: Datagram transport layer security, RFC 4347, in progress, IETF draft-rescorla-dtls-04 5246 (2006)
28. Raza, S., Shafagh, H., Hewage, K., Hummen, R., Voigt, T.: Lithe: Lightweight secure CoAP for the internet of things. Sens. J. IEEE **13**, 3711–3720 (2013)
29. Kushalnagar, N., Montenegro, G., Schumacher, C.: IPv6 over low-power wireless personal area networks (6LoWPANs): overview, assumptions, problem statement, and goals. RFC 4919 (Informational), Internet Engineering Task Force (2007)
30. Hummen, R., Ziegeldorf, J.H., Shafagh, H., Raza, S., Wehrle, K.: Towards viable certificate-based authentication for the internet of things. In: Proceedings of the 2nd ACM workshop on Hot topics on wireless network security and privacy, pp. 37–42. ACM (2013)
31. Heuer, J., Hund, J., Pfaff, O.: Toward the web of things: applying web technologies to the physical world. Computer **48**(5), 34–42 (2015)
32. Gerdes, S., Bergmann, O., Bormann, C.: Delegated CoAP authentication and authorization framework (DCAF). Laryngoscope **108**, 679–682 (1998)
33. Oh, S.W., Kim, H.S.: Decentralized access permission control using resource-oriented architecture for the Web of Things. In: 2014 16th International Conference on Advanced Communication Technology (ICACT), pp. 749–753. IEEE (2014)
34. Jindou, J., Xiaofeng, Q., Cheng, C.: Access control method for web of things based on role and SNS. In: 2012 IEEE 12th International Conference on Computer and Information Technology (CIT), pp. 316–321. IEEE (2012)

35. Bai, G., Yan, L., Gu, L., Guo, Y., Chen, X.: Context-aware usage control for web of things. Secur. Commun. Netw. **7**, 2696–2712 (2014)
36. Barka, E., Mathew, S.S., Atif, Y.: Securing the web of things with role-based access control. In: El Hajji, S., Nitaj, A., Carlet, C., Souidi, E.M. (eds.) C2SI 2015. LNCS, vol. 9084, pp. 14–26. Springer, Heidelberg (2015)
37. Raggett, D.: The web of things: challenges and opportunities. Computer **48**, 26–32 (2015)
38. Cheng, C., Zhang, C., Qiu, X.: A security-enhanced discovery model for WoT system based on reputation. Adv. Inf. Sci. Serv. Sci. **4**, 434–442 (2012)
39. Chang, E., Dillon, T.: Trust, reputation, and risk in cyber physical systems. In: Papadopoulos, H., Andreou, A.S., Iliadis, L., Maglogiannis, I. (eds.) AIAI 2013. IFIP AICT, vol. 412, pp. 1–9. Springer, Heidelberg (2013)
40. Baronti, P., Pillai, P., Chook, V.W., Chessa, S., Gotta, A., Hu, Y.F.: Wireless sensor networks: survey on the state of the art and the 802.15. 4 and ZigBee standards. Comput. Commun. **30**, 1655–1695 (2007)

Searchable Encryption

UC-Secure Dynamic Searchable Symmetric Encryption Scheme

Kaoru Kurosawa$^{(\boxtimes)}$, Keisuke Sasaki, Kiyohiko Ohta, and Kazuki Yoneyama

Ibaraki University, Hitachi, Japan
{kaoru.kurosawa.kk,kazuki.yoneyama.sec}@vc.ibaraki.ac.jp

Abstract. In a dynamic searchable symmetric encryption (SSE) scheme, a client can add/modify/delete encrypted files. In this paper, we first prove a weak equivalence between the UC security and the stand alone security based on the previous work on static SSE schemes. We next show a more efficient UC secure dynamic SSE scheme than before by replacing the RSA accumulator with XOR-MAC to authenticate the index table.

Keywords: Searchable symmetric encryption · UC-security · XOR-MAC

1 Introduction

In the model of searchable symmetric encryption (SSE) schemes, a client stores a set of encrypted files C_j on an untrusted server in the store phase. In the search phase, he can efficiently retrieve some of the encrypted files containing specific keywords, keeping the keywords and the files secret.

The first SSE scheme was proposed by Song et al. [25]. Since then, single keyword search SSE schemes [9,14,16,19,20], dynamic SSE schemes [12,21 24], multiple keyword search SSE schemes [4,5,11,17,18,26] and more [15] have been studied extensively by many researchers.

Curtmola et al. [9,10] gave a rigorous definition of privacy against passive adversaries. Namely a server is an adversary who is honest but curious. They also showed a scheme called SSE2 which is secure against adaptive chosen keyword attacks.

An SSE scheme is called dynamic if the client can add/modify/delete encrypted files. Otherwise it is called static. Kamara et al. [23] constructed a *dynamic* SSE scheme in the random oracle model. Subsequently Kamara et al. [22] showed a parallel and dynamic SSE scheme in the random oracle model.

Cash et al. [12] pointed out that in the scheme of [23], the structure of the added documents is leaked to the server. They then showed a more efficient dynamic SSE scheme than [22] in the random oracle model.

Naveed et al. [24] showed a dynamic SSE scheme which reveals less information to the server than [12,22,23] in the standard model.

© Springer International Publishing Switzerland 2016
K. Ogawa and K. Yoshioka (Eds.): IWSEC 2016, LNCS 9836, pp. 73–90, 2016.
DOI: 10.1007/978-3-319-44524-3_5

In all these works, only the privacy aspect has been considered. However, a malicious server may return incorrect search results to the client, or may delete some encrypted files to save her memory space. Even if the server is honest, a virus, worm, trojan horse or a software bug may delete, forge or swap some encrypted files.

On the other hand, Canetti introduced a notion of universal composability (UC), and proved the UC composition theorem which states that if a protocol Π is UC secure, then its security is preserved under a general protocol composition operation [8].

From this point of view, Kurosawa and Ohtaki showed a UC secure static SSE scheme in [19,20]. In particular, they proved a weak equivalence between the UC security and the stand alone security (the privacy and the reliability.)

Kurosawa and Ohtaki [21] next showed a UC-secure dynamic SSE scheme for the model in which the set of keywords contained in each file do not change. The index table changes only when a new file is added. However, they do not show any equivalence between the UC-security and the stand alone security. Indeed, they did not even define the privacy nor the reliability of dynamic SSE schemes.

The main problem of dynamic SSE schemes is that a malicious server may return some old encrypted file C'_j instead of the current one C_j. They solved this problem by using the RSA accumulator [6,7,13] to time-stamp on both the encrypted files and the index table. However, the RSA accumulator is slow.

In this paper, we first prove a weak equivalence between the UC security and the stand alone security of *dynamic* SSE schemes. Thus, one can focus on the simpler privacy and reliability notion, and yet achieve the strong UC security.

We next show a more efficient UC secure dynamic SSE scheme for the same model as that of [21] by replacing the RSA accumulator with XOR-MAC [3] to authenticate the index table. (Only the encrypted files are authenticated by using the RSA accumulator.) When the client adds a new file, the new index table is authenticated efficiently by using the nice incrementality property of XOR-MAC. Also the client keeps the number of files. This allows us not to time-stamp on the index table. Since XOR-MAC can be implemented by using AES, the proposed scheme is more efficient than [21].

If X is a string, then $|X|$ denotes the bit length of X. If X is a set, then $x \xleftarrow{\$} X$ denotes sampling an element from X at random and assigning it to x.

2   Verifiable Dynamic SSE Scheme

Let $\mathcal{D} = \{D_1, \cdots, D_n\}$ be a set of files and $\mathcal{W} = \{w_1, \cdots, w_m\}$ be a set of keywords. Let $\text{Index} = (e_{i,j})$ be an $m \times n$ binary matrix such that

$$e_{i,j} = \begin{cases} 1 \text{ if a keyword } w_i \text{ is contained in a file } D_j \\ 0 \text{ } otherwise \end{cases}. \tag{1}$$

Let $\mathcal{C} = \{C_1, \cdots, C_n\}$ be a set of encrypted files and $\mathcal{I}$ be an encryption of Index. Let $\text{D}(w)$ be the set of files D_j which contain a keyword w, $\text{C}(w)$ be the set of ciphertexts C_j of $D_j \in \text{D}(w)$ and $\text{List}(w)$ be the set of indexes j of

$D_j \in \mathtt{D}(w)$. Namely $\mathtt{List}(w_i) = \{j \mid e_{i,j} = 1\}$, $\mathtt{D}(w_i) = \{D_j \mid j \in \mathtt{List}(w_i)\}$ and $\mathtt{C}(w_i) = \{C_j \mid j \in \mathtt{List}(w_i)\}$.

For example, let $\mathcal{D} = \{D_1, \cdots, D_5\}$, $\mathcal{W} = \{w_1, w_2\}$ and

$$\mathtt{Index} = \begin{pmatrix} 1\,0\,1\,0\,1 \\ 0\,1\,0\,1\,0 \end{pmatrix}. \tag{2}$$

Then $\mathtt{List}(w_1) = \{1, 3, 5\}$, $\mathtt{D}(w_1) = \{D_1, D_3, D_5\}$, $\mathtt{C}(w_1) = \{C_1, C_3, C_5\}$.

A verifiable dynamic SSE scheme is a protocol between a client and a server such as follows.

(Store phase) The client takes $(n, m, \mathcal{D}, \mathcal{W}, \mathtt{Index})$ as an input. He generates a key K, and computes $(\mathcal{C}, \mathcal{I})$. He then sends $(\mathtt{store}, \mathcal{C}, \mathcal{I})$ to the server, and keeps $(K, \mathtt{state})$, where $\mathtt{state}$ includes (n, m) and some (non-secret) information.

(Update/Search phase) For $i = 1, \ldots, q$, do one of the followings.

- On input $(\mathtt{search}, w)$, where $w \in \mathcal{W}$, the client sends $(\mathtt{search}, t(w))$ to the server. The server finds $\mathtt{C}(w)$ by using $t(w)$, and returns $(\mathtt{C}(w), Tag(w))$ to the client. The client verifies them by using $Tag(w)$ and $(K, \mathtt{state})$. If they are acceptable, then he outputs $\mathtt{D}(w)$.
- On input $(\mathtt{add}, D_{n+1}, \mathtt{e}_{n+1})$, where $\mathtt{e}_{n+1} = (e_{1,n+1}, \ldots, e_{m,n+1})$ is a binary vector, the client sends $(\mathtt{add}, C_{n+1}, \alpha)$ to the server and updates $\mathtt{state}$. The server updates $\mathcal{I}$ based on α, and appends C_{n+1} to $\mathcal{C}$.
- On input $(\mathtt{modify}, i, D_i')$, the client does the following:
    1. The client sends $(\mathtt{get}, i)$ to the server. The server returns (C_i, tag_i). The client outputs $\mathtt{accept}$ or $\mathtt{reject}$ based on tag_i.
    2. If the client outputs $\mathtt{accept}$, then he sends $(\mathtt{modify}, i, C_i', \beta)$ to the server, and updates $\mathtt{state}$.
    3. The server updates $\mathcal{I}$ based on β, and replaces C_i with C_i'.
- On input $(\mathtt{delete}, i)$, the client does the following:
    1. The client sends $(\mathtt{get}, i)$ to the server. The server returns (C_i, tag_i). The client outputs $\mathtt{accept}$ or $\mathtt{reject}$ based on tag_i.
    2. If the client outputs $\mathtt{accept}$, then he sends $(\mathtt{delete}, i, \gamma)$ to the server, and updates $\mathtt{state}$.
    3. The server updates $(\mathcal{C}, \mathcal{I})$ based on γ.

3 Privacy

In this section, we define the privacy of verifiable dynamic SSE schemes. A difference from *static* SSE schemes is that we must consider the leakage from the add/modify/delete protocols.

We allow only the following information is leaked to the server. We call them the minimum leakage because the server learns them in any verifiable dynamic SSE scheme.

In the store phase, n, m and $|D_1|, \ldots, |D_n|$ are leaked from $(\mathcal{D}, \mathcal{W}, \mathtt{Index})$. In the update/modify phase, $(\mathtt{search}, \mathtt{List}(w))$ is leaked from $(\mathtt{search}, t(w))$,

$(\mathsf{add}, |D_{n+1}|)$ is leaked from $(\mathsf{add}, C_{n+1}, \alpha)$, $(\mathsf{modify}, i, |D_i'|)$ is leaked from $(\mathsf{modify}, i, C_i', \beta)$ and (delete, i) is leaked from $(\mathsf{delete}, i, \gamma)$.

The notion of *privacy* requires that the server should not be able to learn any more information than the minimum leakage. Formally, we consider a real game Game_{real} and a simulation game Game_{sim}. At the end of each game, a distinguisher B outputs a bit b.

The real game Game_{real} is played by two PPT players, a distinguisher B and a challenger.

(Store phase) B chooses $(\mathcal{D}, \mathcal{W}, \mathsf{Index})$, and sends them to the challenger. The challenger returns $(\mathcal{C}, \mathcal{I})$.

(Update/Search phase) For $i = 1, \ldots, q$, do: B chooses an input X_i to the client, and sends it to the challenger. The challenger returns Y_i to B, where Y_i is the message(s) that the client sends to the server on input X_i.

The simulation game Game_{sim} is played by three PPT players, a distinguisher B and a challenger and a simulator Sim, where the challenger sends the minimum leakage to Sim. From the minimum leakage, Sim simulates Y_i.

(Store phase)

1. B chooses $(\mathcal{D}, \mathcal{W}, \mathsf{Index})$ and sends them to the challenger.
2. The challenger sends the minimum leakage $m, n, |D_1|, \cdots, |D_n|$ to Sim.
3. Sim computes $(\mathcal{C}', \mathcal{I}')$, and returns them to the challenger.
4. The challenger relays $(\mathcal{C}', \mathcal{I}')$ to B.

(Update/Search phase) For $i = 1, \ldots, q$, do:

1. B chooses an input X_i to the client, and sends it to the challenger.
2. The challenger sends the minimum leakage derived from X_i to Sim.
3. Sim returns Y_i' to the challenger.
4. The challenger relays Y_i' to B.

Then we define the advantage of privacy as

$$\mathsf{Adv}_{\mathsf{Sim}}^{priv}(B) = |\Pr(b = 1 \text{ in } \mathsf{Game}_{real}) - \Pr(b = 1 \text{ in } \mathsf{Game}_{sim})|. \tag{3}$$

Further let $\mathsf{Adv}_{\mathsf{Sim}}^{priv} = \max_B \mathsf{Adv}_{\mathsf{Sim}}(B)$.

Definition 1. *We say that a verifiable dynamic SSE scheme satisfies privacy if there exists a PPT simulator Sim such that $\mathsf{Adv}_{\mathsf{Sim}}^{priv}$ is negligible.*

4   Reliability

In this section, we formulate *reliability* of verifiable dynamic SSE schemes. A difference from *static* SSE schemes is that a malicious server may cheat the client by using the information which she obtained in the add/modify/delete protocols.

Consider the following attack game among three PPT algorithms, the client, A_1 and A_2. (A_1, A_2) is an adversary, and A_2 plays the roll oaf a malicious server. We also assume that A_1 and A_2 can communicate freely.

(Store phase) A_1 chooses $(\mathcal{D}, \mathcal{W}, \mathtt{Index})$ and sends them to the client. The client sends $(\mathcal{C}, \mathcal{I})$ to A_2.

(Update/Search phase) For $i = 1, \ldots, q$, do:

1. A_1 chooses an input X_i to the client, and sends it to the client.
2. The client runs the protocol with A_2 on input X_i.
3. The client sends its output O_i to A_1 unless X_i is $(\mathsf{add}, D, \mathsf{e})$.

We say that the adversary (A_1, A_2) succeeds if the client outputs $\mathtt{D}(w)'$ such that $\mathtt{D}(w)' \neq \mathtt{D}(w)$ for some input (search, w), where $\mathtt{D}(w)$ is the current set of files D_j which contain the keyword w. In this case, we let A_1 output 1. Otherwise A_1 outputs 0.

Then we define the advantage of reliability by

$$\mathsf{Adv}^{auth}(A_1, A_2) = \Pr((A_1, A_2)\,\text{succeeds}).$$

Further let $\mathsf{Adv}^{auth} = \max_{(A_1, A_2)} \mathsf{Adv}^{auth}(A_1, A_2)$.

Definition 2. *We say that a verifiable dynamic SSE scheme satisfies reliability if Adv^{auth} is negligible.*

Further we say that the adversary (A_1, A_2) strongly succeeds if the client accepts $(\mathtt{C}(w)', Tag'(w))$ such that $(\mathtt{C}(w)', Tag'(w)) \neq (\mathtt{C}(w), Tag(w))$ for some input (search, w), or he accepts (C_i', tag_i') such that $(C_i', tag_i') \neq (C_i, tag_i)$ for some $(\mathsf{modify}, i, D_i')$ or (delete, i).

In this case, we let A_1 output 1. Otherwise A_1 outputs 0. Then we define the advantage of strong reliability by

$$\mathsf{Adv}^{sauth}(A_1, A_2) = \Pr((A_1, A_2)\,\text{strongly succeeds}).$$

Further let $\mathsf{Adv}^{sauth} = \max_{(A_1, A_2)} \mathsf{Adv}^{sauth}(A_1, A_2)$.

Definition 3. *We say that a verifiable dynamic SSE scheme satisfies strong reliability if Adv^{sauth} is negligible.*

5   UC Security

In the UC framework of verifiable dynamic SSE schemes Π, the real world and the ideal world of Π are defined. In the ideal world, a real world adversary A can corrupt the server. (We assume that the client is honest.) In the ideal world, the client is replaced with a dummy client and the run of Π is replaced with an ideal functionality $\mathcal{F}_{\mathrm{dSSE}}$. Also there exists the ideal world adversary S.

Then the protocol Π is called UC-secure if no environment $\mathcal{Z}$ can distinguish the real world and the ideal world, where $\mathcal{Z}$ generates the inputs X_i to the client and receives the outputs Y_i. In addition, $\mathcal{Z}$ can interact with A or S in an arbitrary way. In the ideal world, the dummy client relays each input X_i to $\mathcal{F}_{\mathrm{dSSE}}$, and relays each message Y_i from $\mathcal{F}_{\mathrm{dSSE}}$ to $\mathcal{Z}$.

5.1   Ideal Functionality

We define the ideal functionality $\mathcal{F}_{\mathrm{dSSE}}$ as shown in Fig. 1. For a search request on keyword w, $\mathcal{F}_{\mathrm{dSSE}}$ returns $\mathrm{D}(w)$ or reject. For an add request, $\mathcal{F}_{\mathrm{dSSE}}$ appends a new file D_{n+1} to $\mathcal{D}$. For a modify request, $\mathcal{F}_{\mathrm{dSSE}}$ replaces D_i with D_i' or returns reject. For a delete request, $\mathcal{F}_{\mathrm{dSSE}}$ replaces D_i with reject or returns reject. For each request, $\mathcal{F}_{\mathrm{dSSE}}$ leaks only the minimum leakage to an ideal world adversary S.

$\mathcal{F}_{\mathrm{dSSE}}$ provides an ideal world because the ideal world adversary S learns only the minimum leakage and the dummy client receives the correct $\mathrm{D}(w)$ or reject.

Ideal Functionality $\mathcal{F}_{\mathrm{dSSE}}$

Running with the dummy client P_1, and an adversary S.

- Upon receiving (store, $sid, n, m, \mathcal{D}, \mathcal{W}$, Index) from P_1, verify that this is the first input from P_1 with (store, sid).
  If so, store $(n, m, \mathcal{D}, \mathcal{W}, \mathrm{Index})$, and send (store, $n, m, |D_1|, \cdots, |D_n|$) to S. Otherwise ignore this input.
- Upon receiving (search, sid, w) from P_1, send (search, $\mathrm{List}(w)$) to S.
  1. If S returns OK, then send $\mathrm{D}(w)$ to P_1.
  2. If S returns reject, then send reject to P_1.
- Upon receiving (add, sid, D, e) from P_1, append D to $\mathcal{D}$, update n to $n + 1$ and update the $m \times n$ binary matrix Index to the $m \times (n + 1)$ one such that the last column is e^T.
  Then send (add, $|D|$) to S.
- Upon receiving (modify, sid, i, D_i') from P_1, send (modify, $i, |D_i'|$) to S.
  1. If S returns accept, then send accept to P_1. Then replace D_i with D_i'.
  2. If S returns reject, then send reject to P_1.
- Upon receiving (delete, sid, i) from P_1, send (delete, i) to S.
  1. If S returns accept, then send accept to P_1. Then replace D_i with delete.
  2. If S returns reject, then send reject to P_1.

Fig. 1. Ideal Functionality of Dynamic SSE

5.2   UC Security of Dynamic SSE Scheme

Let $\mathrm{P}_{real} = \Pr(\mathcal{Z} \text{ outputs } 1, \text{ in the real world})$, $\mathrm{P}_{ideal} = \Pr(\mathcal{Z} \text{ outputs } 1 \text{ in the ideal world})$ and $\mathrm{Adv}_{\mathsf{S}}^{uc}(\mathcal{Z}, \mathsf{A}) = |\mathrm{P}_{real} - \mathrm{P}_{ideal}|$.

Then we say that a verifiable dynamic SSE scheme securely realizes the ideal functionality $\mathcal{F}_{\mathrm{dSSE}}$ if for any real world adversary A, there exists an ideal world adversary S such that $\mathrm{Adv}_{\mathsf{S}}^{uc}(\mathcal{Z}, \mathsf{A})$ is negligible for any environment $\mathcal{Z}$.

5.3   Weak Equivalence

In this section, we show a similar equivalence for verifiable *dynamic* SSE schemes. The proofs are similar to those of [20], and are given in Appendices.

Theorem 1. *If a verifiable dynamic SSE scheme Π securely realizes $\mathcal{F}_{\text{SSE}}$, then Π satisfies privacy and reliability.*

The real world can be seen as the real game of privacy by looking at $\mathcal{Z}$ as a distinguisher and (client, server, A) as a challenger. The ideal world can be seen as the ideal game of privacy by looking at $\mathcal{Z}$ as a distinguisher, S as a simulator and (dummy-client, $\mathcal{F}_{\text{dSSE}}$) as a challenger. Hence the privacy is satisfied if the protocol is UC-secure.

For an adversary (A_1, A_2) of reliability, consider $\mathcal{Z}$ and A such that $\tilde{A} = (\mathcal{Z}, \mathsf{A}) = (A_1, A_2)$. Then $\tilde{A} = (\mathcal{Z}, \mathsf{A})$ cannot cheat the client if the protocol is UC-secure. Hence the reliability is satisfied.

Theorem 2. *If a verifiable dynamic SSE scheme Π satisfies privacy and strongly reliability, then Π securely realizes $\mathcal{F}_{\text{SSE}}$.*

The proof of Theorem 2 is more complicated. See Appendix B.

6   How to Construct UC-Secure Dynamic SSE

In this section, we show a more efficient UC secure dynamic SSE scheme than [21]. In our scheme, we authenticate **Index** by using a variant of XOR-MAC [3] which has the incrementality property. We authenticate only the encrypted files by using the RSA accumulator.

6.1   Proposed Scheme

We assume that $\mathcal{W} = \{0,1\}^\ell$ for some $\ell = O(\log_2 \lambda)$, where λ is the security parameter. Hence $m = 2^\ell$.

Let $\mathsf{SKE} = (G, E, E^{-1})$ be a symmetric-key encryption scheme. Let $H : \{0,1\}^* \to \{0,1\}^\lambda$ be a collision resistant hash function. For a bit string x, let $[x]_{1\ldots n}$ denote the first n bits of x, and $[x]_n$ denote the nth bit of x.

(Store protocol) The client takes $(\mathcal{D}, \mathcal{W}, \mathbf{Index})$ as an input, where $\mathbf{Index} = (e_{i,j})$ is an $m \times n$ binary matrix defined by Eq. (1).

Let $\pi_k = \pi(k, \cdot)$ be a pseudorandom permutation on $\mathcal{W} = \{0,1\}^\ell$, and $f : \{0,1\}^\lambda \times \{0,1\}^* \to \{0,1\}^\lambda$ and $\mathsf{PRF} : \{0,1\}^\lambda \times \{0,1\}^\ell \to \{0,1\}^L$ be two psuedorandom functions, where L is an upper bound on n (which is the number of files).

(Encryption of $\mathcal{D}$)

The client generates $k_e \leftarrow G(1^\lambda)$ and computes $C_j = E_{k_e}(D_j)$ for $j = 1, \ldots, n$. Let $\mathcal{C} = (C_1, \ldots, C_n)$.

(Encryption of Index)

We authenticate Index by using a variant of XOR-MAC [3].

1. The client chooses k, k' and k_m randomly, where k is a key of π, k' is a key of PRF and k_m is a key of f.
2. Let Table($\cdot$) be an array of size $m = 2^\ell$.

For $i = 1, \ldots, m(= 2^\ell)$, the client computes

$$mac_i = f_{k_m}(0\|w_i\|n) \oplus \sum_{j=1}^{n} e_{i,j} \times f_{k_m}(1\|j),$$

$$X_i = (e_{i,1}, \ldots, e_{i,n}) \oplus [\mathsf{PRF}_{k'}(w_i)]_{1\ldots n},$$

$$\mathsf{Table}(\pi_k(w_i)) = (X_i, mac_i)$$

where $\|$ means concatenation and $\oplus$ means bit-wise XOR.

(Time stamping on C_j)

We use the RSA accumulator [6,7] to time stamp on each C_j.

1. The client generates two large primes $p = 2p' + 1$ and $q = 2q' + 1$ such that p' and q' are also primes. He computes $N = pq$, and generates a generator g of QR_N.
2. For $j = 1, \ldots, n$, the client generates a prime p_j such that

$$p_j = H(j, C_j)2^{u+1} + 2r_j + 1, \tag{4}$$

where u is a large enough parameter, and r_j is randomly chosen from $\{0, \ldots, 2^u - 1\}$.
3. He computes the accumulated value as $Acc = g^{p_1 \times \cdots \times p_n} \bmod N$.
4. For $j = 1, \ldots, n$, he computes the witness of C_j as

$$x_j = Acc^{1/p_j} \bmod N. \tag{5}$$

Finally the client stores $\mathcal{C}$ and

$$\mathcal{I} = (\mathsf{Table}, (N, g), Acc, tag_1 = (p_1, x_1), \ldots, tag_n = (p_n, x_n))$$

to the server. He keeps $K = (k, k', k_e, k_m, p, q)$ and state $= (n, m, Acc)$.

(Search protocol) The client takes a keyword $w \in \mathcal{W}$ as an input.

1. The client sends $t(w) = (\pi_k(w), [\mathsf{PRF}_{k'}(w)]_{1\ldots n})$ to the server.
2. Let $\mathsf{Table}(\pi_k(w)) = (X, mac)$. The server computes $(\hat{e}_1, \ldots, \hat{e}_n) = X \oplus [\mathsf{PRF}_{k'}(w)]_{1\ldots n}$. She then returns $C(w) = \{C_j \mid \hat{e}_j = 1\}$ and

$$Tag(w) = [(\hat{e}_1, \ldots, \hat{e}_n), mac, \{tag_j = (p_j, x_j) \mid \hat{e}_j = 1\}]$$

to the client.

3. The client first verifies if

$$mac = f_{k_m}(0\|w\|n) \oplus \sum_{j=1}^{n} \hat{e}_j \times f_{k_m}(1\|j).$$

Next for each $\hat{e}_j$ such that $\hat{e}_j = 1$, he verifies if p_j is written like Eq. (4) for some r_j and $Acc = x_j^{p_j} \bmod N$.

4. If everything is OK, then he computes $D_j = E^{-1}(C_j)$ for each $\hat{e}_j$ such that $\hat{e}_j = 1$, and outputs $D(w) = \{D_j \mid \hat{e}_j = 1\}$.
Otherwise he outputs reject.

(Add protocol) The client takes a new file D_{n+1} and a binary vector $e = (e_{1,n+1}, \ldots, e_{m,n+1})$ as an input.

Then the client does the following.

1. He computes $C_{n+1} = E_{k_e}(D_{n+1})$, and generates a prime p_{n+1} such that

$$p_{n+1} = H(n+1, C_{n+1})2^{u+1} + 2r_{n+1} + 1, \tag{6}$$

where r_{n+1} is randomly chosen from $\{0, \ldots, 2^u - 1\}$.
2. For $i = 1, \ldots, m$, he computes
$a_i = e_{i,n+1} \oplus [\mathsf{PRF}_{k'}(w_i)]_{n+1}$ and

$$\Delta_{w_i} = f_{k_m}(0\|w_i\|n) \oplus f_{k_m}(0\|w_i\|n+1) \oplus e_{i,n+1} \times f_{k_m}(1\|n+1) \tag{7}$$

and sets $\mathsf{Table}'(\pi_k(w_i)) = (a_i, \Delta_{w_i})$.
3. He sets $x_{n+1} = Acc$, $Acc := Acc^{p_{n+1}} \bmod N$ and $n := n + 1$.
4. He finally sends C_{n+1} and $\alpha = (\mathsf{Table}', tag_{n+1} = (p_{n+1}, x_{n+1}))$ to the server.

The server does the following.

1. She stores (p_{n+1}, x_{n+1}), and updates $\mathcal{C} = (C_1, \ldots, C_n)$ to $\mathcal{C} = (C_1, \ldots, C_n, C_{n+1})$.
2. For $i = 1, \ldots, m$, she updates $\mathsf{Table}(\pi_k(w_i)) = (X_i, mac_i)$ to $\mathsf{Table}(\pi_k(w_i)) = ((X_i, a_i), mac_i \oplus \Delta_{w_i})$.
3. She sets $x_j := x_j^{p_{n+1}} \bmod N$ for $j = 1, \ldots, n$.
She also sets $Acc := Acc^{p_{n+1}} \bmod N$ and $n := n + 1$.

Note that $(X_i, a_i) = (e_{i,1}, \ldots, e_{i,n}, e_{i,n+1}) \oplus [\mathsf{PRF}_{k'}(w_i)]_{1 \ldots n+1}$ and

$$mac_i \oplus \Delta_{w_i} = \{f_{k_m}(0\|w_i\|n) \oplus \sum_{j=1}^{n} e_{i,j} \times f_{k_m}(1\|j)\}$$

$$\oplus \{f_{k_m}(0\|w_i\|n) + f_{k_m}(0\|w_i\|n+1) \oplus e_i \times f_{k_m}(1\|n+1)\}$$

$$= f_{k_m}(0\|w_i\|n+1) \oplus \sum_{j=1}^{n+1} e_{i,j} \times f_{k_m}(1\|j).$$

(Modify protocol) The client takes (i, D_i') as an input.

1. The client sends (get, i) to the server.
2. The server returns $(C_i, tag_i = (p_i, x_i))$ to the client.
3. The client outputs accept if $Acc = x_i{}^{p_i} \bmod N$ and p_i is written like Eq. (4). Otherwise he outputs reject.
4. Suppose that the client outputs accept. Then he computes $C_i' = E_{k_e}(D_i')$, and generates a prime p_i' such that $p_i' = H(i, C_i')2^{u+1} + 2r_i' + 1$ for some $r_i' \in \{0, \ldots, 2^u - 1\}$. He then sends $(i, C_i', \beta = p_i')$ to the server. Finally he updates Acc to $Acc := x_i{}^{p_i'} \bmod N$.
5. The server updates x_j to $x_j^{p_i'/p_i} \bmod N$ for each $j \neq i$ by using the technique of [13] as follows. For $j = 1, \ldots, i-1, i+1, \ldots, n$, the server computes (a, b) such that $ap_i + bp_j = 1$ by using the extended Euclidean algorithm. She then sets

$$x_j := (x_j^a x_i^b)^{p_i'} \bmod N. \tag{8}$$

Finally she updates Acc and p_i to $Acc := x_i{}^{p_i'} \bmod N$ and $p_i := p_i'$.

(Delete protocol) The client takes (i, delete) as an input. Then the delete protocol is the same as the modify protocol with $C_i' = \text{delete}$.

6.2   Privacy of Our Scheme

Theorem 3. *The proposed protocol satisfies privacy if* SKE *is Left-or-Right (LOR) secure [2].*

Proof. We show a simulator Sim such that no distinguisher can distinguish the simulation game Game_{sim} from the real game Game_{real} in the definition of privacy. Our Sim behaves in the same way as the client except for the followings in Game_{sim}.

- Use $0^{|D_j|}$ instead of D_j for all j.
- Use a random string of length n instead of each X_i, and a random bit instead of each a_i.
- Use random strings of length λ instead of each max_i and each Δ_{w_i}.
- In the search phase, Sim first sets $R \leftarrow \emptyset$.

Suppose that Sim is given $\text{List}(w)$ of some $w \in \mathcal{W}$ by the challenger. Then choose $c \leftarrow \{0, 1\}^\ell \setminus R$.

For $j = 1, \ldots, n$, set

$$\hat{e}_j = \begin{cases} 1 \; if \; j \in \text{List}(w) \\ 0 \; if \; j \notin \text{List}(w) \end{cases}$$

Suppose that $\text{Table}(c) = (X, mac)$. Then let $Y \leftarrow (\hat{e}_1, \ldots, \hat{e}_n) \oplus X$ and $t'(w) \leftarrow (c, Y)$. Sim returns $t'(w)$ to the challenger. Finally Sim sets $R \leftarrow R \cup \{c\}$.

Then we consider a series of games $\mathsf{Game}_0, \cdots, \mathsf{Game}_4$ such that $\mathsf{Game}_0 = \mathsf{Game}_{real}$. Let $p_i = \Pr(B$ outputs $b = 1$ in $\mathsf{Game}_i)$.

- Game_1 is the same as Game_0 except for that C_j is replaced with $C'_j = E_{k_e}(0^{|D_j|})$ for $j = 1, \ldots, n$. Then $|p_1 - p_0|$ is negligible because SKE is LOR secure.
- Game_2 is the same as Game_1 except for that each π_k is replaced with a random permutation $\bar{\pi}$. Then $|p_2 - p_1|$ is negligible.
- Game_3 is the same as Game_2 except for that each X_i replaced with random string of length n in the store phase, and each a_i is replaced with a random bit in the add protocol. Then $|p_3 - p_2|$ is negligible because PRF is a pseudorandom function.
- Game_4 is the same as Game_3 except for that each mac_i in the store phase and each Δ_{w_i} in the add protocol are replaced with random strings of length λ. Then $|p_4 - p_3|$ is negligible because f is a pseudorandom function.

It is easy to see that $p_4 = \Pr(b = 1$ in $\mathsf{Game}_{sim})$. Therefore

$$\mathsf{Adv}_{\mathsf{Sim}}^{priv}(B) = |\Pr(b = 1 \text{ in } \mathsf{Game}_{real}) - \Pr(b = 1 \text{ in } \mathsf{Game}_{sim})|$$
$$= |p_0 - p_4| = negligible$$

for any distinguisher B. Therefore the proposed protocol satisfies privacy.

6.3 Strong Reliability of Our Scheme

Theorem 4. *The above dynamic SSE scheme satisfies strong reliability under the strong RSA assumption.*

Let (A_1, A_2) be an adversary in the definition of strong reliability. Suppose that the client has stored $\mathcal{C} = (C_1, \ldots, C_n)$ and

$$\mathcal{I} = (\mathsf{Table}, (N, g), Acc, (p_1, x_1), \ldots, (p_n, x_n))$$

to A_2. Let BAD_1 be the event that A_2 returns (C'_j, p'_j, x'_j) such that $(C'_j, p'_j, x'_j) \neq (C_j, p_j, x_j)$ for some j, and the client outputs accept in the search, modify or delete protocol. Let BAD_2 be the event that A_2 returns an invalid $(\hat{e}'_1, \ldots, \hat{e}'_n, mac')$, and the client outputs accept in the search protocol.

We need to show that BAD_1 or BAD_2 occurs only with negligible probability.

Lemma 1. *For any (A_1, A_2), BAD_1 occurs with negligible probability under the strong RSA assumption.*

Proof. The strong RSA assumption claims that it is hard to find (x, e) such that $y = x^e \bmod N$ for given (N, y), where $y \xleftarrow{\$} Z_N^*$.

Suppose that there exits some (A_1, A_2) such that BAD_1 occurs with nonnegligible probability. We construct an attacker B on the strong RSA assumption as follows. B takes (N, y) as an input, where $y \xleftarrow{\$} Z_N^*$. B sets $(N, g) := (N, y)$. It is easy to see that $g = y$ is a generator of QR_N with probability almost $1/4$.

B runs (A_1, A_2) by playing the role of the client with the above (N, g), where it computes x_j in the store phase by

$$x_j = g^{p_1 \times \cdots \times p_{j-1} \times p_{j+1} \cdots \times p_n} \bmod N$$

instead of Eq. (5). Suppose that A_2 sends (C'_j, p'_j, x'_j) such that $(C'_j, p'_j, x'_j) \neq (C_j, p_j, x_j)$ for some j, and the client outputs accept. Then p'_j is a prime and $Acc = g^{p_0} = (x'_j)^{p'_j}$, where $p_0 = p_1 \times \ldots \times p_n$. Note that $\gcd(p_0, p'_j) = 1$. Now B can break the strong RSA assumption as in [6,7]. B computes $a, b \in Z$ such that $ap_0 + bp'_j = 1$ by the extended Euclidean algorithm and outputs $x = (x'_j)^a g^b$ and p'_j. Then we have $x^{p'_j} = ((x'_j)^a g^b)^{p'_j} = (g^{p_0})^a g^{bp'_j} = g$. Hence the strong RSA assumption is broken with nonnegligible probability. $\qquad\square$

Lemma 2. *For any* (A_1, A_2), BAD$_2$ *occurs with negligible probability if* f *is a pseudorandom function.*

Proof. Suppose that there exits some (A_1, A_2) such that BAD$_2$ occurs with nonnegligible probability. We will construct a distinguisher B which can distinguish between f and the random oracle RO : $\{0,1\}^* \to \{0,1\}^\lambda$.

Let $\mathcal{O}$ denote the oracle $f_{k_m}(\cdot)$ or RO$(\cdot)$. B runs (A_1, A_2) by playing the role of the client, where B computes the values of f by using the oracle $\mathcal{O}$. B finally outputs 1 if BAD$_2$ occurs, and 0 otherwise.

If $\mathcal{O} = f_{k_m}(\cdot)$, then $\Pr(B$ outputs $1) = nonnegligible$ from our assumption.

Suppose that $\mathcal{O} = $ RO$(\cdot)$, and A_2 returns an invalid $(\hat{e}'_1, \ldots, \hat{e}'_n, mac')$ for some $t(w^*) = (\pi_k(w^*), [\mathsf{PRF}_{k'}(w^*)]_{1\ldots n})$ at some point in the search protocol. In the store protocol, suppose that the client received Index $= (e_{i,j})$ from A_1, and stored $mac_1, \ldots, mac_m$ to A_2 such that

$$mac_1 = \mathsf{RO}(0\|w_1\|n) \oplus \sum_{j=1}^n e_{1,j} \times \mathsf{RO}(1\|j), \tag{9}$$

$$\vdots$$

$$mac_m = \mathsf{RO}(0\|w_m\|n) \oplus \sum_{j=1}^n e_{m,j} \times \mathsf{RO}(1\|j) \tag{10}$$

Note that A_2 received the above $(mac_1, \ldots, mac_m)$, but not each value of RO. Further for each value of $(\mathsf{RO}(1\|1), \ldots, \mathsf{RO}(1\|n))$, there exit some $((\mathsf{RO}(0\|w_1\|n), \ldots, \mathsf{RO}(0\|w_m\|n))$ which satisfy Eqs. (9) and (10). This means that $(\mathsf{RO}(1\|1), \ldots, \mathsf{RO}(1\|n))$ are uniformly distributed from a view point of A_2. By using a similar argument, we can see that this is so even if Δ_{w_1} of Eq. (7) is given to A_2 in the Add protocol. (In our protocol, the set of keywords contained in each file do not change. The index table changes only when a new file is added.)

Without loss of generality, let $w^* = w_1$. Then the client accepts $(\hat{e}'_1, \ldots, \hat{e}'_n, mac')$ if

$$mac' = \mathsf{RO}(0\|w_1\|n) \oplus \sum_{j=1}^n \hat{e}_j \times \mathsf{RO}(1\|j). \tag{11}$$

Suppose that $(\hat{e}'_1, \ldots, \hat{e}'_n) = (e_{1,1}, \ldots, e_{1,n})$ and $mac' \neq mac_1$. Then Eq. (11) does not hold clearly from Eq. (9).

Suppose that $(\hat{e}'_1, \ldots, \hat{e}'_n) \neq (e_{1,1}, \ldots, e_{1,n})$. Then it must be that

$$mac' = mac_1 \oplus \sum_{j=1}^{n} u_j \times \mathsf{RO}(1\|j), \tag{12}$$

where $u_j = e_{1,j} \oplus \hat{e}_j$ for $j = 1, \ldots, n$ and $(u_1, \ldots, u_n) \neq (0, \ldots, 0)$. Now Eq. (12) holds with probability $1/2^\lambda$ because $(\mathsf{RO}(1\|1), \ldots, \mathsf{RO}(1\|n))$ are uniformly distributed. Hence the client accepts $(\hat{e}'_1, \ldots, \hat{e}'_n, mac')$ only with negligible probability. Consequently $\Pr(B \text{ outputs } 1) = negligible$. However, this is a contradiction because f is a pseudorandom function. □

Therefore the proposed protocol satisfies strong reliability.

6.4   UC Security

Corollary 1. *Our verifiable SSE scheme securely realizes the ideal functionality $\mathcal{F}_{\mathsf{SSE}}$.*

Proof. This corollary is obtained from Theorems 2, 3 and 4.

7   Hybrid Variant

A major difference between our scheme and that of [21] is how to authenticate the index table Index. Another difference is how to use the RSA accumulator to authenticate encrypted files. In our scheme, the client stores Witness $= \{tag_i = (p_i, x_i) \mid i = 1, \ldots, n\}$ to the server, and the server returns $\{tag_i \mid \hat{e}_i = 1\}$ to the client in the search phase. On the other hand, in [21], the client does not store Witness to the server. Instead, the server computes

$$\pi_C = g^{\prod_{\hat{e}_i=1} p_i} \tag{13}$$

for each search query and returns it to the client. The client verifies if

$$Acc = (\pi_C)^{\prod_{\hat{e}_i=0} p_i}, \tag{14}$$

where the client and the server share the same key k_p of a pseudorandom function to generate primes p_i.

Now we can consider a hybrid variant such that the index table is authenticated by using XOR-MAC, and the encrypted files are authenticated by using the RSA accumulator as shown by Eqs. (13) and (14).

In other words, the hybrid variant is the same as the scheme of [21] except for that the index table is authenticated by using XOR-MAC. Our main scheme is the same as the hybrid variant except for that the encrypted files are authenticated by using Witness.

In the search protocol, our main scheme is the most efficient and our hybrid variant is the second.

In the modify protocol and the delete protocol, on the other hand, the server has to compute $3(n-1)$ exponentiations in our main scheme while the server needs to compute only $(n-1)$ exponentiations in our hybrid variant and in the scheme of [21].

8   Computer Simulation

Figures 2, 3, 4, 5 show our simulation results of search protocols, where we used a laptop computer. In each figure, the horizontal axis shows the number of files n, and the vertical axis shows the running time of the client and the server. The number of keywords is fixed to $m = 20$.

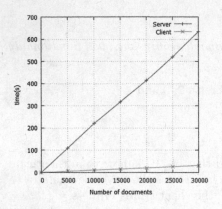

Fig. 2. KO13 [21] with $|D(w)| = 1$.

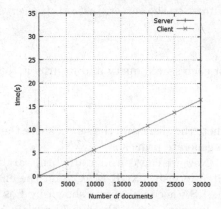

Fig. 3. KO13 [21] with $|D(w)| \simeq n/2$.

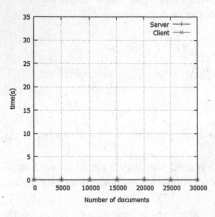

Fig. 4. Main scheme with $|D(w)| = 1$.

Fig. 5. Main scheme with $|D(w)| \simeq n/2$

Figures 2 and 3 are the previous scheme [21], and Figs. 4 and 5 are our main scheme. Each keyword is contained in a single file in Figs. 2 and 4, and it is contained in about $n/2$ files In Figs. 3 and 5.

In Fig. 4, both running times are almost zero. In Fig. 5, the running time of the server is almost zero. From these figures, we can see that our main scheme is much faster than that of [21].

A   Proof of Theorem 1

(Proof of privacy). In the real world, consider an adversary A_0 who corrupts the server in such a way that A_0 sends each message Y_i that the server received from the client to $\mathcal{Z}$. Look at $\mathcal{Z}$ as a distinguisher and (client, server, A) as a challenger. Then this real world can be seen as the real game of privacy.

On the other hand, in the ideal world, there exists an adversary S which sends Y_i' which is almost the same Y_i to $\mathcal{Z}$ because $\mathcal{Z}$ cannot distinguish between the real world and the ideal world from our assumption. Now look at $\mathcal{Z}$ as a distinguisher, S as a simulator and (dummy-client, $\mathcal{F}_{dSSE}$) as a challenger. Then this ideal world can be seen as the ideal game of privacy.

This means that $\mathsf{Adv}_S^{priv}(\mathcal{Z}) = \mathsf{Adv}_S^{uc}(\mathcal{Z}, A_0)$. Therefore we have

$$\mathsf{Adv}_S^{priv} = \max_{\mathcal{Z}} \mathsf{Adv}_S^{priv}(\mathcal{Z}) = \max_{\mathcal{Z}} \mathsf{Adv}_S^{uc}(\mathcal{Z}, A_0) = negligible$$

from our assumption. Hence Π satisfies privacy.

(Proof of reliability). For an adversary (A_1, A_2) of reliability (see Sect. 4), consider an environment $\mathcal{Z}$ and a real world adversary A such that $(\mathcal{Z}, A) = (A_1, A_2)$. Then there exists an ideal world adversary S such that

$$\mathsf{Adv}_S^{uc}(\mathcal{Z}, A) = |\mathrm{P}_{real} - \mathrm{P}_{sim}| = negligible$$

from our assumption.

In the ideal world, $\mathcal{Z}$ never receives $\mathsf{D}(w)'$ such that $\mathsf{D}(w)' \neq \mathsf{D}(w)$ for any (search, w). Therefore

$$\mathrm{P}_{ideal} = \Pr(\mathcal{Z} \text{ outputs } 1) = \Pr(A_1 \text{ outputs } 1) = 0.$$

Hence $\mathrm{P}_{real} = $ negligible. This means that

$$\mathsf{Adv}^{auth}(A_1, A_2) = \mathrm{P}_{real} = negligible.$$

Therefore Π satisfies reliability.

B   Proof of Theorem 2

Fix a real world adversary A who corrupts the server arbitrarily. In the following, we consider a series of games $\mathsf{Game}_0, \cdots, \mathsf{Game}_3$, where Game_0 is the real world. Let $p_i = \Pr(\mathcal{Z} \text{ outputs } 1 \text{ in } \mathsf{Game}_i)$.

(Game$_1$) This game is the same as Game$_0$ except for the following.

In the store phase, the client records $(\mathcal{D}, \mathcal{W}, \mathtt{Index})$ in addition to sending (store, $\mathcal{C}, \mathcal{I}$) to the server.

In the search/update phase:

- If the client takes (add, D, e) as an input from $\mathcal{Z}$, then in addition to sending (add, C_{n+1}, α) to the server, he appends D to $\mathcal{D}$, and updates the $m \times n$ binary matrix $\mathtt{Index}$ to the $m \times (n+1)$ one such that the last column is $\mathbf{e}^T$.

- If the client takes the other type of input from $\mathcal{Z}$, then he sends the (first) message to the server.

1. If A instructs the server to return an invalid $(C'(w), Tag'(w))$ or an invalid (C'_i, tag'_i), then the server returns reject to the client.
   Otherwise the server returns accept to the client.

2. If the client receives reject from the server, then he sends reject to $\mathcal{Z}$.

3. Suppose that the client receives accept from the server.
   - If his input is (search, w), then he sends $D(w)$ to $\mathcal{Z}$.
   - If his input is (modify, i, D'_i), then he replaces D_i with D'_i.
   - If his input is (delete, i), then he replaces D_i with delete.

Let BAD be the event that the client accepts an invalid $(C'(w), Tag'(w))$ or an invalid (C_i, tag_i) in Game$_0$. Then it holds that $|p_0 - p_1| \leq \Pr(\mathsf{BAD})$. Now consider an adversary (A_1, A_2) on the reliability such that $(A_1, A_2) = (\mathcal{Z}, (\mathsf{A}, server))$ in Game$_0$. Then we can see that $\Pr(\mathsf{BAD}) = \mathsf{Adv}^{sauth}(A_1, A_2)$. Therefore we have $|p_0 - p_1| \leq \mathsf{Adv}^{sauth}$.

(Game$_2$) In this game, we modify Game$_1$ as follows. We replace the client with $(client_1, client_2)$ such as follows.

1. Both of $client_1$ and $client_2$ receive the (same) input from $\mathcal{Z}$.
2. $client_2$ sends the (first) message of the client to the server.
3. $client_1$ receives accept or reject from the server, and behaves in the same way as the client does in Game$_1$.

This change is conceptual only. Therefore $p_2 = p_1$.

(Game$_3$) In this game, we modify Game$_2$ as follows. Since Π satisfies privacy from our assumption, there exists a simulator Sim such that $\mathsf{Adv}_{\mathsf{Sim}}^{priv} = negligible$. Now in Game$_3$, $client_2$ plays the role of the challenger in the simulation game of privacy, and sends the minimum leakage to Sim. Sim then sends its outputs (the simulated message) to the server.

Further look at $(\mathcal{Z}, client_1, server, \mathsf{A})$ as a distinguisher of the privacy game. Then Game$_3$ is the simulation game and Game$_2$ is the real game. Therefore it holds that $|p_3 - p_2| \leq \mathsf{Adv}_{\mathsf{Sim}}^{priv}$.

In Game$_3$, $(client_1, clinet_2)$ behaves exactly in the same way as the ideal functionality $\mathcal{F}_{\mathrm{dSSE}}$. Further look at $(\mathsf{A}, server, \mathsf{Sim})$ as the ideal world adversary S. Then Game$_3$ can be seen as the ideal world of the UC framework.

Therefore we have

$$\mathsf{Adv}_{\mathsf{S}}^{uc}(\mathcal{Z}, A) = |p_0 - p_3| \leq \mathsf{Adv}^{sauth} + \mathsf{Adv}_{\mathsf{Sim}}^{priv}$$

for any $\mathcal{Z}$. Finally Adv^{sauth} and $\mathsf{Adv}_{\mathsf{Sim}}^{priv}$ are negligible from our assumption. Hence Π securely realizes $\mathcal{F}_{\mathrm{dSSE}}$.

References

1. Bellovin, S., Cheswick, W.: Privacy-enhanced searches using encrypted bloom filters, Cryptology ePrint Archive, Report 2006/210 (2006). http://eprint.iacr.org/
2. Bellare, M., Desai, A., Jokipii, E., Rogaway, P.: A concrete security treatment of symmetric encryption. In: FOCS 1997, pp. 394–403 (1997)
3. Bellare, M., Guérin, R., Rogaway, P.: XOR MACs: new methods for message authentication using finite pseudorandom functions. In: Coppersmith, D. (ed.) CRYPTO 1995. LNCS, vol. 963, pp. 15–28. Springer, Heidelberg (1995)
4. Ballard, L., Kamara, S., Monrose, F.: Achieving efficient conjunctive keyword searches over encrypted data. In: Qing, S., Mao, W., López, J., Wang, G. (eds.) ICICS 2005. LNCS, vol. 3783, pp. 414–426. Springer, Heidelberg (2005)
5. Byun, J.W., Lee, D.-H., Lim, J.-I.: Efficient conjunctive keyword search on encrypted data storage system. In: Atzeni, A.S., Lioy, A. (eds.) EuroPKI 2006. LNCS, vol. 4043, pp. 184–196. Springer, Heidelberg (2006)
6. Benaloh, J.C., de Mare, M.: One-way accumulators: a decentralized alternative to digital signatures. In: Helleseth, T. (ed.) EUROCRYPT 1993. LNCS, vol. 765, pp. 274–285. Springer, Heidelberg (1994)
7. Barić, N., Pfitzmann, B.: Collision-free accumulators and fail-stop signature schemes without trees. In: Fumy, W. (ed.) EUROCRYPT 1997. LNCS, vol. 1233, pp. 480–494. Springer, Heidelberg (1997)
8. Canetti, R., Security, U.C.: A new paradigm for cryptographic protocols, Cryptology ePrint Archive, Report 2000/067 (2005). http://eprint.iacr.org/
9. Curtmola, R., Garay, J.A., Kamara, S., Ostrovsky, R.: Searchable symmetric encryption: improved definitions and efficient constructions. In: ACM Conference on Computer and Communications Security 2006, pp. 79–88 (2006)
10. Full version of the above: Cryptology ePrint Archive, Report 2006/210 (2006). http://eprint.iacr.org/
11. Cash, D., Jarecki, S., Jutla, C., Krawczyk, H., Roşu, M.-C., Steiner, M.: Highly-scalable searchable symmetric encryption with support for boolean queries. In: Canetti, R., Garay, J.A. (eds.) CRYPTO 2013, Part I. LNCS, vol. 8042, pp. 353–373. Springer, Heidelberg (2013)
12. Cash, D., Jaeger, J., Jarecki, S., Jutla, C.S., Krawczyk, H., Rosu, M.-C., Steiner, M.: Dynamic searchable encryption in very-large databases: data structures and implementation. In: NDSS 2014
13. Camenisch, J.L., Lysyanskaya, A.: Dynamic accumulators and application to efficient revocation of anonymous credentials. In: Yung, M. (ed.) CRYPTO 2002. LNCS, vol. 2442, p. 61. Springer, Heidelberg (2002)
14. Chang, Y.-C., Mitzenmacher, M.: Privacy preserving keyword searches on remote encrypted data. In: Ioannidis, J., Keromytis, A.D., Yung, M. (eds.) ACNS 2005. LNCS, vol. 3531, pp. 442–455. Springer, Heidelberg (2005)
15. Cash, D., Tessaro, S.: The locality of searchable symmetric encryption. In: Nguyen, P.Q., Oswald, E. (eds.) EUROCRYPT 2014. LNCS, vol. 8441, pp. 351–368. Springer, Heidelberg (2014)
16. Goh, E.-J.: Secure indexes. Cryptology ePrint Archive, Report 2003/216 (2003). http://eprint.iacr.org/
17. Golle, P., Staddon, J., Waters, B.: Secure conjunctive keyword search over encrypted data. In: Jakobsson, M., Yung, M., Zhou, J. (eds.) ACNS 2004. LNCS, vol. 3089, pp. 31–45. Springer, Heidelberg (2004)

18. Kurosawa, K.: Garbled searchable symmetric encryption. In: Financial Cryptography 2014, pp. 234–251 (2014)
19. Kurosawa, K., Ohtaki, Y.: UC-secure searchable symmetric encryption. In: Financial Cryptography 2012, pp. 285–298 (2012)
20. The final version of [19]. Cryptology ePrint Archive, Report 2015/251 (2015)
21. Kurosawa, K., Ohtaki, Y.: How to update documents *Verifiably* in searchable symmetric encryption. In: Abdalla, M., Nita-Rotaru, C., Dahab, R. (eds.) CANS 2013. LNCS, vol. 8257, pp. 309–328. Springer, Heidelberg (2013)
22. Kamara, S., Papamanthou, C.: Parallel and dynamic searchable symmetric encryption. In: FC 2013 (2013)
23. Kamara, S., Papamanthou, C., Roeder, T.: Dynamic searchable symmetric encryption. In: ACM Conference on Computer and Communications Security 2012, pp. 965–976 (2012)
24. Naveed, M., Prabhakaran, M., Gunter, C.: Dynamic searchable encryption via blind storage. In: IEEE Security & Privacy 2014
25. Song, D., Wagner, D., Perrig, A.: Practical techniques for searches on encrypted data. In: IEEE Symposium on Security and Privacy 2000, pp. 44–55 (2000)
26. Wang, P., Wang, H., Pieprzyk, J.: Keyword field-free conjunctive keyword searches on encrypted data and extension for dynamic groups. In: Franklin, M.K., Hui, L.C.K., Wong, D.S. (eds.) CANS 2008. LNCS, vol. 5339, pp. 178–195. Springer, Heidelberg (2008)

Simple, Secure, and Efficient Searchable Symmetric Encryption with Multiple Encrypted Indexes

Takato Hirano[1](✉), Mitsuhiro Hattori[1], Yutaka Kawai[1], Nori Matsuda[1],
Mitsugu Iwamoto[2], Kazuo Ohta[2], Yusuke Sakai[3], and Tatsuji Munaka[4]

[1] Mitsubishi Electric Corporation, Kamakura, Japan
Hirano.Takato@ay.MitsubishiElectric.co.jp,
Hattori.Mitsuhiro@eb.MitsubishiElectric.co.jp,
Kawai.Yutaka@da.MitsubishiElectric.co.jp,
Matsuda.Nori@ea.MitsubishiElectric.co.jp
[2] University of Electro-Communications, Chofu, Japan
{mitsugu,kazuo.ohta}@uec.ac.jp
[3] National Institute of Advanced Industrial Science and Technology, Tokyo, Japan
yusuke.sakai@aist.go.jp
[4] Tokai University, Tokyo, Japan
Munaka@tsc.u-tokai.ac.jp

Abstract. In searchable symmetric encryption (SSE), adding documents to a database is an indispensable functionality in real situations, and there are two approaches for executing the process: One approach is to update the encrypted index, and the other is to generate a new encrypted index. The former approach is called dynamic SSE, which has been extensively studied recently due to its importance. The latter approach has an advantage such that it can be directly applied to any existing SSE scheme without degrading its original functionalities, but previous methods are not satisfactory from a viewpoint of security, storage size, or efficiency. In this paper, we propose a simple document adding method that resolve the problem occurred in the latter approach. Our method is quite generic, and therefore can be applied to any existing SSE scheme (e.g. non-dynamic one with useful functionalities). Our key idea is to utilize publicly available information and hash chains in construction of encrypted indexes. In order to exhibit the ability of our method, we present a concrete scheme which is led by applying our method to the well-known and influential scheme SSE-2 (ACM CCS 2006). Thanks to the simplicity of our method, the scheme can be easily proved secure under a naturally generalized setting of the most widely used security model.

Keywords: Searchable symmetric encryption · Document adding · Generic approach · Multiple encrypted indexes · Generalized security model

© Springer International Publishing Switzerland 2016
K. Ogawa and K. Yoshioka (Eds.): IWSEC 2016, LNCS 9836, pp. 91–110, 2016.
DOI: 10.1007/978-3-319-44524-3_6

1   Introduction

1.1   Background

Searchable encryption of symmetric-key type is called *searchable symmetric encryption* or *SSE* and its concrete schemes have been proposed (e.g. [1,3,5–16,18–34]). SSE consists of *document storing process* and *keyword searching process*, and the processes are executed by the same user. In the document storing process, the user encrypts documents and generates an *encrypted index* from the secret key, and the server stores a pair of the encrypted documents (*ciphertexts* hereafter) and the encrypted index. In the keyword searching process, the user generates an encrypted query called *trapdoor* from the secret key and a keyword, and the server searches on the ciphertexts by applying the trapdoor to the encrypted index.

Security models for SSE have been also studied. The security model formalized by Curtmola et al. [11] covers the security of both the document storing process and the keyword searching process, and therefore is widely used in the SSE literature. Curtmola et al. carefully examined unavoidable information leaked from the document storing process and the keyword searching process of a general SSE scheme, and formalized *acceptable leakage information* in SSE. Then, they defined that an SSE scheme is secure if information revealed from the processes of the scheme is at most the acceptable leakage information. Since their security framework is considered practical in current SSE literature, many previous works [1,5–7,9–14,16,18–27,29–34] employ this security model and its slightly modified variants.

1.2   Related Works

The first searchable encryption scheme was proposed in [28], and many concrete schemes have been constructed. In addition to the basic functionalities such as document storing and keyword searching, SSE schemes with other useful functionalities have been proposed [1,3,5–7,9–14,16,18–26,29–34].

The most fundamental functionality is capability of document adding, and therefore SSE schemes with such a functionality have been proposed [5,16,18,19, 22,26,29,31,34]. These schemes employ an index-updating approach: When new documents are added, the encrypted index corresponding the existing documents is updated accordingly.

Another naive approach is to add new documents in a manner totally identical to document storing: When documents are added, it is processed in the same way as document storing, and the processed data (i.e. a new encrypted index and ciphertexts) is stored side-by-side with the existing one. The existing encrypted indexes are therefore unchanged, and still used in the keyword searching process. This approach is obviously more flexible and generic than the index-updating approach, and would be applied to any SSE scheme. A secure method of the approach has been also proposed [8,11] in which an additional secret key is generated in every document adding process.

The SSE schemes with no document adding functionality but other useful ones have been also studied: Examples include supporting multi-user settings [11–13,33], UC-security [21,30], flexible search such as Boolean queries [6, 20,25], fuzzy matching [3,23,24,32], and substring matching [10,14], and efficient locality [1,7].

1.3 Motivation

As mentioned in the above subsection, there are mainly two approaches for enabling document adding in SSE: One is to update the existing encrypted index, and the other is to generate an additional encrypted index.

The former approach is called *dynamic* SSE, which has been extensively studied recently due to its importance, and a lot of concrete schemes have been proposed [5,16,18,19,22,26,29,31,34]. In this paper, we call such SSE *Index-Updatable Dynamic SSE (IU-DSSE)*.

IU-DSSE schemes are capable of not only document adding, but also flexible document updating and deleting. However, due to the structural complexity of the encrypted index of IU-DSSE, it is not easy to apply this approach to ordinary SSE schemes, and thereby modify them into IU-DSSE ones. As a typical example, the encrypted index of the IU-DSSE scheme [18] is constructed by introducing a very complex link-type structure into SSE-1 proposed in [11]. In fact, there are few IU-DSSE schemes with other useful functionalities (e.g. [22,26]).

The latter approach focuses mainly on introducing a document adding functionality to the existing SSE scheme without degrading other useful functionalities that the schemes have already equipped with. The strategy behind this approach is generosity: It should be straightforward to modify non-dynamic but useful SSE mentioned in Sect. 1.2 [1,3,6,7,10–14,20,21,23–25,30,32,33]. Hence, the latter approach is also important in SSE literature, similarly to IU-DSSE. In this paper, we call such SSE *Index-Generatable Dynamic SSE (IG-DSSE)*.

However, as pointed out in [8,11], undesirable information is leaked if the user naively generates encrypted indexes using the same secret key twice. Indeed, meaningful information can be extracted by comparing two of the encrypted indexes or by applying past trapdoors to future encrypted indexes (a.k.a. forward privacy). This is because the security model of [11] and many existing schemes do not care about the information leaked from multiple encrypted indexes.

In order to address this information leakage problem, [8,11] also proposed its countermeasures. The common strategy behind them is to generate a new secret key every time new documents are added. This strategy leads to simple and generic document adding methods which can be applied to all existing SSE schemes. However, the methods [8,11] are not necessarily suitable for the case where the document adding process is conducted frequently. Since additional secret keys are generated every time new documents are added, it is unable to employ secure and lightweight key management solutions such as IC-cards, because they have significant limitation on the storage size. Moreover, in the keyword searching process, the user has to generate a lot of trapdoors each of which corresponds to encrypted indexes stored on the server. Roughly, the number of additional secret keys and the number of trapdoors generated in the methods are both $O(N)$, where N is the number of encrypted indexes stored on the server.

1.4   Our Contribution

In this paper, we propose a simple, secure, and efficient document adding method which can be used to convert any existing SSE scheme to IG-DSSE ones without degrading security and without requiring additional secret keys. The method enables us to apply a document adding functionality to existing non-dynamic but useful SSE schemes mentioned in Sect. 1.2 [1, 3, 6, 7, 10–14, 20, 21, 23–25, 30, 32, 33] without degrading useful functionalities that the schemes have already equipped with.

Our method consists of two ideas. The first one is to embed a unique identifier into each encrypted index. This simple idea brings simple and secure conversion, but at the same time, it leads to inefficiency in trapdoor size. The second one is to use hash chains in order to resolve the inefficiency problem. Generality, Security, and efficiency of our method can be confirmed by using an abstract framework, pointed out in this paper, which can cover all existing SSE schemes.

In order to exhibit the ability of our method, we present a concrete IG-DSSE scheme which is led by applying our method to the well-known and influential scheme SSE-2 proposed by Curtmola et al. [11]. Note that we use a slightly modified SSE-2 (SSE-2' hereafter) which is proposed in this paper and more efficient than original one in regard to the trapdoor size. We show that the IG-DSSE scheme converted from SSE-2' using our method is secure under a "naturally generalized setting" of their security model [11]. Since the security model [11] cannot cover security for IG-DSSE, we also formalize security definitions suitable for IG-DSSE by naturally generalizing the security model, and show their relationships.

Comparison among our method and previous document adding methods is summarized in Table 1. Secret Key Adding and Index Updating methods correspond to [8, 11] and [5, 16, 18, 19, 22, 26, 29, 31, 34], respectively. Key Size and Trapdoor Size mean the number of secret keys and of trapdoors, respectively, where N is that of encrypted indexes stored on the server. ROM means the random oracle model.

Table 1. Comparison among the previous document adding methods and our method

	IU-DSSE	IG-DSSE		
	Index Updating	Naive Adding	Secret Key Adding	Ours
Generality	Low	High	High	High
Security	High	Low	High	High
Key Size	$O(1)$	$O(1)$	$O(N)$	$O(1)$
Trapdoor Size	$O(1)$	$O(1)$	$O(N)$	$O(1)$
Additional Assumption	ROM (almost all schemes)	None	None	ROM

The organization of this paper are as follows. In Sect. 2, we give some notations, and review definitions of SSE. Section 3 is devoted to give the security definitions for IG-DSSE, and to show relationships among them. Our proposal for the document adding method is given in Sect. 4, and a concrete scheme is provided by applying it to SSE-2'. In Sect. 5, we conclude this paper.

2 Preliminaries

2.1 Notations and Basic Cryptographic Primitives

We denote the set of positive real numbers by $\mathbb{R}^+$. We say that a function $\text{negl} : \mathbb{N} \to \mathbb{R}^+$ is negligible if for any (positive) polynomial p, there exists $n_0 \in \mathbb{N}$ such that for all $n \geq n_0$, it holds $\text{negl}(n) < 1/p(n)$. If A is a probabilistic algorithm, $y \leftarrow A(x)$ denotes running A on input x with a uniformly-chosen random tape and assigning the output to y. $A^{\mathcal{O}}$ denotes an algorithm with oracle access to $\mathcal{O}$. If S is a finite set, $s \xleftarrow{u} S$ denotes that s is uniformly chosen from S. We denote the bit length of S by $|S|$, and the cardinality of S by $\#S$. For sequences $\mathbf{s} = (s_1, \ldots, s_m)$ and $\mathbf{s}' = (s_1', \ldots, s_n')$, $\mathbf{s}||\mathbf{s}'$ denotes $(s_1, \ldots, s_m, s_1', \ldots, s_n')$. For $\mathbf{S} = (S_1, \ldots, S_n)$ and $\mathbf{S}' = (S_1', \ldots, S_n')$, where S_i and S_j' are sets, $\mathbf{S} \cup \mathbf{S}'$ denotes $(S_1 \cup S_1', \ldots, S_n \cup S_n')$. For strings a and b, $a||b$ denotes the concatenation of a and b.

We recall the definition of pseudo-random functions. A function $f : \{0,1\}^\lambda \times \{0,1\}^m \to \{0,1\}^n$ is pseudo-random if f is polynomial-time computable in λ, and for any probabilistic polynomial-time (PPT) algorithm $\mathcal{A}$, it holds $|\Pr[1 \leftarrow \mathcal{A}^{f_K(\cdot)}(\lambda) \mid K \xleftarrow{u} \{0,1\}^\lambda] - \Pr[1 \leftarrow \mathcal{A}^{g(\cdot)}(\lambda) \mid g \xleftarrow{u} \text{FUNC}[m,n]]| \leq \text{negl}(\lambda)$, where $\text{FUNC}[m,n]$ is the set of functions mapping $\{0,1\}^m$ to $\{0,1\}^n$. If $m = n$, we say f pseudo-random permutation.

We recall the definition of *left-or-right indistinguishability against the chosen plaintext attack (LOR-CPA)* [2] for symmetric-key encryption. A symmetric-key encryption scheme is secure in the sense of LOR-CPA if for any PPT adversary $\mathcal{A}$, it holds $|\Pr[1 \leftarrow \mathcal{A}^{\text{Enc}_K(\mathcal{LR}(\cdot,\cdot,1))}(1^\lambda) \mid K \leftarrow \text{Gen}(1^\lambda)] - \Pr[1 \leftarrow \mathcal{A}^{\text{Enc}_K(\mathcal{LR}(\cdot,\cdot,0))}(1^\lambda) \mid K \leftarrow \text{Gen}(1^\lambda)]| \leq \text{negl}(\lambda)$, where $\text{Enc}_K(\mathcal{LR}(\cdot,\cdot,b))$ is the left-or-right oracle that takes an input (x_0, x_1) and outputs $C_0 \leftarrow \text{Enc}_K(x_0)$ if $b = 0$ and $C_1 \leftarrow \text{Enc}_K(x_1)$ if $b = 1$.

2.2 Definitions of Ordinary SSE

We recall the definitions of ordinary SSE, formalized in [11].

- Let w be a keyword, and $\Delta \subseteq \{0,1\}^\ell$ be a set of d keywords. We assume that ℓ is small throughout this paper. That is, d and 2^ℓ are polynomial bounded in the security parameter λ. In this paper, we assume $d = 2^\ell$.
- Let $D \in \{0,1\}^*$ be a document (or file), and $\mathbf{D} = (D_1, \ldots, D_n)$ be a document collection. Let $\mathbf{C} = (C_1, \ldots, C_n)$ be a ciphertext collection of $\mathbf{D}$, where C_i is a ciphertext of D_i for $1 \leq i \leq n$. We assume that the ciphertext C_i contain unique identifier (or file name) $id(D_i) \in \{0,1\}^\mu$.

- For $\mathbf{D} = (D_1, \ldots, D_n)$, let $\mathbf{D}(w)$ be a set of identifiers of documents that contain the keyword w. That is, $\mathbf{D}(w) = \{id(D_{i_1}), \ldots, id(D_{i_m})\}$. For a searching sequence $\mathbf{w} = (w_1, \ldots, w_q)$, let $\mathbf{D}(\mathbf{w}) = (\mathbf{D}(w_1), \ldots, \mathbf{D}(w_q))$.

An (ordinary) SSE scheme over a dictionary Δ, SSE = (Gen, Enc, Trpdr, Search, Dec), is defined as follows.

- $K \leftarrow$ Gen(1^λ): is a probabilistic algorithm which generates a secret key K, where λ is a security parameter.
- $(\mathcal{I}, \mathbf{C}) \leftarrow$ Enc$(K, \mathbf{D})$: is a probabilistic algorithm which outputs an encrypted index $\mathcal{I}$ and a ciphertext collection $\mathbf{C} = (C_1, \ldots, C_n)$.
- $t(w) \leftarrow$ Trpdr(K, w): is a deterministic algorithm which outputs a trapdoor $t(w)$ for a keyword w.
- $S(w) \leftarrow$ Search$(\mathcal{I}, t(w))$: is a deterministic algorithm which outputs an identifier set $S(w)$.
- $D \leftarrow$ Dec(K, C): is a deterministic algorithm which outputs a plaintext D of C.

Here, an SSE scheme is correct if for all $\lambda \in \mathbb{N}$, all $w \in \Delta$, all K output by Gen(1^λ), all $\mathbf{D}$, and $(\mathcal{I}, \mathbf{C})$ output by Enc$(K, \mathbf{D})$, it holds Search$(\mathcal{I}, $Trpdr$(K, w)) = \mathbf{D}(w)$ and Dec$(K, C_i) = D_i$ $(1 \leq i \leq n)$.

3   Security Notions and Definitions for IG-DSSE

In this section, we naturally generalize the security notions proposed in [11] and formalize security definitions for IG-DSSE. Also, we discuss limitations of previous document adding methods under our security definitions. Note that we employ the security model [12] more intuitive than [11].

3.1   Naturally Generalized Security Notions

Curtmola et al. proposed the security notions, *history*, *access pattern*, *search pattern*, *trace*, and *non-singular* for ordinary SSE in order to formalize both document storing security and keyword searching security [11]. Here, we generalize the five security notions in a natural way and formalize a new security notion *index adding pattern* so that we formally analyze the security of SSE schemes with executing the Enc algorithm multiple times (i.e. IG-DSSE).

Let $\mathbf{D}^{(i)} = (D_1^{(i)}, \ldots, D_{n_i}^{(i)})$ be the i-th added document collection, and $\mathbf{w}^{(i)} = (w_1^{(i)}, \ldots, w_{q_i}^{(i)})$ be a searching sequence soon after executing the i-th document adding process (i.e. the i-th encrypted index generation process) until just before executing the $(i + 1)$-th one, where i, n_i and q_i are integers. Then, we formalize the new security notions, as follows.

- An i-th *history* $H^{(i)}$ is a tuple $(\mathbf{D}^{(i)}, \mathbf{w}^{(i)})$. We can regard $H^{(i)}$ as sensitive information soon after executing the i-th document adding process until just before executing the $(i + 1)$-th one. A *history* $\mathbf{H}^{(k)}$ is a tuple $(H^{(1)}, \ldots, H^{(k)})$, where $k \in \mathbb{Z}$ and $k \geq 0$.

- The *access pattern* $\alpha(\mathbf{H}^{(k)})$ for a history $\mathbf{H}^{(k)}$ is a set of identifiers obtained from search results on $\mathbf{w}^{(1)}, \ldots, \mathbf{w}^{(k)}$. That is,

$$
\begin{aligned}
\alpha(\mathbf{H}^{(k)}) = (\ &\mathbf{D}^{(1)}(\mathbf{w}^{(1)}), \mathbf{D}^{(1)}(\mathbf{w}^{(2)}), \ldots, \mathbf{D}^{(1)}(\mathbf{w}^{(k)})) \\
\cup (\ &\emptyset^{q_1}, \mathbf{D}^{(2)}(\mathbf{w}^{(2)}), \ldots, \mathbf{D}^{(2)}(\mathbf{w}^{(k)})) \\
\cup (\ &\emptyset^{q_1}, \emptyset^{q_2}, \ldots, \mathbf{D}^{(k)}(\mathbf{w}^{(k)})),
\end{aligned}
$$

where $\emptyset^q$ means a vector $(\emptyset, \ldots, \emptyset)$ of length q. Note that there is no search result $\mathbf{D}^{(2)}(\mathbf{w}^{(1)})$ in the above information since $\mathbf{w}^{(1)}$ is a searching sequence before adding documents $\mathbf{D}^{(2)}$. We see that $\alpha(\mathbf{H}^{(k)})$ would be disclosed to the server.

- For $\mathbf{w}^{(1)}, \ldots, \mathbf{w}^{(k)}$ of a history $\mathbf{H}^{(k)}$, let $\mathbf{w} = \mathbf{w}^{(1)} \| \cdots \| \mathbf{w}^{(k)} = (w_1, \ldots, w_Q)$, where $Q = \sum_{i=1}^{k} q_i$. The *search pattern* $\sigma(\mathbf{H}^{(k)})$ for a history $\mathbf{H}^{(k)}$ is a binary symmetric matrix such that for $1 \le i \le j \le q$, the element in the i-th row and the j-th column is 1 if $w_i = w_j$, and 0 otherwise. Since trapdoors of almost all existing SSE schemes are generated deterministically, this information would be disclosed to the server (i.e. attacker). Furthermore, the server can also number the search sequence $\mathbf{w} = (w_1, \ldots, w_Q)$ from $\sigma(\mathbf{H}^{(k)})$. For example, let $\mathbf{w} = (w_1, w_2, w_3, w_4, w_5) = (a, c, a, a, b)$. Then, the server can compute some appearance sequence $(1, 2, 1, 1, 3)$ from $\sigma(\mathbf{H}^{(k)})$ since one can check $t(w_1) = t(w_3) = t(w_4)$. We call this information *search pattern appearance*, and denote it by $\gamma(\mathbf{w})$. We see that for $\gamma(\mathbf{w}) = (z_1, \ldots, z_J) \in \mathbb{Z}^Q$, it holds $a_i \le d$ for $1 \le i \le Q$, where z_i is a positive integer and d is the cardinality of Δ. Let $\gamma(\mathbf{w})[i] = z_i$ and $\gamma(\mathbf{w})(w)$ be $\gamma(\mathbf{w})[i]$ such that $\mathbf{w}[i] = w$. For example, $\gamma(\mathbf{w})(a) = 1$, $\gamma(\mathbf{w})(b) = 3$, and $\gamma(\mathbf{w})(c) = 2$.

- The *index adding pattern* $\beta(\mathbf{H}^{(k)})$ for a history $\mathbf{H}^{(k)}$ is defined as a sequence $(q_1, \ldots, q_k)$. Since this information is revealed from document adding (i.e. index generation) processes, and therefore would be disclosed to the server.

- Let $|\mathbf{D}^{(i)}|$ be a sequence $(|D_1^{(i)}|, \ldots, |D_{ni}^{(i)}|)$ for $1 \le i \le k$. The *trace* $\tau(\mathbf{H}^{(k)})$ for a history $\mathbf{H}^{(k)}$ is a tuple $(|\mathbf{D}^{(1)}|, \ldots, |\mathbf{D}^{(k)}|, \alpha(\mathbf{H}^{(k)}), \sigma(\mathbf{H}^{(k)}), \beta(\mathbf{H}^{(k)}))$. Roughly speaking, $\tau(\mathbf{H}^{(k)})$ is defined as acceptable leakage information in IG-DSSE.

- A history $\mathbf{H}^{(k)}$ is *non-singular* if (1) there exists at least one history $\mathbf{H}'^{(k)} \ne \mathbf{H}^{(k)}$ such that $\tau(\mathbf{H}^{(k)}) = \tau(\mathbf{H}'^{(k)})$, and if (2) for given $\tau(\mathbf{H}^{(k)})$, $\mathbf{H}'^{(k)}$ can be found in polynomial-time. Hereafter, we assume that all histories considered in this paper are non-singular.

We note that $\mathbf{H}^{(k)}$, $\alpha(\mathbf{H}^{(k)})$, $\sigma(\mathbf{H}^{(k)})$, and $\tau(\mathbf{H}^{(k)})$ are same as the original notions defined in [12] when $k = 1$ (this is the same situation as no document adding process).

Here, let us discuss on our trace. Since ciphertext collections and their corresponding encrypted indexes are stored in the server, then one can know $|\mathbf{D}^{(1)}|, \ldots, |\mathbf{D}^{(k)}|$, and $\beta(\mathbf{H}^{(k)})$ in IG-DSSE. If there exists a tuple $(i, j, h, g) \in \mathbb{Z}^4$ such that $1 \le g \le q_i$, $1 \le h \le q_j$, $1 \le i \le j \le k$, and $t(w_g^{(i)}) = t(w_h^{(j)})$, then the server notices $w_g^{(i)} = w_h^{(j)}$ since trapdoors are deterministically generated.

Hence, $\sigma(\mathbf{H}^{(k)})$ would be leaked from the keyword searching processes of IG-DSSE. Since $\mathbf{w}^{(i)}$ is the searching sequence soon after executing the i-th document adding process until just before executing the $(i+1)$-th one, the search result $\mathbf{D}^{(1)}(\mathbf{w}^{(i)}), \ldots, \mathbf{D}^{(i)}(\mathbf{w}^{(i)})$ would be leaked from the keyword searching processes of IG-DSSE. This information is exactly our access pattern $\alpha(\mathbf{H}^{(k)})$. On the other hand, for $i < j$, the information $\mathbf{D}^{(j)}(\mathbf{w}^{(i)})$ should not be leaked from the keyword searching processes of IG-DSSE since $\mathbf{w}^{(i)}$ is one of the searching sequence before adding $\mathbf{D}^{(j)}$. Therefore, we see that our trace $\tau(\mathbf{H}^{(k)})$ is a natural generalization of the original one defined in [12], and would be acceptable leakage information in IG-DSSE.

3.2 Naturally Generalized Security Definitions

Curtmola et al. proposed the security definitions, *(non-)adaptive indistinguishability* and *(non-)adaptive semantic security* [12]. Their security definitions can formally consider the security for both the document storing process and the keyword searching process in contrast to [8,15,28], and therefore are widely used in SSE literature. Informally, an SSE scheme is secure if information obtained from the processes is (computationally) equal to or less than the original trace (i.e. our trace with $k = 1$).

However, their security definitions cannot formally consider the security for IG-DSSE since the number of encrypted indexes generated in experiments of their security definitions is unique. This means that the security for IG-DSSE is outside of their security definitions although all existing SSE schemes can easily add documents by generating a new encrypted index. This fact is a serious problem for ordinary SSE schemes with no index update functionality.

Therefore, we present a formal security model for SSE with multiple encrypted indexes (i.e. IG-DSSE) by naturally generalizing the security model [12]. In this paper, our security model does not employ the leakage function approach defined in [9] since the approach does not focus on information revealed from leakage functions. This means that we would like to consider the security for IG-DSSE under practical leakage situations similarly to [12]. On the other hand, we can easily consider our security model with this leakage function approach.

Here, we formalize adaptive security definitions for IG-DSSE. Firstly, we give the definition, *adaptive indistinguishability for IG-DSSE (shortly, A-IND for IG-DSSE)*, by modifying adaptive indistinguishability [12]. For $i, j \geq 1$ and $b \in \{0, 1\}$, let $H_b^{(i)} = (\mathbf{D}_b^{(i)}, w_{b,1}^{(i)}, \ldots, w_{b,q_i}^{(i)})$, $\mathbf{t}_{b,0}^{(i)} = \emptyset$, $\mathbf{t}_{b,j}^{(i)} = (t(w_{b,1}^{(i)}), \ldots, t(w_{b,j}^{(i)}))$, $\boldsymbol{v}_{b,0} = \emptyset$, and $\boldsymbol{v}_{b,i} = \{\mathcal{I}_b^{(c)}, \mathcal{C}_b^{(c)}, \mathbf{t}_b^{(c)}\}_{c=1}^i$. We note that the following security definition is the same as the original one when $k = 1$.

Definition 1. *For a security parameter λ and an adversary $\mathcal{A} = (\{\mathcal{A}_0^{(i)}, \ldots, \mathcal{A}_{q_i}^{(i)}\}_{i=1}^k, \mathcal{A}')$ such that $k, q_1, \ldots, q_k \in \mathbb{N}$, consider Experiment 1 of Fig. 1 with the restriction that $\tau(H_0^{(1)}, \ldots, H_0^{(k)}) = \tau(H_1^{(1)}, \ldots, H_1^{(k)})$, where $\mathcal{A}_0^{(1)}(\boldsymbol{v}_{b,0}, st_{\mathcal{A}}) =$*

$$\mathbf{IND}^{\mathrm{adpt}}_{\mathrm{SSE},\mathcal{A}}(\lambda):$$
$\quad K \leftarrow \mathrm{Gen}(1^\lambda)$
$\quad b \stackrel{u}{\leftarrow} \{0,1\}$
$\quad$ for $1 \leq i \leq k$:
$\quad\quad (\mathbf{D}_0^{(i)}, \mathbf{D}_1^{(i)}, st_{\mathcal{A}}) \leftarrow \mathcal{A}_0^{(i)}(v_{b,i-1}, st_{\mathcal{A}})$
$\quad\quad (\mathcal{I}_b^{(i)}, \mathbf{C}_b^{(i)}) \leftarrow \mathrm{Enc}(K, \mathbf{D}_b^{(i)})$
$\quad\quad$ for $1 \leq j \leq q_i$:
$\quad\quad\quad (w_{0,j}^{(i)}, w_{1,j}^{(i)}, st_{\mathcal{A}}) \leftarrow \mathcal{A}_j^{(i)}(v_{b,i-1}, \mathcal{I}_b^{(i)}, \mathbf{C}_b^{(i)}, \mathbf{t}_{b,j-1}^{(i)}, st_{\mathcal{A}})$
$\quad\quad\quad t(w_{b,j}^{(i)}) \leftarrow \mathrm{Trpdr}(K, w_{b,j}^{(i)})$
$\quad b' \leftarrow \mathcal{A}'(v_{b,i}, st_{\mathcal{A}})$
$\quad$ output 1 if $b' = b$, 0 otherwise

Fig. 1. Experiment 1

$\mathcal{A}_0^{(1)}(1^\lambda)$ *as an exception. We say that* SSE *is secure in the sense of A-IND for IG-DSSE if for any PPT adversary* $\mathcal{A} = (\{\mathcal{A}_0^{(i)}, \ldots, \mathcal{A}_{q_i}^{(i)}\}_{i=1}^k, \mathcal{A}')$ *such that* $k, q_1, \ldots, q_k$ *are polynomial in* λ, *it holds* $\Pr[\mathbf{IND}^{\mathrm{adpt}}_{\mathrm{SSE},\mathcal{A}}(\lambda) = 1] \leq 1/2 + \mathrm{negl}(\lambda)$.

Secondly, we give the definition, *adaptive semantic security for IG-DSSE (shortly, A-SS for IG-DSSE)*, by modifying adaptive semantic security [12]. For $i, j \geq 1$, let $\mathbf{w}_j^{(i)} = (w_1^{(i)}, \ldots, w_j^{(i)})$, $H^{(i)} = (\mathbf{D}^{(i)}, \mathbf{w}_{q_i}^{(i)})$, $\mathbf{H}^{(0)} = \emptyset$, $\mathbf{H}^{(i)} = (H^{(1)}, \ldots, H^{(i)})$, $\mathbf{t}_0^{(i)} = \emptyset$, $\mathbf{t}_j^{(i)} = (t(w_1^{(i)}), \ldots, t(w_j^{(i)}))$, $v_0 = \emptyset$, and $v_i = \{\mathcal{I}^{(c)}, \mathbf{C}^{(c)}, \mathbf{t}^{(c)}\}_{c=1}^i$. We note that the following security definition is the same as the original one when $k = 1$.

Definition 2. *For a security parameter* λ, *an adversary* $\mathcal{A} = \{\mathcal{A}_0^{(i)}, \ldots, \mathcal{A}_{q_i}^{(i)}\}_{i=1}^k$ *such that* $k, q_1, \ldots, q_k \in \mathbb{N}$, *and a simulator* $\mathcal{S} = \{\mathcal{S}_0^{(i)}, \ldots, \mathcal{S}_{q_i}^{(i)}\}_{i=1}^k$, *consider Experiment 2 of Fig. 2, where* $\mathcal{A}_0^{(1)}(v_0, st_{\mathcal{A}}) = \mathcal{A}_0^{(1)}(1^\lambda)$ *and* $\mathcal{S}_0^{(1)}(\tau(\mathbf{H}^{(0)}, \mathbf{D}^{(1)}), st_{\mathcal{S}}) = \mathcal{S}_0^{(1)}(\tau(\mathbf{D}^{(1)}))$ *as exceptions. We say that* SSE *is secure in the sense of A-SS for IG-DSSE if for any PPT adversary* $\mathcal{A} = \{\mathcal{A}_0^{(i)}, \ldots, \mathcal{A}_{q_i}^{(i)}\}_{i=1}^k$ *such that* $k, q_1, \ldots, q_k$ *are polynomial in* λ, *there exists a PPT simulator*

$\mathbf{Real}^{\mathrm{adpt}}_{\mathrm{SSE},\mathcal{A}}(\lambda):$	$\mathbf{Sim}^{\mathrm{adpt}}_{\mathrm{SSE},\mathcal{A},\mathcal{S}}(\lambda):$
$\quad K \leftarrow \mathrm{Gen}(1^\lambda)$	$\quad$ for $1 \leq i \leq k$:
$\quad$ for $1 \leq i \leq k$:	$\quad\quad (\mathbf{D}^{(i)}, st_{\mathcal{A}}) \leftarrow \mathcal{A}_0^{(i)}(v_{i-1}, st_{\mathcal{A}})$
$\quad\quad (\mathbf{D}^{(i)}, st_{\mathcal{A}}) \leftarrow \mathcal{A}_0^{(i)}(v_{i-1}, st_{\mathcal{A}})$	$\quad\quad (\mathcal{I}^{(i)}, \mathbf{C}^{(i)}, st_{\mathcal{S}}) \leftarrow \mathcal{S}_0^{(i)}(\tau(\mathbf{H}^{(i-1)}, \mathbf{D}^{(i)}), st_{\mathcal{S}})$
$\quad\quad (\mathcal{I}^{(i)}, \mathbf{C}^{(i)}) \leftarrow \mathrm{Enc}(K, \mathbf{D}^{(i)})$	$\quad\quad$ for $1 \leq j \leq q_i$:
$\quad\quad$ for $1 \leq j \leq q_i$:	$\quad\quad\quad (w_j^{(i)}, st_{\mathcal{A}}) \leftarrow \mathcal{A}_j^{(i)}(v_{i-1}, \mathcal{I}^{(i)}, \mathbf{C}^{(i)}, \mathbf{t}_{j-1}^{(i)}, st_{\mathcal{A}})$
$\quad\quad\quad (w_j^{(i)}, st_{\mathcal{A}}) \leftarrow \mathcal{A}_j^{(i)}(v_{i-1}, \mathcal{I}^{(i)}, \mathbf{C}^{(i)}, \mathbf{t}_{j-1}^{(i)}, st_{\mathcal{A}})$	$\quad\quad\quad (t(w_j^{(i)}), st_{\mathcal{S}}) \leftarrow \mathcal{S}_j^{(i)}(\tau(\mathbf{H}^{(i-1)}, \mathbf{D}^{(i)}, \mathbf{w}_j^{(i)}), st_{\mathcal{S}})$
$\quad\quad\quad t(w_j^{(i)}) \leftarrow \mathrm{Trpdr}(K, w_j^{(i)})$	$\quad$ output $v_k = \{\mathcal{I}^{(i)}, \mathbf{C}^{(i)}, \mathbf{t}^{(i)}\}_{i=1}^k$ and $st_{\mathcal{A}}$
$\quad$ output $v_k = \{\mathcal{I}^{(i)}, \mathbf{C}^{(i)}, \mathbf{t}^{(i)}\}_{i=1}^k$ and $st_{\mathcal{A}}$	

Fig. 2. Experiment 2

$\mathcal{S} = \{\mathcal{S}_0^{(i)}, \dots, \mathcal{S}_{q_i}^{(i)}\}_{i=1}^k$ *such that for any PPT distinguisher* $\mathcal{D}$, *it holds* $|\Pr[\mathcal{D}(v_k, st_\mathcal{A}) = 1 \mid (v_k, st_\mathcal{A}) \leftarrow \mathbf{Real}_{\text{SSE},\mathcal{A}}^{\text{adpt}}(\lambda)] - \Pr[\mathcal{D}(v_k, st_\mathcal{A}) = 1 \mid (v_k, st_\mathcal{A}) \leftarrow \mathbf{Sim}_{\text{SSE},\mathcal{A},\mathcal{S}}^{\text{adpt}}(\lambda)]| \leq \mathtt{negl}(\lambda)$.

Then, we can show the following theorem in the same manner as [12].

Theorem 1. *A-SS for IG-DSSE implies A-IND for IG-DSSE.*

3.3   Limitations of Previous Document Adding Methods

Here, we describe that it is not easy to construct secure IG-DSSE schemes under our security model even if previous document adding methods are used.

Firstly, we discuss the naive document adding method which straightforwardly executes the Enc algorithm in every document adding process. With the naive method, we can directly give the document adding functionality to any ordinary SSE scheme. However, as mentioned in [8,11], undesirable information such as $\mathbf{D}^{(j)}(\mathbf{w}^{(i)})$ $(i < j)$ would be leaked by applying trapdoors generated in past keyword searching processes to future encrypted indexes, although $\mathbf{w}^{(i)}$ is a search sequence before adding the document collection $\mathbf{D}^{(j)}$. Therefore, the schemes with the naive method cannot achieve our security definitions since the undesirable leakage information is over our trace.

Secondly, we discuss previous document adding methods [8,11] that additional secret keys are used in every document adding process. Although the previous methods are simple and generic, they are not desirable approaches when the document adding process is frequently executed. Since additional secret keys are generated in every document adding process, the user cannot employ key management solutions using secure devices such as IC-cards of significantly limited storage size. Additionally, the user has to generate trapdoors depending on the number of encrypted indexes stored on the server. Roughly, the number of additional secret keys and the number of generating trapdoors in the methods are both $O(N)$, where N is the number of encrypted indexes stored on the server. Furthermore, IG-DSSE schemes with additional secret keys are outside of our security model.

4   Specific Construction

In this section, we propose a simple and generic document adding method for constructing secure IG-DSSE schemes, and give a secure IG-DSSE scheme constructed from our document adding method and our proposed variant of SSE-2 [11].

4.1   Our Simple and Generic Document Adding Method

Our document adding method consists of the following two ideas.

The First Idea. We consider a modification that encrypted indexes and trap-doors are generated with the same secret key and additional *public* information, but not with additional secret information. This modification gives a potential solution that one can generate distinct encrypted indexes and trapdoors according to this additional public information even if the same documents are stored or keywords are used. That is, we expect that for a keyword w, a trapdoor $t(w)$ corresponding to an encrypted index $\mathcal{I}$ cannot be applied to other encrypted index $\mathcal{I}'$. In other words, $t(w) \neq t(w)'$, where $t(w)$ and $t(w)'$ are trapdoors corresponding to encrypted indexes $\mathcal{I}$ and $\mathcal{I}'$, respectively. In the previous methods [8,11], this situation is achieved by using distinct secret keys. Fortunately, all existing ordinary SSE schemes [6,7,9–11,13,20,21,24,25,32,33] can accept this modification. Our concrete modification is as follows[1].

We modify the Enc algorithm in such a way that the user firstly generates a unique identifier $id(\mathcal{I})$ of an encrypted index $\mathcal{I}$ before generating $\mathcal{I}$, and after that, the user computes $\mathcal{I}$ from the secret key K and $id(\mathcal{I})$. In this modification, $id(\mathcal{I})$ is the additional public information. For example, we take as $id(\mathcal{I})$ a publicly available global counter. Similarly, we also modify the Trpdr algorithm in such a way that the user computes a trapdoor $t(w)$ corresponding to $\mathcal{I}$ from K and $id(\mathcal{I})$. By using abnormal notations, we can regard an encrypted index $\mathcal{I}$ and a trapdoor $t(w)$ in our modification as $\mathcal{I} = \mathcal{I}(sk, id(\mathcal{I}), w)$ and $t(w) = t(sk, id(\mathcal{I}), w)$, respectively.

As a simple example for achieving the above modification, we can employ $\mathcal{I}(K, id(\mathcal{I}) \parallel w)$ and $t(K, id(\mathcal{I}) \parallel w)$. Then, we observe that each keyword w varies another distinct keywords according to each encrypted index $\mathcal{I}$. That is, a keyword w for an encrypted index $\mathcal{I}$ can be regarded as $id(\mathcal{I}) \parallel w$ which never appear in other encrypted indexes $\mathcal{I}'$. Due to this fact, we would directly employ the original security proof of an existing ordinary SSE scheme since each encrypted index can be considered as independently generated.

In addition to the above explanation, let us further discuss generality and security of the first idea of our method by using the following abstract framework. In general SSE, we can abstractly consider that the encrypted index $\mathcal{I}$ is an array and constructed as $\mathcal{I}[F(sk, w_j)] = \{id(D)\}$ for $w_j \in \Delta$, where F is some secure function such as pseudo-random function or a keyed hash function, Δ is a set of keywords, and $\{id(D)\}$ is a set of identifiers of documents which contain the keyword w_j[2]. Then, $F(sk, w_j)$ can be regarded as the trapdoor of the keyword w_j in this framework. From a document adding point of view, this framework can be further generalized that by introducing a notion of master secret key into SSE, the encrypted index $\mathcal{I}^{(i)}$ generated in the i-th document adding process is constructed as $\mathcal{I}^{(i)}[F'(msk, sk_i, w_j)] = \{id(D^{(i)})\}$ for $w_j \in \Delta$, where F' is some secure function with three inputs, msk is the master secret key, sk_i is the

---

[1] This modification can be also applied to any existing IU-DSSE scheme.

[2] We can further consider another abstract framework $\mathcal{I}[F(sk, w_j)] = \{id(D)\} \oplus G(sk', w_j)$ applicable to e.g. [11,18], where sk' is a secret key and G is some secure function which is used for masking $\{id(D)\}$. Our discussion given in the subsection can be also applied to this framework.

secret key used in the i-th document adding process, and $\{id(D^{(i)})\}$ is a set of identifiers of documents which contain w_j and are added in the i-th document adding process.

In the naive method that each encrypted index is generated with the same secret key, we can regard $msk = sk$, $sk_i = \emptyset$, and $F'(msk, sk_i, w_j) = F'(sk, \emptyset, w_j) = F(sk, w_j)$ in the above framework. In this case, the i-th encrypted index $\mathcal{I}^{(i)}$ and the i'-th one $\mathcal{I}^{(i')}$ obtained from this method can be represented as $\mathcal{I}^{(i)}[F'(msk, \emptyset, w_j)] = \{id(D^{(i)})\}$ and $\mathcal{I}^{(i')}[F'(msk, \emptyset, w_j)] = \{id(D^{(i')})\}$ for $w_j \in \Delta$, respectively. Then, we observe that undesirable information would be leaked from the comparison among the encrypted indexes since $\mathcal{I}^{(i)}$ and $\mathcal{I}^{(i')}$ are constructed as the same values $\{F(msk, \emptyset, w_j)\}_{w_j \in \Delta}$. In the previous methods [8,11], we can regard $msk = \emptyset$, $sk_i \neq sk_j$ and $F'(msk, sk_i, w_j) = F'(\emptyset, sk_i, w_j) = F(sk_i, w_j)$. Then, we observe that the previous methods can add documents without losing security since each $\mathcal{I}^{(i)}$ is constructed from distinct values $\{F'(msk, sk_i, w_j)\}_{w_j \in \Delta}$.

In the first idea of our method, we can regard $msk = sk$, $sk_i = id(\mathcal{I}^{(i)})$, and $F'(msk, sk_i, w_j) = F'(sk, id(\mathcal{I}^{(i)}), w_j) = F(sk_i, id(\mathcal{I}^{(i)}) \parallel w_j)$, where $id(\mathcal{I}^{(i)})$ is the identifier of $\mathcal{I}^{(i)}$ and publicly available information. We observe that our first idea has applicability to existing SSE schemes since it follows the abstract framework. Additionally, while $sk_i(= id(\mathcal{I}^{(i)}))$ is publicly available information in contrast to the previous methods [8,11], our first idea would be still secure if F is a pseudo-random function or a keyed hash function. This means that computing msk or w_j from $F(msk, id(\mathcal{I}^{(i)}) \parallel w_j)$ and $id(\mathcal{I}^{(i)})$ is intractable if F is such a secure function. Actually, all existing SSE schemes use such functions as F, and therefore one can easily construct secure IG-DSSE schemes from our first idea.

The Second Idea. In the above idea, there is still an efficiency problem, similarly to the previous document adding methods [8,11]. Concretely, the number of trapdoors generated in the keyword searching process is $O(N)$, where N is the number of encrypted indexes stored on the server. More precisely, the user has to generate $\{t(sk, id(\mathcal{I}^{(i)}), w)\}_{i=1}^{N}$ in order to search the keyword w. This problem is serious when the document adding process is frequently executed.

In order to address the inefficiency problem, the second idea of our method employs hash chains, which are also used in the IU-DSSE scheme [31]. In this idea, by using hash chains in reverse order, the user computes only a core element which can generate all past trapdoors on a keyword, and the server can generate all trapdoors from the core element. As a result, the second idea can address the inefficiency problem.

Let us also explain generality and security of the second idea by using the same abstract framework used in the explanation of the first idea. In the second idea, the encrypted index $\mathcal{I}^{(i)}$ is modified as $\mathcal{I}^{(i)}[H(H^{M+1-i}(msk \parallel w_j) \parallel id(\mathcal{I}^{(i)}))] = \{id(D^{(i)})\}$, where H is a hash function, $M \in \mathbb{Z}$ is the maximum number of executable document adding processes, and H^i means that the number of hash chains is i (i.e. we run i-times the algorithm of H with an initial value $msk \parallel w_j$). Then, the core element of trapdoors of $w_j \in \Delta$ can be regarded as $H^{M+1-i}(msk \parallel w_j)$ if the total number of executions of the document adding process is i. Indeed, from the core element $H^{M+1-i}(msk \parallel w_j)$ and the unique identifiers, the server can compute the trapdoors

$$H(H^{M+1-i}(msk \parallel w_j) \parallel id(\mathcal{I}^{(i)})) \text{ for } \mathcal{I}^{(i)},$$
$$H(H^{M+1-(i-1)}(msk \parallel w_j) \parallel id(\mathcal{I}^{(i-1)})) \text{ for } \mathcal{I}^{(i-1)},$$
$$\vdots$$
$$H(H^{M+1}(msk \parallel w_j) \parallel id(\mathcal{I}^{(1)})) \text{ for } \mathcal{I}^{(1)}.$$

Therefore, in the keyword searching process, it is sufficient that the user generates only $H^{M+1-i}(msk \parallel w_j)$, instead of $\{F(msk, id(\mathcal{I}^{(i)}), w_j)\}_i$ which are trapdoors in the first idea or the previous methods [8,11]. Thus, the second idea can reduce trapdoor size to constant. From the same argument of the first idea, the second one also has applicability to any existing SSE scheme, and would be secure in the random oracle model. Note that our method using salt hash where msk is publicly opened as a salt, has a critical security issue that one can obtain the hidden keyword w_j from $H^{M+1-i}(msk \parallel w_j)$ by querying concatenation of msk and all candidates $w \in \Delta$ one-by-one.

4.2 SSE-2′ with Our Method

In order to show that our method works very well, we present an IG-DSSE scheme based on SSE-2 [11]. Here, we also propose an efficient variant of SSE-2 (say, SSE-2′) in the sense of trapdoor size, and show the security of SSE-2′ with our method.

SSE-2′ with our method (say, our scheme) generates an encrypted index from the secret key and a non-sensitive unique number generated from a global counter. For example, our scheme sets the identifiers of the i-th generated encrypted index $\mathcal{I}^{(i)}$ and the $(i+1)$-th one $\mathcal{I}^{(i+1)}$ as $id(\mathcal{I}^{(i)}) = i$ and $id(\mathcal{I}^{(i+1)}) = i+1$, respectively.

Let c be a global counter which is public information, set 0 as the initial value. Let $M \in \mathbb{Z}$ be the possible maximum value of c, that is, $c \leq M$. We assume that for any document collection $\mathbf{D} = (D_1, \ldots, D_n)$, its cardinality n is not exceed a pre-defined threshold N. This restriction is not strong since we can divide a large document collection into multiple small document collections whose cardinalities are at most N.

Let $H : \{0,1\}^* \to \{0,1\}^\delta$ be a hash function and SKE be a symmetric-key encryption scheme. Then, we present SSE-2′ with our method, as follows:

- Gen(1^λ): Pick $K_1 \xleftarrow{u} \{0,1\}^\lambda$, generate $K_2 \leftarrow$ SKE.Gen(1^λ), and output $K = (K_1, K_2)$.
- Enc(K, $\mathbf{D}$):
  1. Compute $c = c + 1$.
  2. Compute $C_i = \text{SKE.Enc}_{K_2}(D_i)$ for $1 \leq i \leq n$, and set $\mathcal{C}^{(c)} = (C_1, \ldots, C_n)$.
  3. Let $id(\mathcal{I}^{(c)}) = c$ and $\mathcal{I}^{(c)}$ be an array of size $2^\ell n$.

4. For $1 \leq i \leq 2^{\ell}$:
   (a) Let $\mathbf{D}(w_i) = \{id(D_{i_1}), \ldots, id(D_{i_m})\}$ and $\{i_{m+1}, \ldots, i_n\} = \{1, \ldots, n\} \setminus \{i_1, \ldots, i_m\}$, where $i_{m+1} < \cdots < i_n$.
   (b) Compute $\mathtt{addr}_{i,j} = H(H^{M+1-c}(K_1 \| 0 \| w_i) \| c \| j)$ when $1 \leq j \leq m$ and $H(H^{M+1-c}(K_1 \| 1 \| w_i) \| c \| j)$ when $m+1 \leq j \leq n$.
   (c) Set $\mathcal{I}^{(c)}[\mathtt{addr}_{i,j}] = id(D_{i_j})$ for $1 \leq j \leq n$.
5. Output a tuple $(\mathcal{I}^{(c)}, \mathbf{C}^{(c)})$.

- $\mathtt{Trpdr}(\mathbf{K}, \mathbf{w})$: Compute $t = H^{M+1-c}(K_1 \| 0 \| w)$.
- $\mathtt{Search}(\mathbf{I}, \mathbf{t})$:
  1. Let $S = \emptyset$ and parse $\mathbf{I}$ as $(\mathcal{I}^{(1)}, \ldots, \mathcal{I}^{(c)})$.
  2. For $1 \leq i \leq c$:
     (a) $t_j^{(i)} = H(H^{c-i}(t) \| i \| j)$ for $1 \leq j \leq N$.
     (b) Let $\mathcal{I}^{(i)}[t_j^{(i)}] = id(D_{s_j}^{(i)})$ or $\perp$ for $1 \leq j \leq N$
     (c) Add $id(D_{s_j}^{(i)})(\neq \perp)$ to S for $1 \leq j \leq N$.
  3. Output S.
- $\mathtt{Dec}(\mathbf{K}, \mathbf{C})$: Compute $D \leftarrow \mathtt{SKE.Dec}_{K_2}(C)$ and output D.

Note that H is just a hash function: $\{0,1\}^* \rightarrow \{0,1\}^{\delta}$, but not keyed-hash: $\{0,1\}^{\lambda} \times \{0,1\}^* \rightarrow \{0,1\}^{\delta}$. Nevertheless, we use H like keyed-hash in the trapdoor generating process. Concretely, it takes concatenation of the secret key K_1, the constant value 0, and a keyword w as an input, and outputs $t = H^{M+1-c}(K_1 \| 0 \| w)$. That is, the knowledge of K_1 is required to generate trapdoors. On the other hand, no knowledge of K_1 is required to compute hash chains $H^i(t)$ for $i \geq 2$ if the trapdoor t is given. This computation is a part of the searching process by the server.

Then, we can show that $\mathtt{SSE\text{-}2}'$ with our method is secure if the hash function H is modeled as random oracle. Here, we assume that the parameter k in Definition 2 is bounded (concretely, $k \leq M$) in our security proof, since there is an upper bound for the number of hash chains in our method.

Theorem 2. *Our scheme is secure in the sense of A-SS for IG-DSSE and in the random oracle model if $\mathtt{SKE}$ is LOR-CPA secure.*

Proof. We construct a PPT simulator $\mathcal{S} = \{\mathcal{S}_0^{(i)}, \ldots, \mathcal{S}_{q_i}^{(i)}\}_{i=1}^k$ such that for any PPT adversary $\mathcal{A} = \{\mathcal{A}_0^{(i)}, \ldots, \mathcal{A}_{q_i}^{(i)}\}_{i=1}^k$, the outputs of $\mathbf{Real}_{\mathtt{SSE}, \mathcal{A}}^{\mathrm{adpt}}(\lambda)$ and $\mathbf{Sim}_{\mathtt{SSE}, \mathcal{A}, \mathcal{S}}^{\mathrm{adpt}}(\lambda)$ are computationally indistinguishable. We also simulate random oracle on H in $\mathcal{S}$ by using a hash table $Table_H$.

Let $Table_H$ be a set, and its element denote $(input, output)$, where $input \in \{0,1\}^*$ and $output \in \{0,1\}^{\delta}$. For $Table_H = \{(input_i, output_i)\}_i$, let $Table_H.Input = \{input_i\}_i$, $Table_H.Output = \{output_i\}_i$, and $Table_H[input_i] = output_i$.

Firstly, we construct $\mathcal{S}^{(1)} = (\mathcal{S}_0^{(1)}, \ldots, \mathcal{S}_{q_1}^{(1)})$ as follows.

- $\mathcal{S}_0^{(1)}(\tau(\mathbf{D}^{(1)}))$:
  - Generate $K = (K_1, K_2) \leftarrow \mathtt{Gen}(1^{\lambda})$.
  - Set $Table_H = \emptyset$.
  - Compute $M_1 = 2^{\ell} n_1$ from $\tau(\mathbf{D}^{(1)})$.

- For $1 \leq i \leq M$ and $1 \leq j \leq 2^\ell$, pick $r_j^{(i)} \xleftarrow{u} \{0,1\}^\delta$, and append the following pairs to $Table_H$:

$$(K_1 \| 0 \| 1, r_1^{(M)}), \ldots, (K_1 \| 0 \| 2^\ell, r_{2^\ell}^{(M)}),$$
$$(r_1^{(M)}, r_1^{(M-1)}), \quad \ldots, \quad (r_{2^\ell}^{(M)}, r_{2^\ell}^{(M-1)}),$$
$$\vdots \qquad\qquad\qquad \vdots$$
$$(r_1^{(2)}, r_1^{(1)}), \quad \ldots, \quad (r_{2^\ell}^{(2)}, r_{2^\ell}^{(1)}).$$

- Construct $\mathcal{I}^{(1)}$ of size M_1, as follows. For $1 \leq l \leq n_1$ and $1 \leq j \leq 2^\ell$, pick $R_{l,j}^{(1)} \xleftarrow{u} \{0,1\}^\delta$, and set

$$\mathcal{I}^{(1)}[R_{1,1}^{(1)}] = id(D_1^{(1)}), \; \cdots, \; \mathcal{I}^{(1)}[R_{1,2^\ell}^{(1)}] = id(D_1^{(1)}),$$
$$\vdots \qquad\qquad\qquad \vdots$$
$$\mathcal{I}^{(1)}[R_{n_1,1}^{(1)}] = id(D_{n_1}^{(1)}), \; \cdots, \; \mathcal{I}^{(1)}[R_{n_1,2^\ell}^{(1)}] = id(D_{n_1}^{(1)}).$$

- Compute $C_i^{(1)} \leftarrow \mathsf{SKE.Enc}_{K_2}(0^{|D_i^{(1)}|}) \, (1 \leq i \leq n_1)$, and set $\mathbf{C}^{(1)} = (C_1^{(1)}, \ldots, C_{n_1}^{(1)})$.
- Let $\mathcal{R} = \{R_{1,1}^{(1)}, \ldots, R_{n_1,2^\ell}^{(1)}\}$, and set $st_{\mathcal{S}} = (K, Table_H, \mathcal{R})$.
- Output $(\mathcal{I}^{(1)}, \mathbf{C}^{(1)}, st_{\mathcal{S}})$.
- $\mathcal{S}_j^{(1)}(\tau(\mathbf{D}^{(1)}, \mathbf{w}_j^{(1)}), st_{\mathcal{S}})$ for $1 \leq j \leq q_1$:
  - Check $\gamma(\mathbf{w}_j^{(1)}) = (z_1, \ldots, z_j)$ from $\sigma(\mathbf{D}^{(1)}, \mathbf{w}_j^{(1)})$.
  - Set $t(w_j^{(1)}) = r_{z_j}^{(1)}$.
  - Check $\mathbf{D}^{(1)}(w_j^{(1)}) = \emptyset$ or $\{id(D_{j_1}^{(1)}), \ldots, id(D_{j_m}^{(1)})\} \subseteq \{id(D_1^{(1)}), \ldots, id(D_{n_1}^{(1)})\}$ from $\alpha(\mathbf{D}^{(1)}, \mathbf{w}_j^{(1)})$.
  - If $\mathbf{D}^{(1)}(w_j^{(1)}) \neq \emptyset$, then append the following pairs to $Table_H$:

$$(r_{z_j}^{(1)} \| 1 \| 1, R_{j_1, z_j}^{(1)}), \ldots, (r_{z_j}^{(1)} \| 1 \| m, R_{j_m, z_j}^{(1)}).$$

Note that if there already exist the above pairs in $Table_H$, then this appending process is skipped.
  - Update $st_{\mathcal{S}}$ and output $(t(w_j^{(1)}), st_{\mathcal{S}})$.
- Let $\mathbf{t}^{(1)} = (t(w_1^{(1)}), \ldots, t(w_{q_1}^{(1)}))$, and set $v_1 = \{\mathcal{I}^{(1)}, \mathcal{C}^{(1)}, \mathbf{t}^{(1)}\}$.
- If $\mathcal{A}^{(1)}$ queries a value x to random oracle in order to compute $H(x)$, then $\mathcal{S}^{(1)}$ executes as follows:
  - If $x \in Table_H.Input$, then output $Table_H[x]$.
  - Else, pick $r' \xleftarrow{u} \{0,1\}^\delta$, append a pair (x, r') to $Table_H$, and output r'.

Here, we show that the above simulator $\mathcal{S}^{(1)}$ is valid when $k = 1$. Note that in the real experiment, H's output of any $x \in \{0,1\}^*$ is a uniform-randomly number in $\{0,1\}^\delta$, in the random oracle model. In other words, any existing address of an encrypted index and any hash chain value are generated uniform-randomly, because of following the protocol straightforwardly.

- The probability that K output by $\mathcal{S}^{(1)}$ is the same as the secret key output by the real experiment, is negligible.
- For $1 \leq i, j \leq n_1$, let $C_i^{(1)}$ and $C_j'^{(1)}$ be ciphertexts generated in our simulation $\mathcal{S}^{(1)}$ and the real experiment, respectively. Obviously, $C_i^{(1)}$ is indistinguishable from $C_j'^{(1)}$, because SKE is LOR-CPA secure.
- Any existing address $R_{i,j}^{(1)}$ of the encrypted index $\mathcal{I}^{(1)}$ in our simulation is generated uniform-randomly in $\{0,1\}^\delta$, similarly to the real experiment.
- Since any PPT adversary $\mathcal{A}^{(1)}$ cannot obtain K_1 from $\mathcal{S}^{(1)}$, $\mathcal{A}^{(1)}$ cannot query any hash value $H(K_1 \mathbin\| \cdot \mathbin\| \cdot)$ to random oracle without the knowledge of K_1. From properties of random oracle, $\mathcal{A}^{(1)}$ has no way faster than brute force to find K_1, and cannot compute any inverted value $K_1 \mathbin\| \cdot \mathbin\| \cdot$ from $H^M(K_1 \mathbin\| \cdot \mathbin\| \cdot)$ while $\mathcal{A}^{(1)}$ can obtain the hash values $H^M(K_1 \mathbin\| \cdot \mathbin\| \cdot)$ by querying a keyword to $\mathcal{S}^{(1)}$. Additionally, before knowing a trapdoor $t(w_j^{(1)}) = r_{z_j}^{(1)}$, $\mathcal{A}^{(1)}$ cannot query $r_{z_j}^{(1)} \mathbin\| 1 \mathbin\| \cdot$, in order to compute valid addresses of $\mathcal{I}^{(1)}$ in advance.
- Each trapdoor $t(w_j^{(1)})$ output by $\mathcal{S}^{(1)}$ has no information on the corresponding keyword, and only leakage information $\tau(\mathbf{D}^{(1)}, \mathbf{w}_j^{(1)})$ appears by applying the trapdoor to the encrypted index $\mathcal{I}^{(1)}$.
- Any trapdoor $t(w_j^{(1)})$ in our simulation is generated uniform-randomly in $\{0,1\}^\delta$, similarly to the real experiment. Furthermore, $\mathcal{S}^{(1)}$ can output the same trapdoor thanks to $\gamma(\mathbf{w}_j^{(1)})$, even if $\mathcal{A}^{(1)}$ queries the same keyword used in the past, similarly to the real experiment.

To show that, let $t(w_j^{(1)}) = r_{z_j}^{(1)}$ be a trapdoor output by $\mathcal{S}^{(1)}$ and $\mathbf{D}^{(1)}(w_j^{(1)}) = \{id(D_{j_1}), \ldots, id(D_{j_m})\}$. If $\mathcal{A}^{(1)}$ knows $r_{z_j}^{(1)}$ as $t(w_j^{(1)})$ and queries N values $x_1 = r_{z_j}^{(1)} \mathbin\| 1 \mathbin\| 1, \ldots, x_N = r_{z_j}^{(1)} \mathbin\| 1 \mathbin\| N$ to random oracle, for the first time, in order to compute addresses of $\mathcal{I}^{(1)}$, then $\mathcal{S}^{(1)}$ can find the valid addresses $R_{j_1,z_j}^{(1)}, \ldots, R_{j_m,z_j}^{(1)}$ from $Table_H[x_i]$ for $1 \leq i \leq m$. Further, $\mathcal{S}^{(1)}$ picks $R_{j_{m+1},z_j}'^{(1)}, \ldots, R_{j_N,z_j}'^{(1)} \xleftarrow{u} \{0,1\}^\delta$, appends

$$(r_{z_j}^{(1)} \mathbin\| 1 \mathbin\| m+1, R_{j_{m+1},z_j}'^{(1)}), \ldots, (r_{z_j}^{(1)} \mathbin\| 1 \mathbin\| N, R_{j_N,z_j}'^{(1)})$$

to $Table_H$, and then outputs

$$R_{j_1,z_j}^{(1)} \text{ as } H(x_1), \ldots, R_{j_m,z_j}^{(1)} \text{ as } H(x_m),$$
$$R_{j_{m+1},z_j}'^{(1)} \text{ as } H(x_{m+1}), \ldots, R_{j_N,z_j}'^{(1)} \text{ as } H(x_N).$$

Note that the probability $\Pr[R_{j_i,z_j}'^{(1)} \in Table_H.Output]$ for $m+1 \leq \forall i \leq N$ is negligible probability in δ. Additionally, if $\mathcal{A}^{(1)}$ has already queried the above N values then there exist the pairs $(x_m, R_{j_{m+1},z_j}'^{(1)}), \ldots, (x_N, R_{j_N,z_j}'^{(1)})$ in $Table_H$. Then, $\mathcal{S}^{(1)}$ can skip the above appending and picking processes and merely output the corresponding values from $Table_H$.

From the above arguments, $\mathcal{S}^{(1)}$ can simulate the real experiment, correctly. Therefore, any PPT distinguisher $\mathcal{D}$ cannot distinguish v_1 output by the real experiment from that by $\mathcal{S}^{(1)}$.

For $2 \leq i \leq k$, we similarly construct $\mathcal{S}^{(i)} = (\mathcal{S}_0^{(i)}, \ldots, \mathcal{S}_{q_i}^{(i)})$ as follows.

- $\mathcal{S}_0^{(i)}(\tau(\mathbf{H}^{(i-1)}, \mathbf{D}^{(i)}), st_{\mathcal{S}})$:
  - Compute $M_i = 2^\ell n_i$ from $\tau(\mathbf{H}^{(i-1)}, \mathbf{D}^{(i)})$.
  - Construct $\mathcal{I}^{(i)}$ of size M_i, as follows. For $1 \leq l \leq n_i$ and $1 \leq j \leq 2^\ell$, pick $R_{l,j}^{(i)} \xleftarrow{u} \{0,1\}^\delta$, and set

$$\mathcal{I}^{(i)}[R_{1,1}^{(i)}] = id(D_1^{(i)}), \cdots, \mathcal{I}^{(i)}[R_{1,2^\ell}^{(i)}] = id(D_1^{(i)}),$$
$$\vdots \qquad\qquad\qquad \vdots$$
$$\mathcal{I}^{(i)}[R_{n_i,1}^{(i)}] = id(D_{n_i}^{(i)}), \cdots, \mathcal{I}^{(i)}[R_{n_i,2^\ell}^{(i)}] = id(D_{n_i}^{(i)}).$$

  - Compute $C_j^{(i)} \leftarrow \mathsf{SKE.Enc}_{K_2}(0^{|D_j^{(i)}|})$ $(1 \leq j \leq n_i)$, and set $\mathbf{C}^{(i)} = (C_1^{(i)}, \ldots, C_{n_i}^{(i)})$.
  - Append $R_{1,1}^{(i)}, \ldots, R_{n_i,2^\ell}^{(i)}$ to $\mathcal{R}$.
  - Update $st_{\mathcal{S}}$ and output $(\mathcal{I}^{(i)}, \mathbf{C}^{(i)}, st_{\mathcal{S}})$.
- $\mathcal{S}_j^{(i)}(\tau(\mathbf{H}^{(i-1)}, \mathbf{D}^{(i)}, \mathbf{w}_j^{(i)}), st_{\mathcal{S}})$ for $1 \leq j \leq q_i$:
  - Set $\mathbf{w} = \mathbf{w}^{(1)}||\cdots||\mathbf{w}^{(i-1)}||\mathbf{w}_j^{(i)}$.
  - Check $\gamma(\mathbf{w}) = (z_1, \ldots, z_J)$, where $J = q_1 + \cdots + q_{i-1} + j$.
  - Set $t(w_j^{(i)}) = r_{z_J}^{(i)}$.
  - For $1 \leq l \leq i$, execute as follows:
    * Check $\mathbf{D}^{(l)}(w_j^{(i)}) = \emptyset$ or $\{id(D_{j_1}^{(l)}), \ldots, id(D_{j_{m(l)}}^{(l)})\} \subseteq \{id(D_1^{(l)}), \ldots, id(D_{n_l}^{(l)})\}$, from $\alpha(\mathbf{H}^{(i-1)}, \mathbf{D}^{(i)}, \mathbf{w}_j^{(i)})$.
    * If $\mathbf{D}^{(l)}(w_j^{(i)}) \neq \emptyset$, then append the following pairs to $Table_H$:

$$(r_{z_J}^{(l)} \,||\, l \,||\, 1, R_{j_1, z_J}^{(l)}), \ldots, (r_{z_J}^{(l)} \,||\, l \,||\, m^{(l)}, R_{j_{m(l)}, z_J}^{(l)})$$

    Note that if there already exist the above pairs in $Table_H$, then this appending process is skipped.
  - Update $st_{\mathcal{S}}$ and output $(t(w_j^{(i)}), st_{\mathcal{S}})$.
- Let $\mathbf{t}^{(i)} = (t(w_1^{(i)}), \ldots, t(w_{q_i}^{(i)}))$, and set $v_i = \{\mathcal{I}^{(c)}, \mathbf{C}^{(c)}, \mathbf{t}^{(c)}\}_{c=1}^{i-1} \cup \{\mathcal{I}^{(i)}, \mathbf{C}^{(i)}, \mathbf{t}^{(i)}\}$.
- Similarly to $i = 1$, if $\mathcal{A}^{(i)}$ queries a value x to random oracle in order to compute $H(x)$, then $\mathcal{S}^{(i)}$ executes as follows:
  - If $x \in Table_H.Input$, then output $Table_H[x]$.
  - Else, pick $r' \xleftarrow{u} \{0,1\}^\delta$, append a pair (x, r') to $Table_H$, and output r'.

Here, we show that the above $\mathcal{S}^{(i)}$ for $1 \leq i \leq k$ can simulate correctly.

- $\mathcal{S}$ can easily switch $\mathcal{S}_{q_i}^{(i-1)}$ to $\mathcal{S}_0^{(i)}$ for $2 \leq \forall i \leq k$, by checking the index adding pattern $\beta(\mathbf{H}^{(i+1)})$.

– For the same reason as $i = 1$, the ciphertext collections $(\mathbf{C}^{(1)}, \ldots, \mathbf{C}^{(i)})$ output by the real experiment and our simulation are computationally indistinguishable.

– For the same reason as $i = 1$, the existing addresses of the encrypted indexes $(\mathcal{I}^{(1)}, \ldots, \mathcal{I}^{(i)})$ output by the real experiment and our simulation are computationally indistinguishable.

– For the same reason as $i = 1$, any PPT adversary $\mathcal{A}^{(i)}$ with no knowledge of K_1 cannot query any hash value $H(K_1 \| \cdot \| \cdot)$, and compute any inverted value $K_1 \| \cdot \| \cdot$ from $H^{M+1-i}(K_1 \| \cdot \| \cdot)$ which is appeared by querying a keyword to $\mathcal{S}^{(i)}$. Additionally, before knowing $t(w_j^{(i)}) = r_{z_J}^{(i)}$ for $1 \leq i \leq k$, $\mathcal{A}^{(i)}$ cannot query $r_{z_J}^{(i)} \| \cdot \| \cdot$ to random oracle.

– Each trapdoor $t(w_j^{(i)})$ output by $\mathcal{S}^{(i)}$ has no information on the corresponding keyword, and only leakage information $\tau(\mathbf{H}^{(i-1)}, \mathbf{D}^{(i)}, \mathbf{w}_j^{(i)})$ appears by applying the trapdoor to the encrypted indexes $(\mathcal{I}^{(1)}, \ldots, \mathcal{I}^{(i)})$.

– For the same reason as $i = 1$ and thanks to $Table_H$, $\mathcal{S}$ can output valid addresses of $(\mathcal{I}^{(1)}, \ldots, \mathcal{I}^{(i)})$ from a trapdoor $t(w_j^{(i)})$, similarly to the real experiment.

– Similarly to the real experiment, $\mathcal{S}^{(i)}$ can output $t(w_j^{(i-1)}) = r_{z_J}^{(i-1)}$ from $t(w_j^{(i)}) = r_{z_J}^{(i)}$ for $2 \leq \forall i \leq k$, correctly, by using $Table_H$.

– For the same reason as $i = 1$, the trapdoors $(\mathbf{t}^{(1)}, \ldots, \mathbf{t}^{(i)})$ output by the real experiment and our simulation are computationally indistinguishable.

From the above arguments, $\mathcal{S}^{(i)}$ for $1 \leq i \leq k$ can simulate the real experiment, correctly. Therefore, any PPT distinguisher $\mathcal{D}$ cannot distinguish v_k output by the real experiment from that by $\mathcal{S}$. Thus, our scheme is secure in the sense of A-SS for IG-DSSE.   □

5   Conclusion

In this paper, we have studied the document adding methods for constructing IG-DSSE, and proposed the simple and generic method without degrading security and without requiring additional secret keys. Our method enables us to apply the document adding functionality to existing non-dynamic but useful SSE schemes (e.g. [1,3,6,7,10–14,20,21,23–25,30,32,33]) without degrading useful functionalities that the schemes have already equipped with. Generality, security, and efficiency of our method can be confirmed by using the abstract framework which can cover all existing SSE schemes. We have proposed the naturally generalized definitions of the security model [12], and shown that the IG-DSSE scheme converted from SSE-2′ using our method is secure under the definition in the random oracle model.

A future work of IG-DSSE is to prove security of our document adding method in the standard model. Additionally, our document adding method achieves forward security that past trapdoors cannot be applied to future encrypted indexes, but not backward security that trapdoors cannot be applied to deleted encrypted indexes. Also, protecting against known attacks [4,17] is outside of this paper. Therefore, it is also interesting in constructing document adding methods with backward security or secure against the known attacks.

Acknowledgments. The authors would like to thank the anonymous reviewers for their valuable and helpful comments.

References

1. Asharov, G., Naor, M., Segev, G., Shahaf, I.: Searchable symmetric encryption: optimal locality in linear space via two-dimensional balanced allocations. In: STOC 2016 (2016)
2. Bellare, M., Desai, A., Jokipii, E., Rogaway, P.: A concrete security treatment of symmetric encryption. In: FOCS 1997, pp. 394–403 (1997)
3. Boldyreva, A., Chenette, N.: Efficient fuzzy search on encrypted data. In: Cid, C., Rechberger, C. (eds.) FSE 2014. LNCS, vol. 8540, pp. 613–633. Springer, Heidelberg (2015)
4. Cash, D., Grubbs, P., Perry, J., Ristenpart, T.: Leakage-abuse attacks against searchable encryption. In: ACM CCS 2015, pp. 668–679 (2015)
5. Cash, D., Jaeger, J., Jarecki, S., Jutla, C., Krawczyk, H., Roşu, M., Steiner, M.: Dynamic searchable encryption in very-large databases: data structures and implementation. In: NDSS 2014 (2014)
6. Cash, D., Jarecki, S., Jutla, C., Krawczyk, H., Roşu, M.-C., Steiner, M.: Highly-scalable searchable symmetric encryption with support for boolean queries. In: Canetti, R., Garay, J.A. (eds.) CRYPTO 2013, Part I. LNCS, vol. 8042, pp. 353–373. Springer, Heidelberg (2013)
7. Cash, D., Tessaro, S.: The locality of searchable symmetric encryption. In: Nguyen, P.Q., Oswald, E. (eds.) EUROCRYPT 2014. LNCS, vol. 8441, pp. 351–368. Springer, Heidelberg (2014)
8. Chang, Y.-C., Mitzenmacher, M.: Privacy preserving keyword searches on remote encrypted data. In: Ioannidis, J., Keromytis, A.D., Yung, M. (eds.) ACNS 2005. LNCS, vol. 3531, pp. 442–455. Springer, Heidelberg (2005)
9. Chase, M., Kamara, S.: Structured encryption and controlled disclosure. In: Abe, M. (ed.) ASIACRYPT 2010. LNCS, vol. 6477, pp. 577–594. Springer, Heidelberg (2010)
10. Chase, M., Shen, E.: Substring-searchable symmetric encryption. In: PETS 2015, vol. 2015(2), pp. 263–281 (2015)
11. Curtmola, R., Garay, J., Kamara, S., Ostrovsky, R.: Searchable symmetric encryption: improved definitions and efficient constructions. In: ACM CCS 2006, pp. 79–88 (2006)
12. Curtmola, R., Garay, J., Kamara, S., Ostrovsky, R.: Searchable symmetric encryption: Improved definitions and efficient constructions. J. Comput. Secur. **19**(5), 895–934 (2011)
13. Dong, C., Russello, G., Dulay, N.: Shared and searchable encrypted data for untrusted servers. J. Comput. Secur. **19**(3), 367–397 (2011)
14. Faber, S., Jarecki, S., Krawczyk, H., Nguyen, Q., Rosu, M., Steiner, M.: Rich queries on encrypted data: beyond exact matches. In: Pernul, G., Ryan, P.Y.A., Weippl, E. (eds.) ESORICS 2015. LNCS, vol. 9327, pp. 123–145. Springer, Heidelberg (2015)

15. Goh, E.-J.: Secure indexes. Cryptology ePrint Archive, Report 2003/216 (2003). http://eprint.iacr.org/2003/216
16. Hahn, F., Kerschbaum, F.: Searchable encryption with secure and efficient updates. In: ACM CCS 2014, pp. 310–320 (2014)
17. Islam, M.S., Kuzu, M., Kantarcioglu, M.: Access pattern disclosure on searchable encryption: ramification, attack and mitigation. In: NDSS 2012 (2012)
18. Kamara, S., Papamanthou, C., Roeder, T.: Dynamic searchable symmetric encryption. In: ACM CCS 2012, pp. 965–976 (2012)
19. Kamara, S., Papamanthou, C.: Parallel and dynamic searchable symmetric encryption. In: Sadeghi, A.-R. (ed.) FC 2013. LNCS, vol. 7859, pp. 258–274. Springer, Heidelberg (2013)
20. Kurosawa, K.: Garbled searchable symmetric encryption. In: Christin, N., Safavi-Naini, R. (eds.) FC 2014. LNCS, vol. 8437, pp. 232–249. Springer, Heidelberg (2014)
21. Kurosawa, K., Ohtaki, Y.: UC-secure searchable symmetric encryption. In: Keromytis, A.D. (ed.) FC 2012. LNCS, vol. 7397, pp. 285–298. Springer, Heidelberg (2012)
22. Kurosawa, K., Ohtaki, Y.: How to update documents *Verifiably* in searchable symmetric encryption. In: Abdalla, M., Nita-Rotaru, C., Dahab, R. (eds.) CANS 2013. LNCS, vol. 8257, pp. 309–328. Springer, Heidelberg (2013)
23. Kuzu, M., Islam, M.S., Kantarcioglu, M.: Efficient similarity search over encrypted data. In: IEEE ICDE 2012, pp. 1156–1167 (2012)
24. Li, J., Wang, Q., Wang, C., Cao, N., Ren, K., Lou, W.: Fuzzy keyword search over encrypted data in cloud computing. In: IEEE INFOCOM 2010 (Mini-Conference), pp. 1–5 (2010)
25. Moataz, T., Shikfa, A.: Boolean symmetric searchable encryption. In: ASIACCS 2013, pp. 265–276 (2013)
26. Naveed, M., Prabhakaran, M., Gunter, C.A.: Dynamic searchable encryption via blind storage. In: IEEE S&P 2014, pp. 639–654 (2014)
27. Ogata, W., Koiwa, K., Kanaoka, A., Matsuo, S.: Toward practical searchable symmetric encryption. In: Sakiyama, K., Terada, M. (eds.) IWSEC 2013. LNCS, vol. 8231, pp. 151–167. Springer, Heidelberg (2013)
28. Song, D., Wagner, D., Perrig, A.: Practical techniques for searching on encrypted data. In: IEEE S&P 2000, pp. 44–55 (2000)
29. Stefanov, E., Papamanthou, C., Shi, E.: Practical dynamic searchable encryption with small leakage. In: NDSS 2014 (2014)
30. Taketani, S., Ogata, W.: Improvement of UC secure searchable symmetric encryption scheme. In: Tanaka, K., Suga, Y. (eds.) IWSEC 2015. LNCS, vol. 9241, pp. 135–152. Springer, Heidelberg (2015)
31. van Liesdonk, P., Sedghi, S., Doumen, J., Hartel, P., Jonker, W.: Computationally efficient searchable symmetric encryption. In: Jonker, W., Petković, M. (eds.) SDM 2010. LNCS, vol. 6358, pp. 87–100. Springer, Heidelberg (2010)
32. Wang, C., Ren, K., Yu, S., Urs, K.M.R.: Achieving usable and privacy-assured similarity search over outsourced cloud data. In: IEEE INFOCOM 2012, pp. 451–459 (2012)
33. Yang, Y.J., Ding, X.H., Deng, R.H., Bao, F.: Multi-user private queries over encrypted databases. Int. J. Appl. Cryptography **1**(4), 309–319 (2009)
34. Yavuz, A.A., Guajardo, J.: Dynamic searchable symmetric encryption with minimal leakage and efficient updates on commodity hardware. In: Dunkelman, O., Keliher, L. (eds.) SAC 2015. LNCS, vol. 9566, pp. 241–259. Springer, Heidelberg (2016)

Secure Automata-Based Substring Search Scheme on Encrypted Data

Hiroaki Yamamoto[✉]

Department of Information Engineering, Shinshu University,
4-17-1 Wakasato, Nagano-shi 380-8553, Japan
yamamoto@cs.shinshu-u.ac.jp

Abstract. Symmetric searchable encryption (SSE) is a method which searches encrypted data without decrypting it, and several SSE schemes have been proposed. However, most of them support only exact keyword search. To search for any substring in a document, we must register all substrings of the document in an index. Hence if the length of a document is n, we must register $O(n^2)$ substrings in an index. In this paper, we present a secure and efficient substring search scheme on encrypted documents.

1 Introduction

1.1 Backgrounds

In recent years, remote storage services are rapidly spreading in cloud computing. In such a system, there is often a case where a user wants to protect his/her privacy and sensitive data on a remote server. In the field of information retrieval, the importance of security is increasing. For example, there is a case such that, in a database and an email system, a user wants to make a search without revealing the contents of the stored data to a server. In this case, the standard technique is that a user stores data in an encrypted form. By such encryption, the server cannot know the contents, but a search becomes difficult. Therefore a technique for searching the encrypted data on the server efficiently is desired. Up to now, researches on efficient search techniques for encryption data have been actively done under such a background [6,7,10–13,18–22,24]. In particular, a scheme using symmetric key encryption is called symmetric searchable encryption (SSE). Bösch et al. [4] present a survey of secure searchable encryption including SSE.

1.2 Our Contributions

Most of SSE schemes proposed until now support only exact keyword search, and therefore one of the challenging problems for SSE is to develop a secure search scheme to efficiently search for all substrings appearing in a document. A trivial technique is that we register all substrings occurring in a document

This work was supported by JSPS KAKENHI Grant Number 26330154.

K. Ogawa and K. Yoshioka (Eds.): IWSEC 2016, LNCS 9836, pp. 111–131, 2016.
DOI: 10.1007/978-3-319-44524-3_7

in an index. However, this method generates a huge index because there are $O(n^2)$ substrings in a document of length n. Reducing the size of an index is an important problem. Toward solving this problem, substring search schemes on encrypted data have been proposed in [9,23] recently.

In this paper, we present a new encrypted search scheme that can search for all substrings. In particular, to design a compact and secure index, we use a directed acyclic word graph (DAWG) and a Bloom filter. A DAWG, which is given by [2,3], is a deterministic finite automaton that accepts all substrings of a string. We extend a DAWG for a set of strings. A Bloom filter is a data structure proposed by Bloom [1] and has been applied to many fields such as a network application [5] because of its compactness. We introduce a new data structure called a hierarchical Bloom filter (HBF), and use an HBF to hide the structure of a DAWG. Let $D = \{d_0, \cdots, d_{N-1}\}$ be a set of documents and q be a query of length m. Here a document and a query are defined as a string on an alphabet Σ. Our contributions are as follows. The details are given in Sect. 5.

- We present a new substring searchable symmetric encryption scheme, SUB_SSE, which enables us to search for any substring occurring in a document. The proposed secure index is built by an encrypted DAWG for the set D and an array of states and document IDs. Furthermore, in order to hide the structure of the encrypted DAWG and to reduce the size of the index, we embed the encrypted DAWG into an HBF. By using an HBF, the size of the index for the encrypted DAWG depends only on the number of transitions.
- We introduce a block parameter γ. When making an encrypted index and a trapdoor of a query, documents and queries are encrypted by regarding a block of 2γ consecutive characters as one symbol. By this, we can hide the frequency of each character occurring in a query.
- SUB_SSE finds all documents in which q appears in $O((m/\gamma) \log n_D + |D(q)|)$ time, where $n_D = \sum_{d \in D} |d|$ and $D(q)$ is the set of IDs of documents matching q. Furthermore, the size of the index is $O((\gamma + N)n_D)$. If we construct an inverted index using $O(n^2)$ substrings, the size would become $O(N \times n_D^2)$. We will give a method to improve the size of the index.
- The number of rounds of communication between a user and a server is two. The schemes proposed by [9,23] require two or three rounds. The number of rounds is crucial for efficiency and security.
- Under some restriction, our scheme meets non-adaptive semantic security introduced by Curtmola et al. [8]. In general, a non-adaptive scheme can be more efficient than an adaptive scheme for time and space.

1.3   Related Works

Goh [10] presented an encrypted search scheme using a Bloom filter. His method stores keywords of each document in one Bloom filter and search all documents for a given query. Hence it takes a time proportion to the number of documents. Curtmola et al. [8] presented an encrypted index using an inverted index. They pointed out the drawback of the security models used in Goh [10] and introduced two new security models, a non-adaptive semantic security model and an adaptive semantic security model. They gave two secure search schemes, called SSE-1 and SSE-2. Kamara et al. [17] presented a secure dynamic search scheme by improving Curtmola's inverted index. Their scheme provides an efficient update, but the identifier of each keyword contained in an added documents is leaked. They showed that their scheme meets adaptive semantic security and runs in time proportional to the number of documents matching a query. Hahn and Kerschbaum [13] presented a secure dynamic search scheme with efficient and secure updates. Their scheme does not leak any information concerning keywords of a document when adding or deleting the document. Hence it does not leak the identifier of each keyword. They showed that their scheme meets adaptive semantic security. The search time is proportional to the total number of keywords contained in all documents when a query is searched first, but the second search for the same query is proportional to the number of documents matching the query.

Golle et al. [11] proposed a secure conjunctive keyword search scheme that does not leak even the content of the conjunction of keywords. However, their scheme provides only a restricted search, and is inefficient because it needs exponentiation calculation for every document. The methods [8,13,17] using an inverted index must compute a set intersection when carrying out a conjunctive keyword search. As a more flexible search, Liu et al. [20] first proposed a fuzzy keyword search scheme. They introduced an edit distance between two strings to measure the similarity. Suga et al. [22] gave a search scheme using Bloom filters, which allows us to use wildcard characters. Their methods can make a flexible search but cannot find any substring. These schemes meet non-adaptive semantic security, but can search for a query only by one round of communication.

Table 1. Comparison of substring search schemes. Here m denotes the size of a query, n_D denotes the size of the document collection, N denotes the number of documents, γ is the block parameter, and $\sigma = |\Sigma|$. For simplicity, the security parameter is not included as a factor. The terms *mal-adapt*, *adapt*, and *non-adapt* mean adaptive security for malicious adversaries, adaptive security, and non-adaptive security, respectively.

Scheme	# of rounds	Index size	Server Search time	User Search time	Space	Security
CS-scheme	4	$O(\sigma n_D)$	$O(\sigma m + occ)$	$O(\sigma m + occ)$	$O(m + \sigma + occ)$	mal-adapt
SR-scheme	2	$O(n_D)$	$O(m + occ)$	$O(m + occ)$	$O(m + occ)$	adapt
SUB_SSE (This paper)	2	$O((\gamma + N)n_D)$	$O((m/\gamma) \log n_D + |D(q)|)$	$O(m/\gamma)$	$O(1)$	non-adapt
Scheme-2 (This paper)	3	$O(\gamma n_D)$	$O((m/\gamma) \log n_D + occ)$	$O(m/\gamma + occ)$	$O(occ)$	non-adapt

As for substring search schemes, two schemes [9,23] have been proposed recently. Table 1 gives a comparison of these schemes and our scheme (SUB_SSE). Scheme-2 shows a scheme described in Sect. 5.4. The column "# of rounds" denotes the number of rounds of communication between a user and a server for a search. The search time of the user includes the time to make a trapdoor, but not include the time to decrypt encrypted documents returned from the server. The space of the user denotes the additional space other than space to store a query and a trapdoor. Chase and Shen [9] proposed a method (CS-scheme) based on a suffix tree which is a data structure constructed from all suffixes of a string. Given two strings q and d, CS-scheme finds all occurrences of q in d. Note that the strings d and q correspond to a document and a query in our setting, respectively. Hence if CS-scheme is extended to a set D of documents, then the size of the document collection is n_D. They state an extension of CS-scheme to multiple strings, that is, a document collection. As for the number of rounds of communication, CS-scheme performs three rounds in the protocol given in [9]. However, the user gets encrypted IDs from the serve after the third round. Therefore, for the user to get the documents corresponding IDs from the sever, the user must send decrypted IDs to the server. Hence CS-scheme needs four rounds. The number of rounds in SUB_SSE is two. Let us see the time and space complexity for a search. As for the server, CS-scheme takes $O(\sigma m + occ)$ time, where $\sigma = |\Sigma|$, and SUB_SSE takes $O((m/\gamma) \log n_D + |D(q)|)$. For the document collection D, the factor occ denotes the number of all occurrences of a query as a substring in D. Therefore, in general, $|D(q)| \leq occ$. Thus CS-scheme runs faster than SUB_SSE for the server if σ is small. CS-scheme, however, imposes more work on the user than SUB_SSE because the user must perform decryption or pseudo-random functions $O(\sigma m + occ)$ times on each round other than making a trapdoor. In addition, the user needs $O(m + \sigma + occ)$ additional space to perform some functions. In SUB_SSE, the user performs encryption only once other than making a trapdoor, and takes only $O(m/\gamma)$ time for making a trapdoor. Furthermore, the additional space of the user is $O(1)$. The index size of CS-scheme is $O(\sigma n_D)$, and the index size of SUB_SSE is $O((\gamma + N)n_D)$. Thus SUB_SSE needs more space on the server. We will show a method (Scheme-2) to reduce the index size to $O(\gamma n_D)$ in Sect. 5.4. Scheme-2 uses a tree of equivalence classes defined in [2,3]. As we see in Table 1, although the index size is reduced, the number of rounds, the search time of the server, and the time and space of the user increase. As for security, they introduced a security model for malicious adversaries and proved the security of CS-scheme. As mentioned before, in CS-scheme, the user finally gets encrypted IDs corresponding a query, and decrypts them. SR-scheme and Scheme-2 are also similar. On the other hand, in SUB_SSE (and several schemes proposed previously), the server directly gets IDs matching a query and sends the corresponding encrypted documents to the user. This difference seems to be crucial for security because the user can handle the encrypted IDs freely.

Strizhov and Ray [23] proposed a method (SR-scheme) based on a position heap tree for a string. Since a position heap tree holds positions of substring, SR-scheme also finds all occurrences of a query in a document collection. SR-Scheme takes $O(m + occ)$ time on the server, and the index size is $O(n_D)$. This scheme requires two rounds of communication. SR-scheme also performs a pseudo-random permutation at most $m + occ$ times on the user other than making a trapdoor. Hence the search time and the space of the user are both $O(m + occ)$. As seen in Table 1, they show that SR-scheme meets adaptive semantic security. However, the structure of a position heap tree used as an index is revealed because it constructs an encrypted index by encrypting a node and a edge one by one. CS-scheme and our schemes hide the structure of a tree and an automaton. In addition, since SR-scheme generates the trapdoor of a query by encrypting each character of the query one by one, the adversary can make a new trapdoor from trapdoors used previously. For example, the adversary can make the trapdoor of a query $a_1 a_2 b_3 b_4$ from trapdoors of two queries $a_1 a_2 a_3 a_4 a_5$ and $b_1 b_2 b_3 b_4$ without knowing the secret key. Thus it seems to us that the security is weak a little. SR-scheme is also designed such that the user gets encrypted IDs from the server at the first round, decrypts them and then sends decrypted IDs to the server.

2   Preliminaries

Throughout this paper, Σ denotes an arbitrary finite alphabet, and a document and a query denote a string (word) in Σ^*. The empty string is denoted by ε. For a string $w \in \Sigma^*$, $|w|$ denotes the length of w. If W is a set, then $|W|$ denotes the number of elements of W. For strings $w, x, y, z \in \Sigma^*$, if $w = xyz$, then y is called a substring of w. Let $FACT(w) = \{y \mid y$ is a substring of $w\}$.

We consider the following substring search problem. Let $D = \{d_0, \ldots, d_{N-1}\}$ be the set of N documents. Each document d_i is assigned a unique number $ID(d_i) = i$ called a *document ID*. For a document d, let $n_d = |d|$ and let $n_D = \sum_{d \in D} |d|$. Then the substring search problem is, for a given string q (q is called a *query*), to find all documents d_i such that $q \in FACT(d_i)$. We say that a document d matches a query q (or q matches d) if $q \in FACT(d)$. We define $D(q) = \{ID(d_i) \mid d_i$ matches $q\}$. In this paper, we address a substring search problem using a symmetric encryption scheme. A symmetric encryption scheme is a set of three polynomial time algorithms SKE=(KeyGen, Enc, Dec), where KeyGen(1^λ) takes as an input a security parameter λ and randomly outputs a secret key sk; Enc(sk, d) takes as inputs a secret key sk and a text d, and returns a ciphertext c; Dec(sk, c) takes as inputs a key sk and a ciphertext c, and returns d if sk is the key that is used to produce c. As seen in [13], we consider that a symmetric encryption scheme satisfies chosen-plaintext attack security (CPA-security). For simplicity, by Enc$_{sk}(\cdot)$ we denote an encryption function Enc($sk, \cdot$) with a secret key sk. In addition to a symmetric encryption scheme, we make use of pseudo-random functions $F : \{0,1\}^\lambda \times \{0,1\}^* \to \{0,1\}^\eta$, which are polynomial-time functions that cannot be distinguished from random functions. We write $F_{sk}(x)$ for $F(sk, x)$. Similarly, we use a pseudo-random permutation $\pi : \{0,1\}^\lambda \times \{0,1\}^\eta \to \{0,1\}^\eta$ and write $\pi_{sk}(x)$ for $\pi(sk, x)$. We define a negligible function for a security definition.

Definition 1. *A function f from natural numbers to positive real numbers is negligible in a security parameter λ if for every positive polynomial $p(\cdot)$ and sufficiently large λ, $f(\lambda) < p(\lambda)$.*

The search system consists of two parties, a user and a server. The user is the owner of data and stores data in the server in an encrypted form. The user wants to search encrypted data on the server without revealing the contents of data to the server. We assume that the server is honest but curious. The search system works as follows. Search phase is performed by using two rounds of communication. (1) Setup phase: The user constructs a secure index from the set D of documents and encrypts all documents d_i. After that, the user stores them in the server. (2) Search phase: For a query q, the user makes a trapdoor $T(q)$ of q and sends it to the server. The server finds the set $D(q)$ of IDs of all documents matching q, and returns $\{c_i \mid i \in D(q)\}$ to the user. (3) The user decrypts each c_i and gets the original document d_i.

3   Bloom Filters

A Bloom filter is a data structure proposed by Bloom [1], which consists of a bit sequence and is used for efficiently checking whether $x \in S$ for a set S and an element x. Let BF be a Bloom filter of m bits and let $W = \{w_1, \ldots, w_N\}$ be a set of N strings, $h_1, \ldots, h_k$ be hash functions mapping strings to $[0, m-1]$. Then, for $w_i \in W$, we set all bits at positions $h_1(w_i)$, ..., $h_k(w_i)$ in BF to 1. For any string w, whether $w \in W$ or not is checked as follows. First we compute $h_1(w)$, ..., $h_k(w)$, and then check bits at positions $h_1(w)$, ..., $h_k(w)$ in BF. If all bits are 1, then we decide $w \in W$; otherwise $w \notin W$. The drawback of a Bloom filter is to make an error called *a false positive*, that is, there is a possibility such that for $v \notin W$, all bits at positions $h_1(v)$, ..., $h_k(v)$ are 1. In this case, we get a wrong answer such that $v \in W$. Note that for $w \in W$ we always get a correct answer. Broder and Mitzenmacher [5] analyze the relationship among the size of a Bloom filter, the number of elements, the probability of false positive, and the number of hash functions. They showed that given m_1 and m_2, the probability of false positive becomes minimum when $k = (m_1/m_2)\ln 2$. In this case the false positive rate is approximately $(0.6185)^{m_1/m_2}$. In this paper, we use a hierarchical Bloom filter (HBF) to build a secure index.

4   A Directed Acyclic Word Graph for a Set of Strings

Blumer, Blumer and Haussler [2] gave a directed acyclic word graph (DAWG) for a string $w \in \Sigma^*$, which is a deterministic finite automaton (DFA) that accepts $FACT(w)$. In addition, they gave a linear time on-line algorithm to construct a DAWG for a given string. After that, in [3], they extend a DAWG for a set of strings. We here give definitions and properties of a DAWG. Let $W = \{w_1, \ldots, w_k\}$ be the set of strings on Σ. For any $w = a_1 \cdots a_m \in W$

and $v \in \Sigma^*$, let $end\text{-}set(v, w) = \{i \mid v = a_{i-|v|+1} \cdots a_i\}$. In particular, $end\text{-}set(\varepsilon, w) = \{0, 1, \ldots, m\}$. Then, we define an equivalence class such that strings x and y in Σ^* are equivalent on W if and only if for all $w \in W$, $end\text{-}set(x, w) = end\text{-}set(y, w)$. We give an algorithm BuildDawgSet to construct a DAWG for W in Algorithm 1. BuildDawgSet constructs a DAWG $M(W)$ using the subset construction which is the standard method to translate a nondeterministic finite automaton (NFA) into a DFA (for example, see [14]). Note that this algorithm is simple, but takes more time than linear time algorithms given in [2,3]. Our secure index is constructed using an encrypted DAWG, which is given in the next section. Let $M(W) = (Q, \Sigma, \delta, init, F)$ be a DAWG constructed by Build-DawgSet, where Q is the set of states, δ is the transition function, $init$ is the initial state, and $F = Q$ is the set of final states. Then a state of $M(W)$ corresponds to an equivalence class on W. The following proposition is obtained from the results of [2,3].

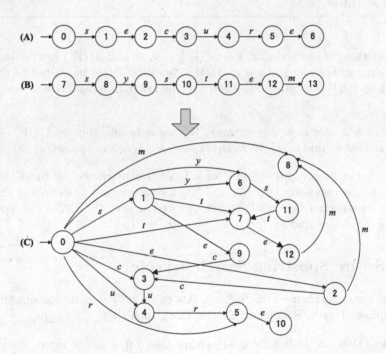

Fig. 1. A DAWG for $\{secure, system\}$

Proposition 1. Let $n_W = \sum_{w \in W} |w|$. Then,

1. the number of states of $M(W)$ is at most $2n_W - 1$, and the number of transitions is at most $3n_W - 4$,
2. for any state of $M(W)$, all the incoming transitions of the state have the same symbol,
3. for any string $v \in \Sigma^*$, $M(W)$ accepts v if and only if there is $w \in W$ such that $v \in FACT(w)$.

Algorithm 1. BuildDawgSet(W)

Input: $W = \{w_1, \ldots, w_k\}$
1: $state \leftarrow 0$
2: **for all** $w_i \in W$ where $w_i = a_{i,1} \cdots a_{i,l_i}$ **do**
3: 　　construct a DFA $M(w_i) = (Q_i, \Sigma_i, \delta_i, init_i, Q_i)$ such that $\Sigma_i = \{a_{i,1}, \ldots, a_{i,l_i}\}$,
　　　$Q_i = \{state, \ldots, state + l_i\}$, $init_i = state$, and for all $j = 1, \ldots, l_i$, $\delta(state + j - 1, a_{i,j}) = state + j$
4: 　　$state \leftarrow state + l_i + 1$
5: **end for**
6: $init \leftarrow state$
7: construct an NFA $M(W) = (Q, \Sigma, \delta, init, Q)$ such that $Q = \{init\} \cup \bigcup_{i \in \{1, \ldots, k\}} Q_i$,
　　$\Sigma = \bigcup_{i \in \{1, \ldots, k\}} \Sigma_i$, $M(W)$ has all transitions of $M(w_i)$, and $\delta(init, \varepsilon) = st$ for all
　　states $st \in Q - \{init\}$
8: translate $M(W)$ into a DFA $DAWG(W)$ using the subset construction
9: number states of $DAWG(W)$ from 0, where the initial state is numbered 0
10: **return** $DAWG(W)$

We say that for any string x, x is $M(W)$ at state st if $M(W)$ reaches state st after reading x. For any state st of $M(W)$, let $WORD(st)$ be the set of strings accepted by $M(W)$ at state st. Then the following proposition also holds for $M(W)$.

Proposition 2. *Let w be any string of W and st be any state of $M(W)$. Then, for any strings v_1 and v_2 in $WORD(st)$, end-set(v_1, w) = end-set(v_2, w)*

Example 1. Let us give an example of a DAWG constructed by BuildDawgSet in Fig. 1. Given two automata (A) and (B) for *secure* and *system*, the DAWG of (C) is constructed by BuildDawgSet. As we can see, the DAWG accepts all substrings of *secure* and *system*.

5　A Secure Substring Search Scheme

Our secure search scheme SUB_SSE consists of six polynomial-time algorithms, (KeyGen, Enc, Trapdr, BuildIndex, Search, Dec), such that

- KeyGen(1^λ) is an probabilistic algorithm that takes as an input a security parameter λ and returns a secret key $SK = (sk_1, sk_2, sk_3, sk_4)$,
- Enc(sk, d) is a probabilistic algorithm that takes as inputs a secret key sk and a document d and returns an encrypted document c, that is, $c = Enc_{sk}(d)$. In particular, Enc$_{sk}(D) = \bigcup_{d \in D} \{Enc_{sk}(d)\}$,
- Trapdr(sk, q) is a deterministic algorithm that takes as inputs a secret key sk and a query q, and returns a trapdoor $T(q)$ of q,
- BuildIndex(SK, D, γ, ν) is a probabilistic algorithm that takes as inputs a secret key sk, a set D of documents and a false positive parameter ν and returns an encrypted index and a set of encrypted documents,

- Search$(T(q), \Pi)$ is a deterministic algorithm that takes as an input a trapdoor $T(q)$ and and an encrypted index Π, and then returns IDs of all documents matching q,
- Dec(sk, c) is a deterministic algorithm that takes as inputs a secret key sk and an encrypted document c and returns the decrypted document d.

In the following, we describe details of Trapdr, BuildIndex, and Search. The proposed secure indexes are constructed by an encrypted DAWG and a hierarchical Bloom filter, which are given in the following sections. In addition to SKE=(KeyGen, Enc, Dec), we use a pseudo-random function $F_{sk_2} : \{0,1\}^* \rightarrow \{0,1\}^{n_1}$, and two pseudo-random permutations $\pi_{sk_3} : \{0,1\}^{n_2} \rightarrow \{0,1\}^{n_2}$ and $\pi_{sk_4} : \{0,1\}^{n_3} \rightarrow \{0,1\}^{n_3}$. In the definition of SUB_SSE, the notation $r \xleftarrow{\$} \{0,1\}^l$ means that we set r to an l-bit string uniformly selected from $\{0,1\}^l$.

5.1   An Encrypted DAWG for a Set of Documents

We here describe how to construct an encrypted DAWG for D. Let $d = a_1 \cdots a_{n_d} \in \Sigma^*$ be a document in D. Let γ be a block parameter such that $1 \leq \gamma \leq max_{d \in D} n_d$ and let a new symbol $\# \notin \Sigma$. Then we define the set $B(d) = \{B(1,d), \ldots; B(\gamma, d)\}$ of block words $B(i,d)$ on d as follows. For any $1 \leq i \leq \gamma$, $B(i,d) = Z_{i,1}\# \cdots \#Z_{i,l_i}$, where $l_i = \lceil (n_d - i + 1)/\gamma \rceil$, and $Z_{i,j} = a_{i+(j-1)\gamma} \cdots a_{i+(j+1)\gamma}$. A string $Z_{i,j}$ is called *a block symbol* and for $(j-1)\gamma \leq k \leq (j+1)\gamma$, if $i + k > n_d$, then we define $a_{i+k} = \#$. Thus a block word $B(i,d)$ is a sequence of block symbols, where block symbols are delimited by $\#$. Note that a block symbol consists of 2γ consecutive characters and the last γ characters of $Z_{i,j}$ overlaps with the first γ characters of $Z_{i,j+1}$. We define the length of a block word $B(i,d)$, denoted by $|B(i,d)|$, to be l_i. Furthermore, for any block word $B(i,d) = Z_1 \# \cdots \# Z_l$, we define $\tilde{B}(i,d)$ as a block word $Z_1 \# \cdots \# Z_{l'}$ such that $l' \leq l$ and $Z_{l'}$ contains a symbol $\#$ but $Z_{l'-1}$ does not contain it. For example, when $d = a_1 a_2 a_3 a_4 a_5 a_6 a_7$ (note that $a_i \in \Sigma$ and $n_d = 7$) and $\gamma = 3$, $B(1,d) = Z_{1,1}\#Z_{1,2}\#Z_{1,3}$ where $Z_{1,1} = a_1 a_2 a_3 a_4 a_5 a_6$, $Z_{1,2} = a_4 a_5 a_6 a_7 a_8 a_9$ and $Z_{1,3} = a_7 a_8 a_9 a_{10} a_{11} a_{12}$, $B(2,d) = Z_{2,1}\#Z_{2,2}$ where $Z_{2,1} = a_2 a_3 a_4 a_5 a_6 a_7$ and $Z_{2,2} = a_5 a_6 a_7 a_8 a_9 a_{10}$, $B(3,d) = Z_{3,1}\#Z_{3,2}$ where $Z_{3,1} = a_3 a_4 a_5 a_6 a_7 a_8$ and $Z_{3,2} = a_6 a_7 a_8 a_9 a_{10} a_{11}$. We have $|B(1,d)| = 3$ and $|B(2,d)| = |B(3,d)| = 2$. Furthermore, $\tilde{B}(1,d) = Z_{1,1}\#Z_{1,2}$, $\tilde{B}(2,d) = Z_{2,1}\#Z_{2,2}$, and $\tilde{B}(3,d) = Z_{3,1}$. Note that $a_8 = a_9 = a_{10} = a_{11} = a_{12} = \#$. Let us define $B(D) = \cup_{d \in D} B(d)$ and $FACT(D) = \cup_{d \in D} FACT(d)$. For $FACT(D)$, we give an algorithm BuildEncDawg to construct an encrypted DAWG $A(D) = (Q, \Sigma, \delta, st, Q)$ in Algorithm 3. In BuildEncDawg, $\#^i$ denotes a string consisting of i $\#$'s. Our secure index, which is given in the next section, is constructed by implementing an encrypted DAWG using Bloom filters. For a block word $B(i,d)$, we define $F_{sk}(B(i,d)) = F_{sk}(Z_{i,1})\# \cdots \#F_{sk}(Z_{i,l_i})$, where $F_{sk}(B(i,d))$ is called *an encrypted block word*. BuildEncDawg constructs a DAWG for the set $CWORD$ of encrypted block words. When constructing an encrypted DAWG, we want to ignore a symbol $\#$ appearing in a block word, because $\#$ is used only as a delimiter. To do this, we give a modified version BuildDawgSetBlock of BuildDawgSet in Algorithm 2.

Algorithm 2. BuildDawgSetBlock(W)

Input: $W = \{C_1, \ldots, C_k\}$
1: $state \leftarrow 0$
2: **for all** $C_i \in W$ where $C_i = X_{i,1}\#\cdots\#X_{i,l_i}$ **do**
3:    construct a DFA $M(C_i) = (Q_i, \Sigma_i, \delta_i, init_i, Q_i)$ such that $\Sigma_i = \{X_{i,1}, \ldots, X_{i,l_i}\}$,
      $Q_i = \{state, \ldots, state + l_i\}$, $init_i = state$, and for all $j = 1, \ldots, l_i$, $\delta(state + j -$
      $1, X_{i,j}) = state + j$
4:    $state \leftarrow state + l_i + 1$
5: **end for**
6: $init \leftarrow state$
7: construct an NFA $M(W) = (Q, \Sigma, \delta, init, Q)$ such that $Q = \{init\} \cup \cup_{i \in \{1, \ldots, k\}} Q_i$,
   $\Sigma = \cup_{i \in \{1, \ldots, k\}} \Sigma_i$, $M(W)$ has all transitions of $M(C_i)$, and $\delta(init, \varepsilon) = st$ for all
   states $st \in Q - \{init\}$
8: translate $M(W)$ into a DFA $DAWG(W)$ using the subset construction
9: number states of $DAWG(W)$ from 0 randomly, where the initial state is numbered
   0
10: **return** $DAWG(W)$

Let $A(D)$ be an encrypted DAWG generated by BuildEncDawg. Then $A(D)$ has the following properties if Fsk is injective. In general, F_{sk} is not always injective, but the provability that $F_{sk}(x) = F_{sk}(y)$ for any $x \neq y$ is very small. Here, for any state st of $A(D)$, we call the symbol in 3 of Proposition 3 *the symbol of st*. Furthermore, note that $A(D)$ ignores # in an encrypted block word given as an input.

Proposition 3. *1. The number of states of $A(D)$ is at most $(2 + 6\gamma)n_D$, and the number of transitions is at most $\gamma(3n_D - 4)$.*
2. For any string $v \in \Sigma^*$, $A(D)$ accepts $F_{sk}(\tilde{B}(1, v))$ if and only if $v \in FACT(D)$.
3. For any state of $A(D)$, all the incoming transitions of the state have the same symbol.

Proof. Let $A'(D)$ be a DAWG obtained at line 6 of BuildEncDawg. Since $\sum_{C_i \in CWORD} |C_i| = n_D$, it follows from Proposition 1 that the number of states of $A'(D)$ is at most $2n_D - 1$ and the number of transitions is at most $3n_D - 4$. $A(D)$ is built by adding at most $2\gamma - 1$ states and $2\gamma - 1$ transitions for each transition of $A'(D)$ in lines 7–21. Therefore the number of states of $A(D)$ is at most $2n_D - 1 + (2\gamma - 1)(3n_D - 4) \leq (2 + 6\gamma)n_D$ and the number of transitions of $A(D)$ is at most $\gamma(3n_D - 4)$. Next let us consider the second property. Let $\tilde{B}(1, v) = Z_{1,1}\#\cdots\#Z_{1,l}$. Then $A'(D)$ can reach a state st by $F_{sk}(Z_{1,1})\#\cdots\#F_{sk}(Z_{1,l-1})$ because $Z_{1,1}, \ldots, Z_{1,l-1}$ do not contain symbol #. For any transition $\delta(st, X) = st'$ of $A'(D)$ such that $X = F_{sk}(Z)$ with $Z = a_1 \cdots a_{2\gamma}$, BuildEncDawg constructs $A(D)$ by adding at most $2\gamma - 1$ transitions by $a_1\#^{2\gamma-1}, \ldots, a_1 \cdots a_{2\gamma-1}\#$ to $A'(D)$. Hence if $A(D)$ accepts $F_{sk}(\tilde{B}(1, v))$, then v is obtained from $Z_{1,1}, \ldots, Z_{1,l}$ and $v \in FACT(D)$. Conversely, if $v \in FACT(D)$, $A(D)$ accepts $F_{sk}(\tilde{B}(1, v))$. It follows that the second

---

Algorithm 3. BuildEncDawg($sk, \gamma, B(D)$)

1: $CWORD \leftarrow \emptyset$
2: **for all** $B(i,d) \in B(D)$ **do**
3:     $C_i \leftarrow F_{sk}(B(i,d)) \; (= F_{sk}(Z_{i,1})\# \cdots \#F_{sk}(Z_{i,l_i}))$
4:     $CWORD \leftarrow CWORD \cup \{C_i\}$
5: **end for**
6: construct a DAWG $A(D) = (Q, \Sigma, \delta, 0, Q)$ using BuildDawgSetBlock($CWORD$).
7: **for all** $st \in Q$ **do**
8:     let $\{X_1, \ldots, X_l\}$ be the set of encrypted block symbols X_i such that $\delta(st, X_i) = st_i$ is defined, and for $1 \leq i \leq l$, let $X_i = F_{sk}(Z_i)$ where $Z = a_{i,1} \cdots a_{i,2\gamma}$.
9:     $\mathcal{X} \leftarrow \{a_{1,1} \cdots a_{1,2\gamma}, \ldots, a_{l,1} \cdots a_{l,2\gamma}\}$
10:     **while** $\mathcal{X} \neq \emptyset$ **do**
11:         get a string $a_{i,1} \cdots a_{i,2\gamma}$ from $\mathcal{X}$
12:         **for** $j = 1$ to $2\gamma - 1$ **do**
13:             $Y_i \leftarrow a_{i,1} \cdots a_{i,j}\#^{2\gamma-j}$ and $\tilde{X} \leftarrow F_{sk}(Y_i)$
14:             **if** there is not a state st' in $A(D)$ such that $\delta(st, \tilde{X}) = st'$ **then**
15:                 make a new state st'
16:                 add st' and $\delta(st, \tilde{X}) = st'$ to $A(D)$
17:             **end if**
18:         **end for**
19:     **end while**
20: **end for**
21: **return** $A(D)$

---

property holds. Since we make a new state so that all the incoming transitions of the state has the same symbol, the third property follows from Proposition 1.

5.2   Constructing a Secure Index

In this section, we present a secure index based on an encrypted DAWG for the set D of documents. Let $A(D) = (Q, \Sigma, \delta, 0, Q)$ be a DAWG for D. We want to hide the structure of $A(D)$. For this purpose, we use a hierarchical Bloom filter (HBF). We define $S_i = \{(j, X) \mid j \in Q, \delta(j, X) = i\}$ for any $i \in Q$ and $S = \cup_{i \in Q} S_i$. Note that the size of S is the number of transitions of $A(D)$ because $A(D)$ is a DFA. We introduce a binary tree T_S, which is called *a state-set tree*, based on S. Let $h_D = \log |Q|$ where we use 2 as the base of a logarithm. Note that we have $|Q| \leq 2n_D - 1$ by Proposition 1. Without loss of generality, we may assume that $|Q|$ is a power of 2, because we can add dummy states p such that $S_p = \emptyset$ to Q. For any level $0 \leq lev \leq h_D$, we define a decomposition of S at a level lev, $S^{lev} = \{S_0^{lev}, S_{2^\alpha}^{lev}, S_{2 \cdot 2^\alpha}^{lev}, \ldots, S_{(2^{lev}-1) \cdot 2^\alpha}^{lev}\}$ as follows. Here, let $\alpha = h_D - lev$.

Definition 2. *1. For all $0 \leq lev \leq h_D$ and $i = 0, 2^\alpha, 2 \cdot 2^\alpha, 3 \cdot 2^\alpha, \ldots, (2^{lev} - 1) \cdot 2^\alpha$, $S_i^{lev} = \cup_{0 \leq j \leq 2^\alpha - 1} S_{i+j}$.*

Then a state-set tree T_S for S is defined as follows. (1) The nodes of a state-set tree T_S consists of S_i^{lev} defined above. (2) The root of T_S is S_0^0. (3) For any

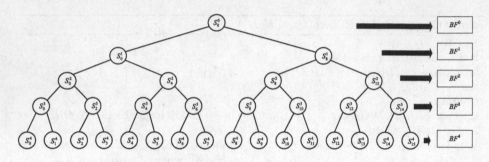

Fig. 2. A state-set tree and a hierarchical Bloom filter

Algorithm 4. BuildIndex(SK, D, γ, ν)

Input: $SK = \{sk_1, sk_2, sk_3, sk_4\}$, $D = \{d_0, \ldots, d_{N-1}\}$

1: $HBF_D \leftarrow \emptyset$
2: $A(D) \leftarrow$ BuildEncDawg($sk_2, \gamma, B(D)$), where $A(D) = (Q, \Sigma, \delta, 0, Q)$ and $h_D = \log|Q|$
3: **for** $lev = 0$ to h_D **do**
4:    $BF_D^{lev} \leftarrow \emptyset$
5:    initialize a Bloom filter BF_D^{lev} of $\nu \times \gamma n_D$ bits,
6:    **for all** $S_i^{lev} \in S^{lev}$ **do**
7:        **for all** $(q, X) \in S_i^{lev}$ **do**
8:            $Y \leftarrow F_X(q||X||i)$,
9:            $p_1 \leftarrow hash_1(Y), \ldots, p_e \leftarrow hash_e(Y)$, and set positions $p_1, \ldots, p_e$ of BF_D^{lev} to 1.
10:       **end for**
11:       randomly select $e(3\gamma n_D - |S|)$ positions of BF_D^{lev} and set them to 1
12:   **end for**
13:   add BF_D^{lev} to HBF_D,
14: **end for**
15: $ctr \leftarrow 0$
16: **for all** $st \in Q - \{0\}$ **do**
17:   $K_1 \overset{\$}{\leftarrow} \{0,1\}^\lambda$, and $naddr \leftarrow \pi_{sk_3}(ctr)$
18:   $\beta_{st} \leftarrow F_{sk_2}(X_{st}||st)$, where X_{st} is the symbol of st.
19:   $\Gamma_1[\pi_{sk_4}(st)] \leftarrow \mathsf{Enc}_{\beta_{st}}(naddr||K_1||X_{st})$
20:   $ctr \leftarrow ctr + 1$
21:   let $D(st) = \{L_1, \ldots, L_k\}$
22:   **for** $i = 1$ to k **do**
23:       $K_{i+1} \overset{\$}{\leftarrow} \{0,1\}^\lambda$
24:       $addr \leftarrow naddr$, $naddr \leftarrow \pi_{sk_3}(ctr)$, and $\Gamma_2[addr] \leftarrow \mathsf{Enc}_{K_i}(L_i||naddr||K_{i+1})$
25:       $ctr \leftarrow ctr + 1$
26:   **end for**
27: **end for**
28: set the remaining entries of Γ_1 and Γ_2 which are not used above to random strings of the same size as the other entries.
29: **return** $\Pi = (HBF_D, \Gamma_1, \Gamma_2)$.

---

i and $0 \leq lev \leq h_D - 1$, if S_i^{lev} is a node of T_S, then S_i^{lev+1} and $S_{i+2^\alpha}^{lev+1}$ are also nodes of T_S, and are the left child and the right child of S_i^{lev}, respectively.

The number i of each node S_i^{lev} is called a node ID of S_i^{lev}. If $lev = h_D$, then, for any i ($0 \leq i \leq 2^{h_D} - 1$), a leaf $S_i^{h_D}$ becomes S_i. We assign one Bloom filter BF_D^{lev} to each level $0 \leq lev \leq h_D$. Hence we use $h_D + 1$ BFs in total to construct an index.

Example 2. Let us give an example of a sate-set tree for a DAWG in Fig. 1. We have $Q = \{0,1,2,3,4,5,6,7,8,9,10,11,12\}$. Then, we add dummy states $13, 14, 15$ so that the number of states becomes 2^4. Thus $h_D = 4$. Furthermore we have $S_0 = \emptyset$, $S_1 = \{(0,s)\}$, $S_2 = \{(0,e)\}$, $S_3 = \{(0,c),(2,c),(9,c)\}$, $S_4 = \{(0,u),(3,u)\}$, $S_5 = \{(0,r),(4,r)\}$, $S_6 = \{(0,y),(1,y)\}$, $S_7 = \{(0,t),(1,t),(11,t)\}$, $S_8 = \{(0,m),(2,m),(12,m)\}$, $S_9 = \{(1,e)\}$, $S_{10} = \{(5,e)\}$, $S_{11} = \{(6,s)\}$, $S_{12} = \{(7,e)\}$, and $S = \cup_{1 \leq i \leq 12} S_i$. Then, the state-set tree obtained from Q is given in Fig. 2. In Fig. 2, Bloom filters BF^0, BF^1, BF^2, BF^3, BF^4 are built for each level. Each node S_i^{lev} of T_S is a subset of S such that
$S_0^0 = \cup_{0 \leq i \leq 12} S_i \subset S_0^1 = \cup_{0 \leq i \leq 7} S_i$, $S_8^1 = \cup_{8 \leq i \leq 12} S_i$,
$S_0^2 = \cup_{0 \leq i \leq 3} S_i$, $S_4^2 = \cup_{4 \leq i \leq 7} S_i$, $S_8^2 = \cup_{8 \leq i \leq 11} S_i$, $S_{12}^2 = S_{12}$,
$S_0^3 = \cup_{0 \leq i \leq 1} S_i$, $S_2^3 = \cup_{2 \leq i \leq 3} S_i$, $S_4^3 = \cup_{4 \leq i \leq 5} S_i$, $S_6^3 = \cup_{6 \leq i \leq 7} S_i$,
$S_8^3 = \cup_{8 \leq i \leq 9} S_i$, $S_{10}^3 = \cup_{10 \leq i \leq 11} S_i$, $S_{12}^3 = S_{12}$, $S_{14}^3 = \emptyset$,
$S_0^4 = S_0$, $S_1^4 = S_1$, $S_2^4 = S_2$, $S_3^4 = S_3$, $S_4^4 = S_4$, $S_5^4 = S_5$, $S_6^4 = S_6$, $S_7^4 = S_7$,
$S_8^4 = S_8$,
$S_9^4 = S_9$, $S_{10}^4 = S_{10}$, $S_{11}^4 = S_{11}$, $S_{12}^4 = S_{12}$, $S_{13}^4 = S_{14}^4 = S_{15}^4 = \emptyset$.

We give an algorithm BuildIndex in Algorithm 4 which constructs an encrypted index using Bloom filters. In BuildIndex, $x \| y$ denotes the concatenation of two strings x and y.

BuildIndex constructs an encrypted DAWG $A(D)$ using BuildEncDawg, and then stores $A(D)$ in an HBF. Since $A(D)$ is constructed from all documents, we cannot know which documents contain a give query. To solve this problem, we prepare two additional arrays Γ_1 and Γ_2. Γ_1 is a look-up table of $(2 + 6\gamma)n_D$ entries from which we can get the starting address of list of $D(q)$ for a query. Γ_2 is an array of $N \times n_D$ entries in which document lists are stored. To build Γ_1 and Γ_2, we use the following lemma of $A(D)$. This lemma is obtained from Proposition 2, and states that if there are more than one string accepted at a state st on $A(D)$, then all of them occur in the same documents. Hence, using Γ_1 and Γ_2, we can get a correct list of IDs of documents matching a given query. Since, by the definition of an encrypted block word, any subword C of an encrypted block word has the original string w such that C is constructed from w, we define $D(C) = D(w)$.

Lemma 1. *For any state st of $A(D)$, let $CWORD(st)$ be the set of encrypted block words accepted by $A(D)$ at state st. Then, for any $C_1, C_2 \in CWORD(st)$, $D(C_1) = D(C_2)$.*

Let st be any state of $A(D)$ and let C be an encrypted block word accepted by $A(D)$. Since every encrypted block word accepted as state st has $D(C)$ by lemma 1, we assign the set $D(C)$ of document IDs to state st. We construct secure an index $\Pi = (HBF_D, \Gamma_1, \Gamma_2)$ using BuildIndex given in Algorithm 4. BuildIndex is given secret keys $SK = (sk_1, sk_2, sk_3, sk_4)$ generated by KeyGen and uses two pseudo-random permutations $\pi_{sk_3}(\cdot)$ with $\eta_2 = \log(n_D \times N)$ and $\pi_{sk_4}(\cdot)$ with $\eta_3 = \log((2 + 6\gamma)n_D)$. Γ_1 and Γ_2 is used to store $D(C)$ assigned to state st in the following manner. Let st be any state of $A(D)$. It follows from Proposition 3 that the symbols of incoming transitions of st are all same. Now we let the symbol of st be X_{st}. Then, we set $\beta_{st} = F_{sk_2}(X_{st}||st)$ and $\Gamma_1[\pi_{sk_4}(st)] = \mathsf{Enc}_{\beta_{st}}(\pi_{sk_3}(ctr)||K_1||X_{st})$. We partition $D(w)$ into $L_1, \ldots, L_k$ such that $|L_1| = \cdots = |L_k|$. For any $1 \le i \le k$, let $addr = \pi_{sk_3}(ctr + j - 1)$ and $\Gamma_2[addr] = \mathsf{Enc}_{K_i}(L_i||\pi_{sk_3}(ctr + j)||K_{i+1})$. It follows from Proposition 3 that the next theorem holds.

Theorem 1. *Let D be a set of documents, and let $\Pi = (HBF_D, \Gamma_1, \Gamma_2)$ be the index built by BuildIndex. Then, the size of HBF_D is $O(\gamma n_D)$, the size of Γ_1 is $O(\gamma n_D)$, and the size of Γ_2 is $O(N \times n_D)$.*

5.3   A Search Algorithm

The Trapdoor of a Query. The algorithm $\mathsf{Trapdr}(sk, q)$ makes the trapdoor $T(q)$ of a query q by $T(q) = F_{sk}(\tilde{B}(1, q))$. We define $|T(q)| = |\tilde{B}(1, q)|$.

Search for $T(q)$. We give a search algorithm Search in Algorithm 5. Search finds documents by communication between a server and a user as follows. Given a trapdoor $T(q) = X_1 \cdots X_l$ for a query q of length m, the server simulates an encrypted DAWG $A(D)$ using the index HBF_D and $T(q)$, where $l = \lfloor m/\gamma \rfloor$. To simulate $A(D)$, the server invokes CheckDoc, which computes states reachable from the initial state of $A(D)$ using a function Trans. Trans recursively performs transitions of $A(D)$ using HBF_D. Furthermore, since $A(D)$ is deterministic, $A(D)$ can reach just one state for $T(q)$ if there is a document matching q. Therefore, if we set the size of HBF_D so that the false positive becomes small enough, then the function Trans runs in $O(h_D)$ time, that is, $O(\log n_D)$ time for each X_i. In addition, the size of $State$ in CheckDoc is bounded by a constant. It follows that CheckDoc runs in $O((m/\gamma) \log n_D)$ time.

Next suppose that the server gets a state st after reading $T(q)$. The server send it to the user and get the key $(\beta_{st}, p_{st}) = (F_{sk_2}(X||st), \pi_{sk_4}(st))$ from the user. The sever extracts document IDs from Γ_1 and Γ_2 using the key (β_{st}, p_{st}). Note that the entry of Γ_1 is encrypted with β_{st} such that $\beta_{st} = F_{sk_2}(X_{st}||st)$ for the symbol X_{st} of state st. The server might have gotten a wrong state st by a false positive of HBF_D. However, the server can know whether the state is correct by checking $X' = X_l$ at line 15 because X_l is the symbol of st. Thus the server can find IDs of all documents matching q. Search takes $O((m/\gamma) \log n_D)$ time to simulate $A(D)$ using HBF_D, and takes $O(|D(q)|)$ time to get document IDs. Furthermore, it uses two rounds of communication. The following theorem follows from Proposition 3.

Algorithm 5. Search($T(q), \Pi$)

Input: $T(q) = X_1 \cdots X_l$, $\Pi = (HBF_D, \Gamma_1, \Gamma_2)$
   Server:
 1: $STATE \leftarrow \mathsf{CheckDoc}(T(q), HBF_D, 0)$
 2: send $STATE$ to the user
   User:
 3: **if** $STATE \neq \emptyset$ **then**
 4:    **for all** $st \in STATE$ **do**
 5:       $\beta_{st} \leftarrow F_{sk_2}(X_l \| st)$ and $p_{st} \leftarrow \pi_{sk_4}(st)$
 6:       add (β_{st}, p_{st}) to KEY
 7:    **end for**
 8:    send KEY to the server
 9: **else**
10:    halt.
11: **end if**
   Server:
12: $MATCH \leftarrow \emptyset$
13: **for all** $(\beta_{st}, p_{st}) \in KEY$ **do**
14:    $(addr, K, X') \leftarrow \mathsf{Dec}_{\beta_{st}}(\Gamma_1[p_{st}])$
15:    **if** $X' = X_l$ **then**
16:       extract $D(q)$ from Γ_2 starting at $\Gamma_2[addr]$
17:       $MATCH \leftarrow D(q) \cup MATCH$
18:    **end if**
19: **end for**
20: **return** $MATCH$

Theorem 2. *For any query q of length m, the algorithm* Search *exactly finds all documents matching q in $O((m/\gamma) \log n_D + |D(q)|)$ time using two rounds of communication.*

5.4 Reducing the Size of the Index

We describe how to reduce the size of the index to $O(\gamma n_D)$. According to Sect. 4, we describe the idea for a non-encrypted DAWG. We call a scheme obtained by this modification a *Scheme-2*, and will give only the outline.

The size of the index $\Pi = (HBF_D, \Gamma_1, \Gamma_2)$ mainly depends on the size of Γ_2. The array Γ_2 holds document IDs to get the document IDs matching a query from a state of a DAWG. Let $W = \{w_1, \ldots, w_k\}$. In Sect. 4, we defined an equivalence relation on Σ^* with respect to W. For any $x \in \Sigma^*$, let $[x]_W$ be an equivalence class to which x belongs. As defined in [2,3], we construct a tree T_W from equivalence classes as follows.

1. The nodes of T_W consist of equivalence classes.
2. The root of T_W is $[\varepsilon]_W$.
3. Let $[x]_W$ be any node of T_W and x be the longest string in $[x]_W$. Then, for any $a \in \Sigma$, if $ax \in FACT(W)$, then $[ax]_W$ is a child of $[x]_W$.

Algorithm 6. CheckDoc(T, HBF, st)

1: $State \leftarrow \{st\}$
2: **for** $i = 1$ to l **do**
3:    $Next \leftarrow \emptyset$
4:    **for all** $st \in State$ **do**
5:        $Next \leftarrow Next \cup \mathsf{Trans}(st, X_i, HBF, 0, 0)$
6:    **end for**
7:    $State \leftarrow Next$
8: **end for**
9: **return** $State$

   Function $\mathsf{Trans}(st, X, HBF, lev, id)$
   {This function computes $\delta(st, X)$}
10: $Y \leftarrow F_X(st\|X\|id)$
11: $p_1 \leftarrow hash_1(Y), \ldots, p_e \leftarrow hash_e(Y)$
12: **if** the bits of all positions $p_1, \ldots, p_e$ in $BF^{lev} \in HBF$ are 1 **then**
13:    **if** $lev = h_D$ **then**
14:        **return** $\{id\}$
15:    **else**
16:        $\alpha \leftarrow h_D - lev$
17:        **return** $\mathsf{Trans}(st, X, HBF, lev + 1, id + 2^\alpha) \bigcup \mathsf{Trans}(st, X, HBF, lev + 1, id)$
18:    **end if**
19: **else**
20:    **return** $\emptyset$
21: **end if**

Let $M(W)$ be the DAWG for W. Recall that a state of $M(W)$ also corresponds to an equivalence class. Hence there is a one-to-one correspondence between a state of $M(W)$ and a node of T_W. We assign a node of T_W to document IDs as follows. Let $[x]_W$ be any node of T_W and x be the longest string in $[x]_W$. Then, if x only appears in w_i as a prefix, then ID i is assigned to node $[x]_W$. We call a node with IDs *an info-node*. As an example, we give T_W for the DAWG of Fig. 1 in Fig. 3. The info-nodes are 1,3,4,5,6,7,8,9,10,11, and 12.

Now, by L_v we denote the set of IDs assigned to a node v, and by $T_W(v)$ we denote the subtree of T_W rooted by v. Furthermore, let us define $L(T_W(v)) = \cup_{v \in V} L_v$, where V is the set of nodes of $T_W(v)$. Then we have the following property.

Proposition 4. *For any string $x \in \Sigma^*$, let x be accepted by $M(W)$ at state st and let v_{st} be the node of T_W corresponding to st. Then, for any $i \in \{1, \ldots, k\}$, x is a substring of w_i if and only if $i \in L(T_W(v_{st}))$.*

We can show that the size of T_W with document IDs is $O(n_W)$. We construct arrays $\tilde{\Gamma}_1$ and $\tilde{\Gamma}_2$ in the following way. First we number the info-nodes of T_W in preorder. For any state st of $M(W)$, $\tilde{\Gamma}_1[st]$ is set to (t_1, t_2) where t_1 and t_2 is the smallest number and the largest number of info-nodes in $T_W(v_{st})$, respectively. The array $\tilde{\Gamma}_2[st]$ is set to $L_{v_{st}}$. In the similar way to Γ_1 and Γ_2, we can construct encrypted $\tilde{\Gamma}_1$ and $\tilde{\Gamma}_2$ for an encrypted DAWG as follows. When constructing

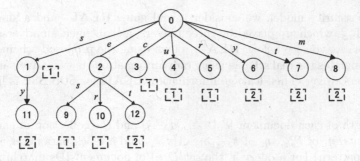

Fig. 3. A tree T_W with assigned IDs for the DAWG given in Fig. 1. The number in a dotted square is the ID of a string assigned to each node. Here $W = \{secure, system\}$ where $ID(secure) = 1$ and $ID(system) = 2$.

encrypted $\tilde{\Gamma}_1$ and $\tilde{\Gamma}_2$, we must pay attention to two points, which are that an encrypted DAWG handles block symbols and extra states are added to an encrypted DAWG.

1. For any state st, set $\tilde{\Gamma}_1[\pi_{sk_4}(st)]$ to encrypted (t_1, t_2, P), where P is the set of states which holds IDs related to a query. The set P can be computed when additional states are added to an encrypted DAWG in BuildEncDawg.
2. For any info-state st, set $\tilde{\Gamma}_1[num(st)]$ to encrypted IDs which is attached to st, where $num(st)$ is the number assigned to st.

We can use encrypted $\tilde{\Gamma}_1$ and $\tilde{\Gamma}_2$ instead of Γ_1 and Γ_2. Since the number of states of an encrypted DAWG is $O(\gamma n_D)$, the size of $\tilde{\Gamma}_1$ and $\tilde{\Gamma}_2$ becomes $O(\gamma n_D)$. Thus we can reduce the size of the index from $O((\gamma + N)n_D)$ to $O(\gamma n_D)$ because the size of HBF_D is also $O(\gamma n_D)$. Proposition 4 states that we can search for a query by computing $L(T_W(v_{st}))$, which is computed using HBF_D, $\tilde{\Gamma}_1$, and $\tilde{\Gamma}_2$. The search is done as follows. The user makes the trapdoor $T(q)$ of a query and sends it the server. The server computes a state st using HBF_D and $T(q)$ and send it to the user. The user sends a key β_{st} to the server. The server gets encrypted IDs from $\tilde{\Gamma}_1$ and $\tilde{\Gamma}_2$, and sends them to the user. Thus, in Scheme-2, the user decrypts encrypted IDs as with CS-scheme and SR-scheme. Therefore Scheme-2 increases the number of rounds, the search time of the server, the time and space of the user. For example, since the size of $L(T_W(v_{st}))$ is $O(occ)$, the search time of the server is $O((m/\gamma) \log n_D + occ)$, and the time of the user is $O(m/\gamma + occ)$.

6 Security Analysis

For the security analysis, we adopt the security model of Curtmola et al. [8]. They define two kinds of security models, a non-adaptive semantic security model and an adaptive semantic security model. We here give the definition of a non-adaptive semantic security model and shows that SUB_SSE meets the non-adaptive semantic security model.

In this security model, we consider a real game $\mathbf{REAL}_{\mathcal{A}}$ and a simulation game $\mathbf{SIM}_{\mathcal{A},\mathcal{S}}$, which are played by three players, a challenger, an adversary and a simulator. As you see below, $\mathbf{REAL}_{\mathcal{A}}$ plays using the proposed scheme, while $\mathbf{SIM}_{\mathcal{A},\mathcal{S}}$ simulates the real scheme using only information that an adversary (that is, a server) can get. Then leakage information $\mathbf{LEAK}$ for SUB_SSE is listed as follows.

- The length of each document $|d_0|, \cdots, |d_{N-1}|$ and the collection of encrypted documents, η_1 of F_{sk_2}, η_2 of π_{sk_3}, η_3 of π_{sk_4}, and a block parameter γ.
- (access pattern) For a query q, the set $D(q)$ of document IDs matching q.
- (search pattern) For a query q, let $T(q) = X_1 \# \cdots \# X_l$. Then $l = |T(q)|$ and information on whether $X_i = X_j$ for any $1 \le i, j \le l$. Since a trapdoor $T(q)$ is deterministic, the adversary can know whether each query q was used in the previous searches.
- (transition pattern) Let $T(q) = X_1 \# \cdots \# X_l$ be trapdoor. Then, the sequence $Trace(T(q)) = (st_0, \cdots, st_l)$ of states such that st_0 is the initial state and for any $1 \le j \le l$, $\delta(st_{j-1}, X_j) = st_j$.

[Non-adaptive semantic security model]

- $\mathbf{REAL}_{\mathcal{A}}(\lambda)$
- The adversary $\mathcal{A}$ chooses (D, Q), where $D = \{d_0, \ldots, d_{N-1}\}$ is the set of documents, $Q = \{q_1, \ldots, q_m\}$ is the set of polynomially many queries. After that, $\mathcal{A}$ sends them to the challenger $\mathcal{C}$.
- $\mathcal{C}$ generates randomly a secret key $SK = (sk_1, sk_2, sk_3, sk_4)$ using $\mathsf{KeyGen}(1^\lambda)$, and builds Π by $\mathsf{BuildIndex}(SK, D, \nu)$, $T(Q)$ by $\mathsf{Trapdr}(sk_2, q_i)$ for $q_i \in Q$, and $\mathsf{Enc}_{sk_1}(D)$, and then $\mathcal{C}$ sends them to $\mathcal{A}$. Here Π is the encrypted index, $T(Q) = \{T(q_1), \ldots, T(q_m)\}$ is the set of trapdoors, and $\mathsf{Enc}_{sk_1}(D)$ is the set of encrypted documents.
- After making searches for $T(Q)$, $\mathcal{A}$ outputs a bit b.

- $\mathbf{SIM}_{\mathcal{A},\mathcal{S}}(\lambda)$
- The adversary $\mathcal{A}$ chooses (D, Q) where $D = \{d_0, \ldots, d_{N-1}\}$ is the set of documents, $Q = \{q_1, \cdots, q_m\}$ is the set of polynomially many, and then $\mathcal{A}$ sends them to the challenger $\mathcal{C}$.
- $\mathcal{C}$ sends leakage information $\mathbf{LEAK}$ to the simulator $\mathcal{S}$.
- $\mathcal{S}$ builds an index Π^*, a set $\{c_0^*, \ldots, c_{N-1}^*\}$ of encrypted documents, trapdoors $T^*(q_1), \ldots, T^*(q_m)$ using $\mathbf{LEAK}$. After that $\mathcal{S}$ sends Π^*, c_i^* and $T^*(q_i)$ to $\mathcal{C}$.
- $\mathcal{C}$ relays them to $\mathcal{A}$.
- After making searches for $T^*(Q)$, $\mathcal{A}$ outputs a bit b.

Let $Q(d)$ be the set of queries q_i such that $ID(d) \in D(q_i)$. We here assume that the set Q of queries asked by $\mathcal{A}$ satisfies the restriction such that for any queries q and q' in Q, $q = q'$ or for any string v with $|v| \ge \gamma$, v appears in at most one of q and q' as a substring. We call this restriction γ-*substring restriction*.

The γ-substring restriction guarantees that $\mathcal{A}$ cannot make a new trapdoor from $T(Q)$. In practical, if we set γ to a value such as $\gamma \geq 8$, then the γ-substring restriction does not seem to be strong.

Definition 3. *We say that a search system meets non-adaptive semantic security with γ-substring restriction if for all probabilistic polynomial time adversaries $\mathcal{A}$, there is a probabilistic polynomial time simulator such that*
$$|Pr(\mathcal{A} \text{ outputs } b{=}1 \text{ in } \mathbf{REAL}_{\mathcal{A}}(\lambda)) - Pr(\mathcal{A} \text{ outputs } b{=}1 \text{ in } \mathbf{SIM}_{\mathcal{A},\mathcal{S}}(\lambda))|$$
is negligible.

Since a symmetric encryption scheme satisfies CPA-security, the following theorem holds.

Theorem 3. *The scheme* SUB_SSE *meets non-adaptive semantic security with γ-substring restriction.*

Proof. We describe a polynomial time simulator $\mathcal{S}$ such that the advantage of any probabilistic polynomial time adversary $\mathcal{A}$ to distinguish between the outputs of $\mathbf{REAL}_{\mathcal{A}}(\lambda)$ and $\mathbf{SIM}_{\mathcal{A},\mathcal{S}}(\lambda)$ is negligible. Let $D = \{d_0, \cdots, d_{N-1}\}$ be a set of documents and $Q = \{q_1, \cdots, q_m\}$ be a set of queries that are asked by $\mathcal{A}$ and satisfies γ-substring restriction. The simulator $\mathcal{S}$ simulates SUB_SSE using **LEAK** as follows.

– Simulating an encrypted index for the set of documents.
  The simulator $\mathcal{S}$ builds an index $\Pi^* = (HBF_D^*, \Gamma_1^*, \Gamma_2^*)$ using **LEAK** as follows.
  1. Let $T(q_i) = X_1\# \cdots \#X_{l_i}$ for each query $q_i \in Q$. For each $1 \leq i \leq m$, $\mathcal{S}$ generates l_i random strings of length η_1, $r_{1,1}^{(i)}, \cdots, r_{1,l_i}^{(i)}$. $\mathcal{S}$ sets $T_i^* = r_{1,1}^{(i)}\# \cdots \#r_{1,l_i}^{(i)}$.
  2. For any document d, let $L_d = n_d - \sum_{q_i \in Q(d)} |T_i^*|$. Let us define $CWORD^*(d) = \{T_i^* \mid q_i \in Q(d)\}$. If $L_d > 0$, then $\mathcal{S}$ generates L_d random strings of length η_1, $r_1, \cdots, r_{L_d}$, and then add $r_1\# \cdots \#r_{L_d}$ to $CWORD^*(d)$. Let $CWORD^*(D) = \cup_{d \in D} CWORD^*(d)$. $\mathcal{S}$ constructs an encrypted DAWG $A^*(D)$ using $CWORD^*(D)$. $\mathcal{S}$ give each state of $A^*(D)$ a unique number according to $Trace(T(q_i))$ so that $Trace(T(q_i)) = Trace(T_i^*)$. After that, $\mathcal{S}$ builds HBF_D^* using $A^*(D)$ in the similar way to BuildIndex. As a result, HBF_D and HBF_D^* have the same false positive rate and the search for T_i^* using HBF_D^* returns a similar answer to the search for $T(q_i)$ using HBF_D.
  3. $\mathcal{S}$ knows $D(st)$ for all states st of $A^*(D)$ such that st is reachable from the initial state by T_i^* $(1 \leq i \leq m)$. Then $\mathcal{S}$ performs lines 15–28 of BuildIndex for $A^*(D)$ using distinct random strings of length η_2 instead of π_{sk_3}, distinct random strings of length η_3 instead of π_{sk_4} and random strings β_{st}^* of length η_1 instead of $\beta_{st} = F_{sk_2}(X_{st}\|st)$, where X_{st} is the symbol of st.
– Simulating an encrypted document. The simulator $\mathcal{S}$ simulates the encryption of d_i by generating a random string of length n_{d_i}.

- Simulating a trapdoor $T^*(q_i)$ and β^*_{st}. S uses T^*_i as $T^*(q_i)$ and β^*_{st} for each state of $A^*(D)$.

We show that an adversary $\mathcal{A}$ cannot distinguish a real world and a simulated world with all but negligible probability.

- The adversary $\mathcal{A}$ cannot distinguish the real index Π and the simulated index Π^*. The size of the real set $CWORD$ of D and the simulated set $CWORD^*(D)$ is same. Furthermore, since T^*_i is embedded in $CWORD^*(d)$ according to $D(q_i)$, $\mathcal{A}$ gets $D(q_i)$ if $\mathcal{A}$ searches for T^*_i using Π^*. Similarly, $\mathcal{A}$ gets $D(q_i)$ if $\mathcal{A}$ searches for $T(q_i)$ using Π. In addition, since Q satisfies γ-substring restriction, $\mathcal{A}$ cannot make a new trapdoor from $T(Q)$. Therefore the indistinguishability of the real Π and the simulated Π^* follows from the pseudo-randomness of F_{sk_2}, π_{sk_3}, and π_{sk_4}.
- The adversary $\mathcal{A}$ cannot distinguish the real trapdoor $T(q)$ and the simulated trapdoor $T^*(q)$ for a query q. $T(q)$ is generated by F_{sk_2}. Hence the indistinguishability of the real trapdoor and the simulated trapdoor follows from the pseudo-randomness of F_{sk_2}.
- The adversary $\mathcal{A}$ cannot distinguish β_{st} and β^*_{st}. Since each state of $A(D)$ has a unique number st, the indistinguishability of $\beta_{st} = F_{sk_2}(X_{st}||st)$ and a random string β^*_{st} follows from the pseudo-randomness of F_{sk_2}.
- For each document, the indistinguishability of the real encrypted document and the simulated document follows from CPA-security of a symmetric encryption scheme.

Thus $\mathcal{A}$ cannot distinguish $\mathbf{REAL}_{\mathcal{A}}$ and $\mathbf{SIM}_{\mathcal{A},\mathcal{S}}$.

7   Conclusions

We proposed a new substring search scheme based on a DAWG for encrypted data. As mentioned in Introduction, we compared schemes proposed previously with our schemes theoretically, but we have not evaluated our schemes experimentally yet. This is one of future work.

Acknowledgments. The author would like to thank the anonymous referees for helpful comments.

References

1. Bloom, B.H.: Space/time trade-offs in hash coding with allowable errors. Comm. ACM **13**, 422–426 (1970)
2. Blumer, A., Blumer, J., Haussler, D.: The smallest automaton recognizing the subwords of a text. Theoretical Comput. Sci. **40**, 31–55 (1985)
3. Blumer, A., Blumer, J., Haussler, D., Mcconnell, R.: Complete inverted files for efficient text retrieval and analysis. J. ACM. **34**(3), 578–595 (1987)

4. Bösch, C., Hartel, P., Jonker, W., Peter, A.: A survey of provably secure searchable encryption. ACM Comput. Surv. **47**(2), 18:1–18:51 (2014)
5. Broder, A., Mitzenmacher, M.: Network applications of bloom filters: a survey. Internet Math. **1**(4), 485–509 (2004)
6. Cao, N., Wang, C., Li, M., Ren, K., Lou, W.: Privacy-preserving multi-keyword ranked search over encrypted cloud data. In: Proceedings of INFOCOM 2011, pp. 829–837 (2011)
7. Chang, Y.-C., Mitzenmacher, M.: Privacy preserving keyword searches on remote encrypted data. In: Ioannidis, J., Keromytis, A.D., Yung, M. (eds.) ACNS 2005. LNCS, vol. 3531, pp. 442–455. Springer, Heidelberg (2005)
8. Curtmola, R., Garay, J., Kamara, S., Ostrovsky, R.: Searchable symmetric encryption: Improved definitions and efficient constructions. J. Comput. Secur. **19**(5), 895–934 (2011)
9. Chase, M., Shen, E.: Substring-searchable symmetric encryption. Proc. Priv. Enhancing Technol. **2015**(2), 263–831 (2015)
10. Goh, E.-J.: Secure indexes. Stanford University Technical report. In: IACR ePrint Cryptography Archive (2003). http://eprint.iacr.org/2003/216
11. Golle, P., Staddon, J., Waters, B.: Secure conjunctive keyword search over encrypted data. In: Jakobsson, M., Yung, M., Zhou, J. (eds.) ACNS 2004. LNCS, vol. 3089, pp. 31–45. Springer, Heidelberg (2004)
12. Hacüigumüs, H., Hore, B., Iyer, B., Mehrotra, S.: Search on encrypted data. Adv. Inf. Secur. **33**, 383–425 (2007)
13. Hahn, F., Kerschbaum, F.: Searchable encryption with secure and efficient updates. In: Proceedings of CCS2014, pp. 310–320 (2014)
14. Hopcroft, J.E., Ullman, J.D.: Introduction to Automata Theory Language and Computation. Addison Wesley, Reading Mass (1979)
15. Katz, J., Lindell, Y.: Introduction to Modern Cryptography, 2nd edn. CRC Press, Boca Raton (2015)
16. Kurosawa, K., Ohtaki, Y.: UC-secure searchable symmetric encryption. In: Keromytis, A.D. (ed.) FC 2012. LNCS, vol. 7397, pp. 285–298. Springer, Heidelberg (2012)
17. Kamara, S., Papamanthou, C., Roeder, T.: Dynamic searchable symmetric encryption. In: Proceedings of CCS 2012, pp. 965–976 (2012)
18. Liu, L., Gai, J.: Bloom filter based index for query over encrypted character strings in database. In: Proceedings of CSIE 2009, pp. 303–307 (2009)
19. Liu, Q., Wang, G., Wu, J.: An efficient privacy preserving keyword search scheme in cloud computing. In: Proceedings of CSE 2009, pp. 715–720 (2009)
20. Li, J., Wang, Q., Wang, C., Cao, N., Ren, K., Lou, W.: Fuzzy keyword search over encrypted data in cloud computing. In: Proceedings of INFCOM 2010, pp. 441–445 (2010)
21. Popa, R.A., Redfield, C.M.S., Zeldovich, N., Balakrishnan, H.: CryptDB: processing queries on an encrypted database. Commun. ACM **55**(9), 103–111 (2012)
22. Suga, T., Nishide, T., Sakurai, K.: Secure keyword search using bloom filter with specified character positions. In: Takagi, T., Wang, G., Qin, Z., Jiang, S., Yu, Y. (eds.) ProvSec 2012. LNCS, vol. 7496, pp. 235–252. Springer, Heidelberg (2012)
23. Strizhov, M., Ray, I.: Substring position search over encrypted cloud data using tree-based index. In: Proceedings of IEEE IC2E 2015, pp. 165–174 (2015)
24. Song, D.X., Wagner, D., Perrig, A.: Techniques for searchers on encrypted data. In: IEEE Symposium on Security and Privacy, pp. 44–55 (2000)
25. Wang, C., Cao, N., Li, J., Ren, K., Lou, W.: Secure ranked keyword search over encryptedcloud data. In: Proceedings of ICDCS 2010, pp. 253–262 (2010)

Cryptanalysis

Related-Key Impossible Differential Analysis
of Full *Khudra*

Qianqian Yang[1,2,3], Lei Hu[1,2(✉)], Siwei Sun[1,2], and Ling Song[1,2]

[1] State Key Laboratory of Information Security,
Institute of Information Engineering, Chinese Academy of Sciences,
Beijing 100093, China
{qqyang13,hu,swsun,lsong}@is.ac.cn
[2] Data Assurance and Communication Security Research Center,
Chinese Academy of Sciences, Beijing 100093, China
[3] University of Chinese Academy of Sciences, Beijing 100049, China

Abstract. *Khudra* is a block cipher proposed by Souvik Kolay and Debdeep Mukhopadhyay in the SPACE 2014 conference which is applicable to Field Programmable Gate Arrays (FPGAs). It is an 18-round lightweight cipher based on recursive Feistel structure, with a 64-bit block size and 80-bit key size. The designers indicated that 18 rounds of *Khudra* provide sufficient security margin for related key attacks. But in this paper, we obtain 2^{16} 14-round related-key impossible differentials of *Khudra*, and based on these related-key impossible differentials for 32 related keys, we launch an attack on the full *Khudra* with data complexity of 2^{63} related-key chosen-plaintexts, time complexity of about $2^{68.46}$ encryptions and memory complexity of 2^{64}. This is the first known attack on full *Khudra*.

Keywords: Lightweight · Block cipher · *Khudra* · Related-key · Impossible differential cryptanalysis

1 Introduction

Recently, lightweight block ciphers, which could be widely adopted in small embedded devices such as RFIDs and sensor networks, are becoming more and more popular. Due to the strong demand from industry, a lot of lightweight block ciphers are proposed in recent years, such as PRESENT [8], LED [12], LBlock [27], PRINCE [9], and another two lightweight block ciphers SIMON and SPECK [2], designed by the U.S. National Security Agency.

Security is crucially important for a cipher, and there are many different attacks on block ciphers. Thus a new cipher must be able to resist all known attacks. Differential cryptanalysis [5] and linear cryptanalysis [23] are two of the most basic and effective attacks on block ciphers. Based on differential cryptanalysis, several variants of differential analysis have been developed, such as related-key attack [3], truncated differential attack [16], boomerang attack [25] and

© Springer International Publishing Switzerland 2016
K. Ogawa and K. Yoshioka (Eds.): IWSEC 2016, LNCS 9836, pp. 135–146, 2016.
DOI: 10.1007/978-3-319-44524-3_8

impossible differential attack [4,6]. Those attacks are chosen plaintext attacks based on a differential distinguisher which uses pairs of plaintexts.

Impossible differential attack, which was independently proposed by Biham *et al.* [4] and Knudsen [15], is one of the well-known attacks on block ciphers [1,19,22,28]. With its development, there are several approaches which have been proposed to derive truncated impossible differentials of block ciphers/structures effectively such as the $\mathcal{U}$-method [14], UID-method [20] and the extended tool of generalized upon to the former two methods by Wu and Wang proposed in Indocrypt 2012 [26]. Unlike traditional differential cryptanalysis, impossible differential attack starts with finding an input difference that results in an output difference with probability 0. It is an attack that aborts wrong key candidates by searching the plaintext-ciphertext pairs which meet the input and output differences of the impossible differential. Related-key attacks [3] allow a cryptanalyst to obtain plaintext-ciphertext pairs by using related but unknown keys. The attacker first searches for possible weaknesses of the encryption and key schedule algorithms, then chooses appropriate relation between keys and makes two encryptions using the related keys expecting to derive the unknown information. Related-key impossible differential attack [13] is a combination of the above two attacks.

Khudra [17] is a new lightweight block cipher which was recently proposed by Souvik Kolay and Debdeep Mukhopadhyay in the SPACE 2014 conference. While there are many lightweight block ciphers designed based on rationales and popular techniques which are suitable for implementation on Application Specific Integrated Circuits (ASICs), few of block ciphers are applicable to Field Programmable Gate Arrays (FPGAs) due to the underlying FPGA architecture. *Khudra* was designed by using new methods and design criteria to enable it capable of operating on FPGAs. It is a 18-round generalized Feistel block cipher with 64-bit block size and 80-bit key size. A recent analysis on the 16-round *Khudra* is a related-key rectangle attack proposed by Ma *et al.* [21]. In [24], Tolba *et al.* presented meet-in-the-middle attacks on 13 and 14 round-reduced *Khudra*. Moreover, Mehmet *et al.* showed a new guess-and-determine type attack on 14-round *Khudra* in [29]. For other attacks, the designers pointed out that full round *Khudra* is secure against some popular attacks, like differential cryptanalysis, linear cryptanalysis, impossible differential attack, differential-linear attack [18], algebraic attack, boomerang type attacks, slide attack [7] and related-key attack.

Our Contribution. Based on the generalized Feistel structure of the block cipher *Khudra*, we obtain 2^{16} related-key impossible differential characteristics for the 14-round *Khudra*. By adding two rounds before and after the impossible differentials respectively, we propose a related-key impossible differential attack on full *Khudra*, with data complexity of 2^{63} chosen-plaintexts, time complexity of about $2^{68.46}$ encryptions and memory complexity of 2^{64}. Shown in Table 1, our work is the first known attack on full *Khudra*.

Organization of this Paper. We briefly describe the *Khudra* block cipher in Sect. 2. In Sect. 3, we obtain 14-round related-key impossible differential characteristics and propose the related-key impossible differential attack on the full *Khudra*. Finally, we conclude this study.

Table 1. Comparison of cryptanalysis results of *Khudra*

Type of crypt-analysis	# Rounds of attacked	Data complexity	Time complexity	Memory complexity	Reference
Meet-in-the-middle	13	2^{51}	$2^{66.11}$	$2^{64.8}$	[24]
Meet-in-the-middle	14	2^{51}	$2^{66.19}$	$2^{64.8}$	[24]
Guess-and-determine	14	2	2^{64}	-	[29]
Related-key rectangle	16	2^{53}	$2^{64.08}$	-	[11]
Related-key rectangle	16	$2^{57.82}$	$2^{78.68}$	-	[21]
Related-key impossible differential	18(full)	2^{63}	$2^{68.46}$	2^{64}	This Paper

2 The *Khudra* Lightweight Block Cipher

2.1 Notation

The following notations are used in this paper:

$\oplus$ bitwise exclusive OR (XOR);

$x\|y$ bit string concatenation of x and y;

P_i the i-th 16-bit word of 64-bit plaintext, $0 \le i < 4$;

C_i the i-th 16-bit word of 64-bit ciphertext, $0 \le i < 4$;

ΔX the XOR difference of X and X';

ΔF_r^i the XOR difference after the i-th F-function of the r-th round, $1 \le i \le 2$.

2.2 Description of *Khudra*

In this section, we give a briefly description of the design of the block cipher *Khudra* and we refer the readers to [17] for more details.

Khudra is a lightweight block cipher suitable for resource-constrained devices. The designers of *Khudra* have shown that many popular techniques for lightweight block ciphers which work on Application Specific Integrated Circuits (ASICs) are not suitable for Field Programmable Gate Arrays (FPGAs). They have identified new methods and design criteria for designing lightweight block ciphers on FPGAs. *Khudra* is based on these guidelines.

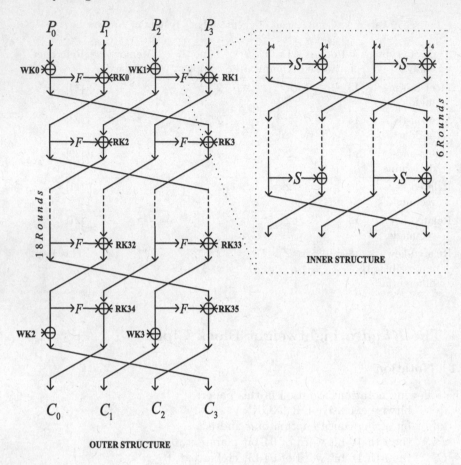

Fig. 1. The structure of Khudra

Khudra is a block cipher using "Generalized type-2 transformations" of Feistel Structure (GFS) on 64-bit blocks and 80-bit keys. The cipher has 18 rounds that each round has two 16×16 *F*-Function. The structure of the cipher is depicted in the left part of Fig. 1, which is called the Outer Structure of the cipher.

The F-function. The F-function has a similar structure adopted in *Khudra*, i.e., the same 4 branch type-2 generalized Feistel Structure. It uses 12 copies of a 4×4 S-box to provide non-linearity, showing the right part of Fig. 1, that is the structure for the F-function as Inner Structure of the cipher. For the F-function, the designers show that there are at least 6 active S-boxes in the differential and linear characteristics and the differential and linear probabilities are 2^{-12}.

The S-box. *Khudra* uses the S-box of the block cipher PRESENT for its higher algebraic degree and low differential and linear probability [8]. The S-box is given in Table 2.

Table 2. S-box of Khudra

x	0	1	2	3	4	5	6	7	8	9	A	B	C	D	E	F
S(x)	C	5	6	B	9	0	A	D	3	E	F	8	4	7	1	2

The Key Schedule. The 80-bit master key for the block cipher *Khudra* is $(k_0, k_1, k_2, k_3, k_4)$, the sizes of $k_i (i = 0, 1, 2, 3, 4)$ are 16-bit. The key scheduling part generates 16-bit round-keys $RKi(0 \leq i < 36)$ and 16-bit whitening keys $WKi(0 \leq i < 4)$, seeing Algorithm 1, where RC_i is the 16-bit round constant and $i_{(6)}$ is the 6-bit representation of the round counter i.

Algorithm 1. Key Scheduling $(k_0, k_1, k_2, k_3, k_4)$

1: $WK0 \leftarrow k_0, WK1 \leftarrow k_1, WK2 \leftarrow k_3, WK3 \leftarrow k_4$;
2: **for** $i = 0$ to 35 **do**
3:    $RCi \leftarrow \{0||i_{(6)}||00||i_{(6)}||0\}$;
4:    $RKi \leftarrow k_{i \bmod 5} \oplus RCi$;
5: **end for**

---

3   Related-Key Impossible Differential Attack on Full *Khudra*

In this section, we describe a related-key impossible differential attack on the full *Khudra*. We give both the related-key impossible differential characteristics and the attack on the full *Khudra* in detail.

3.1   Related-Key Impossible Differential Characteristic of Block Cipher *Khudra*

According to the key schedule of *Khudra*, the difference values of round-keys are cyclic, that is, $\Delta RKi = \Delta RKi \bmod 5$. We acquire the 14-round related-key impossible differential path used for this attack is

$$(\boldsymbol{0}, \boldsymbol{0}, \boldsymbol{0}, \Delta) \stackrel{14}{\nrightarrow} (\Delta, \boldsymbol{0}, \boldsymbol{0}, \boldsymbol{0})$$

where the $\boldsymbol{0}$ denotes 16-bit 0. This path is placed between the 3rd and 16th round of the cipher. The difference of the corresponding related-key is that $\Delta RK5 = \Delta RK10 = \Delta RK15 = \Delta RK20 = \Delta RK25 = \Delta RK30 = \Delta k_0 = \Delta$.

The details of the 14-round related-key impossible differential path are given in Fig. 2. The black color stands for nibbles that have a difference with probability 1 (active nibbles), while white symbolizes nibbles that do not have a difference (passive nibbles). The stripe stands for nibbles that have a same difference we

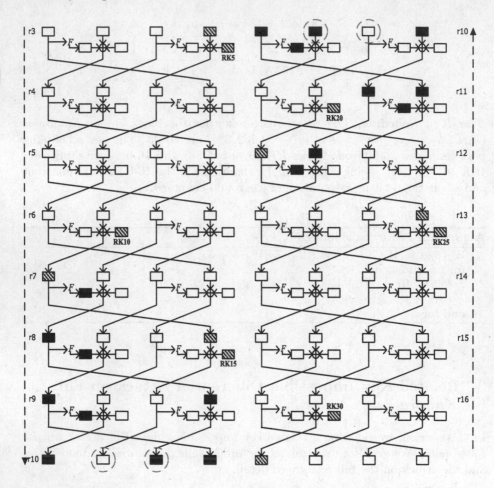

Fig. 2. Related-key impossible differential path for 14-round Khudra.

know. This 14-round related-key impossible differential path combines two paths of probability 1 for which an impossibility occurs after 7 rounds. The nibbles for which the impossibility occurs are the second and the third nibbles from the input of the 10th round.

3.2   Related-Key Impossible Differential Analysis on Block Cipher *Khudra*

To attack the full *Khudra*, we extend these 14-round related-key impossible differentials on rounds 3–16 by adding 2 rounds to the input and 2 rounds to the output. As can be seen in Fig. 3, different colors stand for the different differences.

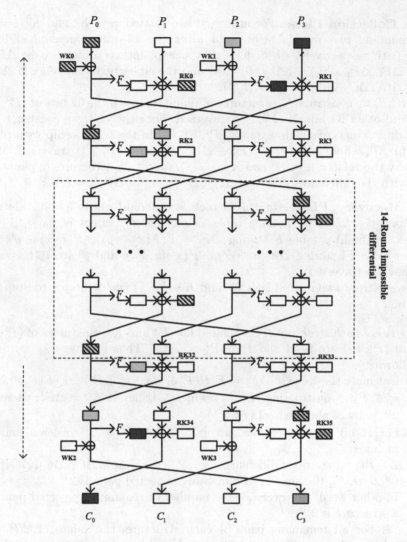

Fig. 3. Related-key impossible differential attack against full Khudra

Choosing $N_r = 32$ related keys, we can obtain $N_\Delta = C_{N_r}^2 \approx (N_r)^2/2 = 2^9$ values of differences of related keys.

$$
\begin{aligned}
K^0 &= K = (k_0, k_1, k_2, k_3, k_4); \\
K^i &= (k_0^i, k_1^i, k_2^i, k_3^i, k_4^i) = K \oplus (\Delta k_0^i, \mathbf{0}, \mathbf{0}, \mathbf{0}, \mathbf{0}) \\
&= (k_0 \oplus \Delta k_0^i, k_1, k_2, k_3, k_4); \\
\Delta K^{ij} &= K^i \oplus K^j = (\Delta k_0^{ij}, \mathbf{0}, \mathbf{0}, \mathbf{0}, \mathbf{0}),
\end{aligned}
\tag{1}
$$

where Δk_0^i is the relation between keys. We call the 32 related keys as $K^i, 0 \le i < 32$.

-Data Collection Phase. For arbitrary two related keys K^i and $K^j (i \neq j)$, by expanding two rounds before and after the 14-round impossible differential path respectively, we deduce that the plaintexts difference is $\Delta P = (\Delta P_0, \Delta P_1, \Delta P_2, \Delta P_3) = (\Delta k_0^{ij}, \mathbf{0}, *, *)$ and the ciphertexts difference is $\Delta C = (\Delta C_0, \Delta C_1, \Delta C_2, \Delta C_3) = (*, \mathbf{0}, \mathbf{0}, *)$.

For K^0, we construct N_s structures of plaintexts with the 32 bits of (P_0^0, P_1^0) fixed and other 32 bits of (P_2^0, P_3^0) traversed. For other K^i, we construct corresponding structure's plaintexts $(P_0^i, P_1^i, P_2^i, P_3^i)$ in the relationship with plaintexts in K^0, where $(P_0^i, P_1^i) = (P_0^0 \oplus \Delta k_0^{0i}, P_1^0)$ and (P_2^i, P_3^i) traversed. With arbitrary two related-keys K^i and K^j $(i \neq j)$, we get N_s structures of plaintexts pairs with the differences $\Delta P^{ij} = (\Delta P_0^{ij}, \Delta P_1^{ij}, \Delta P_2^{ij}, \Delta P_3^{ij}) = (\Delta k_0^{ij}, \mathbf{0}, *, *)$.

-Key Recovery Phase. In this attack, we should guess 64-bit values of $k_0 || k_1 || k_3 || k_4$. Thus we build a table D storing 2^{64} values of $k_0 || k_1 || k_3 || k_4$. Besides, we build a table F storing $\Delta F = F(F(x) \oplus y) \oplus F(F(x) \oplus y')$ and another table F' storing $\Delta F' = F(x) \oplus F(x')(x, x', y$ and y' are 16-bit words and they are traversed).

For arbitrary two related keys K^i and K^j $(i \neq j)$, we do Step 1 to Step 5 as following.

-Step 1. For each structure of the related key K^i and K^j, the values of (P_0^i, P_1) and (P_0^j, P_1) are fixed and $P_0^i \oplus P_0^j = \Delta k_0^{ij}$. Thus for every k_0 we do as following:

(a) Calculate the value of $\Delta F_2^1 = F(F(P_0^i \oplus k_0^i) \oplus k_0^i \oplus P_1) \oplus F(F(P_0^j \oplus k_0^j) \oplus k_0^j \oplus P_1)$. Constructing (P_2^i, P_2^j) which satisfies $\Delta P_2^{ij} = \Delta F_2^1$, there are 2^{16} pairs of plaintexts of (P_2^i, P_2^j).

(b) For 16-bit P_3^i and P_3^j, we can gain $2^{16} \times 2^{32} = 2^{48}$ ordered pairs of plaintexts.

(c) As the ciphertext difference is $\Delta C = (\Delta C_0, \Delta C_1, \Delta C_2, \Delta C_3) = (*, \mathbf{0}, \mathbf{0}, *)$, the number of remaining expected pairs is $2^{48} \times 2^{-32} = 2^{16}$. In other words, for every k_0 the number of remaining expected pairs for a structure is 2^{16}.

-Step 2. For all remaining pairs of each structure, the values of ΔP_3 and (P_2^i, P_2^j) are known. Thus by looking up the table, we get the value of $RK1 = k_1$ satisfying the difference value $\Delta F_1^2 = F(P_2^i \oplus k_1) \oplus F(P_2^j \oplus k_1) = \Delta P_3$. For each pair, there is one expected solution of k_1, thus for every $k_0 || k_1$ the number of remaining expected pairs for a structure is $2^{16} \times 2^{-16} = 1$.

-Step 3. For remaining pairs, the values of $\Delta C_3^{ij} = \Delta C_3^i \oplus \Delta C_3^j$, C_1, C_2 and $(RK35^i = k_0^i, RK35^j = k_0^j)$ are known. Similar to Step 2, by looking up the table, we get the value of $WK3 = k_4$ satisfying the difference $\Delta F_{17}^1 = F(F(C_1 \oplus k_4) \oplus k_0^i \oplus C_2) \oplus F(F(C_1 \oplus k_4) \oplus k_0^j \oplus C_2) = \Delta C_3^{ij}$. Similarly, there is one expected solution of k_4 for each pair, thus for every $k_0 || k_1 || k_4$ the number of remaining expected pairs for a structure is $1 \times 2^{-16} = 2^{-16}$.

-Step 4. For remaining pairs, the values of ΔC_0^{ij} and (C_3^i, C_3^j) are known. Similar to Step 2, by looking up the table, we get the value of $WK2 = k_3$ satisfying the difference $\Delta C_0^{ij} = \Delta F_{18}^1 = F(C_3^i \oplus k_3) \oplus F(C_3^j \oplus k_3)$. By looking up the table we get k_3. There is one expected solution of k_3 for each pair, thus for each $k_0||k_1||k_4||k_3$ the number of remaining expected pairs for a structure is $2^{-16} \times 2^{-16} = 2^{-32}$.

-Step 5. If we find a right pair for the guessing value $k_0||k_1||k_4||k_3$, we delete the corresponding subkey $k_0||k_1||k_4||k_3$ in table D.

-Step 6. For other differences of related-key Δk_0^{ij}, we repeat step 1 to step 5. Ultimately, for each survived candidate in Table D, we compute the seed key by doing an exhaustive search for other 16 bits.

Complexity Analysis. Recently, Boura et al. [10] proposed a generic vision of impossible differential attacks on block ciphers. In their method, they split the cipher in three parts: $E = E_3 \circ E_2 \circ E_1$, in E_2 there is an impossible differential($\Delta_X \nrightarrow \Delta_Y$), see Fig. 4. Δ_X (resp. Δ_Y) is propagated through E_1^{-1} (resp. E_3) with probability 1 to obtain Δ_{in} (resp. Δ_{out}). Thus the differential $(\Delta_X \leftarrow \Delta_{in})$ (resp. $\Delta_Y \leftarrow \Delta_{out}$) is verified with probability $1/2^{c_{in}}$ (resp. $1/2^{c_{out}}$), where c_{in} (resp. c_{out}) is the number of bit-conditions that have to be verified to get Δ_X from Δ_{in} (resp. Δ_Y from Δ_{out}).

Let Δ_X (resp. Δ_Y) denote the input (resp. output) differences of the impossible differential, Δ_{in} (resp. Δ_{out}) denote the set of all possible input (resp. output) differences of the cipher, r_{in} (resp. r_{out}) denote the number of rounds of the differential path (Δ_X, Δ_{in}) (resp. (Δ_Y, Δ_{out})), and r_Δ denotes the number of rounds of the impossible differential.

According to the method of calculating complexity in [10], we get the results of data complexity, time complexity and memory complexity as following.

-*Data Complexity.* In our work, $\Delta_{in} = \Delta P$, $\Delta_{out} = \Delta C$ and $c_{in} = c_{out} = 32$. It follows that for a given key $k_0||k_1||k_4||k_3$, a pair of plaintext-ciphertext already

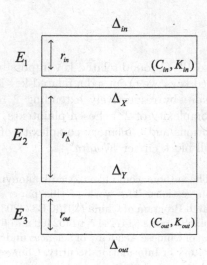

Fig. 4. Generic vision of impossible differential attack

satisfying ΔP and ΔC, the probability that it is the right pair is $2^{-c_{in}} \times 2^{-c_{out}} = 2^{-64}$. Therefore, for N pairs of plaintext-ciphertexts satisfying ΔP and ΔC, the probability that the given key is remaining in the table D is $P = (1 - 2^{-64})^N$.

Because of $\Delta P = (\Delta k_0, \boldsymbol{0}, *, *), \Delta C = (*, \boldsymbol{0}, \boldsymbol{0}, *)$, there are $2^{32} \times 2^{32} \times 2^{-32} = 2^{32}$ ordered pairs of plaintext-ciphertext satisfying ΔP and ΔC for one structure. Taking $N_s = 2^{26}$ such that $N = N_\Delta \times N_s \times 2^{32} = 2^9 \times 2^{26} \times 2^{32} = 2^{67}$, there is $2^{64} \times (1 - 2^{-64})^N = 2^{64} \times (1 - 2^{-64})^{2^{67}} = 2^{52.46}$ values of $k_0||k_1||k_3||k_4$ remaining in table D.

The data complexity is $N_r \times N_s \times 2^{32} = 2^5 \times 2^{26} \times 2^{32} = 2^{63}$ chosen-plaintexts.

-*Time Complexity.* To analyze the time complexity, we will analyze the time complexity in each step. In the data collection phase, the time complexity is 2^{63} full-round encryptions.

In the key recovery phase, building the table F and F' the time complexity is $2^{48} \times 1/18 \times 2 + 2^{32} \times 1/18 \approx 2^{44.83}$. In Step 1. the time complexity is $|k_0| \times N_\Delta \times N_s \times 1/18 \times 2 = 2^{16} \times 2^9 \times 2^{26} \times 1/18 \times 2 \approx 2^{47.83}$. In Step 2, the time complexity is $|k_0| \times N_\Delta \times N_s \times 2^{16} \times 1/18 \times 1/24 = 2^{16} \times 2^{9+26+16} \times 1/18 \times 1/24 \approx 2^{58.25}$. In Step 3, the time complexity is $|k_0||k_1| \times N_\Delta \times N_s \times 1 \times 1/18 \times 1/24 = 2^{32} \times 2^{9+26} \times 1 \times 1/18 \times 1/24 \approx 2^{58.25}$. In Step 4, the time complexity is $|k_0||k_1||k_4| \times N_\Delta \times N_s \times 2^{-16} \times 1/18 \times 1/24 = 2^{48} \times 2^{9+26-16} \times 1/18 \times 1/24 \approx 2^{58.25}$. In Step 6 for the exhaustive searching, the time complexity is $2^{52.46} \times 2^{16} \approx 2^{68.46}$.

Therefore, the total time complexity is $2^{68.46}$ full-round encryptions.

-*Memory Complexity.* For storing the key table D, F and F', the memory complexity is $2^{64}, 2^{48}$ and 2^{32}, respectively. Thus the memory complexity is 2^{64}.

In summary, we propose an attack on full *Khudra* with the data complexity of 2^{63} chosen-plaintexts, time complexity of $2^{68.46}$ encryptions and memory complexity of 2^{64}.

4   Conclusions

In this paper, we acquire 2^{16} 14-round related-key impossible differential characteristics. Using 32 related keys, we proposed a related-key impossible differential attack on the full *Khudra* by respectively extending 2 rounds backward and forward, with a data complexity of 2^{63} chosen plaintexts, a time complexity of $2^{68.46}$ full-round encryptions and a memory complexity of 2^{64}. This is the first known attack on the full block cipher *Khudra*.

Acknowledgements. The authors would like to thank anonymous reviewers for their helpful comments and suggestions. The work of this paper was supported by the National Key Basic Research Program of China (2013CB834203), the National Natural Science Foundation of China (Grants 61472417, 61402469 and 61472415), the Strategic Priority Research Program of Chinese Academy of Sciences under Grant XDA06010702, and the State Key Laboratory of Information Security, Chinese Academy of Sciences.

References

1. Bahrak, B., Aref, M.R.: Impossible differential attack on seven-round AES-128. IET Inf. Secur. **2**, 28–32 (2008)
2. Beaulieu, R., Shors, D., Smith, J., Treatman-Clark, S., Weeks, B., Wingers, L.: The SIMON and SPECK Families of Lightweight Block Ciphers. Cryptology ePrint Archive (2013). https://eprint.iacr.org/2013/404
3. Biham, E.: New types of cryptanalytic attacks using related keys. In: Helleseth, T. (ed.) EUROCRYPT 1993. LNCS, vol. 765, pp. 398–409. Springer, Heidelberg (1994)
4. Biham, E., Biryukov, A., Shamir, A.: Cryptanalysis of Skipjack reduced to 31 rounds using impossible differentials. In: Stern, J. (ed.) EUROCRYPT 1999. LNCS, vol. 1592, pp. 12–23. Springer, Heidelberg (1999)
5. Biham, E., Shamir, A.: Differential cryptanalysis of DES-like cryptosystems. J. Cryptology **4**(1), 3–72 (1991)
6. Biryukov, A.: Impossible differential attack. In: van Tilborg, H.C.A., Jajodia, S. (eds.) Encyclopedia of Cryptography and Security, p. 597. Springer, New York (2011)
7. Biryukov, A., Wagner, D.: Advanced slide attacks. In: Preneel, B. (ed.) EUROCRYPT 2000. LNCS, vol. 1807, pp. 589–606. Springer, Heidelberg (2000)
8. Bogdanov, A.A., et al.: PRESENT: an ultra-lightweight block cipher. In: Paillier, P., Verbauwhede, I. (eds.) CHES 2007. LNCS, vol. 4727, pp. 450–466. Springer, Heidelberg (2007)
9. Borghoff, J., et al.: PRINCE – a low-latency block cipher for pervasive computing applications. In: Wang, X., Sako, K. (eds.) ASIACRYPT 2012. LNCS, vol. 7658, pp. 208–225. Springer, Heidelberg (2012)
10. Boura, C., Naya-Plasencia, M., Suder, V.: Scrutinizing and improving impossible differential attacks: applications to CLEFIA, Camellia, LBlock and SIMON. In: Sarkar, P., Iwata, T. (eds.) ASIACRYPT 2014. LNCS, vol. 8873, pp. 179–199. Springer, Heidelberg (2014)
11. Dai, Y., Chen, S.: Security analysis of Khudra: a lightweight block cipher for FPGAs. Secur. Commun. Netw. (2015)
12. Guo, J., Peyrin, T., Poschmann, A., Robshaw, M.: The LED block cipher. In: Preneel, B., Takagi, T. (eds.) CHES 2011. LNCS, vol. 6917, pp. 326–341. Springer, Heidelberg (2011)
13. Jakimoski, G., Desmedt, Y.: Related-key differential cryptanalysis of 192-bit key AES variants. In: Matsui, M., Zuccherato, R.J. (eds.) SAC 2003. LNCS, vol. 3006, pp. 208–221. Springer, Heidelberg (2004)
14. Kim, J.-S., Hong, S.H., Sung, J., Lee, S.-J., Lim, J.-I., Sung, S.H.: Impossible differential cryptanalysis for block cipher structures. In: Johansson, T., Maitra, S. (eds.) INDOCRYPT 2003. LNCS, vol. 2904, pp. 82–96. Springer, Heidelberg (2003)
15. Knudsen, L.: DEAL - a 128-bit block cipher. In: NIST AES Proposal (1998)
16. Knudsen, L.R.: Truncated and higher order differentials. In: Preneel, B. (ed.) FSE 1995. LNCS, vol. 1008, pp. 196–211. Springer, Heidelberg (1995)
17. Kolay, S., Mukhopadhyay, D.: Khudra: a new lightweight block cipher for FPGAs. In: Chakraborty, R.S., Matyas, V., Schaumont, P. (eds.) SPACE 2014. LNCS, vol. 8804, pp. 126–145. Springer, Heidelberg (2014)
18. Langford, S.K., Hellman, M.E.: Differential-linear cryptanalysis. In: Desmedt, Y.G. (ed.) CRYPTO 1994. LNCS, vol. 839, pp. 17–25. Springer, Heidelberg (1994)

19. Li, R., Sun, B., Li, C.: Impossible differential cryptanalysis of SPN ciphers. IET Inf. Secur. **5**(2), 111–120 (2011)
20. Luo, Y., Lai, X., Zhongming, W., Gong, G.: A unified method for finding impossible differentials of block cipher structures. Inf. Sci. **263**, 211–220 (2014)
21. Ma, X., Qiao, K.: Related-key Rectangle Attack on Round-reduced *Khudra* Block Cipher. Cryptology ePrint Archive, Report 2015/533 (2015). http://eprint.iacr.org/
22. Mala, H., Dakhilalian, M., Shakiba, M.: Impossible differential cryptanalysis of reduced-round Camellia-256. IET Inf. Secur. **5**(3), 129–134 (2011)
23. Matsui, M.: Linear cryptanalysis method for DES cipher. In: Helleseth, T. (ed.) EUROCRYPT 1993. LNCS, vol. 765, pp. 386–397. Springer, Heidelberg (1994)
24. Tolba, M., Abdelkhalek, A., Youssef, A.M.: Meet-in-the-middle attacks on round-reduced Khudra. In: Chakraborty, R.S., Schwabe, P., Solworth, J. (eds.) SPACE 2015. LNCS, vol. 9354, pp. 127–138. Springer, Heidelberg (2015)
25. Wagner, D.: The boomerang attack. In: Knudsen, L.R. (ed.) FSE 1999. LNCS, vol. 1636, pp. 156–170. Springer, Heidelberg (1999)
26. Wu, S., Wang, M.: Automatic search of truncated impossible differentials for word-oriented block ciphers. In: Galbraith, S., Nandi, M. (eds.) INDOCRYPT 2012. LNCS, vol. 7668, pp. 283–302. Springer, Heidelberg (2012)
27. Wu, W., Zhang, L.: LBlock: a lightweight block cipher. In: Lopez, J., Tsudik, G. (eds.) ACNS 2011. LNCS, vol. 6715, pp. 327–344. Springer, Heidelberg (2011)
28. Xue, W., Lai, X.: Impossible differential cryptanalysis of MARS-like structures. IET Inf. Secur. **9**(4), 219–222 (2015)
29. Özen, M., Çoban, M., Karakoç, F.: A guess-and-determine attack on reduced-round Khudra and weak keys of full cipher. Cryptology ePrint Archive, Report 2015/1163 (2015). http://eprint.iacr.org/

On the Division Property of Simon48 and Simon64

Zejun Xiang[1,2], Wentao Zhang[1(✉)], and Dongdai Lin[1]

[1] State Key Laboratory of Information Security, Institute of Information
Engineering, Chinese Academy of Sciences, Beijing, China
{xiangzejun,zhangwentao,ddlin}@iie.ac.cn
[2] University of Chinese Academy of Sciences, Beijing, China

Abstract. Simon is a family of lightweight block ciphers published by
the U.S. National Security Agency (NSA) in 2013. Due to its novel and
bit-based design, integral cryptanalysis on Simon seems a tough job. At
EUROCRYPT 2015 Todo proposed division property which is a generalized integral property, and he applied this technique to searching integral
distinguishers of Simon block ciphers by considering the left and right
halves of Simon independently. As a result, he found 11-round integral
distinguishers for both Simon48 and Simon64. Recently, at FSE 2016
Todo *et al.* proposed bit-based division property that considered each
bit independently. This technique can find more accurate distinguishers,
however, as pointed out by Todo *et al.* the time and memory complexity is bounded by 2^n for an n-bit block cipher. Thus, bit-based division
property is only applicable to Simon32.

In this paper we propose a new technique that achieves a trade-off
between considering each bit independently and considering left and right
halves as a whole, which is actually a trade-off between time-memory and
the accuracy of the distinguishers. We proceed by splitting the state of
Simon into small pieces and study the division property propagations
of circular shift and bitwise AND operations under the state partition.
Moreover, we propose two different state partitions and study the influences of different partitions on the propagation of division property. We
find that different partitions greatly impact the division property propagation of circular shift which will finally result in a big difference on
the length of integral distinguishers. By using a tailored search algorithm for Simon, we find 12-round integral distinguishers for Simon48
and Simon64 respectively, which improve Todo's results by one round
for both variants.

Keywords: Simon · Division property · Integral cryptanalysis

1 Introduction

Due to the security requirements on resource constrained devices such as RFID
tags, lightweight cryptography has been a very hot topic in cryptographic community in the past decade. This situation has motivated a lot of lightweight

© Springer International Publishing Switzerland 2016
K. Ogawa and K. Yoshioka (Eds.): IWSEC 2016, LNCS 9836, pp. 147–163, 2016.
DOI: 10.1007/978-3-319-44524-3_9

block cipher designs, including KATAN/KTANTAN [13], LBlock [21], PRESENT [7], PRIDE [3], PRINCE [8], RECTANGLE [23], SIMON/SPECK [5], to name but a few. SIMON is a family of lightweight block ciphers proposed by Beaulieu *et al.* from the U.S. National Security Agency (NSA) which is tuned for optimal performance in hardware. This family has 10 variants targeting on different security levels with block size varying from 32 to 128 bits and key size varying from 64 to 256 bits.

In this paper, we focus on searching integral distinguishers of SIMON48 and SIMON64. SIMON adopts a Feistel structure with a very compact round function which only uses circular shift, bitwise AND and bitwise XOR operations. However, SIMON was published only with specification, its design criteria and cryptanalysis results were not known to the public. Thus, since its publication, SIMON has received lots of attentions from cryptographic community [1,2,4,6,9–11,15,19,20] in terms of a variety of attack techniques. However, from all these cryptanalytic works, it seems that integral cryptanalysis is not sufficient and well-studied for the SIMON family block ciphers.

Integral attack (or square attack [12]) was initially proposed by Daemen *et al.* at FSE 1997 and formalized later by Knudsen [14] at FSE 2002. The core part of integral attack is to construct an integral distinguisher whose outputs (or some bits of the outputs) have the zero-sum property with respect to a set of carefully chosen input texts. One way to construct an integral distinguisher is to study the propagation characteristics of integral property, e.g., the $\mathcal{A}$ property, the $\mathcal{C}$ property, the $\mathcal{B}$ property and the $\mathcal{U}$ property.

At EUROCRYPT 2015, Todo [17] proposed a generalized integral property–division property and studied the propagation characteristics of division property. Furthermore, he applied division property to SPN and Feistel structures and presented some generalized integral distinguishers without knowing the details of the ciphers except for the algebraic degrees of nonlinear components. Later, Todo [16] applied division property to MISTY1 block cipher and successfully broke full-round MISTY1. In the search of integral distinguishers of Fesitel ciphers, Todo treated the cipher state as the left and right two halves, moreover the Feistel round function was viewed as a big Sbox and he only need to know its algebraic degree. In [17] integral distinguishers of SIMON for each state size are presented. Those distinguishers were searched by viewing the round function of SIMON as an Sbox of algebraic degree two.

Very recently, Todo *et al.* introduced bit-based division property in [18] that considered each bit of SIMON32 independently. As a result they found more accurate integral distinguisher for SIMON32 and confirmed the result in [20]. However, as pointed out in [18], bit-based division property was only applicable to SIMON32, since the time and memory complexity for bit-based division property is upper bounded by 2^n for an n-bit block cipher. For SIMON family with larger block size, this technique is computationally impractical.

1.1 Contributions

If the left and right halves of SIMON are considered independently, the integral distinguishers found are too coarse. However, if bit-based division property is considered, it will be computational impractical for SIMON family with block size larger than 32 bits. In this paper we study a trade-off between time-memory complexity and accuracy of the distinguishers. We split the state into small pieces and investigate the division property propagations of each operation used in SIMON round function. We propose two state partitions and study the corresponding division property propagations. Moreover, we compare these two approaches from both theoretic and experimental aspects. Based on the propagation characteristics of each SIMON operation, a search algorithm for integral distinguishers is presented, and our experimental results show that we can derive 12-round integral distinguishers for both SIMON48 and SIMON64 which improve the results in [17] by one round for both variants. Moreover, we note that our approach is a unified approach, the method with treating each bit independently and the method with treating the left and right halves independently are actually the two limit cases of our state partition.

There are two main contributions in this paper:

(1) We propose two different state partitions to present division property of the state of SIMON. We find that different state partitions have a big impact on the division property propagation with respect to circular shift operation. According to both theoretic and experimental results we illustrate that assigning bits with some fixed interval t (that is the i-th, $(i + t)$-th, $(i + 2t)$-th $\cdots$ bits, with $t \mid n$ and the addition is modular n addition) into a piece is much better than assigning consecutive bits into a piece.
(2) We split the state of SIMON into as many pieces as possible to get a more detailed description of division property of the state, and we study the division property propagations of circular shift and bitwise AND operations which are used in SIMON round function. Moreover, we apply these properties in a search algorithm. As a result, we find 12-round integral distinguishers for both SIMON48 and SIMON64, which is better than Todo's results.

The rest of the paper is organized as follows. Section 2 will present a brief review of SIMON and recall the division property. Section 3 will give two kinds of state partitions and study division property propagations against circular shift and bitwise AND operations. Moreover, our search algorithm and experimental results for SIMON48 and SIMON64 will be presented in this section. At last Sect. 4 comes the summary.

2 Preliminaries

In this section, we first give the description of SIMON family block ciphers, and then we briefly recall division property.

2.1   Description of SIMON

SIMON is a family of Feistel structured lightweight block ciphers with 10 variants targeting on different block sizes and key sizes. The SIMON block cipher with an n-bit word is denoted as SIMON$2n$, which means the block size is $2n$ bits.

The round function used in the Feistel structure of SIMON block ciphers consists of circular shift, bitwise AND and bitwise XOR operations. The structure of one round SIMON encryption is depicted in Fig. 1, where S^i represents a left circular shift by i bits, X_i and Y_i are n-bit words and k_i is the round key. Since the key schedule has no relevance in this paper, we omit the key schedule and refer the readers to [5] for more details.

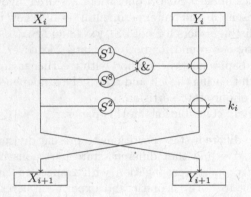

Fig. 1. Feistel structure of SIMON round function

2.2   Division Property

For clarity we first introduce some notations. Denote $\mathbb{F}_2$ the finite field with only two elements, and $\mathbb{F}_2^n$ the n dimensional vector space over $\mathbb{F}_2$. For any $x \in \mathbb{F}_2^n$, the i-th element of x is denoted by $x[i]$ and the Hamming weight of x is calculated as follows:

$$w(x) = \sum_{i=0}^{n-1} x[i].$$

Moreover, let $(\mathbb{F}_2{}^n)^m$ be the m dimensional vector space whose coordinates belong to $\mathbb{F}_2{}^n$. Given $\boldsymbol{x} \in (\mathbb{F}_2^n)^m$, the Hamming weight of $\boldsymbol{x} = (x_0, x_1, \cdots, x_{m-1})$ is defined as $W(\boldsymbol{x}) = (w(x_0), w(x_1), \cdots, w(x_{m-1}))$. Let $\boldsymbol{k} = (k_0, k_1, \cdots, k_{m-1})$ and $\boldsymbol{k}^* = (k_0^*, k_1^*, \cdots, k_{m-1}^*)$ denote two vectors in $\mathbb{Z}^m$ where $\mathbb{Z}^m$ denotes m dimensional vector space over all integers $\mathbb{Z}$. Define $\boldsymbol{k} \succeq \boldsymbol{k}^*$ if $k_i \geq k_i^*$ holds for all $i = 0, 1, \cdots, m - 1$. Otherwise w e write $\boldsymbol{k} \not\succeq \boldsymbol{k}^*$.

Bit Product Function $\pi_u(x)$ and $\boldsymbol{\pi_u(x)}$: For any $u \in \mathbb{F}_2^n$, let $\pi_u(x)$ be a function from $\mathbb{F}_2^n$ to $\mathbb{F}_2$. For any $x \in \mathbb{F}_2^n$, define $\pi_u(x)$ as follows:

$$\pi_u(x) = \prod_{i=0}^{n-1} x[i]^{u[i]}.$$

Let $\boldsymbol{\pi_u}(\boldsymbol{x})$ be a function from $(\mathbb{F}_2^{n_0} \times \mathbb{F}_2^{n_1} \times \cdots \times \mathbb{F}_2^{n_{m-1}})$ to $\mathbb{F}_2$ for all $\boldsymbol{u} \in (\mathbb{F}_2^{n_0} \times \mathbb{F}_2^{n_1} \times, \cdots, \times \mathbb{F}_2^{n_{m-1}})$. For any $\boldsymbol{u} = (u_0, u_1, \cdots, u_{m-1}), \boldsymbol{x} = (x_0, x_1, \cdots, x_{m-1}) \in (\mathbb{F}_2^{n_0} \times \mathbb{F}_2^{n_1} \times, \cdots, \times \mathbb{F}_2^{n_{m-1}})$, define $\boldsymbol{\pi_u}(\boldsymbol{x})$ as follows:

$$\boldsymbol{\pi_u}(\boldsymbol{x}) = \prod_{i=0}^{m-1} \pi_{u_i}(x_i).$$

Definition 1 (Division Property [16]). Let $\mathbb{X}$ be a multiset whose elements take a value of $(\mathbb{F}_2^n)^m$, and $\boldsymbol{k}$ is an m-dimensional vector whose i-th element takes a value between 0 and n. When the multiset $\mathbb{X}$ has the division property $\mathcal{D}_{\boldsymbol{k}^{(0)}, \boldsymbol{k}^{(1)}, \cdots, \boldsymbol{k}^{(q-1)}}^{n,m}$, it fulfills the following conditions: The parity of $\pi_{\boldsymbol{u}}(\boldsymbol{x})$ over all $\boldsymbol{x} \in \mathbb{X}$ is always even when

$$\boldsymbol{u} \in \left\{ (u_0, u_1, \cdots, u_{m-1}) \in (\mathbb{F}_2^n)^m | W(\boldsymbol{u}) \not\succeq \boldsymbol{k}^{(0)}, \cdots, W(\boldsymbol{u}) \not\succeq \boldsymbol{k}^{(q-1)} \right\}.$$

The definition of division property divides all possible values of $(\mathbb{F}_2^n)^m$ into two sets Γ_0 and $\Gamma_?$. For any $\boldsymbol{u} \in \Gamma_0$, the parity of $\pi_{\boldsymbol{u}}(\boldsymbol{x})$ over all $\boldsymbol{x} \in \mathbb{X}$ is always even, and for any $\boldsymbol{u} \in \Gamma_?$ the parity is unknown. However, we are only interested in Γ_0. If Γ_0 is nonempty and there exits a nonzero vector $\boldsymbol{u} \in \Gamma_0$, then according to the definition we have $\bigoplus_{\boldsymbol{x} \in \mathbb{X}} \pi_{\boldsymbol{u}}(\boldsymbol{x}) = 0$ which is a zero-sum property. Furthermore, if $\boldsymbol{u}$ has only one nonzero bit, the parity is exactly the XOR-sum of a certain fixed bit whose position is the same as the nonzero bit of $\boldsymbol{u}$. The steps of constructing an integral distinguisher by division property are to choose a set of plaintexts with some given division property, then trace its propagation through $(r+1)$-round encryption such that Γ_0 for the first time doesn't contain any nonzero vector. In this case, we get an r-round integral distinguisher. Todo presented in [16,17] propagation characteristics of division property for some round function operations, we review some propagation characteristics here which will be used later in this paper.

Proposition 1 (Copy [16]). *Denote $\mathbb{X}$ an input multiset, and let $x \in \mathbb{X}$. The copy function creates (y_1, y_2) from x where $y_1 = x, y_2 = x$. Assuming the input multiset has division property $\mathcal{D}_k^n$. Let $\mathbb{Y}$ be the corresponding output multiset set, then $\mathbb{Y}$ has division property $\mathcal{D}_{(0,k),(1,k-1),\cdots,(k,0)}^{n,n}$.*

Proposition 2 (Compression [16]). *Denote $\mathbb{X}$ an input multiset, let $(x_1, x_2) \in \mathbb{X}$ be an input to the compression function and denote the ouput value by y where $y = x_1 \oplus x_2$. Let $\mathbb{Y}$ be the corresponding output multiset. If input multiset $\mathbb{X}$ has division property $\mathcal{D}_{\boldsymbol{k}}^{n,n}$ where $\boldsymbol{k} = (k_1, k_2)$, then the division property of $\mathbb{Y}$ is $\mathcal{D}_{k_1+k_2}^n$.*

3   Improved Division Property on SIMON48 and SIMON64

In this section, we will study improved division property by cutting the state into small subblocks. In [17] Todo treated the state as two pieces, that is, the left half and the right half which is a rather coarse treatment. However, if we consider bit-based division property as in [18], the time and memory complexity for SIMON48 and SIMON64 will be upper bounded by 2^{48} and 2^{64} respectively, which is impractical for current computing and memory capacity. Thus, we consider cutting the state into small pieces such that the time and memory is feasible. At the meantime, since the state has been cut into pieces, we should get some more accurate integral distinguishers.

After the state partition we study the division property propagation of SIMON round function and construct an algorithm to search integral distinguishers of SIMON. We will propose in this section two different partitions and discuss their influences. Furthermore, we found that different partitions on state bits have different impact on the division property propagation of circular shift operation, and thus this will affect the length of integral distinguishers.

3.1 The First Partition of the State

For SIMON$2n$, both the left and the right halves of the state are n bits, we could cut the state into t-bit pieces where t can divide n, denoted as $t \mid n$. In the following, we assume the state of SIMON is split into t-bit pieces with $t \mid n$.

We present a straightforward partition in this subsection. Denote the left half of the input as X, and the right half as Y. Let $X = a_0 a_1 \cdots a_{n-1}$ where n is the word length and $a_i \in \mathbb{F}_2$ ($i = 0, 1, \cdots, n-1$), moreover, a_0 is the leftmost bit. Similarly, denote $Y = b_0 b_1 \cdots b_{n-1}$ where $b_i \in \mathbb{F}_2$ ($i = 0, 1, \cdots, n-1$) and b_0 is the leftmost bit. The partition adopted in this subsection is to cut the state every t consecutive bits. Thus, the state can be expressed as follows:

$$
\begin{aligned}
(X, Y) &\stackrel{cut}{\Longrightarrow} (a_0 \cdots a_{t-1}, \cdots, a_{n-t} \cdots a_{n-1}, b_0 \cdots b_{t-1}, \cdots, b_{n-t} \cdots b_{n-1}) \\
&\stackrel{def}{=} (x_0, \cdots, x_{\frac{n}{t}-1}, y_0, \cdots, y_{\frac{n}{t}-1})
\end{aligned}
\tag{1}
$$

We can view the state as a vector in $(\mathbb{F}_2^t)^{\frac{2n}{t}}$. In this case, the division property of SIMON is indicated by vectors in $\mathbb{Z}^{\frac{2n}{t}}$ whose coordinates are between 0 and t. We can see from Fig. 1 that one round encryption of SIMON involves copy, circular shift, bitwise AND and compression by bitwise XOR operations. Since **Copy** and **Compression** functions have been studied by Todo and we presented them in **Propositions** 1 and 2. In the following we will propose three propositions to illustrate the propagation characteristics of division property of bitwise AND and circular shift operations which are used in SIMON round functions and some of the proofs are given in Appendix A.

SIMON round function uses bitwise AND operation to provide nonlinearity. Todo [17] viewed all nonlinear components as an Sbox, thus bitwise AND can be viewed as an Sbox with algebraic degree two. We give here a more detailed look at division property propagation with respect to bitwise AND operation.

Proposition 3 (Bitwise AND). *Let $\mathbb{X}$ be an input multiset, and let $\boldsymbol{x} = (x_0, \cdots, x_{\frac{n}{t}-1}, x_0^*, \cdots, x_{\frac{n}{t}-1}^*) \in \mathbb{X}$ where x_i and x_i^* belong to $\mathbb{F}_2^t$. The bitwise*

AND function creates $z = (x_0 \& x_0^*, \cdots, x_{\frac{n}{t}-1} \& x_{\frac{n}{t}-1}^*)$ from x, and let $\mathbb{Z}$ denote the output multiset. If the input multiset has division property $\mathcal{D}_{\boldsymbol{k}}^{t, \frac{2n}{t}}$ where $\boldsymbol{k} = (k_0, \cdots, k_{\frac{n}{t}-1}, k_0^*, \cdots, k_{\frac{n}{t}-1}^*)$, then the output multiset has division property $\mathcal{D}_{\hat{\boldsymbol{k}}}^{t, \frac{n}{t}}$, where $\hat{\boldsymbol{k}} = (\hat{k_0}, \cdots, \hat{k_{\frac{n}{t}-1}})$ and $\hat{k_i} = \max\{k_i, k_i^*\}$.

Actually, in the search algorithm of integral distinguisher we are given an initial set Γ_0 whose vectors result in an even parity, this set Γ_0 will shrink along the encryption procedure and we stop the search algorithm right before it becomes a set only with a zero vector. If we view bitwise AND operation as an Sbox with algebraic degree two, the division property will propagate from $\boldsymbol{k} = (k_0, k_1, \cdots, k_{\frac{n}{t}-1}, k_0^*, k_1^*, \cdots, k_{\frac{n}{t}-1}^*)$ to $\bar{\boldsymbol{k}} = (\bar{k}_0, \bar{k}_1, \cdots, \bar{k}_{\frac{n}{t}-1})$ where $\bar{k}_i = \lceil \frac{k_i + k_i^*}{2} \rceil$.[1] Note that $\bar{k}_i \leq \hat{k}_i$ always holds, and this makes Proposition 3 much better than viewing bitwise AND as an Sbox with algebraic degree two. Since $\hat{\boldsymbol{k}} \succeq \bar{\boldsymbol{k}}$ indicates that $\bar{\boldsymbol{k}}$ will rule out more vectors from the possible values of $\boldsymbol{u}$ for making the parity even, and thus make set Γ_0 smaller.

Another operation adopted in SIMON round function is circular shift which is used to get diffusion across the state. The rotation parameter for SIMON is one, eight and two. We first study division property propagation of circular shift by one bit in terms of the given state partition.

Proposition 4 (Circular Shift by One Bit). *Let $\mathbb{X}$ be the input multiset, and let $\boldsymbol{x} = (x_0, x_1, \cdots, x_{\frac{n}{t}-1}) \in \mathbb{X}$ where x_i belongs to $\mathbb{F}_2^t$ for all $i \in \{0, 1, \cdots, \frac{n}{t} - 1\}$. Denote $x_0 = a_0 a_1 \cdots a_{t-1}, x_1 = a_t a_{t+1} \cdots a_{2t-1}, \cdots, x_{\frac{n}{t}-1} = a_{n-t} a_{n-t+1} \cdots a_{n-1}$ where $a_i \in \mathbb{F}_2$. The circular shift by one bit function $\boldsymbol{x} \lll 1$ creates $\boldsymbol{x}^* = (x_0^*, x_1^*, \cdots, x_{\frac{n}{t}-1}^*)$ where $x_0^* = a_1 a_2 \cdots a_t, x_1^* = a_{t+1} a_{t+2} \cdots a_{2t}, \cdots, x_{\frac{n}{t}-1}^* = a_{n-t+1} a_{n-t+2} \cdots a_{n-1} a_0$. Denote the output multiset by $\mathbb{X}^*$, if the input multiset has division property $\mathcal{D}_{\boldsymbol{k}}^{t, \frac{n}{t}}$ with $\boldsymbol{k} = (k_0, k_1, \cdots, k_{\frac{n}{t}-1})$, the division property of $\mathbb{X}^*$ is $\mathcal{D}_{\boldsymbol{k}^{(0)}, \boldsymbol{k}^{(1)}, \cdots, \boldsymbol{k}^{(q-1)}}^{t, \frac{n}{t}}$ where $\boldsymbol{k}^{(0)}, \boldsymbol{k}^{(1)}, \cdots, \boldsymbol{k}^{(q-1)}$ are all the solutions $(k_0^*, k_1^*, \cdots, k_{\frac{n}{t}-1}^*)$ of the following equations:*

$$
\begin{cases}
k_0^* = k_0 - c_0 + c_1 & 0 \leq k_0^* \leq t, \\
\vdots \\
k_{\frac{n}{t}-2}^* = k_{\frac{n}{t}-2} - c_{\frac{n}{t}-2} + c_{\frac{n}{t}-1} & 0 \leq k_{\frac{n}{t}-2}^* \leq t, \\
k_{\frac{n}{t}-1}^* = k_{\frac{n}{t}-1} - c_{\frac{n}{t}-1} + c_0 & 0 \leq k_{\frac{n}{t}-1}^* \leq t,
\end{cases}
\tag{2}
$$

where $c_i \in \{0, 1\}$.

Since circular shift by one bit will shift the leftmost bit of a piece into another piece, the division property of any two adjacent pieces will interfere with each other. We illustrate this procedure in Fig. 2 where the piece size is 2 bits. For the sake of simplicity we give an illustration on SIMON32, however we note that for SIMON48 and SIMON64 this partition is similar.

---

[1] This result is according to Rule 1 and Rule 5 in [16].

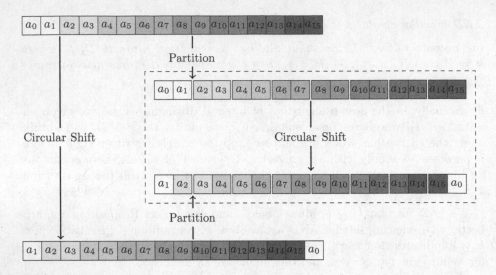

Fig. 2. Left circular shift by one bit regarding the state partition

It is clear that left circular shift by i bits just need to apply the proposition i times. However, note that when the shift offset is a multiple of t, the bitwise circular shift is just a piece-wise circular shift. In this situation, division property propagation is a circular shift of the corresponding coordinates of vectors.

Proposition 5 (Circular Shift by One Piece). *Let $\mathbb{X}$ be the input multiset, and let $\boldsymbol{x} = (x_0, x_1, \cdots, x_{\frac{n}{t}-1}) \in \mathbb{X}$ where x_i belongs to $\mathbb{F}_2^t$. The circular shift by one piece creates $\boldsymbol{x}^* = (x_1, x_2, \cdots, x_{\frac{n}{t}-1}, x_0)$. Denote the output multiset by $\mathbb{X}^*$, if the input multiset has division property $\mathcal{D}_{\boldsymbol{k}}^{t, \frac{n}{t}}$ with $\boldsymbol{k} = (k_0, k_1, \cdots, k_{\frac{n}{t}-1})$, the division property of $\mathbb{X}^*$ is $\mathcal{D}_{\boldsymbol{k}^*}^{t, \frac{n}{t}}$ where $\boldsymbol{k}^* = (k_1, k_2, \cdots, k_{\frac{n}{t}-1}, k_0)$.*

Take SIMON48 as an example, we split the state into 4-bit pieces. In this case, circular shift by one bit applies Proposition 4 once, circular shift by eight bits applies Proposition 5 twice and circular shift by two bits applies Proposition 4 twice.

Note that the difference between Propositions 4 and 5 is Proposition 4 will create approximate (some vectors are invalid when varying the values of each c_i in Eq. 2, since the coordinates of each vectors can only take on values from 0 to t) $2^{\frac{n}{t}}$ vectors from one vector while Proposition 5 creates only one vector from a given vector. Furthermore, each vector imposes a constraint on parity vector $\boldsymbol{u}$, and in general the more vectors, the smaller the size of set Γ_0. In the search algorithm of integral distinguisher we would like to keep Γ_0 shrink as slow as possible along encryption procedure. Thus, we prefer to use Proposition 5. However, the shift offsets of SIMON are one, eight and two, and the greatest common divisor is one. If we use only Proposition 5, we need to set the piece size $t = 1$, which corresponds to bit-based division property.

3.2   The Second Partition of the State

In this subsection we present an improved state partition which do not assign consecutive bits into a piece, on the contrary we assign the bits separated by a given interval into a piece as below.

Assume the piece size is t with $t \mid n$, let X and Y denote the left and right halves of the state respectively, $X = a_0 a_1 \cdots a_{n-1}$ and $Y = b_0 b_1 \cdots b_{n-1}$ are given as in Subsect. 3.1. We cut the state as follows:

$$
\begin{aligned}
X \stackrel{cut}{\Longrightarrow} (\,&a_0 a_{\frac{n}{t}} a_{\frac{2n}{t}} \cdots a_{n-\frac{n}{t}}, \\
&a_1 a_{\frac{n}{t}+1} a_{\frac{2n}{t}+1} \cdots a_{n-\frac{n}{t}+1}, \\
&\cdots, \\
&a_{\frac{n}{t}-1} a_{\frac{2n}{t}-1} a_{\frac{3n}{t}-1} \cdots a_{n-1}) \\
\stackrel{def}{=} (\,&x_0, x_1, \cdots, x_{\frac{n}{t}-1})
\end{aligned}
\tag{3}
$$

$$
\begin{aligned}
Y \stackrel{cut}{\Longrightarrow} (\,&b_0 b_{\frac{n}{t}} b_{\frac{2n}{t}} \cdots b_{n-\frac{n}{t}}, \\
&b_1 b_{\frac{n}{t}+1} b_{\frac{2n}{t}+1} \cdots b_{n-\frac{n}{t}+1}, \\
&\cdots, \\
&b_{\frac{n}{t}-1} b_{\frac{2n}{t}-1} b_{\frac{3n}{t}-1} \cdots b_{n-1}) \\
\stackrel{def}{=} (\,&y_0, y_1, \cdots, y_{\frac{n}{t}-1})
\end{aligned}
\tag{4}
$$

Proposition 6 (Revised Circular Shift by One Bit). *Let* $\mathbb{X}$ *be an input multiset,* $\boldsymbol{x}$ *is an element of* $\mathbb{X}$ *and* $\boldsymbol{x} \in \mathbb{F}_2^n$. *Cut* $\boldsymbol{x}$ *as in Eq. (3) and denoted by* $\boldsymbol{x} \stackrel{def}{=} (x_0, x_1, \cdots, x_{\frac{n}{t}-1})$. *Left circular shift by one bit creates* $\boldsymbol{x}^*$ *with* $\boldsymbol{x}^* = \boldsymbol{x} \lll 1$. *Let* $\mathbb{X}^*$ *denote the output multiset. Cut* $\boldsymbol{x}^*$ *as in (3) and denoted by* $\boldsymbol{x}^* = (x_0^*, x_1^*, \cdots, x_{\frac{n}{t}-1}^*)$. *Then we have* $x_0^* = x_1, x_1^* = x_2, \cdots, x_{\frac{n}{t}-2}^* = x_{\frac{n}{t}-1}, x_{\frac{n}{t}-1}^* = (x_0 \lll 1)$. *Moreover, if the input multiset has division property* $\mathcal{D}_k^{t,\frac{n}{t}}$ *with* $k = (k_0, k_1, \cdots, k_{\frac{n}{t}-1})$, *then the output multiset has division property* $\mathcal{D}_{k^*}^{t,\frac{n}{t}}$ *with* $k^* = (k_0^*, k_1^*, \cdots, k_{\frac{n}{t}-1}^*)$, *where* $k_0^* = k_1, k_1^* = k_2, \cdots, k_{\frac{n}{t}-2}^* = k_{\frac{n}{t}-1}, k_{\frac{n}{t}-1}^* = k_0$.

We give a schematic diagram of this improved state partition, and illustrate the circular shift operation based on the state partition in Fig. 3. For the sake of simplicity, in Fig. 3 we take Simon32 as an example and the piece size $t = 2$. Similarly, this partition is always feasible for Simon48 and Simon64.

Under this new state partition, circular shift by i bits just apply Proposition 6 for i times. Based on this partition, division property propagation of circular shift is just a circular shift of coordinates of the corresponding vectors, thus the number of vectors before and after circular shift will retain the same as we have expected. Note that this new state partition does not influence the division property propagations of bitwise AND and bitwise XOR operations, since unlike circular shift, bitwise AND and bitwise XOR operate on corresponding bits among pieces of *two* words. Thus together with Propositions 1, 2 and 3, division property propagation can be studied under this new state partition.

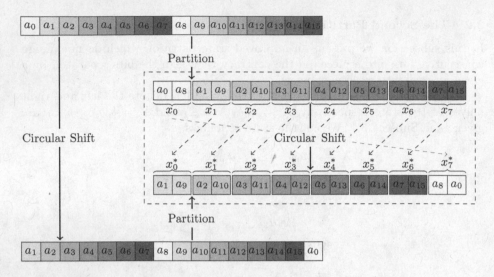

Fig. 3. Left circular shift by one bit regarding improved partition

Comparison Between Two Partitions. Thereafter, we denote the first state partition presented in Subsect. 3.1 as **PartitionI**, denote the second state partition presented in Subsect. 3.2 as **PartitionII**. (1). As described in Subsect. 3.1, if the piece size t satisfies $0 < t < n$ in PartitionI, the use of Proposition 4 is unavoidable and this will create lots of extra vectors, however in PartitionII the number of vectors keep unchanged. Thus, the search algorithm under PartitionI is much more computationally expensive than PartitionII. (2). Since each vector adds a constraint on $\boldsymbol{u}$, PartitionI will create more vectors than PartitionII and this makes the set Γ_0 smaller under PartitionI. Thus, we expect that Γ_0 will shrink fast under PartitionI which will result in a shorter integral distinguisher. (3). In the choice of piece size t, PartitionII only needs $t \mid n$, however PartitionI has to consider the shift offsets and makes the partition use fewer times of Proposition 4. From this point of view PartitionII is much better.

3.3   Search Algorithm and Results

So far we have discussed division property propagations of all operations used in SIMON round function. Given a partition and a multiset of chosen inputs values, assume that the division property of this multiset is $\mathcal{D}_k^{t,\frac{2n}{t}}$ under the given partition, the division property propagation of one round SIMON can be evaluated with the propagation characteristics introduced in the previous two subsections.

Search Algorithm. Now we are ready to give our search Algorithm 1. The algorithm calls four functions:

1. *RoundEval* returns the division property of outputs of one round SIMON given the input division property and partition.

2. **MinSum** returns the minimal sum of coordinates of the given set of vectors. Since the division property can always propagate if the minimal sum of coordinates of all vectors is greater than one which means all the state bits are balanced. Note that if there exist $k^{(i)}$ and $k^{(j)}$ such that $k^{(i)} \succeq k^{(j)}$, then the sum of coordinates of $k^{(i)}$ is greater than the sum of coordinates of $k^{(j)}$. When the minimal sum of coordinates of all vectors in a given set S is greater than one, it is clear that any vector u with $W(u)$ a unit vector will satisfy $W(u) \not\succeq k^{(i)}$, for all $k^{(i)} \in S$. Thus, all state bits are balanced.

3. **SizeReduce** eliminates redundant vectors since redundant vectors provide no useful information. A vector $k^{(i)}$ in $\{k^{(0)}, k^{(1)}, \cdots, k^{(q)}\}$ is called redundant if there exists $k^{(i)} \succeq k^{(j)}$ with $j \neq i$.

4. **MaxCoord** returns the maximal coordinate of the given set S of vectors. If there exists a vector $k^{(i)}$ with one of the coordinates greater than one after SizeReduce, we can choose a vector u whose weight $W(u)$ is a unit vector such that $k^{(i)} \succeq W(u)$. In this case, any vector $k^{(j)} \in S$ will satisfy $W(u) \not\succeq k^{(j)}$, otherwise we have $k^{(i)} \succeq k^{(j)}$ which contradicts with the fact that S has been processed by SizeReduce function. Hence we get a nonzero vector u in Γ_0 which results to an even parity.

Algorithm 1. Integral Distinguisher search of SIMON2n

Require: $n, t, PartitionType$, Initial division property $\mathcal{D}_k^{t, \frac{2n}{t}}$.
Ensure: Round r.

$r \leftarrow 0$

$k_r^{(0)}, k_r^{(1)}, \cdots, k_r^{(q_r)} \leftarrow \boldsymbol{RoundEval}(n, t, ParititonType, \mathcal{D}_k^{t, \frac{2n}{t}})$

while $MinSum(k_r^{(0)}, k_r^{(1)}, \cdots, k_r^{(q_r)}) > 1$ **do**

    $r \leftarrow r + 1$

    $k_r^{(0)}, k_r^{(1)}, \cdots, k_r^{(q_r)} \leftarrow \boldsymbol{RoundEval}(n, t, ParititonType, \mathcal{D}_{k_{r-1}^{(0)}, k_{r-1}^{(1)}, \cdots, k_{r-1}^{(q_{r-1})}}^{t, \frac{2n}{t}})$

end while

$\hat{k}_r^{(0)}, \hat{k}_r^{(1)}, \cdots, \hat{k}_r^{(p_r)} \leftarrow \boldsymbol{SizeReduce}(k_r^{(0)}, k_r^{(1)}, \cdots, k_r^{(q_r)})$

while $MaxCoord(\hat{k}_r^{(0)}, \hat{k}_r^{(1)}, \cdots, \hat{k}_r^{(p_r)}) > 1$ **do**

    $r \leftarrow r + 1$

    $k_r^{(0)}, k_r^{(1)}, \cdots, k_r^{(q_r)} \leftarrow \boldsymbol{RoundEval}(n, t, ParititonType, \mathcal{D}_{\hat{k}_{r-1}^{(0)}, \hat{k}_{r-1}^{(1)}, \cdots, \hat{k}_{r-1}^{(p_{r-1})}}^{t, \frac{2n}{t}})$

    $\hat{k}_r^{(0)}, \hat{k}_r^{(1)}, \cdots, \hat{k}_r^{(p_r)} \leftarrow \boldsymbol{SizeReduce}(k_r^{(0)}, k_r^{(1)}, \cdots, k_r^{(q_r)})$

end while

return r.

The most troublesome problems in the search algorithm are the rapid expansion of vectors created by copy function and circular shift (if PartitionI is adopted). Another problem we have met is that the SizeReduce algorithm which deletes the redundant vectors is very costly as mentioned in [16, 22]. To solve the rapid expansion of vectors, we carefully choose the piece size t to make sure that the number of all possible vectors is of reasonable size and we store all possible vectors in a table. Each time when calculating one step of division property propagation we first mark all the vectors in such a table by 0, then calculate the division property propagation and mark the resulting vectors by 1, thus we can eliminate duplicated vectors. To solve the second problem we do not perform SizeReduce procedure through the search algorithm until there exists a vector whose coordinates add up to one. We found that when such a vector appears SizeReduce can be very efficient.

Results. To compare two state partitions proposed above, we run experiments on SIMON32, and the results are listed in Table 1.

Table 1. Results on SIMON32 with $t = 2$

Target	$\log_2(\sharp\text{texts})$									
	$r=3$	$r=4$	$r=5$	$r=6$	$r=7$	$r=8$	$r=9$	$r=10$	$r=11$	$r=12$
PartitionI	2	3	5	17	25	28	30	-	-	-
PartitionII	-	-	-	2	5	18	22	25	28	30

Table 1 shows that PartitionII gives better results with respect to data and the number of covered rounds. Note that in [18] Todo *et al.* applied bit-based division property on SIMON32, thus, we only use SIMON32 here as an example to illustrate the influences of the two state partitions. Since PartitionII gives better results, in the following we only consider PartitionII. Table 2 lists the longest integral distinguishers we found by PartitionII compared with previous results.

Table 2. Results on SIMON48 and SIMON64(PartitionII)

Cipher	[17]		This paper		
	$\log_2(\sharp\text{texts})$	Round	$\log_2(\sharp\text{texts})$	Round	Piece Size
SIMON48	47	11	47	12	4
SIMON64	63	11	63	12	8

Integral distinguishers found in Table 2 are similar for both SIMON48 and SIMON64. The input structure of SIMON48 (resp. SIMON64) keeps the leftmost bit of the state constant and let the remaining 47 (resp. 63) bits take on all possible values. Then the 24 (resp. 32)-bit word of right half of the state are balanced after 12 (resp. 12) rounds. Based on these distinguishers, integral attack can be launched. For SIMON48, 18- and 19-round SIMON can be attacked with key size 72 bits and 96 bits respectively. For SIMON64, 19- and 20-round SIMON can be attacked with key size 96 bits and 128 bits respectively. Due to the limit of space, we omit the details here.

Complexity of the Algorithm. Given a state partition with piece size t, division property is indicated by vectors in $\{0, 1, \cdots, t\}^{\frac{2n}{t}}$, and the number of such vectors is $(t+1)^{\frac{2n}{t}}$. Thus, the complexity of the algorithm is upper bounded by $(t+1)^{\frac{2n}{t}}$. For SIMON48 we choose $t = 4$, thus the complexity of the algorithm is upper bounded by $5^{12} \approx 2^{27.9}$. Similarly, the complexity for SIMON64 is upper bounded by $2^{25.4}$. We note that the methods used in [17] and [18] for searching integral distinguishers of SIMON family, can be seen as two limit cases of our method by using a state partition. If we set the piece size $t = 1$, this case corresponds to the bit-based division property. In this case, the complexity of the algorithm is upper bounded by 2^{2n}, which is impractical for SIMON with block size larger than 32 bits. On the other hand, if we set $t = n$, that is, the state of SIMON is split into two parts: the left half and right half, and this corresponds to the approach used in [17]. In this case the complexity is upper bounded by $(n + 1)^2$, which is rather small even for SIMON128.

4   Summary and Discussion

In this paper we showed improved division property of SIMON48 and SIMON64 by studying the division property propagations of SIMON round function operations. We first split the state into small pieces in order to get a trade-off between time-memory complexity and accuracy of the distinguishers, and then we studied the division property propagations of bitwise AND and circular shift which are basic operations used in SIMON. Moreover, we found that the state partition has a great influence on the propagation of division property. To be specific, the propagation of division property against circular shift operation. In this paper we presented two state partitions and experimented on SIMON32 to illustrate this influence, the experimental results showed that different state partitions resulted to different data and the number of covered rounds.

Based on the state partition and these propagation characteristics we presented a search algorithm and found 12-round distinguishers for SIMON48 and SIMON64 which improved Todo's results in [17] by one round for both ciphers.

Furthermore, we also applied the search algorithm to SIMON96 and SIMON128. We could only set $t = 16$ and $t = 32$ for SIMON96 and SIMON128 at the present, respectively. As a result, it seemed that the size of t was too large and we could not get better integral distinguishers for SIMON96 and SIMON128 than the results in [17]. However, we believe that the state partition and division property propagations studied in this can help study the division property of SIMON, and we leave it as a future work.

Acknowledgements. We are very grateful to the anonymous reviewers. This work was supported by the National Natural Science Foundation of China (Grant No. 61379138), the "Strategic Priority Research Program" of the Chinese Academy of Sciences (Grant No. XDA06010701).

A   Proofs of Propositions

A.1   Proof of Proposition 3

Proof. The aim is to prove under what conditions the output parity is always even given the input multiset division property. Let $\boldsymbol{u} = (u_0, u_1, \cdots, u_{\frac{n}{t}-1}) \in (\mathbb{F}_2^t)^{\frac{n}{t}}$ and

$$
\begin{aligned}
\bigoplus_{z \in Z} \pi_{\boldsymbol{u}}(z) &= \bigoplus_{z \in Z} \prod_{i=0}^{\frac{n}{t}-1} \pi_{u_i}(z_i) \\
&= \bigoplus_{x \in X} \prod_{i=0}^{\frac{n}{t}-1} \pi_{u_i}(x_i \& x_i^*) \\
&= \bigoplus_{x \in X} \prod_{i=0}^{\frac{n}{t}-1} \pi_{u_i}(x_i) \prod_{i=0}^{\frac{n}{t}-1} \pi_{u_i}(x_i^*) \\
&= \bigoplus_{x \in X} \pi_{(\boldsymbol{u},\boldsymbol{u})}(\boldsymbol{x}).
\end{aligned}
\tag{5}
$$

In order to get an even parity of $\bigoplus_{z \in Z} \pi_{\boldsymbol{u}}(z)$, the parity of $\bigoplus_{x \in X} \pi_{(\boldsymbol{u},\boldsymbol{u})}(\boldsymbol{x})$ must be even. According to the input division property $\mathcal{D}_{\boldsymbol{k}}^{t, \frac{2n}{t}}$, it follows that there must exist $i \in \{0, 1, \cdots, \frac{n}{t}-1\}$ such that $w(u_i) < k_i$ or $w(u_i) < k_i^*$, thus $w(u_i) < \max\{k_i, k_i^*\}$. It's evident to see we need $W(\boldsymbol{u}) \not\succeq \hat{\boldsymbol{k}}$ which completes the proof.

A.2   Proof of Proposition 4

Proof. Let $\boldsymbol{u} = (u_0, u_1, \cdots, u_{\frac{n}{t}-1}) \in (\mathbb{F}_2^t)^{\frac{n}{t}}$, since $\boldsymbol{x}^* = \boldsymbol{x} \lll 1$ we have $\bigoplus_{\boldsymbol{x}^* \in X^*} \pi_{\boldsymbol{u}}(\boldsymbol{x}^*) = \bigoplus_{\boldsymbol{x} \in X} \pi_{\boldsymbol{u} \ggg 1}(\boldsymbol{x})$. Let $\boldsymbol{v} = (v_0, v_1, \cdots, v_{\frac{n}{t}-1}) \in (\mathbb{F}_2^t)^{\frac{n}{t}}$, and $\boldsymbol{v} = \boldsymbol{u} \ggg 1$. It follows that $\bigoplus_{\boldsymbol{x}^* \in X^*} \pi_{\boldsymbol{u}}(\boldsymbol{x}^*) = \bigoplus_{\boldsymbol{x} \in X} \pi_{\boldsymbol{v}}(\boldsymbol{x})$.

In order to prove for any $W(\boldsymbol{u}) \not\succeq \boldsymbol{k}^{(0)}, \boldsymbol{k}^{(1)}, \cdots, \boldsymbol{k}^{(q-1)}$ the corresponding $\boldsymbol{v} = \boldsymbol{u} \ggg 1$ satisfies $W(\boldsymbol{v}) \not\succeq \boldsymbol{k}$, we can prove for any $W(\boldsymbol{v}) \succeq \boldsymbol{k}$ there exists i such that the corresponding $\boldsymbol{u} = \boldsymbol{v} \lll 1$ satisfies $W(\boldsymbol{u}) \succeq \boldsymbol{k}^{(i)}$.

Write the bit string expression of $\boldsymbol{v}$ as $(v[0]v[1] \cdots v[t-1], v[t]v[t+1] \cdots v[2t-1], \cdots, v[n-t]v[n-t+1] \cdots v[n-1])$ with $v[i]$ the i-th bit of $\boldsymbol{v}$. Since $\boldsymbol{u} = \boldsymbol{v} \lll 1$, it is easy to see that

$$
\begin{cases}
w(u_0) &= w(v_0) - v[0] + v[t], \\
\vdots & \\
w(u_{\frac{n}{t}-2}) &= w(v_{\frac{n}{t}-2}) - v[n - 2t] + v[n - t], \\
w(u_{\frac{n}{t}-1}) &= w(v_{\frac{n}{t}-1}) - v[n - t] + v[0].
\end{cases}
\tag{6}
$$

Since $W(\boldsymbol{v}) \succeq \boldsymbol{k}$, it follows that $w(v_i) \geq k_i$ for any $i \in \{0, 1, \cdots, \frac{n}{t} - 1\}$. Thus we have

$$
\begin{cases}
w(u_0) & = w(v_0) - v[0] + v[t] \geq k_0 - v[0] + v[t], \\
\vdots \\
w(u_{\frac{n}{t}-2}) & = w(v_{\frac{n}{t}-2}) - v[n-2t] + v[n-t] \geq k_{\frac{n}{t}-1} - v[n-2t] + v[n-t], \\
w(u_{\frac{n}{t}-1}) & = w(v_{\frac{n}{t}-1}) - v[n-t] + v[0] \geq k_{\frac{n}{t}-1} - v[n-t] + v[0].
\end{cases}
$$
(7)

If the coordinates of $(k_0 - v[0] + v[t], \cdots, k_{\frac{n}{t}-1} - v[n-t] + v[0])$ are between 0 and t, according to (2), there exists i such that $\boldsymbol{k}^{(i)} = (k_0 - v[0] + v[t], \cdots, k_{\frac{n}{t}-1} - v[n-t] + v[0])$. It follows that $W(\boldsymbol{u}) \succeq \boldsymbol{k}^{(i)}$ and we have thus proved the proposition.

However, if the coordinates of $(k_0 - v[0] + v[t], \cdots, k_{\frac{n}{t}-1} - v[n-t] + v[0])$ do not range from 0 to t, we can still find $\boldsymbol{k}^{(i)}$ such that $W(\boldsymbol{u}) \succeq \boldsymbol{k}^{(i)}$. Note that $k_i - v[i * t] + v[(i+1) * t] \leq w(u_i) \leq t$, thus $k_i - v[i * t] + v[(i+1) * t]$ will be invalid only if it happens that $k_i - v[i * t] + v[(i+1) * t] = -1$. If this happens we can deduce that $k_i = 0, v[i * t] = 1$ and $v[(i+1) * t] = 0$, thus bit string $v[0]v[t] \cdots v[\frac{n}{t} - 1]$ can not take on values of all one's or all zero's. We show next how to construct vector $\boldsymbol{k}^{(i)}$ such that $W(\boldsymbol{u}) \succeq \boldsymbol{k}^{(i)}$.

Without loss of generality, we assume that $k_i - v[i * t] + v[(i+1) * t] = -1$ and $v[s * t]v[(s + 1) * t] \cdots v[i * t] = 01 \cdots 1$ with $s < i$. Denote $(k_0 - v[0] + v[t], \cdots, k_{\frac{n}{t}-1} - v[n-t] + v[0]) = \boldsymbol{a}$, thus we have

$$
\begin{cases}
a_j & = k_j - v[j * t] + v[(j+1) * t] \quad \forall j \notin \{s, s+1, \cdots, i\}, \\
a_s & = k_s - 0 + 1 = k_s + 1, \\
a_{s+1} & = k_{s+1} - 1 + 1 = k_{s+1}, \\
\vdots \\
a_i & = k_i - 1 + 0 = -1.
\end{cases}
$$
(8)

We construct $\boldsymbol{b}$ as follows:

$$
\begin{cases}
b_j & = k_j - v[j * t] + v[(j+1) * t] \quad \forall j \notin \{s, s+1, \cdots, i\}, \\
b_s & = k_s - 0 + 0 = k_s, \\
b_{s+1} & = k_{s+1} - 0 + 0 = k_{s+1}, \\
\vdots \\
b_i & = k_i - 0 + 0 = k_i = 0.
\end{cases}
$$
(9)

Since $w(u_s) \geq k_s - v[s*t] + v[(s+1)*t] = k_s - 0 + 1 = a_s > b_s = k_s, w(u_{s+1}) \geq k_{s+1} - v[(s+1)*t] + v[(s+2)*t] = k_{s+1} = a_{s+1} = b_{s+1}, \cdots, w(u_i) \geq 0 = b_i$, thus we have constructed vector $\boldsymbol{b}$ such that $W(\boldsymbol{u}) \succeq \boldsymbol{b}$. If the coordinates of $\boldsymbol{b}$ range from 0 to t, $\boldsymbol{b}$ is a solution of (2) and there exists $\boldsymbol{k}^{(t)}$ such that $\boldsymbol{k}^{(t)} = \boldsymbol{b}$, thus we have proved the proposition. However, If these still exits coordinates of $\boldsymbol{b}$ equal to -1, we can repeat the above process to modify $\boldsymbol{b}$ until we get a valid solution.

References

1. Abdelraheem, M.A., Alizadeh, J., Alkhzaimi, H.A., Aref, M.R., Bagheri, N., Gauravaram, P.: Improved linear cryptanalysis of reduced-round SIMON-32 and SIMON-48. Cryptology ePrint Archive, Report 2015/988 (2015). http://eprint.iacr.org/

2. Abdelraheem, M.A., Alizadeh, J., Alkhzaimi, H.A., Aref, M.R., Bagheri, N., Gauravaram, P., Lauridsen, M.M.: Improved linear cryptanalysis of reduced-round SIMON. Cryptology ePrint Archive, Report 2014/681 (2014). http://eprint.iacr.org/

3. Albrecht, M.R., Driessen, B., Kavun, E.B., Leander, G., Paar, C., Yalçın, T.: Block ciphers-focus on the linear layer (feat. PRIDE). In: Advances in Cryptology-CRYPTO 2014, pp. 57–76 (2014)

4. Ashur, T.: Improved linear trails for the block cipher SIMON. Cryptology ePrint Archive, Report 2015/285 (2015). http://eprint.iacr.org/

5. Beaulieu, R., Shors, D., Smith, J., Treatman-Clark, S., Weeks, B., Wingers, L.: The SIMON and SPECK families of lightweight block ciphers. IACR Cryptology ePrint Archive 2013, p. 404 (2013)

6. Biryukov, A., Roy, A., Velichkov, V.: Differential analysis of block ciphers SIMON and SPECK. In: Cid, C., Rechberger, C. (eds.) FSE 2014. LNCS, vol. 8540, pp. 546–570. Springer, Heidelberg (2015)

7. Bogdanov, A.A., Knudsen, L.R., Leander, G., Paar, C., Poschmann, A., Robshaw, M., Seurin, Y., Vikkelsoe, C.: PRESENT: an ultra-lightweight block cipher. In: Paillier, P., Verbauwhede, I. (eds.) CHES 2007. LNCS, vol. 4727, pp. 450–466. Springer, Heidelberg (2007)

8. Borghoff, J., et al.: PRINCE-A low-latency block cipher for pervasive computing applications. In: Wang, X., Sako, K. (eds.) Advances in Cryptology-ASIACRYPT 2012. LNCS, vol. 7658, pp. 208–225. Springer, Heidelberg (2012)

9. Boura, C., Naya-Plasencia, M., Suder, V.: Scrutinizing and improving impossible differential attacks: applications to CLEFIA, Camellia, LBlock and SIMON. In: Sarkar, P., Iwata, T. (eds.) ASIACRYPT 2014. LNCS, vol. 8873, pp. 179–199. springer, Heidelberg (2014)

10. Chen, H., Wang, X.: Improved linear hull attack on round-reduced Simon with dynamic key-guessing techniques. Cryptology ePrint Archive, Report 2015/666 (2015). http://eprint.iacr.org/

11. Chen, Z., Wang, N., Wang, X.: Impossible differential cryptanalysis of reduced round SIMON. Cryptology ePrint Archive, Report 2015/286 (2015). http://eprint.iacr.org/

12. Daemen, J., Knudsen, L.R., Rijmen, V.: The block cipher SQUARE. In: Biham, E. (ed.) FSE 1997. LNCS, vol. 1267, pp. 149–165. Springer, Heidelberg (1997)

13. De Cannière, C., Dunkelman, O., Knežević, M.: KATAN and KTANTAN — a family of small and efficient hardware-oriented block ciphers. In: Clavier, C., Gaj, K. (eds.) CHES 2009. LNCS, vol. 5747, pp. 272–288. Springer, Heidelberg (2009)

14. Knudsen, L.R., Wagner, D.: Integral cryptanalysis. In: Daemen, J., Rijmen, V. (eds.) FSE 2002. LNCS, vol. 2365, pp. 112–127. Springer, Heidelberg (2002)

15. Mourouzis, T., Song, G., Courtois, N., Christofii, M.: Advanced differential cryptanalysis of reduced-round SIMON64/128 using large-round statistical distinguishers. Cryptology ePrint Archive, Report 2015/481 (2015). http://eprint.iacr.org/

16. Todo, Y.: Integral cryptanalysis on full MISTY1. In: Gennaro, R., Robshaw, M. (eds.) CRYPTO 2015. LNCS, vol. 9216, pp. 413–432. Springer, Heidelberg (2015)

17. Todo, Y.: Structural evaluation by generalized integral property. In: Oswald, E., Fischlin, M. (eds.) EUROCRYPT 2015. LNCS, vol. 9056, pp. 287–314. Springer, Heidelberg (2015)
18. Todo, Y., Morii, M.: Bit-based division property and application to SIMON family. Cryptology ePrint Archive, Report 2016/285 (2016). http://eprint.iacr.org/
19. Wang, N., Wang, X., Jia, K., Zhao, J.: Differential attacks on reduced SIMON versions with dynamic key-guessing techniques. Cryptology ePrint Archive, Report 2014/448 (2014). http://eprint.iacr.org/
20. Wang, Q., Liu, Z., Varıcı, K., Sasaki, Y., Rijmen, V., Todo, Y.: Cryptanalysis of reduced-round SIMON32 and SIMON48. In: Meier, W., Mukhopadhyay, D. (eds.) INDOCRYPT 2014. LNCS, vol. 8885, pp. 143–160. Springer, Heidelberg (2014)
21. Wu, W., Zhang, L.: LBlock: a lightweight block cipher. In: Lopez, J., Tsudik, G. (eds.) ACNS 2011. LNCS, vol. 6715, pp. 327–344. Springer, Heidelberg (2011)
22. Zhang, H., Wu, W.: Structural evaluation for generalized feistel structures and applications to LBlock and TWINE. In: Biryukov, A., Goyal, V. (eds.) INDOCRYPT 2015. LNCS, vol. 9462, pp. 218–237. Springer, Heidelberg (2015)
23. Zhang, W., Bao, Z., Lin, D., Rijmen, V., Yang, B., Verbauwhede, I.: RECTANGLE: a bit-slice lightweight block cipher suitable for multiple platforms. Sci. Chin. Inf. Sci. 58(12), 1–15 (2015)

Practical Analysis of Key Recovery Attack Against Search-LWE Problem

Momonari Kudo[1], Junpei Yamaguchi[1], Yang Guo[1], and Masaya Yasuda[2,3(✉)]

[1] Graduate School of Mathematics, Kyushu University, Fukuoka, Japan
[2] Institute of Mathematics for Industry, Kyushu University,
744 Motooka Nishi-ku, Fukuoka 819-0395, Japan
`yasuda@imi.kyushu-u.ac.jp`
[3] JST, CREST, 4-1-8 Honcho, Kawaguchi, Saitama 332-0012, Japan

Abstract. The security of a number of modern cryptographic schemes relies on the computational hardness of the learning with errors (LWE) problem. In 2015, Laine and Lauter analyzed a key recovery (or decoding) attack against the search variant of LWE. Their analysis is based on a generalization of the Boneh-Venkatesan method for the hidden number problem to LWE. They adopted the LLL algorithm and Babai's nearest plane method in the attack against LWE, and they also demonstrated a successful range of the attack by experiments for hundreds of LWE instances. In this paper, we give an alternative analysis of the key recovery attack. While Laine and Lauter's analysis gives explicit information about the effective approximation factor in the LLL algorithm and Babai's nearest plane method, our analysis is useful to estimate which LWE instances can be solved by the key recovery attack. Furthermore, our analysis enables one to determine a successful range of the attack with practical lattice reduction such as the BKZ algorithm.

Keywords: LWE · Lattice reduction · Babai's nearest plane method

1 Introduction

The LWE problem was introduced by Regev [27], and it is a generalization of the learning parity with noise (LPN) problem [16] into large moduli q. Given an LWE instance (n, q, d, χ), where n and d are positive integers, q a prime, and χ an error distribution on $\mathbb{Z}$. Let $\mathbb{Z}_q$ be a set of representatives of integers modulo q, and $[a]_q \in \mathbb{Z}_q$ denote the reduction of an integer a by modulo q. For a fixed secret vector $\mathbf{s} \in \mathbb{Z}_q^n$, the LWE problem setting involves d LWE samples $(\mathbf{a}_i, [\langle \mathbf{a}_i, \mathbf{s} \rangle + e_i]_q) \in \mathbb{Z}_q^n \times \mathbb{Z}_q$ for $0 \leq i \leq d-1$, where $\mathbf{a}_i$ is uniformly chosen from $\mathbb{Z}_q^n$ at random and e_i sampled from χ for every i. Then two questions are asked in the LWE problem; The decision variant of LWE is to distinguish whether a column vector $\mathbf{u} = (u_0, \ldots, u_{d-1})^T \in \mathbb{Z}_q^d$ is obtained from LWE samples with $u_i = [\langle \mathbf{a}_i, \mathbf{s} \rangle + e_i]_q$ for $0 \leq i \leq d-1$, or uniformly at random from $\mathbb{Z}_q^d$. The search variant of LWE is to recover the secret vector $\mathbf{s}$ from LWE samples.

© Springer International Publishing Switzerland 2016
K. Ogawa and K. Yoshioka (Eds.): IWSEC 2016, LNCS 9836, pp. 164–181, 2016.
DOI: 10.1007/978-3-319-44524-3_10

The LWE problem is proved to be as hard as worst-case lattice problems [9,28]. The hardness of the LWE problem assures the security of modern cryptography. Constructions of schemes such as [25,26,28] are based on the LWE problem. In recent years, the LWE problem has become a central building block to construct encryption schemes with high functionality, such as fully homomorphic encryption [8,10,11] and candidates of multi-linear maps [15]. On the other hand, LWE-based cryptography has been paid much attention as a candidate of post-quantum cryptography [23].

1.1 Practical Attacks Against LWE and Their Analysis

While reductions of LWE to worst-case lattice problems are discussed in [9,21,28], a number of *practical* algorithms have been proposed to solve concrete LWE instances (e.g. see the survey paper [4]). There are two main strategies to solve the LWE problem; reductions of LWE to short integer solutions (SIS) and bounded distance decoding (BDD) (in the other strategies, Arora-Ge method [2,3] using Gröbner bases is known to directly solve the search-LWE problem). In the SIS strategy, the distinguishing attack by Micciancio-Regev [22] is efficient to solve the decision-LWE problem, and the Blum-Kalai-Wasserman (BKW) algorithm [6] might be efficient to solve the decision-LWE problem with extremely large number of samples (see [1] for the complexity of BKW). In the BDD strategy, a key recovery (or decoding) attack is the most basic approach, in which the search-LWE problem is reduced to the closest vector problem (CVP) over a certain lattice (e.g. see [13, Example 19.7.6]). Lindner-Peikert [20] proposed improvements of Babai's nearest plane method [5], which is the most basic method to solve CVP (their improvements were analyzed in [19]). They also studied the key recovery attack using their nearest plane method, and analyzed security estimates for an LWE-based cryptosystem. In 2015, Laine and Lauter [17] analyzed the key recovery attack against the search-LWE problem. Their analysis is based on a generalization of the Boneh-Venkatesan method [7] for the hidden number problem to LWE. In their analysis, they focus on a combination of the LLL algorithm [18] and Babai's nearest plane method. Given an LWE instance (n, q, d, χ), they analyzed that the key recovery attack is successful with overwhelming probability when $q \geq 2^{O(n)}$. They also ran the attack for hundreds of LWE instances, and demonstrated a successful range of the attack.

1.2 Our Contributions

By their experiments, Laine and Lauter [17] analyzed the effective approximation factor in the LLL algorithm for q-ary lattices that arise from LWE samples (see [17, Table 1] for their experimental results). In this paper, we give an alternative analysis of the key recovery attack. Our analysis is heuristic but practical to estimate which LWE instances (n, q, d, χ) can be solved by the key recovery attack against the search-LWE problem. While the complexity of the attack is discussed in [20], our aim is to determine which LWE instances can be solved by the attack. In the key recovery attack, we construct a q-ary lattice Λ from

LWE samples, obtain a reduced basis $\mathbf{B}$ of Λ by lattice reduction, and reduce the search-LWE problem to the closest vector problem (CVP) over Λ. In this paper, we consider the LLL algorithm and the BKZ algorithm with blocksize $\beta = 20$ for the q-ary lattice Λ (in practice, $\beta = 20$ can achieve the best time/quality compromise in the BKZ algorithm). The success of the key recovery attack depends on the shape of the reduced basis $\mathbf{B}$. Let $\mathbf{B}^*$ denote the Gram-Schmidt orthogonalization of $\mathbf{B}$. Our strategy is to analyze the shape of the fundamental domain $\mathcal{P}(\mathbf{B}^*)$ of $\mathbf{B}^*$ in order to determine whether Babai's nearest plane method over the q-ary lattice Λ in the attack is succeeded, or not. Different from Laine and Lauter's analysis, ours is useful to estimate a successful range of LWE instances (n, q, d, χ) by the key recovery attack with practical lattice reduction such as the BKZ algorithm. Note that the output quality of lattice reduction for random lattices is different from that for q-ary lattices in general (in fact, as mentioned in [20, Sect. 4], the last several vectors of $\mathbf{B}^*$ for q-ary lattices are typically very short). Then we evaluate the output quality of the LLL and BKZ algorithms for q-ary lattices by experiments (note that we cannot apply Gama-Nguyen's experimental data [14] for random lattices to q-ary lattices Λ).

Notation. The symbols $\mathbb{Z}$, $\mathbb{Q}$, and $\mathbb{R}$ denote the ring of integers, the field of rational numbers, and the field of real numbers, respectively. For an odd prime number q, we denote by $\mathbb{Z}_q$ a set of representatives of integers modulo q in the interval $(-q/2, q/2)$, that is, $\mathbb{Z}_q = \mathbb{Z} \cap (-q/2, q/2)$. Let $[z]_q \in \mathbb{Z}_q$ denote the reduction of an integer z by modulo q. For two vectors $\mathbf{a} = (a_1, \ldots, a_n)^T$ and $\mathbf{b} = (b_1, \ldots, b_n)^T \in \mathbb{R}^n$, we let $\langle \mathbf{a}, \mathbf{b} \rangle = \sum_{i=1}^n a_i b_i$ denote the inner product between $\mathbf{a}$ and $\mathbf{b}$ (in this paper, we always represent vectors as column vectors). We also let $\|\mathbf{a}\|$ denote the Euclidean norm of $\mathbf{a} \in \mathbb{R}^n$ defined by $\|\mathbf{a}\|^2 = \sum_{i=1}^n a_i^2$.

2 Preliminaries

In this section, we briefly review lattices, lattice reduction, and approximate CVP methods, which are needed in our discussions.

2.1 Lattices

Given two positive integers m and n, let $\mathbf{B} \in \mathbb{R}^{m \times n}$ be a matrix and $\mathbf{b}_i \in \mathbb{R}^m$ denote its i-th column vector for $1 \le i \le n$ (that is, $\mathbf{B} = [\mathbf{b}_1, \ldots, \mathbf{b}_n]$). Denote by

$$\mathcal{L}(\mathbf{B}) = \left\{ \sum_{i=1}^n x_i \mathbf{b}_i : x_i \in \mathbb{Z} \text{ for } 1 \le i \le n \right\}$$

the set of all integral linear combinations of the $\mathbf{b}_i$'s. The set $\mathcal{L}(\mathbf{B})$ is a subgroup of $\mathbb{R}^m$. The subgroup $\mathcal{L}(\mathbf{B})$ is called a *lattice of dimension n* if all $\mathbf{b}_i$'s are linearly independent over $\mathbb{R}$. In this case, the matrix $\mathbf{B}$ is called a *basis* of the lattice. In particular, the lattice $\mathcal{L}(\mathbf{B})$ is said to be of *full-rank* when $m = n$. Every lattice has infinitely many lattice bases; If $\mathbf{B}_1$ and $\mathbf{B}_2$ are two bases, then there exists a unimodular matrix $\mathbf{T} \in \mathrm{GL}_n(\mathbb{Z})$ satisfying $\mathbf{B}_1 = \mathbf{B}_2 \times \mathbf{T}$. Since $\det(\mathbf{T}) = \pm 1$, the value $\sqrt{\det(\mathbf{B}^T \cdot \mathbf{B})}$ is invariant for any basis $\mathbf{B}$, denoted by $\det(L)$. Note $\det(L) = |\det(\mathbf{B})|$ for any basis $\mathbf{B}$ when $m = n$. Given a basis $\mathbf{B}$, we let

$$\mathcal{P}(\mathbf{B}) = \left\{ \sum_{i=1}^{n} x_i \mathbf{b}_i : -\frac{1}{2} < x_i \le \frac{1}{2} \text{ for } 1 \le i \le n \right\}$$

denote its associated half-open parallelepiped. The volume of $\mathcal{P}(\mathbf{B})$ is precisely equal to $\det(L)$.

The Gram-Schmidt orthogonalization of a basis $\mathbf{B} = [\mathbf{b}_1, \ldots, \mathbf{b}_n]$ is the orthogonal family $[\mathbf{b}_1^*, \ldots, \mathbf{b}_n^*]$, recursively defined by

$$\mathbf{b}_i^* = \mathbf{b}_i - \sum_{j=1}^{i-1} \mu_{i,j} \mathbf{b}_j^*, \text{ where } \mu_{i,j} = \frac{\langle \mathbf{b}_i, \mathbf{b}_j^* \rangle}{\|\mathbf{b}_j^*\|^2} \text{ for } 1 \le j < i \le n.$$

Let $\mathbf{B}^* = [\mathbf{b}_1^*, \ldots, \mathbf{b}_n^*] \in \mathbb{R}^{m \times n}$ and $\mathbf{U} = (\mu_{i,j})_{1 \le i,j \le n} \in \mathbb{R}^{n \times n}$, where we set $\mu_{i,i} = 1$ for all i and $\mu_{i,j} = 0$ for $j > i$. Then $\mathbf{B} = \mathbf{B}^* \times \mathbf{U}^T$ and

$$\mathrm{vol}(L) = \prod_{i=1}^{n} \|\mathbf{b}_i^*\|.$$

2.2 Lattice Reduction, Root Hermite Factor, and GSA

Given a basis of a lattice L of dimension n, lattice reduction outputs a basis $\mathbf{B} = [\mathbf{b}_1, \ldots, \mathbf{b}_n]$ of L with short and nearly orthogonal column vectors $\mathbf{b}_1, \ldots, \mathbf{b}_n$. Lattice reduction gives a powerful tool to break lattice-based cryptosystems. The *root Hermite factor* δ of a lattice reduction algorithm is defined by

$$\delta = \|\mathbf{b}_1\| / \det(L)^{1/n}$$

with the output basis $[\mathbf{b}_1, \ldots, \mathbf{b}_n]$ (we assume $\|\mathbf{b}_1\| \le \|\mathbf{b}_i\|$ for all $2 \le i \le n$). This factor gives an index to measure the output quality of a lattice reduction algorithm. In particular, the output quality becomes better as δ is smaller. In the following, we introduce two practical lattice reduction algorithms:

- LLL is a polynomial-time algorithm [18]. Gama-Nguyen's experimental results [14, Fig. 4] show that the root Hermite factor of LLL for random lattices is practically 1.0219^n on average in high dimension $n \ge 100$.
- BKZ is a blockwise generalization of LLL with subexponential complexity [31]. At present, no good upper bound on the complexity is known. BKZ uses a blockwise parameter β, and larger β improves the output quality but increases the running time. In practice, $\beta \approx 20$ can achieve the best time/quality compromise. It follows from [14, Sect. 5.2] that the root Hermite factor with $\beta = 20$ for random lattices is practically 1.0128^n on average.

Geometric Series Assumption (GSA). Except when a lattice has a special structure, practical reduction algorithms output a basis $\mathbf{B} = [\mathbf{b}_1, \ldots, \mathbf{b}_n]$ such that

$$\frac{\|\mathbf{b}_i^*\|}{\|\mathbf{b}_{i+1}^*\|} \approx q \text{ for any } 1 \leq i \leq n-1,$$

that is, $\|\mathbf{b}_i^*\| \approx q^{1-i}\|\mathbf{b}_1\|$ for $1 \leq i \leq n$, where the constant q depends on algorithms (this assumption was introduced by Schnorr [30]). Under GSA, the values $\log_2(\|\mathbf{b}_1\|/\|\mathbf{b}_i^*\|)$'s are on a straight line (e.g. see [30, Figure 1]). According to [18], we have $q \approx 1.02^2 \approx 1.04$ (resp. $q \approx 1.025$) in practice for LLL (resp. BKZ with $\beta = 20$) for random lattices.

2.3   Approximate CVP Methods

Here we introduce typical approximate CVP methods. Let $\mathbf{B} = [\mathbf{b}_1, \ldots, \mathbf{b}_n] \in \mathbb{R}^{n \times n}$ be a basis of a full-rank lattice L of dimension n, and let $\mathbf{t} \in \mathbb{R}^n$ be a target vector. Let $\mathbf{w} \in L$ be the closest lattice vector to $\mathbf{t}$, and $\mathbf{e} = \mathbf{t} - \mathbf{w}$ the error vector.

– Babai's rounding method [5] is a polynomial-time algorithm, which outputs the unique lattice vector $\mathbf{v} \in L$ such that $\mathbf{t} - \mathbf{v}$ is inside the parallelepiped $\mathbf{P}(\mathbf{B})$. The output vector $\mathbf{v}$ is the closest lattice vector $\mathbf{w}$ if and only if $\mathbf{e} \in \mathcal{P}(\mathbf{B})$.
– Babai's nearest plane method is also a polynomial-time algorithm. It outputs the unique lattice vector $\mathbf{v} \in L$ such that $\mathbf{t} - \mathbf{v}$ is inside the parallelepiped $\mathcal{P}(\mathbf{B}^*)$. Then the output vector $\mathbf{v}$ is the closest lattice vector $\mathbf{w}$ if and only if $\mathbf{e} \in \mathcal{P}(\mathbf{B}^*)$. In a typical reduced basis, the output vector of Babai's nearest plane method is closer to $\mathbf{t}$ than the rounding method (but the rounding method is much faster).

3   Search-LWE Problem and Key Recovery Attack

In this section, we first give the formal definition of the search-LWE problem and review the key recovery attack against the search-LWE problem. Let us first present the definition of the search-LWE problem as follows (see also [27]):

Definition 1 (search-LWE). *Let n be a security parameter, q a prime modulus parameter with $r = \lfloor \log_2(q) \rfloor$, and χ an error distribution over $\mathbb{Z}_q$. Let $\mathbf{s} \in \mathbb{Z}_q^n$ denote a fixed secret vector with each entry chosen uniformly at random. Given d LWE samples of the form*

$$\left(\mathbf{a}_i, [\langle \mathbf{a}_i, \mathbf{s}\rangle + e_i]_q\right) \in \mathbb{Z}_q^n \times \mathbb{Z}_q \text{ for } 0 \leq i \leq d-1, \tag{1}$$

where the $\mathbf{a}_i$'s are uniformly chosen at random from $\mathbb{Z}_q^n$ and the e_i's are sampled from χ for all $0 \leq i \leq d-1$. Then the search-LWE problem, denoted "search-LWE$_{n,r,d,\chi}$", is to recover $\mathbf{s}$ from the LWE samples (1).

In practice, the error distribution χ is taken as the discrete Gaussian distribution $D_{\mathbb{Z},\sigma}$ with standard deviation $\sigma > 0$. In this case, we write the search-LWE problem as "search-LWE$_{n,r,d,\sigma}$".

Assumption 1 (Definition 6 of [17]). *In the search-LWE problem with samples* (1), *we assume*

$$[\langle \mathbf{a}_i, \mathbf{s} \rangle + e_i]_q = \langle \mathbf{a}_i, \mathbf{s} \rangle_q + e_i \text{ for } 0 \leq i \leq d - 1. \tag{2}$$

Note that Assumption 1 is required for correct decryption in a number of LWE-based schemes such as [8,10,11]. Under Assumption 1, Laine and Lauter [17] analyzed the key recovery attack against the search-LWE problem.

3.1   Key Recovery Attack Against LWE

In this subsection, we give an outline of the key recovery attack against search-LWE$_{n,r,d,\chi}$ (see [17, Sect. 4] or [13, Example 19.7.6] for the attack). The procedures of the attack can be divided into the following four steps (see [17, Sect. 4] for details): Note that $d > n$ is required for the attack.

Step 1. Given d LWE samples (1) satisfying the condition (2), we first construct an $(n + d) \times d$-matrix

$$\mathbf{C} = \begin{pmatrix} qI_{d \times d} \\ \mathbf{A} \end{pmatrix} \text{ with } \mathbf{A} = [\mathbf{a}_0, \mathbf{a}_1, \dots, \mathbf{a}_{d-1}] \in \mathbb{Z}_q^{n \times d}, \tag{3}$$

where $I_{d \times d}$ is the $d \times d$-identity matrix and we write the d column vectors $\mathbf{a}_i$ for $0 \leq i \leq d - 1$ as columns of the $n \times d$-matrix $\mathbf{A}$.

Step 2. Let $\mathbf{A}_q$ denote the $d \times d$ row-Hermite normal form of the matrix $\mathbf{C}$. Let Λ denote the lattice generated by the rows of $\mathbf{A}_q$, that is, $\Lambda = \mathcal{L}(\mathbf{A}_q^T)$. In other words, Λ is a d-dimensional lattice with basis $\mathbf{A}_q^T$.

Step 3. We then reduce $\mathbf{A}_q$ by lattice reduction (e.g. LLL or BKZ algorithm) to obtain a reduced basis $\mathbf{B}$ of the lattice Λ.

Step 4. Let $\mathbf{u} = (u_0, u_1, \dots, u_{d-1})^T \in \mathbb{Z}_q^d$ with $u_i = [\langle \mathbf{a}_i, \mathbf{s} \rangle + e_i]_q$ for $0 \leq i \leq d-1$. We solve CVP over Λ with instance $(\mathbf{B}, \mathbf{u})$ by adopting a practical CVP-method (e.g. Babai's nearest plane or rounding method). Then the CVP-method with input $(\mathbf{B}, \mathbf{u})$ may output the lattice vector

$$\mathbf{v} = (\langle \mathbf{a}_0, \mathbf{s} \rangle_q, \langle \mathbf{a}_1, \mathbf{s} \rangle_q, \dots, \langle \mathbf{a}_{d-1}, \mathbf{s} \rangle_q)^T \in \Lambda \tag{4}$$

if $\mathbf{B}$ is sufficiently reduced and $\mathbf{u}$ is sufficiently close to $\mathbf{v}$. Once we obtain $\mathbf{v} \in \Lambda$, we can easily recover the secret vector $\mathbf{s} \in \mathbb{Z}_q^n$ from $(\mathbf{A}, \mathbf{v})$.

Here we describe why the above steps can solve search-LWE$_{n,r,d,\chi}$. For each $0 \leq i \leq d - 1$, there exists an integer k_i satisfying $\langle \mathbf{a}_i, \mathbf{s} \rangle_q = \langle \mathbf{a}_i, \mathbf{s} \rangle + qk_i$. Set $\mathbf{w} = (k_0, \dots, k_{d-1}, s_0, \dots, s_{n-1})^T \in \mathbb{Z}^{n+d}$, where write $\mathbf{s} = (s_0, \dots, s_{n-1})^T \in \mathbb{Z}_q^n$ as the secret vector. Since the vector $\mathbf{v}$ defined by (4) is rewritten as $\mathbf{C}^T \cdot \mathbf{w}$, the vector $\mathbf{v}$ is contained in Λ. Moreover, the difference between $\mathbf{u}$ and $\mathbf{v}$ is given by

$$\mathbf{e} = \mathbf{u} - \mathbf{v} = (e_0, e_1, \dots, e_{d-1})^T \in \mathbb{Z}^d \tag{5}$$

under Assumption 1. Recall that each entry e_i is sampled from the error distribution χ, and hence it is considerably small compared to the modulus parameter q in practice. When the norm size of the noise vector $\mathbf{e} \in \mathbb{Z}^d$ is considerably small (that is, when the vector $\mathbf{v}$ is the closest lattice vector to $\mathbf{u}$), we may obtain $\mathbf{v}$ by a CVP-method with input $(\mathbf{B}, \mathbf{u})$ if the basis $\mathbf{B}$ is sufficiently reduced.

3.2   Analysis of [17] on Success Probability of Key Recovery Attack

Laine and Lauter [17] analyzed the success probability of the key recover attack for search-LWE$_{n,r,d,\sigma}$ when the LLL algorithm and Babai's nearest plane method are adopted. In this subsection, we briefly describe their analysis on the success probability of the attack. We begin to recall the following well-known result by Babai [5] (see also [13, Theorem 18.1.6] or [17, Theorem 2]):

Theorem 1 (LLL-Babai). *For an LLL-reduced basis of a lattice L of dimension N, Babai's nearest plane method on $\mathbf{z} \in \mathbb{R}^N$ (with $\mathbf{z} \notin L$) outputs $\mathbf{x} \in L$ such that*

$$\|\mathbf{z} - \mathbf{x}\| < 2^{\mu N} \cdot \|\mathbf{z} - \mathbf{y}\|$$

for all $\mathbf{y} \in L$ and some constant $\mu > 0$. In particular, when we take $\alpha = 3/4$ as the LLL reduction parameter, a value of the effective approximate factor $\mu = 1/2$ is guaranteed in theory. However, significantly smaller μ is expected in practice for any fixed $1/4 < \alpha < 1$.

As in Theorem 1, let μ denote the effective approximate factor when we apply the LLL-Babai algorithm to $(\mathbf{B}, \mathbf{u})$ in the key recovery attack. The analysis in [17, Sect. 4] shows that we can expect to need

$$\log_2(1 - p) + r(d - n) > d \log_2 \left[2 \left(1 + 2^{\mu d} \right) \sigma \sqrt{d} + 1 \right]$$

in order to succeed to solve search-LWE$_{n,r,d,\sigma}$ with probability at least p (see the Eq. (24) in [17]). Furthermore, Laine and Lauter estimate that we expect to have $\mu \leq \mu_{\mathrm{LLL}}$ if the attack for search-LWE$_{n,r,d,\sigma}$ is succeeded, where set

$$\mu_{\mathrm{LLL}} \approx \frac{1}{d} \log_2 \left(\frac{1}{2\sqrt{d}} \cdot \frac{q}{\sigma} \cdot \frac{1}{q^{n/d}} \right).$$

With this estimate, Laine and Lauter measured the effective performance of LLL-Babai by their exhaustive experiments for the search-LWE problem with various LWE instances (n, r, d, σ) (see [17, Table 1] for their experimental results).

4   Our Analysis of Key Recovery Attack

In this section, we give a heuristic but practical analysis of the key recovery attack against search-LWE$_{n,r,d,\sigma}$. While Laine-Lauter's analysis is used to measure the effectiveness of the LLL-Babai algorithm (in particular, the effective approximate factor μ of LLL-Babai can be evaluated by their analysis), our analysis is useful to estimate which instances of search-LWE$_{n,r,d,\sigma}$ can be solved by the key recovery attack with practical lattice reduction and Babai's nearest plane method. In this section, we focus on the key recovery attack with the LLL algorithm and the BKZ algorithm with blocksize $\beta = 20$.

4.1 Our Heuristic Analysis

Let $\mathbf{B} = [\mathbf{b}_1, \ldots, \mathbf{b}_d]$ denote a reduced basis of the lattice Λ of dimension d, obtained in Step 3 of the key recovery attack (recall that we represent vectors as row vectors). We let $\mathbf{B}^* = [\mathbf{b}_1^*, \ldots, \mathbf{b}_d^*]$ denote its Gram-Schmidt orthogonalization (see Subsect. 2.1 for the orthogonalization). Recall that for a target vector $\mathbf{t}$, Babai's nearest plane method on the pair $(\mathbf{B}, \mathbf{t})$ outputs the unique lattice vector $\mathbf{z} \in \Lambda$ such that $\mathbf{t} - \mathbf{z}$ is included in the parallelepiped

$$\mathcal{P}(\mathbf{B}^*) = \left\{ \sum_{i=1}^{d} x_i \mathbf{b}_i^* : -\frac{1}{2} < x_i \leq \frac{1}{2} \text{ for } 1 \leq i \leq d \right\}.$$

Let $\mathbf{e} = \mathbf{u} - \mathbf{v} = (e_0, \ldots, e_{d-1})^T \in \mathbb{Z}^d$ denote the noise vector given by (5). As in [17], we assume that each entry e_i is sampled by the discrete Gaussian distribution $\chi = D_{\mathbb{Z}, \sigma}$. We write $\mathbf{e} = \sum_{i=1}^{d} x_i \mathbf{b}_i^*$ with $x_i \in \mathbb{R}$ for $1 \leq i \leq d$. Then the key recovery attack by Babai's nearest plane method on the instance $(\mathbf{B}, \mathbf{u})$ is succeeded if and only if the noise vector $\mathbf{e}$ is contained in the parallelepiped $\mathcal{P}(\mathbf{B}^*)$ (recall that the attack is succeeded when the vector $\mathbf{v}$ defined by (4) is recovered by Babai's nearest plane method). In other words, the attack is succeeded if and only if $-\frac{1}{2} < x_i \leq \frac{1}{2}$ for all $1 \leq i \leq d$. Since $\langle \mathbf{e}, \mathbf{b}_i^* \rangle = x_i \cdot \|\mathbf{b}_i^*\|^2$ for $1 \leq i \leq d$, we have

$$|x_i| < \frac{1}{2} \iff \frac{|\langle \mathbf{e}, \mathbf{b}_i^* \rangle|}{\|\mathbf{b}_i^*\|^2} < \frac{1}{2}.$$

Moreover, we heuristically have

$$\frac{|\langle \mathbf{e}, \mathbf{b}_i^* \rangle|}{\|\mathbf{b}_i^*\|^2} \approx \frac{\|\mathbf{e}\| \cdot \|\mathbf{b}_i^*\|}{\sqrt{d} \cdot \|\mathbf{b}_i^*\|^2} = \frac{\|\mathbf{e}\|}{\sqrt{d} \cdot \|\mathbf{b}_i^*\|}.$$

We can also estimate $\|\mathbf{e}\| \approx \sigma\sqrt{d}$ since each entry e_i is sampled by the distribution $\chi = D_{\mathbb{Z}, \sigma}$. Then we can estimate that the key recovery attack by Babai's nearest plane method is succeeded if and only if

$$2\sigma < \|\mathbf{b}_i^*\| \text{ for all } 1 \leq i \leq d \iff 2\sigma < \min_{1 \leq i \leq d} \|\mathbf{b}_i^*\|. \tag{6}$$

Then it is the most important in our analysis to precisely evaluate the size of $\min_{1 \leq i \leq d} \|\mathbf{b}_i^*\|$, which depends on lattice reduction.

4.2 Experimental Estimation for $\min \|\mathbf{b}_i^*\|$

If the basis $\mathbf{B} = [\mathbf{b}_1, \ldots, \mathbf{b}_d]$ were obtained by the LLL algorithm or the BKZ algorithm with $\beta = 20$ for a basis of a *random lattice* L, we could estimate from Gama-Nguyen's experimental results [14] for random lattices that in the LLL case, we have

$$\|\mathbf{b}_d^*\| \approx (1.04)^{-(d-1)} \cdot \|\mathbf{b}_1\| \text{ and } \|\mathbf{b}_1\| \approx (1.0219)^d \cdot \mathrm{vol}(L)^{1/d}, \tag{7}$$

or in the case of BKZ with $\beta = 20$, we have

$$\|\mathbf{b}_d^*\| \approx (1.025)^{-(d-1)} \cdot \|\mathbf{b}_1\| \text{ and } \|\mathbf{b}_1\| \approx (1.0128)^d \cdot \text{vol}(L)^{1/d} \tag{8}$$

on average for large $d \geq 100$ (see also Subsect. 2.2 for details). Then we might estimate $\min_{1 \leq i \leq d} \|\mathbf{b}_i^*\| \approx \|\mathbf{b}_d^*\|$ for the random lattice L. However, in the key recovery attack against the search-LWE problem, we need to handle the special lattice Λ defined in Step 2 of the attack. Specifically, the lattice Λ can be rewritten as so-called the *q-ary lattice*

$$\left\{ \mathbf{y} \in \mathbb{Z}^d : \mathbf{y} \equiv \mathbf{A}^T \mathbf{z} \pmod{q} \text{ for some } \mathbf{z} \in \mathbb{Z}^n \right\},$$

where the matrix $\mathbf{A} \in \mathbb{Z}_q^{n \times d}$ is given by (3) in Step 1 of the key recovery attack. Therefore we cannot apply Gama-Nguyen's results to the q-ary lattice Λ. In the following, we give experimental results of LLL and BKZ with $\beta = 20$ for q-ary lattices in order to estimate the size of $\min_{1 \leq i \leq d} \|\mathbf{b}_i^*\|$.

LLL for q-ary Lattices. Here we give experimental results for an LLL-reduced basis $\mathbf{B}$ of the q-ary lattice Λ. Recall that the q-ary lattice Λ has volume $\text{vol}(\Lambda) \approx q^{d-n}$ with overwhelming high probability (e.g. see [20]). Then we set

$$c_{\text{LLL}} = \left(\frac{\min_{1 \leq i \leq d} \|\mathbf{b}_i^*\|}{q^{(d-n)/d}} \right)^{1/d} \tag{9}$$

for the lattice Λ. In other words, we have

$$\min_{1 \leq i \leq d} \|\mathbf{b}_i^*\| = c_{\text{LLL}}^d \cdot q^{(d-n)/d} \approx c_{\text{LLL}}^d \cdot \text{vol}(\Lambda)^{1/d} \tag{10}$$

(cf. by the Eq. (7), we may expect $c_{\text{LLL}} \approx \frac{1.0219}{1.04} \approx 0.982596$ on average for a random lattice). In Figs. 2, 3 and 4, we give experimental results on c_{LLL} for the q-ary lattice Λ. Specifically, in each of Figs. 2, 3 and 4, we show histogram of c_{LLL} for the q-ary lattice Λ with $r = \lfloor \log_2(q) \rfloor = 15, 30$ and 50. For our experiments, we conducted the following procedures for each LWE instance:

1. Given an LWE instance (n, r, d, σ) of the search-LWE problem, we generate d LWE samples (1) satisfying the condition (2).
2. We next construct the $(n + d) \times d$-matrix $\mathbf{C}$ as in (3), and compute its $d \times d$ row-Hermite normal form to obtain $\mathbf{A}_q \in \mathbb{Z}^{d \times d}$ for the q-ary lattice Λ as in Step 2 (that is, $\Lambda = \mathcal{L}(\mathbf{A}_q^T)$).
3. As in Step 3, we reduce $\mathbf{A}_q^T$ by the LLL algorithm to obtain an LLL-reduced basis $\mathbf{B}$ for Λ, and compute its Gram-Schmidt orthogonalization $\mathbf{B}^* = [\mathbf{b}_1^*, \ldots, \mathbf{b}_d^*]$. We compute the value c_{LLL} for the basis $\mathbf{B}$ of Λ.

Implementation and LWE Instances. We implemented the above procedures using Sage [29] (version 6.8). In particular, we used the function "LWE" in Sage for generating LWE samples, and "FP_LLL" for the LLL algorithm with reduction parameter $\alpha = 0.99$ (FP_LLL is the floating point implementation of LLL in the fpLLL library, which is also included in Sage). In our experiments, for LWE instances, we took

$$(n, r, d, \sigma) = \begin{cases} (80, 15, 255, 8/\sqrt{2\pi}), & (100, 15, 300, 8/\sqrt{2\pi}), \\ (80, 30, 255, 8/\sqrt{2\pi}), & (100, 30, 300, 8/\sqrt{2\pi}), \\ (80, 50, 255, 8/\sqrt{2\pi}), & (100, 50, 300, 8/\sqrt{2\pi}). \end{cases} \tag{11}$$

The triples (n, d, σ) of the above LWE instances were used in Laine and Lauter's experiments [17] (see [17, Table 1] for details). For each LWE instance (n, r, d, σ), we calculated the value c_{LLL} 100 times by generating different LWE samples.

Constant for c_{LLL}. Here we shall fix a value of c_{LLL} for the q-ary lattice Λ from our experimental results. Note that c_{LLL} is independent of the parameter σ by the definition (9), namely, c_{LLL} depends on the parameters (n, r, d). W see from Figs. 2, 3 and 4 that c_{LLL} does not depend on n and d, and it depends mainly on $r = \lfloor \log_2(q) \rfloor$. Since Fig. 3 resembles Fig. 4, we estimate that histograms of c_{LLL} are almost the same for all $r \geq 30$. Here we fix

$$c_{LLL} = 0.9775 \tag{12}$$

for any q-ary lattice Λ with $r \geq 15$. This constant is the minimum value in our experimental results (from the left-side of Fig. 4, we see that the minimum value of c_{LLL} is 0.977516). We expect that the minimum value would give a boundary between the success and the failure of the key recovery attack.

BKZ with $\beta = 20$ for q-ary Lattices. Here we give experimental results for a basis **B** reduced by BKZ with $\beta = 20$ of the q-ary lattice Λ. As in the LLL case, we can define c_{BKZ20} by (9). In Figs. 5, 6 and 7, we show histogram of c_{BKZ20} for Λ with $r = \lfloor \log_2(q) \rfloor = 15, 30$ and 50. For our experiments, we took the same LWE instances (11). As in the LLL case, we calculated c_{BKZ20} 100 times for each LWE instance. In our implementation, we used the NTL-implementation BKZ function in Sage, which adapts *full* enumeration as a subroutine for SVP of dimension β (cf. BKZ 2.0 [12] uses *pruned* enumeration). Then we expect that this function could return the best output quality of the BKZ algorithm (cf. BKZ 2.0 is faster). From our experimental results, we fix

$$c_{BKZ20} = 0.9863 \tag{13}$$

for any q-ary lattice Λ (cf. by (8), we may expect $c_{BKZ20} \approx \frac{1.0128}{1.025} \approx 0.9881$ on average for random lattices). As in the LLL case, this constant is the minimum value in our experimental results (from the left-side of Fig. 7, the minimum value of c_{BKZ20} is 0.986257). We expect that the constant is a limit of the BKZ algorithm with $\beta = 20$. We also estimate that larger blocksizes β can make the constant closer to 1 (we run experiments by BKZ with $\beta = 50$, but it takes 1 or 2 months to collect experimental data).

Table 1. Comparison of values $\left(\frac{\min \|\mathbf{b}_i^*\|}{q^{(d-n)/d}}\right)^{1/d}$ for reduced bases $\mathbf{B} = [\mathbf{b}_1, \ldots, \mathbf{b}_d]$ of random lattices and q-ary lattices ($r = \lfloor \log_2(q) \rfloor$)

	LLL	BKZ with $\beta = 20$
random lattices	average: $\frac{1.0219}{1.04} \approx 0.9826$ [14]	average: $\frac{1.0128}{1.025} \approx 0.9881$ [14]
q-ary lattices	average: 0.9789 ($r \geq 30$)	average: 0.9868 ($r \geq 15$)
	minimum: $c_{LLL} = 0.9775$	minimum: $c_{BKZ20} = 0.9863$

Summary. In Table 1, we give a comparison of values $\left(\frac{\min \|\mathbf{b}_i^*\|}{q^{(d-n)/d}}\right)^{1/d}$ for reduced bases $\mathbf{B} = [\mathbf{b}_1, \ldots, \mathbf{b}_d]$ of random lattices and q-ary lattices (as mentioned in [20, Sect. 4], the last several Gram-Schmidt vectors of $\mathbf{B}$ of a q-ary lattice are typically very short).

4.3 Our Estimation and Comparison with Results in [17]

In this subsection, we give an estimation of the boundary between the success and the failure of the key recovery attack against search-LWE$_{n,r,d,\sigma}$. We also compare our estimation with experimental results by Laine and Lauter [17].

Our Estimation. By combining (6) and (10), we can estimate that the key recovery attack against search-LWE$_{n,r,d,\sigma}$ by the LLL algorithm and Babai's nearest plane method is succeeded if and only if (recall $r = \lfloor \log_2(q) \rfloor$ and $d > n$).

$$2\sigma < c_{LLL}^d \cdot q^{(d-n)/d} \iff \log_2(2\sigma) < d \log_2(c_{LLL}) + \frac{r(d-n)}{d}$$

$$\iff r > \left(\frac{d}{d-n}\right) \{\log_2(2\sigma) - d \log_2(c_{LLL})\}. \quad (14)$$

With our constant $c_{LLL} = 0.9775$ by (12), the inequality (14) gives a boundary to determine which LWE instances (n, r, d, σ) can be solved by the key recovery attack with the LLL algorithm and Babai's nearest plane method.

In using BKZ with $\beta = 20$ for the key recovery attack, we use the constant $c_{BKZ20} = 0.9863$ given by (13), instead of c_{LLL} (we expect that larger blocksize β can make the constant of the BKZ algorithm very closer to 1).

Comparison with Experimental Results by [17]. By their exhaustive experiments, Laine and Lauter demonstrated a successful range of LWE instances (n, r, d, σ) by the key recovery attack [17, Table 1]. In their experiments, they fixed $\sigma = 8/\sqrt{2\pi} \approx 3.192$, and used the floating point variant of the LLL algorithm (with reduction parameter $\alpha = 0.99$) in PARI/GP [24].

- For $(n, d) = (200, 500)$, they showed that $r \geq 32$ can be solved (cf. the attack failed for $(n, r, d) = (200, 31, 505)$). In contrast, for such (n, d), our estimation (14) for LLL implies that $r > 31.817$ can be solved.

– For $(n, d) = (350, 805)$, they showed that $r \geq 52$ can be solved (cf. the attack failed for $(n, r, d) = (350, 51, 810)$). In contrast, for such (n, d), our estimation (14) for LLL implies that $r > 51.491$ can be solved.

As in the above comparison, we can verify that our estimation (14) for LLL coincides with all experimental results [17, Table 1]. Therefore we expect that our estimation (14) could give a practical boundary between the success and the failure of the key recovery attack for any LWE instance (n, r, d, σ).

Optimal Number of Samples for Attack. For fixed n and σ, our estimation (14) enables us to obtain the optimal number of LWE samples to solve search-$\mathrm{LWE}_{n,r,d,\sigma}$ by the key recovery attack. In fact, the optimal number $d_{\mathrm{LLL}}^{\mathrm{opt}}$ in using the LLL algorithm is given by

$$d_{\mathrm{LLL}}^{\mathrm{opt}} = \left\lceil n + \sqrt{n^2 + n\left(\frac{c_1}{c_2}\right)} \right\rceil \in \mathbb{Z} \tag{15}$$

where $c_1 = \log_2(2\sigma)$ and $c_2 = -\log_2(c_{\mathrm{LLL}}) = -\log_2(0.9775) > 0$. Note that the optimal number $d_{\mathrm{LLL}}^{\mathrm{opt}}$ minimizes the right-hand side value of our estimation (14). For example, we have the following results on the value $d_{\mathrm{LLL}}^{\mathrm{opt}}$:

– For $(n, \sigma) = (200, 8/\sqrt{2\pi})$, we have $d_{\mathrm{LLL}}^{\mathrm{opt}} = 437$ by (15). For this $d_{\mathrm{LLL}}^{\mathrm{opt}}$, our estimation (14) shows that $r > 31.386$ can be solved by the key recovery attack with the LLL algorithm and Babai's nearest plane method.
– For $(n, \sigma) = (350, 8/\sqrt{2\pi})$, we have $d_{\mathrm{LLL}}^{\mathrm{opt}} = 739$ by (15). As in the above case, for this $d_{\mathrm{LLL}}^{\mathrm{opt}}$, our estimation (14) shows that $r > 51.173$ can be solved.

In using BKZ with $\beta = 20$ for the attack, we obtain the optimal number of samples $d_{\mathrm{BKZ20}}^{\mathrm{opt}}$ as (15) by using $c_{\mathrm{BKZ20}} = 0.9863$ given by (13).

Successful Range of Key Recovery Attack by Our Estimation. In Fig. 1, we show our estimation of the successful range of key recovery attack against search-$\mathrm{LWE}_{n,r,d,\sigma}$. Specifically, we show successful range (n, r) of the attack by LLL and BKZ with $\beta = 20$ with optimal sample number $d = d_{\mathrm{LLL}}^{\mathrm{opt}}$ and $d_{\mathrm{BKZ20}}^{\mathrm{opt}}$, respectively (we set $\sigma = 8/\sqrt{2\pi}$ as in [17]). Since we take the minimum output quality of lattice reduction algorithms for c_{LLL} and c_{BKZ20}, the lines in Fig. 1 give a boundary between success and failure of the attack. For example, in case of $n = 350$, we estimate from Fig. 1 that $r = \lfloor \log_2(q) \rfloor \geq 52$ is solvable by LLL and Babai's nearest plane method, but $r \leq 51$ is unsolvable. Moreover, we estimate that $r \geq 34$ is solvable by BKZ with $\beta = 20$ and Babai's nearest plane method, but $r \leq 33$ is unsolvable.

In Fig. 1, we also show Laine and Lauter's experimental data [17, Table 1] on a successful range of the attack using LLL. We see from Fig. 1 that our estimation for LLL coincides with their experimental data. We plot example parameters (n, r) of LWE-based encryption by Lindner and Peikert [20, Fig. 3] (including two parameters by [22]), in which $\sigma \approx 8$ is used (cf. we take $\sigma = 8/\sqrt{2\pi} \approx 3.192$ for our estimation, and our estimation lines in Fig. 1 move up slightly when we take $\sigma = 8$). In particular, Lindner and Peikert [20] estimate that $(n, r) = (256, 12)$ has the almost same security level as AES-128.

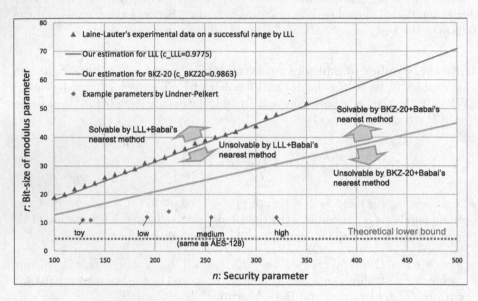

Fig. 1. Our estimation of the successful range (n, r) of the key recovery attack against search-LWE$_{n,d,r,\sigma}$ by LLL and BKZ with $\beta = 20$ ($d = d_{\text{LLL}}^{\text{opt}}$ and $d_{\text{BKZ20}}^{\text{opt}}$, $\sigma = 8/\sqrt{2\pi}$). The theoretical lower bound is given by (16)

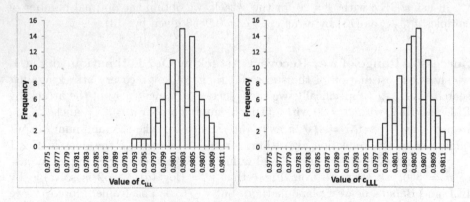

Fig. 2. Histogram of c_{LLL} for the q-ary lattice Λ with $r = \lfloor \log_2(q) \rfloor = 15$ (Left figure: $(n, r, d) = (80, 15, 255)$, average $= 0.981022$, minimum $= 0.979202$, Right figure: $(n, r, d) = (100, 15, 300)$, average $= 0.981115$, minimum $= 0.979587$)

Remark 1. For any reduced basis $\mathbf{B} = [\mathbf{b}_1, \ldots, \mathbf{b}_d]$ of a q-ary lattice Λ, we have

$$\text{vol}(\Lambda) = \prod_{i=1}^{d} \|\mathbf{b}_i^*\| \geq \left(\min_{1 \leq i \leq d} \|\mathbf{b}_i^*\| \right)^d.$$

Hence it follows that $\left(\frac{\min \|\mathbf{b}_i^*\|}{q^{(d-n)/d}} \right)^{1/d} \leq 1$ under the assumption $\text{vol}(\Lambda) = q^{d-n}$. By inequality (14), this gives a theoretical lower bound (note $d > n$)

$$r > \left(\frac{d}{d-n} \right) \cdot \log_2(2\sigma) > \log_2(2\sigma) \tag{16}$$

for the successful range (n, r) of the key recovery attack.

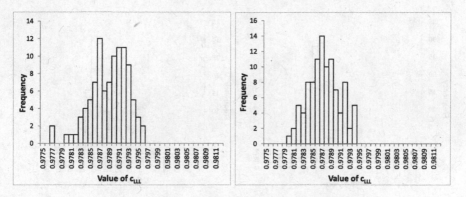

Fig. 3. Same as in Fig. 2, but $r = \lfloor \log_2(q) \rfloor = 30$ (Left figure: $(n, r, d) = (80, 30, 255)$, average $= 0.979594$, minimum $= 0.977674$, Right figure: $(n, r, d) = (100, 30, 300)$, average $= 0.978698$, minimum $= 0.977972$)

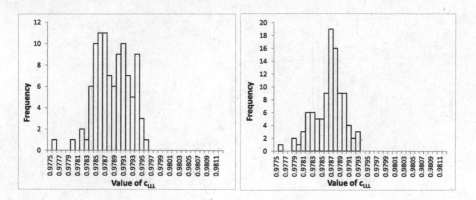

Fig. 4. Same as in Fig. 2, but $r = \lfloor \log_2(q) \rfloor = 50$ (Left figure: $(n, r, d) = (80, 50, 255)$, average $= 0.978815$, minimum $= 0.977516$, Right figure: $(n, r, d) = (100, 50, 300)$, average $= 0.978622$, minimum $= 0.977566$)

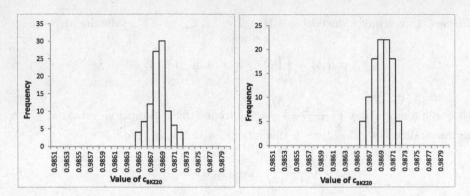

Fig. 5. Histogram of c_{BKZ20} for the q-ary lattice Λ with $r = \lfloor \log_2(q) \rfloor = 15$ (Left figure: $(n, r, d) = (80, 15, 255)$, average = 0.986792, minimum = 0.986414, Right figure: $(n, r, d) = (100, 15, 300)$, average = 0.986873, minimum = 0.986503)

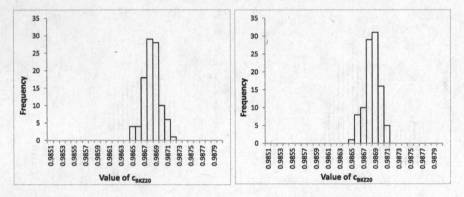

Fig. 6. Same as in Fig. 5, but $r = \lfloor \log_2(q) \rfloor = 30$ (Left figure: $(n, r, d) = (80, 30, 255)$, average = 0.986779, minimum = 0.986402, Right figure: $(n, r, d) = (100, 30, 300)$, average = 0.986798, minimum = 0.986425)

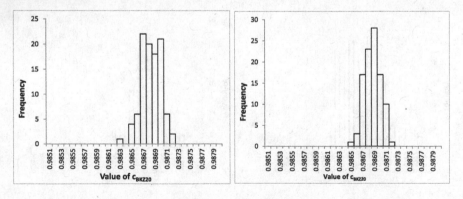

Fig. 7. Same as in Fig. 5, but $r = \lfloor \log_2(q) \rfloor = 50$ (Left figure: $(n, r, d) = (80, 50, 255)$, average = 0.986782, minimum = 0.986257, Right figure: $(n, r, d) = (100, 50, 300)$, average = 0.986824, minimum = 0.986493)

5   Conclusion and Future Work

We gave a heuristic but practical analysis of the key recovery attack against the search-LWE problem. By (14), we estimated successful range of (n, r, d, σ) of the attack by using LLL and BKZ with $\beta = 20$. Different from Laine and Lauter's analysis [19], our estimation (14) enables to determine whether a given LWE instance can be solved, or not. In Fig. 1, we also gave a boundary of (n, r) between success and failure of the attack with optimal d and fixed σ (note that our estimation for the attack with LLL coincides with Laine and Lauter's experimental results [17, Table 1] for $80 \leq n \leq 350$).

Our future work is to analyze the key recovery attack by the BKZ algorithm with larger blocksizes and other CVP methods (e.g. Lindner-Peikert's nearest plane method [20]). In fact, we are now running experiments by BKZ with $\beta = 50$ (but we do not have sufficient experimental data for analysis). In this paper, we focused on a successful range of LWE instances by the key recovery attack. In particular, we did not discuss the complexity of lattice reduction algorithms. In order to evaluate security level of LWE-based schemes, we would like to precisely estimate the complexity of the key recovery attack for the search-LWE problem.

Acknowledgements. This work was supported by CREST, JST. This work was also supported by JSPS KAKENHI Grant Number 16H02830.

References

1. Albrecht, M.A., Cid, C., Faugère, J.-C., Fitzpartrick, R., Perret, L.: On the complexity of the BKW algorithm on LWE. Des. Codes Crypt. **74**, 325–354 (2015)
2. Albrecht, M.A., Cid, C., Faugère, J.-C., Perret, L.: Algebraic algorithms for LWE. IACR ePrint 2014/1018
3. Arora, S., Ge, R.: New algorithms for learning in presence of errors. In: Aceto, L., Henzinger, M., Sgall, J. (eds.) ICALP 2011, Part I. LNCS, vol. 6755, pp. 403–415. Springer, Heidelberg (2011)
4. Albrecht, M.R., Player, R., Scott, S.: On the concrete hardness of learning with errors. J. Math. Cryptology **9**(3), 169–203 (2015)
5. Babai, L.: On Lovász' lattice reduction and the nearest lattice point problem. Combinatorica **6**(1), 1–13 (1986)
6. Blum, A., Kalai, A., Wasserman, H.: Noise-tolerant learning, the parity problem, and the statistical query model. J. ACM **50**(4), 506–519 (2003)
7. Boneh, D., Venkatesan, R.: Hardness of computing the most significant bits of secret keys in Diffie-Hellman and related schemes. In: Koblitz, N. (ed.) CRYPTO 1996. LNCS, vol. 1109, pp. 129–142. Springer, Heidelberg (1996)
8. Brakerski, Z., Gentry, C., Vaikuntanathan, V.: (Leveled) fully homomorphic encryption without bootstrapping. In: Innovations in Theoretical Computer Science-ITCS 2012, pp. 309–325, ACM (2012)
9. Brakerski, Z., Langlois, A., Peikert, C., Regev, O., Stehlé, D.: Classical hardness of learning with errors. In: Theory of Computing-STOC 2013, pp. 575–584, ACM (2013)

10. Brakerski, Z., Vaikuntanathan, V.: Fully homomorphic encryption from ring-LWE and security for key dependent messages. In: Rogaway, P. (ed.) CRYPTO 2011. LNCS, vol. 6841, pp. 505–524. Springer, Heidelberg (2011)

11. Brakerski, Z., Vaikuntanathan, V.: Efficient fully homomorphic encryption from (standard) LWE. In: Foundations of Computer Science-FOCS 2011, pp. 97–106, IEEE (2011)

12. Chen, Y., Nguyen, P.Q.: BKZ 2.0: better lattice security estimates. In: Lee, D.H., Wang, X. (eds.) ASIACRYPT 2011. LNCS, vol. 7073, pp. 1–20. Springer, Heidelberg (2011)

13. Galbraith, S.D.: Mathematics of Public Key Cryptography. Cambridge University Press, Cambridge (2012)

14. Gama, N., Nguyen, P.Q.: Predicting lattice reduction. In: Smart, N.P. (ed.) EURO-CRYPT 2008. LNCS, vol. 4965, pp. 31–51. Springer, Heidelberg (2008)

15. Gentry, C., Gorbunov, S., Halevi, S.: Graph-induced multilinear maps from lattices. In: Dodis, Y., Nielsen, J.B. (eds.) TCC 2015, Part II. LNCS, vol. 9015, pp. 498–527. Springer, Heidelberg (2015)

16. Kearns, M.J., Mansour, Y., Ron, D., Rubinfeld, R., Schapire, R.E., Sellie, L.: On the learnability of discrete distributions. In: Theory of Computing-STOC 1994, pp. 273–282, ACM (1994)

17. Laine, K., Lauter, K.: Key recovery for LWE in polynomial time. IACR ePrint 2015/176 (2015)

18. Lenstra, A.K., Lenstra, H.W., Lovász, L.: Factoring polynomials with rational coefficients. Math. Ann. **261**(4), 515–534 (1982)

19. Liu, M., Nguyen, P.Q.: Solving BDD by enumeration: an update. In: Dawson, E. (ed.) CT-RSA 2013. LNCS, vol. 7779, pp. 293–309. Springer, Heidelberg (2013)

20. Lindner, R., Peikert, C.: Better key sizes (and attacks) for LWE-based encryption. In: Kiayias, A. (ed.) CT-RSA 2011. LNCS, vol. 6558, pp. 319–339. Springer, Heidelberg (2011)

21. Micciancio, D., Peikert, C.: Trapdoors for lattices: simpler, tighter, faster, smaller. In: Pointcheval, D., Johansson, T. (eds.) EUROCRYPT 2012. LNCS, vol. 7237, pp. 700–718. Springer, Heidelberg (2012)

22. Micciancio, D., Regev, O.: Lattice-based cryptography. In: Bernstein, D.J., Buchmann, J., Dahmen, E. (eds.) Post Quantum Cryptography-PQCrypto 2009, pp. 147–191. Springer, Heidelberg (2009)

23. National Institute of Standards and Technology (NIST), Report on post-quantum cryptography. http://csrc.nist.gov/publications/drafts/nistir-8105/nistir_8105_draft.pdf

24. The PARI Group, PARI/GP. http://pari.math.u-bordeaux.fr/

25. Peikert, C.: Public-key cryptosystems from the worst-case shortest vector problem: extended abstract. In: Theory of Computing-STOC 2009, pp. 333–342, ACM (2009)

26. Peikert, C., Waters, B.: Lossy trapdoor functions and their applications. SIAM J. Comput. **40**(6), 1803–1844 (2011)

27. Regev, O.: On lattices, learning with errors, random linear codes, and cryptography. In: Theory of Computing-STOC 2005, pp. 84–93, ACM Press (2005)

28. Regev, O.: On lattices, learning with errors, random linear codes, and cryptography. J. ACM **56**(6), 34 (2009)

29. The Sage Group, SageMath: Open-Source Mathematical SoftwareSystem. http://www.sagemath.org/
30. Schnorr, C.P.: Lattice reduction by random sampling and birthday methods. In: Alt, H., Habib, M. (eds.) STACS 2003. LNCS, vol. 2607, pp. 145–156. Springer, Heidelberg (2003)
31. Schnorr, C.P., Euchner, M.: Lattice basis reduction: improved practical algorithms and solving subset sum problems. Math. Program. **66**, 181–199 (1994)

A Note on Fault Attacks Against Deterministic Signature Schemes (Short Paper)

Alessandro Barenghi and Gerardo Pelosi[(✉)]

Department of Electronics, Information and Bioengineering – DEIB,
Politecnico di Milano, Milano, Italy
{alessandro.barenghi,gerardo.pelosi}@polimi.it

Abstract. Providing sound and fault resilient signature schemes is of crucial importance for the realization of modern secure embedded systems. In this context, the use of standardized discrete logarithm signature primitives such as DSA and ECDSA has been proven frail with respect to failures in the RNG subsystem of a device, leading to the design of deterministic schemes. In this work we analyze the resistance of deterministic signature primitives to fault attacks. We devise an attack strategy relying on a relaxed fault model and show how to efficiently derive the secret key of the deterministic version of both DSA and ECDSA, employing a single correct-faulty signature pair, while we show that the EdDSA algorithm shows structural resistance against such attacks.

1 Introduction

Modern computing systems are increasingly relied upon to perform safety and security critical tasks, such as automotive and industrial control, home automation, and physical access control systems. Among the security requirements of these computing platforms, a crucial one is to be able to prove the authenticity of a given portion of data, or ensuring the authenticity of the issuer of a received command, before it is executed, a task which can be accomplished in a sound fashion by cryptographic signature schemes. While effective in their task, cryptographic signature primitives have proven to be challenging in their adaptation to resource-constrained embedded systems. In particular, a mandatory requirement to ensure the security of signatures is a sound Random Number Generator (RNG). A failure, or malfunctioning, in the RNG of an embedded device may have dire consequences from a security standpoint, as a result of random values with poor entropy being generated. One of the best known security points of failure in the standard discrete logarithm (DL) based signature schemes recommended by the US government in its FIPS 186-4 document, is due to a malfunctioning RNG. In fact, both Digital Signature Algorithm (DSA) and Elliptic Curve DSA (ECDSA) require fresh random values to be drawn each time a new signature is computed. Failure in doing so, and, in particular, reusing the same random value to sign two different messages allows to efficiently retrieve the private signature key from the value of the signatures. This well known frailty has caused multiple security accidents in practice, among which the disclosure of

© Springer International Publishing Switzerland 2016
K. Ogawa and K. Yoshioka (Eds.): IWSEC 2016, LNCS 9836, pp. 182–192, 2016.
DOI: 10.1007/978-3-319-44524-3_11

the binary code signature key from the Playstation 3 console binaries. The need to provide RNG-failure resilient algorithms to perform discrete logarithm based digital signatures has spurred the research community to devise proposals which do not require fresh randomness at each signature computation. To this end, two of the most successful approaches are: deterministic (EC)DSA, as described by Pornin in [9], and EdDSA, proposed by Bernstein et al. in [6]. Both schemes rely on the use of cryptographic hash functions to derive a unique, pseudorandom value for each signature from the message and the private key involved in its computation, although with different strategies. However, when considering an implementation for embedded devices, the attacker model should take into account also the security breaching techniques which can be enacted having physical access to the device. In particular, the so-called *Side-Channel* Attacks (SCAs) are able to extract the secret parameters involved in the computation of a cryptographic algorithm either exploiting the measurement of environmental parameters, such as the energy consumption or deriving its value from incorrect outputs, caused by artificially inserted faults [4]. The former techniques are named passive SCAs, while the latter are called active SCAs, or fault attacks. The randomized (EC)DSA primitive has shown good resistance to both passive and active SCAs: indeed, the fresh randomness drawn at each signature generation profitably enhances its resistance. However, no investigation of the resistance to either passive or active side-channel attacks has been made on deterministic (EC)DSA [9], while EdDSA [6] has been explicitly designed with some degree of resistance to passive SCA, but no investigations concerning its resistance against active attacks have been made. We propose two fault attacks, highlighting how the deterministic (EC)DSA is vulnerable to both, while the EdDSA scheme withstands them due to its inner structure.

2   Background

Fault attacks can be categorized in two large classes, depending on how they exploit the information coming from the induced abnormal behavior of the device [4]. Attacks exploiting the differences in the outputs of both a correct execution of the cryptographic primitive and an erroneous one are known as Differential Fault Analyses (DFAs) [1,5], while techniques exploiting the information coming from the device outputting the correct result even in presence of induced faults are known as safe-error attacks [4]. In this work we will be dealing with the former class of techniques, where the attacker is supposed to be able to alter one of the intermediate values in the computation according to a specific *fault model*. The fault model describes how the intermediate value is altered (bit flips, or stuck-at values), whether the alteration is permanent or not, and what is its entity and position. The viable techniques to achieve the controlled fault injection required to be compliant to a given fault model are derived from common natural fault causes in digital circuits. Altering either the supply voltage or the circuit clock are two of the most widely and more cost-effective techniques [4]. Such techniques cause setup time violations which may lead to mis-storages into the circuit registers, which are modeled as transient bit flips in an intermediate value of the computation. We will be considering two fault models:

Fault model 1: random corruption of a value. In this fault model, an intermediate value of the computation v is assumed to be replaced with an incorrect one $\widetilde{v}$, having the same bit size of v, and chosen at random. This fault model can be caused by any transient data-affecting fault during the computation of v. This corresponds to a fault when the computation of v takes place, without no care on which specific alteration is made, or if it has been caused by the alteration of either the data or control flow. As a consequence of the low precision required by the model, the fault can be injected via particularly cheap workbenches, e.g., simply overclocking the device [4].

Fault model 2: bit/byte flip. This fault model assumes to be able to alter an intermediate value of the computation so that the difference between the correct value v and the erroneous one $\widetilde{v}$ is either a single bit, or a single byte-wide pattern. Consequently, it is possible to describe the faulty value as $\widetilde{v} = v \pm 2^i \varepsilon$, where $0 \le i < \lceil \log_2(v) \rceil, \varepsilon = 1$ for a single bit fault, while $0 \le i < \lceil \log_2(v) \rceil - 8, 1 \le \varepsilon \le 255$ in case of a single-byte wide fault. Since this fault model is more stringent than fault model 1, it is possible to enumerate the differences between the correct and erroneous values. However, inducing such a fault can still be done via simple setup time violations caused by either inserting glitches in the clock or underfeeding the computing platform are known to cause compliant faults [2,3].

2.1 Discrete Logarithm Based Signature Schemes

El Gamal [7] was the first to propose a signature scheme based on the DL problem, which were improved by Schnorr in [12] employing a prime order subgroup. Both DSA and ECDSA specialize Schnorr's scheme stating sets of parameters and were the first schemes able to perform signatures considered legally binding by a government. The recommendations for configuring the DSA and ECDSA algorithms in the US FIPS 186-4 document provide a list of parameters for the use of one among several cyclic algebraic groups, chosen for optimal security and implementation efficiency. Each group $(G, \odot)$ has a fully specified structure, group generator $g \in G$, and prime group order $q = |G|$. Since the input message msg can be a binary string of arbitrary length, a cryptographic hash function H: $\{0,1\}^* \mapsto \mathbb{Z}_q$ is employed to map msg into a properly sized bitstring, which can be interpreted as an element of $\mathbb{Z}_q$. In particular, for the DSA scheme the selected group structure is given by a subgroup of the set of equivalence classes modulo a (large) prime number p, $(\mathbb{Z}_q, \cdot) \subseteq (\mathbb{Z}_p, \cdot)$. The public parameters p, q are recommended to be chosen as $0 < p < 2^L$ and $0 < q < 2^N$, with (L, N) in the following list: (1024, 160), (2048, 224), (2048, 256), and (3072, 256). For the ECDSA scheme, the standard reports the equations of 5 elliptic curves, each of which defined over 5 prime fields $\mathbb{F}_p$ with $\lceil \log_2(p) \rceil \in \{192, 224, 256, 384, 521\}$ bits. Five $\mathbb{F}_{2^m}$ fields with $m \in \{163, 233, 283, 409, 571\}$, are also specified together

---

Algorithm 1. ECDSA and DSA Signature Generation (FIPS 186-4)

Globals. cyclic group, $(\mathrm{G}, \odot)$ with prime order $q=|\mathrm{G}|$;
   a generator of the group, $g \in \mathrm{G}$ (i.e., $\langle g \rangle = (\mathrm{G}, \odot)$);
   a cryptographic hash function, $\mathrm{H} : \{0,1\}^* \mapsto \mathbb{Z}_q$.

ECDSA specific. given a standardized elliptic curve $\mathbb{E}$, the encoding function $f(\cdots)$ outputs an integer number starting from the x-coordinate of an elliptic curve point taken as input, $f(\cdots) \triangleq \mathrm{int}(\mathrm{x-coord}(\cdots))$.

DSA specific. Given a prime finite field $\mathbb{Z}_p$, the encoding function $f(\cdots)$ is the identity map and outputs an integer number greater than 0 and lesser than p, $f(\cdots) \triangleq \mathrm{id}(\cdots)$.

Input: message, msg; private key, $d \in (\mathbb{Z}_q \backslash \{0\}, \cdot)$
Output: signature token, (r, s) with $r, s \in (\mathbb{Z}_q \backslash \{0\}, \cdot)$

1 **begin**
2   **repeat**
3        $k \overset{rand}{\leftarrow} \{2, \ldots, q-1\}$ // $k \in \mathbb{Z}_q$
4        $r \leftarrow f(\mathrm{GROUPEXPONENTIATION}(g, k)) \bmod q$
5        $s \leftarrow (\mathrm{H}(\mathtt{msg}) + r \cdot d) \cdot k^{-1} \bmod q$
6   **until** $r \neq 0$ AND $s \neq 0$
7 **end**
8 **return** (r, s)

---

with the equations of an elliptic curve and a Koblitz curve for each one of them.

Each signature scheme is made of three algorithms: *key generation, signature generation* and *signature verification*. The *key generation* algorithm picks a set of public parameters containing the definition of the group G, its order q and a generator $g \in \mathrm{G}$. Subsequently, a cryptographically strong random integer $d \in \mathbb{Z}_q \backslash \{0\}$ is generated to act as private key, and the public key is computed raising the the generator of the group to the value chosen as the private key, i.e.: $y = \mathrm{GROUPEXPONENTIATION}(g, k)$. The *signature generation* algorithm (see Algorithm 1) takes as input the private key, a message msg, and produces a signature token (r, s), with $r, s \in \mathbb{Z}_q \backslash \{0\}$. The algorithm first draws a cryptographically strong random number $k \in \mathbb{Z}_q \backslash \{0\}$ (line **2**) that must be different in every run of the primitive. A reuse of the same random in multiple signatures allows an attacker to retrieve d solving a set of two simultaneous equations. Subsequently, the group exponentiation is performed and the first portion of the signature, r, is computed as the residue modulo q of either the group exponentiation outcome, for the DSA scheme, or the x-coordinate of the elliptic curve point resulting from the group exponentiation, for the ECDSA scheme (line **4**). Note that, when the elliptic curve is defined over a binary field, the interpretation of the x-coordinate as an integer is also standardized. The second part of the signature token, s, is computed through combining together the hash of the message msg, the value r and the random number k (line **5**). In case either $r = 0$ or $s = 0$ the procedure is re-run with a different k until an admissible signature is obtained.

Algorithm 2. EdDSA Signature generation [6,10]

Data: a prime number $p\equiv1 \bmod 4$; $b=1+\lceil\log_2(p-1)\rceil$, $\mathtt{bin}(\cdot)$: $\mathbb{F}_p\mapsto\{0,1\}^{b-1}$,
  i.e., $z\in\mathbb{F}_p$, $\mathtt{bin}(z)=\langle z_0,z_1,\ldots,z_{b-2}\rangle$ encoded lsb first
  An Edwards curve $\mathbb{E}(\mathbb{F}_p)$ and a cyclic group, $(\langle B\rangle,\odot)$ with generator
  $B\in\mathbb{E}(\mathbb{F}_p)$, and prime order $q=|\langle B\rangle|$, $q<2^b$;
  The binary encoding of a point is defined as: $\mathtt{binP}(\cdot,\cdot)$: $\mathbb{F}_p\times\mathbb{F}_p\mapsto\{0,1\}^b$,
  i.e., $(x,y)\in\langle B\rangle$, $\mathtt{binP}(x,y)=\langle y_0,y_1,\ldots,y_{b-2},x_0\rangle$.
  Hash function $\mathtt{H}:\{0,1\}^* \mapsto \{0,1\}^{2b}$

Input: input message $\mathtt{msg}$, b-bit private key $d\in\{0,1\}^b$, public key
   $A=(x_A,y_A)\in\mathbb{E}(\mathbb{F}_q)$

Output: Signature $\langle\mathtt{bin}(x_R,y_R),s\rangle$ for message $\mathtt{msg}$, where
   $(x_R,y_R)\in\mathbb{E}(\mathbb{F}_q),s\in\mathbb{Z}_q$

1 $\langle h_0,h_1,\ldots h_{2b-1}\rangle \leftarrow \mathtt{H}(d)$ `// encoded lsb first`

2 $a \leftarrow \mathtt{int}(\langle 0,0,0,h_3,h_4,\ldots,h_{b-3},1\rangle) \bmod q$

3 $k \leftarrow \mathtt{int}(\mathtt{H}(\langle h_b,h_{b+1},\ldots h_{2b-1}\rangle\|\mathtt{msg})) \bmod q$

4 $(x_R,y_R) \leftarrow [k]B$

5 $v \leftarrow \mathtt{int}(\mathtt{H}(\mathtt{bin}(x_R,y_R)\|\mathtt{bin}((x_A,y_A))\|\mathtt{msg})) \bmod q$

6 $s \leftarrow (k+a\cdot v) \bmod q$

7 **return** $\langle\mathtt{bin}(x_R,y_R),s\rangle$

2.2   Deterministic Discrete Logarithm Based Signature Schemes

In [8], M'Raihi *et al.* first described how to use hash functions to render Schnorr's
signatures deterministic, and proved that the deterministic signature schema
has at least the same mathematical security guarantees as the one employing
an actual RNG. The deterministic EC(DSA) currently employed in prominent
cryptographic software such as Gnu Privacy Guard (GPG) and ARM mbed TLS
library was proposed by Pornin in the RFC 6979 [9]. In the signature generation
algorithm, instead of picking a random integer $k \in \mathbb{Z}_q^*$ (see line **3** in Algorithm 1),
such a parameter is replaced by a value computed as the outcome of a deterministic pseudo-RNG which is fed with the hash of the input message and the private
key (either SHA-1 or SHA-2) as input [9]. Bernstein *et al.* in [6] proposed the
Edwards-curve Digital Signature Algorithm (EdDSA) as a scheme for speeding
up the generation and verification of elliptic curve based signatures, exploiting
the technique defined in [8] to avoid the requirement for fresh randomness at each
signature. The most relevant modification included in the EdDSA design with
respect to elliptic curve based DL signature schemes is the use of *twisted Edwards*
elliptic curves over a prime field rather than *Weierstrass* elliptic curves employed
in the ECDSA design. A twisted Edwards curve is defined as the set of coordi-
nate pairs over a prime field: $\mathbb{E}(\mathbb{F}_p) = \{(x,y) \in \mathbb{F}_p \times \mathbb{F}_p : -x^2 + y^2 = 1 + \delta x^2 y^2\}$,
where p is a prime number congruent to 1 modulo 4 (i.e., $p\equiv_4 1$) and $\delta \in \mathbb{F}_p$ is
not a square element of the field (i.e., $\left(\frac{\delta}{q}\right) = -1$). The public parameters of the
scheme include a value $b = 1 + \lceil\log_2(p-1)\rceil$ employed to map every element

$z \in \mathbb{F}_p$ into a binary string with $b - 1$ digits, i.e., $\text{bin}(z) = \langle z_0, z_1, \ldots, z_{b-2} \rangle$, where $z_i \in \{0, 1\}, 0 \leq i < b - 1$, and z_0 is assumed to be the least significant bit. Each point of the elliptic curve is encoded as a binary string with length b, exploiting the fact that if a pair of coordinates lie on the curve (i.e., $(x, y) \in \mathbb{E}(\mathbb{F}_p)$), then its x-coordinate can be represented as a single-bit value depending on the encoding convention adopted considering the sign of the following formula: $x = \pm\sqrt{(y^2 - 1)/(\delta y^2 + 1)}$. The set of points of an Edwards curve is endowed with the algebraic structure of a cyclic group by means of a complete internal composition law, i.e., a law characterized by having point addition and point doubling operations computed in the same fashion, as opposed to the common Weierstrass-curve addition law. This feature is remarkably welcome as it removes data-dependent branching in the computation of operation between curve points, effectively suppressing information which could leak on side-channels such as the power consumption. The public parameters of the signature scheme include the generator $\text{B} \in \mathbb{E}(\mathbb{F}_p)$ of a subgroup $\langle \text{B} \rangle$ of the curve points with prime order $q = |\langle \text{B} \rangle|$, having a binary encoding of length b. Finally, a cryptographic hash function, $\text{H} : \{0, 1\}^* \mapsto \{0, 1\}^{2b}$, yielding a $2b$-bit long digest is employed to expand the b-bit private key d onto a larger bit-sized value, and to derive deterministically the scalar coefficient of a scalar-point multiplication from a portion of $\text{H}(d)$ and the input message msg. The private key d is chosen as a random binary string including b bits, i.e., $d \in \{0, 1\}^b$, while the public key A is computed as the scalar-point multiplication, $\text{A} = [a]\text{B}$, of the generator of the group B multiplied by an integer value $0 < a < q$. In particular, the binary encoding of a is defined through selecting some of the bits of the hashed value of the secret key, $\text{H}(d) = \langle h_0, h_1, \ldots, h_{2b-1} \rangle$, converting them into an integer number and computing its residue modulo q: $a = \text{int}(\langle 0, 0, 0, h_3, h_4, \ldots, h_{b-3}, 1 \rangle) \bmod q$. The signature generation algorithm (see Algorithm 2) takes as input the private key, a message msg, and produces a signature token $\langle \text{bin}(x_\text{R}, y_\text{R}), s \rangle$, with $(x_\text{R}, y_\text{R}) \in \mathbb{E}(\mathbb{F}_q)$, and $s \in \mathbb{Z}_q$. The algorithm first computes the $2b$-bit digest of the secret key (line 1), then a value $a \in \mathbb{Z}_q$ is derived through selecting a a subset of the bits of the digest (line 2), while the input message is concatenated with a different subset of the bits of the digest, and hashed again before being converted in an integer value $k \in \mathbb{Z}_q$ (line 3), which is indeed the deterministically computed scalar acting as a coefficient for the group exponentiation, here reported as a scalar-point multiplication. Subsequently, a scalar-point multiplication with the value k and the generator of the subgroup of elliptic curve points is performed (line 4), yielding a point $(x_\text{R}, y_\text{R}) \in \mathbb{E}(\mathbb{F}_p)$. The compressed b-bit binary encoding of such a point, $\text{bin}(x_\text{R}, y_\text{R})$, is returned as the first part of the signature token. The second part of the signature token, $s \in \mathbb{Z}_q$, is computed in two steps: the first one, combines together the message msg, the binary encoding of the public key $\text{bin}(x_\text{A}, y_\text{A})$ and the value $\text{bin}(x_\text{R}, y_\text{R})$ through computing another $2b$-bit digest which is, in turn, converted into a value $v \in \mathbb{Z}_q$ (line 5). The second step, combines the values k, a and v through computing one modular multiplication and one modular addition (line 6): such a strategy saves the computation of a modular inverse, needed in (EC)DSA (line 5, Algorithm 1). A point worth noting is that the private key d is never used directly in the signature computation: instead, it is expanded by means of a cryptographic hash (line **1**, Algorithm 2). Exploiting this computation, EdDSA employs two separate values, obtained splitting the digest in half, to build the public key and generate the pseudorandom scalar for the scalar-point multiplication (line **3**, Algorithm 2). This in turn prevents an attacker from being able to derive the key material required to compute the value k for an arbitrary message, even assuming he knows the value a required for computing the public key.

3   Fault Attacks on Deterministic (EC)DSA

3.1   Random Value Change During Group Exponentiation

Considering the random value change model, we assume the attacker is able to introduce a random fault in the result of the group exponentiation in either deterministic (EC)DSA or EdDSA, i.e., he is able to corrupt the values of r and $\mathtt{bin}(x_R, y_R){=}\rho$, respectively (line **4**, in both Algorithms 1 and 2). We indicate with $\widetilde{r}$ and $\widetilde{\rho}$ the corresponding faulty values, and we assume that the attacker will have access to a correct and faulty signature coming from the same message $\mathtt{msg}$. The attacker will just need to induce a fault in a portion of the computation taking, time-wise, 90 % or more of the overall signature execution time, depending on the efficiency of the arithmetics of the chosen group. As a consequence, even a fault injection setup with extremely poor temporal and spatial accuracy, i.e., not able to inject a fault at a precise time instant or in a specific intermediate value of the group exponentiation computation, will suffice.

Deterministic (EC)DSA. The purpose of the attacker in this case is to recover the value of the secret key d, from the values of the correct signature (r, s) and the erroneous one $(\widetilde{r}, \widetilde{s})$. The attacker is able to build the following simultaneous equation set on $\mathbb{Z}_q^*$ in the unknowns d and k:

$$\begin{cases} s \equiv_q (\mathtt{H(msg)} + d \cdot r) \cdot k^{-1} \\ \widetilde{s} \equiv_q (\mathtt{H(msg)} + d \cdot \widetilde{r}) \cdot k^{-1} \end{cases} \text{ and solve it for } \begin{cases} d \equiv_q \frac{(s-\widetilde{s}) \cdot \mathtt{H(msg)}}{(r \cdot \widetilde{s} - \widetilde{r} \cdot s)} \\ k \equiv_q s^{-1} \cdot (\mathtt{H(msg)} \cdot d + r) \end{cases}$$

The amount of computation required to derive the secret key is negligible, and it is possible, in case an unreliable fault injection technique is being used, to confirm whether the correct values of d and k have been extracted deriving the deterministic k corresponding to the d via the procedure specified in [9], and checking it against the one obtained from the simultaneous equations.

EdDSA. Due to the fact that only the hash of the secret key d is used in the computation of an EdDSA signature, the attacker will not be able to retrieve the original value of d. However, starting from the available signatures (ρ, s) and $(\widetilde{\rho}, \widetilde{s})$ the attacker may compute $\widetilde{v} = \mathtt{int}(\mathtt{H}(\widetilde{\rho}||\mathtt{bin}(x_A, y_A)||\mathtt{msg}))$ from the value of the portion of the erroneous signature $\widetilde{\rho}$, the public key A, and the message $\mathtt{msg}$. Similarly, he computes $v = \mathtt{int}(\mathtt{H}(\rho||\mathtt{bin}(x_A, y_A)||\mathtt{msg}))$ starting from the correct signature values. As a consequence, he will be able to derive the value $a \equiv_q \frac{s-\tilde{s}}{v-\tilde{v}}$, which constitutes the second half of the hash of the secret key value d, for which the correctness can be checked simply deriving the value of the public key A=[a]B. The attacker will also be able to retrieve the value $k \equiv_q s - a \cdot v$ (manipulating line **6**, Algorithm 2) which corresponds to the hash of the second half of the hash of the secret key and the signed message msg (line **3**, Algorithm 2). However, since the value of k depends on both msg and an unknown portion of the hash of d, the attacker will not be able to exploit it to successfully forge a signature for any message different from msg. Note that the retrieval of the value a yields to the attacker the ability of inverting the per-private-key blinding in the base point of the group exponentiation operation.

3.2   Single Bit/Byte Flip in k During the Computation of s

The injection of a single bit/byte flip may still lead to a successful attack when the value change is affecting k, while it is being employed to compute the final signature recombination (line **5** in Algorithm 1, and line **6** in Algorithm 2). We note that, in the case of deterministic DSAs [9], injecting a bit- or byte-sized change in k, even without knowing whether this corresponds to an increase or decrease in its value, is of practical use to lead an attack. This contrasts with the case of the randomized DSAs, where the attacks [11] rely on injecting a fault causing a known change in the value (e.g., zeroing out some bits).

(EC)DSA. Consider the injection of a fault compliant with the single bit/byte flip fault model into the value k so that the computation of the signature recombination is done with an erroneous value $\tilde{k} = k \pm 2^i \varepsilon$, where $0 \le i < \lceil \log_2(v) \rceil, \varepsilon = 1$ for a single bit fault, or $0 \le i < \lceil \log_2(v) \rceil - 8, 1 \le \varepsilon \le 255$ in case of a single byte one. Such a fault induction yields an incorrect value of s, i.e., $\tilde{s} = (\mathrm{H}(\mathrm{msg}) + r \cdot d) \cdot (\tilde{k})^{-1} \bmod q$. Exploiting the knowledge of the erroneous and correct signatures, $(\tilde{r}, \tilde{s})$ and (r, s) respectively, it is possible to note that:

$$\frac{s}{\tilde{s}} \equiv_q \frac{(\mathrm{H}(\mathrm{msg}) + r \cdot d) \cdot k^{-1}}{(\mathrm{H}(\mathrm{msg}) + r \cdot d) \cdot (\tilde{k})^{-1}} \equiv_q \frac{(\mathrm{H}(\mathrm{msg}) + r \cdot d) \cdot k^{-1}}{(\mathrm{H}(\mathrm{msg}) + r \cdot d) \cdot (k \pm 2^i \varepsilon)^{-1}} \equiv_q \frac{k^{-1}}{(k \pm 2^i \varepsilon)^{-1}}$$

Given the limited number of possible values which can be assumed by both i and ε, it is possible to compute a guess for the unknown value of k. We denote as $\hat{k}_{i,\varepsilon}$ the guess on the secret value k given the two values for i and ε. Exploiting this value it is also possible to compute a prediction for the value of the secret key d, as $\hat{d}_{i,\varepsilon} \equiv_q \frac{s \cdot \hat{k}_{i,\varepsilon} - \mathrm{H}(\mathrm{msg})}{r}$, employing the value of r which is known as it is part of the message signature (manipulating the relation in line **5** in Algorithm 1). In order to find out whether a given pair of values for (i, ε) yields the correct predictions for k and d, it is sufficient to either derive the value of k from $\hat{d}_{i,\varepsilon}$ checking it against $\hat{k}_{i,\varepsilon}$, or compute the public (EC)DSA key from $\hat{d}_{i,\varepsilon}$ and check it against the available one. In either case, the attacker will be able to distinguish which is the correct prediction for d and thus effectively retrieve its correct value.

EdDSA. Considering the insertion of single bit or single byte change into the value of k prior to the signature composition, the attacker will obtain an erroneous signature $(\rho, \widetilde{s})$, where $\widetilde{s} \equiv_q (\widetilde{k} + a \cdot v)$ (line **6** in Algorithm 2). It is possible to observe that, besides leaking to the attacker the exact difference between the correct and the erroneous value of $k - \widetilde{k} = \Delta$, which can be obtained as $s - \widetilde{s} \equiv_q \Delta$, nothing else is revealed. In fact, being the information conveyed by the difference between the correct and faulty signature equivalent to the fault value alone, no inference on the secret values a, k, d involved in the signature computation can be made, beyond the ones which are possible to an attacker who receives only a correct signature. As a consequence in this case, with the fault affecting the value k, EdDSA does not reveal any information. The resistance shown by EdDSA to this fault model is a consequence of the choice of combining the value k with the remaining ones involved in the signature via addition, instead of the multiplication employed in the (EC)DSA algorithms.

Table 1. Timing results (in seconds) for the recovery of the private key d under a single bit and single byte change fault model, damaging the value k during the computation of the value s, reported for all cryptographic hash algorithms and group sizes specified in [9]. G denotes the group where the DL problem is instantiated, $q = |G|$.

	$(\lceil \log_2(p) \rceil,$ $\lceil \log_2(q) \rceil)$	Cryptographic Hash Function									
		SHA-1		SHA-2-224		SHA-2-256		SHA-2-384		SHA-2-512	
		bit	byte	bit	byte	bit	byte	bit	byte	bit	byte
DSA over	(1024,160)	0.01	3.81	0.01	4.18	0.01	4.18	0.01	4.45	0.01	4.47
$G \subseteq (\mathbb{Z}_p^*, \cdot)$	(2048,256)	0.08	22.58	0.09	23.76	0.09	23.47	0.09	23.41	0.08	23.15
ECDSA over	(192,192)	0.04	10.53	0.04	11.21	0.04	11.22	0.04	11.61	0.04	11.42
$G \subseteq \mathbb{E}(\mathbb{F}_p)$	(224,224)	0.05	15.14	0.06	15.82	0.06	15.85	0.06	16.23	0.06	16.51
	(256,256)	0.08	22.54	0.09	23.73	0.09	23.46	0.09	23.42	0.09	23.17
	(384,384)	0.20	51.99	0.20	52.83	0.20	52.55	0.20	52.87	0.20	52.75
	(521,521)	0.38	98.24	0.39	100.71	0.39	101.32	0.40	102.20	0.40	102.07

4 Experimental Evaluation

We implemented the key recovery attacks in C, employing the mbedTLS library. The platforms where the benchmarks were run is an Intel Xeon E5-2603v3, clocked at 1.60 GHz, and endowed with 32 GiB DDR4 DRAM. All the benchmarks were compiled with gcc 4.9.3 for and run on a Gentoo Linux 13.0 x86_64. The timings were gathered employing the POSIX primitive clock_gettime and averaged over 100 runs. The key retrievals were performed sequentially on a single core, as all the attacks exploiting achieve satisfactory running times even in this condition. All the reported timings include the computation time required to check the correctness of the retrieved value of d: the check was performed re-deriving the value of k according to the procedure specified in RFC 6979, as we measured it to be significantly faster than re-computing the public key from the value of d. To provide an equal comparison we considered msg to be 64 B in size, which corresponds to the input block size of each one of the considered cryptographic hashes. As a consequence the timing requirements of attacking messages longer than a single block may simply be obtained adding the time required to hash the input message to the ones reported in this work. We note that this does not impact on the practical feasibility of the attacks, as the only underlying assumption is that it is computationally feasible to hash the input message, which is also a requirement to perform the signature in the first place. We report that less than 0.5 ms of computation time is required to retrieve the private key in the first fault model, for all the key sizes and (EC)DSA variants reported in [9]. In all the cases, the key retrieval is performed in less than 0.5 ms of computation, pointing to a high practical feasibility of the attack. Table 1 reports the results of the key retrieval attack performed exploiting faults damaging the value of the deterministically generated k during signature composition, assuming a single bit and single byte fault injection model. Concerning the case of the single bit fault injection, the results show that it is possible to recover the correct value of the secret key in less than 0.5 s for any possible choice of cryptographic hash and cyclic group employed. Relaxing the fault model to be a single faulty byte, in any possible position in the value k leads to recovery times for the private key d below two minutes of computation for any choice of cryptographic hash and cyclic group. We note that, also in this case, a single pair of correct and faulty signatures is enough to retrieve d. The small computational requirements for the key retrieval allow to further relax the fault model, if needed. In fact, considering the possibility of a single 32-bit word of k being faulty in the computation, the expected computation time is of 2.8 to 77 CPU/days, depending on the cryptographic primitive choice. Such requirements are still within the realm of feasibility, considering the parallel nature of the computation, which can easily be split on a large number of CPUs or GPUs.

Acknowledgements. This work was supported in part by the EU grant awarded for the action "Safe Cooperating Cyber-Physical Systems using Wireless Communication – SafeCOP" (ECSEL JU 2015-RIA). Grant agreement no. 692529.

References

1. Barenghi, A., Bertoni, G.M., Breveglieri, L., Pelosi, G., Sanfilippo, S., Susella, R.: A fault-based secret key retrieval method for ECDSA: analysis and countermeasure. J. Emerg. Technol. Comput. Syst. **13**(1) (2016)
2. Barenghi, A., Bertoni, G.M., Breveglieri, L., Pellicioli, M., Pelosi, G.: Fault attack on AES with single-bit induced faults. In: Sixth International Conference on Information Assurance and Security, IAS 2010, Atlanta, GA, USA, 23–25 August 2010. IEEE (2010)
3. Barenghi, A., Bertoni, G.M., Breveglieri, L., Pelosi, G.: A fault induction technique based on voltage underfeeding with application to attacks against AES and RSA. J. Syst. Softw. **86**(7), 1864–1878 (2013)

4. Barenghi, A., Breveglieri, L., Koren, I., Naccache, D.: Fault injection attacks on cryptographic devices: theory, practice, and countermeasures. Proc. IEEE **100**(11), 3056–3076 (2012)
5. Barenghi, A., Breveglieri, L., Koren, I., Pelosi, G., Regazzoni, F.: Countermeasures against fault attacks on software implemented AES: effectiveness and cost. In: 5th Workshop on Embedded Systems Security, WESS 2010. ACM (2010)
6. Bernstein, D.J., Duif, N., Lange, T., Schwabe, P., Yang, B.: High-speed High-security Signatures. J. Cryptographic Eng. **2**(2), 77–89 (2012)
7. El Gamal, T.: A public key cryptosystem and a signature scheme based on discrete logarithms. IEEE Trans. Inf. Theory **31**(4), 469–472 (1985)
8. Vitek, J., Naccache, D., Pointcheval, D., Vaudenay, S.: Computational alternatives to random number generators. In: Tavares, S., Meijer, H. (eds.) SAC 1998. LNCS, vol. 1556, pp. 72–80. Springer, Heidelberg (1999)
9. Pornin, T.: Deterministic Usage of the Digital Signature Algorithm (DSA) and Elliptic Curve Digital Signature Algorithm (ECDSA). IETF RFC 6979 (2013)
10. Josefsson, S., Möller, N.: EdDSA and Ed25519 (2015). https://tools.ietf.org/html/draft-josefsson-eddsa-ed25519-03
11. Schmidt, J., Medwed, M.: A fault attack on ECDSA. In: FDTC 2009, pp. 93–99. IEEE CS (2009)
12. Schnorr, C.: Efficient signature generation by smart cards. J. Cryptology **4**(3), 161–174 (1991)

Permutation and Symmetric Encryption

Lower Bounds for Key Length of k-wise Almost Independent Permutations and Certain Symmetric-Key Encryption Schemes

Akinori Kawachi[1]($\boxtimes$), Hirotoshi Takebe[2], and Keisuke Tanaka[3]

[1] Tokushima University, Tokushima, Japan
kawachi@is.tokushima-u.ac.jp
[2] Kanazawa University, Kanazawa, Japan
[3] Tokyo Institute of Technology and JST CREST, Tokyo, Japan

Abstract. The k-wise almost independent permutations are one of important primitives for cryptographic schemes and combinatorial constructions. Kaplan, Naor, and Reingold showed a general construction for k-wise almost independent permutations, and Kawachi, Takebe, and Tanaka provided symmetric-key encryption schemes that achieve multi-message approximate secrecy and multi-ciphertext approximate non-malleability based on Kaplan et al.'s construction. In this paper, we show lower bounds of key length for these constructions. In particular, they are nearly optimal for k-wise almost independent permutations and multi-message approximate secrecy if the approximation parameter is a constant.

Keywords: k-wise almost independent permutations · Symmetric-key encryption schemes · Approximate secrecy · Non-malleability

1 Introduction

1.1 Background

In the computer science, the k-wise independent permutations are one of important primitives. Roughly speaking, we say that $\{f_s\}_s$ is a collection of k-wise independent permutations if f_s is a permutation for every s and $(f_s(x_1), ..., f_s(x_k))$ is uniformly distributed for any distinct $x_1, ..., x_k$ and a uniformly random key s. It is well known that they have many applications to combinatorial constructions and cryptographic schemes. For example, k-wise independent permutations are applicable to constructions for block ciphers such as DES, as discussed in [1,2]. In spite of the useful properties, explicit constructions of k-wise independent permutations have been unknown so far for $k \geq 4$ (e.g. [3]). Kuperberg, Lovett, and Peled [4] recently showed the existence of a collection of k-wise independent permutations with a polynomial-size description, but efficiently computable constructions are still unknown.

However, approximate independence suffices for such applications in practice, and hence, efficient constructions of k-wise *almost* independent permutations

© Springer International Publishing Switzerland 2016
K. Ogawa and K. Yoshioka (Eds.): IWSEC 2016, LNCS 9836, pp. 195–211, 2016.
DOI: 10.1007/978-3-319-44524-3_12

have been extensively studied [1,5–7]. Informally, for k-wise almost independent permutations $\{f_s\}_s$, the output distribution $(f_s(x_1), ..., f_s(x_k))$ is *statistically close* to the uniform distribution. If the statistical distance is at most ϵ, then we call it by ϵ-dependent (see Definition 1 for the formal definition). Kaplan, Naor, and Reingold [7] provided an efficient general construction of the permutations that achieves short key length, which is almost the same as that of schemes of which only their existence can be shown by the probabilistic argument.

Kawachi, Takebe, and Tanaka [8] recently applied their permutations to efficient constructions for symmetric-key encryption schemes satisfying multi-message approximate secrecy and multi-ciphertext approximate non-malleability. Intuitively, multi-message secrecy means the secrecy for multiple messages encrypted with a single key, and multi-ciphertext non-malleability means the unforgeability of ciphertexts under the situation that an adversary can obtain multiple samples of ciphertexts (for the formal definitions, see Definitions 6 and 9, respectively).

At first glance, the definition of k-message secrecy looks like that of k-wise independence. However, they are slightly different since the output of k-wise independent permutations is uniform, but k-message secrecy does not need such uniformity of ciphertexts. So, while the construction of the encryption schemes just used Kaplan et al.'s permutations directly, the security proofs require tailored analyses for these notions.

1.2   Our Contributions

In this paper, we show lower bounds of the key length for satisfying k-wise almost independence, k-message approximate secrecy, and k-ciphertext approximate non-malleability. We note that the base of logarithms is 2 throughout this paper.

As shown in [7], Kaplan et al.'s construction achieves the following upper bound for the key length of k-wise ϵ-dependent permutations.

Theorem 1 ([7]). *For every $n \in \mathbb{N}$, $1 \leq k \leq 2^n$ and $0 < \epsilon < 1$, there exists a collection of k-wise ϵ-dependent permutations $\mathbf{F}_n = \{f_s : \{0,1\}^n \to \{0,1\}^n\}_{s \in \{0,1\}^m}$ that is computable in polynomial time in n, k, and $\log \epsilon^{-1}$ and whose key length m is at most $O(nk + \log \epsilon^{-1})$.*

They also gave the following existential proof for the permutations with short keys by the probabilistic argument.

Theorem 2 ([7]). *For every $n \in \mathbb{N}$, $1 \leq k \leq 2^n$ and $0 < \epsilon < 1$, there exists a collection of k-wise ϵ-dependent permutations $\mathbf{F}_n = \{f_s : \{0,1\}^n \to \{0,1\}^n\}_{s \in \{0,1\}^m}$ whose key length m is at most $2nk + \log nk + 2\log \epsilon^{-1} + O(1) = O(nk + \log \epsilon^{-1})$.*

Note that Kuperberg et al. [4] gave an existential proof for (0-dependent) k-wise independent permutations with key length of at most $k^{O(1)} + O(nk)$ by the probabilistic argument. This implies that there would exist (efficiently computable) k-wise ϵ-dependent permutations with shorter keys than Kaplan et al.'s construction for small k and ϵ.

For k-wise ϵ-dependent permutations, the lower bound we show is given by the following theorem:

Theorem 3. *If* $\mathbf{F}_n = \{f_s : \{0,1\}^n \to \{0,1\}^n\}_{s \in \{0,1\}^m}$ *is a collection of k-wise ϵ-dependent permutations, then the key length m is at least* $\log(1 - \epsilon) + \log(2^n \cdot (2^n - 1) \cdots (2^n - k + 1))$.

Note that if ϵ is a constant the lower bound is $\Omega(nk)$, which matches to the upper bound in Theorems 1 and 2 up to a constant factor.

As already mentioned, Kawachi et al. [8] constructed symmetric-key encryption schemes satisfying information-theoretically security notions, multi-message approximate secrecy and multi-ciphertext approximate non-malleability, from Kaplan et al.'s efficient construction of k-wise almost independent permutations.

Suppose our message and ciphertext spaces are identically $\{0,1\}^n$ (and thus the encryption function is a permutation over $\{0,1\}^n$) throughout this paper. Informally, we say that a symmetric-key encryption scheme has k-message ϵ-secrecy if the distance between a random message X and its ciphertext $f_S(X)$ is bounded by small ϵ for its encryption function f with a single random key S, and we say that it has k-ciphertext approximate non-malleability if the distance between a random message X and its ciphertext $f_S(X)$ is bounded by small ϵ when given $X_1, ..., X_k, f_S(X_1), ..., f_S(X_k)$ for any k distinct messages $X_1, ..., X_k$ and a random key S.

Using the k-wise ϵ-dependent permutations Kawachi et al. showed an upper bound of the key length for satisfying these security notions in [8].

Theorem 4 ([8]). *For every* $n \in \mathbb{N}$, $0 < \epsilon < 1$ *and* $2 \le k \le 2^n$, *there is a symmetric-key encryption scheme on n-bit messages that achieves k-message ϵ-secrecy and $(k - 1)$-ciphertext ϵ-non-malleability of key length at most* $O(nk + \log \epsilon^{-1})$.

In this paper, we show lower bounds of the key length for these security notions. In particular, we provide the following lower bound for encryption schemes that satisfy k-message ϵ-secrecy, which matches to the upper bound of Kawachi et al. up to a constant factor if ϵ is a constant:

Theorem 5. *For every* $n \in \mathbb{N}$, $0 \le \epsilon < 1$ *and* $1 \le k \le 2^n$, *if a symmetric-key encryption scheme satisfies k-message ϵ-secrecy then the key length is at least* $\log(2^n \cdot (2^n - 1) \cdots (2^n - k + 1)) + \log(1 - \epsilon)$.

We also provide the following lower bound for k-ciphertext ϵ-non-malleability with some natural property:

Theorem 6. *For every* $n \in \mathbb{N}$, $0 \le \epsilon < 1$ *and* $2 \le k \le 2^n$, *if a k-mixing symmetric-key encryption scheme satisfies $(k - 1)$-ciphertext ϵ-non-malleability then the key length is at least* $\log(2^n \cdot (2^n - 1) \cdots (2^n - k + 1)) + \log(1 - \epsilon)$.

The scheme is k-mixing if for every pair of distinct k messages $(m_1, \ldots, m_k)$ and ciphertexts $(c_1, \ldots, c_k)$ there is some key s such that $f_s(m_1) = c_1, \ldots, f_s(m_k) = c_k$ for the encryption function f. As Kawachi et al.'s scheme satisfies for small ϵ, this property would be natural for symmetric-key encryption schemes. As discussed in Sect. 3, a kind of the k-mixing property is required to obtain non-trivial lower bounds of key length for k-ciphertext ϵ-non-malleability. We can also show lower bounds of key length under more relaxed properties. (See Theorem 10.)

1.3 Related Results

Dodis [9] gave another formalization of approximate secrecy by relaxing Shannon's perfect secrecy [10], and showed some relations between his approximate secrecy and key length. He mainly focused on the running time of adversaries, and then formalized this notion based on the indistinguishability of ciphertexts, rather than the distance between messages and ciphertexts such as the definition we adopt in this paper. He also showed the relations among their indistinguishability-based definition and Shannon's original mutual-information-based definition.

Kawachi et al. [11] showed the relations among some information-theoretic security notions. Particularly, they formalized multi-message (approximate) secrecy and multi-ciphertext (approximate) non-malleability we adopt in this paper, and proved that 1-ciphertext perfect non-malleability is equivalent to 2-message perfect secrecy if the message and ciphertext spaces are identical. This demonstrates that Hanaoka's construction [12] of 1-ciphertext perfectly non-malleable scheme is optimal with respect to key length immediately from the tight lower bound of key length in 2-message perfectly secure scheme which can be easily proved. Therefore, our lower bounds for multi-message approximate secrecy and multi-ciphertext approximate non-malleability are natural extensions of theirs. Note that the equivalence between the approximate versions is unknown unlike perfect ones and thus we need to prove lower bounds individually for the two notions.

They also showed that approximate authenticity implies approximate non-malleability. Since it is already known that approximate authenticity can be achieved with $O(\log n)$-bit keys [13], approximate non-malleability can be achieved with the same key length from the result. This seems to conflict our result at first glance, but the implication actually assumes that the non-malleable scheme in [11] from the approximate authenticity is allowed to have an invalid ciphertexts, while our scheme supposes that the message and ciphertext spaces are identical. This difference makes a significant gap in the key length of the approximate non-malleability.

2   Preliminaries

2.1   Definitions

In this section, we define notation and notions by following [8,11].

Notation. Throughout this paper, we represent sets by calligraphic letters (e.g., $\mathcal{X}$), and denote by $|\mathcal{X}|$ the number of elements in the set $\mathcal{X}$. The uppercase letters (e.g., X) mean a random variable, and the lowercase letters mean a specific element in some set (e.g., $x \in \mathcal{X}$). Let $P_X(x)$ be the probability that the random variable takes an element x, i.e., $P_X(x) := \Pr_X[X = x]$. Similarly, we define the joint probability of two random variables X and Y as $P_{XY}(x, y) := \Pr[X = x \wedge Y = y]$. We denote by XY the corresponding random variable defined from the joint probability. The conditional probability is also defined as $P_{X|Y}(x|y) := \Pr[X = x|Y = y]$. $X \cdot Y$ is defined as a random variable according to the probability $P_{X \cdot Y}(x, y) := P_X(x)P_Y(y)$. Therefore, X and Y are independent if and only if $P_{XY}(x, y) = P_{X \cdot Y}(x, y)$.

We denote by $X_{[k]}$ a sequence of k random variables $X_1, \ldots, X_k$ on sets $\mathcal{X}_1, \ldots, \mathcal{X}_k$ and by x_i the i-th element of $x_{[k]} = (x_1, \ldots, x_k) \in \mathcal{X}_1 \times \ldots \times \mathcal{X}_k$. We further define the following notation for sets that have different elements in every coordinates:

$$\mathcal{X}_{\text{diff}}^{\times k} := \{(x_1, \ldots, x_k) \in \mathcal{X}^k : x_i \neq x_j \ (1 \leq \forall i < \forall j \leq k)\}.$$

For a k-tuple $x_{[k]} = (x_1, \ldots, x_k)$ of inputs and function f, we define $f(x_{[k]})$ as $(f(x_1), \ldots, f(x_k))$.

k-wise Almost Independent Permutations. As mentioned in Sect. 1, the k-wise ϵ-dependent permutations are one of basic primitives for many useful applications in combinatorics, cryptography, and others. The formal definition is given as follows.

Definition 1 (k-wise ϵ-dependent Permutations). *Let $\mathbf{F} = \{f_s : \mathcal{X} \rightarrow \mathcal{X}\}_{s \in \mathcal{S}}$ be a collection of permutations and $\epsilon \geq 0$. The collection $\mathbf{F}$ is k-wise ϵ-dependent if for every k-tuple of distinct elements $x_{[k]} := (x_1, \ldots, x_k) \in \mathcal{X}_{\text{diff}}^{\times k}$, the statistical distance between the distribution $f_S(x_{[k]}) := (f_S(x_1), \ldots, f_S(x_k))$ and the uniform distribution over $\mathcal{X}_{\text{diff}}^{\times k}$ is at most ϵ, where S is the uniform random variable on $\mathcal{S}$. That is,*

$$\frac{1}{2} \sum_{y_{[k]} \in \mathcal{X}_{\text{diff}}^{\times k}} \left| \Pr_S[f_S(x_{[k]}) = y_{[k]}] - \frac{1}{|\mathcal{X}_{\text{diff}}^{\times k}|} \right| \leq \epsilon.$$

If $\epsilon = 0$, then the collection $\mathbf{F}$ is said to be k-wise independent.

Kaplan et al. [7] constructed a collection of k-wise ϵ-dependent permutations over $\mathcal{X} = \{0, 1\}^n$ for every $n \in \mathbb{N}$ as given in Theorem 1.

Symmetric-Key Encryption. We next give the formal definition of symmetric-key encryption schemes.

Definition 2 (Symmetric-Key Encryption). *A symmetric-key encryption scheme Σ consists of three algorithms such as $\Sigma = $ (Key-Generation, Encryption, Decryption). Key-Generation picks a key s from a key set $\mathcal{S}$ uniformly at random. Encryption applies an encryption function $f_s : \mathcal{X} \rightarrow \mathcal{Y}$ to a message $m \in \mathcal{X}$ with* *a key s, and then outputs the ciphertext $c = f_s(m) \in \mathcal{Y}$. Decryption applies a decryption function f_s^{-1} to a ciphertext $c \in \mathcal{Y}$, and then outputs $m = f_s^{-1}(c)$ if such a unique $m \in \mathcal{X}$ exists, and $\perp$ otherwise.*

Throughout this paper, we generally denote messages, ciphertexts, and keys by random variables M, C, and S respectively. Also, we suppose that the message and ciphertext spaces are identical, i.e., $\mathcal{X} = \mathcal{Y}$ in this paper, and thus, the encryption and decryption functions are permutations. If C is determined by M with a key $s \in \mathcal{S}$, we write $C = f_s(M)$.

Statistical Distance. In this paper, we often make use of variants of the statistical distance for discussion of security notions. We review the definitions.

Definition 3 (Statistical Distance). *Let X, Y be random variables over $\mathcal{X}$. The statistical distance between X and Y is defined as*

$$d(X, Y) := \frac{1}{2} \sum_{x \in \mathcal{X}} |P_X(x) - P_Y(x)|.$$

For another random variable Z over $\mathcal{Z}$, a variant of the statistical distance that we call the statistical distance between X and Y conditioned on $Z = z$ for $z \in \mathcal{Z}$ is defined as

$$d(X, Y | Z = z) := \frac{1}{2} \sum_{x \in \mathcal{X}} |P_{X|Z}(x|z) - P_{Y|Z}(x|z)|.$$

Moreover, we define the conditional statistical distance as

$$d(X, Y | Z) := \sum_{z \in \mathcal{Z}} P_Z(z) d(X, Y | Z = z).$$

The conditional statistical distance (called by the expected variational distance in [11]) is an "average-case" version of the statistical distance conditioned on $Z = z$ in some sense.

2.2   Security Notions

In this section, we define security notions of secrecy and non-malleability for symmetric-key encryption. These definitions have been already formalized in the literature such as [8,11,12,14,15]. As stated above, our formalization basically follows [8,11]. Let $\Sigma = $ (Key-Generation, Encryption, Decryption) be a symmetric-key encryption scheme.

Secrecy. First, we define secrecy of symmetric-key encryption schemes. Intuitively, secrecy means the undetectability of original messages from the ciphertexts. Since ciphertexts are sent over an insecure channel, an adversary can intercept them and try to derive information on messages. Thus, encryption schemes should satisfy (perfect) secrecy. We review the notion of information-theoretic secrecy defined by Shannon [10].

Definition 4 (Perfect Secrecy [10]). *We say that Σ satisfies perfect secrecy (PS) if for every message random variable M on $\mathcal{X}$ independent from a key random variable S, it holds that the mutual information of M and C is equal to 0, or $I(M; C) = 0$, where $I(M; C)$ denotes the mutual information between random variables M and C.*

We also define the approximate secrecy formalized as in [11] by relaxing the perfect one. In the approximate secrecy, a ciphertext is *almost independent* from the message. We formalize this notion via the statistical distance.

Definition 5 (Approximate Secrecy [11]). *We say that Σ satisfies ϵ-secrecy (ϵ-S) if for every message random variable M on $\mathcal{X}$ independent from a key random variable S, it holds that*

$$d(MC, M \cdot C) \leq \epsilon,$$

where $C := f_S(M)$ is a random variable of the resulting ciphertext.

We note that this notion coincides with the perfect secrecy if $\epsilon = 0$.

The above approximate secrecy is naturally extended to multiple-message secrecy, as defined in [11], which guarantees the approximate secrecy for encryption of multiple messages with a single key.

Definition 6 (k-message Approximate Secrecy [11]). *We say that Σ satisfies k-message ϵ-secrecy (ϵ-S^k) if for every random variable $M_{[k]}$ of distinct k messages on $\mathcal{X}_{\mathrm{diff}}^{\times k}$ independent from a key random variable S, it holds that*

$$d(M_{[k]}C_{[k]}, M_{[k]} \cdot C_{[k]}) \leq \epsilon,$$

where $C_{[k]}$ is the random variable of the ciphertexts obtained by encrypting $M_{[k]}$ with a key S. If $\epsilon = 0$, we then say that the scheme satisfies k-message perfect secrecy (PS^k).

Non-malleability. We next define information-theoretic non-malleability of symmetric-key encryption schemes, formalized by Hanaoka et al. [14] for the first time. Intuitively, non-malleability means the unforgeability of ciphertexts whose decrypting results are meaningfully related to those of already obtained ciphertexts.

Definition 7 (Perfect Non-malleability [14]). *We say that Σ satisfies perfect non-malleability (PNM) if for every message random variable M_1 on $\mathcal{X}$ independent from a key random variable S, and every random variable C_2 on $\mathcal{Y}$ different from $C_1 = f_S(M_1)$ and independent from S given M_1C_1 (i.e., $\Pr[C_1 = C_2] = 0$ and $I(C_2; S|M_1C_1) = 0$), it holds that the mutual information of M_2 and C_2 conditioned on M_1, C_1 is equal to 0 (that is, $I(M_2; C_2|M_1C_1) = 0$), where $M_2 := f_S^{-1}(C_2)$ is a random variable on $\mathcal{X}$ obtained by decrypting C_2 with S.*

In this definition, the random variable C_2 is regarded as a forged cipertext that an adversary chooses by observing C_1. Thus, C_2 should be independent from the key S. The condition $\Pr[C_1 = C_2] = 0$ is necessary for the definition of non-malleability. If it is not posed, an adversary can easily break the non-malleability by simply copying C_1 to C_2 since a trivial relation $M_1 = M_2$ holds. Then, we require the condition to exclude such a trivial attack.

Remark. In this paper, we employ the formalizations of information-theoretic non-malleability from previous works such as [14]. Their formalization seems to be sufficient, but too strong to capture the notion of non-malleability. It would be interesting to study weaker variations of information-theoretic non-malleability.

In [11], the above non-malleability is extended to the following approximate version.

Definition 8 (Approximate Non-malleability [11]). *We say that Σ satisfies ϵ-non-malleability (ϵ-NM) if for every message random variable M_1 on $\mathcal{X}$ independent from a key random variable S, and every random variable C_2 on $\mathcal{Y}$ different from $C_1 = f_S(M_1)$ and independent from S given M_1C_1 (i.e., $\Pr[C_1 = C_2] = 0$ and $I(C_2; S|M_1C_1) = 0$), it holds that*

$$d(M_2C_2, M_2 \cdot C_2|M_1C_1) \le \epsilon,$$

where $M_2 := f_S^{-1}(C_2)$ is a random variable on $\mathcal{X}$ obtained by decrypting C_2 with S.

We note that this coincides with the perfect non-malleability if $\epsilon = 0$.

The above approximate non-malleability can be also extended to a multi-ciphertext version in which an adversary can get multiple ciphertexts. In this context, a variant of the non-malleability on the "worst-case" messages has been proposed in [8], which simplifies the formalization of multi-ciphertext non-malleability.

Definition 9 (k-ciphertext Approximate Non-malleability [8]). *We say that Σ satisfies k-ciphertext worst-case ϵ-non-malleability (ϵ-NM$_*^k$) if every $m_{[k]} := (m_1, \ldots, m_k)$ on $\mathcal{X}_{\mathrm{diff}}^{\times k}$, every $c_{[k]} := (c_1, \ldots, c_k) \in \mathcal{Y}_{\mathrm{diff}}^{\times k}$, and every ciphertext random variable C_{k+1} on $\mathcal{Y} \setminus \{c_1, \ldots, c_k\}$ independent from a key random variable S, it holds that*

$$d(M_{k+1}C_{k+1}, M_{k+1} \cdot C_{k+1}|M_{[k]} = m_{[k]}, C_{[k]} = c_{[k]})$$

$$= \frac{1}{2} \sum_{\substack{m_{k+1} \in \mathcal{X}', \\ c_{k+1} \in \mathcal{Y}'}} \left| P_{M_{k+1}C_{k+1}}(m_{k+1}, c_{k+1}) - P_{M_{k+1}}(m_{k+1})P_{C_{k+1}}(c_{k+1}) \right|$$

$$\le \epsilon,$$

where $\mathcal{X}' := \mathcal{X} \setminus \{m_1, \ldots, m_k\}$, $\mathcal{Y}' := \mathcal{Y} \setminus \{c_1, \ldots, c_k\}$, and a random variable M_{k+1} on $\mathcal{X} \setminus \{m_1, \ldots, m_k\}$ is defined as a decryption of c_{k+1} under the key random variable S, i.e., $M_{k+1} := f_S^{-1}(c_{k+1})$.

Since the equivalence between the notions of Definition 9 and the natural extension of Definition 8 is shown in [8], we refer to the non-malleability of Definition 9 as the "k-ciphertext ϵ-non-malleability."

We note that Kawachi, Portmann, and Tanaka also formalized (1-ciphertext) ϵ-strong non-malleability in the full version of [11], which corresponds to the worst-case of m_1, c_1, and c_2 in our notation. Then their definition is stronger than ours (Definition 9) in the case $k = 1$.

3   Lower Bounds for Key Length

In this section, we discuss lower bounds for key length of k-wise almost independent permutations, and that of symmetric-key encryption schemes when satisfying the security notions defined before.

Before showing the lower bounds for key length, we give a lemma frequently used in the rest of this paper.

Lemma 1. *Let $\mathcal{A}$ and $\mathcal{B}$ be finite sets where $|\mathcal{A}| < |\mathcal{B}|$, let A be the uniform random variable over $\mathcal{A}$, and let $\phi : \mathcal{A} \to \mathcal{B}$ be a function. Then it holds that*

$$\frac{1}{2} \sum_{b \in \mathcal{B}} \left| \Pr_A[\phi(A) = b] - \frac{1}{|\mathcal{B}|} \right| \geq 1 - \frac{|\mathcal{A}|}{|\mathcal{B}|}.$$

Proof. For a function ϕ and $b \in \mathcal{B}$, let $\phi^{-1}(\{b\}) := \{a \in \mathcal{A} \mid \phi(a) = b\}$ and $t := \left| \{ b \in \mathcal{B} \mid |\phi^{-1}(\{b\})| > 0 \} \right|$. Now we notice that

$$t = \sum_{b \in \mathcal{B} : |\phi^{-1}(\{b\})| > 0} 1 \leq \sum_{b \in \mathcal{B} : |\phi^{-1}(\{b\})| > 0} |\phi^{-1}(\{b\})| = |\mathcal{A}|.$$

Hence we obtain

$$\frac{1}{2} \sum_{b \in \mathcal{B}} \left| \Pr_A[\phi(A) = b] - \frac{1}{|\mathcal{B}|} \right|$$

$$= \frac{1}{2} \sum_{b \in \mathcal{B} : |\phi^{-1}(\{b\})| > 0} \left| \Pr_A[\phi(A) = b] - \frac{1}{|\mathcal{B}|} \right| + \frac{1}{2} \sum_{b \in \mathcal{B} : |\phi^{-1}(\{b\})| = 0} \left| \Pr_A[\phi(A) = b] - \frac{1}{|\mathcal{B}|} \right|$$

$$= \frac{1}{2} \sum_{b \in \mathcal{B} : |\phi^{-1}(\{b\})| > 0} \left| \frac{|\phi^{-1}(\{b\})|}{|\mathcal{A}|} - \frac{1}{|\mathcal{B}|} \right| + \frac{1}{2} \sum_{b \in \mathcal{B} : |\phi^{-1}(\{b\})| = 0} \left| 0 - \frac{1}{|\mathcal{B}|} \right|$$

$$= \frac{1}{2} \sum_{b \in \mathcal{B} : |\phi^{-1}(\{b\})| > 0} \left(\frac{|\phi^{-1}(\{b\})|}{|\mathcal{A}|} - \frac{1}{|\mathcal{B}|} \right) + \frac{1}{2} \sum_{b \in \mathcal{B} : |\phi^{-1}(\{b\})| = 0} \frac{1}{|\mathcal{B}|}$$

$$= \frac{1}{2} \left(\frac{|\mathcal{A}|}{|\mathcal{A}|} - \frac{t}{|\mathcal{B}|} \right) + \frac{1}{2} \left(\frac{|\mathcal{B}| - t}{|\mathcal{B}|} \right)$$

$$= 1 - \frac{t}{|\mathcal{B}|} \geq 1 - \frac{|\mathcal{A}|}{|\mathcal{B}|},$$

where the third equality follows from $|\mathcal{A}| < |\mathcal{B}|$, and the last inequality follows from $t \leq |\mathcal{A}|$.   □

3.1 k-wise Almost Independent Permutations

We first prove a lower bound for key length of k-wise ϵ-dependent permutations. Actually, since we will later give a lower bound of key length for symmetric-key encryption schemes with k-message ϵ-secrecy and the k-message ϵ-secrecy can be achieved by k-wise ϵ-dependent permutations with the same key length as in Theorem 4 of [8], we can immediately obtain the lower bound for the permutations from these results. However, since this proof is simpler and contains the basic idea common in all the proofs for secrecy and non-malleability, we present a direct proof for the lower bound.

The following theorem is a more detailed version of Theorem 3.

Theorem 7. *Let* $\mathbf{F} = \{f_s : \mathcal{X} \to \mathcal{X}\}_{s \in \mathcal{S}}$ *be a collection of k-wise ϵ-dependent permutations, where $k \geq 1$ and $0 \leq \epsilon < 1$. Then it holds that $|\mathcal{S}| \geq (1-\epsilon)\left|\mathcal{X}_{\mathrm{diff}}^{\times k}\right|$.*

Proof. Assume that $|\mathcal{S}| < \left|\mathcal{X}_{\mathrm{diff}}^{\times k}\right|$ at first (otherwise the proof is done). Let

$$g(x_1, \ldots, x_k) := \frac{1}{2} \sum_{y_{[k]} \in \mathcal{X}_{\mathrm{diff}}^{\times k}} \left| \Pr_S[f_S(x_{[k]}) = y_{[k]}] - \frac{1}{\left|\mathcal{X}_{\mathrm{diff}}^{\times k}\right|} \right|.$$

Hence we obtain $g(x_1, \ldots, x_k) \geq 1 - \frac{|\mathcal{S}|}{\left|\mathcal{X}_{\mathrm{diff}}^{\times k}\right|}$ by applying Lemma 1 ($\mathcal{S}$ and $\mathcal{X}_{\mathrm{diff}}^{\times k}$ correspond to $\mathcal{A}$ and $\mathcal{B}$ of Lemma 1 respectively).

Since $g(x_1, \ldots, x_k) \leq \epsilon$ by the definition, we obtain $|\mathcal{S}| \geq (1 - \epsilon)\left|\mathcal{X}_{\mathrm{diff}}^{\times k}\right|$.   □

It is easy to see that this theorem immediately provides Theorem 3 if message, ciphertext, and key spaces are bit strings.

3.2   Symmetric-Key Encryption Schemes

Now, we discuss lower bounds of key length for symmetric-key encryption schemes when satisfying multi-message secrecy and multi-ciphertext non-malleability. Let $\Sigma = $ (Key-Generation, Encryption, Decryption) be a symmetric-key encryption scheme. Recall that the message and ciphertext spaces are identical (i.e., $\mathcal{X} = \mathcal{Y}$), and thus, the encryption function is a permutation.

Multi-message Approximate Secrecy. First, we discuss lower bounds of key length with regard to multi-message approximate secrecy. The following theorem is a more detailed version of Theorem 5.

Theorem 8. *Assume $0 \leq \epsilon < 1$ and $1 \leq k \leq |\mathcal{X}|$. If Σ satisfies k-message ϵ-secrecy, then it holds that $|\mathcal{S}| \geq (1 - \epsilon)\left|\mathcal{Y}_{\mathrm{diff}}^{\times k}\right|$.*

Proof. We suppose that $M_{[k]} := (M_1, \ldots, M_k)$ is uniformly distributed over $\mathcal{X}_{\mathrm{diff}}^{\times k}$, i.e., $P_{M_{[k]}}(m_{[k]}) = \frac{1}{\left|\mathcal{X}_{\mathrm{diff}}^{\times k}\right|}$ for every $m_{[k]} := (m_1, \ldots, m_k) \in \mathcal{X}_{\mathrm{diff}}^{\times k}$. Now we give four claims, and then immediately obtain the statement of Theorem 8 by combining them.

Claim 1. *If Σ satisfies k-message ϵ-secrecy, then there exists $m_{[k]}^* \in \mathcal{X}_{\text{diff}}^{\times k}$ such that $\frac{1}{2} \sum_{c_{[k]} \in \mathcal{Y}_{\text{diff}}^{\times k}} \left| P_{C_{[k]}|M_{[k]}}(c_{[k]}|m_{[k]}^*) - P_{C_{[k]}}(c_{[k]}) \right| \leq \epsilon.$*

Claim 2. *It holds $P_{C_{[k]}|M_{[k]}}(c_{[k]}|m_{[k]}) = \Pr_S[f_S(m_{[k]}) = c_{[k]}]$ for every $m_{[k]}$ and every $c_{[k]}$*

Claim 3. *If $M_{[k]}$ is uniformly distributed over $\mathcal{X}_{\text{diff}}^{\times k}$, then $C_{[k]} := f_S(M_{[k]})$ is uniformly distributed over $\mathcal{Y}_{\text{diff}}^{\times k}$, i.e., $P_{C_{[k]}}(c_{[k]}) = \frac{1}{|\mathcal{Y}_{\text{diff}}^{\times k}|}$ for every $c_{[k]}$.*

Claim 4. *Assume there exists $m_{[k]}^* \in \mathcal{X}_{\text{diff}}^{\times k}$ such that*

$$\frac{1}{2} \sum_{c_{[k]} \in \mathcal{Y}_{\text{diff}}^{\times k}} \left| \Pr_S[f_S(m_{[k]}^*) = c_{[k]}] - \frac{1}{|\mathcal{Y}_{\text{diff}}^{\times k}|} \right| \leq \epsilon.$$

Then it holds that $|\mathcal{S}| \geq (1 - \epsilon)|\mathcal{X}_{\text{diff}}^{\times k}|$.

We give the proofs of the above claims.

Proof (Claim 1). Since $M_{[k]}$ is uniformly distributed over $\mathcal{X}_{\text{diff}}^{\times k}$ and Σ satisfies k-message ϵ-secrecy, we obtain

$$d(M_{[k]}C_{[k]}, M_{[k]} \cdot C_{[k]})$$

$$= \frac{1}{2} \sum_{m_{[k]} \in \mathcal{X}_{\text{diff}}^{\times k}, c_{[k]} \in \mathcal{Y}_{\text{diff}}^{\times k}} \left| P_{M_{[k]}C_{[k]}}(m_{[k]}, c_{[k]}) - P_{M_{[k]}}(m_{[k]})P_{C_{[k]}}(c_{[k]}) \right|$$

$$= \frac{1}{2} \sum_{m_{[k]} \in \mathcal{X}_{\text{diff}}^{\times k}} P_{M_{[k]}}(m_{[k]}) \sum_{c_{[k]} \in \mathcal{Y}_{\text{diff}}^{\times k}} \left| P_{C_{[k]}|M_{[k]}}(c_{[k]}|m_{[k]}) - P_{C_{[k]}}(c_{[k]}) \right|$$

$$= \frac{1}{|\mathcal{X}_{\text{diff}}^{\times k}|} \sum_{m_{[k]} \in \mathcal{X}_{\text{diff}}^{\times k}} \frac{1}{2} \sum_{c_{[k]} \in \mathcal{Y}_{\text{diff}}^{\times k}} \left| P_{C_{[k]}|M_{[k]}}(c_{[k]}|m_{[k]}) - P_{C_{[k]}}(c_{[k]}) \right| \leq \epsilon.$$

Hence, there exists $m_{[k]}^* \in \mathcal{X}_{\text{diff}}^{\times k}$ such that $\frac{1}{2} \sum_{c_{[k]} \in \mathcal{Y}_{\text{diff}}^{\times k}} \left| P_{C_{[k]}|M_{[k]}}(c_{[k]}|m_{[k]}^*) - P_{C_{[k]}}(c_{[k]}) \right| \leq \epsilon$ by the averaging argument. $\square$

Proof (Claim 2). By the definition, we obtain

$$P_{C_{[k]}|M_{[k]}}(c_{[k]}|m_{[k]}) = \Pr_{S,C_{[k]},M_{[k]}}[C_{[k]} = c_{[k]} \mid M_{[k]} = m_{[k]}]$$

$$= \Pr_{S,M_{[k]}}[f_S(M_{[k]}) = c_{[k]} \mid M_{[k]} = m_{[k]}]$$

$$= \Pr_{S,M_{[k]}}[f_S(m_{[k]}) = c_{[k]} \mid M_{[k]} = m_{[k]}]$$

$$= \Pr_S[f_S(m_{[k]}) = c_{[k]}],$$

where the last equality follows from the independence of $M_{[k]}$ and S. $\square$

Proof (Claim 3). We obtain $P_{C_{[k]}}(c_{[k]}) = \Pr_{S,M_{[k]}}[f_S(M_{[k]}) = c_{[k]}]$ by the definition. If $M_{[k]}$ is uniformly distributed over $\mathcal{X}_{\mathrm{diff}}^{\times k}$, then $f_s(M_{[k]})$ is uniformly distributed over $\mathcal{Y}_{\mathrm{diff}}^{\times k}$ for every $s \in \mathcal{S}$ since f_s is a permutation. Now S is uniformly distributed over $\mathcal{S}$ independently from $M_{[k]}$. Then, for every $c_{[k]}$, we obtain

$$\Pr_{S,M_{[k]}}[f_S(M_{[k]}) = c_{[k]}] = \sum_s \Pr_{S,M_{[k]}}[S = s \wedge f_s(M_{[k]}) = c_{[k]}]$$

$$= \sum_s \Pr_S[S = s] \Pr_{M_{[k]}}[f_s(M_{[k]}) = c_{[k]}]$$

$$= \sum_s \Pr_S[S = s] \frac{1}{|\mathcal{Y}_{\mathrm{diff}}^{\times k}|} = \frac{1}{|\mathcal{Y}_{\mathrm{diff}}^{\times k}|},$$

where the second equality follows from the independence of $M_{[k]}$ and S.   □

Proof (Claim 4). We fix $m_{[k]} \in \mathcal{X}_{\mathrm{diff}}^{\times k}$ which satisfies the assumption, and let $g(m_{[k]}) := \frac{1}{2} \sum_{c_{[k]} \in \mathcal{Y}_{\mathrm{diff}}^{\times k}} \left| \Pr_S[f_S(m_{[k]}) = c_{[k]}] - \frac{1}{|\mathcal{Y}_{\mathrm{diff}}^{\times k}|} \right|$. Hence we obtain $g(m_{[k]}) \geq 1 - \frac{|\mathcal{S}|}{|\mathcal{X}_{\mathrm{diff}}^{\times k}|}$ by applying Lemma 1 ($\mathcal{S}$ and $\mathcal{Y}_{\mathrm{diff}}^{\times k}$ correspond to $\mathcal{A}$ and $\mathcal{B}$ of Lemma 1 respectively, and $|\mathcal{X}_{\mathrm{diff}}^{\times k}| = |\mathcal{Y}_{\mathrm{diff}}^{\times k}|$). On the other hand, it holds that $g(m_{[k]}) \leq \epsilon$ by the assumption. Therefore, we have $|\mathcal{S}| \geq (1 - \epsilon)|\mathcal{X}_{\mathrm{diff}}^{\times k}|$.

Thus, we obtain the proof of Theorem 8.   □

By Theorem 8, k-message ϵ-secrecy requires key length of $\log(2^n \cdot (2^n - 1) \cdots (2^n - k + 1)) + \log(1 - \epsilon)$ bits if the message, ciphertext, and key spaces of the scheme are defined over bit strings, as stated in Theorem 5.

Multi-ciphertext Approximate Non-malleability. Next, we discuss lower bounds of key length with regard to multi-ciphertext approximate non-malleability. At first, we define the k-mixing property of encryption schemes.

Definition 10. *We say that Σ is k-mixing if for every $m_{[k]} \in \mathcal{X}_{\mathrm{diff}}^{\times k}$ and every $c_{[k]} \in \mathcal{Y}_{\mathrm{diff}}^{\times k}$ there exists s such that $f_s(m_{[k]}) = c_{[k]}$, where $f_s(m_{[k]}) := (f_s(m_1), \ldots, f_s(m_k))$.*

A kind of the k-mixing property is required for non-trivial lower bounds of key length for the non-malleability. We now consider the following unnatural scheme over 1-bit message and cipertext spaces. The encryption function does nothing for a given message, i.e., a ciphertext that the function outputs is always equal to a given message. This scheme obviously needs no key, but it satisfies 1-ciphertext 0-non-malleability. Therefore, we cannot obtain non-trivial lower bounds of key length for general k-ciphertext ϵ-non-malleability without posing natural properties to schemes. Fortunately, this scheme does not satisfy the 1-mixing property, and so, it would be possible to show non-trivial lower bounds for the non-malleability under the k-mixing property.

We actually prove the following theorem, which is a more detailed version of Theorem 6, showing lower bounds of key length for k-mixing schemes that satisfy k-ciphertext ϵ-non-malleability.

Theorem 9. *Assume $1 \leq k < |\mathcal{X}| = |\mathcal{Y}|$ and $0 \leq \epsilon < 1$. If a k-mixing scheme Σ satisfies k-ciphertext ϵ-non-malleability, then it holds that $|\mathcal{S}| \geq (1 - \epsilon) \left| \mathcal{Y}_{\text{diff}}^{\times k+1} \right|$.*

Proof. Basically, we make use of the same strategy as the proof of Theorem 8. We choose a pair $(m_{[k]}^*, c_{[k]}^*) = ((m_1^*, ..., m_k^*), (c_1^*, ..., c_k^*)) \in \mathcal{X}_{\text{diff}}^{\times k} \times \mathcal{Y}_{\text{diff}}^{\times k}$ such that $0 < \left| \{ s \in \mathcal{S} \mid f_s(m_{[k]}^*) = c_{[k]}^* \} \right| \leq \left| \{ s \in \mathcal{S} \mid f_s(m_{[k]}) = c_{[k]} \} \right|$ for every $(m_{[k]}, c_{[k]})$. (Note that there exists a key s such that $f_s(m_{[k]}) = c_{[k]}$ for every $m_{[k]}$ and every $c_{[k]}$ from the k-mixing property.) Let $\mathcal{X}^* := \mathcal{X} \setminus \{c_1^*, ..., c_k^*\}$ and $\mathcal{Y}^* := \mathcal{Y} \setminus \{c_1^*, ..., c_k^*\}$.

Then, for every $C_{[k]}$ over $\mathcal{Y}_{\text{diff}}^{\times k}$, we obtain

$$\frac{1}{2} \sum_{\substack{m_{k+1} \in \mathcal{X}^*, \\ c_{k+1} \in \mathcal{Y}^*}} \left| P_{M_{k+1} C_{k+1}}(m_{k+1}, c_{k+1}) - P_{M_{k+1}}(m_{k+1}) P_{C_{k+1}}(c_{k+1}) \right| \leq \epsilon$$

by the definition of k-ciphertext ϵ-non-malleability. We define $\tilde{\mathcal{S}} := \{ s \in \tilde{\mathcal{S}} \mid f_s(m_{[k]}^*) = c_{[k]}^* \}$ as the subset of the key space $\mathcal{S}$. Then, let $\tilde{S}$ be a random variable uniform over $\mathcal{S}$ conditioned that $f_{\tilde{S}}(m_{[k]}^*) = c_{[k]}^*$. (Hence, $\tilde{S}$ is uniformly distributed over $\tilde{\mathcal{S}}$.)

We suppose that C_{k+1} is uniformly distributed over $\mathcal{Y}^*$, i.e., $P_{C_{k+1}}(c_{k+1}) = \frac{1}{|\mathcal{Y}^*|}$ for every c_{k+1}. Now we give five claims. We can immediately obtain the statement of Theorem 9 by combining them.

Claim 5. *If Σ satisfies k-ciphertext ϵ-non-malleability, then there exists $c_{k+1}^* \in \mathcal{Y}^*$ such that $\frac{1}{2} \sum_{m_{k+1} \in \mathcal{X}^*} \left| P_{M_{k+1}|C_{k+1}}(m_{k+1}|c_{k+1}^*) - P_{M_{k+1}}(m_{k+1}) \right| \leq \epsilon$.*

Claim 6. *It holds that $P_{M_{k+1}|C_{k+1}}(m_{k+1}|c_{k+1}) = \Pr_{\tilde{S}}[f_{\tilde{S}}^{-1}(c_{k+1}) = m_{k+1}]$ for every $m_{k+1} \in \mathcal{X}^*$ and every $c_{k+1} \in \mathcal{Y}^*$*

Claim 7. *If C_{k+1} is uniformly distributed over $\mathcal{Y}_{\text{diff}}^{\times k}$, then M_{k+1} is uniformly distributed over $\mathcal{X}^*$, i.e., $P_{M_{k+1}}(m_{k+1}) = \frac{1}{|\mathcal{X}^*|}$ for every $m_{k+1} \in \mathcal{X}^*$.*

Claim 8. *Assume there exists $c_{k+1}^* \in \mathcal{Y}^*$ such that*

$$\frac{1}{2} \sum_{m_{k+1} \in \mathcal{X}^*} \left| \Pr_{\tilde{S}}[f_{\tilde{S}}^{-1}(c_{k+1}^*) = m_{k+1}] - \frac{1}{|\mathcal{X}^*|} \right| \leq \epsilon.$$

Then it holds that $|\tilde{\mathcal{S}}| \geq (1 - \epsilon) |\mathcal{Y}^*| = (1 - \epsilon) \frac{\left| \mathcal{Y}_{\text{diff}}^{\times k+1} \right|}{\left| \mathcal{Y}_{\text{diff}}^{\times k} \right|}$.

Claim 9. *It holds that $|\mathcal{S}| \geq \left| \mathcal{Y}_{\text{diff}}^{\times k} \right| \cdot \left| \tilde{\mathcal{S}} \right|$ if Σ is k-mixing.*

We give the proofs of the above claims.

Proof (Claim 5). Since C_{k+1} is uniformly distributed over $\mathcal{Y}^*$ and Σ satisfies k-ciphertext ϵ-non-malleability, we obtain

$$d(M_{k+1}C_{k+1}, M_{k+1} \cdot C_{k+1} | M_{[k]} = m_{[k]}, C_{[k]} = c_{[k]})$$

$$= \frac{1}{2} \sum_{m_{k+1} \in \mathcal{X}^*, c_{k+1} \in \mathcal{Y}^*} \left| P_{M_{k+1}C_{k+1}}(m_{k+1}, c_{k+1}) - P_{M_{k+1}}(m_{k+1})P_{C_{k+1}}(c_{k+1}) \right|$$

$$= \frac{1}{2} \sum_{c_{k+1} \in \mathcal{Y}^*} P_{C_{k+1}}(c_{k+1}) \sum_{m_{k+1} \in \mathcal{X}^*} \left| P_{M_{k+1}|C_{k+1}}(m_{k+1}|c_{k+1}) - P_{M_{k+1}}(m_{k+1}) \right|$$

$$= \frac{1}{|\mathcal{Y}^*|} \sum_{c_{k+1} \in \mathcal{Y}^*} \frac{1}{2} \sum_{m_{k+1} \in \mathcal{X}^*} \left| P_{M_{k+1}|C_{k+1}}(m_{k+1}|c_{k+1}) - P_{M_{k+1}}(m_{k+1}) \right| \leq \epsilon.$$

Hence, there exists $c^*_{k+1} \in \mathcal{Y}^*$ such that $\frac{1}{2} \sum_{m_{k+1} \in \mathcal{X}^*} \left| P_{M_{k+1}|C_{k+1}}(m_{k+1}|c^*_{k+1}) - P_{M_{k+1}}(m_{k+1}) \right| \leq \epsilon$ by the averaging argument. □

Proof (Claim 6). By the definition, we obtain

$$P_{M_{k+1}|C_{k+1}}(m_{k+1}|c_{k+1}) = \Pr_{\tilde{S}, M_{k+1}, C_{k+1}} [M_{k+1} = m_{k+1} \mid C_{k+1} = c_{k+1}]$$

$$= \Pr_{\tilde{S}, C_{k+1}} [f_{\tilde{S}}^{-1}(C_{k+1}) = m_{k+1} \mid C_{k+1} = c_{k+1}]$$

$$= \Pr_{\tilde{S}, C_{k+1}} [f_{\tilde{S}}^{-1}(C_{k+1}) = m_{k+1} \mid C_{k+1} = c_{k+1}]$$

$$= \Pr_{\tilde{S}} [f_{\tilde{S}}^{-1}(c_{k+1}) = m_{k+1}].$$

□

Proof (Claim 7). As in the proof of Claim 6, we have $P_{M_{k+1}}(m_{k+1}) = \Pr_{\tilde{S}, C_{k+1}} [f_{\tilde{S}}^{-1}(C_{k+1}) = m_{k+1}]$ by the definition. If C_{k+1} is uniformly distributed over $\mathcal{Y}^*$, then $f_s^{-1}(C_{k+1})$ is uniformly distributed over $\mathcal{X}^*$ for every $s \in \tilde{S}$. From the assumption, C_{k+1} is independent from S, and thus so is C_{k+1} from $\tilde{S}$. Hence, we obtain for every m_{k+1},

$$\Pr_{\tilde{S}, C_{k+1}} [f_{\tilde{S}}^{-1}(C_{k+1}) = m_{k+1}] = \sum_s \Pr_{\tilde{S}, C_{k+1}} [\tilde{S} = s \wedge f_s^{-1}(C_{k+1}) = m_{k+1}]$$

$$= \sum_{s \in \tilde{S}} \Pr_{\tilde{S}} [\tilde{S} = s] \Pr_{C_{k+1}} [f_s^{-1}(C_{k+1}) = m_{k+1}]$$

$$= \sum_{s \in \tilde{S}} \Pr_{\tilde{S}} [\tilde{S} = s] \frac{1}{|\mathcal{X}^*|} = \frac{1}{|\mathcal{X}^*|},$$

where the second equality follows from the independence of C_{k+1} and $\tilde{S}$.

Proof (Claim 8). Basically, we make use of the same strategy as the proof of Theorem 7.

First, we assume that $\left|\tilde{\mathcal{S}}\right| < |\mathcal{X}^*|$. Otherwise we obtain $\left|\tilde{\mathcal{S}}\right| \geq |\mathcal{X}^*| = |\mathcal{Y}^*|$ as a lower bound, and thus, the proof is done.

We fix $c_{k+1}^* \in \mathcal{Y}^*$ which satisfies the assumption, and let $h(c_{k+1}^*) :=$ $\frac{1}{2} \sum_{m_{k+1} \in \mathcal{X}^*} \left| \mathrm{Pr}_{\tilde{S}}[f_{\tilde{S}}^{-1}(c_{k+1}^*) = m_{k+1}] - \frac{1}{|\mathcal{X}^*|} \right|$. Hence we obtain $h(c_{k+1}^*) \geq 1 - \frac{|\tilde{\mathcal{S}}|}{|\mathcal{Y}^*|}$ by applying Lemma 1 ($\tilde{S}$ and $\mathcal{X}^*$ correspond to $\mathcal{A}$ and $\mathcal{B}$ of Lemma 1, respectively.

On the other hand, it holds that $h(c_{k+1}^*) \leq \epsilon$ by the assumption. Therefore, we obtain $\left|\tilde{\mathcal{S}}\right| \geq (1 - \epsilon)|\mathcal{Y}^*| = (1 - \epsilon)\frac{|\mathcal{Y}_{\mathrm{diff}}^{\times k+1}|}{|\mathcal{Y}_{\mathrm{diff}}^{\times k}|}$. $\square$

Proof (Claim 9). For the message $m_{[k]}^*$ defined above, we have

$$|\mathcal{S}| = \left| \bigcup_{c_{[k]}} \{s \in \mathcal{S} \mid f_s(m_{[k]}^*) = c_{[k]}\} \right| = \sum_{c_{[k]}} |\{s \in \mathcal{S} \mid f_s(m_{[k]}^*) = c_{[k]}\}| \geq \left|\mathcal{Y}_{\mathrm{diff}}^{\times k}\right| \cdot \left|\tilde{\mathcal{S}}\right|,$$

where the second equality follows from the fact that for every distinct $c_{[k]}, c_{[k]}'$ the sets $\{s \in \mathcal{S} \mid f_s(m_{[k]}^*) = c_{[k]}\}$ and $\{s \in \mathcal{S} \mid f_s(m_{[k]}^*) = c_{[k]}'\}$ are disjoint, and the last inequality follows from the definitions of $(m_{[k]}^*, c_{[k]}^*)$ and $\tilde{\mathcal{S}}$ and the k-mixing property.

Thus, we obtain $|\mathcal{S}| \geq (1 - \epsilon)\left|\mathcal{Y}_{\mathrm{diff}}^{\times k+1}\right|$, which corresponds to the claimed result of Theorem 9. $\square$

By Theorem 9, if the message, ciphertext, and key spaces of the scheme satisfying $(k-1)$-ciphertext ϵ-non-malleability are defined over bit strings, then the key length is at least $\log(2^n \cdot (2^n - 1) \cdots (2^n - k + 1)) + \log(1 - \epsilon)$ bits, as stated in Theorem 6.

Inspecting the above proof carefully, we can still obtain non-trivial lower bounds of key length for k-ciphertext ϵ-non-malleability even if Σ is not k-mixing.

Definition 11. *We say that Σ is δ-degenerate k-mixing if for every $m_{[k]} \in \mathcal{X}_{\mathrm{diff}}^{\times k}$ we have*

$$\Pr_{C_{[k]}} [\forall s \in \mathcal{S} : f_s(m_{[k]}) \neq C_{[k]}] \leq \delta,$$

where $C_{[k]}$ is uniformly distributed over $\mathcal{Y}_{\mathrm{diff}}^{\times k}$.

Obviously, 0-degenerate k-mixing Σ is k-mixing. The following theorem shows lower bounds of key length for δ-degenerate k-mixing scheme.

Theorem 10. *Assume $1 \leq k < |\mathcal{X}| = |\mathcal{Y}|$ and $0 \leq \epsilon < 1$. If a δ-degenerate k-mixing scheme Σ satisfies k-ciphertext ϵ-non-malleability, then it holds that $|\mathcal{S}| \geq (1 - \epsilon)(1 - \delta) \left|\mathcal{Y}_{\mathrm{diff}}^{\times k+1}\right|$.*

Proof. We choose a pair $(m^*_{[k]}, c^*_{[k]}) \in \mathcal{X}^{\times k}_{\text{diff}} \times \mathcal{Y}^{\times k}_{\text{diff}}$ such that $\left| \{ s \in \mathcal{S} \mid f_s(m^*_{[k]}) = c^*_{[k]} \} \right| \leq \left| \{ s \in \mathcal{S} \mid f_s(m_{[k]}) = c_{[k]} \} \right|$ for every $(m_{[k]}, c_{[k]})$ for which there exists $s \in \mathcal{S}$ such that $f_s(m_{[k]}) = c_{[k]}$. Note that Claims 5, 6, 7 and 8 do not depend on the definition of $(m^*_{[k]}, c^*_{[k]})$ and the k-mixing property. These properties are required only in the proof of Claim 9. Instead of Claim 9 we prove the following alternative claim for δ-degenerate k-mixing property:

Claim 10. It holds that $|\mathcal{S}| \geq (1 - \delta) \left| \mathcal{Y}^{\times k}_{\text{diff}} \right| \cdot \left| \tilde{\mathcal{S}} \right|$ if Σ is δ-degenerate k-mixing.

Proof. For the message $m^*_{[k]}$ defined above, we have

$$
\begin{aligned}
|\mathcal{S}| &= \sum_{c_{[k]} : \exists s : f_s(m^*_{[k]}) = c_{[k]}} \left| \{ s \in \mathcal{S} \mid f_s(m^*_{[k]}) = c_{[k]} \} \right| \\
&\geq (1 - \delta) \left| \mathcal{Y}^{\times k}_{\text{diff}} \right| \cdot \left| \{ s \in \mathcal{S} \mid f_s(m^*_{[k]}) = c^*_{[k]} \} \right| \\
&\geq (1 - \delta) \left| \mathcal{Y}^{\times k}_{\text{diff}} \right| \cdot \left| \tilde{\mathcal{S}} \right|,
\end{aligned}
$$

where the second last inequality follows from the definitions of $(m^*_{[k]}, c^*_{[k]})$ and $\tilde{\mathcal{S}}$ and the δ-degenerate k-mixing property.

By combining Claims 5, 6, 7 and 8 and 10, we obtain the statement of this theorem. □

4   Conclusion

In this paper, we proved lower bounds of the key length for k-wise ϵ-dependent random permutations and relevant symmetric-key encryption schemes, which asymptotically match to the known upper bounds (up to constant factors) if the approximation factor ϵ is a constant. An obvious open question is to close the gap between upper and lower bounds of the key length, e.g., for k-wise ϵ-dependent random permutations. As mentioned in Sect. 1, the existential upper bound $O(nk)$ (for a small k) of Kuperberg et al. [4] for k-wise 0-dependent random permutations implies the possibility of improvements over the best known k-wise ϵ-dependent random permutations of key length $O(nk + \log \epsilon^{-1})$ by Kaplan et al. [7]. It would be quite interesting if one could (even existentially) prove upper bounds less than $O(nk)$ of the key length for k-wise ϵ-dependent random permutations.

Acknowledgements. This work is partially supported by the JSPS Grant-in-Aid for Scientific Research (A) No.16H01705 and the ELC project (Grant-in-Aid for Scientific Research on Innovative Areas MEXT Japan, KAKENHI No. 24106009).

References

1. Naor, M., Reingold, O.: On the construction of pseudorandom permutations: Luby-Rackoff revisited. J. Cryptol. **12**(1), 29–66 (1999)
2. Hoory, S., Magen, A., Myers, S., Rackoff, C.: Simple permutations mix well. Theor. Comput. Sci. **348**(2–3), 251–261 (2005)
3. Cameron, P.J.: Permutation groups. In: Graham, R.L., Grötschel, M., Lovász, L. (eds.) Handbook of Combinatorics, vol. 1, pp. 611–645. MIT Press, Cambridge (1995)
4. Kuperberg, G., Lovett, S., Peled, R.: Probabilistic existence of rigid combinatorial structures. In: Karloff, H.J., Pitassi, T. (eds.) STOC, pp. 1091–1106. ACM (2012)
5. Luby, M., Rackoff, C.: How to construct pseudorandom permutations from pseudorandom functions. SIAM J. Comput. **17**(2), 373–386 (1988)
6. Brodsky, A., Hoory, S.: Simple permutations mix even better. Random Struct. Algorithms **32**(3), 274–289 (2008)
7. Kaplan, E., Naor, M., Reingold, O.: Derandomized constructions of k-wise (almost) independent permutations. Algorithmica **55**(1), 113–133 (2009)
8. Kawachi, A., Takebe, H., Tanaka, K.: Symmetric-key encryption scheme with multi-ciphertext non-malleability. In: Hanaoka, G., Yamauchi, T. (eds.) IWSEC 2012. LNCS, vol. 7631, pp. 123–137. Springer, Heidelberg (2012)
9. Dodis, Y.: Shannon impossibility. In: Smith, A. (ed.) ICITS 2012. LNCS, vol. 7412, pp. 100–110. Springer, Heidelberg (2012). Revisited
10. Shannon, C.: Communication theory of secrecy systems. Bell Syst. Tech. J. **28**(4), 656–715 (1949)
11. Kawachi, A., Portmann, C., Tanaka, K.: Characterization of the relations between information-theoretic non-malleability, secrecy, and authenticity. In: Fehr, S. (ed.) ICITS 2011. LNCS, vol. 6673, pp. 6–24. Springer, Heidelberg (2011)
12. Hanaoka, G.: Some information theoretic arguments for encryption: non-malleability and chosen-ciphertext security (invited talk). In: Safavi-Naini, R. (ed.) ICITS 2008. LNCS, vol. 5155, pp. 223–231. Springer, Heidelberg (2008)
13. Bierbrauer, J., Johansson, T., Kabatianskii, G.A., Smeets, B.J.M.: On families of hash functions via geometric codes and concatenation. In: Stinson, D.R. (ed.) CRYPTO 1993. LNCS, vol. 773, pp. 331–342. Springer, Heidelberg (1994)
14. Hanaoka, G., Shikata, J., Hanaoka, Y., Imai, H.: Unconditionally secure anonymous encryption and group authentication. Comput. J. **49**(3), 310–321 (2006)
15. McAven, L., Safavi-Naini, R., Yung, M.: Unconditionally secure encryption under strong attacks. In: Wang, H., Pieprzyk, J., Varadharajan, V. (eds.) ACISP 2004. LNCS, vol. 3108, pp. 427–439. Springer, Heidelberg (2004)

Privacy Preserving

Privacy-Preserving Wi-Fi Fingerprinting Indoor Localization

Tao Zhang[1]([⊠]), Sherman S.M. Chow[1], Zhe Zhou[1], and Ming Li[2]

[1] Department of Information Engineering, The Chinese University of Hong Kong,
Sha Tin, N.T., Hong Kong
{zt112,sherman,zz113}@ie.cuhk.edu.hk
[2] Department of Computer Science and Engineering, University of Nevada,
Reno, NV 89557, USA
mingli@unr.edu

Abstract. A diversity of indoor localization techniques have become accurate and ready to use. A client first measures its location characteristics, and then calculates its location with the information provided by the localization server. However, this process may reveal the location information of the client or leak the area information stored on the server. This hinders the growth of indoor localization, but there are only a few solutions available in the literature. In this paper, we formulate an adversary model for fingerprint-based indoor localization techniques, and propose a cryptographic scheme to protect the privacy of both parties in a localization process. Our scheme utilizes the current Wi-Fi fingerprint based positioning techniques, including Gaussian radial basis functions and sigmoid kernels.

Keywords: Indoor localization · Location privacy · Wi-Fi fingerprinting · Applied cryptography · Homomorphic encryption

1 Introduction

Nowadays, flourishing with mobile devices, the emerging location-aware devices and location-based services make our daily life easier and more productive. People now are accustomed to locate themselves and find the nearby facilities using location based services via their location-aware mobile devices. However, global positioning system (GPS) may not be always available especially when the satellite signal is blocked indoors. This motivates researches on developing indoor localization techniques [2,10,11,16,17,19–23,26,27].

Wi-Fi fingerprinting based localization technique [2,27] is one of the promising approaches to provide accurate indoor localization. It involves a localization server and a series of measuring units, usually the Wi-Fi access points (APs), deployed in the covered area. With a large set of known matching pair of locations and fingerprints, the localization technique leverages machine learning algorithms to learn their characteristics and decide the location of an unseen fingerprint.

© Springer International Publishing Switzerland 2016
K. Ogawa and K. Yoshioka (Eds.): IWSEC 2016, LNCS 9836, pp. 215–233, 2016.
DOI: 10.1007/978-3-319-44524-3_13

The localization process has two phases, an offline phase and an online decision phase. In the offline phase, the server collects the necessary information of the covered area to construct the fingerprint database and train the decision algorithm. A training data entry can be a tuple of the following: the coordinates of testing positions, and the corresponding signal fingerprint such as the received signal strength indicator (RSSI). The online phase consists of two sub-phases: a measuring phase and a calculation phase. In the measuring phase, a client measures its fingerprint with the help of the measuring units and asks for its current location by requesting the server to perform computation on the fingerprint. This fingerprint can be the result of a site survey of RSSI measurements from multiple APs, or obtained from other measurement techniques. In the calculation phase, the server uses the trained decision algorithm to calculate the location of the client, and sends this location back.

1.1   Privacy Issues in Wi-Fi Fingerprinting

Although Wi-Fi fingerprinting based technique is a promising approach for indoor localization, it reveals the location information of the client to the server. A malicious server can construct the trace of a client with this information, and probably figure out the habits, interests, activities, and relationships of the clients [13,18]. This privacy issue hinders the growth of localization applications [8]. One trivial solution to this problem is to let the clients download the entire fingerprint database and locally perform the computation upon entering the area [9,27]. However, it reveals the location information of the area stored in the server to the clients. Moreover, even if the geographical database is open to the clients, the downloading process degrades user experience. Furthermore, the clients need to download a new database each time when they enter the area, using relatively weak mobile devices.

1.2   Our Contributions

We formulate an adversary model for privacy-preserving indoor localization. In our model, the measuring parties (the localization server and the measuring units) and the clients do not trust each other, and measuring parties may collude to locate clients and track their trajectories. We propose a cryptographic solution to protect both the location privacy of clients and database confidentiality of the server while applying existing Wi-Fi fingerprint-based positioning techniques.

We assume that the localization server performs the training phase by itself. Hence, we only consider the privacy issues of the online location decision phase.

The focus of this paper is Wi-Fi fingerprint-based system. Yet, our framework can also apply to other localization systems such as trilateration positioning or infrared localization systems [21] with minor modification. Our system has the following properties.

- Cryptographic protection: We use encryption to guarantee privacy, instead of a software-based means such as access control[1].
- High efficiency: The decision process is efficient. We utilize additive homomorphic encryption instead of fully homomorphic encryption. Section 6 presents the performance analysis of the proposed scheme.
- No trusted party: Unlike the previous privacy-preserving localization schemes (e.g., [17]), we consider all the involving parties untrusted. We consider both the location privacy of the clients and the data privacy of the server.
- No specialized devices: Our scheme does not require additional specialized devices or significant adjustment of the current infrastructures.

1.3 Related Work

The research on indoor localization has been active for nearly three decades, from the initial context of specialized devices to the current era of pervasive mobile computing. Early localization techniques require the installment of specialized devices for signals other than Wi-Fi such as infrared [21], ultrasound [16,22], and acoustic background spectrum [19]. Wang et al. [20] proposed an indoor localization technique based on the landmarks of the area which does not require pre-knowledge of the area.

A series of researches have been done on inertial localization [10,23,26]. In the pre-Wi-Fi time, RF fingerprinting is used [2,27]. More recent schemes employ Wi-Fi fingerprinting. Fingerprint-based schemes take the advantage of Wi-Fi facilities and require no extra device installation. Rai et al. [17] employed crowdsourcing to minimize the effort of both the clients and the server for location calibration. It is a collaborative approach in which some clients who are willing to reveal their location will interact with a server for localization, and all clients share their locations with other clients as references. To determine the location, each of them will pick neighbors with the strongest signal and measures their distance to locate itself. In other words, clients trust each other regarding location privacy.

Li et al. [11] proposed a localization scheme with privacy. Their design uses k-nearest neighbor (k-NN) algorithm [6] to estimate the client location, which has certain limits. The efficiency of the server side algorithm decreases significantly when compared with the original k-NN indoor localization algorithm without location privacy. The computation on the client side is heavy. We will elaborate this in Sect. 6.

Privacy-preserving machine learning is a hot topic recently. However, most of these researches [1,24,28,29] focus on addressing the privacy issues in the training phase. Our paper focuses on the privacy issues in the decision phase.

Another line of research work considers the privacy issues in location-based services (LBS) [7,12,15,25,31]. These works consider the scenario that the clients have already obtained their own location by some means and need to get LBS

---

[1] Of course, a careful implementation is still required in order not to reveal extra information about user locations.

based on their location without revealing (too much information of) their location to the other parties. We can combine our privacy-preserving localization with these privacy-preserving LSB in practice to provide a complete privacy-preserving solution for LBS applications.

2   Preliminaries

2.1   Notations

We focus on 2-dimensional area for simplicity. The measuring principles and the positioning algorithms are the same for 2-dimensional and 3-dimensional spaces.

We denote the coordinates of the client by (x, y). The signal measurement a client obtains is in the form of a vector $s = (s_1, s_2, \cdots, s_l)$, where s_i is the signal measurement from the measuring unit AP_i, and l is the total number of measuring units deployed in the area. We denote the ciphertext of s_i by S_i, and $S = (S_1, S_2, \cdots, S_l)$.

2.2   Measuring Principle

Received signal strength indicator (RSSI) technique uses the attenuation of emitted signal strength to estimate the distance of the mobile device from the measuring unit [2]. It can serve as a distance measure in localization.

2.3   Positioning Algorithms

There are many full-fledged positioning algorithms available in the literature. This part briefly describes the ones we use in our privacy-preserving indoor localization system.

Support Vector Machine for Regression (SVR). Support vector regression has been used to provide accurate indoor localization [3]. In the training phase, (w, b) is computed by solving the following problem:

$$\text{Minimize}_{w,b,\xi} \quad \frac{1}{2}||w||^2 + C \cdot (\sum_{i=1}^{l} \xi_i)^k$$

$$\text{subject to} \quad \begin{cases} z_i \cdot (\langle w, s \rangle + b) \geq 1 - \xi_i, i = 1, 2, \cdots, l \\ \xi_i \geq 0, i = 1, 2, \cdots, l \\ ||w||^2 \leq c_r \end{cases}$$

where (w, b) is a tunable parameter of the decision function, s is the training data (RSSI from the training set in localization), C and k determine the cost of the constraint violation from the slacks, and c_r limits the coefficient vector. Choosing a proper kernel function $\langle w, s \rangle$ can increase the accuracy of the algorithm. Common kernels include

- Dot product: $\langle w, s \rangle = w \cdot s$
- Gaussian radial basis functions (RBF): $\langle w, s \rangle = e^{-\gamma \|w-s\|^2}$, the parameter γ is chosen with trials in the training phase, while we consider that it is given.
- Sigmoid (hyperbolic tangent): $\langle w, s \rangle = \tanh(\alpha w \cdot s + \beta)$ with parameters α and β, where $\tanh(x) = \frac{e^{2x}-1}{e^{2x}+1}$

Some kernel functions are not efficiently supported by our framework:

- Homogeneous polynomial functions: $\langle w, s \rangle = (w \cdot s)^d$, for a given degree d
- Inhomogeneous polynomial functions: $\langle w, s \rangle = (w \cdot s + 1)^d$ for a given degree d

For a new data s (RSSI from a client), $\langle w, s \rangle + b$ will give the decision result. Burges [4] provides a detailed introduction of machine learning based on support vector machine and the different kernel functions.

2.4 Homomorphic Encryption

Homomorphic encryption allows certain computations on ciphertext(s) without using private key. The homomorphic operation generates a new ciphertext whose plaintext matches the result of the corresponding computations performed on the original plaintext(s).

Paillier Encryption. Paillier encryption [14] is a public-key encryption scheme which supports homomorphic computations for addition of ciphertext pairs (or plaintext-ciphertext pairs), and multiplication of plaintext-ciphertext pairs. It consists of the algorithms $(\mathsf{KeyGen}(), \mathsf{Enc}(), \mathsf{Dec}())$, where $\mathsf{KeyGen}()$ generates the public/private key pairs, $\mathsf{Enc}()$ encrypts a message under the public key, and $\mathsf{Dec}()$ decrypts a given ciphertext using the private key.

$\mathsf{KeyGen}(1^\kappa)$:

1. Choose two κ-bit prime numbers p and q randomly and independently such that $\gcd(pq, (p-1)(q-1)) = 1$, and compute $n = p \cdot q$ and $\lambda = \mathrm{lcm}(p-1, q-1)$.
2. Select $g \xleftarrow{\$} \mathbb{Z}_{n^2}^*$ and compute $\mu = (L(g^\lambda \bmod n^2))^{-1} \bmod n$, where $L(u) = \frac{u-1}{n}$.

Output the public-private key pair $\mathsf{pk} = (n, g)$, $\mathsf{sk} = (\lambda, \mu)$.

$\mathsf{Enc}(\mathsf{pk}, m)$: To encrypt a numeric message $m \in \mathbb{Z}_n$, select $r \xleftarrow{\$} \mathbb{Z}_n^*$ and compute $c = g^m \cdot r^n \bmod n^2$. Output c as the ciphertext.

$\mathsf{Dec}(\mathsf{sk}, c)$: To decrypt a ciphertext c, compute $m = L(c^\lambda \bmod n^2) \cdot \mu \bmod n$.

Homomorphic addition. Multiplication of a plaintext-ciphertext pair or two ciphertexts results in a ciphertext encrypting the addition of the two plaintexts:

$$\mathsf{Dec}(\mathsf{sk}, \mathsf{Enc}(\mathsf{pk}, m_1) \cdot \mathsf{Enc}(\mathsf{pk}, m_2) \bmod n^2) = m_1 + m_2 \bmod n,$$
$$\mathsf{Dec}(\mathsf{sk}, \mathsf{Enc}(\mathsf{pk}, m_1) \cdot g^{m_2} \bmod n^2) = m_1 + m_2 \bmod n.$$

Multiplication of a plaintext with a ciphertext. Raising a ciphertext to the power of a plaintext results in a new one encrypting multiplication of the two plaintexts:

$$\mathsf{Dec}(\mathsf{sk}, \mathsf{Enc}(\mathsf{pk}, m_1)^{m_2} \bmod n^2) = m_1 \cdot m_2 \bmod n.$$

3   System Model

This section gives the system model and our general ideas to construct a privacy-preserving indoor localization system. An indoor localization system involves three parties: a localization server, a set of measuring units, and clients. The localization server and the measuring units can be considered as one entity.

Localization Server is a server holding the Wi-Fi fingerprint database of a target area. It is in charge of the computation of the locations for the clients.

Measuring Units are auxiliary devices deployed in a target area. In a Wi-Fi fingerprint setting, a measuring unit can be a Wi-Fi access point. A measuring unit passively measures the location fingerprint for a client. Our choice in this paper is RSSI, which allows passive measurement.

Clients are the users with mobile devices who want to know their location. A client can collect RSSI from the measuring units and send the RSSI to the server to initiate a localization query.

3.1   Measuring Phase

In this phase, the client needs to communicate with at least three measuring units to create a fingerprint. The client should be anonymous in this phase.

We apply *received signal strength indicator* (RSSI) as our measurement method for fingerprinting the location of the client. RSSI-based measuring technique requires only unilateral communication between the client and the measuring units. This means a measuring unit cannot obtain the fingerprint of a client device. This kind of measurement is inherently anonymous and unlinkable. The measuring units are constantly broadcasting measuring signals. The client does not need to return any message, such as MAC address, IP address, or any other identifying information of the client, to the measuring units for the measurement.

3.2   Calculation Phase at the Server

In this phase, the client sends the collected information pieces to the server for localization. The server uses a Wi-Fi fingerprint based algorithm to compute the result. We then develop a scheme for protecting location privacy of the clients by applying homomorphic encryption, which consists of the following steps:

1. The client generates a public-private key pair for a homomorphic encryption scheme, encrypts the measurement results under the public key, and sends the ciphertexts along with the public key to the localization server.
2. The localization server homomorphically operates on the encrypted measurement results using the information from the Wi-Fi fingerprint database to calculate the location of the client. The localization server returns the resulting ciphertext to the client.
3. The client decrypts the ciphertext from the localization server using the private decryption key to get the location information.

4   Adversary Model

This section discusses the possible adversaries in an indoor localization system. For protecting the location privacy of the client, the localization server and the measuring units are considered as adversaries. On the other hand, for protecting the database of the server, the client is considered as an adversary.

Localization Server. Malicious localization server is the strongest adversary. In a typical system, the final calculation of the location mostly relies on the localization server. This enables the server to know the location information of all the mobile devices, and even construct an approximate trace of a device with multiple localizations.

Measuring Units. The measuring units are indispensable in an indoor localization system, yet they have less power than a malicious localization server in general. The client collects one piece of the measuring result from each unit during localization. Theoretically, it requires at least three measuring units (for a 2-dimensional area, or four for a 3-dimensional area) located in different places. If the communication during measurement is unilateral, the measuring result is inherently secure against curious measuring units. Take RSSI as an example, RSSI is measured at the client device by evaluating the signal strength from each measuring unit without sending any information back. This kind of measurement leaks no information to the measuring units.

If the communication during measurement is bilateral, colluding measuring units are able to obtain the full measuring result of the client, and compute the location with the help of the localization server (which maintains the Wi-Fi fingerprint database). Hence, it is crucial to make the measurements unlinkable or anonymous for measurement techniques involving bilateral communication.

RSSI involves only unilateral communication, so we do not need to discuss the security against measuring units.

Eavesdropper. Eavesdropper has weaker power than the former two kinds of adversaries. It passively eavesdrops on the communication channel between the client and the localization server, and obtains the final result of the localization. Hence, securing the communication channel between the server and the client is necessary for security against the eavesdroppers.

Localization Client. The localization server should protect its database from being exposed. Malicious users can use this information to track the other users or just sell the information for profit.

Definition 1 (Location Privacy). *An adversary colluding with the localization server and the measuring units succeeds in a location privacy attack if after the localization query, the adversary obtains either of the following*

- *the Wi-Fi fingerprint of the querying client;*
- *the location of the querying client.*

A localization system is location privacy-preserving if it resists location privacy attack.

Definition 2 (Data Privacy). *An adversary succeeds in a data privacy attack if after a number of localization queries, it can perform localization on a given Wi-Fi fingerprint with a certain level of accuracy without the help of the localization server. A localization system is data privacy-preserving if it resists data privacy attack.*

This definition of data privacy is strong. Actually, it is known in the literature of Wi-Fi fingerprinting that, the weakness in ensuring data privacy is inherent. Specifically, an adversary can get enough information to construct a decision function with enough rounds of localization processes or collect RSSI-location pairs by itself.

To launch such an attack, there are obstacles for the adversary though. First, the adversary needs a large number of RSSI-location pairs to build a decision function for an area. The number of data entries decides the accuracy of this decision function. Second, even with enough data entries as the training set, the adversary needs to set up the system and perform a training phase involving the collected data entries. For a typical client, the cost of performing the training phase of SVR-based machine learning algorithm is high. Hence, it is resource-consuming for an adversary to perform accurate localization without the help of the server. We thus aim for protection against a weaker version of data privacy attack, where the accuracy requirement on the result of the adversary is lowered.

Definition 3 (Privacy-Preserving Localization). *A localization system is privacy-preserving if it is both data privacy-preserving and location privacy-preserving.*

5   Our Proposed System

This section describes the privacy-preserving indoor localization system.

5.1   Framework

In the measuring phase, the client measures the RSSI from measuring units within the range. In the calculation phase, we use SVR-based algorithm as the positioning algorithm.

A fingerprinting localization implemented with machine learning techniques requires a training phase before it can provide localization service. In the training phase, the system collects enough data of the form $(s, (x, y))$ and uses the data as the training set, where s_i component of the measurement vector s is the RSSI of AP_i at the position of the client. The objective of the training process is to find an optimal tuple (w_x, b_x, w_y, b_y) which fits the training data best, where (w, b) denotes the parameters of a decision function resulting from the training phase as discussed in Sect. 2. The location coordinates are in the form of vectors. Their dimension decides the number of optimization problems to solve. At the end of the training phase, the localization server obtains the resulting (w_x, b_x, w_y, b_y)

tuple and stores it for positioning. For an input fingerprint s, the positioning calculation is $x = \langle w_x, s \rangle + b_x$, $y = \langle w_y, s \rangle + b_y$.

We first give a brief description of the basic Wi-Fi fingerprinting indoor localization without privacy protection.

1. The localization server collects a set of training data which are location-fingerprint pairs. The server trains the decision algorithm with all the APs in the area and obtains (w_x, b_x, w_y, b_y).
2. A client carrying a mobile device enters the area and gets an RSSI fingerprint s from measuring units. The client sends s as plaintext to the server.
3. The localization server receives s and fetches (w_x, b_x, w_y, b_y) to compute $x = \langle w_x, s \rangle + b_x$ and $y = \langle w_y, s \rangle + b_y$. The localization server sends (x, y) to the client as the client's location. The details of computing (x, y) are stated below.
   - **Dot product:** $x = w_x \cdot s + b_x$, $y = w_y \cdot s + b_y$.
   - **RBF:** $x = e^{-\gamma_x(w_x - s)^2} + b_x$, $y = e^{-\gamma_y(w_y - s)^2} + b_y$.
   - **Sigmoid:** $x = \tanh(\alpha_x w_x \cdot s + \beta_x) + b_x$, $y = \tanh(\alpha_y w_y \cdot s + \beta_y) + b_y$.

This basic implementation does not provide any privacy protection for either the location information of clients or the server database. Now we discuss how to provide privacy-preserving localization service.

1. The localization server collects a set of training data which are location-fingerprint pairs. The server first divides the APs into several subsets with size greater than a threshold τ. The server trains the decision algorithm with each AP subset obtains $\{(w_x, b_x, w_y, b_y)_I\}$ for each subset I.
2. A mobile device enters the area and gets an RSSI fingerprint s from measuring units.
3. The client generates a Paillier public-private key pair (pk, sk) and encrypts each s_i in s under pk. The encrypted fingerprint is $S = (S_1, S_2, \cdots, S_l)$, where $S_i = \mathsf{Enc}(\mathsf{pk}, s_i)$. The client sends the encrypted fingerprint and pk to the localization server, and holds the private key sk in secret.
4. The localization server receives S, randomly chooses a common AP subset I of the client's RSSI and the server's database, and fetches $(w_x, b_x, w_y, b_y)_I$ to compute $X = \langle w_x, S \rangle + b_x$ and $Y = \langle w_y, S \rangle + b_y$. The localization server sends (X, Y) to the client.
5. The client receives (X, Y), and computes $x = \mathsf{Dec}(\mathsf{sk}, X)$ and $y = \mathsf{Dec}(\mathsf{sk}, Y)$. The estimated location of the client is (x, y).

5.2 Instantiations

The operations in Step 3 and Step 4 are subject to the kernel function used in SVR. For dot product, the operations are fully supported by simple use of Paillier encryption. For RBF and sigmoid kernels, the operations of the decision function are not fully supported by Paillier encryption, so the clients need to perform more operations than just encrypting the RSSI and decrypting the coordinates.

– **Dot product.** Paillier encryption supports the operation needed for a dot product well. In Step 3, the computation of (X, Y) is

$$X = \prod_{i\in I} S_i^{w_{x,i}} \cdot g^{b_x} \mod n^2, \qquad Y = \prod_{i\in I} S_i^{w_{y,i}} \cdot g^{b_y} \mod n^2.$$

– **RBF.** Paillier encryption does not support exponentiation or ciphertext multiplication. So in Step 3, the computation of S is changed. S now contains $S_{i,1} = \mathsf{Enc}(\mathsf{pk}, -2 \cdot s_i)$ and $S_{i,2} = \mathsf{Enc}(\mathsf{pk}, s_i^2)$, where $i \in [1, l]$. In Step 4, the computation is changed to

$$X^* = \left(\prod_{i\in I}(S_{i,2} \cdot S_{i,1}^{w_{x,i}}) \cdot \prod_{i\in I} g^{w_{x,i}^2}\right)^{-\gamma_x} \cdot g^{-r_x} \mod n^2,$$

$$Y^* = \left(\prod_{i\in I}(S_{i,2} \cdot S_{i,1}^{w_{y,i}}) \cdot \prod_{i\in I} g^{w_{y,i}^2}\right)^{-\gamma_y} \cdot g^{-r_y} \mod n^2,$$

where r_x and r_y are randomly chosen from the plaintext space of Paillier encryption, and $\prod_{i\in I} g^{w_{x,i}^2}$ and $\prod_{i\in I} g^{w_{y,i}^2}$ are pre-computed by the server. The localization server sends this (X^*, Y^*) to the client who computes

$$x^* = \mathsf{Dec}(\mathsf{sk}, X^*), \qquad X' = \mathsf{Enc}(\mathsf{pk}, e^{x^*}),$$
$$y^* = \mathsf{Dec}(\mathsf{sk}, Y^*), \qquad Y' = \mathsf{Enc}(\mathsf{pk}, e^{y^*}).$$

The client sends (X', Y') to the server who computes

$$X = X'^{e^{r_x}} \cdot g^{b_x} \mod n^2, \qquad Y = Y'^{e^{r_y}} \cdot g^{b_y} \mod n^2.$$

The server sends (X, Y) to the client. Finally, the client computes the location coordinates $(x, y) = (\mathsf{Dec}(\mathsf{sk}, X), \mathsf{Dec}(\mathsf{sk}, Y))$.

RBF is quite promising for indoor localization. It provides accurate results, and the computation in the online phase is efficient [3].

– **Sigmoid.** First, the server and the client interact similarly to the case of dot product. After this operation, the client obtains

$$X^* = \left(\prod_{i\in I} S_i^{w_{x,i}}\right)^{\alpha_x} \cdot g^{\beta_x} \cdot g^{-r_x} \mod n^2,$$

$$Y^* = \left(\prod_{i\in I} S_i^{w_{y,i}}\right)^{\alpha_y} \cdot g^{\beta_y} \cdot g^{-r_y} \mod n^2,$$

where r_x, r_y are randomly chosen from the plaintext space of Paillier encryption. Then, the client computes

$$x^* = \mathsf{Dec}(\mathsf{sk}, X^*), \qquad X' = \mathsf{Enc}(\mathsf{pk}, e^{2x^*}),$$
$$y^* = \mathsf{Dec}(\mathsf{sk}, Y^*), \qquad Y' = \mathsf{Enc}(\mathsf{pk}, e^{2y^*}),$$

and sends (X', Y') to the server who randomly chooses r'_x, r'_y and computes

$$X_1 = ((X'^{e^{2r_x}})^{(b_x+1)} \cdot g^{b_x-1})^{r'_x} \mod n^2, \qquad X_2 = (X'^{e^{2r_x}} \cdot g)^{r'_x} \mod n^2,$$
$$Y_1 = ((Y'^{e^{2r_y}})^{(b_y+1)} \cdot g^{b_y-1})^{r'_y} \mod n^2, \qquad Y_2 = (Y'^{e^{2r_y}} \cdot g)^{r'_y} \mod n^2.$$

The server sends (X_1, X_2, Y_1, Y_2) to the client. Finally, the client obtains the coordinates as $(x, y) = \left(\frac{\mathsf{Dec}(\mathsf{sk}, X_1)}{\mathsf{Dec}(\mathsf{sk}, X_2)}, \frac{\mathsf{Dec}(\mathsf{sk}, Y_1)}{\mathsf{Dec}(\mathsf{sk}, Y_2)}\right)$.

As Paillier encryption takes integers only, as the first step the non-integer parameters in our algorithm needs to be rounded. For preserving m decimal places, the parameters are multiplied by 10^m and rounded to the nearest integer. After the calculation, we divide the result by 10^m. This will decrease the accuracy of the system. We rounded the parameters to $m = 10$ decimal places in our experiment (to be described in Sect. 6), and we found the result acceptable.

5.3 Correctness

Below we evaluate the correctness of the homomorphic operation on the cipher-texts for the x-coordinate. The same argument holds for y.

- **Dot product.**

$$X = \prod_{i \in I} S_i^{w_{x,i}} \cdot g^{b_x} \mod n^2$$

$$= \prod_{i \in I} \mathsf{Enc}(\mathsf{pk}, s_i)^{w_{x,i}} \cdot g^{b_x} \mod n^2$$

$$= \prod_{i \in I} \mathsf{Enc}(\mathsf{pk}, s_i \cdot w_{x,i}) \cdot g^{b_x} \mod n^2$$

$$= \mathsf{Enc}(\mathsf{pk}, \sum_{i \in I}(s_i \cdot w_{x,i})) \cdot g^{b_x} \mod n^2$$

$$= \mathsf{Enc}(\mathsf{pk}, \sum_{i \in I}(s_i \cdot w_{x,i}) + b_x).$$

So $\mathsf{Dec}(\mathsf{sk}, X)$ results in $x = \sum_{i \in I} s_i \cdot w_{x,i} + b_x = \boldsymbol{w_x} \cdot \boldsymbol{s} + b_x$.

- **RBF.** In the first round of communication,

$$X^* = (\prod_{i \in I}(S_{i,2} \cdot S_{i,1}^{w_{x,i}}) \cdot \prod_{i \in I} g^{w_{x,i}^2})^{-\gamma_x} \cdot g^{-r_x} \mod n^2$$

$$= (\prod_{i \in I}(\mathsf{Enc}(\mathsf{pk}, s_{i,2}) \cdot \mathsf{Enc}(\mathsf{pk}, s_{i,1})^{w_{x,i}}) \cdot \prod_{i \in I} g^{w_{x,i}^2})^{-\gamma_x} \cdot g^{-r_x} \mod n^2$$

$$= (\prod_{i \in I}(\mathsf{Enc}(\mathsf{pk}, s_i^2 - 2 \cdot w_{x,i} \cdot s_i) \cdot \prod_{i \in I} g^{w_{x,i}^2})^{-\gamma_x} \cdot g^{-r_x} \mod n^2$$

$$= \mathsf{Enc}(\mathsf{pk}, ||\boldsymbol{w_x} - \boldsymbol{s}||^2)^{-\gamma_x} \cdot g^{-r_x} \mod n^2 = \mathsf{Enc}(\mathsf{pk}, -\gamma_x ||\boldsymbol{w_x} - \boldsymbol{s}||^2 - r_x).$$

So $\mathsf{Dec}(\mathsf{sk}, X^*)$ results in $x^* = -\gamma_x ||\boldsymbol{w_x} - \boldsymbol{s}||^2 - r_x$.

In the second round of communication, $X' = \mathsf{Enc}(\mathsf{pk}, e^{x^*})$,

$$X = X'^{e^{r_x}} \cdot g^{b_x} = \mathsf{Enc}(\mathsf{pk}, e^{x^*})^{e^{r_x}} \cdot g^{b_x} \mod n^2$$

$$= \mathsf{Enc}(\mathsf{pk}, e^{-\gamma_x ||\boldsymbol{w_x} - \boldsymbol{s}||^2 - r_x})^{e^{r_x}} \cdot g^{b_x} \mod n^2$$

$$= \mathsf{Enc}(\mathsf{pk}, e^{-\gamma_x ||\boldsymbol{w_x} - \boldsymbol{s}||^2} + b_x).$$

So $\mathsf{Dec}(\mathsf{sk}, X)$ results in $x = e^{-\gamma_x ||\boldsymbol{w_x} - \boldsymbol{s}||^2} + b_x$.

– **Sigmoid.** In the first round of communication,

$$X^* = (\prod_{i \in I} S_i^{w_{x,i}})^{\alpha_x} \cdot g^{\beta_x} \cdot g^{-r_x} \quad \text{mod } n^2$$

$$= (\prod_{i \in I} \mathsf{Enc}(\mathsf{pk}, s_i)^{w_{x,i}})^{\alpha_x} \cdot g^{\beta_x - r_x} \quad \text{mod } n^2$$

$$= \mathsf{Enc}(\mathsf{pk}, \sum_{i \in I} w_{x,i} \cdot s_i)^{\alpha_x} \cdot g^{\beta_x - r_x} \quad \text{mod } n^2$$

$$= \mathsf{Enc}(\mathsf{pk}, \boldsymbol{w}_x \cdot \boldsymbol{s})^{\alpha_x} \cdot g^{\beta_x - r_x} \quad \text{mod } n^2$$

$$= \mathsf{Enc}(\mathsf{pk}, \alpha_x \cdot \boldsymbol{w}_x \cdot \boldsymbol{s} + \beta_x - r_x).$$

So $\mathsf{Dec}(\mathsf{sk}, X^*)$ results in $x^* = \alpha_x \cdot \boldsymbol{w}_x \cdot \boldsymbol{s} + \beta_x - r_x$.

In the second round of communication, $X' = \mathsf{Enc}(\mathsf{pk}, e^{2x^*})$,

$$X_1 = ((X'^{e^{2r_x}})^{(b_x+1)} \cdot g^{b_x-1})^{r'_x} \quad \text{mod } n^2$$

$$= ((\mathsf{Enc}(\mathsf{pk}, e^{2x^*})^{e^{2r_x}})^{(b_x+1)} \cdot g^{b_x-1})^{r'_x} \quad \text{mod } n^2$$

$$= ((\mathsf{Enc}(\mathsf{pk}, e^{2(\alpha_x \cdot \boldsymbol{w}_x \cdot \boldsymbol{s} + \beta_x - r_x)})^{e^{2r_x}})^{(b_x+1)} \cdot g^{b_x-1})^{r'_x} \quad \text{mod } n^2$$

$$= \mathsf{Enc}(\mathsf{pk}, ((b_x+1)e^{2(\alpha_x \cdot \boldsymbol{w}_x \cdot \boldsymbol{s} + \beta_x)} + b_x - 1) \cdot r'_x), \text{ and}$$

$$X_2 = (X'^{e^{2r_x}} \cdot g)^{r'_x} \quad \text{mod } n^2 = (\mathsf{Enc}(\mathsf{pk}, e^{2x^*})^{e^{2r_x}} \cdot g)^{r'_x} \quad \text{mod } n^2$$

$$= (\mathsf{Enc}(\mathsf{pk}, e^{2(\alpha_x \cdot \boldsymbol{w}_x \cdot \boldsymbol{s} + \beta_x - r_x)})^{e^{2r_x}} \cdot g)^{r'_x} \quad \text{mod } n^2$$

$$= \mathsf{Enc}(\mathsf{pk}, (e^{2(\alpha_x \cdot \boldsymbol{w}_x \cdot \boldsymbol{s} + \beta_x)} + 1) \cdot r'_x).$$

As a result,

$$\mathsf{Dec}(\mathsf{sk}, X_1)/\mathsf{Dec}(\mathsf{sk}, X_2)$$
$$= (((b_x+1)e^{2(\alpha_x \cdot \boldsymbol{w}_x \cdot \boldsymbol{s} + \beta_x)} + b_x - 1) \cdot r'_x)/((e^{2(\alpha_x \cdot \boldsymbol{w}_x \cdot \boldsymbol{s} + \beta_x)} + 1) \cdot r'_x)$$
$$= (b_x e^{2(\alpha_x \cdot \boldsymbol{w}_x \cdot \boldsymbol{s} + \beta_x)} + b_x + e^{2(\alpha_x \cdot \boldsymbol{w}_x \cdot \boldsymbol{s} + \beta_x)} - 1)/(e^{2(\alpha_x \cdot \boldsymbol{w}_x \cdot \boldsymbol{s} + \beta_x)} + 1)$$
$$= (e^{2(\alpha_x \cdot \boldsymbol{w}_x \cdot \boldsymbol{s} + \beta_x)} - 1)/(e^{2(\alpha_x \cdot \boldsymbol{w}_x \cdot \boldsymbol{s} + \beta_x)} + 1) + b_x = \tanh(\alpha \boldsymbol{w} \cdot \boldsymbol{s} + \beta).$$

5.4   Limitations

Polynomial kernels (homogeneous or inhomogeneous) require a computation on the feature vector with a high degree. To protect it in our framework, the client is expected to encrypt each monomial (product of s_i in the feature vector $\boldsymbol{s}$) in the polynomial. This puts a relatively high computation burden on the client side.

Although we can transform any function infinitely differentiable at point a into a polynomial function via Taylor expansion: $f(x) = \sum_{n=0}^{\infty} \frac{f^{(n)}(a)}{n!} \cdot (x - a)^n$, we do not use it in our scheme. The approach using Taylor expansion becomes less accurate and less efficient to work with our framework. Taylor expansion is a polynomial containing infinite number of items, accurately operating on it requires the client to provide as much ciphertexts for the server to evaluate this polynomial. In practice, we cannot process on infinite number of ciphertexts, and hence we need to approximate the result by omitting some items with the n value greater than a chosen threshold. Such approximation is closer to the actual value when the threshold is larger and the input x is closer to the chosen point a. The server should not know whether the input metrics x is close to a or not; otherwise, the server learns the approximate location of the client. This makes the scheme less accurate. Moreover, the number of encryption the client computes and the number of ciphertexts sent to the server are linear with the threshold. This makes the scheme less efficient. Hence, we do not use Taylor expansion. Instead, we add extra rounds of communication to adapt our framework to different classification decision functions.

5.5   Security

We present the detailed argument for localization system.

First, the scheme is *location privacy-preserving*. The RSSI is measured at the client side, so measuring units are not aware of this operation.

The RSSI sent to the server is encrypted. The ciphertext is the only component in our system which contains information about the RSSI of the client. For our instantiation for RBF kernel, although the server obtains both $\mathsf{Enc}(\mathsf{pk}, -2s_i)$ and $\mathsf{Enc}(\mathsf{pk}, s_i^2)$, the server still cannot compute s_i. To take advantage of this ciphertext pair, the server may want to test whether a candidate value of s^* fits by testing if $\mathsf{Enc}(\mathsf{pk}, -2s_i)^{-\frac{1}{2}s^*} = \mathsf{Enc}(\mathsf{pk}, s_i^2)$. However, Paillier encryption is probabilistic which essentially disallows such a test. More formally, we can go through a hybrid argument which we replace the encryption one at a time by changing it to an encryption of 0, in which the intermediate hybrids are indistinguishable from the previous one due to the chosen-plaintext security of Paillier encryption. Any distinguisher of two adjacent hybrids can be used as an adversary against Paillier encryption. Eventually, we reach the final game that all ciphertexts are encryption of 0, and hence the scheme is secure.

For the decision phase, measuring units are not involved. The localization server only knows the location result in an encrypted form. To conclude, our system is preserving the privacy of location due to the nature of RSSI measurement and the security of Paillier encryption.

Second, the proposed scheme is *data privacy-preserving*. Each time the client queries for a localization service, the server will randomly choose a subset of APs and use the corresponding $(\boldsymbol{w}, b)$ to calculate the location. If the RSSI of the client involves l APs, there will be $N = \sum_{i=\tau}^{l} C_l^i$ possible decision functions (tuples of $(\boldsymbol{w}, b)$) for each query and the malicious client can only decide which one is used. This appears to be something inherent in existing machine learning-based schemes and location-based services based on k-NN. The number of trials N is too large to exhaust all possibilities.

To recover the decision function with parameter set $(\boldsymbol{w}, b)$, at least $dim(\boldsymbol{w})+1$ distinct queries for the same AP subset need to be executed, where $dim(\boldsymbol{w})$ denotes the dimension of the vector $\boldsymbol{w}$. Implementation with RBF kernel requires one more query for γ, and implementation with sigmoid kernel requires two more queries for α and β. For the decision function of a specific AP subset, the solution resulting from the queries may not be unique where only one of the solutions gives the correct decision function. Furthermore, the probability for an adversary to pick $dim(\boldsymbol{w}) + 1$ queries using the same AP subset from a total of q queries is $C_q^{dim(\boldsymbol{w})+1}/N^{dim(\boldsymbol{w})}$. Hence, it is not computationally feasible for the malicious client to compute any set of $(\boldsymbol{w}, b)$ especially when $N^{dim(\boldsymbol{w})}$ is large.

For our instantiations which require more than one round of interaction between the client and the server, we also add random factors (r_x, r_y, r_x', and r_y') to hide the intermediate results (x^*, y^*, x' and y' respectively). All the intermediate results are in the same distribution as encryption of random plaintext subjects to the correctness guarantee, so the malicious client cannot get any information from the intermediate results.

Alternatively, the malicious client can build up its own decision algorithm by obtaining enough RSSI-location pairs as its training data. The malicious client needs to collect at least the same amount of training data sets to make its decision algorithm as accurate as that of the server. This is also computationally expensive for common malicious clients. Furthermore, the RSSI in the training data set must be collected in the field. If the malicious client fabricates RSSI sets, there must be some combinations which are impossible to appear in the area. The malicious client cannot make sure that the training set is spread in the area evenly and of a desired density. All these issues bring in significant inaccuracy to the decision algorithm.

Finally, we remark that there exist certain side-channel attacks against a privacy-preserving indoor localization system in general. For example, when a mobile device is sending out signals, colluding measuring units can measure the RSSI and generate a fingerprint for that device, which will be sent to the server for an estimated location. However, most side-channel attacks require adjustment on all measuring units, which involves service providers and may not be practical.

6   Performance Evaluation

6.1   Theoretical Complexity Analysis

We first give a complexity comparison of our scheme and that of Li *et al.* [11] under the following parameter setting. The number of APs is l. The size of the chosen AP subset is $l' > \tau$. We let M be the total number of Wi-Fi fingerprint in the server database (which is usually large and increases with the area covered by the localization service). The Wi-Fi fingerprint in the server database is the training set in the scenario of localization. For the scheme of Li *et al.* [11], we use *LocSet* to denote the set of possible location of the client (which increases with time and has the maximum possible size M).

For encryption related operations, *Enc* and *Dec* denote the Paillier encryption and decryption operation respectively, and *Mul* and *Exp* denote the modular multiplication and modular exponentiation respectively. For a Paillier encryption with 1024-bit n, the size of each ciphertext, denoted by L, is 2048 bits.

Analyzing the Scheme of Li *et al.* In the offline stage, the server samples a large number (M) of location-fingerprint pairs and stores them in the fingerprint database. In the measuring phase, the client encrypts its fingerprint as S. The client sends S to the server. Recall that the length of S is l. The client needs to encrypt both s_i and s_i^2 with Paillier encryption for the server to compute the distance, so the computation complexity of the client is $2lEnc$, and the communication complexity is $2l \cdot L$.

In the calculation phase, the server computes the encrypted distance between S and each of the entries stored its database, and sends them back to the client. At the server side, the computation complexity is $M \cdot (l' + 1)Exp + M \cdot (2l'+3)Mul$, and the communication complexity is $M \cdot L$. The client decrypts the encrypted distances, picks k of them with the shortest distance from the queried feature metrics s, retrieves the k coordinates from the meta-data, and computes the average coordinates from them. The computation complexity of the client is $M \cdot Dec$ (or $|LocSet|Dec$ with an enhancement) and $O(M \cdot \log M)$ for finding the k nearest neighbours.

Not all k-NN algorithms can be trivially applied on encrypted data. The state-of-the-art k-NN implementations use locality sensitive hash (LSH) to improve the efficiency when looking for the k nearest neighbours and significantly reduce the complexity in this process. LSH is an algorithm to hash vector from a space of higher dimension to a vector from a space of lower dimension which "preserves" the locality. If the vectors in the domain are close, their result from LSH will remain close in the co-domain. However, LSH cannot be applied directly on encrypted data since a secure encryption should be probabilistic [30]. Hence, the complexity shown in Table 1 cannot be reduced.

The density and the evenness of this sample have a significant impact on the accuracy of the localization, which means M must be big enough. Furthermore, the client needs to privately retrieve the coordinates of the k nearest neighbours. The client either employs a private information retrieval [5] scheme which can be costly or stores the meta-data locally which is not practical.

Analyzing Our Scheme. We use SVR based classification to implement our privacy-preserving localization. The decision phase computation of an SVR based classification is independent of M, while that of a k-NN based classification is linear with M (or $|LocSet|$, the size of a subset of the training set) without LSH. The computation complexity of our design only depends on l (the dimension of the feature metrics) which can be as small as 4 according to the experiment result shown in Fig. 2. The independence of M makes our design much more efficient.

In the measuring phase, implementation with RBF kernel requires the computation of the second norm of s and w, so both s_i and s_i^2 are encrypted for each i. The computation complexity in this phase is $2l$ encryptions and the communication complexity is $2l \cdot L$. Implementation with sigmoid kernel requires only the encryption of s_i, so the computation complexity is l encryptions and the communication complexity is $l \cdot L$. Table 1 shows a complexity comparison of our scheme and Li *et al.* [11]. It shows that our scheme is more efficient.

Table 1. Complexity comparison

Algorithms	Phase	Computation		Communication
		Client	Server	(in bits)
RBF	Measuring	$2lEnc$	*nil*	$2lL$
	Calculation	$4Dec + 2Enc$	$(2l' + 4)Exp + (4l' + 4)Mul$	$6L$
Sigmoid	Measuring	$lEnc$	*nil*	lL
	Calculation	$6Dec + 2Enc$	$(2l' + 8)Exp + (2l' + 6)Mul$	$8L$
Li *et al.* [11]	Measuring	$2lEnc$	*nil*	$2lL$
	Calculation	$|LocSet|Dec$	$M(l' + 1)Exp + M(2l' + 3)Mul$	ML

6.2   Experimental Performance Evaluation

We evaluated the performance of our SVR based indoor localization scheme. We have implemented RBF kernel instantiation. The offline phase runs for only one time. Our evaluation focuses on the online phase which is repeatedly performed.

We implemented our scheme in python3 with scikit-learn extension for SVR. We used 1024-bit Paillier encryption as the homomorphic encryption. The test

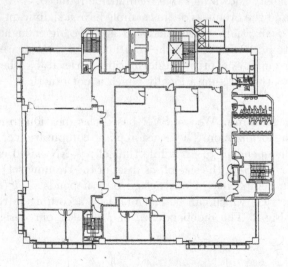

Fig. 1. Building layout

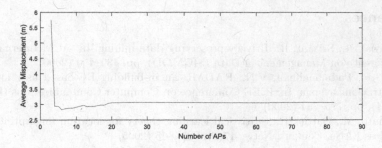

Fig. 2. Number of APs versus Average Misplacement

machine is a Dell OptiPlex 9010 running Linux Ubuntu version 12.04.4 system with dual CPU (3.40 GHz), 1 GB RAM. We conducted the experiment in a building with the floor plan as shown in Fig. 1. The density of the training data was low. One sample was taken every 2 m in the building.

Figure 2 shows the relationship between the number of APs and the misplacement of the calculated location. According to Fig. 2, the variation of AP number does not have strong effect on the result when AP number is greater than 4. This phenomenon confirms to the theory of trilateration. So we can choose a very small l to improve the efficiency.

7   Conclusion and Future Directions

We study the privacy issues of indoor localization, and formulate the corresponding threat model. We propose practical schemes for privacy-preserving indoor localization based on our model. The proposed privacy-preserving indoor localization schemes use homomorphic encryption to protect the location privacy of the client and the data privacy of the server.

Since we only use additive instead of fully homomorphic encryption for higher efficiency, some positioning algorithms such as polynomials kernels (homogeneous or inhomogeneous) cannot be efficiently covered by our framework. Advanced machine learning algorithms (*e.g.*, neural networks) may provide higher accuracy in certain circumstances. Advancement in fully homomorphic encryption may make it more practical to apply these algorithms on encrypted data.

Acknowledgement. Sherman Chow is supported by the Early Career Scheme and the Early Career Award (CUHK 439713), and General Research Funds (CUHK 14201914) of the Research Grants Council, University Grant Committee of Hong Kong. Ming Li is supported by US National Science Foundation grant (CNS-1566634).

References

1. Agrawal, R., Srikant, R.: Privacy-preserving data mining. In: ACM International Conference on Management of Data (SIGMOD), pp. 439–450 (2000)
2. Bahl, P., Padmanabhan, V.N.: RADAR: an in-building RF-based user location and tracking system. In: IEEE Conference on Computer Communications (INFOCOM), pp. 775–784 (2000)
3. Brunato, M., Battiti, R.: Statistical learning theory for location fingerprinting in wireless LANs. Comput. Netw. 47(6), 825–845 (2005)
4. Burges, C.J.C.: A tutorial on support vector machines for pattern recognition. Data Min. Knowl. Discov. 2(2), 121–167 (1998)
5. Chor, B., Kushilevitz, E., Goldreich, O., Sudan, M.: Private information retrieval. J. ACM 45(6), 965–981 (1998)
6. Cover, T.M., Hart, P.E.: Nearest neighbor pattern classification. IEEE Trans. Inf. Theor. 13(1), 21–27 (1967)
7. Gedik, B., Liu, L.: Location privacy in mobile systems: a personalized anonymization model. In: International Conference on Distributed Computing Systems (ICDCS), pp. 620–629 (2005)
8. Gruteser, M.: Indoor localization: ready for primetime? In: International Conference on Mobile Computing and Networking (MobiCom), pp. 375–376 (2013)
9. LaMarca, A., Chawathe, Y., Consolvo, S., Hightower, J., Smith, I., Scott, J., Sohn, T., Howard, J., Hughes, J., Potter, F., Tabert, J., Powledge, P.S., Borriello, G., Schilit, B.N.: Place lab: device positioning using radio beacons in the wild. In: Gellersen, H.W., Want, R., Schmidt, A. (eds.) PERVASIVE 2005. LNCS, vol. 3468, pp. 116–133. Springer, Heidelberg (2005)
10. Leppäkoski, H., Collin, J., Takala, J.: Pedestrian navigation based on inertial sensors, indoor map, and WLAN signals. Signal Process. Syst. 71(3), 287–296 (2013)
11. Li, H., Sun, L., Zhu, H., Lu, X., Cheng, X.: Achieving privacy preservation in Wi-Fi fingerprint-based localization. In: IEEE Conference on Computer Communications (INFOCOM), pp. 2337–2345 (2014)
12. Liu, X., Liu, K., Guo, L., Li, X., Fang, Y.: A game-theoretic approach for achieving k-anonymity in location based services. In: IEEE Conference on Computer Communications (INFOCOM), pp. 2985–2993 (2013)
13. Ma, L., Teymorian, A.Y., Cheng, X.: A hybrid rogue access point protection framework for commodity Wi-Fi networks. In: IEEE Conference on Computer Communications (INFOCOM), pp. 1220–1228 (2008)
14. Paillier, P.: Public-key cryptosystems based on composite degree residuosity classes. In: Stern, J. (ed.) EUROCRYPT 1999. LNCS, vol. 1592, pp. 223–238. Springer, Heidelberg (1999)
15. Peddinti, S.T., Saxena, N.: On the limitations of query obfuscation techniques for location privacy. In: International Conference on Ubiquitous Computing (UbiComp), pp. 187–196 (2011)
16. Priyantha, N.B., Chakraborty, A., Balakrishnan, H.: The cricket location-support system. In: International Conference on Mobile Computing and Networking (Mobicom), pp. 32–43 (2000)
17. Rai, A., Chintalapudi, K.K., Padmanabhan, V.N., Sen, R.: Zee: zero-effort crowdsourcing for indoor localization. In: International Conference on Mobile Computing and Networking (Mobicom), pp. 293–304 (2012)
18. Shokri, R., Theodorakopoulos, G., Boudec, J.L., Hubaux, J.: Quantifying location privacy. In: IEEE Symposium on Security and Privacy (S&P), pp. 247–262 (2011)

19. Tarzia, S.P., Dinda, P.A., Dick, R.P., Memik, G.: Indoor localization without infrastructure using the acoustic background spectrum. In: International Conference on Mobile Systems, Applications, and Services (MobiSys), pp. 155–168 (2011)
20. Wang, H., Sen, S., Elgohary, A., Farid, M., Youssef, M., Choudhury, R.R.: No need to war-drive: unsupervised indoor localization. In: International Conference on Mobile Systems, Applications, and Services (MobiSys), pp. 197–210 (2012)
21. Want, R., Hopper, A., Falcao, V., Gibbons, J.: The active badge location system. ACM Trans. Inf. Syst. **10**(1), 91–102 (1992)
22. Ward, A., Jones, A., Hopper, A.: A new location technique for the active office. IEEE Pers. Commun. **4**(5), 42–47 (1997)
23. Woodman, O., Harle, R.: Pedestrian localisation for indoor environments. In: International Conference on Ubiquitous Computing (UbiComp), Seoul, Korea, pp. 114–123, 21–24 September 2008
24. Xu, K., Yue, H., Guo, L., Guo, Y., Fang, Y.: Privacy-preserving machine learning algorithms for big data systems. In: IEEE International Conference on Distributed Computing Systems (ICDCS), pp. 318–327 (2015)
25. Yang, D., Fang, X., Xue, G.: Truthful incentive mechanisms for k-anonymity location privacy. In: IEEE Conference on Computer Communications (INFOCOM), pp. 2994–3002 (2013)
26. Yang, Z., Wu, C., Liu, Y.: Locating in fingerprint space: wireless indoor localization with little human intervention. In: International Conference on Mobile Computing and Networking (Mobicom), pp. 269–280 (2012)
27. Youssef, M., Agrawala, A.K.: The Horus WLAN location determination system. In: International Conference on Mobile Systems, Applications, and Services (MobiSys), pp. 205–218 (2005)
28. Yu, H., Jiang, X., Vaidya, J.: Privacy-preserving SVM using nonlinear kernels on horizontally partitioned data. In: ACM Symposium on Applied Computing (SAC), pp. 603–610 (2006)
29. Yuan, J., Yu, S.: Privacy preserving back-propagation neural network learning made practical with cloud computing. IEEE Trans. Parallel Distrib. Syst. **25**(1), 212–221 (2014)
30. Zhao, Y., Chow, S.S.M.: Privacy preserving collaborative filtering from asymmetric randomized encoding. In: Böhme, R., Okamoto, T. (eds.) FC 2015. LNCS, vol. 8975, pp. 459–477. Springer, Heidelberg (2015)
31. Zhong, G., Goldberg, I., Hengartner, U.: Louis, Lester and Pierre: three protocols for location privacy. In: Borisov, N., Golle, P. (eds.) PET 2007. LNCS, vol. 4776, pp. 62–76. Springer, Heidelberg (2007)

Formal Policy-Based Provenance Audit

Denis Butin$^{(\boxtimes)}$, Denise Demirel, and Johannes Buchmann

TU Darmstadt, Darmstadt, Germany
{dbutin,ddemirel,buchmann}@cdc.informatik.tu-darmstadt.de

Abstract. Data processing within large organisations is often complex, impeding both the traceability of data and the compliance of processing with usage policies. The chronology of the ownership, custody, or location of data—its provenance—provides the necessary information to restore traceability. However, to be of practical use, provenance records should include sufficient expressiveness by design with a posteriori analysis in mind, e.g. the verification of their compliance with usage policies. Additionally, they ought to be combined with systematic reasoning about their correctness. In this paper, we introduce a formal framework for policy-based provenance audit. We show how it can be used to demonstrate correctness, consistency, and compliance of provenance records with machine-readable usage policies. We also analyse the suitability of our framework for the special case of privacy protection. A formalised perspective on provenance is also useful in this area, but it must be integrated into a larger accountability process involving data protection authorities to be effective. The practical applicability of our approach is demonstrated using a provenance record involving medical data and corresponding privacy policies with personal data protection as a goal.

1 Introduction

Data *provenance* [10,29,30] has been defined disparately, for instance as the origin and history of data or as process-related metadata. It is often associated with the semantic web [19], used as a tool to facilitate content curation by restoring trustworthiness in the quality of digital data, or providing replication recipes [16]. In this work, we adopt the W3C perspective on provenance as *(...) a record that describes the people, institutions, entities and activities, involved in producing, influencing, or delivering a piece of data or a thing* [24]. Hence the key idea of provenance—as taken up here—is to paint a comprehensive picture clarifying the life cycle of data, from its creation to its destruction, including the way it is used, and how other data is derived or linked from it.

This makes provenance valuable to verify compliance with usage policies when sensitive data is collected, stored, and processed by several entities within enterprises or governmental institutions. In such large networks, data flow easily becomes opaque, making simple audit methods—such as log analysis limited to a single component—insufficient and leading to failure to comply with usage policies. Here provenance has the potential to underpin accountability, i.e. each data processing entity must not only comply with data protection rules, but *actively*

K. Ogawa and K. Yoshioka (Eds.): IWSEC 2016, LNCS 9836, pp. 234–253, 2016.
DOI: 10.1007/978-3-319-44524-3_14

demonstrate compliance[1]. This allows an auditor to detect failures within the system. Furthermore, these usage policy rules can be part of the provenance data, making it possible to globally declare them and to prevent inconsistencies. Thus, provenance allows to build powerful audit tools for large networks, such as hospitals and research institutions. In addition, systems using cloud computing typically involve multiple entities, and can therefore benefit from this approach.

An important class of usage policies addresses the privacy of sensitive data [20]. In the context of accountability, such *privacy policies* are often modelled as machine-readable sets of rules in a formally specified privacy policy language such as PPL [32]. While the idea of using provenance as a tool to audit the compliance with privacy regulations is not new, so far formal approaches have been lacking. Both the consistency of provenance records and their compliance with associated privacy policies ought to be stated precisely to pave the way for automated analyses. Some aspects such as the enforcement of processing purposes are not fully amenable to automation, but provenance records allow to collect enough information for complementary manual verification.

Contribution. We present a formal framework modelling provenance events and their compliance with respect to usage policies. We first introduce usage policies and model them as tuples including forwarding policies, authorised purposes for different types of operations, deletion delays, and linking and derivation policies (Sect. 2.1). A data category is not necessarily always associated with the same usage policy. The relevant policy depends on the component and on the log events under consideration. Afterwards, we model provenance records as sequences of discrete events. Each record refers to a single data subject, e.g. a patient in the eHealth scenario, but can accommodate an arbitrary number of entities and processed data categories. The granularity of the events is chosen in accordance with the policies (Sect. 2.2). Next, we establish additional notation (Sect. 3.1) and formalise the correctness (Sect. 3.2) and compliance of logs of provenance events when dealing with privacy policies (Sect. 3.3). Correctness pertains to the internal consistency of the provenance record, independently of the usage policies under consideration. Conversely, compliance relates to the relation between the provenance record and the associated usage policies. This formalisation can serve as a basis for a posteriori provenance analysis by an auditor. Next, we discuss the limitations of the approach when dealing with privacy policies and show how it can be included in a global accountability process (Sect. 4). We consider the case of privacy separately because the guarantees at stake are especially critical when personal data is involved. Furthermore, the application of provenance records to this use case immediately raises the question of whether logging creates additional privacy risks. We show under which conditions our framework for provenance-based auditing is applicable to privacy policies. The framework

---

[1] In the scope of accountability as a data protection principle [3], this proof-of-compliance requirement is not limited to high-level statements of intent, but is often seen as incorporating a practical level as well, i.e. concrete data handling actions [9].

is then evaluated through a scenario involving personal medical data processed among different entities (Sect. 5). Finally, we provide a review of related work (Sect. 6) and offer our conclusions (Sect. 7).

2   Usage Policies and Provenance Events

In this section we introduce the concept of usage policies and provenance events. We refer to an entity collecting or processing data as *component*. In the scope of this paper, a *usage policy* is assumed to be a machine-readable set of rules regarding the use of data. Depending on the scenario under consideration, the values of usage policies are assigned either by a component, or by a data subject[2] if the processed data is of personal nature. With respect to the data processed, a *data category* is a designation of the type of data in natural language, i.e. postal address. By *purpose*, we mean the finality or goal of an operation. Each event is assigned one or two timestamps, corresponding to the start and (if applicable) end of the event.

2.1   Usage Policies for Provenance

To evaluate provenance records systematically, we introduce a formalisation of usage policies. Alternatively, policies can be described involving text in natural language. However, this approach presents usability challenges, especially in the subcase of privacy policies [28].

Furthermore, most existing machine-readable policy languages [20] have limited expressiveness, often impeding automated compliance checking [8]. Thus, to the best of our knowledge, our method is the first to provide sufficient expressiveness to be used in conjunction with provenance records, by covering the broad range of provenance activities.

A number of data handling operations used here are absent from usual policy languages (such as PPL [32]), but essential to provenance modelling. Provenance events will be formalised later (Sect. 2.2), but it is already helpful to introduce these operations intuitively in this section to put the usage policies elements in context.

In the W3C PROV ontology [21], *derivation*, is defined as "a transformation of one entity into another". We use *linking* to refer to the combination of different categories of data from a single source. The *forwarding* of data refers to the sending of data from one component to another, with the assumption that the original component also retains control of the data.

We now define provenance usage policies formally in terms of constraints for deletion, forwarding, linking, derivation, and use for specific purposes.

---

[2] In practice, data subjects may delegate the power of negotiating policies to a third party they trust.

Definition 1 (Usage Policy). *Provenance usage policies are defined as tuples:*

$$\mathcal{P} = D_g \times D_{rf} \times Fw \times Li \times De \times P_{use} \times P_{der}$$

and address rules for deletion, forwarding, linking, derivation, and authorised purposes. These usage policy components are defined as follows:

D_g *The global deletion delay* D_g *is the maximal delay after which data of any category must have been deleted. Time is measured from the initial collection of each piece of data. This deletion does not need to be requested explicitly— the policy specifies that it should happen unconditionally. However, earlier deletion may occur following an explicit request.*

D_{rf} *The request fulfilment delay* D_{rf} *is the maximal delay for components to fulfil requests, e.g. deletion requests. The delay is measured from the timestamp corresponding to the start of the requested event. We do not account for delays between the moment the request is sent and the moment it is received by the component(s) holding the data.*

Fw *The forwarding policy* Fw *is a pair* (rest, List). *Possible values for* rest *are* $\perp$ *(data may be forward to any component),* $\top$ *(data may be forwarded to no other component),* bl *(a list of forbidden components is declared) and* wl *(a list of authorised components is declared). If* rest $= \perp$ *or* rest $= \top$, *the set* List *must be empty. If* rest $=$ bl, *the set* List *is a blacklist of components, i.e. to no component on the list may be forwarded any data. If* rest $=$ wl, List *is a whitelist of components, i.e. any data may be forwarded to any components on the list.* List *then contains identifiers of all components for which data forwarding is forbidden or permitted, respectively.*

Li *The linking policy* Li *is a set of pairs limiting the linking of different data categories by components. If two data categories are in the same pair of this set, pieces of data of these categories may never be linked.[3] This policy component can be used to restrict profiling [4] based on correlation.*

De *The derivation policy* De *is a set of data categories. Data categories in* De *may never be used to derive new data. This policy component can be used, for instance, to prevent the derivation of personal data from perturbed data [25].*

P_{use} *The authorised use purposes* P_{use} *are a set of pairs (data category, acceptable purpose for use).*

P_{der} *The authorised derivation purposes* P_{der} *are a set of pairs (data category, acceptable purpose for derivation).*

Purposes are assumed to be taken from a fixed ontology, i.e. a centralised taxonomy, as in PPL [32]. The adequacy of using a purpose ontology is discussed in Sect. 4.

As an illustration, we describe in turn the components of a concrete usage policy π:

---

[3] For instance, a linking policy can prevent de-anonymisation.

- $\pi.\mathsf{D_g} = 3$ months—data of any category must be deleted within 3 months after its collection;
- $\pi.\mathsf{D_{rf}} = 1$ day—requests received by components must be fulfilled within one day;
- $\pi.\mathsf{Fw} = (\mathsf{wl}, \mathsf{List})$ with $\mathsf{List} = \{\mathsf{Hospital}, \mathsf{ResearchInstitute}\}$—a (white)list of authorised components is declared: data of any category may be forwarded to the components $\mathsf{ResearchInstitute}$ and $\mathsf{Hospital}$. No data exports to other components are allowed;
- $\pi.\mathsf{Li} = \{(\mathsf{Treatment}, \mathsf{Status}), (\mathsf{ID}, \mathsf{Drug})\}$—pieces of data with respective categories $\mathsf{Treatment}$ and Status may never be linked, directly or indirectly. Otherwise, information about the stage of a disease may be extrapolated. In addition, pieces of data with respective categories ID and Drug may never be linked, directly or indirectly, so as not to reveal which patient is taking which drug;
- $\pi.\mathsf{De} = \{\mathsf{Frequency}, \mathsf{Risk}, \mathsf{Drug}\}$—new data may never be derived from pieces of data with category $\mathsf{Frequency}$, Risk, or Drug, directly or indirectly. This prevents that sensitive information about the frequency, e.g. of treatments or hospital visits, the risk of getting a certain disease, or drugs taken by a patient is extracted;
- $\pi.\mathsf{P_{use}} = \{(\mathsf{Treatment}, \mathsf{Logistic}), (\mathsf{ID}, \mathsf{Marketing})\}$—data with category $\mathsf{Treatment}$ may be used (directly or indirectly) only for the purpose $\mathsf{Logistic}$. This allows, for instance, hospitals to reserve operating theaters for patients. Data with category ID, e.g. the name, address, and family status of patients, may be used (directly or indirectly) only for the purpose $\mathsf{Marketing}$. Data of other categories may not appear in Use events;
- $\pi.\mathsf{P_{der}} = \{(\mathsf{History}, \mathsf{Statistic})\}$—Data with category $\mathsf{History}$ may be derived from (directly or indirectly) only for the purpose $\mathsf{Statistic}$, to allow statistical evaluation of medical data. Data of other categories may not appear as the first argument of a Derive event.

2.2   Provenance Events

The usage policies defined above allow to define requirements that must be fulfilled by components when processing data. Their compliance with these policies can be evaluated using the available provenance data. However, to this end, provenance information ought to be represented in a unified way.

Provenance is often visualised as a graph. Instead, we model it as a sequence of discrete events, i.e. $\lambda = \{\lambda_1, \ldots, \lambda_n\}$, allowing us to reason over sets of such events. Since all events include timestamps, they can be represented a posteriori in a chronological fashion. However, log indexes are not assumed to be ordered chronologically, i.e. $i < j$ does not imply that λ_i occurred before λ_j.

Definition 2 (Provenance Events). *Let $\boldsymbol{Pu}$ be a purpose ontology, seen as a set of purposes in natural language. Let $\mathbb{P}(\boldsymbol{Pu})$ be the power set of $\boldsymbol{Pu}$. Similarly, $\boldsymbol{Ca}$ is an ontology of data categories and $\mathbb{P}(\boldsymbol{Ca})$ is its power set. Furthermore, let*

C be a set of components. For all events and independently, $\Theta \in \mathbb{P}(\boldsymbol{Ca})$, $\rho \in \boldsymbol{Pu}$, $P \in \mathbb{P}(\boldsymbol{Pu})$, $C, C' \in \boldsymbol{C}$, and the parameters t, s, and e are timestamps. While t marks the start of discrete events, s and e is used to specify the start and end time for the Use event, which occurs over a time period. Data circulates together with its associated usage policy $\pi \in \mathcal{P}$; we follow the sticky policy approach advocated by Pearson [27]. In a sequence of discrete events $\lambda = \{\lambda_1, \ldots, \lambda_n\}$ a single event λ_i for $i \in [1, n]$ can be one of the following provenance events:

(Acquire, Θ, C, π, P, t) A set of data with a corresponding set of data categories Θ was collected by a component C for a set of specific purposes P. The values of the data do not appear in the event, only its categories. In addition, this event contains the usage policy π set for the collected data and a timestamp t.

(Use, Θ, C, ρ, R, s, e) This event marks the use of a set of data categories Θ, e.g. {Postal address, Age group} by a component C. Reason R is a justification of the single chosen purpose designation ρ in natural language. The timestamps s and e mark the start and the end of this event. Note that for this to be meaningful Θ must be a subset of previously collected data categories.

(Export, Θ, C, C', π, P, t) A set of data, with a corresponding set of data categories Θ, was sent by component C to component C' at time t. The associated usage policy is π and the data export was performed for a specific set of purposes P.

(Link, $\theta, \theta', \theta'', C, \pi, \rho, R, t$) At time t component C linked two data elements with categories θ and θ'. The result is a single piece of data with category θ'', now available to component C. θ'' does not have to be new, but it may be (i.e. has not appeared before). This event also contains a reason R justifying the single chosen purpose designation ρ. The usage policy π is associated with the new data.

(Derive, $\theta, \theta', C, \pi, \rho, R, t$) At time t, component C derived data with category θ' from data with category θ. In addition, the event contains reason R, the corresponding single purpose ρ, and a usage policy π.

(ReqRemove, Θ, t) At time t, total deletion of the set of data categories Θ was requested. Removal requests are assumed to be sent simultaneously to all components relevant to the set of data categories under consideration.

(Remove, Θ, C, t) The set of data categories Θ were deleted by component C at time t.

As an example, consider the event $\lambda_1 = $ (Export, {Treatment, ID, Status}, Hospital, ResearchInstitute, π_1, {Logistic, Statistic}, 2016-05-12T12:17) and the event $\lambda_2 = $ (Link, Frequency, Treatment, Risk, ResearchInstitute, π_2, Statistic, Correlation study, 2016-05-20T12:14). In λ_1, a data set with categories Treatment, ID, and Status is forwarded from the component Hospital to the component ResearchInstitute. The associated usage policy π_1 restricts how the component ResearchInstitute can use the forwarded data set, but is not relevant for this event. The purposes Logistic and Statistic are provided for this data export, and the timestamp of the event is 2016-05-12T12:17. In λ_2, component ResearchInstitute links two pieces of data with respective categories Frequency and Treatment. The result of this linking is a piece of data with category Risk. The usage policy now associated with Risk for the component ResearchInstitute is π_2, which, again, restricts how the research institute can use the forwarded data set, but is not relevant for this event. The provided reason for this linking operation is Correlation study, meant to justify the included purpose designation Statistic, and the last parameter 2016-05-20T12:14 is, again, the timestamp.

3   Formalising Correctness and Compliance

Having defined both usage policies and provenance events enables two types of checks:

- Provenance correctness: a number of conditions must be fulfilled for provenance information to be coherent, independently of any usage policy. Sanity checks are possible and can be seen as a category of minimal guarantees.
- Compliance of provenance with usage policies: the compliance of recorded provenance can be analysed with regard to the predefined policies.

In the following, we first establish some useful definitions in Sect. 3.1, followed by rules for internal correctness of logs in Sect. 3.2 and rules for the compliance of logs with usage policies in Sect. 3.3.

3.1   Definitions

Some formalism is needed to model both aspects: the correctness of logs, and their compliance with usage policies. Let $\lambda = \{\lambda_1, \ldots, \lambda_n\}$ be a log of n provenance events and $i \in [1, n]$.

Definition 3 (Event type). *Let EvType be the function mapping an event to its type. That is, if $X \in \{$Acquire, Use, Export, Link, Derive, ReqRemove, Remove$\}$ and $\lambda_i = (X, \ldots)$, then $\mathrm{EvType}(\lambda_i) = X$.*

Definition 4 (Event time). *EvTime is defined as the function returning the starting time of an event. $\mathrm{EvTime}(\lambda_i) = s$, if $\mathrm{EvType}(\lambda_i) = \mathrm{Use} \wedge \lambda_i = (\mathrm{Use}, \ldots, s, e)$. $\mathrm{EvTime}(\lambda_i) = t$, if $\mathrm{EvType}(\lambda_i) \neq \mathrm{Use} \wedge \lambda_i = (\mathrm{EvType}(\lambda_i), \ldots, t)$. We assume that different events always feature different starting times, i.e. $\lambda_i \neq \lambda_j \implies \mathrm{EvTime}(\lambda_i) \neq \mathrm{EvTime}(\lambda_j)$.*

Definition 5 (Active component). *$\mathrm{Active}(\lambda_i)$ is the acting component for a given event, i.e.*

$$\begin{cases} \lambda_i = (\mathrm{Acquire}, \Theta, C, \pi, P, t) \implies \mathrm{Active}(\lambda_i) = C \\ \lambda_i = (\mathrm{Use}, \Theta, C, \rho, R, s, e) \implies \mathrm{Active}(\lambda_i) = C \\ \lambda_i = (\mathrm{Export}, \Theta, C, C', \pi, P, t) \implies \mathrm{Active}(\lambda_i) = C \\ \lambda_i = (\mathrm{Link}, \theta, \theta', \theta'', C, \pi, \rho, R, t) \implies \mathrm{Active}(\lambda_i) = C \\ \lambda_i = (\mathrm{Derive}, \theta, \theta', C, \pi, \rho, R, t) \implies \mathrm{Active}(\lambda_i) = C \\ \lambda_i = (\mathrm{Remove}, \Theta, C, t) \implies \mathrm{Active}(\lambda_i) = C \end{cases}$$

The active component is undefined for `ReqRemove`, since this event is not initiated by any component but triggered externally.

Definition 6 (Set of controllers). $\mathrm{Control}(\lambda, \theta)$ *is the set of components that have gained control over data with category θ in log λ, i.e.* $\mathrm{Control}(\lambda, \theta) = \{C \mid \exists\ \lambda_i \in \lambda, \Theta, \theta', \theta'', \pi, \rho, P, R, t, C' \mid (\ \theta \in \Theta\ \wedge (\lambda_i = (\texttt{Acquire}, \Theta, C, \pi, P, t) \vee \lambda_i = (\texttt{Export}, \Theta, C', C, \pi, P, t))) \vee \lambda_i = (\texttt{Derive}, \theta', \theta, C, \pi, \rho, R, t) \vee \lambda_i = (\texttt{Link}, \theta', \theta'', \theta, C, \pi, \rho, R, t)\}.$

Definition 7 (Associated data categories). *The function* $\mathrm{DataCat}$ *takes as input an event different from* `ReqRemove` *or* `Remove` *and returns the set of data categories appearing in the event, in any form:*

- $\lambda_i = (\texttt{Acquire}, \Theta, \dots) \vee \lambda_i = (\texttt{Use}, \Theta, \dots) \vee \lambda_i = (\texttt{Export}, \Theta, \dots) \implies \mathrm{DataCat}(\lambda_i) = \Theta.$
- $\lambda_i = (\texttt{Link}, \theta, \theta', \theta'', \dots) \implies \mathrm{DataCat}(\lambda_i) = \{\theta, \theta', \theta''\}.$
- $\lambda_i = (\texttt{Derive}, \theta, \theta', \dots) \implies \mathrm{DataCat}(\lambda_i) = \{\theta, \theta'\}.$

Definition 8 (Descended data categories). *The function* $\mathrm{Dsc}(\lambda, \theta)$ *returns the set of data categories generated from the data category θ, directly or indirectly, through linking or derivation. It is defined recursively as follows:*

$$
\begin{cases}
\theta \in \mathrm{Dsc}(\lambda, \theta) \\
\lambda_i = (\texttt{Derive}, X, \theta', C, \pi, \rho, R, t)\ \wedge X \in \mathrm{Dsc}(\lambda, \theta) \implies \theta' \in \mathrm{Dsc}(\lambda, \theta) \\
\lambda_i = (\texttt{Link}, X, X', \theta', C, \pi, \rho, R, t)\ \wedge X \in \mathrm{Dsc}(\lambda, \theta) \implies \theta' \in \mathrm{Dsc}(\lambda, \theta) \\
\lambda_i = (\texttt{Link}, X, X', \theta', C, \pi, \rho, R, t)\ \wedge X' \in \mathrm{Dsc}(\lambda, \theta) \implies \theta' \in \mathrm{Dsc}(\lambda, \theta)
\end{cases}
$$

Definition 9 (Relative strength of usage policies). *Let π and π' be two usage policies as defined in Definition 1. π' is said to be stronger or equal than π, denoted $\pi' \geq \pi$, if all of the following conditions hold: (1) $\pi'.\mathsf{D_g} \leq \pi.\mathsf{D_g}$; (2) $\pi'.\mathsf{D_{rf}} \leq \pi.\mathsf{D_{rf}}$; (3) $\pi'.\mathsf{Fw} = (\top, \varnothing) \vee \pi'.\mathsf{Fw} = \pi.\mathsf{Fw} = (\bot, \varnothing) \vee (\pi'.\mathsf{Fw} = (\mathsf{bl}, \mathsf{List}') \wedge \pi.\mathsf{Fw} = (\mathsf{bl}, \mathsf{List}) \wedge \mathsf{List} \subseteq \mathsf{List}') \vee (\pi'.\mathsf{Fw} = (\mathsf{wl}, \mathsf{List}') \wedge \pi.\mathsf{Fw} = (\mathsf{wl}, \mathsf{List}) \wedge \mathsf{List}' \subseteq \mathsf{List})$; (4) $\pi.\mathsf{Li} \subseteq \pi'.\mathsf{Li}$; (5) $\pi.\mathsf{De} \subseteq \pi'.\mathsf{De}$; (6) $\pi'.\mathsf{P_{use}} \subseteq \pi.\mathsf{P_{use}}$; (7) $\pi'.\mathsf{P_{der}} \subseteq \pi.\mathsf{P_{der}}$. In particular, $\pi = \pi' \iff \pi \geq \pi' \wedge \pi' \geq \pi$.*

Definition 10 (Extracting the usage policy associated with a data category). *The usage policy relevant for a data category θ depends both on the component C under consideration and on the latest relevant event of the log $\lambda = \{\lambda_1, \dots, \lambda_n\}$. We define $\lambda_*(\lambda, \theta, C)$ to be the latest event defining a usage policy for θ. It is the event such that $\mathrm{EvTime}(\lambda_*(\lambda, \theta, C)) = \max\{t \mid \exists\ \lambda_i \in \lambda, \Theta, \theta_1, \theta_2, C, C', \pi, P, \rho, R \mid (\lambda_i = (\texttt{Acquire}, \Theta, C, \pi,\ P, t) \wedge \theta \in \Theta) \vee (\lambda_i = (\texttt{Export}, \Theta, C', C, \pi, \rho, R, t) \wedge\ \theta \in \Theta) \vee \lambda_i = (\texttt{Link}, \theta_1, \theta_2, \theta, C, \pi, \rho, R, t) \vee \lambda_i = (\texttt{Derive}, \theta_1, \theta, C, \pi, \rho,\ R, t)\}$. Based on the value of this event λ_*, we now define the associated usage policy $\pi_*(\lambda, \theta, C)$ as follows.*

$$\begin{cases} \lambda_* = (\texttt{Acquire}, \Theta, C, \pi, P, t) \Longrightarrow \pi_* = \pi \\ \lambda_* = (\texttt{Export}, \Theta, C', C, \pi, \rho, R, t) \Longrightarrow \pi_* = \pi \\ \lambda_* = (\texttt{Link}, \theta_1, \theta_2, \theta, C, \pi, \rho, R, t) \Longrightarrow \pi_* = \pi \\ \lambda_* = (\texttt{Derive}, \theta_1, \theta, C, \pi, \rho, R, t) \Longrightarrow \pi_* = \pi' \end{cases}$$

Since different events feature different timestamps (Definition 4), λ_* and consequently π_* are uniquely defined for a given triple (λ, θ, C).

The following correctness and compliance rules are stated $\forall \, \lambda_i \in \lambda$.

3.2 Rules for Internal Correctness of Logs

Correctness rules ensure the internal consistency of event logs and are independent of the associated usage policy.

(Cor1) For every Use or Export event and for every data category appearing in the event the data was acquired, derived, or linked somewhere. Note that we only consider "complete" provenance histories. $\lambda_i = (\texttt{Use}, \Theta, C, \rho, R, t, e) \ \vee \ \lambda_i = (\texttt{Export}, \Theta, C, C', \, \pi, P, t) \Longrightarrow \forall \, \theta \, \in \, \Theta, \exists \, \lambda_j \, \in \, \lambda, C'', \Theta', \theta_1, \theta_2, \theta_3, \rho', P', R', t, \, \pi' \mid (\lambda_j = (\texttt{Acquire}, \Theta', C'', \pi', \, P', t') \ \wedge \ \theta \in \Theta') \vee \lambda_j = (\texttt{Derive}, \theta_1, \theta, C'', \pi', \rho', R', t') \vee \lambda_j = (\texttt{Link}, \theta_2, \theta_3, \theta, C'', \pi', \rho', R', t') \wedge (\, t' < t).$

(Cor2) A similar rule holds for Derive events: $\lambda_i = (\texttt{Derive}, \theta, \theta', C, \pi, \rho, R, t) \Longrightarrow \exists \, \lambda_j \in \lambda, \Theta, C', \pi', \rho', P', t', \theta'', R', \theta_1, \theta_2 \mid (\lambda_j = (\texttt{Acquire}, \Theta, C', \pi', P', t') \wedge \theta \in \Theta) \vee \lambda_j = (\texttt{Derive}, \theta'', \theta, C', \rho', R', t') \vee \lambda_j = (\texttt{Link}, \theta_1, \theta_2, \theta, C', \pi', \rho', \, R', t') \wedge (t' < t).$

(Cor3) Similar rules hold for both source arguments of Link events:
- $\lambda_i = (\texttt{Link}, \theta, \theta', \theta'', C, \pi, \rho, R, t) \Longrightarrow \exists j, \Theta, C', \pi', \rho', P', t', R', \theta_1, \theta_2, \theta_3 \mid (\lambda_j = (\texttt{Acquire}, \Theta, C', \pi', P', t') \wedge \theta \in \Theta) \vee \lambda_j = (\texttt{Derive}, \theta_1, \theta, C', \pi', \rho', R', t') \vee \lambda_j = (\texttt{Link}, \theta_2, \theta_3, \theta, C', \pi', \rho', R, t') \wedge (t' < t).$
- $\lambda_i = (\texttt{Link}, \theta, \theta', \theta'', C, \pi, \rho, R, t) \Longrightarrow \exists j, \Theta, C', \pi', \rho', P', t', R', \theta_1, \theta_2, \theta_3 \mid (\lambda_j = (\texttt{Acquire}, \Theta, C', \pi', P', t') \wedge \theta' \in \Theta) \vee \lambda_j = (\texttt{Derive}, \theta_1, \theta', C', \pi', \rho', R', t') \vee \lambda_j = (\texttt{Link}, \theta_2, \theta_3, \theta', C', \pi', \rho, R', t') \wedge (t' < t).$

(Cor4) For non-instantaneous events (i.e. data use), starting and ending timestamps are well-formed: $\lambda_i = (\texttt{Use}, \Theta, C, \rho, R, s, e) \Longrightarrow s < e.$

(Cor5) Successive data derivations exhibit monotonous timestamps: $\lambda_i = (\texttt{Derive}, \theta, \theta', C, \pi, \rho, R, t) \wedge \lambda_j = (\texttt{Derive}, \theta', \theta'', C', \pi', \rho', R', t') \wedge i \neq j \wedge \lambda_j \in \lambda \Longrightarrow t' > t.$

(Cor6) For a given component, the usage policies for a partial log λ of log λ' associated with a given data category are consistent, i.e. the policy may not become weaker. $\lambda \subseteq \lambda' \Longrightarrow \pi_*(\theta, C, \lambda') \geq \pi_*(\theta, C, \lambda).$

(Cor7) Data of a given category is not processed in any form after the data with this category has been removed: $\lambda_i = (\texttt{Remove}, \Theta, C, t) \wedge \lambda_j \in \lambda \wedge \theta \in \Theta \wedge \theta \in \text{DataCat}(\lambda_j) \wedge \text{EvType}(\lambda_j) \in \{\texttt{Use}, \texttt{Export}, \texttt{Link}, \texttt{Derive}\} \Longrightarrow \text{EvTime}(\lambda_j) < t.$

(Cor8) No data forwarding is permitted once a removal request has been received, even before the request fulfilment delay is reached: $\lambda_i = (\mathtt{ReqRemove}, \Theta, t) \wedge \theta \in \Theta \wedge \lambda_j \in \lambda \wedge \lambda_j = (\mathtt{Export}, \Theta', C, C', \pi, P, t') \Longrightarrow \theta \notin \Theta' \vee t' < t$.

(Cor9) Similarly, no data use may start after a removal request has been sent: $\lambda_i = (\mathtt{ReqRemove}, \Theta, t) \wedge \theta \in \Theta \wedge \lambda_j \in \lambda \wedge \lambda_j = (\mathtt{Use}, \Theta', C, \rho, R, s, e) \Longrightarrow \theta \notin \Theta' \vee s < t$.

(Cor10) Likewise, new data may not be derived from data for which deletion has already been requested: $\lambda_i = (\mathtt{ReqRemove}, \Theta, t) \wedge \theta \in \Theta \wedge \lambda_j \in \lambda \wedge \lambda_j = (\mathtt{Derive}, \theta, \theta', C, \pi, \rho, R, t') \Longrightarrow t' < t$.

(Cor11) The new usage policy affecting data generated by linking must be stronger or equal than the policies associated with each of the source data elements: $\lambda_i = (\mathtt{Link}, \theta_1, \theta_2, \theta, C, \pi, \rho, R, t) \wedge \lambda_j = (\mathtt{Acquire}, \Theta_1, C, \pi_1, P, R', t') \wedge \theta_1 \in \Theta_1 \wedge \lambda_k = (\mathtt{Acquire}, \Theta_2, C, \pi_2, P', R'', t'') \wedge \theta_2 \in \Theta_2 \Longrightarrow \pi \geq \pi_1 \wedge \pi \geq \pi_2 \wedge t' < t \wedge t'' < t$.

(Cor12) A similar property holds for derived data: $\lambda_i = (\mathtt{Derive}, \theta, \theta', C, \pi, \rho, R, t) \wedge \lambda_j = (\mathtt{Acquire}, \Theta, C, \pi', P, R', t') \wedge \theta \in \Theta \Longrightarrow \pi \geq \pi' \wedge t' < t$.

Definition 11 (Correctness). *A log λ is said to be correct if all correctness properties Cor1 ... Cor12 hold for λ.*

To illustrate this notion, consider the following example log $\lambda = \lambda_1 \ldots \lambda_7$:

λ_1: (Acquire, {Treatment, ID, Frequency}, Hospital, π_2, {Logistic, Statistic}, 2016-05-01T08:07)

λ_2: (Use, {Treatment, ID}, Hospital, Logistic, Patient registration mandatory, 2016-05-01T10:25, 2016-05-09T17:54)

λ_3: (Export, {Treatment, ID, Frequency}, Hospital, ResearchInstitute, π_1, {Logistic, Statistic}, 2016-05-12T12:17)

λ_4: (Link, ID, Treatment, History, ResearchInstitute, π_1, Statistic, Insurance billing requested, 2016-05-14T22:33)

λ_5: (Derive, History, Frequency, ResearchInstitute, π_1, Statistic, Quantitative research, 2016-05-18T09:41)

λ_6: (Use, {Treatment, Frequency}, ResearchInstitute, Logistic, Workflow optimisation, 2016-05-19T14:41, 2016-05-19T15:03)

λ_7: (Link, Frequency, Age, Risk, ResearchInstitute, π_1, Statistic, Correlation study, 2016-05-20T12:14)

λ is not correct, since Cor3 is violated. No acquisition, derivation or linking event yielding data category Age, appearing in λ_7, is part of λ. Thus, Age cannot be linked with Frequency in λ_7.

Note that provenance for a category of data may not necessarily extend over the entire data life cycle. In particular, the fact that the data may not have been deleted at the end of a log does not falsify the correctness of the log. From this perspective, the existence of deletion events become policy-dependent and is therefore covered by compliance rules, not by correctness rules.

3.3   Rules for Compliance of Logs with Usage Policies

Compliance rules depend on the values of associated usage policies.
Global and requested data deletion

(Com1) The global deletion delay D_g of usage policy $\pi_*(\lambda, \theta, C)$ extracted as defined in Definition 10 holds for all categories of data. No category of data can therefore appear in a log λ after the expiration of this global delay:

- $\lambda_i = (\texttt{Acquire}, \Theta, C, \pi, P, t) \wedge \theta \in \Theta \wedge \theta \in \text{DataCat}(\lambda_j) \wedge \lambda_j \in \lambda \wedge$
  $\text{Active}(\lambda_j) = C \Longrightarrow \text{EvTime}(\lambda_j) - t < \pi_*(\lambda, \theta, C).D_g$.
- $\lambda_i = (\texttt{Export}, \Theta, C, C', \pi, P, t) \wedge \theta \in \Theta \wedge \theta \in \text{DataCat}(\lambda_j) \wedge \lambda_j \in \lambda \wedge$
  $\text{Active}(\lambda_j) = C' \Longrightarrow \text{EvTime}(\lambda_j) - t < \pi_*(\lambda, \theta, C).D_g$.
- $\lambda_i = (\texttt{Link}, \theta', \theta'', \theta, C, \pi, \rho, R, t) \wedge \theta \in \text{DataCat}(\lambda_j) \wedge \lambda_j \in \lambda \wedge$
  $\text{Active}(\lambda_j) = C' \Longrightarrow \text{EvTime}(\lambda_j) - t < \pi_*(\lambda, \theta, C).D_g$.

(Com2) Deletion requests are fulfilled in a delay compatible with the associated policy's request fulfilment delay D_{rf}: $\lambda_i = (\texttt{ReqRemove}, \Theta, t) \wedge \theta \in \Theta \Longrightarrow$
$\forall C \in \text{Control}(\lambda, \theta), \exists \lambda_j \in \lambda, \Theta', t' \mid \lambda_j = (\texttt{Remove}, \Theta', C, t') \wedge \theta \in \Theta' \wedge$
$t' - t < \pi_*(\lambda, \theta, C).D_{rf}$.

Data forwarding

(Com3) If all forwarding is forbidden, no data exports are allowed to take place: $\pi_*(\lambda, \theta, C).\text{Fw} = (\top, \varnothing) \wedge \lambda_j \in \lambda \wedge \text{EvTime}(\lambda_j) \geq$
$\text{EvTime}(\lambda_*(\lambda, \theta, C)) \wedge \theta \in \text{DataCat}(\lambda_j) \Longrightarrow \text{EvType}(\lambda_j) \neq \texttt{Export}$,
where $\lambda_*(\lambda, \theta, C)$ is the latest event defining a usage policy for θ (see Definition 10).

(Com4) If the associated forwarding policy defines a whitelist, all data exports are destined to components on the list: $\lambda_i = (\texttt{Export}, \Theta, C, C', \pi, P, t) \wedge$
$\theta \in \Theta \wedge \pi_*(\lambda, \theta, C).\text{Fw} = (\text{wl}, \text{List}) \wedge \text{EvTime}(\lambda_i) \geq \text{EvTime}(\lambda_*(\lambda, \theta, C)) \Longrightarrow C' \in \text{List}$.

(Com5) In case a blacklist is defined by the associated forwarding policy, no data exports towards components in the list take place: $\lambda_i = (\texttt{Export}, \Theta, C, C', \pi, P, t) \wedge \theta \in \Theta \wedge \pi_*(\lambda, \theta, C).\text{Fw} = (\text{bl}, \text{List}) \wedge$
$\text{EvTime}(\lambda_i) \geq \text{EvTime}(\lambda_*(\lambda, \theta, C)) \Longrightarrow C' \notin \text{List}$.

Data linking

(Com6) If the first data category in the argument list of a $\texttt{Link}$ event also appears directly or indirectly in the data category set of the associated linking policy, then the second data category in the argument list of the event may not appear directly or indirectly in the same set of the linking policy: $\lambda_i = (\texttt{Link}, \theta', \theta'', \theta, C, \pi, \rho, R, t) \wedge \exists A \in \pi_*(\lambda, \theta, C).\text{Li} \mid \theta_A \in A \wedge \theta' \in \text{Dsc}(\lambda, \theta_A) \wedge \text{EvTime}(\lambda_i) \geq \text{EvTime}(\lambda_*(\lambda, \theta, C)) \Longrightarrow \forall \theta'_A \in A \mid \theta'_A \neq \theta_A, \theta'' \notin \text{Dsc}(\lambda, \theta'_A)$.

Data derivation

(Com7) Data categories in the associated derivation policy may neither be used to directly derive new data, nor indirectly: $\lambda_i = (\texttt{Derive}, \theta', \theta'', C, \pi, \rho, R, t) \;\wedge\; \theta' \in \text{Dsc}(\lambda, \theta) \wedge \text{EvTime}(\lambda_i) \geq \text{EvTime}(\lambda_*(\lambda, \theta, C)) \Longrightarrow \theta \notin \pi_*(\lambda, \theta, C).\text{De}.$

Purposes for data use and derivation

(Com8) Only data categories for which use is authorised for a specific purpose appear in Use events: $\lambda_i = (\texttt{Use}, \Theta, C, \rho, R, s, e) \;\wedge\; \theta' \in \Theta \;\wedge\; \theta' \in \text{Dsc}(\lambda, \theta) \wedge \text{EvTime}(\lambda_i) \geq \text{EvTime}(\lambda_*(\lambda, \theta, C)) \Longrightarrow (\theta, \rho) \in \pi_*(\lambda, \theta, C).\text{P}_{\text{use}}.$

(Com9) Similarly, data is only derived, directly or indirectly, for purposes authorised by the associated derivation policy: $\lambda_i = (\texttt{Derive}, \theta', \theta'', C, \pi, \rho, R, t) \;\wedge\; \theta' \in \text{Dsc}(\lambda, \theta) \wedge \text{EvTime}(\lambda_i) \geq \text{EvTime}(\lambda_*(\lambda, \theta, C)) \Longrightarrow (\theta, \rho) \in \pi_*(\lambda, \theta, C).\text{P}_{\text{der}}.$

We can now define compliance for an entire log of provenance events:

Definition 12 (Compliance). *A log λ is said to be compliant if all compliance properties* Com1 ... Com9 *hold for λ.*

To illustrate this notion, we first show in Sect. 4 the applicability of our framework to privacy accountability, and then provide an example in Sect. 5.

4 Applicability to Privacy Accountability

We now discuss under which conditions our framework can be applied to the particular case of personal data protection. We argue that, while provenance can be of great benefit here, special care must be taken due to the sensitive nature of the involved data. Furthermore, it is necessary to combine the framework with a global accountability process, since not all verification aspects can be automated. In the following we use the wording introduced in Sect. 2, making three exceptions. We refer to an entity collecting or processing data as *data controller*, following the usual European terminology. Since personal data is usually assigned to an individual, we call this data owner *data subject*. Furthermore, to reflect the specificities of dealing with personal data, the *usage policies* under consideration are named *privacy policies*.

Motivation. The large-scale dissemination of personal data rightfully causes grave concerns. As data subjects are not informed clearly about the processing and distribution of their data, loss of control prevails [22]. The case of outsourced medical data is particularly problematic. It combines highly sensitive categories of personal data with strong data sharing incentives for data controllers such as hospitals, pharmacies, research institutes, and private firms [6]. With an audit-centric approach, provenance can be not only a tool for (non-personal) data processing fault detection, but can also help restoring some clarity to data subjects regarding the whereabouts of their personal data. In this specific context, provenance can support privacy, and more precisely accountability [7].

Policies. One specificity of privacy-oriented scenarios is the choice of the applicable policies. Even for a given data processing use case, a one-size-fits-all approach is not possible here. Privacy preferences are a matter of personal choice, since data subjects exhibit varying levels of sensitivity with respect to data protection, leading some privacy frameworks to incorporate different trust models corresponding to typical user profiles [14].

Time. In addition, temporal aspects become indispensable in the privacy case. While provenance models do not always include time [23], our framework incorporates this aspect. Once a data subject requests deletion of their data, the applicability of this decision depends on a clear distinction between prior and ulterior events. Note that also other established models, such as PROV-O [21], include temporal aspects.

Logs. A common concern about privacy protection through log auditing is that the log itself may become a threat to privacy. One mitigating feature of our framework is the fact that only data categories, not actual values, are logged. This reduces the threat of leaks to metadata. However, even metadata is known to be potentially sensitive [18]. This raises the question of secure log storage for which solutions do exist [5].

Process integration. The provenance record constitutes the evidence at the centre of the accountability process, but the panoramic view provided by provenance records goes hand in hand with limited guarantees about their trustworthiness. Since numerous entities are involved, there can be no mapping, realised in a controlled environment, between system events and log items. Adopting an external view as we do, provenance records cannot be guaranteed to match actual system processing. For such a decentralised perspective, inclusion in a wider process is critical and pressure on entities to declare data handling truthfully must come from a different direction. The legal implementation of the principle of accountability, a core principle in the recently adopted European General Data Protection Regulation [15], would help to address this issue. Contributing to correct provenance records is a way for data controllers to be accountable to data subjects.

Processing purposes in the privacy case. Another specificity of privacy-oriented use cases is the central importance of stated data processing purposes. Since personal data is involved, processing purposes are actually data handling *finalities*. Declaring such finalities is legally required in the European Union. It is demanded that the purpose designations be in line with actual processing purposes, but the verification of this coupling is not amenable to automation. We assumed the existence of a purpose ontology, but in the case of personal data protection, no convincing real-world and broadly accepted equivalent of such an ontology exists. As a result, there is a realistic risk of data controllers employing purpose designations abusively, stretching commonly accepted meanings to give the appearance of compliance. Data Protection Authorities such as the UK ICO, the Swedish Data Inspection Board, or the French CNIL can play an active role in enforcing a reasonable mapping between processing purposes and involved categories of personal data. Principles such as the legitimacy of processing finalities have already been put forward in this context [2]. More stringent and systematic checks must be enforced for data subjects to fully trust declared processing purposes.

5 Evaluation: A Medical Scenario

To evaluate our formal model, we describe a scenario involving medical data about an individual. Real provenance logs involving multiple components are expected to be much more complex than this simple example.

Personal data from the patient is processed by health professionals from three different organisations on different occasions. The data controllers involved are a hospital Hospital, a research institute ResearchInstitute, and a pharmacy Pharmacy. The following categories of personal data are involved: a patient's full name ID, treatment Treatment, treatment frequency Frequency, status of

$\pi_1.\mathsf{D_g} = 3$ months
$\pi_1.\mathsf{D_{rf}} = 1$ day
$\pi_1.\mathsf{Fw} = (\mathsf{wl}, \mathsf{List})$
$\mathsf{List} = \{\mathsf{Hospital},$
$\mathsf{ResearchInstitute}\}$
$\pi_1.\mathsf{Li} = \{(\mathsf{Treatment}, \mathsf{Status}),$
$(\mathsf{ID}, \mathsf{Drug})\}$
$\pi_1.\mathsf{De} = \{\mathsf{Frequency}, \mathsf{Risk}, \mathsf{Drug}\}$
$\pi_1.\mathsf{P_{use}} = \{(\mathsf{Treatment}, \mathsf{Logistic}),$
$(\mathsf{ID}, \mathsf{Logistic}),$
$(\mathsf{Frequency}, \mathsf{Logistic}),$
$(\mathsf{History}, \mathsf{Logistic}),$
$(\mathsf{Status}, \mathsf{Logistic})\}$
$\pi_1.\mathsf{P_{der}} = \{(\mathsf{History}, \mathsf{Statistic})\}$

$\pi_2.\mathsf{D_g} = 6$ months
$\pi_2.\mathsf{D_{rf}} = 2$ days
$\pi_2.\mathsf{Fw} = (\mathsf{wl}, \mathsf{List})$
$\mathsf{List} = \{\mathsf{Hospital},$
$\mathsf{ResearchInstitute},$
$\mathsf{Pharmacy}\}$
$\pi_2.\mathsf{Li} = \{(\mathsf{Treatment}, \mathsf{Status}),$
$(\mathsf{ID}, \mathsf{Drug})\}$
$\pi_2.\mathsf{De} = \{\mathsf{Frequency}, \mathsf{Drug}\}$
$\pi_2.\mathsf{P_{use}} = \{(\mathsf{Treatment}, \mathsf{Marketing}),$
$(\mathsf{Treatment}, \mathsf{Logistic}),$
$(\mathsf{ID}, \mathsf{Logistic}),$
$(\mathsf{Frequency}, \mathsf{Logistic}),$
$(\mathsf{History}, \mathsf{Logistic}),$
$(\mathsf{Status}, \mathsf{Logistic})\}$
$\pi_2.\mathsf{P_{der}} = \{(\mathsf{History}, \mathsf{Statistic}),$
$(\mathsf{ID}, \mathsf{Logistic}),$
$(\mathsf{Treatment}, \mathsf{Business})\}$

Fig. 1. Example privacy policies π_1 and π_2.

the treated pathology Status, medical history History, drug group Drug, and risk categorisation Risk. Used purpose designations include logistics Logistic, statistics Statistic, business operations Business and marketing Marketing. Let π_1 and π_2 be two privacy policies, with values as in Fig. 1 (the process leading to the definition of these values is beyond the scope of this scenario).

Note that $\pi_1 \geq \pi_2$, but $\neg\pi_2 \geq \pi_1$, i.e. π_1 is strictly stronger than π_2. We now consider the log $\lambda = \lambda_1 \ldots \lambda_{15}$ in Fig. 2. Its corresponding provenance graph is depicted in Fig. 3.

λ_1: (Acquire, {Treatment, ID, Status}, Hospital, π_2, {Logistic, Statistic}, 2016-05-01T08:07)

λ_2: (Use, {Treatment, ID}, Hospital, Logistic, Patient registration mandatory, 2016-05-01T10:25, 2016-05-09T17:54)

λ_3: (Export, {Treatment, ID, Status}, Hospital, ResearchInstitute, π_1, {Logistic, Statistic}, 2016-05-12T12:17)

λ_4: (Link, ID, Status, History, ResearchInstitute, π_1, Statistic, Insurance billing requested, 2016-05-14T22:33)

λ_5: (Derive, History, Frequency, ResearchInstitute, π_1, Statistic, Quantitative research, 2016-05-18T09:41)

λ_6: (Use, {Treatment, Frequency}, ResearchInstitute, Logistic, Workflow optimisation, 2016-05-19T14:41, 2016-05-19T15:03)

λ_7: (Link, Frequency, Treatment, Risk, ResearchInstitute, π_1, Statistic, Correlation study, 2016-05-20T12:14)

λ_8: (Export, {Treatment}, Hospital, Pharmacy, π_2, {Logistic}, 2016-05-22T16:37)

λ_9: (Derive, Treatment, Drug, Pharmacy, π_2, Business, Stock estimation, 2016-05-22T23:12)

λ_{10}: (ReqRemove, {ID, Status}, 2016-06-02T18:23)

λ_{11}: (Remove, {ID, Status}, ResearchInstitute, 2016-06-03T10:46)

λ_{12}: (Remove, {ID, Status}, Hospital, 2016-06-03T11:17)

λ_{13}: (Remove, {Treatment}, Hospital, 2016-06-17T15:40)

λ_{14}: (Remove, {Treatment, History, Frequency, Risk}, ResearchInstitute, 2016-07-02T08:35)

λ_{15}: (Remove, {Treatment}, Pharmacy, 2016-07-25T04:32)

Fig. 2. The provenance log $\lambda = \lambda_1 \ldots \lambda_{15}$ for our example.

This log is correct, since it is straightforward to verify that Cor1 ... Cor12 are all respected. However, log λ is not compliant with respect to the involved privacy policies. Indeed, the Link event in λ_7 contradicts Com6. The latest policy-defining event, as in Definition 10, for the data category Risk for the data controller ResearchInstitute is $\lambda_*(\lambda, \text{Risk}, \text{ResearchInstitute}) = \lambda_7$ = (Link, Frequency, Treatment, Risk, ResearchInstitute, π_1, Statistic, Correlation study, 2016-05-20T12:14). As a consequence, the associated privacy policy is $\pi_*(\lambda, \text{Risk}, \text{ResearchInstitute}) = \pi_1$. Now recall Definition 8,

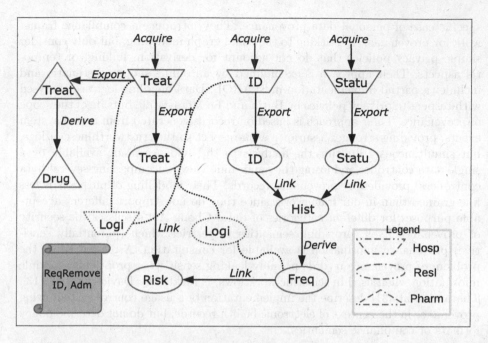

Fig. 3. A provenance record graph depicting the log from Fig. 2. Timestamps and Remove events have been omitted for clarity. Different shapes symbolise different data controllers, as shown in the legend. Dotted lines represent Use events. Some of the used identifiers are abbreviations.

and notice that $\text{Dsc}(\lambda, \text{Treatment}) = \{\text{Treatment}, \text{Risk}, \text{Drug}\}$ because of the linking in λ_7 and the derivation in λ_9. On the other hand, $\text{Dsc}(\lambda, \text{Status}) = \{\text{Status}, \text{History}, \text{Frequency}, \text{Risk}\}$ because of the linking in λ_4, the derivation in λ_5 and the second linking in λ_7. We have $\text{Frequency} \in \text{Dsc}(\lambda, \text{Status})$, and Frequency is the first data category being linked by λ_7. Furthermore, Treatment $\in \text{Dsc}(\lambda, \text{Treatment})$ and Treatment is the second data category being linked by this same event.

Since $(\text{Treatment}, \text{Status}) \in \pi_1.\text{Li} = \pi_*(\lambda, \text{Risk}, \text{ResearchInstitute})$, Com6 is violated and global compliance does not hold as a consequence (Definition 12).

6   Related Work

The W3C specifies constraints [11] for the PROV data model [24], both for correctness and compliance. Since the PROV data model strives for maximal generality, it is more suited to the semantic web than to the scenario of data processing within an organisation. A high-level discussion (without concrete modelling) of the use of provenance records to support accountability via privacy policies can be found in work by Gil and Fritz [17]. Aldeco-Pérez and Moreau zoom into the specific case of personal data provenance. They introduce a compliance framework for provenance [1], sticking to the usual graph modelling, but only consider simple privacy policies that do not account for derivation, linking, or temporal aspects. Their approach is exemplified by an online shopping scenario and includes a partial implementation in SPARQL. Data handling logs are analysed with respect to privacy policies by Butin and Le Métayer [9], outside of the scope of provenance. Their approach is based on records generated from actual system events, providing stronger assurance with respect to the trustworthiness of logs, but simultaneously limiting the analysis to the evidence made available by a single data controller and losing the panoramic view (encompassing several data controllers) provided by provenance records. Their modelling of purposes is less fine-grained than in our framework, since they do not support different acceptable purposes for different categories of data. Chong [12] discusses the security of provenance itself, providing semantics to restrict which (potentially sensitive) provenance information is available for consultation. A related issue, the problem of provenance records possibly leaking sensitive or proprietary module information when used in scientific workflows, is tackled by Davidson et al. [13]. Tharaud et al. [31] describe the implementation of a usage control system using provenance in the context of electronic health records, but do not describe policy formats or compliance semantics.

7   Conclusion

We have introduced a formal correctness and compliance framework for provenance, based on a linear view of provenance events and the definition of sticky usage policies. The presented format for policies and rules for correctness and compliance are not meant to be exhaustive or applicable to all scenarios. However, our framework serves as a basis allowing to include other policy components and event types. For instance, authorised purposes can be defined for other event types as well, such as data linking; and more fine-grained policy components can be considered e.g. for data forwarding or derivation. As an example, one could restrict the target data categories of data derivation instead of the source categories. Therefore, the choices presented here in terms of policy components, event types, and rules should only be seen as an instantiation of the framework.

We discussed the possibility of applying our approach to the special case of personal data processing, and pointed out the necessity of combining the formal framework with a global accountability approach involving pressure from data protection authorities and new legal tools. A scenario involving the processing of medical data by different, communicating data controllers was used to exemplify the framework. The use of such a compliance framework is only meaningful within a wider accountability process, since provenance records cannot be intrinsically trustworthy. In combination with such an accountability process it can however contribute to increase transparency about personal data handling, ultimately benefiting data subjects.

Future work. In privacy-oriented scenarios, while unconditionally enforcing the global correctness of provenance records seems out of reach, a certification-based approach in coordination with data protection authorities could help improve the accuracy of records provided by data controllers, ultimately leading to differentiated levels of assurance for data handling evidence. Taking into account varying levels of data quality in a provenance-based compliance framework could lead to a more granular analysis of global correctness and compliance. Another open question is how the global provenance record is aggregated securely from the different involved components when they are not all trusted. It would also be interesting to estimate the complexity of correctness and compliance checking. Finally, modelling correctness and compliance rules in a theorem prover like Isabelle/HOL [26] would provide additional guarantees in term of overall consistency.

Acknowledgments. This work has been co-funded by the DFG as part of project "Long-Term Secure Archiving" within the CRC 1119 CROSSING. In addition, it has received funding from the European Union's Horizon 2020 research and innovation program under Grant Agreement No 644962. The authors thank Fanny Coudert for insights about purpose ontologies.

References

1. Aldeco-Pérez, R., Moreau, L.: A provenance-based compliance framework. In: Berre, A.J., Gómez-Pérez, A., Tutschku, K., Fensel, D. (eds.) FIS 2010. LNCS, vol. 6369, pp. 128–137. Springer, Heidelberg (2010)
2. Article 29 Data Protection Working Party: Opinion 8/2001 on the processing of personal data in the employment context (2001). http://ec.europa.eu/justice/data-protection/article-29/documentation/opinion-recommendation/files/2001/wp48_en.pdf
3. Article 29 Data Protection Working Party: Opinion 3/2010 on the principle of accountability (2010). http://ec.europa.eu/justice/policies/privacy/docs/wpdocs/2010/wp173_en.pdf
4. Article 29 Data Protection Working Party: Advice paper on essential elements of a definition and a provision on profiling within the EU General Data Protection Regulation (2013). http://ec.europa.eu/justice/data-protection/article-29/documentation/other-document/files/2013/20130513_advice-paper-on-profiling_en.pdf
5. Bellare, M., Yee, B.S.: Forward Integrity for Secure Audit Logs. Technical report University of California at San Diego (1997)
6. Bertino, E., Ooi, B.C., Yang, Y., Deng, R.H.: Privacy and ownership preserving of outsourced medical data. In: Aberer, K., Franklin, M.J., Nishio, S. (eds.) Proceedings of the 21st International Conference on Data Engineering, ICDE 2005, pp. 521–532. IEEE Computer Society (2005)
7. Bier, C.: How usage control and provenance tracking get together – a data protection perspective. In: IEEE Symposium on Security and Privacy Workshops, pp. 13–17. IEEE Computer Society (2013)
8. Butin, D., Chicote, M., Le Métayer, D.: Log design for accountability. In: 2013 IEEE Security & Privacy Workshop on Data Usage Management, pp. 1–7. IEEE Computer Society (2013)

9. Butin, D., Le Métayer, D.: Log analysis for data protection accountability. In: Jones, C., Pihlajasaari, P., Sun, J. (eds.) FM 2014. LNCS, vol. 8442, pp. 163–178. Springer, Heidelberg (2014)
10. Cheney, J.: A formal framework for provenance security. In: Proceedings of the 24th IEEE Computer Security Foundations Symposium, CSF 2011, pp. 281–293. IEEE Computer Society (2011)
11. Cheney, J., Missier, P., Moreau, L.: Constraints of the PROV Data Model. Technical report, W3C (2013). https://www.w3.org/TR/prov-constraints/
12. Chong, S.: Towards semantics for provenance security. In: Cheney, J. (ed.) Proceedings of the First Workshop on the Theory and Practice of Provenance, TaPP 2009. USENIX (2009)
13. Davidson, S.B., Khanna, S., Roy, S., Stoyanovich, J., Tannen, V., Chen, Y.: On provenance and privacy. In: Milo, T. (ed.) Proceedings of the 14th International Conference Database Theory, ICDT 2011, pp. 3–10. ACM (2011)
14. Decroix, K.: Model-Based Analysis of Privacy in Electronic Services. Ph.D. thesis, KU Leuven, Faculty of Engineering Science (2015)
15. European Commission: Regulation (EU) 2016/679 of the European Parliament and of the Council of 27 April 2016 on the protection of natural persons with regard to the processing of personal data and on the free movement of such data, and repealing Directive 95/46/EC (General Data Protection Regulation). Official Journal of the European Union 59 (2016). http://eur-lex.europa.eu/eli/reg/2016/679/oj
16. Foster, I.T., Vöckler, J., Wilde, M., Zhao, Y.: The virtual data grid: a new model and architecture for data-intensive collaboration. In: First Biennial Conference on Innovative Data Systems Research (CIDR) (2003)
17. Gil, Y., Fritz, C.: Reasoning about the appropriate use of private data through computational workflows. In: Intelligent Information Privacy Management, Papers from the 2010 AAAI Spring Symposium, Technical Report SS-10-05. AAAI (2010)
18. Greschbach, B., Kreitz, G., Buchegger, S.: The devil is in the metadata – new privacy challenges in Decentralised Online Social Networks. In: Tenth Annual IEEE International Conference on Pervasive Computing and Communications, PerCom 2012, Workshop Proceedings, pp. 333–339. IEEE Computer Society (2012)
19. Hartig, O.: Provenance information in the web of data. In: Bizer, C., Heath, T., Berners-Lee, T., Idehen, K. (eds.) Proceedings of the WWW 2009 Workshop on Linked Data on the Web, LDOW 2009. CEUR Workshop Proceedings, vol. 538. CEUR-WS.org (2009). http://ceur-ws.org/Vol-538/ldow2009_paper18.pdf
20. Kumaraguru, P., Lobo, J., Cranor, L.F., Calo, S.B.: A survey of privacy policy languages. In: Workshop on Usable IT Security Management (USM 2007): Proceedings of the 3rd Symposium on Usable Privacy and Security. ACM (2007)
21. Lebo, T., Sahoo, S., McGuinness, D.: PROV-O: The PROV Ontology. Technical report, W3C (2013). https://www.w3.org/TR/prov-o/
22. Madden, M., Rainie, L., Zickuhr, K., Duggan, M., Smith, A.: Public Perceptions of Privacy and Security in the Post-Snowden Era. Pew Research Center (2014). http://www.pewinternet.org/2014/11/12/public-privacy-perceptions/
23. Moreau, L., Clifford, B., Freire, J., Futrelle, J., Gil, Y., Groth, P., Kwasnikowska, N., Miles, S., Missier, P., Myers, J., Plale, B., Simmhan, Y., Stephan, E., den Bussche, J.V.: The open provenance model core specification (V1.1). Future Gener. Comput. Syst. 27(6), 743–756 (2011)
24. Moreau, L., Missier, P.: PROV-DM: The PROV Data Model. Technical report, W3C (2013). https://www.w3.org/TR/prov-dm/

25. Okkalioglu, B.D., Okkalioglu, M., Koç, M., Polat, H.: A survey: deriving private information from perturbed data. Artif. Intell. Rev. **44**(4), 547–569 (2015)
26. Paulson, L.C. (ed.): Isabelle – A Generic Theorem Prover. LNCS, vol. 828. Springer, Heidelberg (1994)
27. Pearson, S., Mont, M.C.: Sticky policies: an approach for managing privacy across multiple parties. IEEE Comput. **44**(9), 60–68 (2011)
28. Proctor, R.W., Ali, M.A., Vu, K.P.L.: Examining usability of web privacy policies. Int. J. Hum. Comput. Interact. **24**(3), 307–328 (2008)
29. Ram, S., Liu, J.: A new perspective on semantics of data provenance. In: Freire, J., Missier, P., Sahoo, S.S. (eds.) Proceedings of the First International Workshop on the Role of Semantic Web in Provenance Management (SWPM 2009). CEUR Workshop Proceedings, vol. 526. CEUR-WS.org (2009). http://ceur-ws.org/Vol-526/InvitedPaper_1.pdf
30. Sultana, S., Bertino, E.: A comprehensive model for provenance. In: Groth, P., Frew, J. (eds.) IPAW 2012. LNCS, vol. 7525, pp. 243–245. Springer, Heidelberg (2012)
31. Tharaud, J., Wohlgemuth, S., Echizen, I., Sonehara, N., Müller, G., Lafourcade, P.: Privacy by data provenance with digital watermarking – a proof-of-concept implementation for medical services with electronic health records. In: Echizen, I., Pan, J., Fellner, D.W., Nouak, A., Kuijper, A., Jain, L.C. (eds.) Proceedings of the Sixth International Conference on Intelligent Information Hiding and Multimedia Signal Processing (IIH-MSP 2010), pp. 510–513. IEEE Computer Society (2010)
32. Trabelsi, S., Njeh, A., Bussard, L., Neven, G.: PPL engine: a symmetric architecture for privacy policy handling. In: W3C Workshop on Privacy and Data Usage Control (2010)

Recipient Privacy in Online Social Networks (Short Paper)

Filipe Beato[1], Kimmo Halunen[2(✉)], and Bart Mennink[1]

[1] Department of Electrical Engineering, ESAT/COSIC, KU Leuven, and iMinds,
Leuven, Belgium
{filipe.beato,bart.mennink}@esat.kuleuven.be
[2] VTT Technical Research Centre of Finland Ltd., Oulu, Finland
kimmo.halunen@vtt.fi

Abstract. Alongside the intensive growth of Online Social Networks (OSNs), privacy has become an important concept and requirement when sharing content online, leading users to enforce privacy often using encryption when sharing content with multiple recipients. Although cryptographic systems achieve common privacy goals such as confidentiality, key privacy, and recipient privacy, they have not been designed aiming at dynamic types of networks. In fact, the interactive nature of OSNs provides adversaries new attack vectors against privacy, and in particular against recipient privacy. We present the notion of frientropy, and argue that privacy of recipients is maintained in OSNs provided that the social graph has a high frientropy, besides the conventional recipient privacy notion. We compute the frientropy for various theoretical settings, and discuss its implications on some practical settings.

Keywords: Recipient privacy · Entropy · Online Social Networks

1 Introduction

In today's networked and interactive world privacy has become a focal point of research, and it is debated over several disciplines, such as law, philosophy, technology, and cryptography. Privacy-enhancing technologies have been developed and both lauded and critiqued by experts, politicians, and other interested parties. Although finding a suitable definition for privacy is a very hard task, in modern cryptography the requirement of privacy is resumed to provable security and privacy definitions. In general, notions such as k-anonymity [16] and anonymity sets [14] have been used to make explicit mathematical formulations on anonymity. In the public key cryptography setting, Bellare *et al.* defined the notion of public key anonymity as *key privacy* [6], so that an adversary cannot distinguish which key was used for the encryption and thus cannot identify the user from the ciphertext. Later, Barth *et al.* [2] extended this notion for the multiple user setting by *recipient privacy*, such that to achieve privacy of the recipients on broadcast encryption, the adversary cannot distinguish the identities in the authorized recipient set. The concept has been generalized by Libert *et al.* [13],

© Springer International Publishing Switzerland 2016
K. Ogawa and K. Yoshioka (Eds.): IWSEC 2016, LNCS 9836, pp. 254–264, 2016.
DOI: 10.1007/978-3-319-44524-3_15

and relaxed by Fazio and Perera [11] with the outsider recipient privacy notion, towards outsiders and not against authorized users, i.e., insiders.

At the same time, with the enormous growth of interactive services such as Online Social Networks (OSNs), different privacy paradigms have been introduced, allowing users to share content with multiple entities which may interact with replies, likes, and comments. Yet, the above notions of recipient privacy have not been designed for dynamic systems, and become void and difficult to maintain, as each reply gives away the identity of at least one of the recipients, and subsequently compromises the privacy of the whole recipient set in the adversarial model. In fact, current definitions are designed for scenarios where the data is conveyed through some content distribution system and accessed by different users, and not published on interactive centralized platforms susceptible to single replies revealing the users in the set. Hence, current definitions assume that adversaries are not able to gain information of the set by observing interactions in the communications within the set, which is unrealistic for OSNs.

In this paper, we take a look at the problem of *recipient privacy* when applied to interactive platforms, used in cases where the aim of the cryptographic scheme is to enable anonymous and confidential communications between several entities over a potentially malicious platform with interactive properties, such as OSNs. This notion has been used by practical tools, such as Scramble! [5], aiming at protecting the privacy and secrecy of the content shared in OSNs [3,4]. We begin by demonstrating the shortcomings (Sect. 3) of the existing recipient privacy definitions when applied to interactive platforms such as OSNs, as the security and privacy assumptions as well as the proofs of previous constructions can be broken in a straightforward fashion. Hence, in order to re-define the notion of recipient privacy with interactive properties we introduce the novel notion of *frientropy* (Sect. 4), apply it to complete and threshold sets of recipients and discuss the practical impact of frientropy (Sect. 5). Then we present a new interactive recipient privacy definition along with the notion of membership queries (Sect. 6). We argue that the new notion presents a more suitable definition when applied to interactive platforms and that solely the encryption of the message content does not suffice to provide privacy of recipients of messages against realistic adversaries in the OSN setting. Finally, we discuss our results in the new setting and conclude with future research topics.

2 Private Broadcast Encryption

For any $n \in \mathbb{N}$, let $\{0,1\}^n$ denote the set of bit strings of length n, and $\{0,1\}^*$ the set of bit strings of arbitrary length. For two strings x and y, $x \parallel y$ denotes their concatenation and $x \oplus y$ their bitwise XOR. The notation $x \xleftarrow{\$} X$ indicates that x is selected uniformly at random from the finite set X and $x \xleftarrow{\mathcal{X}} X$ that x is selected from X according to some arbitrary probability distribution $\mathcal{X}$ over X. For any two sets X and Y, we define the union by $X \cup Y = \{z : z \in X \vee z \in Y\}$, the intersection as $X \cap Y = \{z : z \in X \wedge z \in Y\}$, and the empty set by $\emptyset$.

In broadcast encryption, a sender broadcasts an encrypted message to multiple people, so that only a pre-selected set $S \subseteq U$ is able to decrypt, where U is the universe (e.g., the set of all people being active on an OSN). The goal of private broadcast encryption is to keep the pre-selected set of recipients S private, such that from the ciphertext it should be impossible to infer anything about the intended recipients. The security of private broadcast encryption is conventionally split into key privacy and recipient privacy.

Public key anonymity, or key privacy, was defined by Bellare *et al.* [6] as the indistinguishability property of the public keys used for encryption.

Definition 1 (Key Privacy, Bellare *et al.* [6]). *A public key encryption scheme* $C \leftarrow Enc_{pk}(m)$, *is key private if any bounded adversary $\mathcal{A}$, with access to the list of public keys $\{pk_1, \ldots, pk_n\}$, is not able to distinguish the output C_b of* $Enc_{pk_b}(m)$ *when using some pk_x and pk_y, s.t., $b \in \{x, y\}$ and $x, y \in \{1, \ldots, n\}$, with non-negligible probability:*

$$|\Pr[\mathcal{A}(pk_x, pk_y, m, C_x) = 1] - \Pr[\mathcal{A}(pk_x, pk_y, m, C_y) = 1]| \leq \epsilon.$$

Recipient privacy was defined by Barth *et al.* [2], and defines for any two recipient sets S_0 and S_1 the hardness for an $\mathcal{A}$ to distinguish between a ciphertext for the recipient set S_0, and S_1, given that $|S_0| = |S_1|$ and that $\mathcal{A}$ does not possess the secret keys of any users in $U \backslash (S_0 \cap S_1)$. A generalization to anonymous broadcast encryption (and where the challenge message may be different for both sets, if $|S_0 \cap S_1| = 0$) is given by Libert *et al.* [13].

Definition 2 (Recipient Privacy, Barth *et al.* [2]). *A broadcast encryption scheme* $\Pi \leftarrow \{Setup, KeyGen, Encrypt, Decrypt\}$ *provides recipient privacy if a PPT adversary $\mathcal{A}$ wins the following game with the challenger Ch, only with negligible probability:*

Init: *Ch runs* params $\leftarrow$ Setup(λ), *and gives $\mathcal{A}$ the resulting* params. *$\mathcal{A}$ outputs $S_0, S_1 \subseteq U$, such that $|S_0| = |S_1|$.*

Setup: *Ch generates keys $(pk_i, sk_i) \leftarrow$ KeyGen(params, i) for each recipient $i \in U$, and sends pk_i for each $i \in U$ and sk_i for each $i \in S_0 \cap S_1$ to $\mathcal{A}$.*

Phase 1: *$\mathcal{A}$ adaptively issues decryption queries $q_1 = (C, i)$ for any $i \in U$, and Ch returns* Decrypt(params, sk_i, C).

Challenge: *$\mathcal{A}$ gives Ch a message m. The Ch picks a random bit $b \in \{0, 1\}$ and runs $C' \leftarrow$ Encrypt(params, $\{i | i \in S_b\}, m$), and sends C' to $\mathcal{A}$.*

Phase 2: *$\mathcal{A}$ adaptively issues decryption queries $q_2 = (C, i)$, s.t., $C \neq C'$.*

Guess: *$\mathcal{A}$ outputs a guess $b' \in \{0, 1\}$.*

The adversary wins if $b = b'$, and we define $\mathsf{Adv}_{\mathcal{A}}^{RecPriv} = |\Pr[b = b'] - \frac{1}{2}|$.

3   Practical Shortcomings of Recipient Privacy

The common definition of recipient privacy was designed to protect the identities of the recipients in content sharing systems, such as shared filesystems. Nowadays, OSNs have become very popular media for sharing content and distributing information. One key element of the OSNs is that they collect and process all the data that the users post on the OSN, thus OSNs cannot be considered a trusted third party in the communications and should be incorporated into the adversarial model. Hence, posting information encrypted to enhance privacy is a valid strategy and can be done, for example, with the help of Scramble! [5]. However, the above notion of recipient privacy does not stand against the OSN and the dynamic nature of the OSNs. Let $\Pi \leftarrow$ {Setup, KeyGen, Encrypt, Decrypt} be a recipient private broadcast encryption scheme and S and S' be two sets of identities with $|S| = |S'|$ with corresponding (sets of) keys. Now, the encryption of some message m is done with either of these sets and the adversary needs to distinguish between $\mathtt{Encrypt}_S(\mathtt{m})$ and $\mathtt{Encrypt}_{S'}(\mathtt{m})$. Recipient privacy guarantees that the adversary has only a negligible probability for achieving this by performing decryption queries to chosen ciphertexts. However, if the adversary is able to observe subsequent transactions between the communicating parties in the communications channel or OSN, e.g., likes or comments, the adversary can easily break the privacy of the recipients under the recipient privacy definition.

For example, if the adversary chooses two sets of recipients such that $S \cap S' = \emptyset$, then a single like, comment or reply to the message compromises the recipient privacy property for the *whole set of recipients*. That is, a single person in the set can (inadvertently) compromise the privacy for the whole set. If the user $u \in S$ comments on the message, the adversary can see this and knows immediately which set (S or S') was used to encrypt and thus also the identities of the remaining members of the set. This type of observation is usually not even limited to the OSN provider, but can be done also by other members of the OSN or even publicly, e.g., Twitter. Thus the notion of recipient privacy can lead to a false sense of privacy in OSNs, where at least the OSN and quite possibly also other potential adversaries can observe such interactions.

In fact, even if $S \cap S' \neq \emptyset$ and even if there are more than two sets from which the adversary needs to distinguish, any comment from a person that is member of only a single set breaks recipient privacy for the other members of the set. Even if the revealed identity is included in many different sets, those sets that the identity is *not in* can be excluded as possibilities and thus distinguishing becomes easier for the adversary. After a few comments from different identities, the adversary can probably make a good guess on the set of recipients. Avoiding statistical inference from the pattern of communications is very difficult and the very facts that there (a) exists a lot of interaction between people in social networks, and (b) this interaction is usually observable, make recipient privacy fairly hard to accomplish in real systems.

It is also worth noting that even strong schemes, such as the ones presented in [12], cannot protect against this type of inference. The anonymity and unlinkability properties shown in [12] protect against an adversary that gains access to the credentials, but not against an adversary that observes interaction between the profile content and possible recipients. Thus, the adversary can use statistical inference on the social graph to attack the privacy of users.

Furthermore, it can be argued that even in the original intended use cases of content distribution systems, there are many ways in which the adversary could learn the actual recipients of the broadcast messages. The adversary could gain access to the system logs that may contain information on who has gotten hold of the message and whether or not they have been successful in decrypting it. Of course, this requires much more effort than in the OSN setting, but ultimately it leads to the same situation that the adversary learns some members of the recipient set and can try to infer the others from social graphs such as organizational charts, and others.

More generally, encrypting the content of the replies and comments does not protect against this type of privacy attack. As the observation is based on the metadata (i.e. who is communicating with whom etc.) of the communications, the adversary does not need access to the actual content. On the other hand, this attack does not reveal anything about the content of the messages either, so the secrecy of the content is protected even if the privacy of the recipients is violated. Consequently, these observations do not highlight issues in the conventional security definitions (such as the one on recipient privacy), but rather, identify a need for a formalism of the amount of entropy provided by the set of recipients. We will address this issue in the following sections.

4   Frientropy

To take into account the interactive nature of OSNs as content sharing platforms, we argue that an additional security property is needed on top of traditional recipient privacy. At a high level, this security property, which we dub *frientropy*, captures the case that your pool of friends has a sufficiently high level of entropy. We first need a definition of (conditional) min-entropy [1].

Definition 3 ((Conditional) Min-Entropy). *Let X be a random variable. The min-entropy of X is defined as $H_\infty(X) = -\log_2(\max_x \Pr[X = x])$. We define the conditional min-entropy of X based on Y as $H_\infty(X \mid Y) = -\log_2(\max_x \Pr[X = x \mid Y])$, where $\log_2(0) := -\infty$ and $H_\infty(X \mid \text{false}) := \infty$ by default.*

We are now ready to define "frientropy." Recall that $\mathcal{U}$ defines the universe. Denote its power set by $\mathbb{P}(\mathcal{U})$, and let $\mathbb{B} \subseteq \mathbb{P}(\mathcal{U}) \setminus \{\emptyset\}$ be a set of subsets of $\mathcal{U}$ such that $\emptyset \notin \mathbb{B}$. For $i = 1, \ldots, |\mathcal{U}|$, write $\mathbb{B}_i \subseteq \mathbb{B}$ to be the set of subsets of size exactly i. Frientropy informally captures the amount of randomness a set of subsets $\mathbb{B}$ offers even if some users disclosed themselves. Note that, in practical settings, $\mathbb{B}$ corresponds to all possible friend groups in an OSN. As such, the sets of recipients are heavily dependent on the communication patterns and social graphs of users. The randomness of a set $\mathcal{B} \in \mathbb{B}$ to appear will be captured by an arbitrary probability distribution $\mathcal{X}$.

Definition 4 (Frientropy). *Let $\mathcal{X}$ be a probability distribution over the power set of $\mathbb{B}$. Let $0 \leq \kappa \leq |\mathcal{U}|$, and let $\mathcal{R} \subseteq \mathcal{U}$ be a set of size $|\mathcal{R}| = \kappa$. Let $\Phi = (\Phi_1, \ldots, \Phi_{|\mathcal{U}|}) \geq (0, \ldots, 0)$. The set $\mathbb{B}$ has κ-frientropy Φ if for each $i = 1, \ldots, |\mathcal{U}|$,*

$$H_\infty(\mathcal{B} \mid \mathcal{R} \subseteq \mathcal{B}) \geq \Phi_i, \tag{1}$$

where $\mathcal{B} \xleftarrow{\mathcal{X}} \mathbb{B}_i$.

The definition is intuitively captured as follows: we consider the case where $\mathcal{R}$ is a set of users that revealed themselves as being part of a certain unknown set, and the frientropy of $\mathbb{B}$ than captures the amount of randomness offered by all sets that include $\mathcal{R}$. Note that a separation of the frientropy into the different sizes of the sets in $\mathbb{B}$ makes sense, given that in broadcast encryption the size of the set of recipients is known.

One should also note that frientropy is of a dual nature to the measures of anonymity presented by Diaz *et al.* [9] and extended by Serjantov and Danezis [15] and Tóth *et al.* [17]. These measures are centered around the anonymity of a sender or (usually a single) recipient of a message in some mix network that tries to hide the identity of the senders and recipients from observers and provide a metric for the anonymity of recipients. Frientropy provides a metric for the people associated with some known recipients of a message and is thus different from the previous measures.

4.1   Frientropy for Complete Sets

As a simple example, we will compute the frientropy in case $\mathbb{B}$ is a complete set, and the probability distribution is the uniform distribution: $\mathcal{B} \xleftarrow{\$} \mathbb{B}$.

Proposition 1. *Consider* $\mathbb{B} = \mathbb{P}(\mathcal{U}) \backslash \{\emptyset\}$ *to be the set of all non-empty subsets of* $\mathcal{U}$, *and let* $\mathcal{X}$ *be the uniform distribution. Let* $0 \le \kappa \le |\mathcal{U}|$. *The set* $\mathbb{B}$ *has* κ-*frientropy* $\Phi = (\Phi_1, \ldots, \Phi_{|\mathcal{U}|})$, *where*

$$\Phi_i = \begin{cases} \infty & \text{if } 1 \le i < \kappa, \\ \log_2\left(\binom{|\mathcal{U}|-\kappa}{i-\kappa}\right) & \text{if } i \ge \kappa. \end{cases}$$

Proof. Let $\mathcal{R} \subseteq \mathcal{U}$ be a set of size $|\mathcal{R}| = \kappa$. Note that if $i < \kappa$, then $\mathcal{R} \subseteq \mathcal{B}$ cannot be satisfied as $\mathcal{B} \xleftarrow{\$} \mathbb{B}_i$, and we have $H_\infty(\mathcal{B} \mid \text{false}) = \infty$ by default. For $i \ge \kappa$, it is an easy exercise to see that

$$H_\infty(\mathcal{B} \mid \mathcal{R} \subseteq \mathcal{B}) = -\log_2(\max_{b \in \mathbb{B}_i} \Pr[\mathcal{B} = b \mid \mathcal{R} \subseteq \mathcal{B}]) = -\log_2\left(\frac{1}{|\{\mathcal{B} \in \mathbb{B}_i \mid \mathcal{R} \subseteq \mathcal{B}\}|}\right)$$

$$= \log_2(|\{\mathcal{B} \in \mathbb{B}_i \mid \mathcal{R} \subseteq \mathcal{B}\}|) = \log_2\left(\binom{|\mathcal{U}| - \kappa}{i - \kappa}\right) =: \Phi_i,$$

as $\mathcal{R}$ fixes κ elements in $\mathcal{B}$, and the remaining $i - \kappa$ elements can be any of the $|\mathcal{U}| - \kappa$ remaining values in $\mathcal{U}$.   □

The result reminds of the celebrated Erdös-Ko-Rado (EKR) theorem [10]. At a high-level, this theorem centers around the problem of determining maximum families $\mathbb{B}$ of λ-subsets of a set $\mathcal{U}$ such that any two sets have at least μ elements in common, and shows that $|\mathbb{B}| \le \binom{|\mathcal{U}|-\mu}{\lambda-\mu}$ for large enough $\mathcal{U}$. Various variants of the EKR theorem have appeared, all differing in the conditions put on the set (see [7,8] for a discussion). However, the seemingly apparent connection between the EKR theorem and Proposition 1 is merely coincidence, as in our case we focus on the (much simpler) problem of determining the number of sets $\mathcal{B}$ with $\mathcal{R} \subseteq \mathcal{B}$ for a given $\mathcal{R}$. Further, while the EKR theorem targets the derivation of an upper bound, we are effectively aiming for strong lower bounds on the size of $\mathbb{B}$.

4.2 Frientropy for Threshold Sets

A practically more interesting case is where $\mathbb{B} \subseteq \mathbb{P}(\mathcal{U}) \backslash \{\emptyset\}$ is incomplete, in which case the frientropy will naturally decrease. Indeed, if a user $u \in \mathcal{U}$ appears in exactly one set in $\mathcal{B} \in \mathbb{B}$, then $\mathbb{B}$ has 1-frientropy $\Phi_{|\mathcal{B}|} = 0$, which can be seen by taking $\mathcal{R} = \{u\}$. This leads to the definition of appearance in and the threshold of $\mathbb{B}$.

Definition 5. *Let* $\mathbb{B} \subseteq \mathbb{P}(\mathcal{U}) \backslash \{\emptyset\}$. *For a* $u \in \mathcal{U}$, *define its appearance in* $\mathbb{B}$ *by* $\text{appear}_{\mathbb{B}}(u) = |\{\mathcal{B} \in \mathbb{B} \mid u \in \mathcal{B}\}|$. *Define the threshold of* $\mathbb{B}$ *as*

$$\tau_{\mathbb{B}} := \min_{\substack{u \in \mathcal{U}, \\ \text{appear}_{\mathbb{B}}(u) > 0}} \text{appear}_{\mathbb{B}}(u). \tag{2}$$

Informally, the appearance of u in $\mathbb{B}$ is the number of sets in $\mathbb{B}$ that include u, and the threshold of $\mathbb{B}$ determines the minimal non-trivial appearance of any u. We are now ready to derive the following result.

Proposition 2. *Consider any* $\mathbb{B} \subseteq \mathbb{P}(\mathcal{U}) \backslash \{\emptyset\}$, *and let* $\mathcal{X}$ *be the uniform distribution. Let* $0 \leq \kappa \leq |\mathcal{U}|$. *The set* $\mathbb{B}$ *has* κ-*frientropy* $\boldsymbol{\Phi} = (\Phi_1, \ldots, \Phi_{|\mathcal{U}|})$, *where*

$$\Phi_i = \begin{cases} \infty \text{ if } 1 \leq i < \kappa, \\ \log_2 \left(\max\{1, |\mathbb{B}_i| - (|\mathbb{B}_i| - \tau_{\mathbb{B}_i})\kappa\}\right) \text{ if } i \geq \kappa. \end{cases}$$

Proof. Let $\mathcal{R} \subseteq \mathcal{U}$ be a set of size $|\mathcal{R}| = \kappa$. The case $i < \kappa$ is as in Proposition 1. For $i \geq \kappa$, we can similarly compute

$$H_\infty(\mathcal{B} \mid \mathcal{R} \subseteq \mathcal{B}) = -\log_2(\max_{b \in \mathbb{B}_i} \Pr[\mathcal{B} = b \mid \mathcal{R} \subseteq \mathcal{B}]) = \log_2\left(|\{\mathcal{B} \in \mathbb{B}_i \mid \mathcal{R} \subseteq \mathcal{B}\}|\right),$$

provided $|\{\mathcal{B} \in \mathbb{B}_i \mid \mathcal{R} \subseteq \mathcal{B}\}| > 0$. (Note that if this set were of size 0, we would necessarily have $\mathcal{R} \not\subseteq \mathcal{B}$ and thus $H_\infty(\mathcal{B} \mid \text{false}) = \infty$. We could henceforth discard this case.) This leaves us at the problem of determining a lower bound for the following problem: given κ elements $\mathcal{R}$, each of which appears in at least $\tau_{\mathbb{B}_i}$ sets $\mathcal{B} \in \mathbb{B}_i$, what is the number of sets $\mathcal{B} \in \mathbb{B}_i$ that include all elements from $\mathcal{R}$? A simple pigeonhole-principle-like computation shows that

$$|\{\mathcal{B} \in \mathbb{B}_i \mid \mathcal{R} \subseteq \mathcal{B}\}| \geq |\mathbb{B}_i| - (|\mathbb{B}_i| - \tau_{\mathbb{B}_i})\kappa,$$

as every of the κ elements in $\mathcal{R}$ eliminates at most $|\mathbb{B}_i| - \tau_{\mathbb{B}_i}$ sets in $\mathbb{B}_i$. Along with above-mentioned non-emptyness assumption on this set, we can put

$$\Phi_i := \log_2\left(\max\{1, |\mathbb{B}_i| - (|\mathbb{B}_i| - \tau_{\mathbb{B}_i})\kappa\}\right)$$

as stated. $\qquad \square$

A simple sanity check shows that if $\mathbb{B}$ is complete, the quantity in the $\log_2$-term of Proposition 2 reads $|\mathbb{B}_i| - (|\mathbb{B}_i| - \tau_{\mathbb{B}_i})\kappa = \binom{|\mathcal{U}|}{i} - \left(\binom{|\mathcal{U}|}{i} - \binom{|\mathcal{U}|-1}{i-1}\right)\kappa$, which is slightly worse than $\binom{|\mathcal{U}|-\kappa}{i-\kappa}$ of Proposition 1.

5   Frientropy in Practice

In [2] it is suggested that making the set $\mathcal{S}$ always of fixed size using dummy identities could provide some added security against privacy violations. This would mean that if the average size of the recipient set is some $n \in \mathbb{N}$, then during encryption the set $\mathcal{S}$ would be filled up to n with dummy identities or $\mathcal{S}$ would be divided into separate sets of size n and the last one would be filled with dummies. The suggestion is supported by Proposition 2, as it shows that the frientropy increases if for all i we have $\tau_{\mathbb{B}_i} \lesssim |\mathbb{B}_i|$. The adding of dummy friends could be done in such a way that the dummies are selected uniformly at random from the set $\mathcal{U}$ and added to the set $\mathcal{S}$. These dummy friends would not receive the "real" key, but a random string of bits.

However, this approach suffers from various caveats: first off, dummies would neither communicate nor participate in the discussion and the adversary could use this information to her advantage. Secondly, dummy identities should not and would not be able to access the contents, but this leads to the situation where those recipients selected as dummies would know that they are in fact dummies. In this case, the recipient privacy can only be assured for outsiders and not insiders. Care is needed to resolve these issues and support the use of dummy tweaks in a proper way. In addition, the task of the adversary would now be to distinguish real recipients from dummy ones, or if there are any dummy recipients in a given set of recipients.

Statistics show that an average OSN user on, e.g., Facebook, has 350 friends.[1] Furthermore, some statistics show that the average recipient set of group messages to be about 15 people. We remark, however, that the dynamic character of these networks causes the sets of recipients to vary over time, and this may influence the amount of frientropy and the level of privacy.

6   Membership Query Security

As noted earlier, the previous versions of recipient privacy do not take into account the nature of communications between possible recipients, and especially in the OSN setting this leads to diminishing privacy for the recipients. We will next present a stronger form of recipient privacy. It allows for the adversary to make also *membership* queries on the set of recipients in addition to the traditional decryption queries. A membership query tests whether a given u is in the set $\mathcal{S}$ used to encrypt the message.

---

[1] http://www.statista.com/statistics/232499/americans-who-use-social-networking-sites-several-times-per-day (read 2016-06-13).

One might think that this type of adversary is unrealistic and too powerful even in the OSN setting. However, as an example, think about a sysadmin on some content distribution system. In a well-maintained and -operated system, the sysadmin would probably have access to all kinds of logs and system information of even individual machines (of certain users). Thus, the sysadmin could (a) know who has downloaded the content, and (b) infer (through timing, power consumption, or some other form of side-channel/social engineering) whether or not some of these people were able to correctly decrypt the content. In this sense, the power of such queries is not an unrealistic assumption for adversaries both in OSNs and in the original scenarios of recipient privacy.

Definition 6 (Membership Query Security). *Let $n \geq 1$, and let $\mathbb{B}_n \subseteq \mathbb{P}(\mathcal{U})$ be a set of subsets of $\mathcal{U}$ of size n. Let $\mathcal{X}$ be a probability distribution. The set provided membership query security if a PPT adversary $\mathcal{A}$ wins the following game with the challenger Ch, only with negligible probability:*

> **Init:** Ch *chooses a set* $S \overset{\mathcal{X}}{\leftarrow} \mathbb{B}_n$.
> **Phase 1:** $\mathcal{A}$ *adaptively issues κ membership queries. A single membership query $M(u)$ reveals if $u \in S$, i.e., $M(u) = \texttt{true}$ iff $u \in S$ and $\texttt{false}$ otherwise. Denote by $\mathcal{Q}$ the set of all users u for which $\mathcal{A}$ issues a query $M(u)$, and by $\mathcal{R}$ the set $\{u \in \mathcal{Q} : M(u) = \texttt{true}\}$.*
> **Guess:** $\mathcal{A}$ *outputs a guess* $S' \in \mathbb{B}_n$.

The adversary wins if $S' = S$, and we define $\mathsf{Adv}_{\mathcal{A}}^{\mathrm{MemQ}} = \Pr[S = S']$.

It is clear to see that membership query security is closely related to frientropy.

Proposition 3. *Let κ, $n \geq 1$. Consider any $\mathbb{B} \subseteq \mathbb{P}(\mathcal{U})$ consisting of subsets of $\mathcal{U}$ of size n. Assume that $\mathbb{B}$ has κ-frientropy Φ. Let $\mathcal{X}$ be the uniform distribution. For any adversary $\mathcal{A}$ making κ membership queries, we have* $\mathsf{Adv}_{\mathcal{A}}^{\mathrm{MemQ}} \leq 2^{-\Phi_\kappa}$.

Proof. Note that any set of κ membership queries reveals a set of at most κ revealed users, as in the worst case all queries yield $\texttt{true}$. Denote these κ users by $\mathcal{R}$. The goal of the adversary $\mathcal{A}$ now is to guess $S \in \mathbb{B}_n$ given that $\mathcal{R} \subseteq S$. Its success probability is, by definition, at most $2^{-\Phi_\kappa}$. $\qquad\square$

A more strict version would have the adversary guess for a single user $u \in S \setminus \mathcal{R}$ and restrict that $\mathcal{R} \subset S$ is a proper subset. It is easy to see that the notion of privacy against this adversary is stronger than that of the above game. The second way to amend the game would be to take into account the existence of dummy friends. The challenger would choose two sets S and $\mathcal{D}$ with $\mathcal{D} \subset S$, where $\mathcal{D}$ represents the chosen dummies (if any). This would mean that the adversary would also output two sets S' and $\mathcal{D}'$ as guesses, with $|S'| = |S|$ and $\mathcal{D}' \subset S'$, where $\mathcal{D}'$ is the adversary's guess for the dummies. In this game we can also model weak and strong membership queries, where the weak one is as in the above game and the strong gives the adversary also the information whether or not $u \in \mathcal{D}$, if $u \in S$. The analysis of these variations is out of the scope of this paper and a possible venue for future research.

7   Conclusion

The traditional recipient privacy definitions fall short in providing provable security in OSN settings. The issue can be salvaged by requiring a high enough "frientropy," meaning that if one of the recipients gets disclosed, the other recipients (its "friends") remain mostly anonymous. Admittedly, sets of recipients are in practice not random; if a user u appears in only a few social groups, and it reveals itself as being a receiver of a message, the remaining set of recipients, conditioned on the fact that u appears in this group, has a very low entropy, and a way to resolve this is by using dummy friends.

References

1. Alwen, J., Dodis, Y., Wichs, D.: Leakage-resilient public-key cryptography in the bounded-retrieval model. In: Halevi, S. (ed.) CRYPTO 2009. LNCS, vol. 5677, pp. 36–54. Springer, Heidelberg (2009)
2. Barth, A., Boneh, D., Waters, B.: Privacy in encrypted content distribution using private broadcast encryption. In: Di Crescenzo, G. (ed.) FC 2006. LNCS, vol. 4107, pp. 52–64. Springer, Heidelberg (2006)
3. Beato, F.: Private information sharing in online communities. Ph.D. Thesis, Katholieke Universiteit Leuven, Leuven (2015)
4. Beato, F., Ion, I., Capkun, S., Preneel, B., Langheinrich, M.: For some eyes only: protecting online information sharing. In: CODASPY 2013, pp. 1–12. ACM (2013)
5. Beato, F., Kohlweiss, M., Wouters, K.: Scramble! your social network data. In: Fischer-Hübner, S., Hopper, N. (eds.) PETS 2011. LNCS, vol. 6794, pp. 211–225. Springer, Heidelberg (2011)
6. Bellare, M., Boldyreva, A., Desai, A., Pointcheval, D.: Key-privacy in public-key encryption. In: Boyd, C. (ed.) ASIACRYPT 2001. LNCS, vol. 2248, p. 566. Springer, Heidelberg (2001)
7. Chung, F.R.K., Graham, R.L., Frankl, P., Shearer, J.B.: Some intersection theorems for ordered sets and graphs. J. Comb. Theor., Ser. A $\mathbf{43}$(1), 23–37 (1986)
8. Deza, M., Frankl, P.: Erdös-Ko-Rado theorem - 22 years later. SIAM J. Algebraic Discrete Methods $\mathbf{4}$(4), 419–431 (1983)
9. Díaz, C., Seys, S., Claessens, J., Preneel, B.: Towards measuring anonymity. In: Dingledine, R., Syverson, P. (eds.) PET 2002. LNCS, vol. 2482, pp. 54–68. Springer, Heidelberg (2003)
10. Erdös, P., Ko, C., Rado, R.: Intersection theorems for systems of finitesets. Q. J. Math. $\mathbf{12}$(1), 313–320 (1961)
11. Fazio, N., Perera, I.M.: Outsider-anonymous broadcast encryption with sublinear ciphertexts. In: Dingledine, R., Syverson, P. (eds.) PKC 2012. LNCS, vol. 7293, pp. 225–242. Springer, Heidelberg (2012)
12. Günther, F., Manulis, M., Strufe, T.: Cryptographic treatment of private user profiles. In: Danezis, G., Dietrich, S., Sako, K. (eds.) FC 2011 Workshops 2011. LNCS, vol. 7126, pp. 40–54. Springer, Heidelberg (2012)
13. Libert, B., Paterson, K.G., Quaglia, E.A.: Anonymous broadcast encryption: adaptive security and efficient constructions in the standard model. In: Fischlin, M., Buchmann, J., Manulis, M. (eds.) PKC 2012. LNCS, vol. 7293, pp. 206–224. Springer, Heidelberg (2012)

14. Pfitzmann, A., Köhntopp, M.: Anonymity, unobservability, and pseudonymity – a proposal for terminology. In: Federrath, H. (ed.) Designing Privacy Enhancing Technologies. LNCS, vol. 2009, pp. 1–9. Springer, Heidelberg (2001)
15. Serjantov, A., Danezis, G.: Towards an information theoretic metric for anonymity. In: Dingledine, R., Syverson, P. (eds.) PET 2002. LNCS, vol. 2482, pp. 41–53. Springer, Heidelberg (2003)
16. Sweeney, L.: k-anonymity: a model for protecting privacy. Int. J. Uncertainty Fuzziness Knowl. Based Syst. **10**(5), 557–570 (2002)
17. Tóth, G., Hornák, Z., Vajda, F.: Measuring anonymity revisited. NordSec 2004, 85–90 (2004)

Hardware Security

Deep-Learning-Based Security Evaluation on Authentication Systems Using Arbiter PUF and Its Variants

Risa Yashiro[✉], Takanori Machida, Mitsugu Iwamoto, and Kazuo Sakiyama

Department of Informatics, The University of Electro-Communications,
1-5-1 Chofugaoka, Chofu, Tokyo 182-8585, Japan
{yashiro,machida,mitsugu,sakiyama}@uec.ac.jp

Abstract. Fake integrated circuit (IC) chips are in circulation on the market, which is considered a serious threat in the era of the Internet of Things (IoTs). A physically unclonable function (PUF) is expected to be a fundamental technique to separate the fake IC chips from genuine ones. Recently, the arbiter PUF (APUF) and its variants are intensively researched aiming at using for a secure authentication system. However, vulnerability of APUFs against machine-learning attacks was reported. Upon the situation, the double arbiter PUF (DAPUF), which has a tolerance against support vector machine (SVM)-based machine-learning attacks, was proposed as another variant of APUF in 2014. In this paper, we perform a security evaluation for authentication systems using APUF and its variants against Deep-learning (DL)-based attacks. DL has attracted attention as a machine-learning method that produces better results than SVM in various research fields. Based on the experimental results, we show that these DAPUFs could be used as a core primitive in a secure authentication system if setting an appropriate threshold to distinguish a legitimate IC tags from fake ones.

Keywords: Physically unclonable function · Machine-learning attack · Deep learning · Authentication

1 Introduction

1.1 Background

In recent years, fake integrated circuit (IC) chips have become a serious problem because the Internet of Things (IoTs), which heavily relies on IC chips, has spread in the world. Physically unclonable function (PUF) [12] is expected to be a solution to prevent the distribution of such fake IC chips. PUF is a function that provides an output, or response, related to the physical variations of a physical object that are unintentionally generated in the manufacturing process, when an input, or challenge, is given. According to [14], PUFs are classified into two groups; weak PUFs and strong PUFs. In general, weak PUFs have

© Springer International Publishing Switzerland 2016
K. Ogawa and K. Yoshioka (Eds.): IWSEC 2016, LNCS 9836, pp. 267–285, 2016.
DOI: 10.1007/978-3-319-44524-3_16

a small challenge space, and their responses are expected to be stable for the purpose of identification (ID) or secret-key generation. On the contrary, strong PUFs have a large challenge space, which is suitable for challenge-response-based authentication systems.

Arbiter PUF (APUF) proposed in [4] is a kind of strong PUFs [14]. APUF explores a time difference between two signals that propagate through configurable signal paths. In [8], the first report of machine-learning-based modeling attack for APUF is summarized by Lim. It is pointed out that APUF delay difference, i.e., response can be expressed by a formula. Then the modeling attacks are applied for various PUFs to study the required number of CRPs and computed times as discussed by Rührmair et al., in 2010 [14].

In response to the results in [8], N-XOR APUF, which has N APUFs and generates a one-bit response by XORing their outputs, is proposed as a countermeasure against the machine-learning attacks by Suh and Devadas in 2007 [15]. It has been recognized that the difficulty of machine-learning attacks rises exponentially with the number of XORs. However, Becker shows that XOR APUF, which would be computationally infeasible to attack, can be broken in linear time using its inherent unreliability response [3]. From the results, it is figured out that the tolerance of APUF itself should be improved against the machine-learning attack.

As an approach for increasing the difference of responses among chips, i.e., uniqueness, double arbiter PUF (DAPUF) is proposed by Machida et al. [9]. Although the enhancement of uniqueness is not directly linked to a high tolerance for the machine-learning attack, their evaluation results reveal that DAPUF shows a better tolerance than the conventional XOR APUF under the same hardware cost [10,11]. They consider the security evaluation with support vector machines (SVMs) using training data of 1,000 CRPs.

1.2 Contributions

This paper extends the security evaluation of [13] so that the feasibility of DAPUF-based authentication system could be discussed. We employ Deep learning (DL), which is said to be the best machine-learning method as of now in the research field of image recognition based on the benchmark test [1], because DL is considered a promising method to evaluate the security of PUFs strictly. To our best knowledge, no studies have evaluated the security of PUF-based authentication system with DL[1]. We firstly show that DAPUF is tolerant not only against SVM-based attacks, but against DL-based attacks, with up to 50,000 training data. Secondly, we discuss the feasibility of an authentication system that utilizes 256-bit response obtained from a DAPUF to clarify that a legitimate prover can be distinguished from fake ones cloned by an attacker using DL. Finally, we demonstrate that 3-1 DAPUF is the best choice in the use of a PUF-based authentication system from our experiments using a Xilinx® Virtex-5®.

---

[1] Preliminary evaluation results on APUF, 2-1 DAPUF, and 3-1 DAPUF using DL is reported in [13].

2   Arbiter PUF and Its Variants

Here, we briefly introduce APUF and its variants, i.e., XOR-APUF and DAPUF.

2.1   Arbiter PUF

Figure 1 shows the block diagram of APUF. APUF consists of two-line circuits, n-stage selector pairs, and two input signals that are simultaneously provided to the first selector pairs. The route where the two signals are propagated is determined by an n-bit challenge, $\vec{C} = (c_1, c_2, \ldots, c_n)$. If a challenge bit is 0, the two signals go straight, and if the challenge bit is 1, the signals are crossed as shown in Fig. 2. At the last stage, two signals are provided to an arbiter, e.g., SR (Set-Reset)-Latch, and one-bit response r is obtained as output. The value of the response, $r = 1$ or 0, is determined by which signal arrives at the arbiter faster.

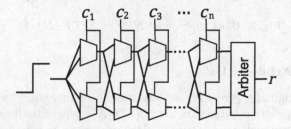

Fig. 1. Block diagram for APUF

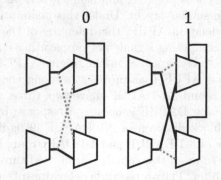

Fig. 2. Signal path determined by a challenge bit

2.2   XOR Arbiter PUF

In [15], the so-called N-XOR APUF is proposed, where N is the number of APUFs. The N one-bit responses from the N APUFs are XORed to generate one-bit response r. XOR PUF is expected to be more resistant to the machine-learning attacks compared to APUF although the hardware cost increases. The block diagram of 2-XOR APUF is depicted in Fig. 3.

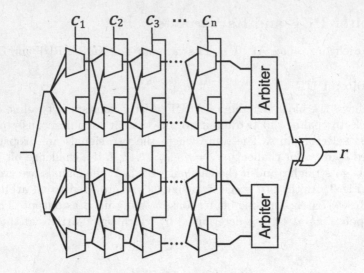

Fig. 3. Block diagram of N-XOR APUF ($N = 2$)

2.3   Double Arbiter PUF

DAPUF was originally proposed as a technique to increase the uniqueness of APUF on field-programmable gate array (FPGA)s, where the layout conditions are tightly constrained, i.e., balanced place and route is significantly difficult. In case of DAPUF, module instantiation can be assumed at the layout level, i.e., reproduction of APUF is possible, and hence it is expected that all APUFs have the same or quite similar layout. Under this assumption, even if there is an unbalanced wiring delay in APUF, the difference of the wiring bias can be cancelled out because competing signals are propagating on the same route in the case of DAPUF. Namely, a signal in the original APUF competes against a signal in a duplicated APUF that propagates along the same route as the original APUF. 2-1, 3-1, and 4-1 DAPUFs have two, three, and four duplicated APUFs, respectively. Each DAPUF generates a response by XORing multiple one-bit outputs. The block diagram of 2-1 DAPUF [9] is illustrated in Fig. 4, and the schematic view of 3-1 DAPUF and 4-1 DAPUF are illustrated in Fig. 5.

In DAPUF, arrival times of two signals transmitted through the same route are compared by the arbiter. The propagation delay time of each signal is denoted by ◯ and △. Suppose that APUFs have an imbalanced layout. Therefore, it is natural to have ① compete with ② and ③, to enhance the performance of the 3-1 DAPUF. For instance, even if ⓘ $<$ △ for i $=$ 1, 2, 3, it is expected that ①, ②, and ③ are similar values as well as △, △, and △. That is, pairs of (①, ②), (②, ③), and (③, ①) are input to three arbiters. The same arbitration is done for (△, △), (△, △), and (△, △). Hence, 3-1 DAPUF outputs 6 bits in total, and 4-1 DAPUF outputs 12 bits. One-bit response is generated by XORing these outputs.

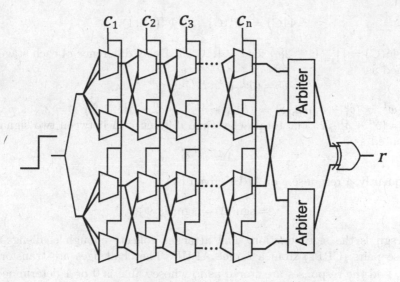

Fig. 4. Block diagram of 2-1 DAPUF

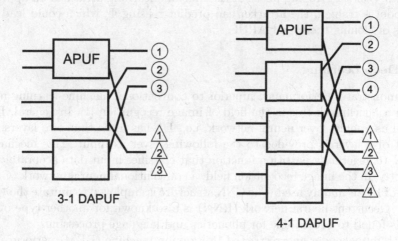

Fig. 5. Schematic view of 3-1 and 4-1 DAPUFs

3 Machine Learning

3.1 Machine-Learning Attacks for Arbiter PUF

We follow the notation for modeling the APUF as defined in [14]. Suppose that the attacker can use external information, i.e., CRPs, and tries to make a model related to the internal information of APUF, i.e., delay time at each stage. Let c_l be the l-th bit challenge out of n bits. If $c_l = 0$, the delay time is represented as δ_l^0. If $c_l = 1$, the delay time is denoted as δ_l^1. $\vec{\Phi}$ is so-called challenge vector, which is expressed as

$$\vec{\Phi}(\vec{C}) = (\Phi^1(\vec{C}), \dots, \Phi^n(\vec{C}), 1), \tag{1}$$

where $\Phi^l(\vec{C}) = \prod_{i=l}^{n}(1 - 2c_i)$ for $l = 1, \dots, n$. Delay difference of each stage, $\vec{w}$, is defined as

$$\vec{w} = (w^1, w^2, \dots, w^n, w^{n+1}), \tag{2}$$

where $w^1 = (\delta_1^0 - \delta_1^1)/2$, $w^i = (\delta_{i-1}^0 + \delta_{i-1}^1 + \delta_i^0 - \delta_i^1)/2$ for $i = 2, \dots, n$, and $w^{n+1} = (\delta_n^0 - \delta_n^1)/2$. The total delay time difference Δ between two signals is represented as

$$\Delta = \vec{w}^T \vec{\Phi}. \tag{3}$$

Consequently, a response r of APUF given by

$$r = \mathrm{sgn}(\Delta) = \mathrm{sgn}(\vec{w}^T \vec{\Phi}), \tag{4}$$

where sgn is the sign function. The attacker collects enough challenge-and-response pairs (CRPs) from a target APUF. The challenges are transformed into $\vec{\Phi}$, and the responses are stored as r, whose value is 0 or 1 determined by the sign of Δ. Then, the attacker provides $\vec{\Phi}$ and r to generate a model that classifies $\vec{\Phi}$ in the training phase of the machine-learning attack. If an appropriate model is trained, the attacker can predict r using $\vec{\Phi}$, which could lead to a success of cloning the target APUF.

3.2 Deep Learning

DL demonstrates performance superior to conventional machine-learning methods on a benchmark test in the field of image recognition [1]. In general, DL is defined as a multi-layer neural network, i.e., DL has more than two layers. The output of a layer is provided to the following layer as input. This mechanism enables to generate a partition function that classifies input data accurately and efficiently. In the image recognition field, a convolutional neural network (CNN), a type of DL, is mainly used. The CNN structure is employed to imitate the visual cortex. Recurrent neural network (RNN) is also known for another type of DL. RNN is found to be suitable for phonetics and language processing.

Both autoencoder and restricted Boltzmann machine (RBM) perform unsupervised learning to extract feature of input data. Although the autoencoder can be operated more simply than RBM, the performance is not better than RBM. A denoising autoencoder, proposed in 2008, is a type of autoencoder that could achieve an equivalent performance to RBM [16] The denoising autoencoder adds noise to input, and learns the way to reducing the noise by comparing with the original input. Stochastic gradient descent (SGD) is used in the optimization process to accelerate the learning speed. It can also decrease errors such that input data are not classified correctly, by updating the parameter in the partition function. We employ a Python-based tool, Pylearn2 [5], where the denoising autoencoder is embedded by default.

4   Security Evaluation of PUF

4.1   Experimental Environment

In this paper, it is assumed that an attacker has a legitimate PUF, and its CRPs can be obtained. The attacker tries to make a PUF clone using the machine-learning attack, where the CRPs are given as training data. Figure 6 depicts an overview of PUF data collection in our experiments. MATLAB generates a challenge, c, for sending to PUF, and collects the corresponding response, r, from PUF. APUF, 2-1 DAPUF, 3-1 DAPUF, 4-1 DAPUF, 2-XOR APUF, and 3-XOR APUF are implemented on a Xilinx® Virtex-5® FPGA XC5VLX30, and their CRPs are obtained via an RS-232C cable for the machine-learning training and test. All PUFs are based on 64 stages.

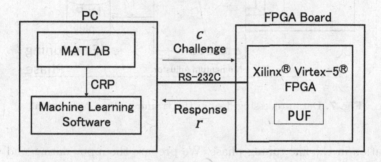

Fig. 6. Collection of PUF CRPs

Xilinx® ISE® design suite 13.2 is used for the logic synthesis and the floorplanning. The functionality of PUF logic is written in Verilog format, and the layout constraints in the floorplanning is specified in a user constraints file (UCF). UCF plays an important role especially when implementing DAPUF on FPGA because the layout of the instantiated APUFs should follow the same arrangement. A part of Verilog code and UCF for 3-1 DAPUF is described in Appendix A.

Table 1. Pylearn2 parameters in the pre-training phase

Layer	nvis	nhid	corruption_level	batch_size	max epochs
1	65	100	0.1	5	100
2	100	500	0.2	10	100
3	500	20	0.2	10	100

In our experimental setting, DL has four layers, including a three-layer denoising autoencoder (pre-training phase), and one logistic regression (fine-tuning phase), as shown in Fig. 7. The pre-training phase performs unsupervised learning to find a law of the input data. The three-layer denoising autoencoder in the pre-training phase generates a partition function that leads to an accurate

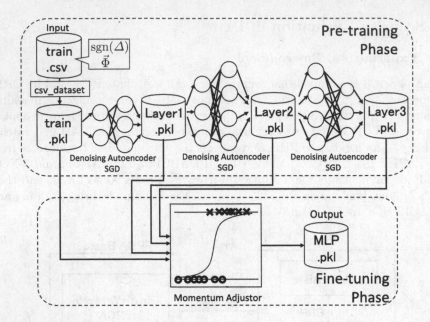

Fig. 7. Data processing flow in the training phase of Pylearn2

classification in the fine-tuning phase. We prepare the input data r and $\vec{\Phi}$ (see Sect. 3.1) written in the CSV format, train.csv, and it is converted into the PKL format, train.pkl, using csv_dataset. 50,000 CRPs are prepared as training data, and 10,000 additional CRPs are also prepared for the test phase.

Denoising autoencoder and SGD of each layer are written with YAML. The YAML file is prepared based on the YAML tutorial [2]. Notice that we do not have to modify the Python code in Pylearn2, but program the YAML file in combination with the Python codes. The YAML file of the third layer used in our experiments is described in Appendix B as an example[2]. Table 1 shows the Pylearn2 parameters in the pre-training phase. The logistic regression that is called momentum adjuster in Pylearn2 is used in the fine-tuning phase, and takes the outputs from the pre-training phase to classify $\vec{\Phi}$. The parameter of max_epochs changed to 150 in fine-tuning phase YAML code.

The performance of the machine-learning attack is measured with a prediction rate that is a success rate of predicting unknown responses from given challenges. Figure 8 shows the data processing flow in the test phase of Pylearn2. Firstly, we input $\vec{\Phi}$ obtained for the test phase in the CSV format as test.csv, and it is converted into the PKL format. Secondly, the resultant data in the training phase, MLP.pkl, is used to calculate r' or clone response. Thirdly, the response r' is compared with r from the original PUF. By repeating the above-mentioned procedures for 10,000 times for different challenges, the prediction rate is derived finally.

---

[2] transformer_dataset descriptions at the beginning of the YAML file are not needed in the first-layer YAML code.

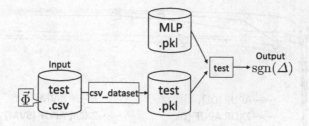

Fig. 8. Data processing flow in the test phase of Pylearn2

4.2 Experimental Results

Figure 9 shows the results of the machine-learning attacks for APUF and XOR APUF. The prediction rates are all greater than 90 %, when the attacker uses more than 5,000 CRPs. It is clear that these PUFs do not tolerate both SVM-based[3] and DL-based attacks. Figure 10 shows the results of the machine-learning attacks for DAPUFs. Approximately 90 % of 2-1 DAPUF responses are predicted. However, 3-1 DAPUF and 4-1 DAPUF are more resistant compared to the conventional APUF, XOR APUF, and 2-1 DAPUF. The machine-learning attacks can predict the responses of 3-1 DAPUF and 4-1 DAPUF with probabilities of approximately 68 % and 62 %, respectively. 3-1 DAPUF has a slightly weaker tolerance than 4-1 DAPUF. However, the steadiness of 4-1 DAPUF was about 35 % as reported in [11].

From the results, DL is considered a strong machine learning for the purpose of attacking all PUFs. XOR APUF of the same cost can be attacked much easier than DAPUF not only by SVM, but also by DL. However, DL needs more training data than SVM to make good classifier. When using more than 10,000 training data, the prediction rates of each PUF are almost unchanged against SVM-based attacks. On the other hand, the prediction rates of DAPUF are dependent on the amount of training data for DL-based attacks.

Table 2 summarizes the PC pacification used in machine-learning attack, and Table 3 shows the machine-learning time for the amount of the training data.

Table 2. PC used in machine-learning attack

OS	CPU	Memory	Processor	Clock
Ubuntu 14.04	Intel® Xeon®	64 GB	8 cores	2.67 GHz

Table 3. Training time

Training data	1000	5000	10000	20000	30000	40000	50000
SVM	0.19 s	5.98 s	41.22 s	3 m 14 s	7 m 22 s	13 m 16 s	21 m 8 s
DL	3 m 40 s	18 m 51 s	38 m 33 s	57 m 32 s	1 h 26 m 20 s	1 h 56 m 33 s	2 h 24 m 42 s

---

[3] SVM-light [7] is used as machine-learning tool.

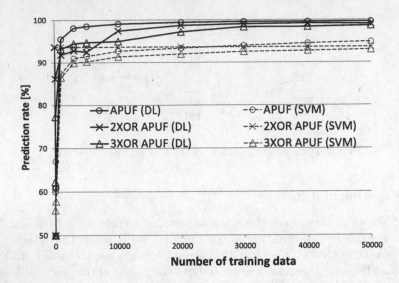

Fig. 9. Results of machine-learning attacks for APUF and XOR APUF.

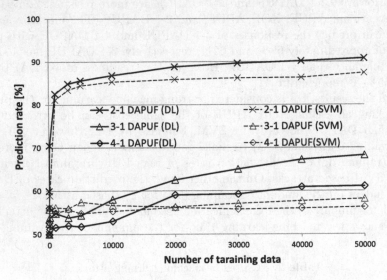

Fig. 10. Results of machine-learning attacks for DAPUF

The training time increases according to the amount of training data. DL needs more training time than SVM. When using 50,000 training data, SVM takes 21 min and 8 s. DL takes 2 h, 24 min, and 42 s. The effect of this time difference is due to the pre-training phase.

In conclusion, it is found that 3-1 and 4-1 DAPUF have a tolerance against DL-based attacks. Hence, we will discuss, in the next section, the feasibility of these DAPUFs for the purpose of authentication.

5   Security Evaluation for PUF-Based Authentication System

In this section, an authentication system using DAPUF is discussed to evaluate its security at the application level. In the system configuration phase, CRPs of a legitimate PUF are stored in the verifier's database. The verifier sends n randomly chosen challenges to the prover. The prover returns n-bit response based on the challenges. Subsequently, the verifier checks the rate of bits coinciding with the stored data out of n bits. If the rate exceeds a threshold value in the unit of bit, the system accepts the prover. For a quantitative evaluation, we define *secure-operation margin* M that indicates the feasibility of secure authentication systems as

$$M = nU \times (1 - S - P), \tag{5}$$

where n, P, S, and U are the number of response bits from PUF or prover, the prediction rate, the steadiness, and the uniqueness, respectively. The number of response bits should be determined with considering the PUF uniqueness U that is defined in [6][4]. Because the verifier has to give up the bits coincidentally matched with other provers. More precisely, we focus on $nU = 256$ bits because the feasibility of a one-to-many authentication system is of concern rather than one-to-one matching in this paper[5]. The verifier has to ignore nS bits because S is the percentage of unstable bits. Furthermore, nUP bits cannot be used for authentication. This is because the attacker can predict P % responses out of nU bits. When M is positive and large enough, the verifier can set a threshold. If M is less than zero, the attacker can break the authentication system with a clone. Figure 11 illustrates the relationship among these metrics.

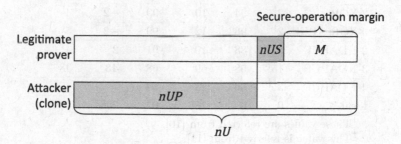

Fig. 11. Secure operation margin.

---

[4] Instead of using the average value for U with several devices, the minimum value should be used in ideal for the purpose of considering the worst case for the secure-operation margin.

[5] In the case of one-to-one matching verification using PUF CRPs, we can set $U = 1$ since uniqueness is not related to the authentication performance.

The prediction rates against APUF, 2-XOR APUF and 3-XOR APUF are all high enough to diminish the authentication performance. In addition, the percentages of uniqueness are also all low, and therefore n tends to be large.

According to [11], approximately 8 %, 15 %, and 35 % of responses from 2-1 DAPUF, 3-1 DAPUF and 4-1 DAPUF, respectively, are not stable. In this paper, we assume the worst case that is the responses predicted by the attacker are unrelated with the responses that affect the steadiness. The next section discusses the performance of the authentication system using these PUFs based on the machine-learning attack along with the steadiness of the responses.

5.1 Security Evaluation for Authentication System

Table 4 shows the secure-operation margin for the APUF-, XOR-APUF-, and DAPUF-based authentication system. In the case for the authentication system using 2-1 DAPUF, approximately 235 bits out of 256 bits are stable since the steadiness of 2-1 DAPUF is approximately 8 % [11]. When using SVM, the attacker can predict approximately 225 bits because the prediction rate is approximately 88 % and there is a 10-bit margin. The attacker with DL can predict approximately 91 % of 256 bits, i.e., approximately 233 bits can be predicted. Therefore, the secure-operation margin M is estimated to be 2 bits.

Table 4. Secure-operation margin for the APUF-based authentication system ($nU = 256$)

	S [%]	SVM		DL		U [%]
		P [%]	M [bit]	P [%]	M [bit]	
APUF	$1^\dagger$	95	10	100	-3	$4^\dagger$
2-XOR	$2^\dagger$	94	10	99	-2	$4^\dagger$
3-XOR APUF	$2^\dagger$	93	12	99	-2	$5^\dagger$
2-1 DAPUF	$8^\dagger$	88	10	91	2	$4^\dagger$
3-1 DAPUF	$15^\dagger$	58	69	68	**43**	$48^\dagger$
4-1 DAPUF	$35^\ddagger$	56	23	62	7	$49^\ddagger$
Ideal	0	0	256	0	256	50

†These values are referred from [10].
‡This value is referred from [11].
S is rounded up, and U is truncated to make a strict evaluation for M.

In case for 3-1 DAPUF, approximately 217 bits out of 256 bits are stable, because of its 15 % steadiness [11]. The attacker can predict approximately 58 %, i.e., 148 bits, and the margin is 69 bits using SVM. The attacker with DL can predict approximately 68 %, i.e., approximately 174 bits can be predicted. From Eq. (5), the margin is calculated as 43 bits.

4-1 DAPUF returns approximately 166-bit stable response, because the steadiness of 4-1 DAPUF is approximately 35 % [11]. The attacker with SVM can predict approximately 143 bits out of 256 bits. Hence, there exists a 23-bit margin. The attacker with DL can predict approximately 62 %, i.e., 159 bits, which leads to an 8-bit margin.

Note that the attacker needs to train each prover when the uniqueness is high. In other words, when the uniqueness is low, the attacker may train multiple distinct provers only with a single prover. 4-1 DAPUF has a best performance in this regard because the uniqueness is closest to the ideal value.

5.2 Discussion

It is revealed that 3-1 DAPUF has an enough margin to distinguish the legitimate prover from cloned ones. The authentication system using 3-1 DAPUF can be realized with a threshold set to around 200 bits. In contrast, in the case for 2-1 DAPUF and 4-1 DAPUF, the margin is only 3 bits and 8 bits, respectively, which indicates that the authentication system would have an insufficient margin. In conclusion, it is figured out that 3-1 DAPUF is the most suitable for the authentication system in our experiments. However, if the verifier excludes unstable responses to improve the steadiness, 4-1 DAPUF could be used for authentication system, and might outperform 3-1 DAPUF. Further, if there exists a better DL model for 3-1 DAPUF, the prediction rate would be higher and affect the results.

6   Conclusions and Future Work

In this paper, we demonstrated a DL-based cloning attack against DAPUF. DAPUF was considered new design approach for enhancing the PUF tolerance against machine-learning attacks. Our experiments using Xilinx® Virtex-5® FPGAs clarified that 3-1 DAPUFs and 4-1 DAPUFs had a higher tolerance for the machine-learning attacks with DL compared to a conventional XOR APUF. In a challenge-response authentication system using APUF and its variants, the verifier was able to distinguish a legitimate PUF from clones as for 3-1 DAPUF. Future work includes DAPUF implementation on an application-specific integrated circuit (ASIC) to perform DL-based attacks with a sufficient amount of PUFs and training data.

Appendix A: Pseudo Verilog Code and User Constraint File of 3-1 DAPUF for Xilinx® Virtex-5® (XC5VLX30)[6]

```
// Verilog Part
/****************** 3-1 DAPUF Module begin ******************/
module 3_DAPUF(clk, rst_n, idata_reg, esig, Answer);

input              clk;        // Clock signal
input              rst_n;      // Reset signal
input     [63:0]   idata_reg;  // 64-bit challenge
input              esig;       // Input signal
output             Answer;     // 1-bit response

reg                Answer_reg;
wire               a0, ... , a64, b0, ... , b64, c0, ... , c64;
wire               d0, ... , d64, e0, ... , e64, f0, ... , f64;
wire               res_a, res_b, res_c, res_d, res_e, res_f;

/****************** Generate Input Signal begin ******************/
FDCE #(
.INIT(1'b0)  // Initial value of register (1'b0 or 1'b1)
) sig_reg_a (
.Q(a0),       // Data output
.C(clk),      // Clock input
.CE(1'b1),    // Clock enable input
.CLR(1'b0),   // Asynchronous clear input
.D(esig)      // Data input
);

FDCE #(
.INIT(1'b0)  // Initial value of register (1'b0 or 1'b1)
) sig_reg_b (
.Q(c0),       // Data output
.C(clk),      // Clock input
.CE(1'b1),    // Clock enable input
.CLR(1'b0),   // Asynchronous clear input
.D(esig)      // Data input
);

/****************** The First Selector Chain begin ******************/
MUXF7 MUX_000(.O(a1), .I0(a0), .I1(a0), .S(idata_reg[0]));
// synthesis attribute keep of a1 is true;
MUXF7 MUX_001(.O(b1), .I0(c0), .I1(c0), .S(idata_reg[0]));
// synthesis attribute keep of b1 is true;
MUXF7 MUX_002(.O(a2), .I0(a1), .I1(b1), .S(idata_reg[1]));
// synthesis attribute keep of a2 is true;
```

---

[6] The copyrights to full versions of the pseudo code and the constraint file belong to The University of Electro-Communications, Japan, and their authorship is attributed to K. Sakiyama, T. Machida, and M. Iwamoto.

```
MUXF7 MUX_003(.O(b2), .I0(b1), .I1(a1), .S(idata_reg[1]));
// synthesis attribute keep of b2 is true;
...
MUXF7 MUX_126(.O(a64), .I0(a63), .I1(b63), .S(idata_reg[63]));
// synthesis attribute keep of a64 is true;
MUXF7 MUX_127(.O(b64), .I0(b63), .I1(a63), .S(idata_reg[63]));
// synthesis attribute keep of b64 is true;

/****************** The Second Selector Chain begin ******************/
MUXF7 MUX_128(.O(c1), .I0(a0), .I1(a0), .S(idata_reg[0]));
// synthesis attribute keep of c1 is true;
MUXF7 MUX_129(.O(d1), .I0(c0), .I1(c0), .S(idata_reg[0]));
// synthesis attribute keep of d1 is true;
...
MUXF7 MUX_254(.O(c64), .I0(c63), .I1(d63), .S(idata_reg[63]));
// synthesis attribute keep of c64 is true;
MUXF7 MUX_255(.O(d64), .I0(d63), .I1(c63), .S(idata_reg[63]));
// synthesis attribute keep of d64 is true;

/****************** The Third Selector Chain begin ******************/
MUXF7 MUX_256(.O(e1), .I0(a0), .I1(a0), .S(idata_reg[0]));
// synthesis attribute keep of e1 is true;
MUXF7 MUX_257(.O(f1), .I0(c0), .I1(c0), .S(idata_reg[0]));
// synthesis attribute keep of f1 is true;
...
MUXF7 MUX_382(.O(e64), .I0(e63), .I1(f63), .S(idata_reg[63]));
// synthesis attribute keep of e64 is true;
MUXF7 MUX_383(.O(f64), .I0(f63), .I1(e63), .S(idata_reg[63]));
// synthesis attribute keep of f64 is true;

/****************** Generate Response begin ******************/
SRFF SRFF_0(.S(a64), .R(c64), .Q(res_a));
// synthesis attribute keep of res_a is true;
SRFF SRFF_1(.S(c64), .R(e64), .Q(res_b));
// synthesis attribute keep of res_b is true;
SRFF SRFF_2(.S(e64), .R(a64), .Q(res_c));
// synthesis attribute keep of res_c is true;
SRFF SRFF_3(.S(b64), .R(d64), .Q(res_d));
// synthesis attribute keep of res_d is true;
SRFF SRFF_4(.S(d64), .R(f64), .Q(res_e));
// synthesis attribute keep of res_e is true;
SRFF SRFF_5(.S(f64), .R(b64), .Q(res_f));
// synthesis attribute keep of res_f is true;

assign Answer = Answer_reg;

always @(posedge clk or negedge rst_n) begin
if (~rst_n) begin
Answer_reg <= 1'b0;                // Reset
end
```

```
else begin
Answer_reg <= res_a^res_b^res_c^res_d^res_e^res_f;
end
end

endmodule

/****************** SR Latch Module begin *****************/
module SRL(S, R, Q);
input S,R;
output Q;
wire QB;

NAND2 NAND_0(.I0(S), .I1(QB), .O(Q));
// synthesis attribute keep of Q is true;
NAND2 NAND_1(.I0(R), .I1(Q), .O(QB));
// synthesis attribute keep of QB is true;
endmodule

//UCF Part
/****************** The First Selector Chain begin *****************/
#The First Selector Chain begin
INST "MUX_000" BEL = F7BMUX;
...
INST "MUX_127" BEL = F7BMUX;

INST "MUX_000" LOC = SLICE_X14Y76;
INST "MUX_001" LOC = SLICE_X15Y76;
...
INST "MUX_126" LOC = SLICE_X14Y13;
INST "MUX_127" LOC = SLICE_X15Y13;

/****************** The Second Selector Chain begin *****************/
#The Second Selector Chain begin
INST "MUX_128" BEL = F7BMUX;
...
INST "MUX_255"BEL = F7BMUX;

INST "MUX_128" LOC = SLICE_X16Y76;
INST "MUX_129" LOC = SLICE_X17Y76;
...
INST "MUX_254" LOC = SLICE_X16Y13;
INST "MUX_255" LOC = SLICE_X17Y13;

/****************** The Third Selector Chain begin *****************/
INST "MUX_256" BEL = F7BMUX;
...
INST "MUX_383" BEL = F7BMUX;

INST "MUX_256" LOC = SLICE_X18Y76;
```

```
INST "MUX_257" LOC = SLICE_X19Y76;
...
INST "MUX_382" LOC = SLICE_X18Y13;
INST "MUX_383" LOC = SLICE_X19Y13;

/***************** Input Signal begin *****************/
INST "sig_reg_a" BEL = BFF;
INST "sig_reg_b" BEL = AFF;
INST "sig_reg_a" LOC = SLICE_X16Y77;
INST "sig_reg_b" LOC = SLICE_X16Y77;

/***************** SR Latch begin *****************/
INST "SRL_0/NAND_0" BEL = C6LUT;
...
INST "SRL_5/NAND_1" BEL = C6LUT;

INST "SRL_0/NAND_0" LOC = SLICE_X14Y12;
INST "SRL_0/NAND_1" LOC = SLICE_X16Y12;
INST "SRL_1/NAND_0" LOC = SLICE_X16Y11;
INST "SRL_1/NAND_1" LOC = SLICE_X18Y11;
INST "SRL_2/NAND_0" LOC = SLICE_X18Y10;
INST "SRL_2/NAND_1" LOC = SLICE_X14Y10;
INST "SRL_3/NAND_0" LOC = SLICE_X15Y12;
INST "SRL_3/NAND_1" LOC = SLICE_X17Y12;
INST "SRL_4/NAND_0" LOC = SLICE_X17Y11;
INST "SRL_4/NAND_1" LOC = SLICE_X19Y11;
INST "SRL_5/NAND_0" LOC = SLICE_X19Y10;
INST "SRL_5/NAND_1" LOC = SLICE_X15Y10;
```

Appendix B: Third-Layer YAML Code for Pylearn2 [2]

```
!obj:pylearn2.train.Train{
dataset: &train !obj:
pylearn2.datasets.transformer_dataset.TransformerDataset{
raw: !pkl:"train.pkl",
transformer: !obj:pylearn2.blocks.StackedBlocks{
# Changed from the default
layers: [ !pkl:"Layer1.pkl", !pkl:"Layer2.pkl" ]
}
},
model: !obj:pylearn2.models.autoencoder.DenoisingAutoencoder{
nvis: 500,                            # Changed from the default
nhid: 20,                             # Changed from the default
irange: 0.05,
corruptor: !obj: pylearn2.corruption.BinomialCorruptor{
corruption_level: 0.2,                # Changed from the default
},
act_enc:"tanh",
act_dec: null,    # Linear activation on the decoder side.
```

```
},
algorithm: !obj:pylearn2.training_algorithms.sgd.SGD{
learning_rate: 1e-3,
batch_size: 10,                              # Changed from the default
monitoring_batches: 1,
monitoring_dataset: *train,
cost:
!obj:pylearn2.costs.autoencoder.MeanSquaredReconstructionError{},
termination_criterion:
!obj:pylearn2.termination_criteria.EpochCounter{
max_epochs: 100,                             # Changed from the default
},
},
save_path:"Layer3.pkl",
save_freq: 1
}
```

References

1. ImageNet Large-Scale Visual Recognition Challenge (2012). http://image-net.org/challenges/LSVRC/2012/
2. YAML for Pylearn2. http://deeplearning.net/software/pylearn2/yaml_tutorial
3. Becker, G.T.: The gap between promise and reality: on the insecurity of XOR arbiter PUFs. In: Güneysu, T., Handschuh, H. (eds.) CHES 2015. LNCS, vol. 9293, pp. 535–555. Springer, Heidelberg (2015)
4. Gassend, B., Clarke, D.E., van Dijk, M., Devadas, S.: Silicon physical random functions. In: Proceedings of the 9th ACM Conference on Computer and Communications Security, CCS 2002, pp. 148–160 (2002)
5. Goodfellow, I.J., Warde-Farley, D., Lamblin, P., Dumoulin, V., Mirza, M., Pascanu, R., Bergstra, J., Bastien, F., Bengio, Y.: Pylearn2: a machine learning research library (2013). arXiv preprint: arXiv:1308.4214
6. Hori, Y., Yoshida, T., Katashita, T., Satoh, A.: Quantitative and statistical performance evaluation of arbiter physical unclonable functions on FPGAs. In: Proceedings of 2010 International Conference on Reconfigurable Computing and FPGAs, ReConFig 2010, pp. 298–303 (2010)
7. Joachims, T.: SVM light. http://svmlight.joachims.org/
8. Lim, D.: Extracting secret keys from integrated circuits. Master's thesis, Massachusetts Institute of Technology (2004)
9. Machida, T., Yamamoto, D., Iwamoto, M., Sakiyama, K.: A new mode of operation for arbiter PUF to improve uniqueness on FPGA. In: Proceedings of the 2014 Federated Conference on Computer Science and Information Systems, FedCSIS 2014, pp. 871–878 (2014)
10. Machida, T., Yamamoto, D., Iwamoto, M., Sakiyama, K.: Implementation of double arbiter PUF and its performance evaluation on FPGA. In: Proceedings of the 20th Asia and South Pacific Design Automation Conference, ASP-DAC 2015, pp. 6–7 (2015)
11. Machida, T., Yamamoto, D., Iwamoto, M., Sakiyama, K.: A new arbiter PUF for enhancing unpredictability on FPGA. Sci. World J. **2015**, 13 (2015)
12. Pappu, R., Recht, B., Taylor, J., Gershenfeld, N.: Physical one-way functions. Science **297**(5589), 2026–2030 (2002)

13. Yashiro, R., Machida, T., Iwamoto, M., Sakiyama, K.: Security evaluation of double arbiter PUF using deep learning. In: Proceedings of the IEICE General Conference, A-7-13 (2016). (in Japanese)
14. Rührmair, U., Sehnke, F., Sölter, J., Dror, G., Devadas, S., Schmidhuber, J.: Modeling attacks on physical unclonable functions. In: Proceedings of the 17th ACM Conference on Computer and Communications Security, CCS 2010, pp. 237–249 (2010)
15. Suh, G.E., Devadas, S.: Physical unclonable functions for device authentication and secret key generation. In: Proceedings of the 44th Design Automation Conference, DAC 2007, pp. 9–14 (2007)
16. Vincent, P., Larochelle, H., Bengio, Y., Manzagol, P.: Extracting and composing robust features with denoising autoencoders. In: Proceedings of the 25th International Conference on Machine Learning, ICML 2008, pp. 1096–1103 (2008)

Post-quantum Cryptography

On the Security and Key Generation of the ZHFE Encryption Scheme

Wenbin Zhang[✉] and Chik How Tan

Temasek Laboratories, National University of Singapore, Singapore, Singapore
{tslzw,tsltch}@nus.edu.sg

Abstract. At PQCrypto'14 Porras, Baena and Ding proposed a new interesting construction to overcome the security weakness of the HFE encryption scheme, and called their new encryption scheme ZHFE. They provided experimental evidence for the security of ZHFE, and proposed the parameter set $(q, n, D) = (7, 55, 105)$ with claimed security level 2^{80} estimated by experiment. However there is an important gap in the state-of-the-art cryptanalysis of ZHFE, i.e., a sound theoretical estimation for the security level of ZHFE is missing. In this paper we fill in this gap by computing upper bounds for the Q-Rank and for the degree of regularity of ZHFE in terms of $\log_q D$, and thus providing such a theoretical estimation. For instance the security level of ZHFE(7,55,105) can now be estimated theoretically as at least 2^{96}. Moreover for the inefficient key generation of ZHFE, we also provide a solution to improve it significantly, making almost no computation needed.

Keywords: Post-quantum cryptography · Multivariate public key cryptography · HFE · ZHFE

1 Introduction

Multivariate public key cryptography (MPKC) [DGS06] is a candidate of post-quantum cryptography to resist future quantum computers. MPKC uses multivariate polynomials to represent its public key, and its security is backed on the fact that solving a random multivariate quadratic polynomial system is NP-hard [GJ79]. Since 1980s there have been many multivariate public key schemes constructed, but unfortunately most of them have been broken. One of the most important schemes is Patarin's Hidden Field Equations (HFE) encryption scheme [Pat96] which uses a low degree univariate polynomial F over the degree n extension field of $\mathbb{F}_q$ to construct the public key $P = T \circ F \circ S$ where S, T are two invertible affine transformations over $\mathbb{F}_q^n$. Though Patarin's original HFE has been broken [KS99, Cou01, FJ03, GJS06, DH11, BFP13], it has been developed into a big family. Some of its variants remain unbroken till now, for example HFEv for encryption and HFEv- for signature [PCG01, DY13, PCY+15].

In 2014 Porras, Baena and Ding [PBD14a, PBD14b] proposed a very interesting extension of HFE for encryption to overcome the security weakness of HFE.

© Springer International Publishing Switzerland 2016
K. Ogawa and K. Yoshioka (Eds.): IWSEC 2016, LNCS 9836, pp. 289–304, 2016.
DOI: 10.1007/978-3-319-44524-3_17

The public key of their construction is $P = T \circ (F_1, F_2) \circ S$, where the central map (F_1, F_2) consists of two *high* degree univariate polynomials F_1, F_2 with a built-in trapdoor. The trapdoor is that two linear combinations of all the Frobenius powers $(F_1)^{q^i}, (F_2)^{q^i}, 0 \le i \le n-1$, are shifted by X, X^q respectively and then added up to a secret *low* degree polynomial Ψ. They called their encryption scheme ZHFE and showed that it is relatively efficient on decryption, but is very inefficient to generate the private key.

ZHFE uses a low degree polynomial Ψ as the trapdoor function and thus belongs to the HFE family. So those attacks on HFE, including direct algebraic attack [FJ03] and the Kipnis-Shamir MinRank attack (KS attack) [KS99, BFP13], might also be applicable to ZHFE and should be investigated carefully. In [PBD14a, PBD14b], experimental method was used to verify the security of ZHFE against the two types of attacks by looking at the computation time and memory consumed for relatively small parameters. The experiment also computed two important characters, the degree of regularity [DG10] and the quadratic rank (Q-Rank) [DH11], of the polynomial system which can determine the security. Based on the experiment results, they found that for relatively small parameters, instances of ZHFE match well with random instances, and thus concluded by guessing that both the degree of regularity and Q-Rank increases as the number of variables increases so that ZHFE is secure. They also recommended a practical parameter set ZHFE(7,55,105) and guessed that its security level is greater than 2^{80}.

Later on Perlner and Smith-Tone [PST16] at PQCrypto'16 provided an additional cryptanalysis for ZHFE. They considered differential attack and Isomorphism of Polynomials attack [WP05], and found that the two attacks are not applicable to ZHFE. They also tried to consider the degree of regularity and the Q-Rank, but the "Q-Rank" they defined is simply the usual rank rather than the one of [DH11, PBD14a, PBD14b]. Due to this issue of terminology, they did not came out a valid theoretical estimation for the two important characters.

Hence it is still missing in the state-of-the-art cryptanalysis of ZHFE the very much desired theoretical estimation for the degree of regularity, Q-Rank and thus for the security level of ZHFE. In this paper we fill in this gap by first computing an upper bound for the Q-Rank of ZHFE which is $\lfloor \log_q D \rfloor + 3$ if $q > 2$ and $\lfloor \log_2 D \rfloor + 4$ if $q = 2$. We then use this upper bound to compute an upper bound for the degree of regularity of ZHFE which is $\frac{1}{2}(q-1)(\lfloor \log_q D \rfloor + 3) + 2$ if $q > 2$ and $\frac{1}{2}\lfloor \log_2 D \rfloor + 4$ if $q = 2$. Hence we obtain the missing theoretical result for the security of ZHFE, and as a consequence, we improve the guessed security level 2^{80} of ZHFE(7,55,105) to a theoretically estimated level 2^{96}. In addition, we find that the Q-Rank and the degree of regularity of the instances in the experiment of [PBD14a, PBD14b] are still (much) less than the upper bound. This explains why the tested ZHFE instances performed the same as random instances.

In this paper we also consider the key generation of ZHFE. The original method for generating the private key of ZHFE [PBD14a, PBD14b] need to solve a large linear system for the about n^3 coefficients of the secret F_1, F_2, and is very time-consuming with complexity $O(n^{3\omega})$. Recently a new paper of

Baena et al. [BCE+16] at PQCrypto'16 was devoted to improve the generation method and reduced the complexity to $O(n^{2\omega+1})$ by carefully studying the structure in the coefficients of F_1, F_2. However we find a very simple solution to the key generation which requires only very little computation, i.e., $O(\log_q D)$ $\mathbb{F}_q$-additions, and thus we can generate the private key almost immediately.

This paper is organized as follows. We first review the design of ZHFE in Sect. 2 and its state-of-the-art cryptanalysis in Sect. 3. We then present our new security analysis in Sect. 4 and our efficient solution to the key generation in Sect. 5. Finally we conclude this paper in Sect. 6.

2   The ZHFE Encryption Scheme

In this section, we shall recall Porras et al.'s novel encryption scheme ZHFE [PBD14a, PBD14b].

2.1   Design of the Core Map

Let $\mathbb{K}$ be a degree n extension of $\mathbb{F}_q$ and $\phi : \mathbb{K} \to \mathbb{F}_q^n$ the canonical isomorphism of vector spaces over $\mathbb{F}_q$. Firstly, we describe how to generate the core map of the scheme which consists of two high degree polynomials over $\mathbb{K}$,

$$F_1(X) = \sum a_{ij} X^{q^i+q^j} + \sum b_i X^{q^i} + c, \quad F_2(X) = \sum a'_{ij} X^{q^i+q^j} + \sum b'_i X^{q^i} + c'$$

whose coefficients will be determined later. Pick four linearized polynomials $L_{kl}(Y) = \sum_{i=0}^{n-1} u_{kl;i} Y^{q^i}$, $(1 \leq k, l \leq 2)$, with coefficients chosen randomly from $\mathbb{K}$. Then define

$$\Psi(X, F_1, F_2) = X \cdot [L_{11}(F_1) + L_{12}(F_2)] + X^q \cdot [L_{21}(F_1) + L_{22}(F_2)]. \quad (1)$$

Choose a positive integer D. The coefficients of F_1, F_2 are required to satisfy

$$\deg \Psi(X, F_1(X), F_2(X)) \leq D. \quad (2)$$

By this degree restriction, a very large linear system can be obtained for the coefficients of F_1, F_2, and any nonzero solution gives a pair of F_1, F_2. Then compute

$$\Psi_D(X) = \Psi(X, F_1(X), F_2(X))$$

$$= \sum_{0 \leq i \leq 1} \sum_{q^i+q^j+q^k \leq D} a''_{ijk} X^{q^i+q^j+q^k} \sum_{q^i+q^j \leq D} b''_{ij} X^{q^i+q^j} + \sum_{q^i \leq D} c''_i X^{q^i}. \quad (3)$$

Secondly, we describe how to invert the central map (F_1, F_2). Given any $Y_1, Y_2 \in \mathbb{K}$, since F_1, F_2 are of high degree, it is expected infeasible in general to solve

$$\begin{cases} F_1(X) = Y_1 \\ F_2(X) = Y_2 \end{cases} \quad (4)$$

directly. It is shown in [PBD14a, PBD14b] that Eq. (4) can be solved with the help of $\Psi_D(X) = \Psi(X, Y_1, Y_2)$; i.e., solutions to (4) are also solutions to

$$\Psi_D(X) - \Psi(X, Y_1, Y_2) = 0. \tag{5}$$

Since the degree of Eq. (5) is bounded by a relatively small D, Eq. (5) can be solved efficiently using Berlekamp's algorithm, then each solution can be checked whether it is also a solution to the original equation (4).

2.2   The ZHFE Encryption Scheme

We can now describe the ZHFE encryption scheme. Its public map is

$$P = T \circ (\phi \times \phi) \circ (F_1, F_2) \circ \phi^{-1} \circ S : \mathbb{F}_q^n \to \mathbb{F}_q^{2n}$$

where $S : \mathbb{F}_q^n \to \mathbb{F}_q^n$ and $T : \mathbb{F}_q^{2n} \to \mathbb{F}_q^{2n}$ are two randomly chosen invertible affine transformations.

Public Key. The public key includes $\mathbb{F}_q$ and the polynomial map $P(x_1, \ldots, x_n)$.
Private Key. The private key includes Ψ, D, Ψ_D and S, T.
Encryption. The ciphertext of a plaintext $(x_1, \ldots, x_n) \in \mathbb{F}_q^n$ is obtained by computing $(y_1, \ldots, y_{2n}) = P(x_1, \ldots, x_n)$.
Decryption. A given ciphertext $\mathbf{y}$ is decrypted as follows:
  1. Compute $(w_1, \ldots, w_{2n}) = T^{-1}(\mathbf{y})$.
  2. Compute $(Y_1, Y_2) = (\phi^{-1}(w_1, \ldots, w_n), \phi^{-1}(w_{n+1}, \ldots, w_{2n}))$;
  3. Substitute (Y_1, Y_2) into Eq. (5), solve it by Berlekamp's algorithm, and let $\mathcal{Z}$ be the set of solutions.
  4. For each $X \in \mathcal{Z}$, compute $S^{-1}(\phi(X))$ and check whether it is a solution to $P(\mathbf{x}) = \mathbf{y}$. Each solution is a candidate for the plaintext — additional redundant information must be added to determine which candidate is the correct plaintext.

In [PBD14b], parameters $(q, n, D) = (7, 55, 105)$ is suggested for ZHFE and its security level is claimed to be greater than 2^{80} with more features listed below.

Public key	Private key	Encryption time	Decryption time	Claimed security
66 KB	11 KB	0.024 s	0.427 s	2^{80}

A drawback of ZHFE is the low efficiency of generating the secret F_1, F_2. In the rest of this paper, we will discuss the security and key generation of ZHFE.

3   Review of Cryptanalysis of ZHFE

ZHFE uses a low degree polynomial over the extension field $\mathbb{K}$ over $\mathbb{F}_q$ as the trapdoor, and thus it belongs to the HFE family. It may further be regarded as a Multi-HFE with two branches, but there is a significant difference. The usual HFE and Multi-HFE use one or more polynomials over the extension field $\mathbb{K}$ which are of low degree (thus of low rank) as the core map. This low degree (low rank) is exactly the weakness of HFE and Multi-HFE. To overcome this weakness, ZHFE [PBD14a, PBD14b] is designed to use two high degree polynomial maps F_1, F_2 over $\mathbb{K}$ as its core map. The trapdoor is that, F_1, F_2 are related to a secret low degree map Ψ (1), which will be inverted, instead of inverting F_1, F_2, for decryption. This design is intended to increase the degree and rank of the core map to improve its security.

There are two types of attacks on the family of HFE schemes, i.e. direct algebraic attack [FJ03] and the Kipnis-Shamir MinRank Attack (KS attack) [KS99, BFP13]. The security of ZHFE against the two attacks was analyzed in [PBD14a, PBD14b], and then a few other attacks were also considered in [PST16]. In this section, we shall review the cryptanalysis of ZHFE from [PBD14a, PBD14b, PST16] and point out an important gap which is missing there.

3.1   Direct Algebraic Attacks

Direct algebraic attacks, such as F_4 [Fau99], F_5 [Fau02] and XL [CKPS00] try to solve the polynomial equation $P(\mathbf{x}) = \mathbf{y}$ directly, where P is the public polynomial map, and is applicable to all multivariate public key cryptosystems. The complexity of direct algebraic attacks is characterized by the degree of regularity of the polynomial system which is informally the highest degree achieved in the process of computing the Gröbner basis, cf. [DG10]. The degree of regularity has been a powerful tool for investigating the security of the HFE family [DG10, DH11, DY13, PCY+15] and it has deep connection with another notion, the quadratic rank of the polynomial system [DH11].

We shall recall the notion of quadratic rank (Q-Rank for short) [DH11] in the following. The rank $\text{Rank}(f)$ of a quadratic function $f = \sum a_{ij}x_ix_j + \sum b_ix_i + c :$ $\mathbb{F}_q^n \to \mathbb{F}_q$ is defined as the rank of its associated quadratic form $\sum a_{ij}x_ix_j$. For a polynomial map $F = (f_1, \ldots, f_m) : \mathbb{F}_q^n \to \mathbb{F}_q^m$, its Q-Rank is defined as the minimal rank of all nonzero linear combination of $f_1, \ldots, f_m$,

$$\text{Q-Rank}(F) = \min\{\text{Rank}(f) \mid f \in Span_{\mathbb{F}_q}(f_1, \ldots, f_m), f \neq 0\}$$

where $Span_{\mathbb{F}_q}(f_1, \ldots, f_m)$ is the linear space over $\mathbb{F}_q$ spanned by $f_1, \ldots, f_m$. For polynomial

$$F(X) = \sum a_{ij}X^{q^i+q^j} + \sum b_iX^{q^i} + c,$$

over $\mathbb{K}$, its rank is also defined as the rank of its associated quadratic form $\sum a_{ij}X_iX_j$ where $X_i = X^{q^i}$. In addition, its Q-Rank is defined as the minimal rank of all its nonzero linear combinations of all the Frobenius powers F^{q^i} of F. Noting the equivalence between the multivariate representation and univariate representation of a polynomial, the two definitions of rank and Q-Rank are also equivalent [BFP13].

Ding and Hodges [DH11] found that the degree of regularity d_{reg} of a polynomial F is bounded by

$$d_{reg}(F) \leq \frac{(q-1)\text{Q-Rank}(F)}{2} + 2 \leq \frac{(q-1)(\lfloor \log_q(D-1) \rfloor + 1)}{2} + 2 \quad (6)$$

if Q-Rank$(F) > 1$. As a consequence, they [DH11] found that inverting HFE systems is polynomial on n if D, q are fixed, and is quasi-polynomial on n if D is of the scale $O(n^\alpha)$. Therefore, to estimate the security level of ZHFE against direct algebraic attacks, it is very important to understand well its degree of regularity and Q-Rank.

A practical experimental approach to test the security strength of a scheme against direct algebraic attacks is to compute some instances and compare with random instances for relatively small parameters. One can do so by computing the Gröbner basis and comparing the time and memory needed, and calculating the degree of regularity and see how it changes as the parameters change. In [PBD14a, PBD14b], experiments were conducted to compute the Gröbner bases of instances of ZHFE and random instances using the F_4 function of MAGMA. Their experiments included instances with $q = 2, n \leq 40$ and $q = 7, n \leq 25$. They found that those relatively small instances of ZHFE match very well with random instances on time, memory and the degree of regularity. Based on the experiment results they concluded that ZHFE would perform generally as random instances against direct algebraic attack, and especially the degree of regularity would grow as n grows.

However, only experiments is not sufficient to guarantee the security level as only a small range of parameters are tested. Theoretical estimation of the degree of regularity and thus of the complexity is necessary, as it can ensure what will happen for parameters beyond the range that can be practically tested. Unfortunately such theoretical estimation is missing in [PBD14a, PBD14b]. This is an important gap which should be filled in.

3.2   The Kipnis-Shamir MinRank Attack

In 1999 Kipnis and Shamir [KS99] proposed an attack to recover the secret key of HFE. Their attack relies on the fact that the core map of HFE has a small rank and thus can be converted into the MinRank Problem.

The MinRank Problem: Let $\mathbb{K}$ be a finite field and $M_1, \ldots, M_m$ $t \times t$ matrices over $\mathbb{K}$. Given a positive integer $r \leq t$, find scalars $\lambda_1, \ldots, \lambda_m$, not all zero, such that

$$\text{Rank}(\lambda_1 M_1 + \cdots + \lambda_m M_m) \leq r.$$

It is well known that this is generally an NP-hard problem, but if r is small, then the MinRank problem is not too hard to compute. Kipnis and Shamir [KS99] proposed a method to solve the MinRank problem for small r and thus gave an attacking method to HFE though not breaking it.

In 2013, Bettale, Faugère and Perret improved the KS attack significantly and break HFE and multi-HFE [BFP13]. They showed that the rank of HFE also gives the Q-Rank of the public polynomial map, then reduced the Min-Rank problem from the extension field $\mathbb{K}$ to the much smaller field $\mathbb{F}_q$ and thus reduced the complexity considerably. The complexity of their improved KS attack is estimated as $O(n^{(r+1)\omega})$ where r is the Q-Rank of the HFE scheme, and thus breaks HFE with practical parameters. Their attack also breaks multi-HFE with k branches with complexity $O(n^{k(r+1)\omega})$. Therefore the Q-Rank of the polynomial system is not only important for the degree of regularity and direct algebraic attack, but also determines the security level against Bettale, Faugère and Perret's (BFP's for short) KS attack.

In [PBD14b], the Q-Rank of the suggested parameter set ZHFE(7,55,105) is showed by experiments to be greater than 3. However for the case that whether the Q-Rank is 4, their experiment did not stop but reached the set time limit and memory limit. Based on this experiment result, it was then guessed in [PBD14b] that for ZHFE: (1) *the Q-rank grows as n grows*; (2) *the Q-rank is independent of D*; (3) *in principle there seems no obvious way to recover Ψ*.

Later on [PST16] tried to analyze the Q-Rank of ZHFE for $q > 2$. However, it should be clarified that the "Q-Rank" of a polynomial $F = \sum a_{ij} X^{q^i + q^j}$ over $\mathbb{K}$ in [PST16, Sect. 3] is defined as the rank of the matrix of the associated quadratic form, while the "Q-Rank" of F defined here and in [PBD14a, PBD14b] is the minimal rank of all nonzero linear combinations of all the Frobenius powers F^{q^i} of F. Namely the "Q-Rank" of [PST16] is *NOT* the "Q-Rank" defined here and in [PBD14a, PBD14b]. In [PST16, Subsect. 3], they noticed that the rank of $L_{11}(F_1) + L_{12}(F_2)$ is no more than $\lceil \log_q D \rceil + 2$, and then claimed that the rank of (F_1, F_2) is bounded by $\lceil \log_q D \rceil + 2$ if L_{ij} are nonsingular, and can be increased easily by choosing singular L_{ij} with small co-rank; but due to their definition, they did not conclude the Q-Rank of ZHFE. Therefore, theoretical analysis of the Q-Rank of ZHFE and the security of ZHFE against BFP' KS attack is still missing in [PST16].

3.3   Other Attacks

[PST16] also considered a few other attacks. They computed the differential symmetry of the secret Ψ and found no evidence to attack ZHFE by the symmetry. They then further proved that Ψ does not have nontrivial differential invariant and thus differential attack is not applicable to ZHFE. The number of equivalent and nonequivalent keys are estimated in [PST16], and found to be large enough to prevent the IP-based equivalent key attacks [WP05].

4   New Security Analysis of ZHFE

From the preceding review on current cryptanalysis of ZHFE, [PBD14a, PBD14b] showed convincing experimental results to support that ZHFE is like random systems against direct algebraic attack for relatively small parameters, but lacked a theoretical analysis. For BFP's KS attack, their experiment results only showed that the Q-Rank of ZHFE(7,55,105) is greater than 3, and again theoretical analysis on the Q-Rank is lacked. [PST16] found that a few other attacks are not applicable to ZHFE and also considered the rank of ZHFE — but unfortunately not the Q-Rank. Therefore a thorough theoretical analysis on the Q-Rank of ZHFE is still missing in the cryptanalysis of ZHFE, but is necessary to ensure the security level of ZHFE.

In this section, we shall fill this gap. We will first deduce a linear system determining the two maps

$$\bar{F}_1 = L_{11}(F_1) + L_{12}(F_2), \quad \bar{F}_2 = L_{21}(F_1) + L_{22}(F_2).$$

which unexpectedly turns out to be so simple that no computation is needed to solve it. We then apply this technical result to give an upper bound for the Q-Rank of ZHFE. Finally we apply this upper bound to give the missing theoretical estimation on the security of ZHFE against direct algebraic attack and BFP's KS attack.

4.1   Computing $L_{11}(F_1) + L_{12}(F_2)$ and $L_{21}(F_1) + L_{22}(F_2)$

Here we shall compute the conditions for the coefficients of

$$\bar{F}_1 = L_{11}(F_1) + L_{12}(F_2), \quad \bar{F}_2 = L_{21}(F_1) + L_{22}(F_2)$$

to satisfy the degree restriction (2) on Ψ. Since the two cases (1) $q > 2$ and (2) $q = 2$ are different, we shall deal with them separately.

First Case: $q > 2$. Write

$$\bar{F}_1(X) = \sum_{0 \le i \le j \le n-1} \bar{a}_{ij} X^{q^i + q^j} + \sum_{0 \le i \le n-1} \bar{b}_i X^{q^i} + \bar{c}$$

$$\bar{F}_2(X) = \sum_{0 \le i \le j \le n-1} \bar{a}'_{ij} X^{q^i + q^j} + \sum_{0 \le i \le n-1} \bar{b}'_i X^{q^i} + \bar{c}'$$

Then by calculation, we have

$$\Psi(X, F_1, F_2) = \sum_{1 \le i \le j \le n-1} \bar{a}'_{ij} X^{q + q^i + q^j} + \sum_{2 \le i \le j \le n-1} \bar{a}_{ij} X^{1 + q^i + q^j} + \sum_{1 \le i \le n-1} \bar{b}'_i X^{q + q^i}$$

$$+ \sum_{1 \le j \le n-1} (\bar{a}_{1j} + \bar{a}'_{0j}) X^{1 + q + q^j} + \sum_{1 \le j \le n-1} \bar{a}_{0j} X^{2 + q^j} + \sum_{2 \le i \le n-1} \bar{b}_i X^{1 + q^i}$$

$$+ \bar{a}'_{00} X^{2+q} + (\bar{b}_1 + \bar{b}'_0) X^{1+q} + \bar{c}' X^q + \bar{a}_{00} X^3 + \bar{b}_0 X^2 + \bar{c} X. \qquad (7)$$

Notice that the highest degree is of the form $q + 2q^{n-1}$. So we shall separate the degree range by $q + 2q^{s-1} < D \le q + 2q^s, 1 \le s \le n-1$. Then $\deg \Psi(X, F_1, F_2) \le q + 2q^s$ if and only if

$$\begin{cases} \bar{a}_{ij} = 0, & 2 \le i < j, \ j > s \\ \bar{a}'_{ij} = 0, & 1 \le i < j, \ j > s \\ \bar{a}_{0j} = 0, \bar{a}'_{0j} = -\bar{a}_{1j}, \ j > s \\ \bar{b}_i = 0, \bar{b}'_i = 0, & i > s \end{cases} \tag{8}$$

Therefore, to find $\bar{F}_1, \bar{F}_2$, we just need to solve this system of linear equations whose solution is already obvious and does not need any computation. In other words, the two secret maps are

$$\bar{F}_1 = \sum_{1 \le j \le n-1} \bar{a}_{1j} X^{q+q^j} + \sum_{0 \le i \le j \le s, i \ne 1} \bar{a}_{ij} X^{q^i + q^j} + \sum_{0 \le i \le s} \bar{b}_i X^{q^i} + \bar{c} \tag{9}$$

$$\bar{F}_2 = \sum_{0 \le j \le n-1} \bar{a}'_{0j} X^{1+q^j} + \sum_{1 \le i \le j \le s} \bar{a}'_{ij} X^{q^i + q^j} + \sum_{0 \le i \le s} \bar{b}'_i X^{q^i} + \bar{c}' \tag{10}$$

where the coefficients can be arbitrarily chosen with the only restriction

$$\bar{a}'_{0j} = -\bar{a}_{1j}, \quad j > s.$$

The secret Ψ_D is then computed by (7) requiring only $s+1 \approx \log_q D$ $\mathbb{F}_q$-additions.

Second Case: $q = 2$. Write

$$\bar{F}_1(X) = \sum_{0 \le i < j \le n-1} \bar{a}_{ij} X^{2^i + 2^j} + \sum_{0 \le i \le n-1} \bar{b}_i X^{2^i} + \bar{c}$$

$$\bar{F}_2(X) = \sum_{0 \le i < j \le n-1} \bar{a}'_{ij} X^{2^i + 2^j} + \sum_{0 \le i \le n-1} \bar{b}'_i X^{2^i} + \bar{c}'$$

Notice that there is no $\bar{a}_{ii}, \bar{a}'_{ii}$ since $X^{2^i + 2^i} = X^{2^{i+1}}$. By computation,

$$\Psi(X, F_1, F_2) = \sum_{1 \le i < j \le n} \bar{a}'_{ij} X^{2+2^i+2^j} + \sum_{2 \le i < j \le n} \bar{a}_{ij} X^{1+2^i+2^j} + \sum_{2 \le i \le n} (\bar{a}_{1i} + \bar{a}'_{0i}) X^{1+2+2^i}$$

$$+ \sum_{2 \le i \le n-1} (\bar{a}_{0i} + \bar{b}'_i) X^{2+2^i} + \sum_{3 \le i \le n-1} \bar{b}_i X^{1+2^i} + (\bar{a}'_{01} + \bar{b}_2) X^5$$

$$+ (\bar{a}_{01} + \bar{b}'_1) X^4 + (\bar{b}_1 + \bar{b}'_0) X^3 + (\bar{b}_0 + \bar{c}') X^2 + \bar{c} X. \tag{11}$$

The highest degree is of the form $2 + 2^{n-2} + 2^{n-1}$. So we shall separate the degree range by $2 + 2^{s-2} + 2^{s-1} < D \le 2 + 2^{s-1} + 2^s$, $2 \le s \le n-1$. Then $\deg \Psi(X, F_1, F_2) \le 2 + 2^{s-1} + 2^s$ if and only if

$$\begin{cases} \bar{a}_{ij} = 0, & 2 \le i < j, \ j > s \\ \bar{a}'_{ij} = 0, & 1 \le i < j, \ j > s \\ \bar{a}'_{0j} = \bar{a}_{1j}, \bar{b}'_j = \bar{a}_{0j}, \bar{b}_j = 0, \ j > s \end{cases} \tag{12}$$

So we already solve the two secret maps

$$\bar{F}_1 = \sum_{j=2}^{n-1} \bar{a}_{1j} X^{2+2^j} + \sum_{j=1}^{n-1} \bar{a}_{0j} X^{1+2^j} + \sum_{2 \leq i < j \leq s} \bar{a}_{ij} X^{2^i+2^j} + \sum_{0 \leq i \leq s} \bar{b}_i X^{2^i} + \bar{c}$$

(13)

$$\bar{F}_2 = \sum_{j=0}^{n-1} \bar{a}'_{0j} X^{1+2^i} + \sum_{j=0}^{n-1} \bar{b}'_j X^{2^i} + \sum_{1 \leq i < j \leq s} \bar{a}'_{ij} X^{2^i+2^j} + \bar{c}'$$

(14),

where the coefficients are arbitrarily chosen with the only restriction

$$\bar{a}'_{0j} = \bar{a}_{1j}, \quad \bar{b}'_j = \bar{a}_{0j}, \quad j > s$$

The secret Ψ_D is then computed by (11) requiring only $2s + 2 \approx 2 \log_2 D$ $\mathbb{F}_2$-additions.

4.2   Upper Bound for the Q-Rank of ZHFE

Notice that $\bar{F}_1, \bar{F}_2$ can have maximum degree $q + q^{n-1}$ and $1 + q^{n-1}$ respectively. Although their maximum degree can be this high, their ranks are still small.

Theorem 1. *We have the following upper bound on the Q-Rank of ZHFE(q, n, D):*

1. *If $q > 2$, $D \leq q + 2q^s$, then*

$$Q\text{-}Rank\ (ZHFE) \leq s + 2 \leq \lfloor \log_q D \rfloor + 3.$$

2. *If $q = 2$, $D \leq 2 + 2^{s-1} + 2^s$, then*

$$Q\text{-}Rank\ (ZHFE) \leq s + 3 \leq \lfloor \log_2 D \rfloor + 4,$$

Proof. From the calculation in Subsect. 4.1, if $q > 2$ is odd, the associated symmetric matrices of the quadratic forms of $\bar{F}_1, \bar{F}_2$ are

$$\begin{pmatrix} \bar{a}_{00} & \bar{a}_{01}/2 & \cdots & \bar{a}_{0s}/2 & & \\ \bar{a}_{01}/2 & \bar{a}_{11} & \cdots & \bar{a}_{1s}/2 & \cdots & \bar{a}_{1,n-1}/2 \\ \vdots & \vdots & & \vdots & & \\ \bar{a}_{0s}/2 & \bar{a}_{1s}/2 & \cdots & \bar{a}_{ss} & & \\ & \vdots & & & & \\ & \bar{a}_{1,n-1}/2 & & & & \end{pmatrix}, \quad \begin{pmatrix} \bar{a}'_{00} & & \cdots & \bar{a}'_{0s}/2 & \cdots & \bar{a}'_{0,n-1}/2 \\ & \ddots & & \vdots & & \vdots \\ \bar{a}'_{0s}/2 & & \cdots & \bar{a}'_{ss} & & \\ & \vdots & & & & \\ \bar{a}'_{0,n-1}/2 & & & & & \end{pmatrix}$$

respectively. If $q > 2$ even, the two matrices are

$$\begin{pmatrix} 0 & \bar{a}_{01} & \cdots & \bar{a}_{0s} & & \\ \bar{a}_{01} & 0 & \cdots & \bar{a}_{1s} & \cdots & \bar{a}_{1,n-1} \\ \vdots & \vdots & & \vdots & & \\ \bar{a}_{0s} & \bar{a}_{1s} & \cdots & 0 & & \\ & \vdots & & & & \\ & \bar{a}_{1,n-1} & & & & \end{pmatrix}, \quad \begin{pmatrix} 0 & & \cdots & \bar{a}'_{0s} & \cdots & \bar{a}'_{0,n-1} \\ & \ddots & & \vdots & & \vdots \\ \bar{a}'_{0s} & & \cdots & 0 & & \\ & \vdots & & & & \\ \bar{a}'_{0,n-1} & & & & & \end{pmatrix}$$

respectively, with zero diagonal. It is then obvious that

$$\mathrm{Rank}(\bar{F}_1) \le s+2 \quad \text{and} \quad \mathrm{Rank}(\bar{F}_2) \le s+2.$$

If $q = 2$, the two matrices are

$$\begin{pmatrix} 0 & \bar{a}_{01} & \cdots & \bar{a}_{0s} & \cdots & \bar{a}_{0,n-1} \\ \bar{a}_{01} & 0 & \cdots & \bar{a}_{1s} & \cdots & \bar{a}_{1,n-1} \\ \vdots & \vdots & & \vdots & & \\ \bar{a}_{0s} & \bar{a}_{1s} & \cdots & 0 & & \\ \vdots & \vdots & & & & \\ \bar{a}_{0,n-1} & \bar{a}_{1,n-1} & & & & \end{pmatrix}, \quad \begin{pmatrix} 0 & \cdots & \bar{a}'_{0s} & \cdots & \bar{a}'_{0,n-1} \\ \vdots & & \vdots & & \\ \bar{a}'_{0s} & \cdots & 0 & & \\ \vdots & & & & \\ \bar{a}'_{0,n-1} & & & & \end{pmatrix}$$

respectively. Then it is also obvious that their ranks are $\le s+3$ and ≤ 2 respectively.

$$\mathrm{Rank}(\bar{F}_1) \le s+3 \quad \text{and} \quad \mathrm{Rank}(\bar{F}_2) \le s+2.$$

Since $\bar{F}_1, \bar{F}_2$ are linear combinations of the Frobenius powers of F_1, F_2, the Q-Rank of (F_1, F_2) is bounded above by the ranks of $\bar{F}_1, \bar{F}_2$. Therefore we have the first part of the claimed upper bound for the Q-Rank of ZHFE.

Notice that for $q+2q^{s-1} < D \le q+2q^s$ or $2+2^{s-2}+2^{s-1} < D \le 2+2^{s-1}+2^s$, we have $s-1 < \log_q D < s+1$, thus $\lfloor \log_q D \rfloor = s-1$ or $\lfloor \log_q D \rfloor = s$. So $s \le \lfloor \log_q D \rfloor + 1$ and the second part of the claimed upper bound follows immediately.

As an example, for ZHFE(7,55,105), $105 = q + 2q^s$ where $q = 7$ and $s = 2$, so its Q-Rank $r \le 4$. From [PBD14b], the Q-Rank of ZHFE(7,55,105) $r > 3$, so $r = 4$. This example shows that the above estimation is tight.

From this result, we see that the Q-rank of ZHFE is independent on n, but dependent on the degree D of the secret Ψ. Moreover, we will show next how to apply BFP's KS attack [BFP13] to recover the secret Ψ. Therefore the three guesses of [PBD14b] on the Q-Rank, summarized in Subsect. 3.2 of this paper, are incorrect. In addition, we remark that the upper bound on the rank of $\bar{F}_1, \bar{F}_2$ when $q > 2$ was also noticed in [PST16], but they did not use it to conclude an upper bound for the Q-Rank of ZHFE. Instead, they concluded that they can choose L_{ij} and F_1, F_2 to make (F_1, F_2) have high rank. The reason is that they defined the Q-Rank as the usual rank.

4.3 BFP's KS Attack

As pointed out in [PBD14b], ZHFE can be regarded as a simple case of multi-HFE with two branches, i.e., $\mathbb{K}^2 \to \mathbb{K}^2$, $(X_1, X_2) \mapsto (F_1(X_1), F_2(X_2))$. Based on this viewpoint, we next sketch how to apply BFP's KS attack [BFP13] to attack ZHFE by recovering $\bar{F}_1, \bar{F}_2$ and Ψ, and estimate its complexity.

$\bar{F}_1$ has high degree $q + q^{n-1}$ but small Q-Rank (bounded by $s+2$ if $q = 2$ and $s+3$ if $q > 3$), and $\bar{F}_2$ also has high degree $1 + q^{n-1}$ but small Q-Rank bounded by $s + 2$. So the first step is to apply BFP's KS attack to compute $\bar{F}_1, \bar{F}_2$. Since there are two branches, the complexity is $O(n^{2(r+1)\omega})$ in terms of $\mathbb{F}_q$ operations. So the complexity of the first step is, $O(n^{(2s+6)\omega})$ if $q > 2$ for small q, and $O(n^{(2s+8)\omega})$ if $q = 2$.

Next recovering Ψ can be done with the simple relation

$$\Psi = X\bar{F}_1 + X^q\bar{F}_2.$$

More explicitly, once we have found two linearly independent G_1, G_2 with rank $s + 2$ (if $q > 2$ and $s + 3$ if $q > 3$) and $s + 2$ respectively, then $\bar{F}_1, \bar{F}_2$ are linear combinations of the Frobenius powers of G_1, G_2, and thus there are coefficients such that

$$\Psi(X, G_1, G_2) = X(u_1 G_1 + u_2 G_1^q + \cdots + u_n G_1^{q^{n-1}} + v_1 G_2 + v_2 G_2^q \cdots + v_n G_2^{q^{n-1}})$$

$$+ X^q(u_{n+1} G_1 + u_{n+2} G_1^q + \cdots + u_{2n} G_1^{q^{n-1}} + v_{n+1} G_2 + v_{n+2} G_2^q + \cdots + v_{2n} G_2^{q^{n-1}})$$

satisfies the degree condition $\deg \Psi \leq D$. So to recover Ψ, we can just find these coefficients by solving an overdefined linear system with $4n$ variables. Such a linear system can be solved using only part of its relations, say $8n$ of them, and thus the complexity is $O(n^3)$.

Therefore the complexity of BFP's KS attack is dominated by the first step of recovering $\bar{F}_1, \bar{F}_2$, and thus is estimated as

$$O(n^{2(r+1)\omega}) = \begin{cases} O(n^{(2s+6)\omega}) \approx O(n^{(2\lfloor \log_q D \rfloor + 8)\omega}), & \text{if } q > 2, \\ O(n^{(2s+8)\omega}) \approx O(n^{(2\lfloor \log_2 D \rfloor + 10)\omega}), & \text{if } q = 2, \end{cases}$$

in terms of $\mathbb{F}_q$ operations. Notice that this complexity is polynomial on n but exponential on $\log_q D$. This seems not so satisfying as it is not exponential on n and that D is small in practice, but it is still secure enough for practical parameters. For example, if choosing $\omega = 2$, the security level of ZHFE(7,55,105) against BFP's KS attack is estimated as at least 2^{138}. As comparison, the HFE system with the same set of parameters $(q, n, D) = (7, 55, 105)$ has Q-Rank 3 and its security level against BFP's KS attack is $n^{(r+1)\omega} = 55^{4\omega} = 2^{46}$. The key improvement of ZHFE is that it has bigger Q-Rank 4 and it has two branches, i.e. its number of equations double that of HFE.

4.4   Direct Algebraic Attacks

By Ding and Hodges' formula [DH11] for the degree of regularity, we have the following consequence of Theorem 1.

Theorem 2. *Let d_{reg} be the degree of regularity of the public polynomial map P of ZHFE(q, n, D).*

1. If $q > 2$, $D \leq q + 2q^s$, then

$$d_{reg} \leq \frac{(q-1)(s+2)}{2} + 2 \leq \frac{(q-1)(\lfloor \log_q D \rfloor + 3)}{2} + 2.$$

2. If $q = 2$, $D \leq 2 + 2^{s-1} + 2^s$, then

$$d_{reg} \leq \frac{s+3}{2} + 2 \leq \frac{\lfloor \log_2 D \rfloor + 4}{2} + 2 = \frac{1}{2}\lfloor \log_2 D \rfloor + 4.$$

For instance, the degree of regularity of ZHFE(2,n,500) is bounded by 8, and the one of ZHFE(7,n,105) is bounded by 14. In the experiment of [PBD14a, PBD14b], the highest degree of regularity achieved for the tested instances is 5 for ZHFE(2,n,500) in [PBD14a] and 6 for ZHFE(7,n,105) in [PBD14b], both of which are only about half of our upper bounds. This explains why the tested instances were like random instances when being solved by direct algebraic attack, and suggests that if bigger parameters exceeding the upper bound were tested, we might see significant drop on computation time compared to random instances. This will require more powerful computer and/or more time to do the experiment, but such bigger parameters should be tested in the future.

Comparing with the upper bound for the degree of regularity of HFE (6),

$$d_{reg}(\text{HFE}) \leq \frac{(q-1)(\lfloor \log_q(D-1) \rfloor + 1)}{2} + 2,$$

we see the upper bound for ZHFE is more than the one for HFE with difference

$$(q-1) \quad \text{if } q > 2, \quad \text{and} \quad \frac{3}{2} \quad \text{if } q = 2.$$

Therefore ZHFE(q, n, D) can be more secure than HFE(q, n, D) if q is bigger. It should be noted that a little change of the degree of regularity can result a difference on the complexity by a factor of a few thousand. For instance, following [DY13, PCY+15], the security of HFE(7,55,105) and ZHFE(7,55,105) against direct algebraic attacks F_4, F_5 can be estimated as

$$C_{F_4/F_5}(\text{HFE } (7,55,105)) \geq 3\tau T^2 = 3\binom{55}{2}\binom{55}{11}^2 \geq 2^{85.7}$$

$$C_{F_4/F_5}(\text{ZHFE } (7,55,105)) \geq 3\tau T^2 = 3\binom{55}{2}\binom{55}{14}^2 \geq 2^{96}$$

respectively. Namely both HFE(7,55,105) and ZHFE(7,55,105) are practically secure against direct algebraic attacks. However it should be noted that their security level against BFP's KS attack is 2^{46} and 2^{138} respectively. Hence our theoretical estimation for the security level of ZHFE(7,55,105) is at least 2^{96}.

5 Improving the Key Generation of ZHFE

The private key F_1, F_2, Ψ of ZHFE are defined subject to the following condition

$$\deg \Psi = \deg(X \cdot [L_{11}(F_1) + L_{12}(F_2)] + X^q \cdot [L_{21}(F_1) + L_{22}(F_2)]) \leq D.$$

Thus to generate F_1, F_2, one need to solve a large linear system derived from the vanishing coefficients of Ψ. Notice that this linear system has the coefficients of F_1, F_2 as the variables whose number is about n^3. The method of [PBD14a, PBD14b] solves F_1, F_2 with complexity $O(n^{3\omega})$ which is very high as it may take several days to generate a practical key. Later on another paper [BCE+16] is devoted to improve the key generation and reduces the complexity to $O(n^{2\omega+1})$. Here we shall propose a solution to improve the key generation which requires only little computation and is almost immediate.

Recall that in Subsect. 4.1, we have computed

$$\bar{F}_1 = L_{11}(F_1) + L_{12}(F_2), \quad \bar{F}_2 = L_{21}(F_1) + L_{22}(F_2).$$

and expressed them in terms of (9), (10) if $q > 2$, and (13), (14) if $q = 2$, whose coefficients can be arbitrarily chosen *without* any computation. In addition, the secret Ψ_D is computed by (7) if $q > 2$ and (11) if $q = 2$ which requires only very *little* computation, i.e., about $\log_q D$ if $q > 2$, or $2\log_2 D$ if $q = 2$, additions of $\mathbb{F}_q$ elements.

Our solution then is to forget F_1, F_2, L_{ij}, but regard $\bar{F}_1, \bar{F}_2$ as two individual maps, and use the pair $(\bar{F}_1, \bar{F}_2)$ as the core map of ZHFE instead of (F_1, F_2). So the public map becomes

$$P = T \circ (\phi \times \phi) \circ (\bar{F}_1, \bar{F}_2) \circ \phi^{-1} \circ S : \mathbb{F}_q^n \to \mathbb{F}_q^{2n}$$

and in the decryption step, we solve the following equation

$$\Psi_D(X) - (XY_1 + X^q Y_2) = 0$$

instead of Eq. (5), while the rest of the scheme remain the same. Namely we redesign the Ψ of ZHFE as

$$\Psi = X\bar{F}_1 + X^q \bar{F}_2.$$

instead of (1), and use $(\bar{F}_1, \bar{F}_2)$ as the core map instead of (F_1, F_2). With this simple change, the original time-consuming key generation of ZHFE now becomes almost immediate with very little computation, i.e., about $\log_q D$ $\mathbb{F}_q$-additions if $q > 2$, or $2\log_2 D$ $\mathbb{F}_2$-additions if $q = 2$. We remark that our new design may be regarded as equivalent to the original one. This is because that $(\bar{F}_1, \bar{F}_2)$ is a linear transformation of (F_1, F_2), and 'if this linear transformation is nonsingular, then (F_1, F_2) is also a linear combination of $(\bar{F}_1, \bar{F}_2)$. If one still wants to compute (F_1, F_2) then just compute the inverse of the linear transformation with complexity $O(n^\omega)$, better than the improvement $O(n^{2\omega+1})$ of [BCE+16].

One may concern if this change affects the security of ZHFE, but we claim that it does not. From the security analysis in the preceding section, we see that to attack ZHFE, one actually does not need to recover F_1, F_2 and the four linear maps L_{ij}, but only need $\bar{F}_1, \bar{F}_2$ which are sufficient to recover the secret Ψ. Namely the two maps F_1, F_2 and the four linear maps L_{ij} actually do not matter, and what matters is $\bar{F}_1, \bar{F}_2$. So the security analysis is not changed and thus our redesign of ZHFE does not change the security.

6   Conclusion

ZHFE is a new novel extension of the HFE encryption scheme and is designed to overcome the security weakness of HFE. There has been cryptanalysis of ZHFE and especially experimental evidence for its security, however a sound theoretical estimation of its security is still missing. We filled in this gap in this paper by providing such a theoretical estimation for the security of ZHFE. We achieved this goal by first computing for the Q-Rank of $ZHFE(q, n, D)$ an upper bound which is $\lfloor \log_q D \rfloor + 3$ if $q > 2$ and $\lfloor \log_2 D \rfloor + 4$ if $q = 2$. We then estimated the security level, in terms of $\mathbb{F}_q$ operations, of ZHFE against Bettale, et al.'s improved Kipnis-Shamir MinRank attack as $O(n^{(2\lfloor \log_q D \rfloor +8)\omega})$ for small $q > 2$, and $O(n^{(2\lfloor \log_2 D \rfloor +10)\omega})$ for $q = 2$, where $2 \leq \omega \leq 3$ depends on the Gaussian elimination algorithm chosen. For instance the security level of ZHFE(7,55,105) against this attack is estimated as at least 2^{138}. We further applied our upper bound on the Q-Rank to give an upper bound for the degree of regularity of ZHFE which is $\frac{(q-1)(\lfloor \log_q D \rfloor +3)}{2} + 2$ if $q > 2$ and $\frac{1}{2}\lfloor \log_2 D \rfloor + 4$ if $q = 2$. Consequently the security level of ZHFE(7,55,105) against the direct algebraic attack F_4 is estimated as at least 2^{96}. Therefore we conclude that ZHFE does increase the degree of regularity and Q-Rank of HFE and thus improve the security to have practical and secure parameters. The security estimation here may still be improved, and more refined analysis and experiment should be carried out in the future to have a more solid estimation.

Moreover we also provided a solution to improve the inefficient key generation of ZHFE. The original key generation of ZHFE is very time-consuming with complexity $O(n^{3\omega})$ and is later improved to $O(n^{2\omega+1})$ by Baena et al. However our solution requires very little computation, i.e., $O(\log_q D)$ $\mathbb{F}_q$-additions, and thus can generate the private key almost immediately.

Acknowledgment. The authors would like to thank the anonymous reviewers of PQCrypto'16 for their valuable comments on an early version of this paper, and the anonymous reviewers of IWSEC'16 for their helpful comments on this paper. The first author would like to thank the financial support from the National Natural Science Foundation of China (Grant No. 61572189).

References

[BCE+16] Baena, J.B., Cabarcas, D., Escudero, D.E., Porras-Barrera, J., Verbel, J.A.: Efficient ZHFE key generation. In: Takagi, T., et al. (eds.) PQCrypto 2016. LNCS, vol. 9606, pp. 213–232. Springer, Heidelberg (2016). doi:10.1007/978-3-319-29360-8_14

[BFP13] Bettale, L., Faugère, J.C., Perret, L.: Cryptanalysis of HFE, multi-HFE and variants for odd and even characteristic. Des. Codes Cryptogr. **69**(1), 1–52 (2013)

[CKPS00] Courtois, N.T., Klimov, A.B., Patarin, J., Shamir, A.: Efficient algorithms for solving overdefined systems of multivariate polynomial equations. In: Preneel, B. (ed.) EUROCRYPT 2000. LNCS, vol. 1807, p. 392. Springer, Heidelberg (2000)

[Cou01] Courtois, N.T.: The security of hidden field equations (HFE). In: Naccache, D. (ed.) CT-RSA 2001. LNCS, vol. 2020, p. 266. Springer, Heidelberg (2001)

[DG10] Dubois, V., Gama, N.: The degree of regularityof HFE systems. In: Abe, M. (ed.) ASIACRYPT 2010. LNCS, vol. 6477, pp. 557–576. Springer, Heidelberg (2010)

[DGS06] Ding, J., Gower, J.E., Schmidt, D.S.: Multivariate public key cryptosystems. In: Advances in Information Security, vol. 25. Springer (2006)

[DH11] Ding, J., Hodges, T.J.: Inverting HFE systems is quasi-polynomial for all fields. In: Rogaway, P. (ed.) CRYPTO 2011. LNCS, vol. 6841, pp. 724–742. Springer, Heidelberg (2011)

[DY13] Ding, J., Yang, B.-Y.: Degree of regularity for HFEv and HFEv-. In: Gaborit, P. (ed.) PQCrypto 2013. LNCS, vol. 7932, pp. 52–66. Springer, Heidelberg (2013)

[Fau99] Faugére, J.-C.: A new efficient algorithm for computing Gröbner bases (F_4). J. Pure Appl. Algebra **139**, 61–88 (1999)

[Fau02] Faugére, J.-C.: A new efficient algorithm for computing Gröbner bases without reduction to zero (F_5). In: ISSAC 2002 Proceedings of the International Symposium on Symbolic and Algebraic Computation, pp. 75–83. ACM, New York (2002)

[FJ03] Faugère, J.-C., Joux, A.: Algebraic cryptanalysis of hidden field equation (HFE) cryptosystems using Gröbner bases. In: Boneh, D. (ed.) CRYPTO 2003. LNCS, vol. 2729, pp. 44–60. Springer, Heidelberg (2003)

[GJ79] Garey, M.R., Johnson, D.S.: Computers and Intractability: A Guide to the Theory of NP-Completeness. Freeman, W. H (1979)

[GJS06] Granboulan, L., Joux, A., Stern, J.: Inverting HFE is quasipolynomial. In: Dwork, C. (ed.) CRYPTO 2006. LNCS, vol. 4117, pp. 345–356. Springer, Heidelberg (2006)

[KS99] Kipnis, A., Shamir, A.: Cryptanalysis of the HFE public key cryptosystem by relinearization. In: Wiener, M. (ed.) CRYPTO 1999. LNCS, vol. 1666, p. 19. Springer, Heidelberg (1999)

[Pat96] Patarin, J.: Hidden fields equations (HFE) and isomorphisms of polynomials (IP): two new families of asymmetric algorithms. In: Maurer, U.M. (ed.) EUROCRYPT 1996. LNCS, vol. 1070, pp. 33–48. Springer, Heidelberg (1996)

[PBD14a] Porras, J., Baena, J., Ding, J.: New candidates for multivariate trapdoor functions. Cryptology ePrint Archive, Report 2014/387 (2014). http://eprint.iacr.org/2014/387

[PBD14b] Porras, J., Baena, J., Ding, J.: ZHFE, a new multivariate public key encryption scheme. In: Mosca, M. (ed.) PQCrypto 2014. LNCS, vol. 8772, pp. 229–245. Springer, Heidelberg (2014)

[PCG01] Patarin, J., Courtois, N.T., Goubin, L.: QUARTZ, 128-bit long digital signatures. In: Naccache, D. (ed.) CT-RSA 2001. LNCS, vol. 2020, p. 282. Springer, Heidelberg (2001)

[PCY+15] Petzoldt, A., Chen, M.-S., Yang, B.-Y., Tao, C., Ding, J.: Design principles for HFEv- based multivariate signature schemes. In: Iwata, T., Cheon, J.H. (eds.) ASIACRYPT 2015. LNCS, vol. 9452, pp. 311–334. Springer, Heidelberg (2015). doi:10.1007/978-3-662-48797-6_14

[PST16] Perlner, R., Smith-Tone, D.: Security analysis and key modification for ZHFE. In: Takagi, T. (ed.) PQCrypto 2016. LNCS, vol. 9606, pp. 197–212. Springer, Heidelberg (2016). doi:10.1007/978-3-319-29360-8_13

[WP05] Wolf, C., Preneel, B.: Equivalent keys in HFE, C*, and variations. In: Dawson, E., Vaudenay, S. (eds.) Mycrypt 2005. LNCS, vol. 3715, pp. 33–49. Springer, Heidelberg (2005)

Cryptanalysis of a Public Key Cryptosystem Based on Diophantine Equations via Weighted LLL Reduction (Short Paper)

Jintai Ding[1], Momonari Kudo[2(✉)], Shinya Okumura[3(✉)], Tsuyoshi Takagi[4], and Chengdong Tao[5]

[1] University of Cincinnati, Cincinnati, USA
[2] Graduate School of Mathematics, Kyushu University, Fukuoka, Japan
m-kudo@math.kyushu-u.ac.jp
[3] Institute of Systems, Information Technologies and Nanotechnologies, Fukuoka, Japan
s-okumura@isit.or.jp
[4] Institute of Mathematics for Industry, Kyushu University, Fukuoka, Japan
[5] South China University of Technology, Guangzhou, China

Abstract. Okumura proposed a candidate of post-quantum cryptosystem based on Diophantine equations of degree increasing type (DEC). Sizes of public keys in DEC are small, e.g., 1,200 bits for 128 bit security, and it is a strongly desired property in post-quantum erea.

In this paper, we propose a polynomial time attack against DEC. We show that the one-wayness of DEC is reduced to finding special (relatively) short vectors in some lattices. The usual LLL algorithm does not work well for finding the most important target vector in our attack. The most technical point of our method is to heuristically find a special norm called a weighted norm to find the most important target vector. We call this method *"weighted LLL algorithm"* in this paper. Our experimental results suggest that our attack can break the one-wayness of DEC for 128 bit security with sufficiently high probability.

Keywords: Post-quantum cryptosystem · Weighted LLL reduction · Diophantine equation

1 Introduction

Post-quantum cryptography is now receiving a great amount of attention. Many candidates of post-quantum cryptosystems (PQC) have been proposed up to the

The full version [12] is available from IACR Cryptology ePrint Archive, 2015/1229.
S. Okumura—Research conducted while at Institute of Mathematics for Industry, Kyushu University.

K. Ogawa and K. Yoshioka (Eds.): IWSEC 2016, LNCS 9836, pp. 305–315, 2016.
DOI: 10.1007/978-3-319-44524-3_18

present, e.g., lattice-based cryptosystems, code-based cryptosystems and multi-variate public key cryptosystems (see [7,11]). However, these PQC require public keys of large sizes, and thus it is important task that we find computationally-hard problems for constructing PQC with public keys of small sizes.

The Diophantine problem is well-known to be a hard problem (see [13]) and has been expected to be used to construct PQC. (The Diophantine problem here means that given multivariate polynomials with integer coefficients, find common rational zeros of them.) In fact, a public key cryptosystem [20] and key exchange protocols [6,17,29] based on the difficulty of the Diophantine problem have been already proposed. However, the one-wayness of the cryptosystem [20] is broken [10], and the protocols [6,17,29] are said to be impractical [17, Proposition 2].

The Diophantine problem is generalized to problems over arbitrary rings. The Algebraic Surface Cryptosystem (ASC) [4] is based on the difficulty of the Diophantine problem over global function fields which is proved to be unsolvable in general [24,27]. In [4], it is analyzed that we may use public keys of sizes of about only 500 bits. However, the one-wayness of ASC is broken by the ideal decomposition attack [15].

Okumura [23] proposed a public key cryptosystem based on the difficulty of solving Diophantine equations of degree increasing type over $\mathbb{Z}$ (see Sect. 3 in this paper for the definition of a polynomial of degree increasing type). We refer to the cryptosystem as DEC for short. In [23, Remark 3.2], Okumura shows that Diophantine equations of degree increasing type are generally unsolvable. DEC is proposed as a number field analogue of ASC and a candidate of PQC. In DEC, a polynomial $X \in \mathbb{Z}[x_1, \ldots, x_n]$ of degree increasing type is used as a public key, and a vector $(a_1, \ldots, a_n) \in \mathbb{Z}^n$ satisfying $X(\frac{a_1}{d}, \ldots, \frac{a_n}{d}) = 0$ for some $d \in \mathbb{Z}$ is used as a secret key (see Sect. 3.2). The main ideas to avoid the analogues of all attacks [15,18,26,28] against ASC (and the previous versions [1–3] of ASC) are to twist a plaintext by using some modular arithmetic and to use some random polynomials with large coefficients in the encryption process. In [23, Sect. 4], it is analyzed that by the above ideas, the number of possible parameters increases, and thus finding the correct plaintext will become infeasible. In addition, the reason why polynomials of degree increasing type are adopted in DEC is to decode a plaintext uniquely even if the plaintext is twisted.

Another advantage of DEC is that sizes of public keys are small, e.g., about 1,200 bits with 128 bit security (see [12, Remark 3.5.1 (3)]), as desired in post-quantum cryptography. Note that well-known efficient candidates of PQC [21,22,25] require public keys whose sizes are about 10 times larger than 1,200 bits to achieve 128 bit security. Thus it is important to analyze the security of DEC.

Our Contribution

In this paper, we propose an attack against DEC. We show that the one-wayness of DEC is transformed to a problem of finding special relatively short vectors in lattices obtained from a public key and a ciphertext. Using three polynomials as a ciphertext allows us to construct linear systems. One can recover a plaintext by finding appropriate solutions of the linear systems, and thus this point is one of the weakness of DEC. Our attack can be divided roughly into three steps, and our experimental results in Sect. 5 show that the key point of our attack is whether a first step of our attack succeeds or not.

The lattice obtained in the first step of our attack has low rank, (e.g., 3-rank in many cases), and thus finding a target vector in the lattice seems to be performed by basis reduction such as the LLL algorithm [19]. However, in [12, Sect. 4.3], we show an example that the usual LLL algorithm fails in finding the target vector in the first step. Our heuristic analysis on the failure of the example is as follows: the target vector is not necessarily shortest in the lattice of low rank but only some entries are relatively small, i.e., the target vector is a relatively short vector with entries of unbalanced sizes.

In order to deal with such situations, we apply the *weighted LLL algorithm*, which is the LLL algorithm with respect to a special norm called *weighted norm* for some weight, to our attack. We find heuristically a new weighted norm so that the target vector becomes (nearly) shortest in some lattice of low rank with respect to this new norm (see Sect. 2 for weighted norms). Note that using other well-known norms in the LLL algorithm does not seem to be effective in finding the target vector (see [12, Sect. 4.3]). Our method can be also viewed as changing the scale of a lattice to carefully control the entries of a LLL reduced basis of the lattice. Such a method has been used in Coppersmith's method [9] (see also [16, Chap. 19]) and in [14]. In particular, we consider 2-power integers to define weighted norms and to use the knowledge of the bit length of entries of our target vector, such as [14] (it is possible to know the bit length of entries of our target vector, and this point is the second weakness of DEC).

Our experimental results in Sect. 5 show that one can find correct vectors in the first step with probability being about from 70 to 90 % for the recommended parameters in Sect. 3 via the weighted LLL algorithm. Moreover, experimental results also show that one can break the one-wayness of DEC with probability being about from 20 to 40 %. From this and complexity analysis on our attack (see [12, Sect. 5]), we infer that our attack can break DEC with sufficiently high probability in polynomial time for all practical parameters.

Notation. For a finite subset Λ of $\mathbb{Z}^n$ and a polynomial $f(x_1, \ldots, x_n) = f(\underline{x}) = \sum_{\underline{i} \in \Lambda} f_{\underline{i}} \underline{x}^{\underline{i}} \in \mathbb{Z}[\underline{x}]$ ($\underline{x}^{\underline{i}} := x_1^{i_1} \cdots x_n^{i_n}$ for $\underline{i} := (i_1, \ldots, i_n)$), we set $\Lambda_f := \{\underline{i} \in \Lambda \mid f_{\underline{i}} \neq 0\}$. We denote by w_f the total degree of f. For $\underline{i} \in \Lambda_f$, we write $c_{\underline{i}}(f)$ as the coefficient of the monomial $\underline{x}^{\underline{i}}$ in f. We set $H(f) := \max_{\underline{i} \in \Lambda_f} |c_{\underline{i}}(f)|$. We define $\mathbf{f} := \left(c_{\underline{i}_1}(f), \ldots, c_{\underline{i}_{\#\Lambda_f}}(f) \right)$ if we set Λ_f as $\{\underline{i}_1, \ldots, \underline{i}_{\#\Lambda_f}\}$.

2   Description of Weighted LLL Reduction

In this section, we define weighted norms and weighted lattices, and give the weighted LLL algorithm.

2.1 Definition of Weighted Lattice

The formal definitions of weighted norms and weighted lattices are as follows:

Definition 1. For $\mathbf{w} = (w_1, \ldots, w_m) \in (\mathbb{R}_{>0})^m$, we define the norm $\| \cdot \|_{\mathbf{w}}$ on $\mathbb{R}^m$ by $\|\mathbf{a}\|_{\mathbf{w}} := ((a_1 w_1)^2 + \cdots + (a_m w_m)^2)^{1/2}$ $(\mathbf{a} = (a_1, \ldots, a_m) \in \mathbb{R}^m)$. Then we call it the *weighted norm* for $\mathbf{w}$. We define a *weighted lattice* for $\mathbf{w}$ in $\mathbb{R}^m$ as a lattice endowed with the weighted norm for $\mathbf{w}$. For any lattice $\mathcal{L} \subset \mathbb{R}^m$ and $\mathbf{w} \in (\mathbb{R}_{>0})^m$, we denote $\mathcal{L}$ by $\mathcal{L}^{\mathbf{w}}$ if we consider $\mathcal{L}$ as a weighted lattice for $\mathbf{w}$.

Let $\mathcal{L} \subset \mathbb{R}^m$ be a lattice and $\mathbf{w} = (w_i)_{1 \leq i \leq m} \in (\mathbb{R}_{>0})^m$ a vector. We set W as the diagonal matrix whose (i,i)-entry coincides with w_i for each $1 \leq i \leq m$. We define the isomorphism $f_W : \mathbb{R}^m \to \mathbb{R}^m$ by $\mathbf{x} \mapsto \mathbf{x}W$. Then for any $\mathbf{x} \in \mathcal{L}^{\mathbf{w}}$, $\mathbf{x}$ is a shortest vector in $\mathcal{L}^{\mathbf{w}}$ if and only if $\mathbf{x}W$ is a shortest vector in $f_W(\mathcal{L})$ with respect to the Euclidean norm. This means that we can find a shortest vector in $\mathcal{L}^{\mathbf{w}}$ if we find a shortest vector in $f_W(\mathcal{L})$ with respect to the Euclidean norm.

2.2 Weighted LLL Reduction

We here define a weighted LLL reduced basis and give an algorithm to find it.

Definition 2. Let $\mathcal{L}$, W and f_W be as in Sect. 2.1. We call an ordered basis $\mathcal{B} = \{\mathbf{b}_1, \ldots, \mathbf{b}_n\}$ of the lattice $\mathcal{L}$ a *weighted LLL reduced basis* of $\mathcal{L}$ if $f_W(\mathcal{B}) = \{\mathbf{b}_1 W, \ldots, \mathbf{b}_n W\}$ is an LLL reduced basis of $f_W(\mathcal{L})$ with respect to the Euclidean norm.

Algorithm 1. *Input*: a vector $\mathbf{w} \in (\mathbb{R}_{>0})^m$ and a basis $\mathcal{B} = \{\mathbf{b}_1, \ldots, \mathbf{b}_n\}$ of a lattice $\mathcal{L} \subset \mathbb{R}^m$.
Output: a weighted LLL reduced basis $\mathcal{B}' = \{\mathbf{b}_1', \ldots, \mathbf{b}_n'\}$ of $\mathcal{L}$.

(1) Compute the basis $\{\mathbf{b}_1 W, \ldots, \mathbf{b}_n W\}$ of $f_W(\mathcal{L})$ (W and f_W are as above).
(2) Compute an LLL reduced basis $\mathcal{B}^{\mathbf{w}} = \{\mathbf{b}_1^{\mathbf{w}}, \ldots, \mathbf{b}_n^{\mathbf{w}}\}$ of $f_W(\mathcal{L})$ with respect to the Euclidean norm by using $\{\mathbf{b}_1 W, \ldots, \mathbf{b}_n W\}$.
(3) Compute $\mathbf{b}_i' := \mathbf{b}_i^{\mathbf{w}} W^{-1}$ $(1 \leq i \leq n)$, and return $\mathcal{B}' = \{\mathbf{b}_1', \ldots, \mathbf{b}_n'\}$.

In our cryptanalysis (Sect. 4), the most important vector is not necessarily a shortest vector in a lattice of low rank but only some entries are relatively small. In order to find such a vector, we use the weighted LLL algorithm which can carefully control the entries of a weighted LLL reduced basis.

3 Overview of DEC

In this section, we give a brief review of DEC (see [23, Sect. 3] for details). DEC has been expected to be one of candidates of post-quantum cryptosystems which has public keys of small sizes, e.g., about 1,200 bits (see [12, Remark 3.5.1(3)]) with 128 bit security. Note that 1,200 bits is about 10 times smaller than sizes of public keys of efficient candidates of PQC [21, 22, 25].

3.1   Polynomials of Degree Increasing Type

Polynomials of degree increasing type which play a central role in DEC.

Definition 3. *A polynomial $X(\underline{x}) \in \mathbb{Z}[\underline{x}] \smallsetminus \{0\}$ is of degree increasing type if a map $\Lambda_X \to \mathbb{Z}_{\geq 0}$; $(i_1, \ldots, i_n) \mapsto \sum_{k=1}^{n} i_k$ is injective.*

Let $X(\underline{x})$ be a polynomial in $\mathbb{Z}[\underline{x}] \smallsetminus \{0\}$. If X is of degree increasing type, then Λ_X is a totally ordered set by the following order $\succ$: for two elements $(i_1, \ldots, i_n)$ and $(j_1, \ldots, j_n)$ in Λ_X, we have $(i_1, \ldots, i_n) \succ (j_1, \ldots, j_n)$ if $i_1 + \cdots + i_n > j_1 + \cdots + j_n$. Throughout this paper, for a polynomial X of degree increasing type, we endow Λ_X with the total order described above.

Now, we describe only the Key Generation and the Encryption processes of DEC according to [23] since only these two processes are needed to describe our attack (for the decryption, see [23, Sect. 3.4]). Note that although in [23] the security parameter is not suggested, here let us set the security parameter λ.

3.2   Key Generation

Secret Key : A vector $\underline{a} := (a_1, \ldots, a_n) \in \mathbb{Z}^n$.
Public Key : (1) An integer d with $\gcd(a_i, d) = 1$ for all i.
   (2) An integer e with $\gcd(e, \varphi(d)) = 1$, where φ is the Euler function.
   (3) An irreducible polynomial $X \in \mathbb{Z}[\underline{x}]$ of degree increasing type with $X(a_1/d, \ldots, a_n/d) = 0$ and $\sharp \Lambda_X \leq w_X$.

For a choice of X and sizes of a_i, e, d and N $(1 \leq i \leq n)$, see [12, Sect. 3.5].

3.3   Encryption

Plaintext : A polynomial $m \in \mathbb{Z}[x_1, \ldots, x_n]$ with $\Lambda_m = \Lambda_X$, $1 < c_{i_1, \ldots, i_n}(m) < d$ and $\gcd(c_{i_1, \ldots, i_n}(m), d) = 1$ for all $(i_1, \ldots, i_n) \in \Lambda_m$.

Encryption Process:

(1) Choose a random integer $N \in \mathbb{Z}_{>0}$ uniformly such that $Nd > 2^\lambda H(X)$. For an upper bound of N, see [12, Sect. 3.5].
(2) Construct the twisted plaintext $\tilde{m}(\underline{x}) \in \mathbb{Z}[\underline{x}]$ by putting $\Lambda_{\tilde{m}} := \Lambda_m$ and $c_{\underline{i}}(\tilde{m}) := c_{\underline{i}}(m)^e \pmod{Nd}$ $(0 < c_{\underline{i}}(\tilde{m}) < Nd, \underline{i} \in \Lambda_{\tilde{m}})$.
(3) Choose a random $f(\underline{x}) \in \mathbb{Z}[\underline{x}]$ uniformly such that $\Lambda_f = \Lambda_X$ and $H(\tilde{m}) < c_{\underline{k}}(f) < Nd$ and $\gcd(c_{\underline{k}}(f), d) = 1$, where $\underline{k}$ is the maximal element in Λ_f.
(4) Choose random polynomials $s_j(\underline{x}), r_j(\underline{x}) \in \mathbb{Z}[\underline{x}]$ uniformly with $\Lambda_X = \Lambda_{s_j} = \Lambda_{r_j}$ for $1 \leq j \leq 3$ so that $|c_{\underline{i}}(s_j)|$ and $|c_{\underline{i}}(r_j)|$ have the same bit length as $|c_{\underline{i}}(X)|$ and $|c_{\underline{i}}(f)|$ for each $\underline{i} \in \Lambda_X$, respectively.
(5) Put cipher polynomials $F_1(\underline{x})$, $F_2(\underline{x})$ and $F_3(\underline{x})$ as follows:

$$F_j(\underline{x}) := \tilde{m}(\underline{x}) + s_j(\underline{x})f(\underline{x}) + r_j(\underline{x})X(\underline{x}) \quad (1 \leq j \leq 3).$$

Finally, send $(F_1(\underline{x}), F_2(\underline{x}), F_3(\underline{x}), N)$.

4   Attack Against DEC via Weighted LLL Reduction

In this section, we present an attack against DEC. Main ideas of our attack are the following: (1) Reduce the one-wayness of DEC to finding some appropriate vectors by linearization technique. (2) Find the most important vector for our attack by Algorithm 1 described in Sect. 2.2.

4.1   Algorithm of Our Attack

In this subsection, we write down an algorithm of our attack against DEC (see [12, Sect. 4, Sect. 5] for a more detailed description and complexity analysis of our algorithm below).

Recall from Sects. 3.2 and 3.3 that a public key and a ciphertext are $(d, e, X) \in \mathbb{Z}^2 \times (\mathbb{Z}[\underline{x}])$ and $(F_1, F_2, F_3, N) \in (\mathbb{Z}[\underline{x}])^3 \times \mathbb{Z}$, respectively. Let $m \in \mathbb{Z}[\underline{x}]$ be a plaintext. Note that $F_j = \tilde{m} + s_j f + r_j X$ for $1 \leq j \leq 3$, where $\tilde{m}$, f, s_j and r_j are the twisted plaintext and random polynomials chosen uniformly according to Sect. 3.3, respectively. We fix $\Lambda_X = \{\underline{i}_1, \ldots, \underline{i}_q\}$ with $\underline{i}_1 \succ \cdots \succ \underline{i}_q$, where the total order $\succ$ on Λ_X is given in Sect. 3.1. Let $\underline{k}$ be the maximal element in Λ_X. Note that it is sufficient for recovering the plaintext m to recover $\tilde{m}$, and that $\Lambda_X = \Lambda_m = \Lambda_{\tilde{m}} = \Lambda_f = \Lambda_{s_j} = \Lambda_{r_j}$ for $1 \leq j \leq 3$. This condition allows us to assume $\Lambda_{F_1} = \Lambda_{F_2} = \Lambda_{F_3}$. The algorithm of our attack is as follows:

Algorithm 2. *Input*: a public key (d, e, X) and a ciphertext (F_1, F_2, F_3, N). *Output*: a twisted plaintext $\tilde{m}$.

> *Step 1*: Determination of $s'_j := s_j - s_{j+1}$ for $j = 1$ and 2
>> *Step 1-1*: Put $F'_j := F_j - F_{j+1}$, $r'_j := r_j - r_{j+1}$ and $g := s'_2 r'_1 - s'_1 r'_2$ for $j = 1$ and 2. Solve the linear system obtained by comparing the coefficients of the equality $s'_2 F'_1 - s'_1 F'_2 = gX$. Let $\mathcal{L}'_1$ be the nullspace and $\{\mathbf{u}'_1, \mathbf{u}'_2, \mathbf{u}'_3\}$[1] a lattice basis of $\mathcal{L}'_1$.
>> *Step 1-2*: Let $\mathbf{u}_i$ be the vector consisting of the 1-$(2\sharp\Lambda_X)$-th entries of $\mathbf{u}'_i$ for $1 \leq i \leq 3$. Let $H(X) := \max_{1 \leq j \leq q} |c_{\underline{i}_j}(X)|$, where $c_{\underline{i}_j}(X)$ is the non-zero coefficient of X for each $\underline{i}_j \in \Lambda_X$ (see Sect. 3.1). Put $w'_j = 2^{\left\lfloor \log_2 \left(\frac{H(X)}{c_{\underline{i}_j}(X)} \right) \right\rfloor}$ for $1 \leq j \leq q$. We then set $\mathbf{w} := (w'_1, \ldots, w'_q, w'_1, \ldots, w'_q)$. Execute Algorithm 1 for the weight $\mathbf{w}$ to the lattice $\mathcal{L}_1 := \langle \mathbf{u}_1, \mathbf{u}_2, \mathbf{u}_3 \rangle_\mathbb{Z}$, and then obtain $\mathbf{s}'_1$ and $\mathbf{s}'_2$.
> *Step 2*: Fixing of a candidate of f
>> *Step 2-1*: Solve the linear system $\mathbf{v}B = \mathbf{b}$ obtained by comparing the coefficients of the equalities $F'_j = s'_j f + r'_j X$ for $j = 1$ and 2, where B is a $(3\sharp\Lambda_X \times \sharp\Lambda_{X^2})$-matrix. Let $\mathbf{v}_0$ be a solution of $\mathbf{v}B = \mathbf{b}$, $\mathcal{L}_2$ the nullspace of $\mathcal{L}_2$ and $\{\mathbf{v}_1\}$ a lattice basis of $\mathcal{L}_2$. Note that if $\gcd(X, s'_1) = 1$, then the rank of $\mathcal{L}_2$ is always equal to 1, see [12, Remark 4.1.4].

---

[1] We may assume rank $(\mathcal{L}'_1) = $ rank $(\mathcal{L}_3) = 3$ (see [12, Remark 6.0.1]).

Step 2-2: Let $\mathbf{v}'_0 := \mathbf{v}_0 - \lfloor \langle \mathbf{v}_0, \mathbf{v}_1 \rangle / \langle \mathbf{v}_1, \mathbf{v}_1 \rangle \rceil \mathbf{v}_1$ be the other solution of $\mathbf{v}B = \mathbf{b}$. Let $\mathbf{v}''_0$ be the vector consisting of the 1-($\sharp \Lambda_X$)-th entries of $\mathbf{v}'_0$. Construct $f' \in \mathbb{Z}[\underline{x}]$ so that $\mathbf{f}' = \mathbf{v}''_0$, where recall that $\mathbf{f}' := (c_{\underline{i}_1}(f), \ldots, c_{\underline{i}_q}(f))$. Experimentally $\mathbf{v}'_0$ provides the polynomial closer to the correct f than $\mathbf{v}_0$ in many cases.

Step 3: Recovery of $\tilde{m}$

Step 3-1: Solve the linear system $\mathbf{w}C = \mathbf{c}$ obtained by comparing the coefficients of the equality $F_1 = \tilde{m} + s_1 f' + r_1 X$, where C is a $(3\sharp \Lambda_X \times \sharp \Lambda_{X^2})$-matrix. Let $\mathbf{w}_0$ be a solution of $\mathbf{w}C = \mathbf{c}$, $\mathcal{L}_3$ the nullspace of C and $\{\mathbf{w}_1, \mathbf{w}_2, \mathbf{w}_3\}^6$ a lattice basis of $\mathcal{L}_3$, where we take $\mathbf{w}_3$ so that its 1-$\sharp \Lambda_X$-th entries are equal to 0, see [12, Remark 4.1.4].

Step 3-2: Execute Babai's nearest plane algorithm [5] to find a closest vector $\mathbf{z}$ in the lattice $\mathcal{L}'_3 := \langle \mathbf{w}_1, \mathbf{w}_2 \rangle_{\mathbb{Z}}$ to $\mathbf{w}_0 + \mathbf{w}_3$ (see [12, Remark 4.1.7] for the reason of using Babai's nearest plane algorithm). Obtain $\mathbf{s}_1$ as the vector consisting of the $(\sharp \Lambda_X + 1)$-2$\sharp \Lambda_X$-th entries of $\mathbf{w}_0 + \mathbf{w}_3 - \mathbf{z}$.

Step 3-3: Solve the linear system $\mathbf{x}H = \mathbf{h}$ obtained by comparing the coefficients of the equality $F_1 - \tilde{m} - s_1 f' = rX$, where the coefficients of $\tilde{m}$ and r are variables and H is a $(2\sharp \Lambda_X \times \sharp \Lambda_{X^2})$-matrix. Let $\mathbf{x}$ be a solution of $\mathbf{x}H = \mathbf{h}$. Let $\mathbf{r}'$ be the vector consisting of the entries corresponding to r of $\mathbf{x}$. Then we obtain a polynomial r' whose coefficients coincide with those of r except the constant part, i.e., $r = r' + t$ for some $t \in \mathbb{Z}$. We can compute t by using modular arithmetic and the fact that the coefficient $c_{\underline{k}}$ of X is divisible by d. Finally output $\tilde{m}$.

Remark 1. It may be effective to use Babai's nearest plane algorithm with respect to a weighted norm and to search a desired vector $\mathbf{s}_1$ by adding some vectors in $\mathcal{L}'_3$. However, we will see in Sect. 5, our attack can break the one-wayness of DEC with sufficiently high probability. Thus we omit these processes.

5   Experimental Results on Our Attack

We show some pieces of experimental results[2] on our attack described in Sect. 4 against DEC for $n = 4$, i.e., the number of variables of a public key X is is equal to 4 (see [12, Table 1] for complete experimental results). We conducted experiments for parameters recommended in [12, Remark 3.5.1] which can let the DEC have 128 bit security.

Experimental Procedure

Given parameters w_X and $\sharp \Lambda_X$, we repeat the following procedure 100 times:

1. Make a secret key and a public key (see Sect. 3.2).
2. Using the public key constructed above, make a ciphertext (see Sect. 3.3).
3. Execute Algorithm 2 for the above public key and the ciphertext.

---

[2] We use a standard note PC with 2.60 GHz CPU (Intel Corei5), 16 GB memory and Mac OS X 64 bit. We implemented the attack in Magma V2.21-3 [8].

In the second step above, we construct a public key X such that $2^{99} \leq |c_{\underline{i}}(X)| < 2^{100}$ for all $\underline{i} \in \Lambda_X \setminus \{\underline{k}, \underline{0}\}$, where $\underline{k}$ is the maximal element in Λ_X with respect to the order described in Sect. 3.1. In order to show the effect of the weighted LLL algorithm on our cryptanalysis, we also execute another version of Algorithm 2. (The other version of Algorithm 2 here means that the usual LLL algorithm is adopted in Step 1-2 of Algorithm 2 instead of the weighted LLL algorithm.) We count the number of successes and time if $\tilde{m}$ or $-\tilde{m}$ are recovered.

Table 1 shows our experimental results. In Step 1 of Table 1, we show the number of successes only if we succeed in recovering the target vector $(\mathbf{s}'_1, \mathbf{s}'_2)$ or $-(\mathbf{s}'_1, \mathbf{s}'_2)$ (see Step 1 of Algorithm 2 in Sect. 4.1). In Step 3 of Table 1, we show the number of successes only if a twisted plaintext $\tilde{m}$ or $-\tilde{m}$ is recovered.

From Step 1 in Table 1, we see that the weighted LLL algorithm found the target vector in Step 1 with probability being about from 70 to 90%, while the usual LLL algorithm could not find the target vector at all. From Step 3 in Table 1, we see that our attack with the weighted LLL algorithm could recover $\tilde{m}$ or $-\tilde{m}$ with probability being about from 20 to 40%, while another attack with the usual LLL algorithm could not recover $\tilde{m}$ or $-\tilde{m}$ at all. Thus we consider that using the weighted LLL algorithm plays a central role of our attack, and that the success probability of Step 3, that is the success probability of our attack, with the weighted LLL algorithm is sufficiently high for practical cryptanalysis.

Table 1. Experimental results on Algorithm 2 in Sect. 4.1 against DEC with four variables of 128 bit security. We did experiments according to Experimental Procedure described in the beginning of Sect. 5. "Ave. Time" means the average of time for performing our attack. (We show the timing data in successful cases.)

Recommended parameters for DEC ([12, Remark 3.5.1])			Experimental results						
Total degree of a public key X	Number of monomials of X	The maximum sizes of the coefficients of X except its constant and maximal terms	Number of successes of Attack Algorithm / 100						
			Method for lattice reduction in Step 1						
			Usual LLL			Weighted LLL			
			Step 1	Step 3	Ave. Time	Step 1	Step 3	Ave. Time	
10	3	100	0	0	-	75	29	0.02s	
10	4	100	0	0	-	78	26	0.03s	
10	5	100	0	0	-	80	36	0.04s	
10	6	100	0	0	-	83	31	0.07s	
10	7	100	0	0	-	82	34	0.08s	
10	8	100	0	0	-	95	40	0.11s	
10	9	100	0	0	-	87	36	0.20s	
10	10	100	0	0	-	91	38	0.27s	

From the viewpoint of the efficiency of the key generation, encryption and decryption of DEC, the parameters in Table 1 are practical (see also Tables 4, 5 and 6 in Sect. 6 of [23]). These experimental results suggest that our attack with the weighted LLL algorithm can break the one-wayness of DEC efficiently for practical parameters with sufficiently high probability.

6 Conclusion

In this paper, we proposed an attack against the one-wayness of the public key cryptosystem based on Diophantine equations of degree increasing type (DEC). It is showed in this paper that the one-wayness of DEC can be transformed to the problem of finding certain relatively shorter vectors in lattices of low ranks obtained by linearization techniques. Our most important target vector is not necessarily shortest in a lattice of low rank but only some entries are relatively small. The usual LLL algorithm with respect to well-known norms does not seem to work well for finding such vectors in our attack.

The most technical point of our attack is to change the norm in the LLL algorithm from the Euclidean norm to a weighted norm which is not widely used in cryptography yet. Our heuristic analysis suggests that the most important target vector becomes a (nearly) shortest vector with respect to a weighted norm for some weight chosen appropriately. Moreover, the most important target vector is a vector in a lattice of 3-rank in many cases. Therefore, the weighted LLL algorithm, which is the LLL algorithm with respect to the weighted norm, is applied to our attack. From experimental results on our attack, we proved that by choosing an appropriate weight, our attack with the weighted LLL algorithm can break the one-wayness of DEC with sufficiently high probability for all practical parameters under some assumptions.

Acknowledgements. The authors thank anonymous referees for careful reading our manuscript and for giving helpful comments. The authors also thank Steven Galbraith, Masaya Yasuda and Shun'ichi Yokoyama for helpful comments. This work was supported by CREST, JST.

References

1. Akiyama, K., Goto, Y.: An algebraic surface public-key cryptosystem. IEICE Tech. Rep. **104**(421), 13–20 (2004)
2. Akiyama, K., Goto, Y.: A public-key cryptosystem using algebraic surfaces. In: Proceedings of PQCrypto, pp. 119–138 (2006). http://postquantum.cr.yp.to/
3. Akiyama, K., Goto, Y.: An improvement of the algebraic surface public-key cryptosystem. In: Proceedings of 2008 Symposium on Cryptography and Information Security, SCIS 2008, CD-ROM, 1F1-2 (2008)
4. Akiyama, K., Goto, Y., Miyake, H.: An algebraic surface cryptosystem. In: Jarecki, S., Tsudik, G. (eds.) PKC 2009. LNCS, vol. 5443, pp. 425–442. Springer, Heidelberg (2009)
5. Babai, L.: On Lovász' lattice reduction and the nearest lattice point problem. Combinatorica **6**(1), 1–13 (1986). (Preliminary version in STACS 1985)

6. Bérczes, A., Hajdu, L., Hirata-Kohno, N., Kovács, T., Pethö, A.: A key exchange protocol based on Diophantine equations and S-integers. JSIAM Lett. **6**, 85–88 (2014)
7. Bernstein, D.J., Buchmann, J., Dahmen, E. (eds.): Post-Quantum Cryptography. Springer, Heidelberg (2009)
8. Bosma, W., Cannon, J., Playoust, C.: The Magma algebra system. I. The user language. J. Symbol. Comput. **24**(3–4), 235–265 (1997)
9. Coppersmith, D.: Small solutions to polynomial equations, and low exponent RSA vulnerabilities. J. Cryptology **10**(4), 233–260 (1997). Springer
10. Cusick, T.W.: Cryptoanalysis of a public key system based on Diophantine equations. Inf. Process. Lett. **56**(2), 73–75 (1995)
11. Ding, J., Gower, J.E., Schmidt, D.S.: Multivariate Public Key Cryptosystems. Advances in Information Security, vol. 25. Springer, US (2006)
12. Ding, J., Kudo, M., Okumura, S., Takagi, T., Tao, C.: Cryptanalysis of a public key cryptosystem based on Diophantine equations via weighted LLL reduction, IACR Cryptology ePrint Archive, 2015/1229 (2015)
13. Davis, M., Matijasevič, Y., Robinson, J.: Hilbert's tenth problem, Diophantine equations: positive aspects of a negative solution. In: Mathematical Developments Arising from Hilbert Problems, pp. 323–378. American Mathematical Society, Providence (1976)
14. Faugère, J.-C., Goyet, C., Renault, G.: Attacking (EC)DSA given only an implicit hint. In: Knudsen, L.R., Wu, H. (eds.) SAC 2012. LNCS, vol. 7707, pp. 252–274. Springer, Heidelberg (2013)
15. Faugère, J.-C., Spaenlehauer, P.-J.: Algebraic cryptanalysis of the PKC'2009 algebraic surface cryptosystem. In: Nguyen, P.Q., Pointcheval, D. (eds.) PKC 2010. LNCS, vol. 6056, pp. 35–52. Springer, Heidelberg (2010)
16. Galbraith, S.D.: Mathematics of Public Key Cryptography. Cambridge University Press, Cambridge (2012)
17. Hirata-Kohno, N., Pethö, A.: On a key exchange protocol based on Diophantine equations. Infocommun. J. **5**(3), 17–21 (2013). Scientific Association for Infocommunications (HTE)
18. Iwami, M.: A reduction attack on algebraic surface public-key cryptosystems. In: Kapur, D. (ed.) ASCM 2007. LNCS (LNAI), vol. 5081, pp. 323–332. Springer, Heidelberg (2008)
19. Lenstra, A.K., Lenstra, H.W., Lovász, L.: Factoring polynomials with rational coefficients. Math. Ann. **261**(4), 515–534 (1982). Springer
20. Lin, C.H., Chang, C.C., Lee, R.C.T.: A new public-key cipher system based upon the diophantine equations. IEEE Trans. Comput. **44**(1), 13–19 (1995). IEEE Computer Society Washington, DC, USA
21. Lyubashevsky, V., Peikert, C., Regev, O.: On ideal lattices and learning with errors over rings. In: Gilbert, H. (ed.) EUROCRYPT 2010. LNCS, vol. 6110, pp. 1–23. Springer, Heidelberg (2010)
22. Misoczki, R., Tillich, J.P., Sendrier, N., Barreto, P.S.L.M.: MDPC-McEliece: new McEliece variants from moderate density parity-check codes. In: Proceedings of the IEEE International Symposium on Information Theory (2013)
23. Okumura, S.: A public key cryptosystem based on diophantine equations of degree increasing type. Pac. J. Math. Ind. **7**(4), 33–45 (2015). Springer, Heidelberg
24. Pheidas, T.: Hilbert's Tenth Problem for fields of rational functions over finite fields. Inventiones Math. **103**(1), 1–8 (1991). Springer

25. Tao, C., Diene, A., Tang, S., Ding, J.: Simple matrix scheme for encryption. In: Gaborit, P. (ed.) PQCrypto 2013. LNCS, vol. 7932, pp. 231–242. Springer, Heidelberg (2013)
26. Uchiyama, S., Tokunaga, H.: On the security of the algebraic surface public-key cryptosystems (in Japanese). In: Proceedings of 2007 Symposium on Cryptography and Information Security, SCIS 2007, CD-ROM, 2C1-2 (2007)
27. Videla, C.R.: Hilbert's Tenth Problem for rational function fields in characteristic 2. Proc. Am. Math. Soc. **120**(1), 249–253 (1994). American Mathematical Society
28. Voloch, F.: Breaking the Akiyama-Goto cryptosystem. In: Contemporary Mathematics, Arithmetic, Geometry, Cryptography and Coding Theory, vol. 487, pp. 113–118. American Mathematical Society, Providence (2007)
29. Yosh, H.: The key exchange cryptosystem used with higher order Diophantine equations. Int. J. Netw. Secur. Appl. J. **3**(2), 43–50 (2011)

Paring Computation

Faster Explicit Formulae for Computing Pairings via Elliptic Nets and Their Parallel Computation

Hiroshi Onuki[1]($\boxtimes$), Tadanori Teruya[2], Naoki Kanayama[3],
and Shigenori Uchiyama[1]

[1] Tokyo Metropolitan University, 1-1, Minami-Ohsawa, Hachioji,
Tokyo 192-0372, Japan
onuki-hiroshi@ed.tmu.ac.jp, uchiyama-shigenori@tmu.ac.jp
[2] National Institute of Advanced Industrial Science and Technology,
2-4-7 Aomi, Koto-ku, Tokyo 135-0064, Japan
tadanori.teruya@aist.go.jp
[3] University of Tsukuba, 1-1-1 Tennodai, Tsukuba, Ibaraki 305-8573, Japan
kanayama@risk.tsukuba.ac.jp

Abstract. In this paper, we discuss computations of optimal pairings over some pairing-friendly curves and a symmetric pairing over supersingular curves via elliptic nets. We show that optimal pairings can be computed more efficiently if we use twists of elliptic curves and give formulae for computing optimal pairings via elliptic nets of these twist curves. Furthermore, we propose parallel algorithms for these pairings and estimate the costs of these algorithms in certain reasonable assumptions.

Keywords: Optimal pairing · Symmetric pairing · Tate pairing · Elliptic net · Parallel computation

1 Introduction

Recently, Miller's algorithm [4] has been widely used for computing pairings. In 2007, Stange [8] defined elliptic nets and proposed an alternative method for computing pairings based on them. In 2011, Ogura et al. [5] gave formulae for computing variants of the Tate pairing.

In recent years, multi-core processors have become widely available, so parallel algorithms have become important. Parallel pairing computation algorithms have been proposed. Aranha et al. [1] and Onuki et al. [6] proposed parallel algorithms based on the Miller's algorithm and elliptic nets, respectively.

In [6], Onuki et al. focused on the optimal pairing over Barreto-Naehrig (BN) curves [2]. They proposed a parallel algorithm for computing this pairing using an elliptic net and showed that this is expected to be computed more efficiently when one uses a twist of a BN curve.

In this paper, we generalize the method proposed by Onuki et al. [6] to optimal pairings over other curves and a symmetric pairing over supersingular curves over finite prime fields. We give explicit conditions on elliptic curves for applying

© Springer International Publishing Switzerland 2016
K. Ogawa and K. Yoshioka (Eds.): IWSEC 2016, LNCS 9836, pp. 319–334, 2016.
DOI: 10.1007/978-3-319-44524-3_19

our method for optimal pairings. For the curves that satisfy these conditions, we give formulae for computing optimal pairings via elliptic nets of these twist curves and propose parallel algorithms for these pairings. Furthermore, we show that our method for optimal pairings can be applied for a symmetric pairing over supersingular curves over finite prime fields.

The remainder of this paper is organized as follows: Sect. 2 recalls the necessary background on pairings, twists of elliptic curves and elliptic nets. Section 3 gives the conditions in which our method can be applied and explains it using twists of elliptic curves. In Sect. 4, we propose a technique that reduces the cost for computing elliptic nets. Section 5 describes our parallel algorithms and their performance analysis. Finally, Sect. 6 concludes the paper.

2   Preliminaries

2.1   Basic Facts

First, we recall the definition of the embedding degree and its basic properties.

Definition 1. *Let q be a prime power, r an integer prime to q. Then the smallest positive integer k that satisfies $r \mid q^k - 1$ is called the **embedding degree** of r with respect to q.*

In other words, the embedding degree is the smallest integer k such that $\mathbb{F}_{q^k}$ contains the set of roots of unity μ_r.

Lemma 1 ([7, **Corollary III.8.1.1.**]). *Let E be an elliptic curve defined over a field K and $m \in \mathbb{N}$. Then*

$$E[m] \subseteq E(K) \Rightarrow \mu_m \subseteq K.$$

Proposition 1 ([10, **Proposition 5.5**]). *Let E be an ellitpic curve define over a finite field $\mathbb{F}q$, r a prime which is prime to q and k the embedding degree of r with respect to q. If $r \mid \#E(\mathbb{F}q)$ and $k > 1$ then k is the smallest integer such that $E[r] \subseteq E(\mathbb{F}_{q^k})$.*

2.2   Pairings

Tate Pairing

Theorem 1 ([10, **Theorem 11.8**]). *Let E be an elliptic curve defined over a finite field $\mathbb{F}q$ and n an integer such that $n \mid q-1$. Then there are non-degenerate bilinear pairings:*

$$\langle \cdot \, , \, \cdot \rangle_n : E(\mathbb{F}q)[n] \times E(\mathbb{F}q)/nE(\mathbb{F}q) \rightarrow \mathbb{F}q^*/\mathbb{F}q^{*n},$$

$$\tau_n : E(\mathbb{F}q)[n] \times E(\mathbb{F}q)/nE(\mathbb{F}q) \rightarrow \mu_n,$$

where for $P \in E(\mathbb{F}q)[n]$, $Q \in E(\mathbb{F}q)$,

$$\tau_n(P, Q \bmod nE(\mathbb{F}q)) = \langle P, Q \bmod nE(\mathbb{F}q) \rangle_n^{\frac{q-1}{n}}.$$

Definition 2. *We call* $\langle \cdot, \cdot \rangle_n$ *of Theorem 1 the* **Tate pairing** *and* τ_n *the* **reduced Tate pairing**.

We denote $\langle P, Q \bmod nE(\mathbb{F}q) \rangle_n$ and $\tau_n(P, Q \bmod nE(\mathbb{F}q))$ by $\langle P, Q \rangle_n$ and $\tau_n(P, Q)$, respectively.

It is known that one can represent the Tate pairing in the Miller function [4] $f_{n,P}$.

Theorem 2 ([10, **Proof of Theorem 11.3**]). *Let E be an elliptic curve defined over a finite field $\mathbb{F}q$, n an integer such that $n \mid q - 1$ and π the q-th power Frobenius map on E. For $P \in E(\mathbb{F}q)[n], Q \in E(\mathbb{F}q)/nE(\mathbb{F}q)$, let D be a divisor of degree 0 such that $\mathrm{sum}(D) = Q$ and $P, O \notin \mathrm{supp}(D)$. Then*

$$\langle P, Q \rangle_n = f_{n,P}(D) \bmod \mathbb{F}q^{*n}, \tag{1}$$

$$\tau_n(P, Q) = f_{n,P}(D)^{\frac{q-1}{n}}. \tag{2}$$

If the Miller function is normalized in an appropriate uniformazer, the Tate pairing can be represented more simply.

Proposition 2. *In Theorem 2, Assume that $P \neq Q$ and the Miller function $f_{n,P}$ is normalized at O in a uniformizer u_O such that $u_O(Q) \neq 0, \infty$. Then*

$$\langle P, Q \rangle_n = f_{n,P}(Q) \bmod \mathbb{F}q^{*n}. \tag{3}$$

Optimal Pairings. The remainder of this subsection, let E be an elliptic curve over a finite field $\mathbb{F}q$, π the q-th power Frobenius map on E, r a prime that is prime to q and that divide $\#E(\mathbb{F}q)$, and k an embedding degree of r with respect to q. And we assume $k \geq 2$. Then, from Proposition 1, $E[r] \subseteq E(\mathbb{F}_{q^k})$ and it is well-known that as a linear map on $E[r]$, eigenvalues of π are 1 and q. We define $G_1 = E[r] \cap \ker(\pi - [1])$ and $G_2 = E[r] \cap \ker(\pi - [q])$.

Let f be the Miller function. And we assume these are normalized at O in a uniformizer which does not have zero or pole at points in G_1 except O.

Theorem 3 ([9]). $\lambda = mr$ with $r \nmid m$ and write $\lambda = \sum_{i=0}^{l} c_i q^i$ then

$$a_{[c_0,...,c_l]} : G_2 \times G_1 \to \mu_r, \ (Q, P) \mapsto \left(\prod_{i=0}^{l} f_{c_i, Q}(P)^{q^i} \prod_{i=0}^{l-1} g_{[s_i]Q, [c_i q^i]Q}(P) \right)^{\frac{q^k - 1}{r}}$$

with $s_i = \sum_{j=i}^{l} c_j q^j$, defines a bilinear pairing. Furthermore, if

$$mkq^{k-1} \not\equiv ((q^k - 1)/r) \sum_{i=0}^{l} i c_i q^{i-1} \bmod r.$$

then the pairing is non-degenerate.

In the above theorem, the pairing is called optimal if it is non-degenerate and $\max_i \{\log_2 c_i\} \leq \frac{\log_2 r}{\varphi(k)} + \log_2 k$, where φ is Euler's totient function.

Symmetric Pairing over Supersingular Curve. Let $\mathbb{F}p$ be a finite prime field of characteristic not 2 or 3, r a prime such that $r \mid \#E(\mathbb{F}p)$ and $r^2 \nmid \#E(\mathbb{F}p)$ and δ a distorsion map on $E[r]$. Then it is well-known that the symmetric paring e_r on $E(\mathbb{F}p)[r]$ defined in the following is non-degenerate:

$$e_r(P, Q) = \tau_r(P, \delta(Q)).$$

2.3   Twist

Definition 3. *Let E be an elliptic curve define over a field K. A **twist** of E is an elliptic curve E' isomorphic to E over $\bar{K}$. The set of twists of E, modulo K-isomorphism, is denoted **Twist**(E/K).*

Definition 4. *Let E be an elliptic curve over a field K and E' a twist of E. The **degree of a twist** E' is $\min\{[L : K] \mid$ there is an isomorphism $: E' \to E$ defined over $L\}$.*

Twist(E/K) has a group structure (see [7, X.2].) and satisfies the following proposition.

Proposition 3 ([7, **Proposition X.5.4**]). *Let K be a field of characteristic not 2 or 3, and E an elliptic curve over K. Then Twist(E/K) is canonically isomorphic to K^*/K^{*n}, where $n = 2$ if $j(E) \neq 0, 1728$, $n = 4$ if $j(E) = 1728$, and $n = 6$ if $j(E) = 0$.*

It is known that there exits the twist E' of $E/\mathbb{F}q$ such that a point of the q-eigenspace G_2 corresponds a point in E' whose coordinate is in a smaller field.

Theorem 4 ([3]). *Let E be an ellitic curver over $\mathbb{F}q$, r a prime which is prime to q and dividing $\#E(\mathbb{F}q)$ and k the embedding degree of r with respect to q. Let n be defined in Proposition 3, $d' = \gcd(q - 1, n)$, $d = \gcd(k, d')$ and $e = k/d$. Assume $k > 2$.*

Then $E/\mathbb{F}q^e$ has the twist E' of degree d such that

- $r \mid \#E'(\mathbb{F}q^e)$.
- $\phi(E'(\mathbb{F}q^e) \cap E'[r]) = E[r] \cap \ker(\pi - [q])$, *where ϕ is the isomorphism $: E' \to E$ and π is the q-th power Frobenius map on E.*

Furthermore E' is unique up to $\mathbb{F}q^e$-isomorphism.

2.4   Elliptic Net

In this subsection, we recall the definition of elliptic nets by Stange [8], representations of pairing via elliptic nets by [5, 8] and how to compute elliptic nets.

Definition 5. *Let A be a finitely generated free abelian group, R integral domain. an* **elliptic net** *is a map $W : A \to R$ satisfying the following recurrence relation for $p, q, r, s \in A$:*

$$W(p + q + s)W(p - q)W(r + s)W(r)$$
$$+W(q + r + s)W(q - r)W(p + s)W(p)$$
$$+W(r + p + s)W(r - q)W(q + s)W(q) = 0. \qquad (4)$$

Stange constructed an elliptic net associated to an elliptic curve E over K which is a subfield of $\mathbb{C}$ or a finite field and $P_1, \ldots, P_n$ which are points of E with $P_i \neq O$ for all i and $P_i \neq \pm P_j$ for all $i \neq j$. This elliptic net is a map $\mathbb{Z}^n \to K(P_1, \ldots, P_n)$, where $K(P_1, \ldots, P_n)$ is the field generated by adjoining the coordinates of $P_1, \ldots, P_n$ to K. For the details of the construction, see [8]. We denote an elliptic net associated to an elliptic curve E and its points $P_1, \ldots, P_n$ by $W_{P_1, \ldots, P_n; E}$.

One important property of elliptic nets is relation with division polynomials.

Proposition 4. *Let E be an elliptic curve over a subfield of $\mathbb{C}$ or a finite field and $P_1, \ldots, P_n \in E$. Let ψ_m be the m-th division polynomial of E. Then*

$$W_{P_1, \ldots, P_n; E}(m, 0, \ldots, 0) = \psi_m(P_1). \qquad (5)$$

In particular, the coordinate of $[m]P$ can be represented by $W_{P;E}(n - 2)$, $\ldots, W_{P;E}(n + 2)$. (For explicit formulae, see [5].)

Stange showed that the reduced Tate pairing could be represented by an elliptic net.

Theorem 5 ([8]). *Let E be an elliptic net defined over a finite field $\mathbb{F}q$ and m a positive integer such that $\mu_m \subseteq \mathbb{F}q$. For $P \in E(\mathbb{F}q)[m]$ and $Q \in E(\mathbb{F}q)$ with $P \neq \pm Q$,*

$$\langle P, P \rangle_m = \frac{W_{P;E}(m + 2)W_{P;E}(1)}{W_{P;E}(m + 1)W_{P;E}(2)}, \qquad (6)$$

$$\langle P, Q \rangle_m = \frac{W_{P,Q;E}(m + 1, 1)W_{P,Q;E}(1, 0)}{W_{P,Q;E}(m + 1, 0)W_{P,Q;E}(1, 1)}. \qquad (7)$$

In the following, we state the method to compute an elliptic net $W_{P,Q;E}$ proposed by Stange.

First we define a block of an elliptic net.

Definition 6. *For an elliptic net $W : \mathbb{Z}^2 \to R$, a* **block of W centred on k** *is a set (see Fig. 1.)*

$$\{W(k - 3, 0), \ldots, W(k + 4, 0), W(k - 1, 1), W(k, 1), W(k + 1, 1)\}.$$

The following proposition allows us to compute a block of an elliptic net inductively.

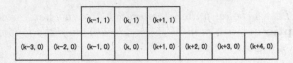

Fig. 1. Block centred on k

Proposition 5 ([8]). *Let $W : \mathbb{Z}^2 \to R$ be an elliptic net such that $W(0,1) = W(1,0) = 1$ and $W(2,0)$, $W(1,1)$, $W(-1,1)$, $W(2,-1) \in R^*$. Then*

$$
\begin{aligned}
W(2k-1,0) &= W(k+1,0)W(k-1,0)^3 \\
&\quad -W(k-2,0)W(k,0)^3,
\end{aligned} \tag{8}
$$

$$
\begin{aligned}
W(2k,0) &= (W(k,0)W(k+2,0)W(k-1,0)^2 \\
&\quad -W(k,0)W(k-2,0)W(k+1,0)^2)/W(2,0),
\end{aligned} \tag{9}
$$

$$
\begin{aligned}
W(2k-1,1) &= (W(k+1,1)W(k-1,1)W(k-1,0)^2 \\
&\quad -W(k,0)W(k-2,0)W(k,1)^2)/W(1,1),
\end{aligned} \tag{10}
$$

$$
\begin{aligned}
W(2k,1) &= W(k-1,1)W(k+1,1)W(k,0)^2 \\
&\quad -W(k-1,0)W(k+1,0)W(k,1)^2,
\end{aligned} \tag{11}
$$

$$
\begin{aligned}
W(2k+1,1) &= (W(k-1,1)W(k+1,1)W(k+1,0)^2 \\
&\quad -W(k,0)W(k+2,0)W(k,1)^2)/W(-1,1),
\end{aligned} \tag{12}
$$

$$
\begin{aligned}
W(2k+2,1) &= (W(k+1,0)W(k+3,0)W(k,1)^2 \\
&\quad -W(k-1,1)W(k+1,1)W(k+2,0)^2)/W(2,-1).
\end{aligned} \tag{13}
$$

Given a block centred on k, we can compute a block centred on $2k$ or $2k+1$ by using this proposition. We call these algorithms Double and DoubleAdd respectively. For the detail of algorithms and the initial values of W, see [8].

Ogura et al. [5] showed that the pairing in Theorem 3 could be represented by an elliptic net.

Theorem 6 ([5]). *Let $a_{[c_0,\ldots,c_l]}$ be a bilinear pairing in Theorem 3. Then*

$$
a_{[c_0,\ldots,c_l]}(Q, P) = \left(\prod_{i=0}^{l} \left(\frac{W_{Q,P;E}(c_i,1)}{W_{Q,P;E}(c_i,0)} \right)^{q^i} \prod_{i=0}^{l-1} g_{[s_i]Q,[c_i q^i]Q}(P) \right)^{\frac{q^k-1}{r}}.
$$

From Proposition 4 and the fact that $[c_i q^i]Q = \pi^i([c_i]Q)$, if given blocks of $W_{Q,P;E}$ centred on c_i for $i = 1,\ldots,l$, $g_{[s_i]Q,[c_i q^i]Q}(P)$ can be computed by operations of $\mathbb{F}q$ and Frobenius map on $\mathbb{F}q$ and the number of these operations does not depend on q, r, c_i.

3   Optimal Pairing via Elliptic Net of Twist Curve

3.1   Motivation and Conditions

In this section, we consider computing optimal pairings on elliptic curves defined over finite fields via elliptic nets associated to twists of these curves.

Throughout this section, $\mathbb{F}q$ is a finite field with q elements of characteristic not 2 or 3, E is an elliptic curve defined over $\mathbb{F}q$, and π is the q-th power Frobenius map on E.

If E has an optimal pairing $a_{[c_1,...,c_l]} : G_1 \times G_2 \to \mu_r$, then from Theorem 6, we can compute the optimal pairing by computing blocks centred on c_i for $i = 1, \ldots, l$ of the elliptic net $W_{Q,P;E}$. Therefore, we focus on computing the block centred on some c_i.

Motivation. First, we explain why we use a twist of a curve instead of an original curve.

From Proposition 5 and the values of a block centred on 1 (see [8].), it can be shown that values of $W_{Q,P;E}(n,0)$ do not depend on the coordinates of P. So these are in the field in which the coordinates of Q are.

We assume E has an optimal pairing: $G_2 \times G_1 \to \mu_r$. Although $Q \in G_2 \subseteq \mathbb{F}_{q^k}$, there may exist a twist of E such that the image of G_2 in the twist is contained in a smaller field. If such a "good" twist E' and the isomorphism $\phi : E' \to E$ exist, $W_{\phi^{-1}(Q),\phi^{-1}(P);E'}(n,0)$ are in a proper subfield of $\mathbb{F}_{q^k}$. Therefore in this situation, the elliptic net of the twist curve can be computed more easily than that of the original curve. The aim of this section is to consider computing an optimal pairing via an elliptic net of the twist curve.

Conditions. We summarize conditions in which a "good" twist exists. Let r be a prime that is prime to q. We define integers (k, n, d', d, e) as follows:

$$k : \text{the embedding degree of } r \text{ with respect to } q,$$

$$n = \begin{cases} 2 \text{ if } j(E) \neq 0, 1728, \\ 4 \text{ if } j(E) = 1728, \\ 6 \text{ if } j(E) = 0, \end{cases}$$

$$d' = \gcd(q-1, n),$$

$$d = \gcd(k, d'),$$

$$e = k/d.$$

Then we consider the following conditions **1.** $r \mid \#E(\mathbb{F}q)$, **2.** $k \geq 2$ and **3.** $d \geq 2$.

When conditions 1 and 2 are satisfied, from Proposition 1, $E[r]$ is decomposed to 1 and q-eigenspace of π (we denote these by G_1 and G_2, respectively). In this situation, $G_2 \subseteq E(\mathbb{F}_{q^k})$ and we can consider a pairing $a_{[c_0,...,c_l]} : G_2 \times G_1 \to \mu_r \subseteq \mathbb{F}_{q^k}$ defined in Theorem 3. Furthermore, from Theorem 4, there exists the twist E' of degree d of E such that the image of G_2 in E' is contained in $E'(\mathbb{F}_{q^e})$.

In addition, if condition 3 is satisfied, $\mathbb{F}_{q^e}$ is a proper subfield of $\mathbb{F}_{q^k}$. Therefore, an elliptic net of E' can be computed more easily than that of E.

In the remainder of this section, we assume that E and r satisfy the above conditions. Also, let (k, n, d', d, e) be the integers defined above. Moreover, we assume that $a_{[c_0,...,c_l]}$ is optimal.

3.2   Elliptic Net of Twist Curve

Let $E'/\mathbb{F}q^e$ be the twist of degree d of E such that $r \mid \#E(\mathbb{F}q^e)$ and $\phi : E' \to E$ the isomorphism defined over $\mathbb{F}_{q^k}$. We can take $\xi \in \mathbb{F}_{q^k}$ such that $\phi(x,y) = (\xi^2 x, \xi^3 y)$. Notice that for $i = 1, \ldots, d-1$, $\xi^i \notin \mathbb{F}q^e$ and $\xi^d \in \mathbb{F}q^e$ since the degree of twist E' is d.

We show a relation between elliptic nets of E and E'.

Proposition 6. *Let $P, Q \in E'$ and $s \in \mathbb{Z}$. Then*

$$W_{Q,P;E'}(s,0) = \xi^{s^2-1} W_{\phi(Q),\phi(P);E}(s,0), \tag{14}$$

$$W_{Q,P;E'}(s,1) = \xi^{s^2-s} W_{\phi(Q),\phi(P);E}(s,1). \tag{15}$$

Proof. It follows immediately by induction on s.   □

Theorem 7. *Let $P, Q \in E'$ and $s \in \mathbb{Z}$. Then*

$$\left(\frac{W_{\phi(Q),\phi(P);E}(s,1)}{W_{Q,P;E}(s,0)} \right)^{\frac{q^k-1}{r}} = W_{Q,P;E'}(s,1)^{\frac{q^k-1}{r}}. \tag{16}$$

Proof. From Proposition 6,

$$\left(\frac{W_{\phi(Q),\phi(P);E}(s,1)}{W_{\phi(Q),\phi(P);E}(s,0)} \right)^{\frac{q^k-1}{r}} = \left(\xi^{s-1} \frac{W_{Q,P;E'}(s,1)}{W_{Q,P;E'}(s,0)} \right)^{\frac{q^k-1}{r}}. \tag{17}$$

From the fact $W_{Q,P;E'}(s,0)$, $\xi^d \in \mathbb{F}q^e$, and $(q^e - 1)d \mid \frac{q^k-1}{r}$, it follows that $W_{Q,P;E'}(s,0)^{\frac{q^k-1}{r}} = 1$ and $\xi^{\frac{q^k-1}{r}} = 1$. This completes the proof of the theorem.   □

4   Modified Elliptic Net

In this section, we define a modified elliptic net for promoting the efficiency of computation of Double and DoubleAdd.

Definition 7. *Let $W : \mathbb{Z}^2 \to R$ be an elliptic net satisfying $W(0,1) = W(1,0) = 1$, $W(-1,1) \in R^*$. Then we define a **modified elliptic net** $\tilde{W}$ of W as follows:*

$$\tilde{W}(s,t) = W(-1,1)^{st} W(s,t). \tag{18}$$

Proposition 7. *A modified elliptic net is an elliptic net.*

Proof. It follows from substituting (18) into (4).   □

Let E be an elliptic curve and $P = (x_1, y_1), Q = (x_2, y_2) \in E$ and both are not O, $P \neq \pm Q$, and $[2]P - Q \neq O$. In the computation of Double or DoubleAdd, this modification changes $W(-1,1)$ from $(x_1 - x_2)$ to 1 and $W(1,1)$ from 1 to $(x_1 - x_2)$. After this modification, the cost of computing Double for a modified elliptic net is the same as that for an original elliptic net and the cost of computing DoubleAdd for a modified elliptic net is the cost of one multiplication less than that for an original elliptic net.

The following propositions show that we can use a modified elliptic net instead of an original elliptic net for computing pairings.

Proposition 8. *Let E be an elliptic curve defined over a finite field $\mathbb{F}q$ and m an integer such that $m \mid q - 1$. Let $P \in E(\mathbb{F}q)[m]$ and $Q \in E(\mathbb{F}q)$ with $P \neq \pm Q$. Then*

$$\frac{W_{P,Q;E}(m+1,1)W_{P,Q;E}(1,0)}{W_{P,Q;E}(m+1,0)W_{P,Q;E}(1,1)} \equiv \frac{\tilde{W}_{P,Q;E}(m+1,1)\tilde{W}_{P,Q;E}(1,0)}{\tilde{W}_{P,Q;E}(m+1,0)\tilde{W}_{P,Q;E}(1,1)} \mod \mathbb{F}q^{*m}.$$

(19)

Proof. By the definition of $\tilde{W}$, it follows that the ratio of both sides is equal to $W(-1,1)^m$. $\quad\square$

Proposition 9. *We use the notation in Sect. 3.2. Then*

$$\left(\prod_{i=0}^{l} W_{Q,P;E'}(c_i,1)^{q^i}\right)^{\frac{q^k-1}{r}} = \left(\prod_{i=0}^{l} \tilde{W}_{Q,P;E'}(c_i,1)^{q^i}\right)^{\frac{q^k-1}{r}}.$$

(20)

Proof

$$\prod_{i=0}^{l} \tilde{W}_{Q,P;E'}(c_i,1)^{q^i} = \prod_{i=0}^{l} W(-1,1)^{c_i q^i} W_{Q,P;E'}(c_i,1)^{q^i}$$

$$= W(-1,1)^{rm} \prod_{i=0}^{l} W_{Q,P;E'}(c_i,1)^{q^i}$$

Therefore $W(-1,1)$ vanishes by the exponentiation by $\frac{q^k-1}{r}$. $\quad\square$

5   Parallelizing

5.1   Parallelization Strategy

In this section, we consider parallelizing the computation of an elliptic net of a twist of an elliptic curve for computing a pairing over this curve. Our strategy for the parallelization is to distribute elements of the block of the elliptic net to each processor.

On a parallel algorithm, its running time depends on the cost of the process that has the highest cost. So we mean this cost by the cost of a parallel algorithm.

5.2   Extending the Block

In this subsection, we describe the extended block method proposed by Onuki et al. [6] and explain how this method can be applied for computing the pairings satisfying the conditions that are stated in Sect. 3.1.

Let E and r be an elliptic curve and a prime number that satisfy the conditions in Sect. 3.1 and have an optimal pairing $a_{[c_0,...,c_l]} : G_1 \times G_2 \rightarrow \mu_r$ and the k, d, e integers defined in Sect. 3.1. Let E' be the twist of degree d of E over $\mathbb{F}q^e$ such that $r \mid \#E'(\mathbb{F}q^e)$ and $\phi : E' \rightarrow E$ the isomorphism.

As we stated in Sect. 3.2, for $P \in \phi^{-1}(G_1)$, $Q \in \phi^{-1}(G_2)$, if we have $W_{Q,P;E'}$ then we can compute the optimal pairing $a_{[c_0,...,c_l]}$. In the following we denote $W_{Q,P;E'}$ by W.

On the twist, the cost of computing $W(n,1)$ is more expensive than that of $W(n,0)$ because $W(n,0) \in \mathbb{F}_{q^e}$ and $W(n,1) \in \mathbb{F}_{q^k}$. Therefore we focus on computing $W(n,1)$.

Equations (12) and (13) in Proposition 5 contain one additional multiplication by the inverse element, whereas Eqs. (10) and (11) do not. (Because $W(1,1) = 1$. In an extended block, we do not use a modified elliptic net but an original elliptic net). Therefore if we can use only (10) and (11) for computing $W(n,1)$, then we can reduce one multiplication in the parallel algorithm.

For this, we extend a block of an elliptic net.

Definition 8. *For an elliptic net $W : \mathbb{Z}^2 \to R$, an **extended block of W centred on k** is a set given by adjoining $W(k+2,1)$ and $W(k+3,1)$ to a block of W centred on k. (see Fig. 2.)*

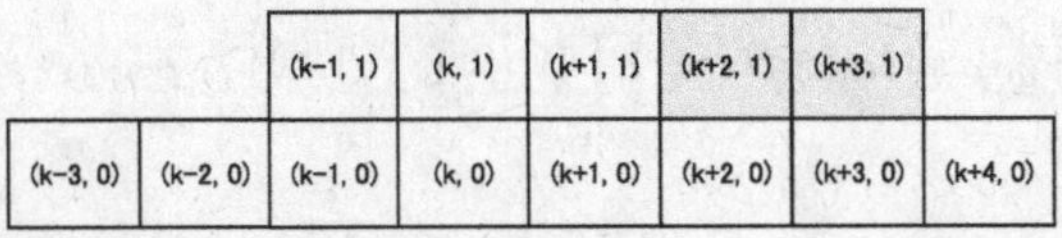

		(k−1, 1)	(k, 1)	(k+1, 1)	(k+2, 1)	(k+3, 1)	
(k−3, 0)	(k−2, 0)	(k−1, 0)	(k, 0)	(k+1, 0)	(k+2, 0)	(k+3, 0)	(k+4, 0)

Fig. 2. Extended block centred on k

Using an extended block, we can compute the block centred on $2k$ or $2k+1$ from the block centred on k without (12), (13). The algorithm for this is shown in Algorithm 1.

The additional initial values in an extended block centred on 1 are as follows:

$$W(3,1) = (W(2,1)W(2,0)^2 - W(3,0)W(1,1)^2)/W(-1,1), \qquad (21)$$

$$W(4,1) = W(1,1)W(3,1)W(2,0)^2 - W(3,0)W(2,1)^2. \qquad (22)$$

5.3 Costs of Field Operations

In this section, we estimate the costs of operations on finite fields. We take a base finite field and estimate the costs of operations on its extension fields based on its costs. For computing a pairing via a twist curve, this base field is $\mathbb{F}_{q^e}$ and a target extension field of the estimation is $\mathbb{F}_{q^k}$. As we stated in Sect. 2.3, the degree of this extension d is 2, 3, 4 or 6.

For simplicity, we estimate the costs of operations by the number of multiplication on a base field.

In the remainder of this section, we denote a base field by $\mathbb{F}q$.

Algorithm 1. Double and DoubleAdd for Extended Block

Input: Extended block V centred at k of an elliptic net satisfying $W(1,0) = W(0,1) = 1$, values $A = W(2,0)^{-1}$, $G = W(1,1)^{-1}$ and boolean add

Output: Extended block centred at $2k$ if $add == 0$ and centred at $2k+1$ if $add == 1$

1: **for** $i = 0$ to 2 **do**
2:     $S_0[i] \leftarrow V[1, i+1]^2$
3:     $P_0[i] \leftarrow V[1, i]V[1, i+2]$
4: **end for**
5: **for** $i = 0$ to 5 **do**
6:     $S[i] \leftarrow V[0, i+1]^2$
7:     $P[i] \leftarrow V[0, i]V[0, i+2]$
8: **end for**
9: **if** $add == 0$ **then**
10:     **for** $i = 0$ to 3 **do**
11:         $V[0, 2i] \leftarrow S[i]P[i+1] - S[i+1]P[i]$
12:         $V[0, 2i+1] \leftarrow (S[i]P[i+2] - S[i+2]P[i])A$
13:     **end for**
14:     **for** $i = 0$ to 1 **do**
15:         $V[1, 2i] \leftarrow (P_0[i]S[i+1] - S_0[i]P[i+1])G$
16:         $V[1, 2i+1] \leftarrow P_0[i]S[i+2] - S_0[i]P[i+2]$
17:     **end for**
18:     $V[1, 4] \leftarrow (P_0[2]S[3] - S_0[2]P[3])G$
19: **else**
20:     **for** $i = 0$ to 3 **do**
21:         $V[0, 2i] \leftarrow (S[i]P[i+2] - S[i+2]P[i])A$
22:         $V[0, 2i+1] \leftarrow S[i+1]P[i+2] - S[i+2]P[i+1]$
23:     **end for**
24:     **for** $i = 0$ to 1 **do**
25:         $V[1, 2i] \leftarrow P_0[i]S[i+2] - S_0[i]P[i+2]$
26:         $V[1, 2i+1] \leftarrow (P_0[i+1]S[i+2] - S_0[i+1]P[i+2])G$
27:     **end for**
28:     $V[1, 4] \leftarrow P_0[2]S[4] - S_0[2]P[4]$
29: **end if**
30: **return** V

Definition 9. *We define as follows:*

    m : *the cost of multiplication on* $\mathbb{F}q$,

     s : *the cost of squaring on* $\mathbb{F}q$,

   m_d : *the cost of multiplication on* $\mathbb{F}q^d$,

    s_d : *the cost of squaring on* $\mathbb{F}q^d$,

m_{d_1,d_2} : *the cost of multiplying an element of* $\mathbb{F}q^{d_1}$ *by one of* $\mathbb{F}q^{d_2}$ *with* $\mathbb{F}q^{d_2} \subseteq \mathbb{F}q^{d_1}$.

We assume that $d \mid q - 1$. In the computing of a pairing over a twist, this assumption is always satisfied.

In the case $d = 2, 3$, we take $D \in \mathbb{F}q^*$ such that $X^d - D \in \mathbb{F}q[X]$ is irreducible over $\mathbb{F}q$ and represents $\mathbb{F}q^d = \mathbb{F}q[\xi]/(\xi^d - D)$. We denote the cost of multiplying

Table 1. Estimation of costs of multiplications

d	Multiplication	Squaring	Squaring (special case)
2	$3m + \tilde{m}$	$3s + \tilde{m}$	$2m$
3	$6m + 2\tilde{m}$	$6s + 2\tilde{m}$	$5m + \tilde{m} + 2\tilde{m}'$
4	$3m_2 + \tilde{m}_2 = 6m + 4\tilde{m}$	$3s_2 + \tilde{m}_2 = 6s + 4\tilde{m}$	$2m_2 = 4m$
6	$3m_3 + \tilde{m}_3 = 18m + 7\tilde{m}$	$3s_3 + \tilde{m}_3 = 18s + 7\tilde{m}$	$2m_3 = 12m + 4\tilde{m}$

D by an element of $\mathbb{F}q$ by $\tilde{m}$. In the case D is a special element, $\tilde{m}$ is less than m. For example, when $4 \nmid q - 1$ and $d = 2$, if we take $D = -1$, then multiplying D is a change of sign and a replacement of coefficients.

In the case $d = 4, 6$, by replacing $\mathbb{F}q$ by $\mathbb{F}q^2$ or $\mathbb{F}q^3$, one can apply the algorithm for $d = 2, 3$. I.e., we represent $\mathbb{F}q^d = \mathbb{F}q^i[\xi]/(\xi^{d/i} - D)$ with $D \in \mathbb{F}q^i$, $i = 2$ or 3. We denote the cost of multiplying D by an element of $\mathbb{F}q^i$ by $\tilde{m}_i$.

Multiplying an element of a field by one of an element of its subfield can be expressed by multiplications of the subfield of the number of the degree of extension. Therefore

$$m_{d_1,d_2} = \frac{d_1}{d_2} m_{d_2}.$$

In the above setting, we estimated the costs of field operations. See Table 1.

5.4   Algorithms and Costs

First, we consider the computation of an optimal pairing. As we will note later, a special case in an optimal pairing can be applied for computing a symmetric pairing over a supersingular curve defined over a finite prime field.

Let E be an elliptic curve, r a prime satisfying the conditions in Sect. 3.1, and k, d, e integers defined in that section. Let π be the q-th power Frobenius map on E, $G_1 = E[r] \cap \ker(\pi - [1])$, and $G_2 = E[r] \cap \ker(\pi - [q])$. Furthermore, let E' be the twist of degree d of E such that $r \mid \#E'(\mathbb{F}q^e)$ and $\phi : E' \to E$ the isomorphism over $\mathbb{F}_{q^k}$.

For $P \in \phi^{-1}(G_1)$ and $Q \in \phi^{-1}(G_2)$, we give algorithms for computing Double and DoubleAdd on the elliptic net $W_{Q,P;E'}$ with $d = 2, 3, 4, 6$ and estimate these costs. Algorithms are shown in Appendix A. We consider the cases in which the number of processors is 1, 4, 8 or the smallest number that gives the minimal cost of the parallel algorithm. We use an extended block if we have enough processors for using it, otherwise we use an original block of a modified elliptic net. In our estimation, we ignore the costs except multiplications of fields and use estimations in Sect. 5.3. Furthermore, we assume there exists a representation such that the cost of multiplying by D can be ignored.

The costs of parallel algorithms are summarized in Tables 2 and 3.

Table 2. Cost of Double by parallel algorithm

d	Single	4 processors	8 processors	Number of processors with minimal cost	Minimal cost
2	$45m + 6s$	$13m$	$8m$	16	$5m$
3	$61m + 6s$	$18m$	$\max\{10m + 3s, 12m\}$	12	$9m$
4	$66m + 6s$	$19m$	$14m$	12	$10m$
6	$104m + 6s$	$36m$	$30m$	10	$24m$

Table 3. Cost of DoubleAdd by parallel algorithm

d	Single	4 processors	8 processors	Number of processors with minimal cost	Minimal cost
2	$46m + 6s$	$\max\{13m, 3s + 11m\}$	$8m$	16	$5m$
3	$61m + 6s$	$18m$	$\max\{10m + 3s, 12m\}$	12	$9m$
4	$66m + 6s$	$19m$	$14m$	12	$10m$
6	$110m + 6s$	$42m$	$30m$	10	$24m$

Supersingular. We can apply the algorithms and these estimations with $d = 2$ for a symmetric pairing over a supersingular curve. However, in the case $j(E) = 0$, since x-coordinate of Q is not in $\mathbb{F}p$, the estimation of the cost of Double is the same as that of DoubleAdd in Table 3.

6   Conclusion

In this paper, we introduced faster formulae for computing optimal pairings via elliptic nets using twists of curves and gave the conditions for applying the formulae. Furthermore, we proposed parallel algorithms for computing the pairings via these formulae and estimated the costs of these algorithms. In the most efficient case, we can reduce the cost of a parallel algorithm to 10 % of that of a single processor algorithm by using 16 processors. We showed that these algorithms can also be applied for a symmetric pairing over supersingular curves. The implementation of these parallel algorithms is expected in future work.

Acknowledgments. We would like to thank the anonymous referees for valuable suggestions. This work was supported by a research grant from the KDDI Foundation A study on improvement of pairing-based cryptography, a Grant-in-Aid for Scientific Research(C) (24540135) and a research grant from NTT Secure Platform Laboratories.

A   Parallel Algorithms

We give parallel algorithms and estimations of these costs for each $d = 2, 3, 4, 6$. We use notations in Algorithm 1 in the following. In the following tables, "proc." and "sync." means processor and synchronization of each processor respectively (Tables 4, 5, 6, 7, 8, 9, 10, 11, 12, 13, 14 and 15).

Table 4. Parallel algorithm for 4 processors ($d = 2$)

proc. 1	$P[i]$ $(i = 0, 1, 2)$							
proc. 1	$P[i]$ $(i = 0, 1, 2)$				$V[0, i]$ $(i = 0, 1, 2, 3)$			
proc. 2	$P[i]$ $(i = 3, 4, 5)$	sync.			$V[0, i]$ $(i = 4, 5, 6, 7)$			
proc. 3	$S[i]$ $(i = 0, 1, 2)$		P_0	sync.	$V[1, 2 - 2add], P_0 S[2 + add]$	sync.	$V[1, 1]$
proc. 4	$S[i]$ $(i = 3, 4, 5)$		S_0		$V[1, 2add], S_0 P[2 + add]$		

Table 5. Parallel algorithm for 8 processors ($d = 2$)

proc. 1	$P[i]$ $(i = 0, 1, 2)$			$V[0, i]$ $(i = 0, 1)$		
proc. 2	$P[i]$ $(i = 3, 4, 5)$			$V[0, i]$ $(i = 2, 3)$		
proc. 3	$S[i]$ $(i = 0, 1, 2)$			$V[0, i]$ $(i = 4, 5)$		
proc. 4	$S[i]$ $(i = 0, 1, 2)$	sync.		$V[0, i]$ $(i = 6, 7)$		
proc. 5	P_0			$V[1, 1]$		
proc. 6	S_0			$V[1, 2 - 2add]$		
proc. 7				$P_0 S[1 + 3add]$	sync.	$V[1, 2add]$
proc. 8				$S_0 P[1 + 3add]$		

Table 6. Parallel algorithm for 16 processor ($d = 2$)

proc. 1-6	$P[i], S[i]$	sync.			$V[0, i]$			
proc. 7,8					$V[0, i]$			
proc. 9-14	$P_0[i], S_0[i]$		sync.		$S_0[i]P[j]$ or $P_0[i]S_0[j]$	sync.	$V[1, i]$
proc. 15,16					$S_0[i]P[j]$ or $P_0[i]S_0[j]$		

Table 7. Parallel algorithm for 4 processors ($d = 3$)

proc. 1	$P[i], S[i]$ $(i = 0, 1, 2)$	sync.		$V[0, i]$ $(i = 0, 1, 2, 3)$
proc. 2	$P[i], S[i]$ $(i = 3, 4, 5)$			$V[0, i]$ $(i = 4, 5, 6, 7)$
proc. 3	P_0		sync.	$V[1, 2add]$
proc. 4	S_0			$V[1, 1], V[1, 2 - 2add]$

Table 8. Parallel algorithm 8 processors $(d = 3)$

proc. 1	$P[i], S[i]$ $(i = 0, 1, 2)$	sync.	$V[0, i]$ $(i = 0, 1, 2)$
proc. 2	$P[i], S[i]$ $(i = 3, 4, 5)$		$V[0, i]$ $(i = 3, 4, 6)$
proc. 3	$P_0[0]$		$V[0, i]$ $(i = 5, 7)$
proc. 4	$P_0[1]$		$V[1, 0]$
proc. 5	$P_0[2]$	sync.	$V[1, 1]$
proc. 6	$S_0[0]$		$V[1, 2]$
proc. 7	$S_0[1]$		$V[1, 3]$
proc. 8	$S_0[2]$		$V[1, 4]$

Table 9. Parallel algorithm for 12 processors $(d = 3)$

proc. 1	$P[0], S[0]$				$V[0, i]$ $(i = 1, 3)$		
proc. 2	$P[1], S[1]$	sync.			$V[0, i]$ $(i = 5, 7)$		
proc. 3	$P[2], S[2]$				$V[0, i]$ $(i = 0, 2, 4, 6)$		
proc. 4-6	$P_0[i]$		sync.		$S_0[i]P[j]$	sync.	$V[1, i]$
proc. 7-12	$S_0[i]$				$S_0[i]P[j]$ or $P_0[i]S[j]$		$V[1, i]$

Table 10. Parallel algorithm for 4 processors $(d = 4)$

proc. 1	$P[i], S[i]$ $(i = 0, 1, 2)$			$V[0, i]$ $(i = 0, 1, 2, 3, 4)$			
proc. 2	$P[i], S[i]$ $(i = 3, 4, 5)$	sync.	$V[0, i]$ $(i = 5, 6, add)$	$P_0 S[2 + add]$	sync.	$V[1, 1]$
proc. 3	P_0		$V[1, 2 - 2add], S_0 P[2 + add]$			
proc. 4	S_0		$V[1, 2add]$			

Table 11. Parallel algorithm for 8 processors $(d = 4)$

proc. 1	$P[i], S[i]$ $(i = 0, 1, 2)$	sync.	$V[0, i]$ $(i = 0, 1, 2)$
proc. 2	$P[i], S[i]$ $(i = 3, 4, 5)$		$V[0, i]$ $(i = 3, 4, 6)$
proc. 3	$P_0[0]$		$V[0, i]$ $(i = 5, 7)$
proc. 4	$P_0[1]$		$V[1, 0]$
proc. 5	$P_0[2]$	sync.	$V[1, 1]$
proc. 6	$S_0[0]$		$V[1, 2]$
proc. 7	$S_0[1]$		$V[1, 3]$
proc. 8	$S_0[2]$		$V[1, 4]$

Table 12. Parallel algorithm for 12 processor $(d = 4)$

proc. 1	$P[0], S[0]$				$V[0, i]$ $(i = 1, 3)$		
proc. 2	$P[1], S[1]$	sync.			$V[0, i]$ $(i = 5, 7)$		
proc. 3	$P[2], S[2]$				$V[0, i]$ $(i = 0, 2, 4, 6)$		
proc. 4-6	$P_0[i]$		sync.		$S_0[i]P[j]$	sync.	$V[1, i]$
proc. 7-12	$S_0[i]$				$S_0[i]P[j]$ or $P_0[i]S[j]$		$V[1, i]$

Table 13. Parallel algorithm for 4 processors $(d = 6)$

proc. 1	$P[i], S[i]$ $(i = 0, 1, 2)$		$V[0, i]$ $(i = 0, 1, 2, 3)$			$V[1, 1]$		
proc. 2	$P[i], S[i]$ $(i = 3, 4, 5)$	sync.	$V[0, i]$ $(i = 4, 5, 6, 7)$	sync.		$V[1, 2add]$		
proc. 3	P_0				$P_0 S[2 + add]$	sync.	$V[1, 2 - 2add]$
proc. 4	S_0				$S_0 P[2 + add]$		

Table 14. Parallel algorithm for 8 processors $(d = 6)$

proc. 1	$P[i], S[i]$ $(i = 0, 1, 2)$		$V[0,i]$ $(i = 0, 1, 2, 3)$	
proc. 2	$P[i], S[i]$ $(i = 3, 4, 5)$		$V[0,i]$ $(i = 4, 5, 6, 7)$	
proc. 3	$P_0[0]$			
proc. 4	$P_0[1]$	sync.	$V[1,0]$	
proc. 5	$P_0[2]$		$V[1,1]$	
proc. 6	$S_0[0]$		$V[1,2]$	
proc. 7	$S_0[1]$		$V[1,3]$	
proc. 8	$S_0[2]$		$V[1,4]$	

Table 15. Parallel algorithm for 10 processors $(d = 6)$

proc. 1	$P[0], P[1], S[0]$		$V[0,i]$ $(i = 0, 1)$		$S_0[i]P[j]$ or $P_0[i]S[j]$		$V[1,i]$
proc. 2	$P[2], P[3], S[1]$	sync.	$V[0,i]$ $(i = 0, 1)$		$S_0[i]P[j]$ or $P_0[i]S[j]$		$V[1,i]$
proc. 3	$P[4], S[2], S[3]$		$V[0,i]$ $(i = 0, 1)$	sync.	$S_0[i]P[j]$ or $P_0[i]S[j]$	sync.	$V[1,i]$
proc. 4	$P[5], S[4], S[5]$		$V[0,i]$ $(i = 0, 1)$		$S_0[i]P[j]$ or $P_0[i]S[j]$		$V[1,i]$
proc. 5-7			$P_0[i]$		$S_0[i]P[j]$ or $P_0[i]S[j]$		$V[1,i]$
proc. 8-10			$S_0[i]$		$S_0[i]P[j]$ or $P_0[i]S[j]$		$V[1,i]$

References

1. Aranha, D.F., Knapp, E., Menezes, A., Rodríguez-Henríquez, F.: Parallelizing the Weil and tate pairings. In: Chen, L. (ed.) IMACC 2011. LNCS, vol. 7089, pp. 275–295. Springer, Heidelberg (2011)

2. Barreto, P.S.L.M., Naehrig, M.: Pairing-friendly elliptic curves of prime order. In: Preneel, B., Tavares, S. (eds.) SAC 2005. LNCS, vol. 3897, pp. 319–331. Springer, Heidelberg (2006)

3. Hess, F., Smart, N., Vercauteren, F.: The eta pairing revisited. IEEE Trans. Inf. Theory **52**, 4595–4602 (2006)

4. Miller, V.: The Weil pairing, and its efficient calculation. J. Cryptol. **17**, 235–261 (2004)

5. Ogura, N., Kanayama, N., Uchiyama, S., Okamoto, E.: Cryptographic pairings based on elliptic nets. In: Iwata, T., Nishigaki, M. (eds.) IWSEC 2011. LNCS, vol. 7038, pp. 65–78. Springer, Heidelberg (2011)

6. Onuki, H., Teruya, T., Kanayama, N., Uchiyama, S.: The optimal ate pairing over the Barreto-Naehrig curve via parallelizing elliptic nets. JSIAM Lett. **8**, 9–12 (2016)

7. Silverman, J.H.: The Arithmetic of Elliptic Curves. Springer, New York (1992)

8. Stange, K.E.: The tate pairing via elliptic nets. In: Takagi, T., Okamoto, E., Okamoto, T., Okamoto, T. (eds.) Pairing 2007. LNCS, vol. 4575, pp. 329–348. Springer, Heidelberg (2007)

9. Vercauteren, F.: Optimal pairings. IEEE Trans. Inf. Theor. **56**, 455–461 (2010)

10. Washington, L.C.: Elliptic Curves: Number Theory and Cryptography. Chapman and Hall/CRC, Boca Raton (2008)

Author Index

Printed in the United States
By Bookmasters